second edition

DESIGN OF COMPUTER DATA FILES

second edition

Owen Hanson

Director of the Centre for Business Systems Analysis
The City University, London

PITMAN

PITMAN PUBLISHING
128 Long Acre, London WC2E 9AN

© Owen J Hanson 1988

First edition published in Great Britain 1982
Reprinted 1983, 1984, 1986, 1987
Second edition published in Great Britain 1988

British Library Cataloguing in Publication Data
Hanson, Owen
    Design of computer data files.——2nd ed.
    1. Data base management   2. System design
    3. File organization (Computer science)
    I. Title
    001.64'42   QA76.9.D3

ISBN 0-273-02530-9 (cased)
ISBN 0-273-02964-9 (paper)

All rights reserved. No part of this publication may be reproduced, stored in a retrieval system, or transmitted, in any form or by any means, electronic, mechanical, photocopying, recording and/or otherwise without the prior written permission of the publishers or a licence permitting restricted copying issued by the Copyright Licensing Agency Ltd., 33–34 Alfred Place, London WC1E 7DP. This book may not be lent, resold, hired out or otherwise disposed of by way of trade in any form of binding or cover other than that in which it is published, without the prior consent of the publishers.

Printed and bound in Great Britain

Contents

1 **An introduction to file design** 1
  1.1 Fundamentals 1
  1.2 Data files 2
  1.3 Data records 4
  1.4 Data fields 5
  1.5 File organization 6
  1.6 Accessing data files 8
  1.7 Data file terminology 9
  1.8 Computer storage 10
  1.9 File processing 12
  Conclusion 18
  References 18
  Revision questions 18

2 **Review of backing storage devices** 20
  2.1 Introduction 20
  2.2 Magnetic tape 20
  2.3 Magnetic disk 31
  2.4 Semiconductor memory devices 46
  2.5 Mass storage devices 47
  2.6 Bubble memory 49
  2.7 Optical or laser disk storage 50
  2.8 Care of magnetic media 51
  Conclusion 52
  References 52
  Revision questions 53

3 **Choice and design of record formats** 55
  3.1 Introduction 55
  3.2 Physical records 55
  3.3 Logical records 59
  3.4 Overall run timing 63
  Conclusion 68
  References 68
  Revision questions 69

4 **Blocking and buffering** 70
  4.1 Introduction 70
  4.2 Blocks on magnetic tape 71
  4.3 Blocks on magnetic disk 75
  4.4 General blocking considerations 82
  4.5 Limitations on block size 82
  4.6 General tape blocking considerations 95
  4.7 General blocking considerations for magnetic disk and other track-oriented devices 96
  4.8 Use of buffers 98
  Conclusion 102
  References 102
  Revision questions 103

5 **Sequential file organization** 106
  5.1 Introduction 106
  5.2 Batching 107
  5.3 Sorting 108
  5.4 Choice of storage medium 109
  5.5 Optimizing magnetic tape file handling 110
  5.6 Sequential files on direct access devices 116
  5.7 Disk versus tape—the effect of hit rate 123

vi Contents

    Conclusion 141
    References 141
    Revision questions 142

6 Direct file organization 144
6.1 Introduction 144
6.2 Self-indexing 145
6.3 Algorithmic addressing 153
6.4 Methods of randomizing 156
6.5 Testing for successful randomization 166
6.6 Minimizing the effect of synonyms 172
6.7 Practical considerations in setting up direct files 209
    Conclusion 215
    References 215
    Revision questions 217

7 Indexed sequential files 219
7.1 Introduction 219
7.2 File structure 220
7.3 Indexes 220
7.4 Additions 232
7.5 Addition techniques 238
7.6 Data format 244
7.7 File packing 246
7.8 Sequential processing 249
7.9 Direct processing 258
7.10 The impact of software on indexed sequential files 263
    Conclusion 270
    References 271
    Revision questions 272

8 File organization for multiple-key processing 273
8.1 Introduction 273
8.2 File types 274
8.3 Record reference 281
8.4 Additions and alterations 283
8.5 Storage requirements 284
    Conclusion 285
    References 286
    Revision questions 287

9 Choice of file organization 288
9.1 Introduction 288
9.2 Reference facility required 289
9.3 Type of access required 290
9.4 Hit rate 291
9.5 The effect of size on design 293
9.6 Expected life 295
9.7 Growth 296
9.8 Volatility 296
9.9 Run integration 297
9.10 Data integrity and backup 297
9.11 Analysis of the criteria 300
9.12 Run timings 300
9.13 Sequential versus indexed sequential 300
9.14 Indexed sequential versus direct 308
    Conclusion 315
    References 315
    Revision questions 316

10 Accuracy, integrity and security 318
10.1 Introduction 318
10.2 Accuracy and integrity during processing 319
10.3 Physical file security 327
10.4 Recovery in batch systems 330
10.5 Recovery in on-line systems 343
10.6 Run controls 350
10.7 Bucket processing 351
10.8 Duplicate facilities 351
10.9 Complete system failure 352

10.10 Security
considerations   354
Conclusion   355
References   355
Revision questions   356

Appendix 1   Curves plotting accesses to synonyms against packing density   358

Appendix 2   Hit record distribution on disk   362

Appendix 3   Response time as a function of device utilization   368

Appendix 4   Useful prime numbers   368

Appendix 5   Extended synonym table   373

Appendix 6   The effect of chaining and tagging synonyms on search times   384

Appendix 7   A detailed example of the results of storing synonyms using consecutive spill   393

Appendix 8   Handling smooth and random access curves   397

Additional questions   403
Index   415

Preface to the second edition

The welcome given to the first edition of this book has led me to prepare a second edition, which is intended to be both easier to read than the original book, and to incorporate a great deal of new work. As databases have become more important, the need to optimize database performance has grown; for that reason, the design of the underlying physical file structures has become more, rather than less, important since the first edition was published. With that in mind, I have included a number of new topics in this edition.

Additions to this edition have been influenced by several reviewers. James Lee Johnson, in the *Journal of Computer-Based Instruction*, suggested the inclusion of some material on tree structures, while D. C. Lindsey in *Computer Bulletin* felt that balanced trees, content-addressable file storage devices and order-preserving hashing mechanisms should be covered. I agree, and have added these and related topics. In making changes, I have used the report by Jay F. Nunamaker and others—'Information Systems Curriculum Recommendations for the 80s: Undergraduate and Graduate Programs'—in *CACM* of November 1982, as a guide. The content of this book covers some of their recommended syllabuses IS1 and IS4, and most of IS2.

A further source of assistance has been our own student body at the City University, London. I am indebted to many past students for their help in pointing out and correcting mistakes in the first edition, and without it this book would not have been complete. The staff of the Centre for Business Systems Analysis, and the many manufacturers who have helped me, were thanked in the first edition; I repeat that thanks now.

Finally, I should like to acknowledge my debt to Cosette Avakian, who did so much of the hard work in transferring the text onto disk. The intention has been to provide both professional file designers and advanced students of data file design with a single authoritative source of information on file design. I leave my readers to decide how far I have succeeded.

Owen Hanson
The Centre for Business Systems Analysis,
April 1987

Preface to the first edition

This book has taken shape over a number of years, during which time the author has worked both in the data processing industry and in education. Over this period it has become clear that the practitioner and the student of data processing have a choice between books that cover file design at an elementary level and original papers covering individual topics in considerable depth. There has been no single source to which file designers could turn to get details of all the considerations involved in their work at a satisfactory level, while referring them to original sources where appropriate.

Two queries might well be raised about the need for such a book. The first is that more and more computer users are turning to database systems for their information-handling needs; the second is that optimized file design is no longer important because the cost of processing equipment is now well below that of the programmers, operators and systems analysts who service it.

The first of these points is certainly true, and may explain the number of excellent books now available on database systems, in comparison with the lack of satisfactory books on file design generally. However, most installations still employ standard file organization techniques. In addition, database systems use the principles described here in handling the actual retrieval of information, so that a thorough knowledge of file organization techniques provides a necessary introduction to database technology.

The second point is rather harder to justify. True, the cost of data processing staff has risen significantly in comparison with that of hardware, and is still rising. However, it is just as easy for the file designer to design an efficient file as an inefficient one; there can hardly be an argument for lack of knowledge in file and systems designers as this could lead to faulty and suspect processing of information and the acquisition of more hardware than is actually required. Thus, however expensive data processing staff become in comparison with computing equipment, employers will expect their staff to be competent and well-informed. More knowledge will be needed in the future rather than less.

This book is intended to provide the file designer with a single source of information that sets a new standard both in identifying and discussing the factors that influence file design, and in the provision of design aids.

The author would like to thank the many people who have helped to make the book possible. These include colleagues and students in IBM (UK) Ltd, IBM (Regional Office East and Central Europe), and the staff and students of the Centre for Business Systems Analysis of The City University. In particular, John Reed of IBM and John Watt of the University of Aston have contributed many helpful suggestions, while Norman Revell of The City University has worked closely with the author in developing much of the material presented here.

Thanks are also due to IBM (UK) Ltd, ICL, CDC, Honeywell, Burroughs, NCR, Memorex Corporation, Ampex Memory Products, Storage Technology Ltd, BASF and all the other companies who provided details of their products, and to the many authors upon whose work the book is based.

Owen Hanson
The Centre for Business Systems Analysis,
March 1981

Introduction

File design is one of a large number of factors that have to be taken into account in producing an efficient data-processing system. The reasons for its importance have been discussed in the Preface. This book deals specifically with file design techniques and considerations: other factors such as the cost of programming involved in design work, the availability of the required design skills, or the facilities provided by a particular programming language may all be equally important in a given installation. To take account of these other factors and put the subject in perspective, a brief discussion of file design in the context of data processing as a whole is given in Chapter 1.

This book is intended both as a teaching aid for students of data-processing and systems analysis, and as a reference book for the practising designer. References to original sources provide the reader with a full bibliography of key documents. The book's aims are to:

> bring together all the up-to-date considerations in the design of computer data files;
> provide an overall methodology of file design, independent of any particular manufacturer's hardware or software, and of current technology;
> present essential data for file designers in order to speed and simplify their task;
> be a fully documented teaching/learning text for file designers.

The body of the book divides naturally into three parts. The first four chapters cover subjects that are a prerequisite for an understanding of file design. The main file organization techniques are dealt with in the next four chapters, while the last two chapters examine areas that depend on a detailed knowledge of all the preceding text. A number of reference tables that are too large to be conveniently presented in the body of the book are placed at the end of the book. Chapter groupings are as follows.

Prerequisites

  Chapter 1   —   An introduction to file design
  Chapter 2   —   Review of backing storage devices

Chapter 3 — Choice and design of record formats
Chapter 4 — Blocking and buffering

File organization techniques

Chapter 5 — Sequential file organization
Chapter 6 — Direct file organization
Chapter 7 — Indexed sequential files
Chapter 8 — File organization for multiple-key processing

Overall topics

Chapter 9 — Choice of file organization
Chapter 10 — Accuracy, integrity and security

Reference data

Appendixes
Index.

The table of contents given at the beginning of the book shows all major subject headings dealt with, but for the convenience of readers a comprehensive index is also provided.

References which can be used to provide further information on many detailed areas dealt with are listed at the end of each chapter. Reference numbers given in the text point to the appropriate member of the list *within* the chapter; in some cases this means that a reference will appear in more than one list and it will usually have a different number in each separate list.

Questions, many of which have been set in the examinations for the MSc in business systems analysis and design and the postgraduate diploma in systems analysis offered by The City University Business School, London, are also given at the end of each chapter. It is hoped that they will provide a nucleus of revision and teaching material for courses in this field.

1 An introduction to file design

1.1 Fundamentals

Every business has to keep records, if only for legal purposes. Sometimes these records have to be presented in a standardized form, such as accounts laid out using the double-entry system. More often they can be arranged in any way that suits the user.

Business records are of little use unless they can be referred to quickly, to provide information when it is required. Most businesses will hold records that are used for a series of different jobs: some will show what goods are in stock, while others are a record of the orders from customers or the cash position. For easy handling, these different sets of records are divided into groups that are all of the same kind. In pre-computing days a set of records was often kept in a single ledger, or book, with entries in the book representing individual transactions. This was usually called a *file*.

Manual records, gathered into a single file, are easy to refer to. If an invoice file is used mainly to answer queries about individual orders, for example, it will usually be arranged in ascending order of invoice numbers. A small business might only insist on orders received during a particular day being entered on the same sheet of a ledger; this relies on the fact that few pages would have to be examined to find any particular record. However, it is generally quicker to use a value that is unique, such as the invoice number, to identify the required record.

In computer systems it is essential to be able to recognize any particular record in a file, rather than to rely on finding it in a group of similar records equivalent to a page of information. For this reason some convenient value such as the invoice, stock or customer number is used as an *identifier* or *key* to the record. Often it is sufficient to arrange all the records in the file in ascending key order; any particular record can then be found by searching through the file until the required key is found. In other cases a more complicated arrangement may be necessary; a new order from a customer might lead to the need to check that all outstanding orders for the customer have already been dispatched, or that all previous invoices sent to the customer have been paid. The most convenient arrangement of records to allow such a check to be made quickly is often to hold all the records for a particular customer together; in a manual system they might be written on the same ledger sheet in date order, while in a computer system the invoices might be arranged in customer number order, and in invoice number order as a secondary key. Much of the rest of this book will examine how best to store records so that they can be retrieved quickly and efficiently when necessary.

From the discussion above it is clear that the concepts of files, records, reference keys and the storage of records in a planned manner that makes later retrieval of information easy were already in use long before computers appeared on the scene. Business records have always been vital; the use of computers has made a more carefully planned approach to the storage and handling of these records essential. In return, new possibilities for the presentation, cross-referencing and analysis of business information have been opened up. To achieve this, information has to be stored in carefully designed files that allow rapid and efficient processing.

A great deal of the nomenclature used in data-processing is based on pre-computer practice, and in order to explain the use of terminology in this book many of the most important terms are defined and explained in this chapter.

1.2 Data files

Records that hold information about similar items of data are usually grouped together into a **file**. On occasions it may be convenient or necessary to group together dissimilar records in a 'miscellaneous' type of file. However, processing of such files is slow and limited, and they will not be considered further. The more usual type of file is one composed of the customer records of a company, the personnel records of employees or some other logically consistent grouping. A further type of file is one composed of all the *changes* to an existing file; new orders to be added to an accounts receivable file, for example, and payments to be recorded in settlement of those orders.

At least four types of file, composed of similar or related records, can be distinguished. They are master files, update files, reference files, and historical or archive files.

Master files

These files are made up of permanent or semi-permanent sets of records containing information that may be *updated* by addition, deletion or changing of data. Individual records may be *added* or *deleted*, e.g. when a new customer is gained, or an old one is lost, but the file itself remains a part of the overall information processing system. Such a file is sometimes called a *dynamic file*[1].

Update files

These are composed of sets of changes to a master file. Fields or records in a master file may be changed, added or deleted using an update file. Although these files are often retained for a period for security reasons (see Chapter 10) they are basically used only once. This, and the fact that every record in the file is processed in this single run, affects the methods of file organization that are appropriate for update files. This is discussed in Chapter 9 (*see* p. 291). These files are also known as *changes files* and *transaction files*.

Reference files

Price lists, actuarial tables and other forms of reference data make up files that are similar to master files, but require much less alteration due to additions, deletions and changes. The information in them is relatively *static*. The main consideration in designing such files is that the data they contain should be available with as little delay as possible, and this requires an appropriate file organization (*see* Chapter 9).

Historical or Archive files

When a system has been redesigned so that a master file is no longer required, or when records in a file have not been referred to in any way for some specified period (say three years), the whole file, or those parts of it that are no longer active, may be transferred to a historical file. The considerations here are that the data should be stored in a compact, organized form so that it can be referred to when needed. Immediate access speed will no longer be important as some delay will be acceptable to the user, and the most usual storage medium is magnetic tape. Optical or laser disk seems likely to replace tape in the near future.

Early systems often omitted to provide historical records. This can be annoying for the customer who completed a hire-purchase or credit transaction satisfactorily some years previously, but has to obtain new references because no record was kept. It can equally reduce the effectiveness of a new business campaign if the results of previous surveys or contacts were not retained. Now that cheap, massive storage facilities are available there is little excuse for not keeping adequate historical data.

Because of the limitations imposed on the organization of such files by the need for cheap, compact storage and the lack of urgency in referring to them, they will not be considered specifically in future chapters. They can be handled as is described for other files, and are in a sense merely 'old' master files.

Files are made up of records; some definitions relating to records are given below.

1.3 Data records

All the items of information that refer to a single customer, stock line or other basic logical unit of a particular job are held as a single entity described as a **record**. Records can be of *fixed length* or *variable length*. If a record is of fixed length, it is likely that all the items contained in the record will also be of fixed length. A record may be variable in length because some of its fields are of variable length, or because it contains a variable number of fields. A special form of variable-length record, known as *undefined*, is available in some computer systems. The reasons for deciding on fixed, variable or undefined record formats are given in Chapter 3 (*see* pp. 59 to 68).

Records are often *blocked*, i.e. stored in groups of more than one record. This is usually done to save space on magnetic tape or disk, or to increase the speed with which the records can be processed. As the decision to block records and the choice of block size can have a dramatic effect on file processing, blocking is considered in detail in Chapter 4. Blocks appear as shown in Fig. 1.1.

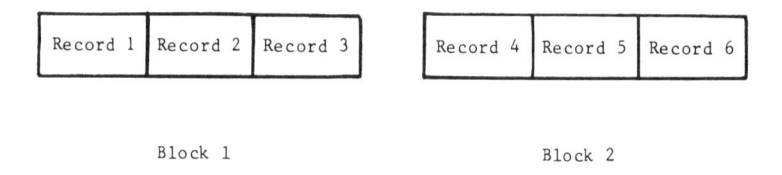

Record 1	Record 2	Record 3		Record 4	Record 5	Record 6

          Block 1   Block 2

Fig. 1.1 Fixed-length blocks of three records each.

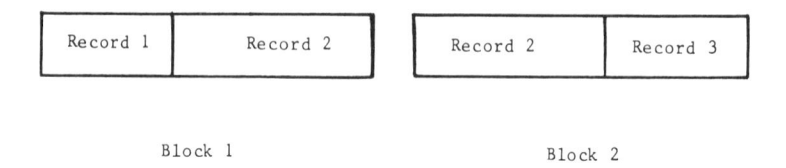

Record 1	Record 2		Record 2	Record 3

          Block 1   Block 2

Fig. 1.2 Fixed-length blocks with spanned records. Some file-handling software requires the spanned record to occupy all the first block and does not load other records into spare space in later blocks.

In some cases it is convenient to store records in the *spanned* form. This means that part of a record is held in one block and part in another, as shown in Fig. 1.2. This form of record storage is very useful in the case where a few records are much larger than the average in a file. Rather than provide a very large input-output area that would only be filled by these few unusual records, it is more efficient to split up the records themselves into parts.

1.4 Data fields

Records are made up of data fields, each of which holds one separate item of the record. These items of information can be referred to separately, and will be held in a particular place in a record. Each item is called a **field** or **data field**. In a personnel record, for example, these fields might include:

personnel number;
name;
age;
sex;
marital status;
address;
date of joining the company;
present position;
previous position(s);
present rate of pay;
special skills, etc.

The most important field in a record is generally its reference key, which was defined earlier. In the example above the 'personnel number' would probably be selected as the key field. In some cases two or more fields may be used, separately or in combination, to identify the required record; an example might be department code and departmental personnel number.

The **field length** will depend upon the medium on which the information is held. On a punched card the field length is usually measured by the number of columns it takes up, although occasionally the card may be processed in half-columns. On a magnetic disk or tape the field length will usually be defined as a number of *bytes* (eight bits), *characters* (usually six or eight bits) or *words* (these may be twenty-four, thirty-two, thirty-six, forty-eight or sixty bits in length in different computer systems). In a few cases a field may be one or more *bits* (binary digits) of a character. If this is so, special programming techniques are used to select the bits required from the complete characters.

Field lengths may be *fixed* or *variable*. All stock numbers will usually contain the same number of digits, so a stock number field is likely to be of fixed length. A name field may be either fixed—in which case room must be left to store most possible names, very long ones being truncated—or variable, allowing just sufficient space for each name. The first alternative is wasteful of space but reduces programming problems. The second saves space at the expense of program complexity. The 'previous position' field in the personnel record shown above needs to be repeated a variable number of times, depending on how many positions the person has held in the company. Factors that determine whether the overall record is of fixed or variable format will be discussed in Chapter 3 (*see* p. 59).

1.5 File organization

In order to be able to reference a desired record in a file it is usually helpful to have the records arranged in some predictable way. This requires some sort of pattern or organization, and the arrangements of records that are dealt with in this book are given below.

Serial files

In this case, records are not arranged in any organized way; this would apply when records are being input into a sort program, for example. The only way in which the records can be logically processed is serially, i.e. in the order in which they have been stored on the device; hence the name of the serial file 'organization'.

Sequential files

The output from a sort program will be arranged in an ascending or descending sequence of records, based on the contents of one or more control or key fields such as personnel or stock numbers. The sort may be in alphabetic, numeric or alphanumeric sequence. Most sequential files are sorted into ascending key sequence.

In order to access a record it is now only necessary to search through the file, starting from the beginning, until the desired key is found. If a higher key is detected before the record is found, then there is either a sequence error or the record is not in the file. In most cases the file is checked for sequence errors by the file organization software during loading, so usually the reason the record is not found is that it is not in the file.

It is of interest to compare sequential and serial files for average serial search times. For both types of file, a *successful search* in which the record is found will require that half the file is searched on average. However, if the record is not found, the sequential file will still demand an average search of only half the file before a higher key is detected, while the serial file has to be searched from start to finish. More rapid search techniques are available for sequential files, and they are described in Chapter 5 (*see* p. 118); serial file searching cannot be speeded up because there is no underlying order in the records that can be exploited.

Sequential files are used in many data processing applications, but they are not efficient when used in enquiry systems because the address of any record is not usually directly obtainable from its key; it is only possible to locate a record by using the overall record key sequence. This has led to the development of other file organization techniques.

Direct or random files

When an enquiry is made the system is usually presented with a record *key* such as a personnel number. However, the *address* of the record on the backing storage device is needed in order to retrieve it. To do this there has to be some connection between the key and the address and the ways in which this can be arranged are discussed in Chapter 6. The file organization is described as *direct* to indicate that it is possible to retrieve a record directly by using its key, without considering the position of this key in the overall key sequence. It is sometimes described as *random*, because the records are not usually stored in a sequence but randomized to individual storage positions. As discussed in Chapter 6 (*see* p. 157), there is usually an underlying pattern in the way in which records are stored, even though the sequence is not obvious if the record keys are printed out in their stored order. Any underlying pattern can have a marked effect on the efficiency of direct files, and for this reason the term 'random' will not be used further to describe the direct file organization technique.

A well-designed direct file will give a more rapid response to random enquiries than any other type of file. However, there is no substitute for knowledge and careful planning in the design of such a file; each individual case differs from every other, if only slightly, so that manufacturers' software cannot carry out the majority of the work for the file designer. As the ultimate performance of an enquiry system is limited by the average time required to access any given record, efficient design provides a significantly better enquiry-throughput potential than inefficient design. Users who employ database software or other file organization techniques for enquiry systems may find their programming effort reduced, and may also obtain security benefits. However, the maximum throughput of their system will be very much lower than would be the case if they used a directly organized file.

Many applications require both a sequential and a direct processing capability. Although direct files can be processed sequentially, the resultant run times will be far longer than would be achieved using a sequential file. Conversely, a sequentially organized file will give a relatively poor performance for direct retrieval. This has led to the development of a further standard type of file that can provide both retrieval methods.

Indexed sequential files

A file that is loaded in key sequence, but can be accessed directly by the use of one or more indices, is known as an indexed sequential file. This is, in many ways, a compromise file organization technique. It is usually slower than a sequential file for sequential retrieval, and access times for direct retrieval are greater than for a well-designed directly organized file.

The advantages of this type of file are that it can handle the requirements of mixed-access applications very much better than the other two types of file organization, and that most manufacturers provide the user with comprehensive software to aid the file designer. Thus the design effort involved in using this type of file organization is far less than that required for direct files. However, the design of indexed sequential files can still be significantly improved by careful planning (*see* Chapter 7).

The general nature of manufacturers' software, reflecting the generality of the routines they have to provide to cover the needs of all likely users, has led to software houses offering 'improved' versions of indexed sequential files that can provide benefits in some conditions. This also is discussed in Chapter 7.

The file organization techniques described above cover most typical data processing requirements. There are a number of other specialized techniques suited to particular applications, and some of the more important of these are discussed in Chapter 8.

1.6 Accessing data files

Even though a file is *organized* in a particular way, this does not prevent it being *accessed* in a different way. Any of the three most frequently used types of file:

sequential;
indexed sequential;
direct;

can be accessed, i.e. referred to, directly, serially or sequentially. A direct file may be printed out serially in order to discover just what records are present in the file or to check the pattern of key distribution in the file. It can be printed out sequentially by supplying keys in sequential order, and so accessing the records in that order. A sequential file can be accessed directly by searching through the whole file for a given key, and only providing information from that record. The system or run designer is thus able to refer to records in any given order without concern for the file organization adopted, except that there may be a considerable loss of efficiency. The description of various forms of file access is as follows.

Update

A record is updated when one or more fields is changed by the addition or subtraction of information. In the general sense, updating also includes some of the following definitions[1], but they are given here for completeness and because they will be used later.

Addition

When a new record is added to a file it is an addition. It will be fitted into its correct place in the key sequence of a sequential or indexed sequential file. In the case of a direct file the record will be stored after its key has been examined and transformed in some appropriate way into an address.

Deletion

When a record is removed from a file it is said to be deleted. On direct access devices the record is often not physically removed as this might then require an average of half the file to be moved up to fill the vacant space. The record may be *tagged* for deletion by setting an indicator in a suitable field, and removed when the file is next reorganized or when an appropriate opportunity occurs such as moving the record into an overflow area. In magnetic tape files, however, the deletion takes place at once as a new file is created on each run.

Accessing

This word is used in two senses. The first is that of referring to a record without changing it in any way. The second, which is adopted in this book, describes reference to a record whether it is to be updated, deleted or used only for reference.

1.7 Data file terminology

Hit

A hit is a record that needs to be accessed; in a sequential file that is being updated it corresponds to a master record for which there is an update. Non-hit records are those for which there is no update.

Hit rate (or hit ratio)

The hit rate in a particular run is defined as:

$$\frac{\text{number of records accessed}}{\text{number of records in the file}}$$

Hit rate is usually quoted as a percentage. It is likely to vary from run to run, and often in other ways, e.g. in a weekly or seasonal cycle. Some authors use the term *activity ratio* for hit rate[2]. It is generally agreed, though, that it is a very useful parameter in file design[3]. Its application to file design is considered in later chapters.

Fan-in/Fan-out ratio

This is defined as:

$$\frac{\text{number of accesses}}{\text{number of records hit}}$$

It is a measure of the number of times each hit record is accessed; cases where this affects file design will be given and discussed in subsequent chapters.

Volatility

This is a measure of the changes in a file with time. It is the ratio:

$$\frac{\text{number of additions} + \text{number of deletions}}{\text{number of records in the file at the start}}$$

A highly volatile file may not repay the same degree of design analysis as a more static file, because conclusions drawn from the earlier set of records making up the file may no longer apply to the later set; thus the designer needs to know how volatile the file is, or at least to have some idea of its likely values.

Growth rate

In allowing space for a file it is essential to know whether the file is growing in size and if so by how much. In planning for the expansion of a file, the strategy adopted for deletions is important. Where space is made available by deletions, only the *real growth* of the file needs to be considered, i.e. additions minus deletions. This allows the designer to provide just enough space for the actual growth expected.

If deletions are merely tagged for later removal, the *apparent growth* will be the total of all additions, and on reorganization the file will become smaller due to deletions. However, in this case the designer will have to allow sufficient space for the file at its largest, i.e. before deletions have been removed.

1.8 Computer storage

A number of different terms are used to describe the storage facilities available in computer systems. The definitions used in this book will be as follows.

Main storage

This is the storage situated in the central processing unit of a computer. It is also sometimes described as *primary storage*[4], *primary memory*[5] or *immediate access storage*. Main storage may be organized into a hierarchy of segments of varying access speeds. These segments may use a variety of different storage media, although MOS (metal oxide semiconductor) chips are now the most common. The operation of main storage is outside the scope of this book, although readers should be aware that single operations can usually be carried out in times of the order of 1–200 nanoseconds. More details of the make-up, operation and speed of main storage are available elsewhere[6, 7].

Main storage is used to hold programs, data for immediate processing, and control information. Because of its high-speed handling of information it would be a desirable storage medium for data files, but as yet the cost of the required quantity of such storage with its necessary accessing and control circuitry makes this impracticable. In addition, it provides temporary rather than permanent storage, as anybody who has lost data due to a power failure or some similar problem will know. The need for large-capacity file storage is met by the means described below.

Backing storage

Information such as that held in data files is only brought into main storage when it is required. At other times it is held on magnetic tape or direct access devices such as magnetic disks or mass storage devices. Backing storage is also known as *secondary storage*[4] or *secondary memory*[5]. Choice of backing storage has a major effect on the cost, speed and design of files; in principle they could be held on punched cards or paper tape, but because of the slow rate at which data can be read from or punched into them, these media are not normally used for anything other than entering data into the system. For this reason files are most often stored on magnetic tapes, disks or mass storage devices, all of which are capable of transferring data rapidly to and from the central processing unit, and are able to hold large quantities of information.

The way in which a storage device operates will affect the speed with which any given record can be located in a file held on the device. Magnetic tapes are serial devices in that a file has to be traversed record by record to locate any given record. If a tape is positioned so that the first record in the file is available and the required record is the last one on the tape, it will take one or more minutes to reach it. Meanwhile many other records in the file will have passed under the reading heads, even though they were not required.

Magnetic disks and mass storage devices were designed to allow the user to refer to any given record directly without having to traverse unwanted records. There will still be some delay in locating a desired record, due to the way the device operates mechanically, but this delay will be between a fiftieth of a second and eleven seconds, rather than one or more minutes. For this reason they are described as direct access devices.

In assessing the use that can be made of a particular device, the designer needs to know the average time it will take to access a record. This is shown

12 Design of computer data files

Table 1.1 Typical values of the factors given at the top of each column, and discussed in the text. (ms = milliseconds, k = 1000, M = 1 000 000.)

Device	Average direct access time	Average sequential access time	Typical data transfer rates
Magnetic tape	1–3 minutes	2–10 ms	150 k–3.0 M characters per second
Magnetic disk (moving heads)	16–70 ms	8–12 ms (Can be improved by file design)	800 k–3.0 M characters per second
Magnetic disk (fixed heads)	2.5–10 ms	2.5–10 ms	1.5–3.0 M characters per second
Semiconductor 'disks'	0.3–0.4 ms	0.3–0.4 ms	1.5–4.0 M characters per second

as the *average direct access time* in Table 1.1. The *average sequential access time*, also given in Table 1.1, is less generally used. It gives a measure of the time required to access a record when a file is being processed sequentially. The *data transfer rate* indicates how fast data is transferred after the record has already been located. It does not include any access time. Table 1.1 shows typical values of these three measures of performance for a number of commonly used devices.

The operation of backing storage devices and the speed with which data held on them can be located and transferred into main storage are described in detail in Chapter 2.

1.9 File processing

Users very often ask for 'immediate' access to information. The file designer has to decide whether this need is a real one—as when counter staff are answering customer requests by accessing a computer data file—or is an expression of the user's sense of urgency. In the first case the system must be designed to cater for continual enquiries and will basically be a direct access application. In the second, very occasional enquiries might be answered directly but most users will have to expect a delay in handling their requests.

The reasons the file designer is likely to advise against providing a direct access file unless it is fully justified are these. First, a greater throughput of processing is possible if records are processed sequentially rather than directly—this is looked at in more detail in Chapter 5 (*see* p. 107). Second, data security is simply and comprehensively arranged in sequentially organized files, while more careful planning is needed if directly organized files are to be made as secure (*see* Chapter 10 for details).

It was pointed out earlier that any file, however it is organized and on whatever device it is stored, can be accessed directly. The average direct access time, or average time to reach a record held on any part of the device, is given in Table 1.1. From this it is clear that a file held on magnetic tape would only be referenced directly in exceptional circumstances. A wait of one to three minutes for the answer to an urgent request is not in itself unreasonable. However, the fact that this implies a throughput of only twenty to sixty enquiries an hour makes magnetic tape an unsatisfactory medium to hold a file that is intended for any significant volume of direct references.

Average sequential access times are also given in Table 1.1. These show the average time it will take to retrieve the next record available on the file. Magnetic tape compares very well with direct access devices in this mode of retrieval, which is why it is so widely used to store sequentially organized files. The occasions when tape is not a suitable medium to hold a sequential file are examined in detail in Chapter 5 (*see* p. 109).

Sequential processing

If a master file is arranged in ascending (or descending) key order, any required record in the file can be located by running through the records until the required key is found. In order to cut down the length of the search for each new record, a group of updates will need to be collected and sorted into the same key order as the master file before updating is carried out. This implies a wait until a large enough group of updates has accumulated.

Sometimes updates quite naturally occur in groups—an example of this is the morning or afternoon delivery of mail. Payments will be received in a random order in the day's mail and thus they make up a natural group, or *batch*, of updates. Telephone enquiries for insurance quotes, on the other hand, occur in chronological order and may be given priority for that reason or on some other basis, perhaps probable value. If batches of these enquiries are made up, a large batch will mean a longer average wait for an answer, so batch size will be a compromise between rapid answering of queries, which would require small batches, and processing efficiency, which is enhanced if batches are large. The effect of batch size is shown in Fig. 1.3.

Batch processing is a two-stage process. The updates have first to be sorted into order and are then used to update the master file. This is shown in Fig. 1.4. Although sequential updating of a master file appears simple, there can be problems in designing a run. Dwyer[8] pointed out that the order in which additions, updates and deletions are applied to a file can be crucial, as an addition must precede updates to or deletion of a given record. Inglis[9] discussed the case in which a record may be treated by some users as if it had been deleted and replaced, while others believe it to be in its original state. Levy[10] presents an alternative solution to sequential file updating that is particularly suited to modular programs. In addition to run design con-

14 Design of computer data files

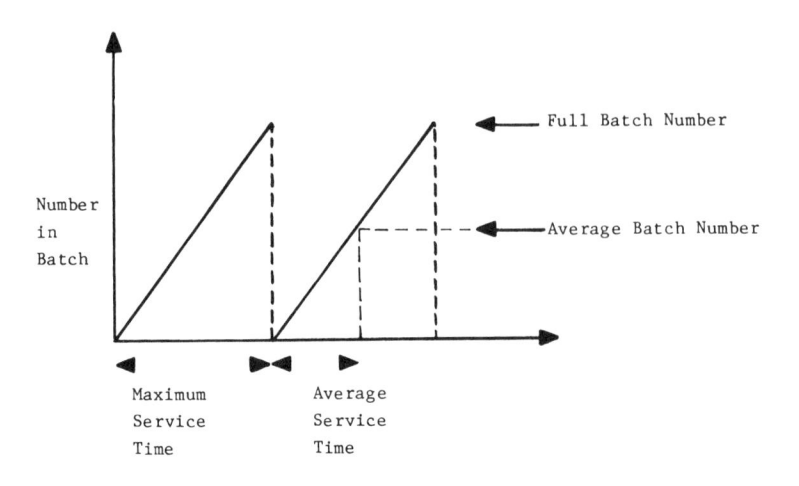

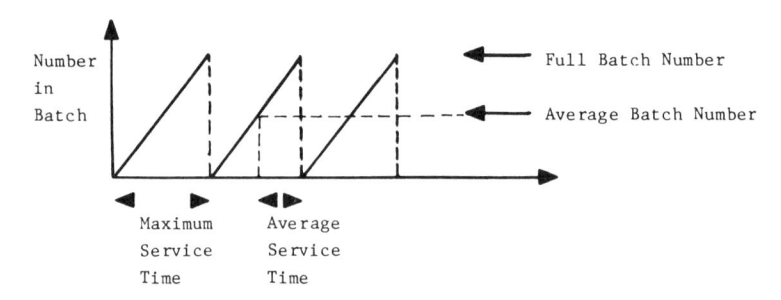

Fig. 1.3 The average number in the batch is the number of references to the file that are being held up on average at any one time due to the batching process. In the same way, the average service time is the time a reference to the file will have to wait on average before it is serviced. The smaller batch number provides a shorter average and maximum enquiry time. Because it allows a higher throughput of work, the file designer will usually decide on as large a batch size as is acceptable to the users.

siderations, a number of steps can be taken to optimise sequential file processing; they are examined in Chapter 5.

Direct processing

This is a great deal simpler in concept than batch processing. There is no need to wait for batches to be built up, because updates or enquiries can be handled as they arise. This allows the user to get a very rapid response, so long as the system can handle the total volume of enquiries input to it. We shall see later that the ability of the system to handle peak loads, as well as the average load throughout the day, becomes a vital factor in design.

An introduction to file design 15

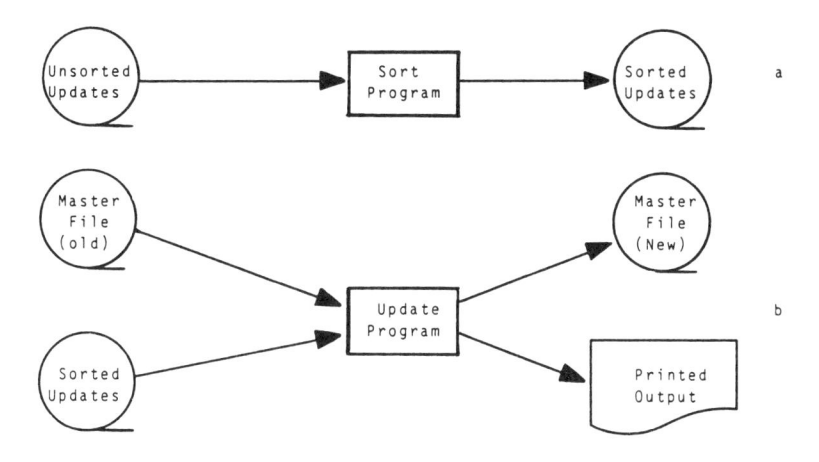

Fig. 1.4 Batch processing, showing the two-stage nature of the update procedure. (a) The unsorted input is sorted into master file order. (b) The master file is updated using the sorted updates, producing the output required by the user.

This mode of processing is used in enquiry systems and considerably enhances system performance in some other cases. An example of this might be accounts prepared on the basis of orders which are sorted into customer number sequence and run against a customer master list. If this job is to be carried out using sequential files, it becomes a four-stage process. First, the unsorted orders have to be sorted into item order, so that prices can be inserted from a price list—which is usually held in stock item order—and the total cost of price times quantity, less any discount, and plus any tax or other addition, can be calculated. This is followed by re-sorting the priced orders into customer number order, to allow production of invoices from the orders and the customer file. The process is shown in Fig. 1.5.

An alternative is to provide a prices file that can be referenced directly during the updating run, cutting the four stages of a sequential system to two, as the orders have only to be sorted into customer number order. This is shown in Fig. 1.6.

This process can be cut to a single stage if the customer file is also capable of being directly processed. The form of the run is shown in Fig. 1.7; note that, although an individual customer invoice may well be prepared more quickly than in the earlier runs, the system may not be able to handle so many customers. Direct processing is a simpler-looking process than batch processing, but it does not follow that it is always more suitable. It often happens that batching small numbers of updates before processing will improve the performance of an indexed sequential file, and sometimes this can also apply to direct files. This is discussed in later chapters.

16 Design of computer data files

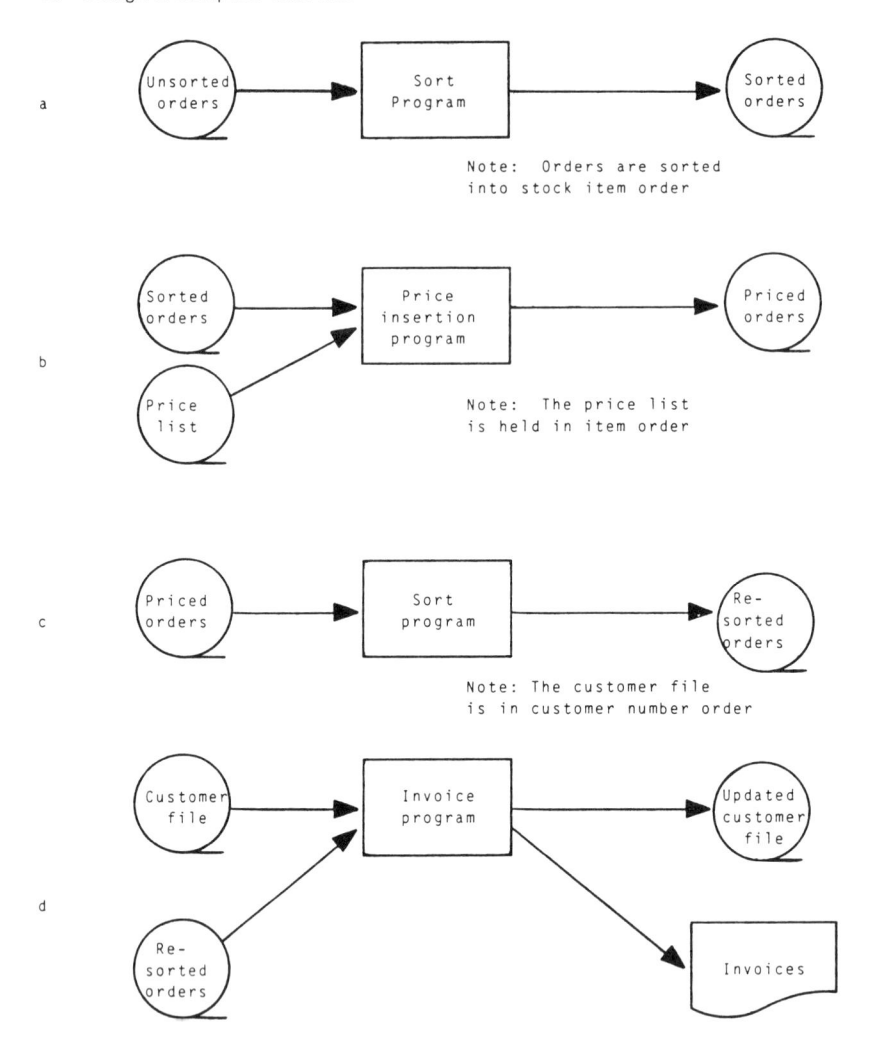

Fig. 1.5 An invoicing run using sequential files only. (a) Orders are sorted to stock item order. (b) Prices are recorded on orders, and totals may be calculated, in preparation for the invoicing run. (c) Orders are re-sorted into customer number order. (d) Invoices are prepared for despatch to customers.

As pointed out earlier, the three main file organization techniques in use are:

sequential;
indexed sequential;
direct.

Of these, the sequential technique is useful only for sequential processing

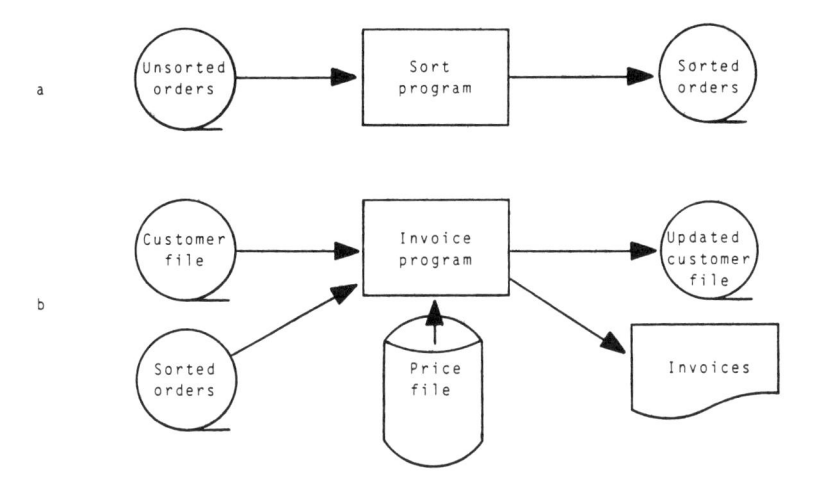

Fig. 1.6 By storing prices on a file that can be accessed directly, two runs are saved in comparison with the process shown in Fig. 1.5. (a) Orders are sorted into customer number order. (b) Orders are matched with customer records, and the prices are inserted by direct reference to the price list. Invoices are produced for each customer for whom there is an order, while updated or unchanged customer records are used as appropriate to provide the new version of the customer file.

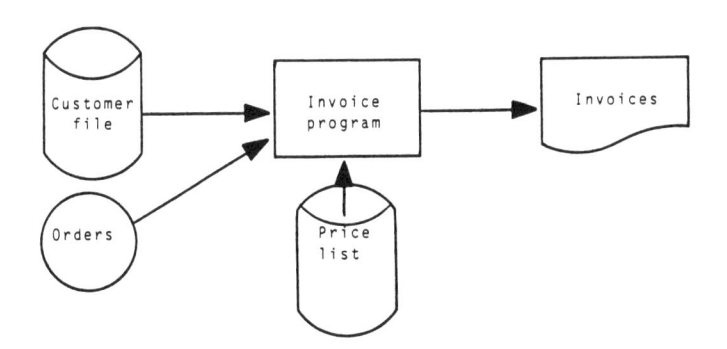

Fig. 1.7 As the price list and the customer file are both directly accessible, the complete process can be carried out in a single process. Note that the updated customer records are usually placed in their original positions, and records that are not required are not read.

and very limited enquiries. Direct organization is only used for direct accessing of files, with very occasional sequential processing. Indexed sequential files provide a useful compromise, as both sequential and direct processing of files organized in this way can be fairly efficient. These techniques are examined in detail in Chapters 5, 6 and 7, and the way in which the file designer chooses between them is discussed in Chapter 9.

Conclusion

In this chapter most of the concepts that are involved in a general study of file design have been defined or described. More specific concepts necessary in the discussion of individual file organization techniques will be introduced and defined in the appropriate chapters.

References

1. *Basic Training in Systems Analysis*, edited by Alan Daniels and Donald Yeates, Pitman (for NCC), 1971, Chapter 5.
2. *A Dictionary of Computers*, by Anthony Chandor, Penguin, 1970.
3. 'File design fallacies', by S. J. Waters, *Computer Journal*, Vol. 15, No. 1, pp. 1–4.
4. *Introduction to Operating System Design*, by A. N. Habermann, Science Research Associates, 1976.
5. *Software Systems Principles*, by Peter Freeman, Science Research Associates, 1975.
6. *Digital Computer Fundamentals*, by Thomas C. Bartee, McGraw-Hill, 1977.
7. *Microchip Technology: the past and the future*, by Charles Kerridge, John Wiley and Sons, 1983.
8. 'One more time—how to update a master file', by Barry Dwyer, *CACM*, Vol. 24, No. 1, January 1981, pp. 3–8.
9. 'Updating a master file-yet one more time', by J. Inglis, *CACM*, Vol. 24, No. 5, May 1981, p. 299.
10. 'Modularity and the sequential file update problem', by Michael R. Levy, *CACM*, Vol. 25, No. 6, June 1982, pp. 362–367.

Revision questions

1 What do you understand by the terms: file; record; data field; master file; update file; reference file; archive file; fixed-length record; variable-length record; undefined record; blocked and unblocked records; bit; character; byte; word; field; field length; serial file; sequential file; direct file; indexed sequential file; accessing files; update; addition; deletion; hit rate; fan in; fan out; volatility; growth rate; main storage; backing storage; batch; batch number; service time; average direct access time; average sequential access time; data transfer rate; batch processing; direct processing?

2 Explain the meaning of *field length* applied to records stored on: punched cards; magnetic tape; magnetic disk; visual display units (VDUs).

3 Set out the main file organizations, and the possible methods by which they can be accessed. Make clear the differences between accessing and file organization and explain how they are related.

4 What types of storage do you know of? Discuss the cost, speed and usage of the types you have described.

5 Where do many terms used in file handling come from? Describe the way in which business records were kept before the advent of computers.

6 Describe and discuss batch processing, emphasizing the advantages and disadvantages of this procedure.

7 Describe direct processing. What form of file organization is required to allow a file to be processed directly? When is it worth processing a file directly, and when not?

8 Explain the types of file you would expect to find in a batch processing run. Draw a diagram of the process as you understand it.

9 Explain the types of file you would expect to find used in an invoicing run. Give three alternative run diagrams showing how the process can be carried out.

10 Why is it important to arrange that additions, updates and deletions are handled in the correct sequence? Give a number of sequences, some correct and some not, explaining why they are correct or otherwise.

2 Review of backing storage devices

2.1 Introduction

An understanding of the way in which backing storage devices operate and the speeds at which they transfer data is essential to the file designer. This brief review brings together data on all the most important devices, to assist the designer in obtaining optimum results.

The devices most used today are magnetic disk and magnetic tape. Coverage in this chapter is intended to explain the way in which they operate, how to calculate the time required to access and process records stored on them, and the range of devices available.

Magnetic drums have not been supplied as new equipment since 1985, when Sperry-Univac dropped them. As the timing considerations for this type of device are related to those for disk storage, they have not been dealt with here. By contrast, floppy disks are discussed because of their growing importance in word processing, data preparation and microcomputer systems. Cassette tapes are discussed for the same reasons. In addition, IBM's latest mainframe tape device—the 3480—uses cassettes.

The advent of very large integrated file systems and of databases has led to the growing use of mass storage devices. For this reason a section is included on them. Optical disks and semiconductor 'disks' are steadily becoming more important, and they too are reviewed below.

The earliest widely used storage device was magnetic tape, and a survey[1] in 1978 showed that only 9 per cent of users were reducing their purchases of tapes, while 45 per cent were increasing their usage. Since then the move to fixed rather than removable disks has meant that tape provides the most convenient backup medium for remote data storage. In addition, the advent of the IBM 3480 and the Memorex 6520 tape cache processor mark an updating of tape technology. Thus it is still very important, and will be examined first.

2.2 Magnetic tape

The main reasons for the continuing popularity of magnetic tape are that it is:

cheap—a full-size tape costs only $10–20;

compact—a single tape can hold as much data as several hundred boxes of cards—over 200 megabytes of data for the 3480.

convenient—modern tapes are easily loaded, and can be stored in racks or cupboards designed to hold large number of reels or 3480 cassettes when they are not in use.

The main drawback of tape is that it can only be referenced serially, but it is such a convenient medium for storing serial and sequential files and for security dumps that it is still used in most large computer installations. Only microcomputer systems use an alternative—floppy disks—because large volumes of storage are not usually required in such installations. Even in this case hard disks are often backed up using tape cassettes, and in business installations this practice is likely to grow.

Physical characteristics

Most tapes are half an inch wide, about one and a half thousandths of an inch thick and 300, 600, 1200 or 2400-feet long. Tapes used to store data files are generally of the 2400 foot length; shorter tapes are useful for user or software program storage. The reels used are 6.25, 7.00, 8.50 or 10.50 inches in diameter depending on tape length; the standard reel size is the last of these. The 3480 uses cassettes that are roughly 1 inch thick, 4 inches deep and 5 inches wide, containing 500 feet of tape.

The recording medium is usually a thin layer of ferrous oxide, although some modern tapes use either chromium dioxide or a mixture of the two. This is held on a tough, flexible plastic base (usually Mylar) by an adhesive or binder. The properties of the tape depend on the base material, the coating, the binder and the coating process. Care of tape for optimum performance is important, and is discussed later in this chapter.

Earlier tapes were loaded manually, but many installations now use cartridges that hold the tape and provide automatic threading. If these are not available, tape guides to simplify and speed threading are often available.

Recording data

Characters are usually written in parallel, meaning that the six or eight bits of the character and its associated parity bit make up a single strip across the tape, which is consequently described as seven- or nine-track. Some cassette tapes record bits serially, but those likely to hold files of any size use the parallel recording mode. The 3480 records on 18 tracks across the half-inch width of the tape.

The format of a character on an IBM nine-track tape is shown in Fig. 2.1.

Three modes of recording are in common use. The first is called NRZI, short for *non-return to zero on ones* (or 'Invert'). In this mode a one bit is

22 Design of computer data files

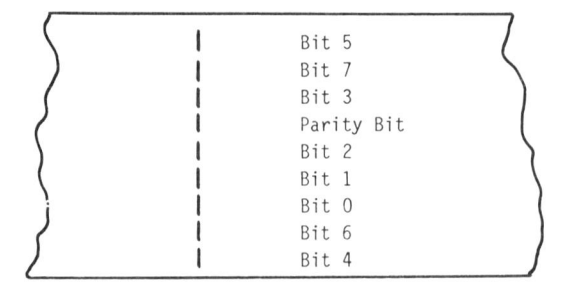

```
⎫             |    Bit 5      ⎧
 ⎬            |    Bit 7      
 ⎬            |    Bit 3      ⎬
 ⎬            |    Parity Bit 
 ⎬            |    Bit 2      ⎬
 ⎬            |    Bit 1      
 ⎬            |    Bit 0      ⎬
 ⎬            |    Bit 6      
⎭             |    Bit 4      ⎩
```

Fig. 2.1 A single nine-bit character on an IBM tape. Note the arrangement of bits. Those bits that are most frequently changed magnetically are stored in the centre of the tape to minimize the possibility of mechanical damage due to contact with the reel, thus leading to mis-reads.

represented by a change of magnetic polarity and a zero bit by no change. Although NRZI mode is widely used, it has led to problems caused by magnetic dust. The process of reading and writing tapes leads to some of the magnetic coating being abraded from the surface, so that a great deal of magnetic dust is present on and around the tape. Particles are attracted to the magnetized spots on the surface, take up a magnetic charge and appear to the read/write heads to be a one bit in a position that would otherwise be recognized as a zero bit, or the reverse.

To counter this problem, *phase-encoded* tapes (PE for short) are widely used, although they require more expensive drives or controllers. In this mode a one bit is indicated by a given level of magnetization, a zero bit by a second level, and both of these differ from the blank reading. Only levels of magnetization within fixed limits are recognized as bits, while all other levels are treated as noise and ignored. Some tapes use a modified form of PE called group coded recording, or GCR.

Phase-encoded tapes usually require a synchronization signal at the start and end of each block of data. For example, the 8809 tape unit used in IBM's 4300 and 8100 series computers requires forty-one-byte blocks arranged as shown in Fig. 2.2.

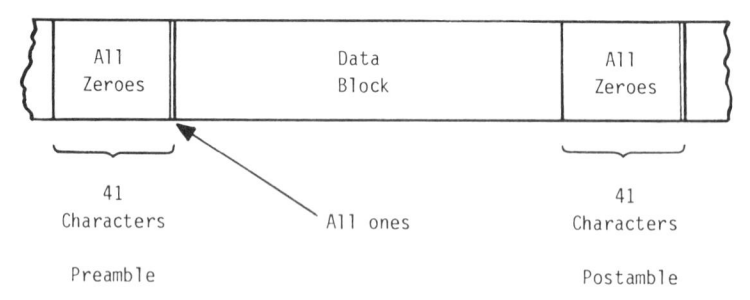

```
⎧   All    ‖              ‖   All    ⎫
⎨  Zeroes  ‖  Data Block  ‖  Zeroes  ⎬
⎩          ‖              ‖          ⎭
      ⎯⎯⎯⎯⎯⎯⎯⎯                ⎯⎯⎯⎯⎯⎯⎯⎯
         41                      41
      Characters    All ones   Characters

        Preamble               Postamble
```

Fig. 2.2 The preamble and postamble synchronization fields are made up of forty-one bytes, the first forty being all zeros and the last all ones.

As many installations still have files or data stored on both types of tape, or may require to be able to read tapes from other sources, it is usual for at least some versions of PE tape drives to have a feature that allows them to read and write in NRZI and in seven-track as well as nine-track format. If a nine-track tape is used in seven-track format, two potential bit storage positions are wasted for each character position. Honeywell's MTU 0400, 0500 and 0600 drives, and ICL's MT-320T in compress-expand mode exploit this by using all the bit positions, so achieving a higher character transfer rate and storage density for seven-bit characters. The arrangement is shown in Fig. 2.3.

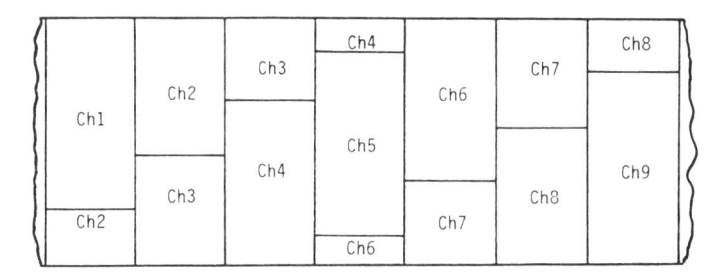

Fig. 2.3 Storage of nine 7-bit characters in the same space as seven 9-bit characters.

Characters are recorded so that there are 200, 556, 800, 1600, 3200 or 6250 characters per inch of tape. This is known as *recording density*. Lower densities may be used for tapes or cassettes that provide low transfer rates of data to or from main storage. The cassette tapes used with the IBM 3480 are stored at 38 000 bytes per inch.

Reading and writing data

Magnetic tape can only be read or written on when it is travelling at a fixed speed. This varies from about 75 to 200 inches per second for most tape drives, although cassette tapes may require a much lower speed.

When the tape starts from rest it cannot be accelerated instantaneously to the required speed. Some time will elapse, and a certain length of tape will be traversed, before the operating speed is reached. This leads to the presence of an *inter-block gap* between each block of data, as shown in Fig. 2.4.

Typically these gaps will be 0.6 inch on nine-track tapes and 0.75 inch on seven-track; higher-density tapes have IBGs (inter-block gaps) of around 0.3 inch, while the 3480 has an effective IBG of 0.08 inch, and slow or lower-density tapes may have larger gaps.

Because the space taken up by IBGs is wasted, in the sense that no useful data is stored in it, manufacturers attempt to keep these gaps as small as

24 Design of computer data files

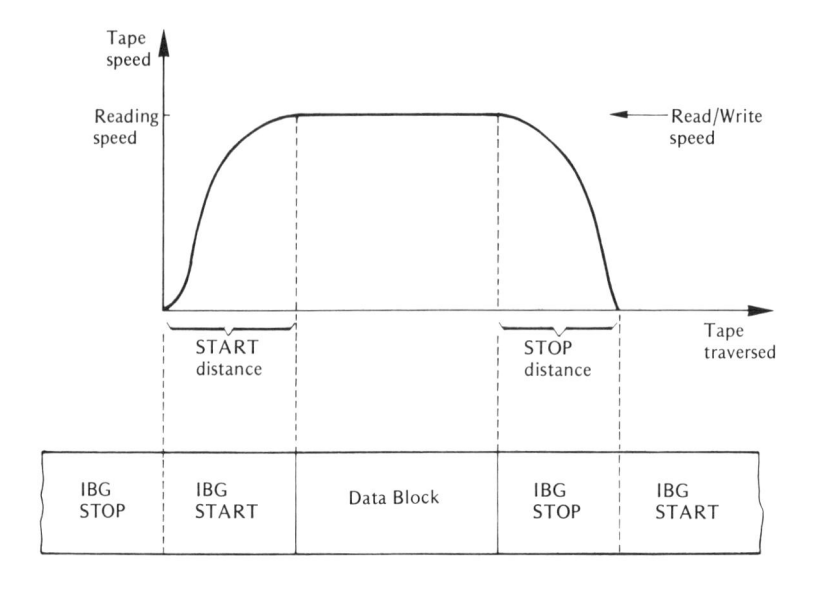

Fig. 2.4 The relationship between tape read–write operations and the size of inter-block gaps.

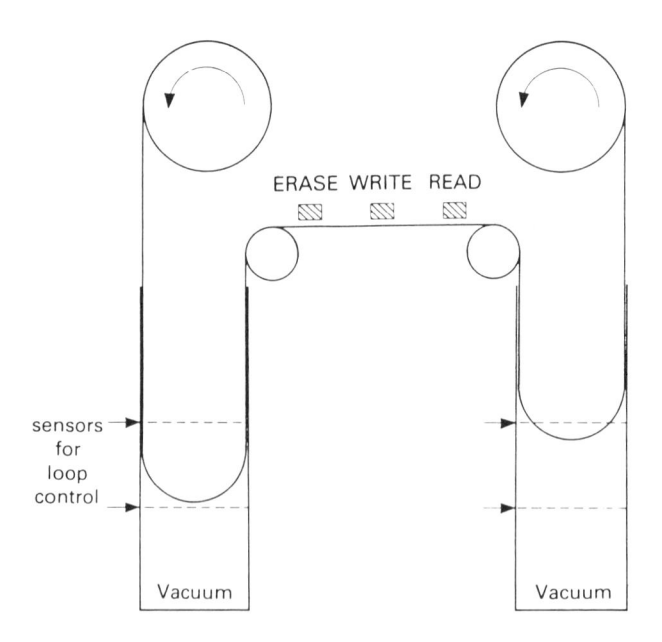

Fig. 2.5 A simplified diagram of a conventional tape drive, showing vacuum loops, loop control and read, write and erase heads.

possible. The familiar vacuum loops shown in Fig. 2.5 are provided to isolate the small length of tape being read or written at any time from the relatively bulky feed and take-up reels. Provision of these loops means that only a short length of tape has to be accelerated or stopped, and the weight of the reels does not affect the process; the capstans that do this have air bearings to minimize friction.

The importance of these precautions is emphasized by the fact that accelerations and decelerations of more than 1000 g occur during starting and stopping of the tape. The loops provide a 'reservoir' of tape; when they grow too large or small, electronic sensors stop or start the reels to correct the loop size.

Some modern tape drives such as the IBM 8809 and the NCR 7330 are more compact than older drives. This is achieved by using electronic control of tape motion and dispensing with loops. The tapes are top-mounted, as shown in Fig. 2.6. However, apart from the 3480 these are relatively slow tapes with a transfer rate in *normal operating mode*, i.e. starting and stopping between data blocks, of 20 000 bytes per second A different mode, known as *streaming* is available to transfer data to and from main storage at 160 000 bytes per second. Even at this transfer rate, the tape speed is as low as 100 inches per second. Because there are no vacuum loops it is not possible to use a high tape-traverse speed, and the start time after a stop is relatively long. The 3480 is one of these microcomputer controlled tapes, and achieves very high performance—despite a tape passing speed of only 79 inches per second—due to the 38 000 bytes per inch it is possible to store on the chromium dioxide coated tape (conventional tapes use iron oxides).

So long as the next read or write command is given before a certain critical point is reached, which depends on the tape drive in use, IBGs will be traversed at reading speeds. For this reason tape read commands should be issued as early as possible in the sequence of the processing program. If this critical point is passed before the read command is given, a longer start time may be required. Some manufacturers arrange that the tape accelerates to a speed greater than that required and then slows down to operating speed, so giving a more rapid start time and avoiding loss of time due to missing the critical point. For example, Univac's Uniservo tapes show a difference between traverse and start-stop times; some of IBM's tapes show a similar difference, while others do not.

Rewinding of tapes is carried out at higher speeds than reading or writing. Even so, a full rewind will take nearly a minute, and it can be as long as three minutes for some drives. Unloading, i.e. removing the tension on the tape and the vacuum loops, usually adds some time to this. Overall performance figures for a number of drives are given in Table 2.1.

The data transfer speeds quoted in manufacturers' publications refer to reading or writing at operating speeds, and are sometimes described as *instantaneous data transfer speeds*. The need to traverse IBGs means that these speeds can never be achieved in practice for a file made up of many

26 Design of computer data files

Table 2.1 The figures given here show the range of values that can be expected from tape drives available at present. A large part of the tape market is made up of IBM or plug-compatible tape drives. Users are generally able to start from the figures given for an IBM tape drive, and compare the performance of all the competing models; the same process applies for Univac tapes, although there are fewer alternative suppliers.

Tape type			Vacuum-loop tapes Various versions of the 3420					Non-loop tapes		
								8809	3480-11	3480-22
Transfer rate (kbytes per second)			60	120	160	320	1250	20/160	1500	3000
Inter-block gap (inches)	PE NRZI		0.6 0.75	0.6 0.75	0.6 0.75	0.6	0.3	0.6	0.08	0.08
IBG traverse time (ms)	non-stop start-stop		8–14 8–20	6–10 9–10	5–8 8	3–5 3–8	1.5 1.5	6 48	1.1 1.1	1.1 1.1
Rewind times (seconds)			50–180	50–120	36–120	36–60	45–65	156	48	48

Fig. 2.6 IBM 8809 showing top mounting.

separate blocks of data, and the actual speeds reached depend on record size and numbers of records in a block. Blocking factors also affect the quantity of data that can be held on a tape, and their effect is relatively greater on high-density tapes, so blocking is very important in tape operations; the effects of blocking are analysed in Chapter 4.

Tape drives

The device that holds the tape while it is in operation is called a *drive* (IBM), a *controller* (ICL), a *deck* (NCR), a *unit* (Unisys) or some similar name, and there is considerable overlap of nomenclature. For example, an IBM drive or set of drives requires a control unit: usually such a control unit is able to control up to eight drives.

The drive will contain a number of magnetic heads to carry out various functions. The tape usually first comes under an *erase head* that is used during write operations to remove any previously recorded data on the tape, ensuring that no unwanted information appears in the newly written record. The *write head* comes next and the *read head* last so that it can be used to read back data that has just been written, carry out a comparison with the data in main storage, and ensure that there has been no error during writing. The position of these heads was shown in Fig. 2.5.

Error checking

As a basic precaution against unintentional destruction of data, most tape drives arrange that tapes can only be written on if a *write protect ring* has been inserted in the reel—the mnemonic is 'no ring, no write'. Other systems require that the ring is removed to allow writing on the tape.

The outside edge of a tape is subjected to more physical stress than the centre, due to handling, touching the sides of reels, etc. So far as possible the bits that are most frequently altered magnetically are placed in the centre of the tape, so that maximum magnetic stress occurs at the places that are least physically stressed. The arrangement shown in Fig. 2.1 was decided upon as a result of a statistical analysis of the frequency with which particular bit positions are magnetically altered in IBM systems.

As explained earlier, dust causes most tape-read problems. To get over this the response of tape drives to a read error is to go through a cycle of attempts to read, followed by a cleaning cycle and further attempts to read. In the IBM 8809 tape drives, four read attempts are followed by a cleaning cycle; ten of these cycles are tried, after which some read operations are terminated and an error message is generated. Other read operations initiate a procedure known as *read-opposite-recovery*. This checks if the tape can be read backward instead of forward. Other tape drives try cycles of ten reads followed by a cleaning operation, the eleven steps being repeated ten times before a read error is registered.

All single-bit errors can be corrected in flight, that is during the read operation, by the use of parity bits. Checking using the parity bit included in each character is often called VRC or *vertical redundancy checking*. In addition an even parity character is recorded at the end of each block of data, referred to as LRC or *longitudinal redundancy checking*. This character is built up by treating the bits in each track of the block as part of a very long single field, and ensuring that an even number of bits are 'on' by setting the state of the bit in the LRC character to achieve this. This is shown in Fig. 2.7.

Tape format

The start and end of a tape are indicated either by a reflective spot or band on the tape, usually placed twelve to fifteen feet from the end to allow for threading on the reels, or by a hole in the tape. This latter method is usually used for cassettes.

This start marker may be followed by a *format identification burst* that indicates the recording mode (PE or NRZI) used for the tape and is separated from the first block of data by a normal inter-block gap.

If more than one file is stored on a tape the files are separated by a *tape mark*. The size and nature of this will depend on the system—in IBM's 8809 tape, for example, it consists of a 128-byte field.

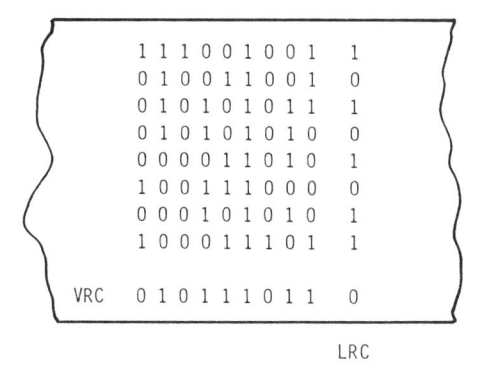

```
      1 1 1 0 0 1 0 0 1   1
      0 1 0 0 1 1 0 0 1   0
      0 1 0 1 0 1 0 1 1   1
      0 1 0 1 0 1 0 1 0   0
      0 0 0 0 1 1 0 1 0   1
      1 0 0 1 1 1 0 0 0   0
      0 0 0 1 0 1 0 1 0   1
      1 0 0 0 1 1 1 0 1   1
VRC   0 1 0 1 1 1 0 1 1   0
                  LRC
```

Fig. 2.7 An example of a short data block (nine bytes) with its associated VRC and LRC characters. Most modern tapes store far more error detection and correction data than this, and the user should check the facilities offered by any particular system before purchase.

Software functions

Commands are usually provided to allow the user to *forward space* a file (FSF), *backspace* a file (BSF), forward space one block or *n* blocks (FSB), or backward space one or more blocks (BSB). These operations are carried out at rewind speeds, and allow relatively rapid reference within a file, or from file to file, if the 'address', i.e. the block number, of a required block is known. The 3480 has a high-speed search facility; while the search goes on the drive is disconnected from the CPU, and the data is stored in a 512 Kbyte buffer attached to the tape drive as soon as it has been retrieved.

Reading backwards is possible on many systems, so avoiding the need to rewind the tape. In this case records or blocks are read backwards, but they are provided to the user program in the usual form as if read forwards. A file that is read backwards is read in descending key order if the records were stored in ascending key order when the file was created.

Shared channels/control units

Most tape drives can be accessed via two or more channels if the appropriate switching circuits are provided. A *two-channel switch* allows two input-output operations to be carried out at the same time. Alternatively, it allows one tape drive to be used as a link between two computers, as shown in Fig. 2.8. Modern control units can also generally be attached to two channels; this can be used either to allow two tape drives to operate at the same time— one reading while the other writes, for example—or to connect the control unit to two different computers. This process can be extended to arrange for a string of tapes to be connected to up to eight channels on each of two machines, although no more than two tapes can operate in a single string at any one time.

30 Design of computer data files

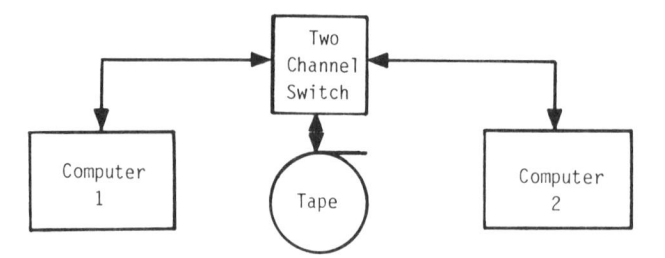

```
                    ┌──────────┐
         ┌─────────▶│   Two    │◀─────────┐
         │          │ Channel  │          │
         │    ┌────▶│  Switch  │          │
         │    │     └──────────┘          │
         ▼    │          ▲                ▼
   ┌────────┐ │          │          ┌────────┐
   │Computer│ │       ╭─────╮       │Computer│
   │   1    │ │      │ Tape  │      │   2    │
   └────────┘ │       ╰─────╯       └────────┘
              │          │
              └──────────┘
```

Fig. 2.8 Multiple control switches can be added to allow further overlap of operations and the ability to access any tape drive through any separate channel. Such facilities are only justified if large numbers of tape drives are installed, but can increase flexibility in complex systems.

Tape cassettes

These drives are useful to input files or data from key-to-tape stations, to input and store software and to output files, usually when they are to be sent to a remote location. Many of these tapes store data in parallel across the tape, as with larger drives. Others, of which the NCR 7621 is an example, store data serially. This device records 800 bits, i.e. 100 bytes, per inch, transfer data at 750 bytes per second, and can store a maximum of 338 400 bytes on a 282-foot tape. In microcomputer applications cassette tapes are widely used to back up hard disks of capacity 10 to 60 Mbytes, rather than using large numbers of floppy disks. The 3480 cassette tape drive is discussed below.

Recent developments in tape technology

Some years ago users were led to believe that 'all data online' was a sensible and realistic aim. In practice, many users did not need to have instant access to all their data, and were not prepared to pay for a facility they did not need. In addition, the emphasis put on fixed disk installations by the manufacturers left users with little option but to retain some tape drives, if only to provide backup. Now that it is clear that magnetic tapes still play a vital role in modern computer installations, improved facilities are appearing. Two of these are discussed below.

The IBM 3480 Cartridge Tape Drive This device achieves a much higher density of data storage than previous tapes by the use of thin film read/write heads, and a chromium dioxide magnetic coating rather than ferric oxide. This allows the tape traverse speed to be reduced to 79 inches per second, compared with 200 on the 3420 model 8; this in turn has made it possible to control tape movement with a digital servo-mechanism, eliminating the need for capstans and vacuum columns. These changes make the device more compact than earlier high-performance tape drives, and is claimed to improve reliability. A stacking mechanism that allows five cassettes to be pre-mounted and read without operator intervention, and the small size of the cassettes, increase the value of the 3480 as a sequential file storage device, and for backup tasks.

A further innovation is the provision of a 512 Kbyte solid state buffer that is shared by all the tape drives in action at a given time. This allows multiple data blocks to be transferred from the tape to the buffer, or the reverse, while the application program handles blocks one at a time. Improvements in tape performance and channel usage are claimed to result.

The Memorex 6520 Tape Cache Processor This device provides the benefits of a solid state buffer for users who have conventional vacuum column tape drives. The buffer size is 1 Mbyte, and buffered operation will allow data transfer to or from the host computer at channel speeds. Error recovery procedures are also carried out by the 6520, increasing the CPU time available for other jobs.

The device also offers a data compaction facility, which the user can invoke by additions to job control language statements. An average data compaction rate of at least 50 per cent is claimed, with some archive data being compacted by 90 per cent to one-tenth of its original volume. Taking the figure of 50 per cent, this would effectively increase instantaneous data transfer speeds to double the rated speed for the device, and would much reduce the space taken up by the data on the tape. In neither case would the overall tape performance be quite doubled, as the IBG size is not altered (see Chapter 4 for a full discussion of effective tape transfer rates). Tape data compression techniques for archiving, if this device is *not* available, are discussed in reference[2].

2.3 Magnetic disk

Although magnetic tapes are very cost effective in applications that suit them, such as processing high hit-rate files, providing backup and archive storage, their use is limited. One disk can be handled logically as if it were several separate devices, which is particularly useful for sorting; disks can easily be maintained in good condition, while tapes require careful planning and more regular maintenance, if they are to give low error rates consistently. In addition, sequential processing, to which magnetic tapes are suited, is relatively less important now that enquiry systems and databases are in common use. For all of these reasons, the most widely used input-output devices today are magnetic disks.

Physical characteristics

The recording medium used on disks is ferric oxide, or a chromic oxide–ferric oxide mixture. Most disks are about 14 inches in diameter, and made of aluminium coated with a magnetic recording medium. This medium contains needle-like magnetic particles that are aligned during manufacture so that they lie roughly in the direction of motion of the disk and thus produce as much magnetization as possible during use. (See reference[3] for further details of this process.) Floppy disks are usually 5.25 inches or 3.5 inches in diameter, and made of flexible material that is about 0.03 inches in thickness.

Disks rotate about a central spindle and data is recorded on concentric tracks. Writing and reading of data is carried out by read-write heads that float on an air cushion just above the surface of the disk; in many modern disks 'takeoff' and 'landing' areas are provided separately from the data storage areas, as contact between surface and head is unavoidable at these times. The separation between head and surface is so small that atmospheric dust can cause the two to jam, and damage both. To avoid this the air in disk drives is filtered, and contamination of this filtered air has to be kept to a minimum. Floppy disks are an exception, as there is contact between the head and the disk surface not only when the device starts or stops but also during normal operation.

Data storage

Data is recorded serially by bit, so that an eight-bit byte is strung along a track as shown in Fig. 2.9.

Parity bits are not written on the disk; instead, a number of check bytes is appended to the end of each field as shown in Fig. 2.9. This saves disk space if data fields are long; the break-even length is sixteen bytes for two check bytes, and thirty-two for four check bytes. For longer fields than these more data is stored than would be possible if parity bits were held. In addition, the *cyclic check bytes* also provide a more effective method of locating and correcting errors, based on treating the whole data field as a single polynomial, than does parity checking.

Data stored on the innermost track of a disk is packed as tightly as possible. If the read-write heads are of normal ferrite construction, this will limit the number of bits per inch to about 6500, and the separation between adjacent tracks to about one and a half thousandths of an inch. The track separation is usually expressed as the number of tracks per inch—in this case about 670. When thin-film heads are used, these figures are increased to around 16 000 bits per inch, and 1000 tracks per inch.

For all other tracks than the innermost, the determining factor in recording and recognizing a bit is *time*. Within limits the physical size of the bit is not important, it is the time for which it is available to the read-write heads that defines a bit position. For this reason the data capacity of an inner

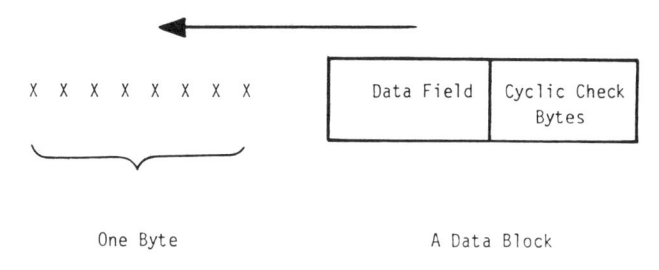

```
         ←─────────────
                              ┌─────────────┬──────────────┐
X  X  X  X  X  X  X  X        │ Data Field  │ Cyclic Check │
                              │             │    Bytes     │
_____/       └─────────────┴──────────────┘


       One Byte                       A Data Block
```

Fig. 2.9 Arrangement of bytes along the track of a disk.

track is as great as that of an outer one; the physical size of the bits is smaller, but their angular separation is the same. This has not been true of all disk devices. Bryant disks provided three zones, those further from the spindle holding more data than the nearer ones. However, users would expect a gramophone record to hold as much music on an inner groove as on an outer one, so the concept of equal angular separation being the most important factor in data storage is not unusual in everyday devices.

Data reference

Any data on a track can be reached by movement of the read-write heads to the track, followed by rotation of the disk. Even if the precise position of the data is known, it can be assumed that, on average, the disk will have to make half a rotation before the data is located, since it is impossible to control the part of the track over which the head will be positioned when it first reaches the track, so that the search can start. In addition to this, software often requires the start of the track to be located first, followed by a search for the desired record. In this case the average length of the search will be a full revolution of the disk.

If a read-write head is not positioned over the correct track when the record is requested, the search cannot commence until the head has moved to this track. This takes a time that depends on the number of tracks to be traversed before the required track is reached. Figures are given in Table 2.2 for the minimum, average and maximum time that head movement will take for a number of devices; capacity, rotational delay and transfer rates for these devices are also given.

Disk organization and addressing

Most devices use *packs* of disks to increase the available storage area. The top surface of the top disk and the bottom surface of the bottom disk are protectively coated and do not hold data. Tracks on the remaining disks are accessed by a group of read-write heads known collectively as an *access comb*. This comb moves as a unit, so that after any particular track has been

34 Design of computer data files

Table 2.2 The figures in this table present performance data for IBM disks and their plug-compatible competitors. Only the most advantageous competitive figures have been given, and it does not always follow that the same device is quoted in every PCM figure that is compared with a given IBM device.

		Device Type																		
		3330-1 and 3330-11		3340		3344		3350		3370		3375		3380		3380E		2305	
		IBM	PCM	IBM	PCM	IBM	PCM	IBM	PCM	IBM	PCM	IBM	PCM	IBM	PCM	IBM	PCM	IBM	PCM
Capacity (megabytes)		100	317	70	70	280	280	317	635	571	571	819	819	2520	2520	5040	5040	11.2	716.8*
Rotational delay (milliseconds)		8.4	8.4	10.1	10.1	10.1	10.1	8.4	8.4	10.1	10.1	10.1	10.1	8.3	8.3	8.3	8.3	2.5	0.4
Head movement (milliseconds)	min.	10	7	10	7	10	7	10	4	5	5	4	4	3	3	3	3	nil	nil
	avg.	30	27	25	20	25	20	25	20	20	20	19	19	16	16	16	16	nil	nil
	max.	55	50	50	50	50	50	50	45	40	40	38	38	30	30	30	30	nil	nil
Transfer rate (kbytes/s)		806	806	885	885	885	885	1198	1198	1859	1859	1859	1859	3000	3000	3000	3000	3000	4000
Fixed heads?		no	no	0.5 Mb	0.5 Mb	1.0 Mb	1.0 Mb	1.1 Mb	1.1 Mb	no	no	no	no	no	no	no	no	11.2 Mb	n/a
Fixed disk?		no	no	no	no	yes	yes	yes	yes	yes	yes	yes	yes	yes	yes	yes	yes	yes	n/a
Removable pack?		yes	yes	yes	yes	no	no	no	yes†	no	no	no	no	no	no	no	no	no	n/a

PCM = Plug-compatible model
* This is a semiconductor device formatted to appear to be a magnetic disk. In its own 'native' format it can store up to 768 megabytes of data.
† These packs are removable only to recover data after a device failure

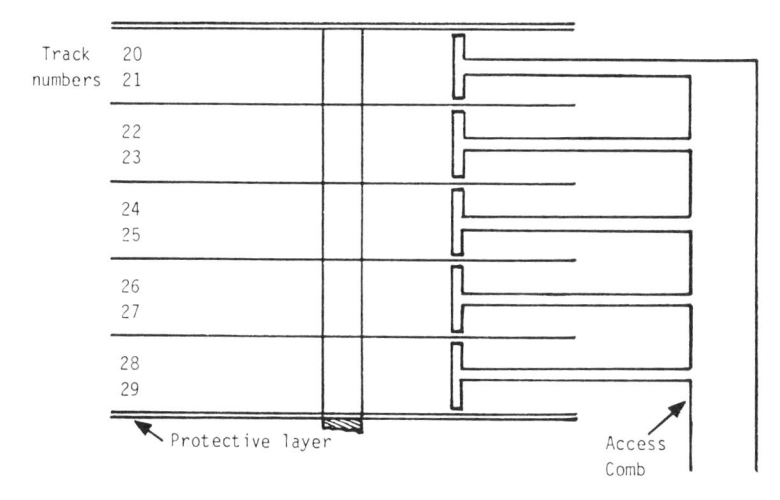

Fig. 2.10 Storage of sequential files on consecutive tracks of a cylinder.

accessed, one track on each surface is available to the read-write heads without head movement. For this reason a pack is regarded as being made up of a set of *cylinders* and the addressing system treats the tracks that make up a cylinder as being a sequence of addresses: this might be tracks 20, 21, 22, ... 29 as shown in Fig. 2.10. Sequential files are stored on the consecutive tracks in a cylinder rather than on adjacent tracks, in order to reduce head movements during sequential processing of records.

Many removable disk packs use a further complete surface for functions such as *rotational position sensing*, which will be described later. This is the reason that some packs made up of eleven disks have nineteen rather than twenty data storage surfaces. Others devote the entire top and bottom disks to protective functions, and so provide only nineteen out of a potential twenty-four surfaces for data storage.

Data storage formats

Data is stored in two basic formats on disk. These are *sector mode* and *free format*. Sectors, which are used on floppy disks, ICL's 1900 series, IBM's 3310 and 3370 and NCR's 6530 amongst others, provide a fixed number of data storage areas on each track; an alternative name for this format is *fixed block architecture*, or FBA. In free format the user decides how many separate data storage areas to define; this is often described as *count-key-data*, or CKD format. A more detailed discussion of these formats, and the blocking considerations involved in their use, is given in Chapter 4 (see p. 75).

Disk defects

During manufacture there is a possibility of small flaws arising on the surfaces of disks. When these surfaces are used to store data, the flaws prevent correct use of the affected track. Most disks provide a number of *alternate tracks* that can be used in place of these defective tracks. They are shown in capacity data as figures such as 200+3, when there are three alternate tracks. This makes up for the loss of data storage space, but time is still lost because the alternate tracks are physically situated in 'spare' cylinders, so that a head movement will be required to write or retrieve data, followed by a further head movement back to the prime data track.

The affected area on a disk, whether arising during manufacture or caused by damage in service, is often limited in size. For this reason it is wasteful to abandon a complete track because a small part of it is faulty. Disks such as IBM's 3310 or 3370 provide less alternate tracks than previous models but include a spare sector on each track. This can be used if a single sector on the track becomes inoperative, avoiding head movement to an alternative storage area. A related technique is applied on the 3380, but modified as the device is not sector formatted.

Most of these small faults occur in manufacture, and alternate sectors or tracks are allocated before delivery. If such limited faults occur in service they may be removed merely by cleaning the disk pack: if not, customer engineers can usually allocate alternate data storage areas. Serious in-service crashes will lead to the scrapping of a disk pack, and such damage cannot be catered for by providing alternate tracks.

Types of disk device

Floppy disks These were originally developed by IBM for software storage, and are unique amongst disks in that contact between head and surface is intended. For this reason the disks are flexible and rotate relatively slowly—see Table 2.3 for typical transfer rates, rotation speeds, etc. A discussion of the actual file access times involved in floppy usage is given by Pechura and Schoeffler[4]. Many of the floppies available use only one surface and thus only one read-write head. However, variations that allow for two-sided operation and double density data recording are also widely used. Thus storage capacities of about 0.25, 0.5, 1.0 and 1.25 Mbytes may be quoted. There are in addition 3.5 inch diameter disks known as *minifloppies*: a single-sided, single density version of these will store about 160 Kbytes. As intense development is taking place in the manufacture of floppy disks at present, the figures given in Table 2.3 should be used only as a general guide.

Floppy disks are held in an envelope at all times, and they are read through a 'window' in it. A further envelope is provided for storage when the disk is not in use. These provide some protection against dust, grease and other contaminants but the disks are also vulnerable to damage from pressure. Labels should be written separately and then stuck on, to avoid

Table 2.3 Note that there may be wide variations from these figures in any particular case; however, they represent typical values at the end of 1986. (SS = single sided, DS = double sided, SD = single density, DD = double density.)

		3.5-inch disks			5.25-inch disks		
		SSSD	SSDD	DSDD	SSSD	SSDD	DSDD
Capacity (Kbytes)		160	320	640	310	625	1250
Data transfer rate (kbits/sec)		125	250	250	250	250	500
Access time (milliseconds)	min.	3	3	3	3	3	3
	avg.	70	70	70	95	95	95
Rotational speed (rpm)		300	300	300	300	300	300

damage due to pen pressure. Floppies should be stored upright and when used they should be smoothly and gently inserted into drives to avoid misalignment of the read-write head or heads. These precautions will minimize problems, but it is inevitable that small irregularities on the surface will occasionally lead to the head bouncing off the surface, giving read errors. The life of these disks is limited, and it is essential not to keep them running when they are not required, and to hold copies of all important data files stored on them.

Removable disk packs Although they are not chronologically the first, disk drives using removable packs of disks provided the bulk of direct access storage between the early 1960s and the late 1970s. The advantage of removable packs was that total storage was not limited, even though only a certain amount could be on-line at any time. This gradually became less important as the capacity of disk devices increased from 2 million characters per pack on the IBM 1311 to 200 million on the IBM 3330 Model 11. At this stage it was estimated by CDC that there were only about three mount/dismount operations per disk drive each shift; this is often advanced as a reason for the switch by manufacturers to fixed disks.

The protective function of the top and bottom surfaces of a pack has already been mentioned. To exclude dust a plastic cover is provided, which is shown in Fig. 2.11. It can only be removed by screwing the spindle into its holder and so excluding dust and dirt; to avoid contamination of the air inside the drive unit it should be open for the minimum time possible while a pack is mounted.

The importance of excluding dust is emphasized by the illustration in Fig. 2.12. Even smoke particles are considerably larger than the 0.5–3 μm (10^{-6} metres) separation between the head and the magnetic coating of the

38 Design of computer data files

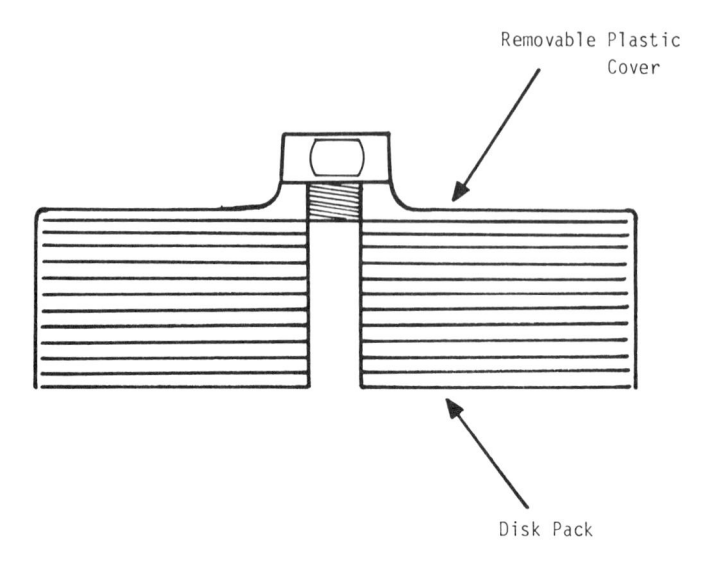

Fig. 2.11 The set of disks that makes up a removable disk pack is protected by a cover when it is not mounted on a disk drive.

disk. This very small separation means that the least distortion of the pack or drive spindle, which can happen if loading is careless, will cause a single or multiple head-crash, i.e. contact between the head and surface, which may lead to loss of data, removal of the magnetic layer or serious damage to head and surface. In the early use of IBM's 2314 drives and similar devices a number of serious cases of damage to multiple units occurred, but improved engineering and more resistant magnetic coatings have substantially reduced these problems. However, the tolerances required in modern disks, as head 'flying' height has been reduced to improve disk capacity, have become so demanding that two other techniques are now used to reduce design problems.

Winchester technology disks One of the problems caused by the very small 'flying' separation of disks and heads shown in Fig. 2.12 is that there is occasional contact between heads and disks during starting and stopping. This causes a build-up of dirt and oxide from the disk surface on the heads. As the main requirement in increasing data storage density is to reduce this separation still further, a new solution was required. 'Winchester' technology disks represent one such solution; a mean time between failures of 5000 to 10 000 hours, which is achieved by many of these disks, shows how successful the approach has been.

Dirt can be almost entirely excluded by arranging that a sealed unit includes both disk pack and access comb. The disk surface has been toughened to reduce oxide loss due to contact, and in fact contact during starting and stopping periods is planned for; the heads are in contact with the

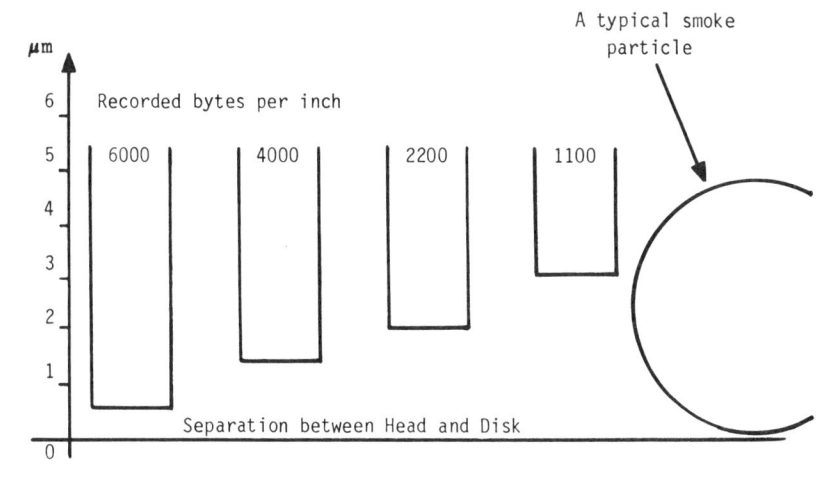

Fig. 2.12 Recording density depends on the distance between head and disk surface. This is now very much less than the diameter of a typical smoke particle.

surface for one third to one half a revolution, but the contact areas are not data-storage tracks. This provides a stable 'flight', with planned contact at 'landing' and 'take off' replacing occasional unplanned contact.

A necessary modification has been to reduce the load on the heads. At flying speeds the air flow between disk and surface provides a 'lift', or separating force, that pushes the heads well away from the surface if it is not checked. To balance this lift, the heads are loaded. Conventional heads have a loading of 40–60 grams, which is not acceptable for the planned contact periods. Hence Winchester heads are loaded to only 8–10 grams. This implies a smaller lift, which can only be achieved if the heads are smaller than conventional heads. The Winchester head was introduced in 1973 by IBM and used in the 3340 disk drive. This innovation allowed a greater number of bits to be stored per inch, and higher data transfer rates to be achieved. Further details are given in reference[5].

Heads made using thin film technology, fabricated by deposition of a spiral conductor on to a silicon substrate[3], were first incorporated in the IBM 3370, and the same company also uses these heads in the 3375 and 3380 disk drives. Data storage density can be increased on each track by a factor of 50 per cent in comparison with the earlier Winchester heads, and the number of tracks per inch perpendicular to the direction of rotation can also be made greater. This largely explains the improvement in disk performance in recent years.

Two approaches have been taken to these disks. The first is to make disk packs removable, so providing the user with unlimited potential direct access storage. This was adopted by IBM in their 3340 removable modules, by NCR in the 6560 and International Memories Inc. in their 7710 'hard' disk used in microcomputer systems. Because it contains both heads and

40 Design of computer data files

disks, the main difficulty is the relatively high cost of each module by comparison with conventional removable disk packs. This led to usage being limited, particularly in the mainframe market, and little development of these devices has taken place.

The second approach is to provide very large storage capacity, sealed and non-removable *fixed disks*. Interestingly, IBM gives the user this option in the 3344 drive that can be used in the same storage complex as the 3340, using the same disk controller. By employing both types of drive, the user has the benefits of removable storage for archiving or backup, and of large-volume non-removable storage capacity. The NCR 6560 is an example of twin drives suited to mini and microcomputers, one being fixed, the other removable for duplication and backup.

The first device offered only as a fixed disk was the 3350. This has been very widely used, and large numbers are still in service. It has been followed, in chronological order, by the 3370, 3375 and 3380 drives; a double-density version of the 3380 (the 3380E) is now available. Fixed disks offer two major advantages. The first is that a large number of disks can be mounted on a single spindle to provide massive storage capacity. Such a pack would be too heavy to remove. The second is that any problems arising during manufacture due to small divergencies from design dimensions can be adjusted without fear of later mis-matches, as the unit will not be used in combination with separately manufactured equipment in the way that a disk pack has to be. Details of the performance of these disks are given in Table 2.2 on page 34.

Fixed-head disks These disks have one or more read/write heads per track. This poses a problem in placement of the heads, which is usually solved by placing them in banks around the perimeter of the disk. However, as there is at least one head per track, access times no longer include an element for head movement. This markedly reduces the time taken to retrieve data. The adjustment of so many heads makes it virtually impossible to arrange for the pack to be removable. Sometimes more than one head per track is provided;

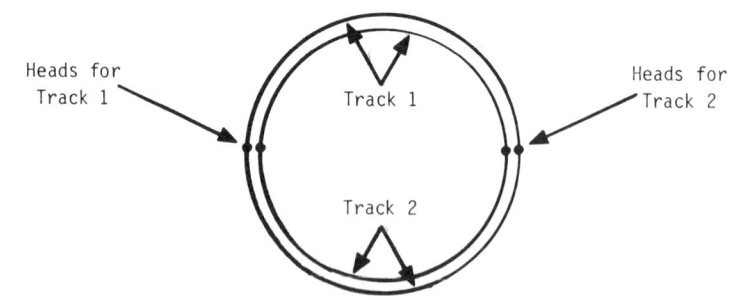

Fig. 2.13 When there are two heads per track a byte is regarded as being made up of pairs of bits on adjacent tracks, and the logical track is regarded as being half of the physical track in length but two tracks in width.

if there are two heads per track, a byte is regarded as being made up of pairs of bits on adjacent tracks, and the logical track is regarded as being half of the physical track in length, but two tracks in width (see Fig. 2.13).

The advantages of this 'zero access' disk storage are so great for page data sets, transient operating system functions and indexes that the 3340, 3344 and 3350 disks offer some fixed-head storage as an option—the first five cylinders of a 3340, the first two of a 3344 and the first two of a 3350. This provides 0.5, 1.0 and 1.1 Mbytes of storage respectively for which no seek is required, so rotational delay is the only time lost in retrieving a record. At present no such option is offered for the 3380.

Timing considerations

The various types of disk reviewed above may be met by users, and new versions are being announced at frequent intervals. It is essential to study the details of any given disk system if its capabilities are to be fully exploited; generally, the most important elements of timing will be those discussed below.

Head movement   This will be determined by the number of cylinders to be traversed to reach the required record, starting from the present position of the access comb. Table 2.2 gives a minimum, average and maximum head movement time for most devices. Minimum is the traverse to an adjacent cylinder. Average is the figure to use if nothing is known about the relative positions of the heads before and after the movement. Maximum is the figure to use to get a 'worst possible' time. It is not typical, as it can only occur in moving from the first to the last cylinder on the pack, or the reverse.

Rotation time   This cannot be reduced except by providing multiple heads per track. However, modern disks have the rotational position sensing option, which allows the disk to search for a given record without using either the input-output channel or the CPU until the disk has rotated to within about 3° of the desired record. At this stage the channel and control unit become busy, but up to that time they are available to other devices. On a device revolving at 3600 rotations per minute the average time that the channel is busy is reduced on average from 8.3 milliseconds—half a rotation—to 0.25 milliseconds. However, if the operation that is at present using the channel does not finish in time, a further rotation will be required before this operation can start. It is one of the advantages offered by the semiconductor memory devices discussed below that they do not run this risk.

Record transfer time   This cannot be reduced in most cases, but incorrect blocking or poor file design will involve the transfer of a great deal of unwanted data, unnecessarily increasing this element of file timing. This is discussed in detail in the chapters on the various file organization techniques.

Disk searching facilities

Often the address of a record on disk is known, and all that is required to retrieve it is to move the head to the required track, wait until the start of the record is detected and read it in. On other occasions the given address is only the start of a search for the record, and in this case the available search commands and record or block formats are very important. The alternatives are usually as follows:

1. As explained above, disks may hold records in fixed-length sectors (this is often known as *fixed block architecture* or FBA), or in a format that does not separate key and data, often called the *count-data* (CD) *format*. Another widely used name for this is the *embedded key format*. The user has no option here; if there is no index, records or blocks have to be read into main storage before they can be examined to see if the desired record has been retrieved. This often leads to loss of revolutions, and so time. FBA and CD formats are described in detail in Chapter 3.
2. The records are held with a separate key. This is the *count-key data format* offered in many IBM systems including the most recent disks, the 3375 and 3380. Using this format the search for a desired key is carried out by the disk control unit. The channel is not busy until the required record is located, and until this occurs the search can continue at rotation speeds. This provides a much faster search than the embedded key format described in section 1 above, but it uses more disk space. For this reason it is usually an alternative, and the more suitable format is chosen in any given case. This format is examined in the next chapter, and its effect on disk storage capacity is discussed in Chapter 4 (see p. 75).
3. For some purposes it is convenient to start a search at a given point and continue it until the whole cylinder has been examined. This is called a *multiple track search*, and it is available on many systems. It usually requires the separate key format. In addition, it is important to ensure that the whole of the first track is searched; this usually requires a seek to the start of the track, followed by the multiple track search command. Failure to ensure that this first track search has been completed may mean missing the record on its expected home track, followed by a lengthy and fruitless search.

Systems considerations

Disks can be used to join two, four and sometimes more systems, by fitting the appropriate switching mechanisms. They are also widely used for storage of operating systems and virtual storage operation. Both these last applications will be allocated space on a fixed head disk with one or more heads per track if it is available; this is because such a disk does not require head movements and so allows rapid retrieval of data at all times. A full review of disk system design considerations is given in reference[6].

As a result of developments at present in progress it is probable that future disks will offer up to twice as high a data density on any given track, and up to ten times more tracks per inch, than present devices. A report on the mainframe disks available at present[7] shows that these offer up to 24 000 bytes per inch, 1000 tracks per inch and transfer rates as high as 3 Mbytes/sec. Fujitsu and Ibis offer maximum data transfer rates of around 9.6 and 12 Mbytes/sec, by arranging that a byte is made up of bits recorded on several tracks. These developments should ensure the future of disks as the main direct access devices for some time to come. Several typical disk drives are shown in Fig. 2.14.

Content addressable disk devices

The CAFS-ISP (content addressable file storage information search processor) offered by ICL is unique in that it searches records on the basis of the values of combinations of data fields, rather than for a single key (compare disk searching facilities, section 2 on page 42). This device uses dedicated hardware in the disk controller to carry out complex searches of disk at full rotation speeds, and selects out only the relevant records to transfer to main storage. It can search sequential (called 'serial' by ICL), indexed sequential and database files in character, numeric or text form, and is able to handle queries based on a combination of up to fifteen separate criteria for different fields that, in total, can take up 256 or less bytes. Individual bits of a field can be 'masked' and not used in the search.

The 'criteria' can consist of Boolean expressions of up to sixteen terms—in a simple or nested arrangement of AND, OR and NOT conditions—and a record can be selected only if all the conditions are satisfied, or if some proportion such as two out of four conditions are met. This last is a *Quorum search*, and can be modified so that each condition has a weighted score, and a record is retrieved if some minimum total score is reached.

The device costs between $35 000 and $70 000 when added to an existing installation, and up to 80 Gbytes of disk can be searched using a number of CAFS-ISP modules on a 2966-based mainframe, or 900 Gbytes on the larger series 39 machines. Various software packages are available to exploit the device, notably Querymaster for terminal users, Relational and Direct CAFS Interfaces for writers of new programs, and CAFS search option for existing programs. The system can provide a great deal of statistical data, such as the number of records in a file meeting the given criteria, the maximum and minimum values of a particular field found in the whole file, and providing totals of the value of a given field in all the 'hit' records in the file.

44 Design of computer data files

Fig. 2.14 Some typical direct access devices.

IBM 3480 Magnetic Tape Subsystem

A view of the cassette storage area of the IBM 3850 mass storage system

Review of backing storage devices **45**

IBM 3880 Storage Control Model 1

IBM 3330 Disk Storage

CAFS is particularly effective for relatively complex search criteria, such as occur in information retrieval systems; these will be examined in Chapter 8. It is not advantageous for retrieval of records on prime key alone, nor is it suited to following pointer chains from record to record. In a suitable system, however, it offers a hardware 'preprocessor' facility that can greatly reduce the load on I–O channels, and accelerate the answering of complex queries. It also allows indexes to be less complex, as the CAFS-ISP carries out much of the searching and matching required; this reduces both index searching time and the space required for indexes.

Shortcomings of disk

There are two major areas in which alternative devices can provide more effective direct retrieval than disk. The first is that of very rapid access. Semiconductor storage that emulates disks is available, and several of these devices are described below. The second is that of volume. Although the capacity of modern disks is very high, some applications require still greater capacity. This is provided by mass storage devices.

2.4 Semiconductor memory devices

The STC 4305 solid-state disk was introduced in 1978; the latest version is the 4325. It is plug-compatible with the IBM 2305 fixed-head disk, which means that it can replace the 2305-2 without requiring any alterations to the system. The user can regard it as a 2305 that accesses information about seven times faster, holds much more data, costs less and is claimed to need considerably less space and power. These devices are useful either as the 'front-end' of a set of disks holding master files, or as the secondary storage to hold libraries, catalogs, indices or work files. In either case they will show a significant improvement over fixed-head disks, as can be seen from Table 2.4. The 2325 can emulate either a 2305-2 or a 3380, as can most of the other devices. The Memorex 6880 also emulates the 3350, which is useful for page data sets.

Both the Memorex and NAS devices have backup magnetic disk storage, and in the event of a power failure the contents of the semiconductor disk are transferred to the magnetic disk before total failure occurs. Several of these devices have standard or optional standby power supplies that will maintain operation for some time, rather than only until data transfer to a magnetic disk is complete. A number of devices can transfer data via two or four channels simultaneously, and so achieve a very high total data transfer rate—shown in Table 2.4 as *(two channels) or †(four channels). The Intel FAST-3825 loses some storage capacity when used in IBM simulation mode, as against the potential capacity when it is used as a device in its own right,

Review of backing storage devices 47

Table 2.4 These details of semiconductor 'disks' indicate the high performance they can provide. This may be enhanced by a range of special features, described in manufacturer's literature.

	STC 4305 Model 3	Model 6	NAS 7900	Memorex 6880	Intel FAST–3825
Capacity (Mbytes)	12–48	12–768	512 max	128–512 (32–128 if 2305)	11.2–720 (768 in native mode)
Access time (ms)	0.6	0.3		0.3	0.4
Data transfer (Mbytes/sec)	1, 1.5, 3	(6*)	3 (12†)	3 (12†)	1.5–3 (4*)
Emulates:	All models emulate the 3380 and 2305-2			3350 also	

Notes: * indicates simultaneous data transfer using 2 channels.
† indicates simultaneous data transfer using 4 channels.

which is described as *native mode*. The Memorex 6880 has a much smaller capacity in 2305-2 emulation mode than when used in 3350 or 3380 mode. The figures are given in brackets in the capacity row of Table 2.4.

A recent development is the provision of semiconductor *cache memory* as a front-end to disk storage. IBM's 3880-21 provides an 8, 16, 32, 48 or 64 Mbyte cache that is intended to accelerate paging or swapping of data between the CPU and 3350s by up to ten times. It cannot be used with 3380 disks. The 3880-23 has an 8, 16, 32, 48 or 64 Mbyte cache storage that operates with the 3380 to improve data handling speeds during file processing.

These devices, rather like the semiconductor disks described above, are aimed at solving the most obvious problem in using disks at present. This is that disk capacity has increased almost sixfold in the last decade, but disk average access times have only reduced by about 40 per cent of their values in 1972. When more than one program in the computer is using the same disk, this can lead to serious waste of time due to *contention*, which is a description of the situation when the disk access mechanism is constantly moving to different parts of the disk, to meet simultaneous data requests from different programs. As the capacity of a disk increases so does the likelihood of contention, because it will hold more files. Cache storage, holding large volumes of active data, provides a way of reducing the effects of contention. (See reference[5] for further discussion.)

2.5 Mass storage devices

In order to combine the enormous total storage capacity of a library of magnetic tapes with the speedy retrieval capabilities of disk, some manufacturers now offer mass storage systems. Although the time required to access

48 Design of computer data files

any given item of data may be relatively long, it is very much less than that involved in retrieving a tape from a manually controlled library, and the huge capacities now available should remove the need for such libraries in all but the largest installations.

Three of the best known mass storage devices are the Braegen 7110 ATL (automated tape library), the Control Data 38500 and the IBM 3850. The first of these stores and organizes tapes, and is physically large, because the device housing stands behind all the tape drives, and has room to allow operator access and to store thousands of tapes. The other two operate on the principle of using disks to hold data while it is referenced, with a mass storage capacity based on tape cartridges for long-term storage.

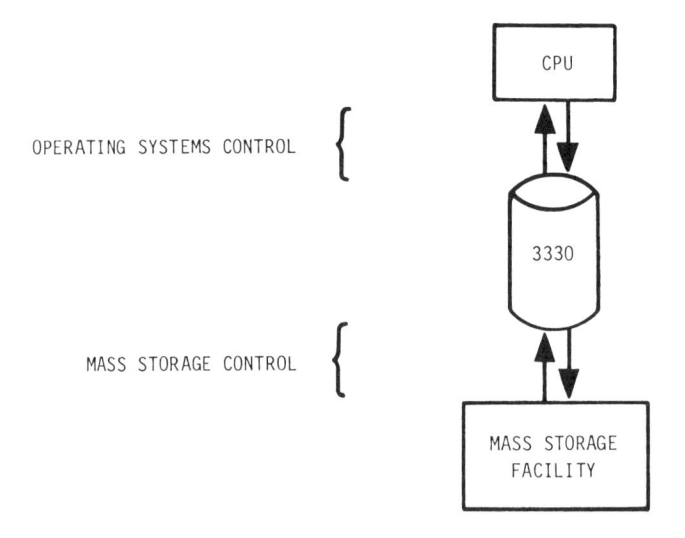

Fig. 2.15 Requests for disk usage come from the CPU, but retrieval of data from the MSF is under mass storage control.

IBM's 3850 mass storage system is based on a combination of 3330 disks and tape cartridges, each able to hold up to 50 million bytes of information; this appears as shown in Fig. 2.15. The cartridges are always handled in pairs; the capacity of a pair is equivalent to a complete 3330 model 1, or half a 3330 model 11.

The total capacity of a 3850 can be as high as 472 billion bytes. Although pairs of tape cartridges hold the contents of a 3330 model 1 disk, any given disk 'drive' defined by the user can be as small as eight cylinders of the 3330. Thus a large number of 'virtual' drives can be simulated by a single actual device. The state of any given virtual drive is monitored and controlled by the mass storage control, which also *stages*, i.e. transfers data from tape to disk when it is needed, and transfers back on to tape any data that has been altered and is no longer required on disk.

The CDC 38500 starts with smaller storage volumes than the 3850 (16 Gbytes as against 35 Gbytes), can be added to in smaller increments, does not require dedicated disk drives and accesses data rather faster than the IBM device. It is therefore a direct competitor with a number of significant advantages. Specifically, the tape cartridges hold 8 Mbytes as against 50, and data transfers are geared to 1 Mbyte units rather than two. This is justified on the grounds that a CDC survey showed only one file in three to be larger than a megabyte in size. Larger files can be allocated more space in 1 Mbyte increments.

The Braegen 7110 provides an automated tape library that can load tapes of many types. Its main advantages are that tapes are not mislaid or lost, and tape library staff can be kept to a minimum. By comparison with manual mounting its speed is only marginally better than that of an operator who is waiting to mount a tape, but additional delays do not occur, as happens when an operator has other urgent duties. User companies claim large savings in personnel and storage costs.

For all these devices, timing from first requirement of a cartridge to data available on disk is relatively slow (see Table 2.5). However, the advantage of holding enormous quantities of data in an organized and readily available form, and the possibility of planning operations so that timings can be regarded as similar to those of a 3330, mean that these devices have much to offer users.

Table 2.5 Performance figures for mass storage devices.

	Braegen 7110	*IBM 3850*	*CDC 38500*
Capacity range	802 to 7775 tape reels	35 000–472 000 Mbytes	16 000–1 000 000 Mbytes
Data access time (seconds)	15–20 to mount tape	8–13 (the total speed range)	7.5 (average)

2.6 Bubble memory

For some time it was thought that bubble memories might supersede disks. The main reasons why this has not happened are those of data capacity, which is very low, and a data transfer rate that is also relatively slow at present, but much nearer to that of disk than the capacity. Only the access time is better. Typical ranges for these properties are:

Capacity: 92 000 to 1 310 720 bits
Transfer rate: 50 000 to 5 000 000 bits per second
Access time: 2.4 to 40 ms (most in range 4–7 ms).

These figures do not imply a rapid expansion in use of bubble memory at the expense of disk[8], as at one time seemed possible. In fact, the problem that larger capacity can only be achieved by accepting a slower access speed, coupled to the ever-improving performance of magnetic disk, make it unlikely that bubble memory will ever become an important storage device in mainframe installations. The main exception is in very difficult environmental conditions; the lack of moving parts makes bubble memory very suitable for military or shop-floor uses, and it seems that these will remain the major application areas. Wright[9] has given a very useful description of the mode of operation of bubble memories, and of the file structures suited to their use.

2.7 Optical or laser disk storage

In recent years a number of disk devices in which data is stored by using lasers to burn pits into the surface of a metal disk have become available. The metal is often tellurium or a tellurium alloy, as its heat-conducting properties are suitable for the application. This technique allows very large quantities of data to be stored on a single disk surface—a gigabyte is typical, and potentially much larger storage volumes are likely to be achieved in the future. Disk diameters are 4.7 to 12 inches.

The drawback of this technique is that data cannot be changed after it has been written. For this reason such storage is often described as WORM, write once, read many (times), or as CDROM, compact disk ROM. Development work on erasable optical disks has concentrated on phase changes such as reflective to transparent, or magneto-optic techniques that depend on phase changes to the surface that are detectable under polarised light. Up to the beginning of 1987 no commercial erasable product had become available; when such a device does appear, it will be a potential competitor to magnetic disk.

Several WORM devices are already offered for use with microcomputers, notably on the IBM Personal System/2. The IBM 3363 optical disk drive provides 200 Mbytes of permanent storage on a 5.25 inch removable disk. Up to eight such devices can be on-line, so 1.6 Gbytes of WORM storage can be used at any one time, while the archive storage capacity is unlimited. Further details are available from IBM literature[10, 11]. At present no such device has been made available for mainframe use, although STC has announced one. Typical performance figures for the devices already available are as follows:

    Capacity: about 1 Gbyte per surface; the largest claimed capacity is 3.6 Gbytes on a double-sided disk of 12 inch diameter.
    Access time: 1–4 ms track-to-track, 150 to 350 ms on average.
    Transfer rate: from 150 Kbytes to 1.25 Mbytes per second.

Uses of the present devices include archive storage, for which the claimed life of data stored optically is ten years, as against three for magnetic tape, and the storage of mixed media, that is a mixture of text and diagrams. When reusable disks become available, the potential applications will grow greatly in number. However, access times will have to be drastically reduced if the present importance of magnetic disk is to be threatened. Rathmann[12] has examined the data structures suited to optical disk storage, particularly in respect of database software.

2.8 Care of magnetic media

The performance of magnetic tapes and disks can be enhanced, and their useful lives extended, by a combination of care and control. This starts with environmental factors. The temperature should be kept between 15°C and 38°C while these media are in use and the relative humidity between 8 per cent and 80 per cent. For storage over long periods the temperature need only be held between −40°C and +60°C.

On arrival both the packaging and the disk pack or tape reel should be examined for signs of physical damage. Storage should be spacious and clean and no pack or reel should be stored on top of another. Many installations note the number of times a disk or tape has been mounted, and the number of errors observed while the medium was in use. Errors are often analysed under the headings hard and soft; a *soft error* is one that is corrected by the device itself, while a *hard error* leads to manual intervention because the device cannot resolve it.

Disk drives should be inspected at regular intervals to ensure that the spindles are not misaligned. Disk packs may be cleaned using specialized equipment after a specified number of mounts, to remove specks of grease or other contaminants. If there is any reason to believe that the pack may have been damaged, devices are available that inspect the disk surfaces for scratches, dents or distortion of the surface. The user can purchase one or both types of equipment, or have the work done by a bureau or specialist company.

Tapes are more subject to damage than disks, and greater savings can be made by good management. They should be cleaned regularly to remove the debris that arises from the abrasion caused by reading and writing. At the same time they should be rewound to equalize the tension through the tape.

Most tape problems occur at the start of the tape, because this is the most used part of it, and many users arrange for cleaning after ten mounts. Persistent errors can often be removed by cutting off the first fifty or so feet of the tape. Three types of tape inspection device are current[13]. A *cleaner* cleans and rewinds the tape. A *certifier* cleans and reads or writes on the tape and stops if it fails, to allow for manual cleaning. A *tester* records where it was not possible to read or write, but does not stop when it finds an error.

Den Danske Bank, a large Danish bank, reject all tapes that have more than one hard error or a very few soft errors per month. As a result this installation is able to claim that in their case tapes are more reliable than disks. While it is unlikely that most installations will have the same success, their record shows what can be achieved by tight control.

Conclusion

In this chapter the available file storage devices have been reviewed. Optimization of data storage on these devices is discussed in Chapter 4, while the effect of the physical operation of these devices on file design is considered in the chapters devoted to each technique; an understanding of the way data is stored can lead to improved performance and cost savings.

References

Many manufacturers' manuals were consulted in preparing this review, but only a few specific references have been cited.

1. *All About EDP Media and Suppliers*, Datapro Research Corporation, October 1978, Report 70J 200-01.
2. 'File archival techniques using data compression', by Michael Pechura, *CACM*, Vol. 25, No. 9, November 1982, pp. 605–609.
3. 'Disk storage technology', by Robert M. White, *Scientific American*, August 1980, pp. 112–121.
4. 'Estimating file access times of floppy disks', M. A. Pechura and J. D. Schoeffler, *CACM*, Vol. 26, No. 10, October 1983, pp. 754–763.
5. 'Winchester disks', *Systems International*, May 1980, pp. 45–48.
6. 'Planning secondary storage systems', by Owen Hanson, *Proc. 1st Pan Pacific Computer Conf.*, Melbourne, Sept. 1985, Vol. 2, pp. 1600–1616.
7. *All About Mainframe Disk Drives*, Datapro Research Corporation, May 1986, Report 70D6 001LD-101, 14 pages.
8. *Bubble Memories*, Systems International, May 1980, pp. 40–42.
9. 'Some file structure considerations pertaining to magnetic bubble memory', by William E. Wright, *Comp. Jnl.*, Vol. 26, No. 1, 1983, January, pp. 43–51.
10. *Announcements Summary Letter Number C87-06*, published by IBM, 2 April 1987.
11. *IBM 3363 Optical Disk Drive*, published by IBM, Plet No. ZG87-0166, April 1987.
12. 'Dynamic data structures on optical disks', by Peter Rathmann, *IEEE Jnl.*, 1984.
13. *All About Magnetic Tape and Disk Pack Maintenance Equipment*, Datapro Research Corporation, September 1985, Report 70D6 001LN-101, 17 pages.

Revision questions

1 What do you understand by the terms: disk; tape; floppy disk; cassette; mass storage device; 7-track tape; 9-track tape; NRZI; phase encoding; preamble; postamble; synchronization signal; compress-expand mode; recording density; IBG (inter-block gap); traverse time; vacuum loop; streaming mode; rewinding; tape drives; erase head; write head; read head; write protect ring; tape error checking; in flight; VRC; LRC; tape mark; FSF; BSF; FSB; BSB; read backwards; shared channels; data transfer rate; cyclic check bytes; track capacity; head positioning; head movement; disk pack; access comb; cylinders; rotational position sensing; sector mode; free format; alternate tracks; spare sectors; two-sided; double density; removable packs; Winchester disks; fixed disks; fixed-head disks; rotation time; record transfer time; virtual drives; bubble memory; disk cleaning; disk inspecting; tape cleaning; tape certifier; tape tester; FBA; CD; CKD; CAFS.

2 How is data recorded on magnetic tapes? Give reasons for the precise arrangement of bits.

3 Why is PE recorded information less likely to be corrupted than data recorded in NRZI format? What is the purpose of providing vacuum loops in tape drives? How is it that some drives do not have such loops, and what effect might this have on their performance?

4 Describe the precautions taken to ensure that data recorded on tapes is not corrupted.

5 What is the main purpose for which tape cassettes are used?

6 How is data recorded on magnetic disks?

7 Describe the process of retrieving a record stored on disk.

8 How and why are the tracks on a disk addressed? Would this apply to semiconductor storage?

9 How does the operation of a floppy disk differ from that of conventional disks? What effect does this have on the data handling characteristics of these disks?

10 What do you consider to be the advantages and disadvantages of removable disks by comparison with fixed disks?

11 Explain the differences between Winchester disks and earlier removable disks.

54 Design of computer data files

12 What considerations determine the time taken to retrieve a record from a disk?

13 When might a mass storage device be advantageous? You should explain the basis of choice in comparison with a large capacity disk, emphasizing what is lost and gained. How does an optical disk compare with them both?

14 Why do you think that bubble memory is not much used for file storage, and when is it justified?

15 Make clear the reasons that tape is liable to be affected by magnetic dust, and explain how you would minimize errors in tape usage over a long period.

16 How do errors arise in disk operations? Outline the precautions that can be taken to reduce these errors.

17 When would you expect CAFS-ISP to provide enhanced performance over conventional disks, and when not? Justify your conclusions by considering the software and hardware components of the system.

3 Choice and design of record formats

3.1 Introduction

It was pointed out in Chapter 1 that data files are made up of records. The format of those records has an effect on the speed and efficiency of file processing. The influence of record format is analysed in this chapter so that the file designer can take it into account at the design stage.

The format in which a record is stored can affect both the time taken to read or write the record and the time required to process it. The first of these can be altered more by changes in format than the second, but in certain cases both elements of the total time required to process a record can be optimized. The formats available for individual records or blocks of records are examined in this chapter, while the overall considerations involved in blocking and buffering records are dealt with in the next chapter.

Records can be regarded in two different ways. On a backing storage device, a record or group of records is stored as a single discrete *physical record* or block. The device does not recognize the difference between a single record and a set of blocked records. On a tape unit, a physical record is bounded by inter-block gaps at each end, and check data usually follows the physical record. Somewhat the same applies on disk, and the possible formats are discussed in detail below. The individual records that make up a block are described as *logical records* because each is a logical entity that is processed separately from all the others. The transfer of physical records between main and backing storage is carried out in units of one physical block. When a number of logical records is blocked to form a single physical record, the separation of the block into distinct logical records for processing in main storage is the job of the user program or manufacturers' software.

3.2 Physical records

Record types

There are three types of physical record:
    fixed length;
    variable length;
    undefined.

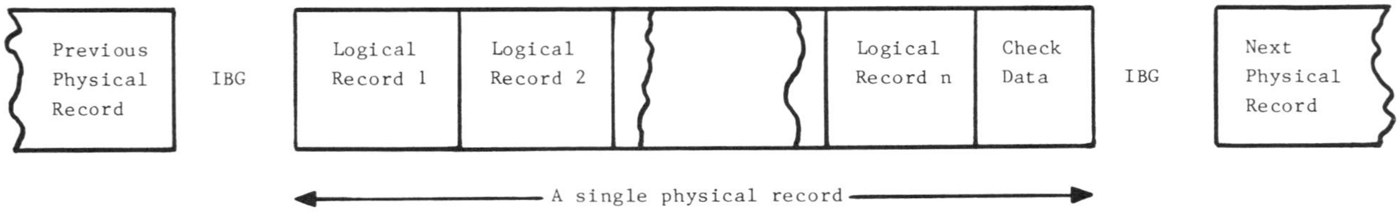

56 Design of computer data files

Fig. 3.1 The format of a physical record on magnetic tape.

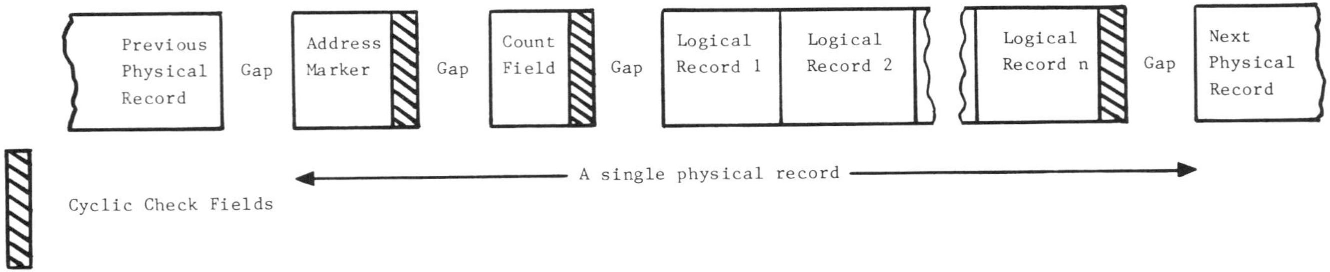

Fig. 3.2 The format of a physical record on disk in count-data format.

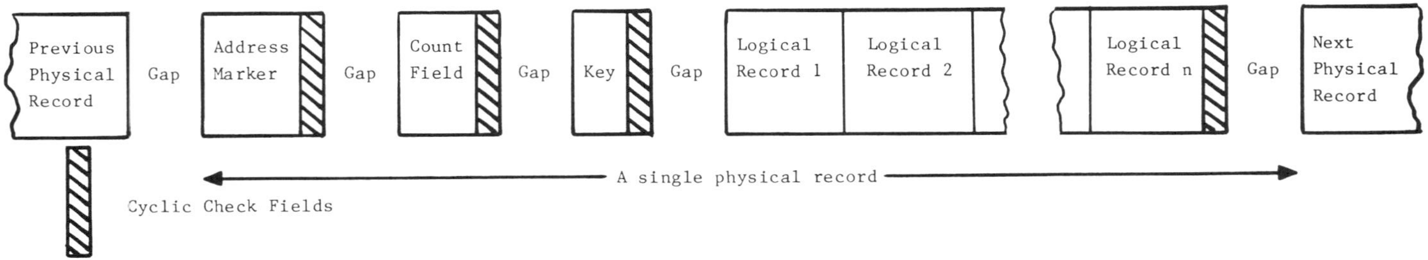

Fig. 3.3 A physical record stored on disk in count-key-data format

Fixed-length physical records may contain one or more logical records, as explained earlier. However, the block is transferred into main storage as a single entity and the user has only to specify the length of the block to allow the software to complete the transfer.

Variable-length records usually contain a length field both for the block and for each record; their format is described in detail later. The programmer has to ensure that any input-output (or I–O) areas are large enough to contain the largest variable-length record in a given file, including its length fields. As the record will have been written when the file was created, the maximum required length is usually known. Records written on disk will require a length to be specified. When records are read into main storage, the record length is provided by the software from the information in the count field, which is described below. The programmer must still allocate a large enough I–O area to hold any record on the file, although some software will warn if a record is oversize and refuse to read it unless a larger I–O area is allocated.

Undefined records are a form of variable-length record without the format restrictions imposed on variable-length records. The programmer need not provide length fields except the overall length of the record. When an undefined record is read into main storage its length is provided by the software, usually in a specified register. All other handling of the record is the responsibility of the programmer; it is treated by manufacturer's software as if it were unblocked. This format is helpful when reading data from a 'foreign' tape, for which no record format details are known.

Magnetic tape format

The reason for inter-block gaps between records on tape was explained in the previous chapter (see p. 23). The block itself is stored with each logical record in the same form as it is held in main storage. Check data is not transferred to main storage when a physical record is read. It is created and used by the device control unit, to ensure that the information in the data block is correctly stored, read and written. A typical block is shown in Fig. 3.1.

Magnetic disk formats

Most manufacturers provide two different record formats on disk. The first of these, called the *count-data format*, is shown in Fig. 3.2; it allows for two separate fields that make up the data record.

The *count field* serves as the 'address' of the record in that it holds its cylinder, head and record reference in addition to a count of the number of data characters in the following field. The count field thus provides a data record length for variable-length record processing, and an address on the device for reference by record position. The field holding the block of logical records is known as the *data field*, and contains only the records themselves including their keys. The size of the physical record is limited only by the maximum capacity of a data track, and in some systems it is possible to store a record on more than one track. This means that it is not practical to provide a buffer in the device control unit large enough to hold data records of any possible size, so that data has to be transferred without delay when it is available, or a disk revolution is lost.

A variant of this format is used on microcomputer systems, ICL's 1900 series disks and IBM's 3310 and 3370 disks. The user is provided with fixed-size sectors, usually of 128 or 512 byte capacity, in which data can be stored. This arrangement of storage is known as FBA, *fixed block architecture*. It has the advantage that a buffer can be provided in the control unit because the size of each data block is known. In general this allows for more rapid data transfer, and less time-critical handling of input-output operations. The main drawback is that maximum block size is restricted and the actual record size may not match well with the sector size; this leads to waste of direct access storage space. Both the count and data fields are still stored on the disk, but the user may not be aware of the existence of the count field, as it is used only by manufacturer's software.

A selective search on a given data key is not possible using the count-data format, as the whole block of logical records has to be read into main storage before the keys are available for processing. In order to allow selective searching for a particular key, a second format known as the *count-key-data format* is provided. This is shown in Fig. 3.3 and allows for a separate *key field*.

If only one logical record is held in the data field, its key is held separately in the key field, and the two are combined in the I-O operation to form a complete record in main storage. This saves space by not duplicating the key. In the more usual case, where the data field holds a block of logical records, the last—and therefore highest—key in the block is also stored separately in the key field. This format is useful whenever the key of a desired record is known, as the search for the record can be carried out by the device control unit, leaving the channel and main storage free until the record is found. Applications of this technique are discussed later.

Some manufacturers do not provide the count-key-data format. This applied with ICL's 1900 series devices, and in this case the user was able to retrieve records selectively using their keys because a key-to-address conversion table was provided in the software. However, reference to a separate table requires considerable additional processing time. It should be remembered that, if ICL's CAFS-ISP is available, embedded keys *can* be searched without reference to an index.

Choice and design of record formats 59

3.3 Logical records

Record types

Logically, records may be handled in five formats:

fixed-length unblocked;   variable-length unblocked;
fixed-length blocked;   variable-length blocked;
                          undefined.

Fixed-length records Unblocked records will be available for processing as soon as they have been read, and the programmer will not require software assistance. On the other hand, *blocked records* will normally be deblocked and made available to the programmer by software. There are two widely used methods of handling such records. The first is to move each record in turn into a work area in which all processing is carried out. This is called the *move mode* of operation. It is shown, with the associated physical operations, in Fig. 3.4.

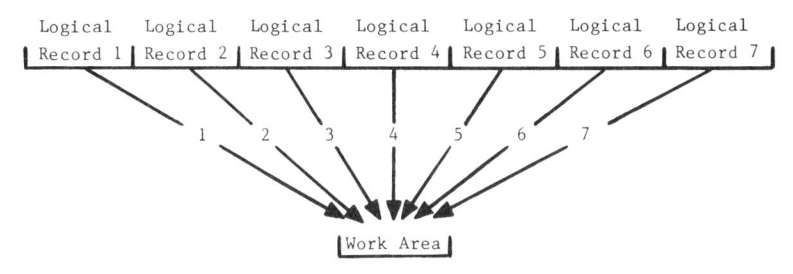

Fig. 3.4 In the move mode of deblocking records are transferred to the work area in sequence.

In the move mode of deblocking, each record is transferred to the work area in turn. Steps 2–7 involve transfer of a single record to the work area. Steps 1, 8, ... ($7n+1$) require the reading of a data block into main storage, followed by transfer of the first record to the work area.

The second method of deblocking is to provide the programmer with an index register containing the address of the record that is currently being

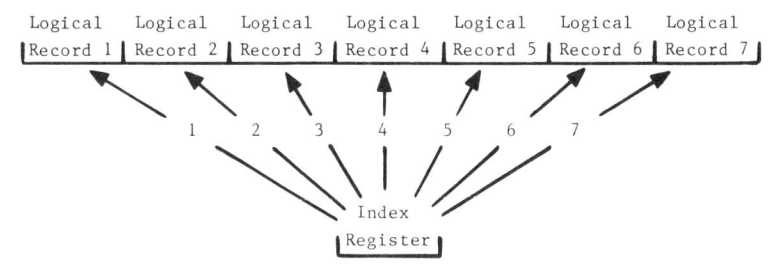

Fig. 3.5 In the locate mode of deblocking the index register points to each record in turn.

60 Design of computer data files

A single record

| BL | RL | Data record |

←— RL —→

←—— BL ——→

Blocked records

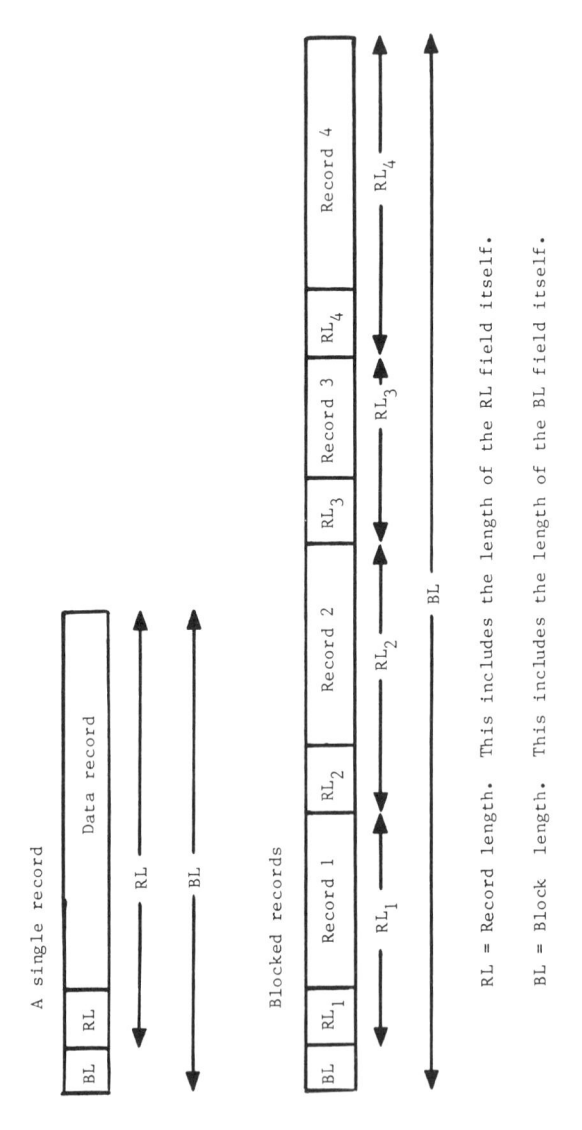

| BL | RL₁ | Record 1 | RL₂ | Record 2 | RL₃ | Record 3 | RL₄ | Record 4 |

←— RL₁ —→ ←— RL₂ —→ ←— RL₃ —→ ←— RL₄ —→

←——————————— BL ———————————→

RL = Record length. This includes the length of the RL field itself.

BL = Block length. This includes the length of the BL field itself.

Fig. 3.6 The arrangement of **BL** and **RL** fields is the same for blocked and unblocked variable-length records for compatibility.

processed. It does not involve moving the record, nor the use of a work area, and is called the *locate mode* of operation. It is shown in Fig. 3.5.

The locate mode of deblocking involves a physical transfer of data only when a new block of records is required. Otherwise an index register is used to point to each record of the block in turn. Apart from duplication of the key of the last record in each block when the count-key-data format is used, processing of fixed-length records does not involve the use of additional space over and above actual record size. The processing time involved in blocking and deblocking is also relatively limited.

Variable-length records In order to handle the input and deblocking of data records for the user, manufacturers' software requires information on the length of blocks and records. When variable-length records are created, the software will usually write this information in the record in the correct format for later re-input, based on information supplied by the program as records are written. The format of variable-length records and blocks used in IBM software is shown in Fig. 3.6. Similar formats are used by other manufacturers.

Both move and locate modes of deblocking can be employed in handling variable-length records. In most cases the input-output area and the work area (if used) will not be completely filled, as they must be large enough to hold the largest record or block in the file. However, blocking a number of variable-length records produces a less variable block size than that of the individual records. In some cases spanned records can be used to reduce the physical block size required to handle very large records, so cutting the I–O area size required. Handling spanned records is often the responsibility of the user; if it is a software function it will add to processing time. In any case the blocking, deblocking and moving or indexing of variable-length records requires more processing time than equivalent functions for fixed-length records, as the length fields have to be created during writing, and are used to de-block records during reading. Main storage space is also less efficiently filled, and the effect of these points on choice of format will be discussed later (see p. 67).

Undefined records The only software requirement for these records is that the user has to supply a length before the record can be written to a backing storage device. When they are read in, the record length will be provided by the software, usually in a general-purpose register. All blocking or deblocking is carried out by the user. Thus the software time costs are relatively minor, but the user is opting to program not only the processing of the record but also the housekeeping associated with that processing. Generally the undefined record format is used only when handling non-standard variable-length records or data that originated from some other computer system.

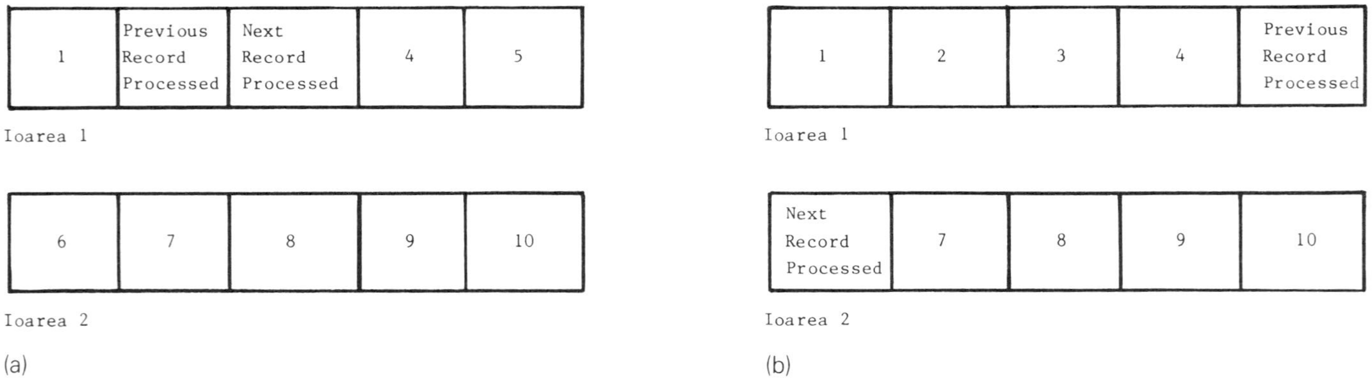

62 Design of computer data files

Fig. 3.7 The relationship between LIOCS and PIOCS when blocked records are handled using double buffers. Whether blocks are single or double buffered, PIOCS is only required when a new block is referred to or a complete block is written out. (a) As there is no change of block, LIOCS only is involved; PIOCS is not required in this process. (b) LIOCS switches to the next record in logical sequence. As one block has now been completely processed, PIOCS reads in a new block (or writes out an old one). If only a single buffer is used, PIOCS is invoked before LIOCS to make the next record available.

Record handling

The manufacturers' software that handles transfer of physical records to and from backing storage is required only when a new block of logical records has to be read or written. By contrast, every individual logical record will call on deblocking software. In IBM systems this has led to the terms *physical input-output control system*, or PIOCS, and *logical input-output control system*, or LIOCS. In most cases the user program will provide two or more input-output areas so that the records in one will be deblocked and processed while the other is written from or read into. The use of two or more such areas is called double or multiple buffering, and it is discussed in more detail in Chapter 4 (see p. 101). The relationship between LIOCS and PIOCS is shown in Fig. 3.7.

3.4 Overall run timing

On input, the time taken to complete a run depends on the times taken to locate the required record, to transfer it to main storage, and to process it. On output, the same three constituents will make up the overall time required to deal with any given record. Looking at each of these stages in more detail, *input-output time* will be made up of:
   seek time on disk, or start time for a tape;
   data transfer time;
while *processing time* will consist of:
   blocking, de-blocking, initiating I-O transfers, etc.;
   record processing.

The objective of designing record formats is to minimize these times as far as possible while not degrading the performance of the files they are held in. This depends on a number of factors, including the way in which the computer in question operates. This has changed with each generation of computers, and the general evolution is given below.

Early computers did not overlap I-O and internal operations, and the computer alternated between handling I-O and processing operations. Because of this, each time element was minimized independently, and there was no trade-off between I-O and CPU timing.

Some second-generation computers allowed I-O and CPU operations to take place simultaneously. This meant that the time taken to complete a processing run would depend on the slower of the two constituents, I-O and CPU processing. Details of overlap during the reading and processing of records are given in Chapter 4 (see p. 99), and shown in Fig. 4.9. When the two constituents take an equal time the run is said to be *balanced*.

If the computer is carrying out a single task only, the aim of the file designer will be to increase the speed of the more time-consuming constituent in order to balance the run. For example, Fig. 3.8 (a) and (b) show unbalanced runs with longer processing and I-O times respectively. Figs. 3.8

64 Design of computer data files

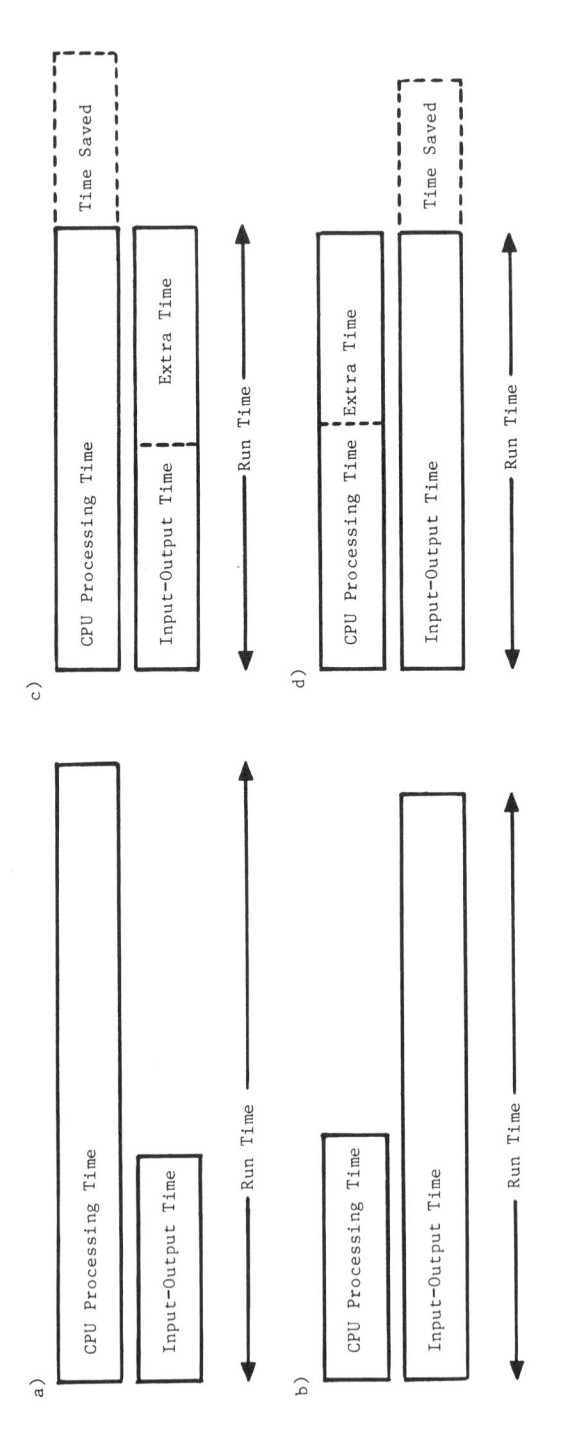

Fig. 3.8 Runs (a) and (b) are unbalanced and one or other constituent determines the overall run time. Correct design of record format and blocking factors can sometimes convert such runs into balanced runs, as shown in (c) and (d). Note that the balanced run time is usually nearer to the longer constituent time than the shorter one.

(c) and (d) show these same runs balanced by altering the record format and blocking factor to speed up the slower constituent.

Nowadays it is very unusual for a computer to be running only a single program at a time. Generally a number of programs will be active at any given moment, and the file designer will wish to minimize the *overall* I–O and CPU times of the system. As it is often not possible to forecast which programs will be run at the same time, the aim of record format and blocking decisions will be to optimize the performance of each individual constituent that makes up run times. Operations staff will ensure as far as possible that the group of programs being run at any given time is in balance overall; the individual programs no longer need to be balanced. This avoids the situation where a very large increase in I–O time—that might be caused by using unblocked records, for example—would be justified if it decreased CPU processing time by a much smaller amount than the increase in I–O time, but produced a balanced run. In a modern multiprogramming system, only changes that will reduce the overall time of I–O and CPU operations are normally worthwhile. (This would not hold if all the programs in an installation were I–O bound or CPU bound. In this case the situation would be similar to that for a computer providing overlap between I–O and CPU operations, and running a single program.)

To examine the effect of record format more closely, we need to look at the elements that make up input-output and processing time.

Input-output time

This is made up of two parts:

1 Record location time The time spent in making a record available, whether it is the start time of a magnetic tape unit or the head movement and/or track search time on a magnetic disk, can be overlapped with both CPU processing and other I–O operations on different devices. Hence this time is sometimes not very significant. It is also more dependent on the file organization than any other factor, and much of the rest of this book aims to help file designers to minimize the time wasted in locating desired records.

2 Data transfer time This can only be reduced by increasing the speed of transfer or reducing the size of the data record. The first possibility depends on the use of a faster device; the second can be affected by record format. The actual transfer of data will occupy a device and a data channel for some time, making them unavailable to other programs and information files. Thus if the time taken to transfer data is critical the file designer should examine record format.

Processing time

This again is made up of two parts:

1 Housekeeping

Operations such as blocking or deblocking records, processing requests for transfers of data to or from backing storage, and locating fields in variable-length records are known as housekeeping. They can add significantly to total processing times. Reducing the number of records in a block will increase the number of separate requests for physical transfer of data that have to be made, and so add to processing time. If blocks are reduced to single records this may be worthwhile in some circumstances, as no blocking or deblocking will be necessary. Otherwise it will not pay. Blocking is looked at in more detail in Chapter 4.

The choice of variable-length records will considerably increase housekeeping times, as each field will have to be identified and located. This is dealt with below.

2 Record processing

The basic disciplines of processing cannot be altered by record format, but move, edit, compare and other operations can be simplified. Hence format should be looked at if processing time is causing a problem.

The way in which overall processing time can be affected by altering record format is considered under the following headings:

record length;
layout;
variable/fixed format;
file size.

Record length Unless actual data transfer time is a problem, it is desirable to provide room in a record for all present requirements and some spare space for possible future modifications. This means that records will tend to be larger than is strictly necessary. This is true when name and address fields are made large enough to contain the longest name and address in the file, even though this is wasteful in most cases. Variable-length records are often avoided in this way at the expense of extra space in most records.

The designer should look out for the situation in which a slightly increased record size will lead to a dramatic increase in file size. This would happen if card records just exceeded eighty characters or if a tape file required an extra reel of tape. In such cases it may be worth restricting record size. However, improved blocking will often offer a way of reducing the impact of increased length without reducing record size (see Chapter 4).

Layout If name and address fields are held in spaced form it is possible simply to move information to a print area and avoid the need for editing;

this saves processing time at the expense of space. Decimal fields can be held with the exact number of leading or trailing zeros for correct positioning, thus speeding numeric operations. Codes can be held in binary, to save space and testing time, even though they will usually be input in numeric form.

The relative position of fields is also important. Few modern computers can provide as much improvement by positioning alone as was achieved in the IBM 1400 series computers by *chaining*[1]. However, two fields that are to be moved together, or used as a composite search or sort key, are best stored together. If one of these is to be used for arithmetic operations it should be stored in the first half-word of a byte-and-word-oriented computer such as IBM System/370, and processed using half-word instructions. This arrangement might be as shown in Fig. 3.9.

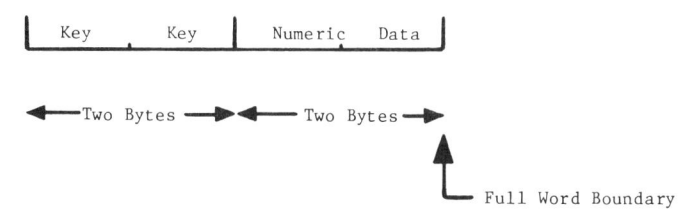

```
| Key    Key    | Numeric   Data |
←— Two Bytes —→←— Two Bytes —→
                ↑
                └— Full Word Boundary
```

Fig. 3.9 Two fields that are to be moved together or used as a composite search or sort key are stored together. If one of these is to be used for arithmetic operations it should be stored in the first half-word of a byte-and-word-oriented computer and processed using half-word instructions.

The numeric field can be used for half-word calculations and moved or compared with the key in other operations. Similar packing arrangements can be achieved with other character- or word-oriented computers.

Duplication of fields can sometimes be useful. This might apply where the same information is needed in different forms—a name used both as part of a name and address field and separately as a key would be an example of this.

In general, layout changes are likely to be used to speed processing at the expense of space, although in some cases careful design can improve both.

Variable or fixed format The main reason to decide on a variable format is that record reading time has to be reduced; thus, an I–O bound file may well use a variable-length format. This choice has been examined in detail by Montgomery[2], who has given guidelines as to the time wasted by deciding on fixed-length format. In addition, the designer should first look at the possibility of storing the file on a direct access device and skip-sequentially processing it. This is examined in later chapters.

The prerequisite for using variable-length records or blocks is that a significant saving in I–O time will be achieved, as there will certainly be an increase in CPU housekeeping time. Thus variable format is normally only

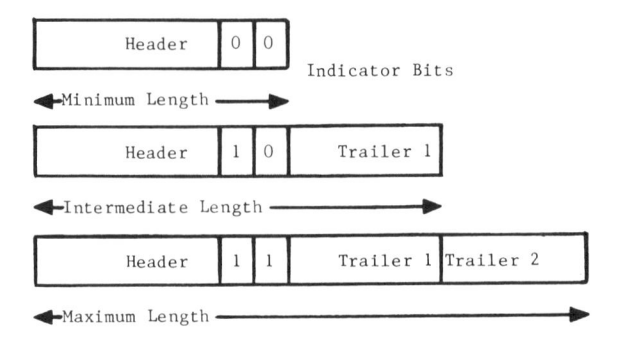

```
    ┌─────────┬─┬─┐
    │ Header  │0│0│
    └─────────┴─┴─┘
                   Indicator Bits
◄─Minimum Length──►

    ┌─────────┬─┬─┬──────────┐
    │ Header  │1│0│ Trailer 1│
    └─────────┴─┴─┴──────────┘
◄─Intermediate Length──────►

    ┌─────────┬─┬─┬──────────┬──────────┐
    │ Header  │1│1│ Trailer 1│ Trailer 2│
    └─────────┴─┴─┴──────────┴──────────┘
◄─Maximum Length──────────────────────►
```

Fig. 3.10 This arrangement will minimize the analysis required to identify the fields in a record, and thus limit the additional housekeeping time involved.

useful for a large file. In addition, many fields should be dropped from many records to justify the work involved. The ideal case is a low-activity tape file that for other reasons cannot be held on a direct-access device.

When variable-length records are used it is best to restrict the number of formats to two or three: in effect, a header record in all cases with one or more additional groups of fields when required. It must also be remembered that, if very large maximum record sizes are allowed for, a very large I–O area will be required in main storage although it will not always be filled. The arrangement might be as shown in Fig. 3.10.

File size It has already been pointed out above that small files should not hold variable-length records. In general, the stress will be on reducing processing time for small files and I–O time for large files. Even in the latter case it must be remembered that space may be needed for later modification, so it is not wise to cut record size to the absolute minimum.

Conclusion

Record and block formats have been defined in this chapter, and their effect on run times has been examined. Although the record format is often left to the programmer, it can be of benefit to the file designer to include it in the design calculations. There is seldom a justification for drastic alteration of formats to produce a balanced run, but overall efficiency can be improved in almost every file by optimized design.

References

1. *Systems Operation Reference Manual, IBM 1440 Data Processing System*, IBM Manual No. A24-3116.

2. 'Designing magnetic tape files for variable-length records', by Tony Y. Montgomery, *Management Informatics*, Vol. 3, No. 6, 1974, pp. 271–276.

Revision questions

1 What is meant by the terms 'logical record' and 'physical record'? Explain the types of format each of these can take up, and their relationship.

2 Describe and draw the format of a physical record on magnetic tape.

3 Why are there a number of formats available on magnetic disk? Describe and draw them.

4 What are the usual methods of deblocking a block of records? Explain the advantages and drawbacks of any method you describe.

5 Distinguish between the software requirements of fixed, variable and undefined logical records. Discuss the size of any input-output areas required by these types of format and make clear how fully they will be used.

6 What are the stages that make up the overall processing time for a logical record? Describe each of these stages in detail, indicating the effect each might have on the overall time.

7 Explain the significance of the term 'balanced run'. Make clear the difference in the application of this concept for a computer system that is running a single program and one that is running multiple programs.

8 How and when would you use the length of a record to affect the overall run time for the records?

9 What effect does record layout have on the overall run time for a record?

10 Distinguish between the situations in which you might choose to hold records in variable- and in fixed-length format.

11 Why does file size have a rather different influence on the methods you might use to exploit format effects than the other factors discussed here?

12 Who is generally responsible for record formats? Why should the file designer take an interest in record formats?

4 Blocking and buffering

4.1 Introduction

Individual records in information files are often quite small. If the file has been adapted from a card file, the records may be only eighty characters in length, and changes or update records are often considerably smaller than this. If these small records are stored separately on magnetic tape or disk files this usually has several undesirable effects. These are that, because of the relatively large gaps between these small records:

effective data transfer rate is slowed up;
time is wasted in traversing the inter-record gaps;
additional backing storage space is required.

One way to reduce the impact of small records is to group them together into blocks. This was discussed in general terms in Chapter 3 (see p. 59); the precise results of blocking depend on the actual tape or disk being used. In this chapter the file designer is shown how to calculate the optimum blocking factor in the general case. Specific data on a number of widely-used information storage devices, that can be used in these calculations, are given in Chapter 2.

Blocking on tape is rather different in effect from blocking on disk. For this reason the first section of the chapter deals with magnetic tape blocking in detail, and the second section with magnetic disk and similar devices. In a general sense it emerges that large blocks are usually advantageous whatever the storage medium, but that there are exceptions.

This is followed by a discussion of the limitations imposed on block size by factors such as limited available main storage or the operating system being used. The next section looks at those cases in which large blocks are not useful, under the heading Block Activity (see p. 83). The section on competing files (see p. 89) discusses the very common case in which limited main storage space has to be shared between several files. Algorithms to aid decisions on the optimum allocation of main storage space are given and the designer is shown how to use them in typical situations.

Blocking improves the overall speed of data transfer and reduces the demand for backing storage in most cases, but it does mean that in a single I–O operation the actual transfer of data will take longer as the quantity of data to be transferred is now greater. Thus the delay between the time that the central processing unit issues a read command and the time that the record is available in main storage, which is already significant, is further increased. This can be improved by the use of one or more buffers, usually in main storage, into which records are read before they are processed. The *principle of buffering* is that during reading the contents of one I–O buffer can be processed while the other buffer (if there are only two) is being filled with the next data block. If the operation being carried out is a write, one buffer is written to disk or tape while the next block is assembled in the other. Processing and input or output alternate between the buffers, and it is possible to overlap I–O operations with processing, so saving a great deal of time. A detailed description of the operation of buffers is given under Use of Buffers (see p. 98) later in this chapter.

4.2 Blocks on magnetic tape

When data is written on to a magnetic tape, or read from it, the tape has to be moving at a constant speed. In between reading or writing records the tape is stationary. Because the tape takes some time to reach its constant reading–writing speed and some time to slow down again, there is inevitably a gap between blocks of data. This gap is typically 0.3 or 0.6 inches in length, although some of the faster tape drives available have smaller gaps than this. The way in which the gap arises was explained in Chapter 2 (see p. 23).

The presence of a set of gaps between the records in effect reduces the packing density of the data on the tape. Manufacturers quote maximum transfer rates for data between a tape drive and main storage, but because of these gaps the *effective transfer rate* is always lower. Just how much lower is clear from Fig. 4.1 and Table 4.1, in which the effective transfer rates for tapes with data recording densities of 800, 1600 and 6250 characters per inch are shown. It is assumed that the first two tapes have 0.6 inch inter-block gaps, the last has 0.3 inch IBGs, and there is no lost time due to start-stops other than traversing the IBGs at reading speed. Values in the table are calculated on the basis that to read a physical record the device has to traverse the record itself and a single IBG. The results are typical of many devices, and are used to illustrate the general principles of blocking.

The very dramatic reduction in effective transfer rate caused by small records, as compared with the rate quoted by the manufacturer, makes it obvious that blocking of small records will be advisable. This is particularly important if the run is input-output bound as the effective transfer rate then determines overall run time.

A reduced transfer rate reflects the fact that an increased length of tape is required to hold the file. This is not important in itself, as magnetic tape is a very cheap storage medium, but it does become significant if the file spills on to a second, third or nth reel of tape, as this will lead to an extra reel change,

72 Design of computer data files

and so further time loss. This is one case in which the IBM 3480 tape drive, with a hopper holding up to six further cassettes, is superior to earlier tape drives. Table 4.2 shows the number of data records that can be stored on a 2400-foot tape, making the same assumptions about data density and interblock gaps as before. From Table 4.2 and Fig. 4.2 it is clear that a larger data block size leads to a very marked increase in data stored on a single tape. This increase is more pronounced the higher the packing density.

The effect of data block size on the quantity of data stored on a single 2400-foot tape is illustrated by Fig. 4.2. It should also be noted that the capacity of a tape depends more on block size than on data density for short blocks, so high-data-density tapes should be used for files that are to be stored in large blocks only, to avoid inefficiency.

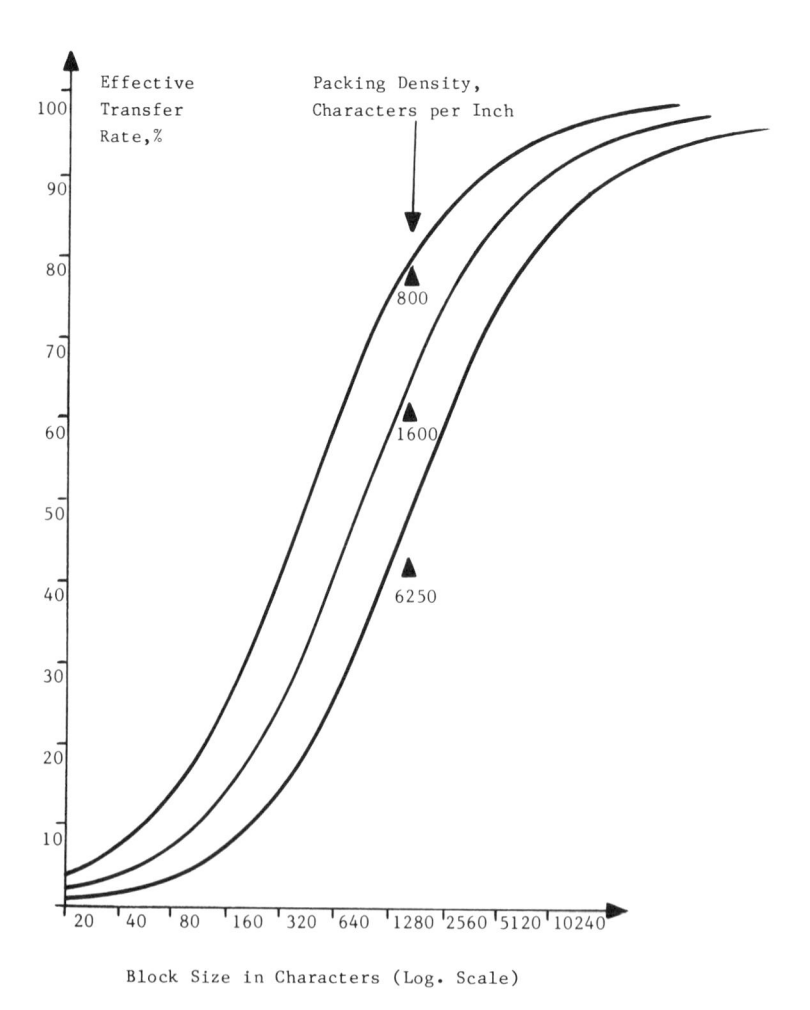

Fig. 4.1 The effect of block size on the actual transfer rate achieved.

Table 4.1 The figures tabulated give the effective data transfer rate as a percentage of the maximum data transfer rate.

Record length (characters)	Packing density (characters per inch) 800	1600	6250
20	4.0	2.0	1.1
40	7.7	4.0	2.1
80	14.3	7.7	4.1
160	25.0	14.3	7.9
320	40.0	25.0	14.6
640	57.1	40.0	25.4
1 280	72.7	57.1	40.6
2 560	84.2	72.7	57.7
5 120	91.4	84.2	73.2
10 240	95.2	91.4	84.5
20 480	97.7	95.2	91.6
40 960	98.8	97.7	95.6

Table 4.2 The figures tabulated show the number of full data blocks of the size shown that can be stored on 2400 feet of magnetic tape at packing densities stated, and the total number of data characters held on the tape in millions of characters.

Block length (characters)	Packing density (characters per inch)					
	800		1600		6250	
	No. of blocks	Total data	No. of blocks	Total data	No. of blocks	Total data
20	46 080	0.922	47 020	0.940	94 916	1.900
40	44 307	1.772	46 080	1.843	93 994	3.760
80	41 142	3.291	44 307	3.545	92 071	7.366
160	36 000	5.760	41 142	6.583	88 452	14.152
320	28 800	9.216	36 000	11.520	82 004	26.241
640	20 571	13.165	28 800	18.432	71 570	45.805
1 280	13 090	16.755	20 571	26.331	57 052	73.027
2 560	7 578	19.400	13 090	33.510	40 586	103.900
5 120	4 114	21.064	7 578	38.799	25 732	131.748
10 240	2 149	22.006	4 114	42.127	14 857	152.136
20 480	1 099	22.508	2 149	44.012	8 051	164.884
40 960	555	22.733	1 099	45.015	4 202	172.114
Maximum	1	23.040	1	46.080	1	180.000

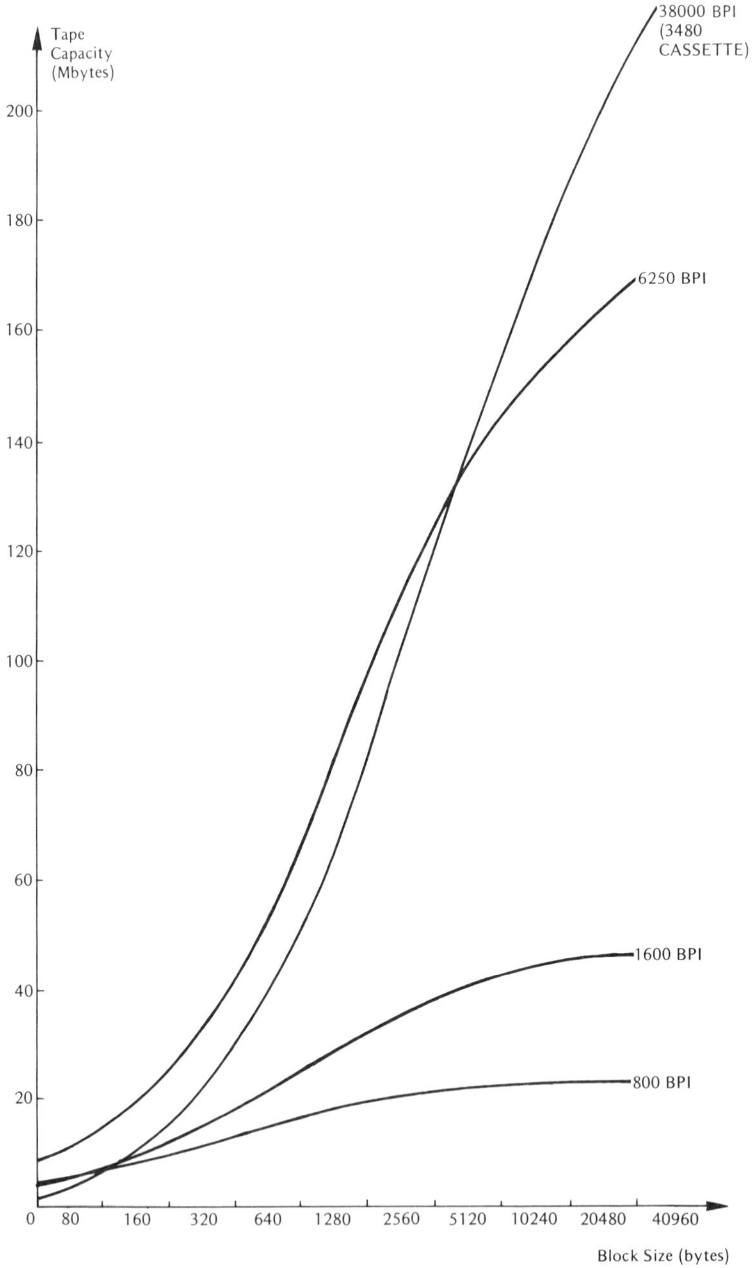

74 Design of computer data files

Fig. 4.2 The curves show the effect of data block size on the storage capacity of magnetic tapes. The 3480 uses a cassette tape that is much shorter than the other tapes shown (500 feet), but has a capacity comparable with 6250 bpi tapes of 2400 feet in length.

Magnetic tape processing is generally based on the sequential or serial processing of every record on the tape, whether it is updated or not. It is possible to backward or forward space through records or files, but this is only done when processing work files during a sort or other operation that requires intermediate backing storage.

Because the input record is written out on to a new tape, every record has to be read, and it is not possible to save time during the reading of data itself. However, the use of larger blocks cuts down the number of inter-block gaps that have to be spaced over, and any overall saving in the *tape passing time* for this file—the time required just to read the records on tape—is due to this. Although such a saving does not sound significant it can in fact be very marked; this is not surprising, as the effect of using very small block sizes has already been demonstrated in Figs. 4.1 and 4.2. The actual savings that can be achieved by correct blocking are discussed later under the heading Competing Files (see p. 89).

4.3 Blocks on magnetic disk

This section deals specifically with magnetic disk storage, but the principles apply equally to drums, data-cells and other devices for which storage is based on a fixed-length track. There are a number of fundamental differences between tape and disk:

1. The device does not stop between the reading or writing of records.
2. The inter-block gap is relatively small.
3. The fixed length of track means that block sizes affect both the efficient storage of information on a track and the number of IBGs. This leads to some smaller block sizes being more efficient than some larger ones.
4. It is normal to update records in place on disk, i.e. to read in a record, modify it and write it back into the same position (this is not possible without extra programming precautions if records are variable in length). For this reason only records that are to be updated need to be read: a low hit-rate file may therefore be better left with one or few records per block, to avoid reading records that are not required.
5. Records can be selectively read into main storage using a separate key that is compared with the required key. The format that is used for this mode of operation was discussed in Chapter 3 (see p. 57).

The points listed above lead to a number of differences between the performance of disk and that of tape. Looking first at the amount of data that can be stored on a single track of a disk device, there are two widely used methods of arranging data storage. The first is that of allowing the user to choose any record size from about five characters to the full length of the track; the second is to provide a number of sectors of fixed size on the track and allow the user to fill them in any way that is required.

76 Design of computer data files

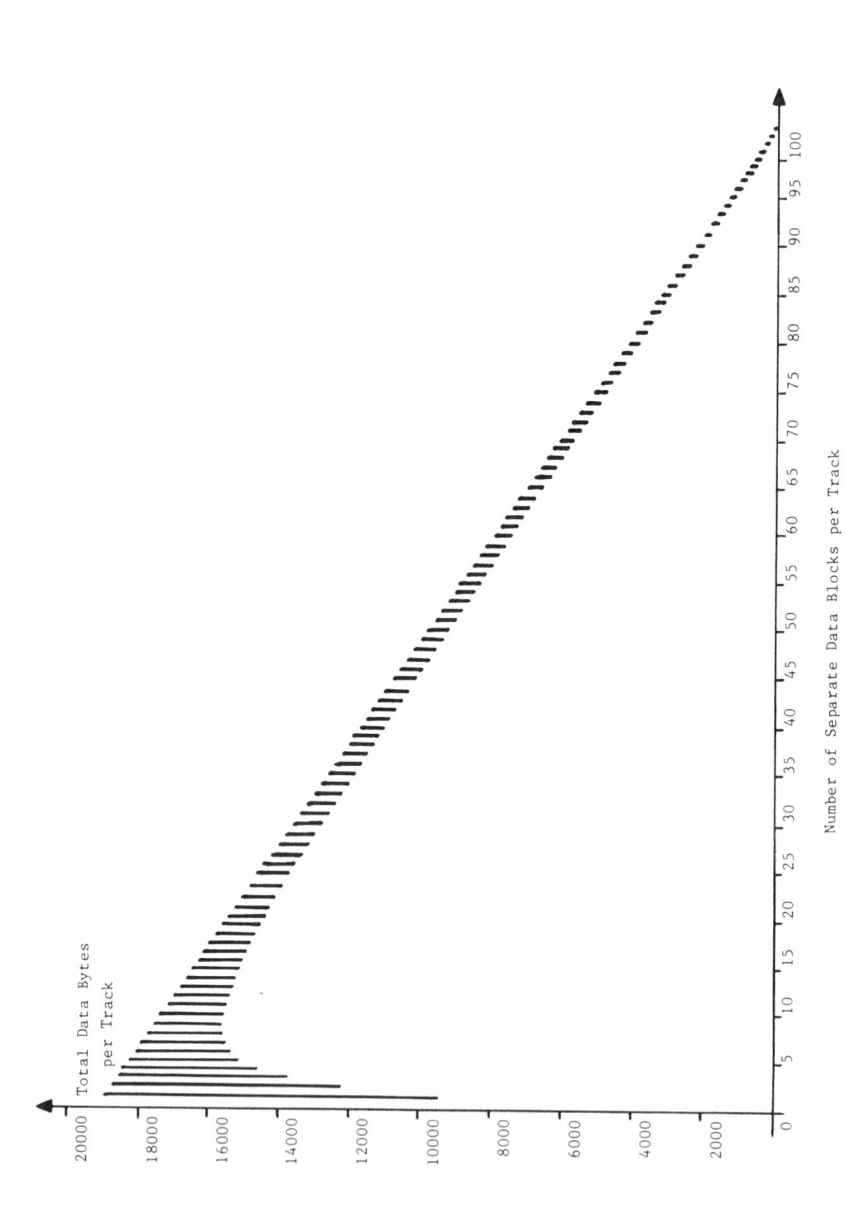

Fig. 4.3 This shows the maximum and minimum number of bytes stored on a single track of an IBM 3350 disk for 1, 2, 3 . . . 100 data blocks per track. The top of each line shows the *best* possible choice of block size and the bottom of each line shows the *worst* possible choice while storing as many blocks as will fit on the track.

The first method gives a very wide choice of record or block size. It is convenient to look at a particular device, and the IBM 3350 is a good example to take. If records or blocks are formatted with separate keys, up to 18 987 bytes can be stored on a single 3350 track. The amount of data actually stored will depend both on block size and on how well the chosen record or block size fits the track: two records of size 9360 bytes (including keys) can be stored on a single track, but only one of size 9361. This is because the end of the second record would overlap the start of the track and overwrite control information. Although this is an extreme example, the principle applies for records of all sizes. Thus, in choosing a block size, the first step is to check which sizes fit well on the disk and which do not. Information on this is available in a number of IBM publications[1,2], and the results of plotting that data for the 3350 are shown in Fig. 4.3. The upper end of each vertical line corresponds to a 'perfect' choice, while the lower end shows the worst choice that can be made if the user wishes to use direct access space efficiently.

In deciding on a blocking factor for records, it is wise to choose a block size that is near the upper end of each line rather than near the lower end. Take the example of 100-character records to be stored with separate keys on an IBM 3350. The number of blocks that can be held on a single track for various blocking factors is given in Table 4.3. If block sizes are small, increasing the blocking factor increases the quantity of data stored on the track. However, blocks of nine records are no better than blocks of eight, while blocks of fourteen records are less efficient than blocks of thirteen. This is even more marked for blocks of nineteen, twenty-two, twenty-five, thirty, thirty-six, forty-six, sixty-two and ninety-four records, as these choices are at or near the lower end of lines in Fig. 4.3. Poor choices are marked with an asterisk.

The result of using a larger basic record size is also shown in Table 4.3. With 600-byte records stored singly, twenty-two can be stored per track. Even if records are blocked in a single huge block, this is only improved to thirty-one records per track, and some intermediate sizes—blocks of sixteen, seventeen, eighteen, nineteen, twenty and twenty-one—are poorer choices than leaving the records unblocked.

These examples demonstrate the care that has to be taken in choosing blocking factors on track-oriented storage. With care very good results can be obtained. Without it the designer may produce a file that is both inefficient—because of the need to read in relatively large blocks of data when accessing a single record—and poorly packed.

The second approach to disk storage allocation is that of providing addressable fixed sectors on the track. This applied to the earlier IBM 1311 disk, which was divided into twenty addressable sectors, each containing 100 characters, for most purposes. ICL use a similar system for their EDS 8, 30, 60, 100 and 200 disk storage devices, although the EDS 100 and 200 can be used in byte mode with record sizes chosen by the user, when attached to the

78 Design of computer data files

Table 4.3 This Table shows the result of choosing various blocking factors for 100 and 600 byte records stored on an IBM 3350 disk. For any given record size it is important to choose a blocking factor that optimizes disk usage.

Blocking Factor	Record size 100 bytes					Record size 600 bytes				
	Block size (bytes)	Blocks per track	Records per track	Total data per track	Percentage of maximum	Block size (bytes)	Blocks per track	Records per track	Total data per track	Percentage of maximum
1	100	52	52	5 200	27.4	600	22	22	13 200	69.5
2	200	41	82	8 200	43.2	1 200	13	26	15 600	82.2
3	300	33	99	9 900	52.1	1 800	9	27	16 200	85.3
4	400	28	112	11 200	59.0	2 400	7	28	16 800	88.5
5	500	25	125	12 500	65.8	3 000	5	25	15 000*	79.0
6	600	22	132	13 200	69.5	3 600	4	24	14 400*	75.8
7	700	19	133	13 300	70.0	4 200	4	28	16 800	88.5
8	800	18	144	14 400	75.8	4 800	3	24	14 400*	75.8
9	900	16	144	14 400	75.8	5 400	3	27	16 200	85.3
10	1 000	15	150	15 000	79.0	6 000	3	30	18 000	94.8
11	1 100	14	154	15 400	81.1	6 600	2	22	13 200*	69.5
12	1 200	13	156	15 600	82.2	7 200	2	24	14 400	75.8
13	1 300	12	156	15 600	82.2	7 800	2	26	15 600	82.2
14	1 400	11	154	15 400*	81.1	8 400	2	28	16 800	88.5
15	1 500	10	150	15 000*	79.0	9 000	2	30	18 000	94.8
16	1 600	10	160	16 000	84.3	9 600	1	16	9 600*	50.6
18	1 800	9	162	16 200	85.3	10 800	1	18	10 800	56.9
19	1 900	8	152	15 200*	80.1	11 400	1	19	11 400	60.0
21	2 100	8	168	16 800	88.5	12 600	1	21	12 600	66.4
24	2 400	7	168	16 800	88.5	14 400	1	24	14 400	75.8
25	2 500	6	150	15 000*	79.0	15 000	1	25	15 000	79.0
29	2 900	6	174	17 400	91.6	17 400	1	29	17 400	91.6
30	3 000	5	150	15 000*	79.0	18 000	1	30	18 000	94.8
31	3 100	5	155	15 500	81.6	18 600	1	31	18 600	98.0
35	3 500	5	175	17 500	92.2					
45	4 500	4	180	18 000	94.8					
61	6 100	3	183	18 300	96.4					
93	9 300	2	186	18 600	98.0					
189	18 900	1	189	18 900	99.5					

* Poor choices of block size

larger 2900 series computers. The EDS 8, which employs the same type of disk packs as the IBM 2311, is described elsewhere[3]. ICL 1900 series computers use six-bit characters, and each track of an EDS 8 provides the user with eight hardware blocks, each able to contain up to 512 characters of data. (This is equivalent to choosing an eight-record format for an IBM 2311 track; eight 384-byte records can be held on a single 2311 track[1], but these are eight-bit bytes, and the number of bits stored in a single hardware block [8×384 or 6×512] is the same for 2311 and EDS 8. The difference is that the 2311 user can store more data by choosing to use larger physical records.)

A record or block size of 512 characters may not be convenient for the user, so ICL operating systems allow a *bucket* of one, two, four or eight blocks to be defined in which data records are stored. Although the user can logically handle record blocks of 512, 1024, 2048 or 4096 six-bit characters in this way, the data is still physically stored in 512-character hardware blocks. No increase, either in maximum data transfer rate or track storage capacity, is achieved by increasing the blocking factor. The main objective of blocking is thus to fill the hardware blocks as efficiently as possible. If basic record size is 200 characters, for example, blocks of two records at maximum would fit in 512-character buckets, while blocks of five records would fit into buckets of 1024 characters. Larger buckets would not improve this data packing density, and so would not be justified on storage efficiency grounds.

The fixed sector concept has been extended to the ICL EDS 30 and 60, using 15×512 character blocks per track, and to the EDS 100 and 200 with 25×512 character blocks per track. As these devices rotate at 3600 revolutions per minute, the maximum data transfer rate for an EDS 100 or 200, including traversing gaps, is 25×512×60, or 768 000 six-bit characters per second. This rate is achieved if every physical block is fully packed; the actual transfer rate can be calculated by finding the packing density in these blocks. The range possible is shown in Fig. 4.4—obviously a user would aim to achieve a high packing density, and so keep at the top end of this range.

The ranges of actual transfer rate shown in Fig. 4.4 are maxima. It is assumed that spare space has been left on a track only when there is not sufficient room to store a further record.

For comparison, the actual transfer rates achieved on an IBM 3330 disk, including traversing gaps, for block sizes such that one to thirty blocks can be held on the track, are given in Table 4.4. The minimum figures show block sizes for which a further block is just not able to fit on the track; even lower figures would be obtained if the track were not filled as far as possible. The bounded area in Fig. 4.4 shows the range of actual transfer rates obtainable. This wide range, much of which is above the rates obtained from an EDS 100 or 200, is due to the greater user choice provided by this method of storage organization. (However, an EDS 100 or 200 used with an ICL 2900 computer is organized like a 3330 and so performs exactly analogously.) The reader should note that Fig. 4.4 shows figures for records stored without separate keys. It is also important to bear in mind that the physical transfer of data takes place at 806 000 bytes per second; the figures given in Table 4.4 and Fig. 4.4 are lower than this because they show the effect of inter-block gaps on the instantaneous transfer rate that is the figure usually quoted by manufacturers.

Table 4.4 The figures tabulated show the effect of the number of blocks per track on the maximum and minimum quantities of data that can be stored on the track, and the upper and lower limits of transfer rate that can be achieved between the disk and main storage. The device is a 3330.

Number of blocks per track	Maximum data per track	Minimum data per track	Maximum transfer rate	Minimum transfer rate
1	13 030	6 448	781 800	386 880
2	12 894	8 508	773 640	510 480
3	12 759	9 471	765 540	568 260
4	12 624	9 996	757 440	599 760
5	12 490	10 300	749 400	618 000
6	12 354	10 476	741 240	628 560
7	12 216	10 577	732 960	634 620
8	12 080	10 624	724 800	637 440
9	11 943	10 638	716 580	638 280
10	11 810	10 620	708 600	637 200
11	11 671	10 593	700 260	635 580
12	11 544	10 536	692 640	632 160
13	11 401	10 478	684 060	628 680
14	11 270	10 402	676 200	624 120
15	11 130	10 320	667 800	619 200
16	10 992	10 240	659 520	614 400
17	10 863	10 149	651 780	608 940
18	10 728	10 044	643 680	602 640
19	10 583	9 956	634 980	597 360
20	10 460	9 840	627 600	590 400
21	10 311	9 744	618 660	584 640
22	10 186	9 636	611 160	578 160
23	10 051	9 522	603 060	571 320
24	9 912	9 408	594 720	564 480
25	9 775	9 300	586 500	558 000
26	9 646	9 178	578 760	550 680
27	9 504	9 072	570 240	544 320
28	9 380	8 932	562 800	535 920
29	9 222	8 816	553 320	528 960
30	9 090	8 700	545 400	522 000

Blocking and buffering **81**

Transfer Rate, Bytes per Second

800000

700000

600000

500000 — Actual transfer rates for the IBM 3330, and the ICL EDS 200 used with a 2900 series computer, will lie within the area bounded by the two lines shown.

400000

300000 — Actual transfer rates for the EDS 200 used with a 1900 series computer will lie on this line. The maximum is decided by the choice of 25 blocks per track; it is usually quoted in characters per second, but is shown here in bytes per second for comparison.

200000

100000

0   5   10   15   20   25   30

Number of Physical Blocks per Track.

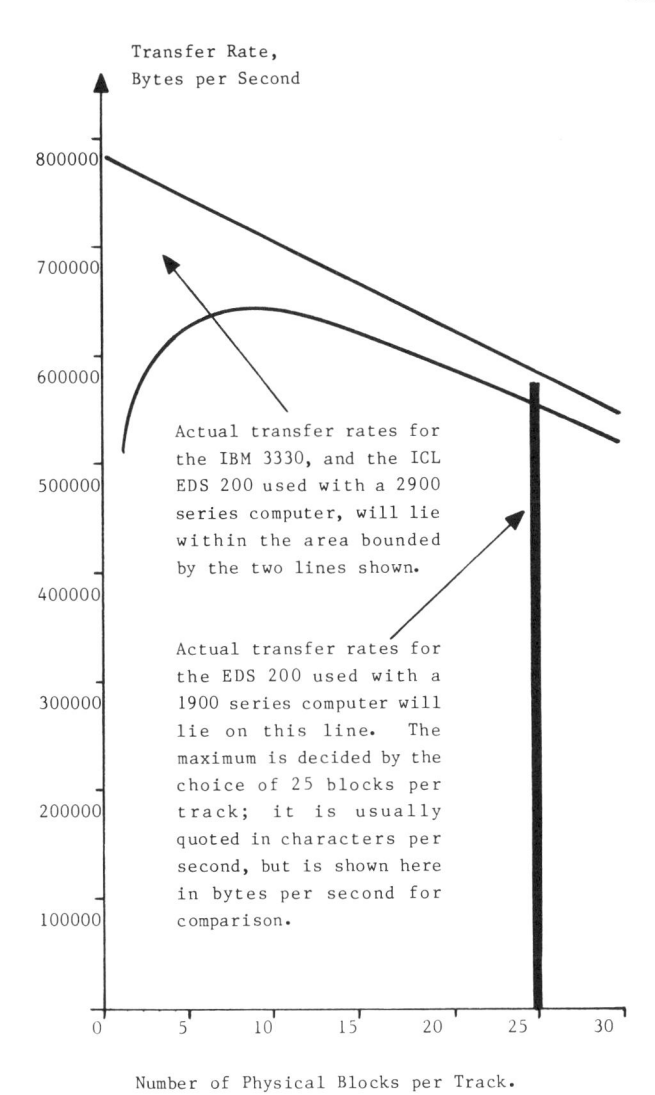

Fig. 4.4 Figures are calculated on the basis that space is left unused on a track only if there is no room to store a further record.

4.4 General blocking considerations

From the discussion above it is clear that the file designer will usually aim to block records to be stored on magnetic tape in blocks that are as large as possible. Records to be stored on track-oriented direct access devices will also often be blocked, but the choice of block size is more critical if the device performance is to be optimized. However, for some direct access applications a large block size is not appropriate. This is discussed in the section on block activity later in the chapter (see p. 83).

In cases where the largest possible data block is desired, a number of factors may limit the blocking factor that the file designer decides on. These are discussed below.

4.5 Limitations on block size

Available main storage

The absolute limit to the size of a block is the amount of main storage available to the program using the file. This will be modified by the number of buffers, so that a double-buffered file will have an absolute limit half the size of a single-buffered file, and so on. If there are pressing reasons to increase block size beyond the limit imposed by available main storage, the file designer will have to arrange for a larger main storage partition in fixed-partition machines. Variable partition size or virtual storage systems may avoid any absolute limit, but even in this case there is a risk of considerable delay due to transfers of data between the disk areas allocated to virtual storage, and main storage. There is still a need to aim for input-output area sizes that are likely to be available without causing unnecessary paging in and out from backing storage.

Programs using the same file

If a file—usually a master file—is used by a number of different programs, each of these programs will impose a different *absolute limit* on the input-output area size available to the file. The smallest of these sizes will become the absolute limit to the block size used for the file. It has been suggested[4] that it would be possible to read different-sized blocks of data from a given file, irrespective of the physical size of the data blocks on the magnetic file storage medium. It was proposed that PIOCS (physical input-output control system) should be used to read blocks of records smaller than the blocks on the file. In principle this can be done, as can the reverse procedure of reading more than one physical block of records in a single I-O operation. In IBM terminology this relies on command and data chaining of CCWs (channel command words), and thus depends on the programmer working at a more detailed level than is usual. The main problem is that of arranging for record and block sizes that lend themselves to suitable breakdown without requiring spanned record handling in one or more programs.

For example, a block of twenty-four records could be read in ones, twos, threes, fours, sixes, eights and twelves apart from the complete block, but fives, sevens, nines, etc., would involve more complicated procedures. The choice of twenty-four as a number of records per block is particularly favourable because it has so many divisors. It is seldom possible to choose block sizes on this basis, using numbers such as twelve, twenty-four, thirty-six and sixty while avoiding ten, fifteen and others lacking sufficient divisors. In addition, there may well be problems due to the location of check data at the *end* of data blocks, while this method depends on transferring only part of the block into or out of main storage.

Apart from using some such technique as described above[4], the file designer has to accept that the absolute limit on block size is set by the most restrictive program using a file. Other constraints may reduce the maximum block size possible still further.

Operating system implications

Files designed to operate under virtual storage conditions will be affected by the page size used by the operating system. IBM's VSAM, for instance, uses pages of 2048 bytes for most purposes. A block of records would be better just within the limits of 2048, 4096, 6144, etc., rather than just outside them, so requiring the transfer of an extra page. In this case the largest block that can be handled by MVS is 32 Kbytes. If the user wishes to handle larger blocks, they must be created using PIOCS.

Other operating systems such as ICL's George III have lower limits. Tape blocks are restricted to 512 words of four characters each, i.e. a maximum size of 2048 characters; disk buckets can be up to 4096 characters in size, but the user is warned that the most efficient size is 2048 characters and that larger blocks will be handled by splitting into 2048 character units for processing by the operating system.

Constraints of this sort will sometimes force the user to employ smaller blocks than would otherwise be desirable.

Block activity

Large blocks offer increased actual data transfer rates and better packing density; they have another effect that is undesirable for skip-sequential processing. This is that, as more records are brought together to form a block, it becomes more likely that a large block of records will have to be accessed in order to update only a single record. For tape processing this is not significant, as every record will have to be read in any case. On disk, unwanted records can be 'skipped'—hence the term skip-sequential. In this case large blocks can be counter-productive, as they increase the number of unwanted records that have to be read in, and so tend to push the application towards an input-output bound condition. In general, the percentage of the blocks in a file that is hit is known as the *block hit rate*, and sometimes the *block activity*, to avoid confusion with hit rates. Block activity will generally be used in this book.

The extent to which blocking of records will increase the effective hit rate for the file depends on the distribution of hits through the file. This distribution is often either unknown, or reasonably random; for this reason the random case will be examined first.

Random updates Assume that the records in a file can be referenced only once in a given run. Then, when blocks containing n records have on average a number of hits h, the probability that any single record in a block will not be accessed is $(1 - h/n)$, and hence the probability p_N that no record in the block will be accessed is:

$$p_N = \left[1 - \left(\frac{h}{n} \right) \right]^n \tag{4.1}$$

This is the first term of the binomial expansion giving the probabilities that $0, 1, 2, \ldots n$ records in the block will be accessed. The probability p_A that *one or more* records will be accessed, and thus that the block must be read in, will therefore be:

$$p_A = 1 - \left[1 - \left(\frac{h}{n} \right) \right]^n \tag{4.2}$$

Although the binomial method of calculating probabilities is relatively accurate (a discussion of its limitations can be found elsewhere[5]) it has the disadvantage that a fresh calculation has to be carried out for each block size. As the number of records in the block rises, the binomial expression in equation (4.1) for the probability that no records will be accessed tends towards the limit set by the expression:

$$p_N = e^{-h} \tag{4.3}$$

and the expression in equation (4.2) for the probability that the block will need to be accessed tends to the limit:

$$p_A = 1 - e^{-h} \tag{4.4}$$

Equations (4.3) and (4.4) do not depend on the number of *records* per block n, but on the number of *hits* per block, h. They represent the case when n is large, and give a fairly accurate forecast of the proportion of blocks that need to be accessed for values of n greater than ten. A number of theoretical ways of calculating these values has been reviewed[5]. In practice these yield the same results as those presented here.

Equation (4.2) has been used to calculate the probability that any given block will be accessed for a range of average hits per block from 0.01 to 8.00

Table 4.5 The figures tabulated show the probability p_A that a block with the expected number of hits shown will be accessed. The expected number of hits is the *average* for the whole file, so these figures are calculated on the assumption of a random hit distribution. In processing a large number of blocks, p_A will indicate the proportion of blocks accessed in the file.

Hits per block	\multicolumn{9}{c}{Number of records per block}
	1	2	3	5	10	15	20	50	∞
0.01	0.010	0.010	0.010	0.010	0.010	0.010	0.010	0.010	0.010
0.02	0.020	0.020	0.020	0.020	0.020	0.020	0.020	0.020	0.020
0.03	0.030	0.030	0.030	0.030	0.030	0.030	0.030	0.030	0.030
0.06	0.060	0.059	0.059	0.059	0.058	0.058	0.058	0.058	0.058
0.10	0.100	0.098	0.097	0.096	0.096	0.095	0.095	0.095	0.095
0.20	0.200	0.190	0.187	0.185	0.183	0.182	0.182	0.182	0.181
0.30	0.300	0.278	0.271	0.266	0.263	0.261	0.261	0.260	0.259
0.40	0.400	0.360	0.349	0.341	0.335	0.333	0.332	0.331	0.330
0.50	0.500	0.438	0.421	0.410	0.401	0.399	0.397	0.395	0.393
0.60	0.600	0.510	0.488	0.472	0.461	0.458	0.456	0.453	0.451
0.70	0.700	0.578	0.549	0.530	0.516	0.512	0.510	0.506	0.503
0.80	0.800	0.640	0.606	0.582	0.566	0.561	0.558	0.554	0.551
0.90	0.900	0.698	0.657	0.629	0.611	0.605	0.602	0.597	0.593
1.00	1.000	0.750	0.704	0.672	0.651	0.645	0.642	0.636	0.632
1.10		0.798	0.746	0.711	0.688	0.681	0.677	0.671	0.667
1.20		0.840	0.784	0.746	0.721	0.714	0.710	0.703	0.699
1.30		0.878	0.818	0.778	0.752	0.743	0.739	0.732	0.727
1.40		0.910	0.848	0.807	0.779	0.770	0.766	0.758	0.753
1.50		0.938	0.875	0.832	0.803	0.794	0.790	0.782	0.777
1.60		0.960	0.898	0.855	0.825	0.816	0.811	0.803	0.798
1.70		0.978	0.919	0.875	0.845	0.835	0.831	0.823	0.817
1.80		0.990	0.936	0.893	0.863	0.853	0.848	0.840	0.835
1.90		0.998	0.951	0.908	0.878	0.869	0.864	0.856	0.850
2.00		1.000	0.963	0.922	0.893	0.883	0.878	0.870	0.865
2.25			0.984	0.950	0.922	0.913	0.908	0.900	0.895
2.50			1.000	0.969	0.944	0.935	0.931	0.923	0.918
2.75				0.982	0.960	0.952	0.948	0.941	0.936
3.00				0.989	0.972	0.965	0.961	0.955	0.950
4.00				1.000	0.994	0.990	0.989	0.985	0.982
5.00					0.999	0.998	0.997	0.995	0.993
6.00					1.000	1.000	0.999	0.998	0.997
7.00							1.000	0.999	0.999
8.00								1.000	1.000

and for block sizes from one to fifty records. The figures are given in Table 4.5. Equation (4.4) has been used to predict the results for an infinite block size; for all practical purposes a block size of fifty records is indistinguishable from 'infinite', and even block sizes of ten or more records show maximum errors of no more than 5 per cent. This is the reason that the curve derived from equation (4.4) has been recommended as a design tool in the author's previous work[6]. The divergence of predictions from this curve for smaller block sizes is shown in Fig. 4.5.

An average number of hits per block of 1.00 would mean that if records were unblocked every record would have to be read. Only three-quarters of two-record blocks need to be read in, and this drops to less than two out of three for blocks containing six or more records. This implies that larger blocks *reduce* the need to read in data records. However, when the effect of blocking records with a fixed *record* hit rate is investigated, as against a fixed number of hits per *block*, the real effect of blocking becomes clear. Fig. 4.6 shows the percentage of blocks that has to be read as a function of *record* hit rate and records per block. The description *block activity* is given to these percentages, to distinguish them from average hits per block.

Fig. 4.6 presents the results of blocking decisions in a form that allows the user to determine block activity for any blocking factor chosen, by drawing a horizontal line through the record hit rate and reading off block activities at the intercepts. The results of blocking in a specific case are shown in Table 4.6. When record hit rate is 0.01 or one hit record in every hundred, only one record per hundred has to be read if records are unblocked. With increasing block size, block activity increases until over 99 per cent of blocks containing 512 records have to be read.

The figures in Table 4.6 are derived from those in Table 4.5 and demonstrate the burden, in terms of inactive records that have to be read, which is imposed by blocking low activity records in large blocks. No attempt has been made to provide a comprehensive table, as any figures required can be taken from Table 4.5 or calculated using equations (4.2) or (4.4).

It is clear from the data provided that there will be occasions when the file designer will choose not to use large blocks on disk, and so avoid the high block activity this causes if record accesses are random. In some cases the pattern of accesses will be known and the figures derived above will not be appropriate. Two of the most common patterns are considered below.

Grouped updates If most of the records to be accessed are in groups the objection to large blocks is very much reduced. Most blocks would remain inactive and the benefits of blocking would make it likely that the file designer would choose blocks that would use disk as efficiently as possible. It was explained above why this does not always mean choosing the *largest* feasible blocking factor on disk. When active records can be identified beforehand they can be blocked in groups, and so provide large blocks with a

Blocking and buffering 87

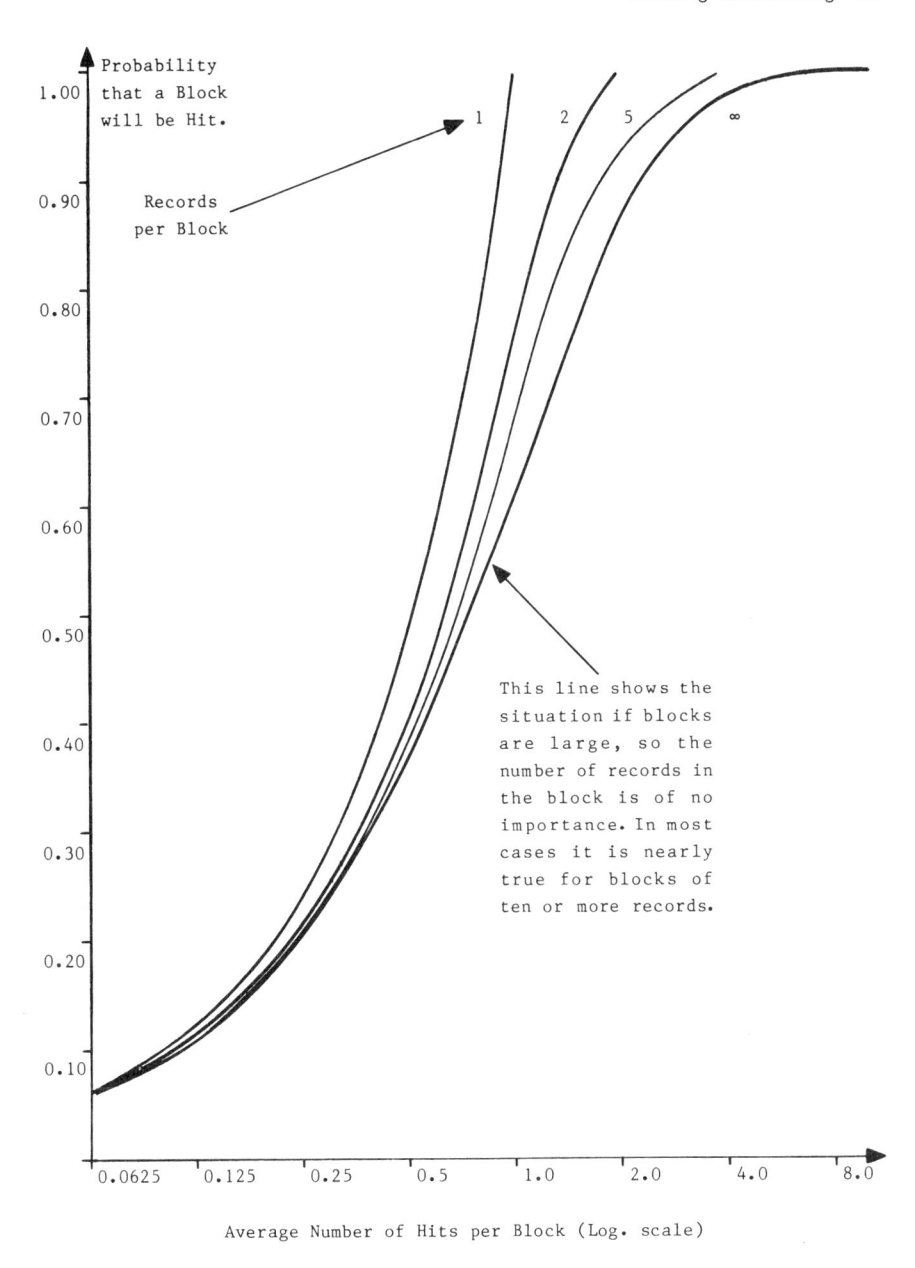

Fig. 4.5 For any given average number of hits per block, an increase in the number of records per block reduces the probability that a given block will be hit.

88 Design of computer data files

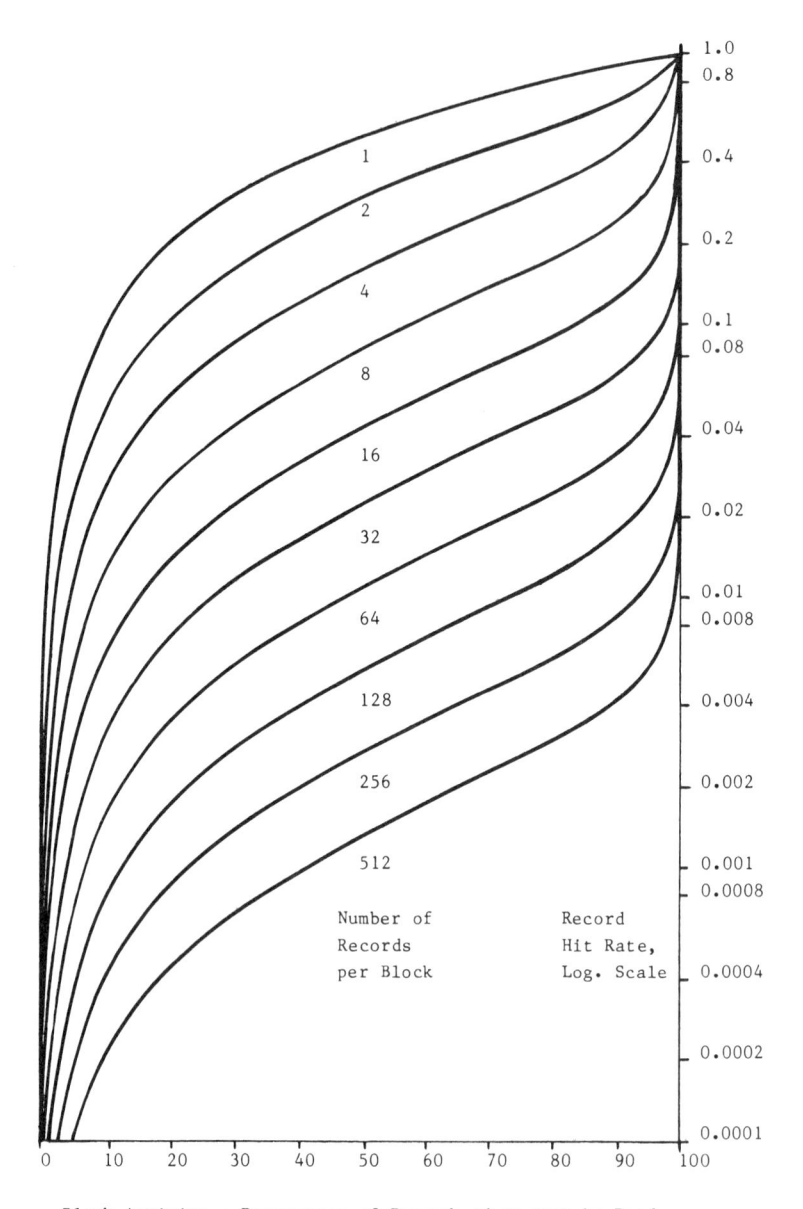

Fig. 4.6 This diagram shows the relationship between record hit rate, the number of records in a block, and the percentage of the blocks in the file that has to be read. For single records it is the same as the hit rate, while for multiple record blocks it is the same as the block hit rate, or block activity. These curves only apply for a random hit distribution.

Table 4.6 The figures in column two of the Table show how the proportion of a file that has to be read during updating is affected by blocking factor.

Block size	Block activity (%)	Average hits per block
1	1.0	0.01
2	2.0	0.02
3	3.0	0.03
4	3.9	0.04
5	4.9	0.05
8	7.7	0.08
10	9.6	0.10
15	14.0	0.15
16	14.9	0.16
20	18.2	0.20
32	27.5	0.32
50	39.5	0.50
64	47.4	0.64
100	63.4	1.00
128	72.4	1.28
200	86.6	2.00
256	92.4	2.56
400	98.2	4.00
512	99.4	5.12

very high *record* hit rate. The usual situation is less clear-cut than this, but is still better than for random updates.

Regular updates If every fifth, tenth, . . . nth record is accessed, the effects of blocking can be precisely calculated. Increases in block activity will tend to be stepwise, and it is often advisable to choose small blocks. However, such a regular pattern is both unusual and, if it does occur, easy to plan for in other ways that are dealt with later in the book (see Chapter 5 on Sequential Files, for example).

Most update patterns are mixtures of the special cases dealt with above and the safest approach is to treat them as random. Even if block activity considerations do not limit the size of the blocks employed, there is usually competition between files for the available space in main storage, and this is discussed in the following section.

Competing files

The absolute limit to block sizes for any file has already been discussed.

Usually, the file designer has to consider the needs of several files when deciding on blocking factors. As with the reasons for blocking itself, the considerations for disk and tape are rather different.

Optimum blocking of magnetic tape files It was pointed out earlier that the actual data read from a tape file is not reduced by blocking. The saving is in the number of inter-block gaps, and several authors[7,8,9] have proposed methods of reducing their effects to a minimum.

In many installations all the tapes used by a program will have the same IBG timings, and the objective of blocking will be to minimize the number of IBGs that have to be traversed. However, some installations use more than one type of tape drive, and if some tape drives provide shorter traverse times than others used by the program, the objective will be to minimize the *time* taken to traverse all the IBGs, rather than their number. Thus the objective is always to minimize the sum:

$$\sum_{i=1}^{n} T_i N_i \qquad (4.5)$$

where N is the number of inter-block gaps with a traverse time of T, and i takes the values $1, \ldots n$, for n different sets of inter-block timings.

The factors the file designer has to take into account in reducing IBG traverse time to a minimum are:

space available for input-output areas;
number of records in each file;
record size;
the number of buffers used for each file.

By using the numerical values of these factors, it is possible in most cases to calculate an optimal set of block sizes for each file that will make significant savings in IBG traverse time.

1 *Single-buffered files*
An algorithm has been developed[7,9] that can be used to calculate the theoretical optimum blocking factors for a number of files competing for limited space. For single-buffered files with fixed-length records this is:

$$B_i = \frac{S(R_i/C_i)^{\frac{1}{2}}}{\sum_{i=1}^{n} (R_i C_i)^{\frac{1}{2}}} \qquad (4.6)$$

where

B_i is the blocking factor for file i;
S is the space available in main storage;

R_i is the number of records in file i; and
C_i is the length of the records in file i.

This expression *does* give the optimal solution, but it suffers from the practical difficulty that the solutions obtained are usually not integers. As blocks have to be made up of whole numbers of records, truncation of the results obtained has been suggested[7]. In some cases this leads to poor and even invalid results, and a program is available that searches for an optimal integer solution, using the theoretical optimal solution as a starting point[8]. This gives good results, but the file designer is usually not able to wait for program runs of this sort; two further procedures are presented below.

In cases where only three files have to be dealt with, and one file has very small records, the needs of this file can be adequately handled by providing space for blocks of ten to twenty records. The remaining two files can be treated by starting with single record blocks of the one file and maximum blocking of the other and trying all possible solutions. Taking an example analysed elsewhere by the author[6], suppose that an update run uses files that are made up in the following way:

file 1—100 000 records of 250 characters;
file 2—30 000 records of 300 characters;
file 3—30 000 records of 25 characters.

If there are 2500 character storage positions available for this program in main storage, and file 3 is blocked in tens, it requires only 250 storage positions and contributes only 3000 IBGs to the run time. This leaves 2250 storage positions for the other two files, which can be blocked in the combinations shown in Table 4.7.

The best solution is to block file 1 in fives and file 2 in threes. This leaves one hundred character storage spaces available; to use this space, file 3 is blocked in fourteens, giving the optimal solution—a total of 32 143 IBGs, and so a time of 32 143T due to IBG traverses. Fig. 4.7 shows the magnitude of the improvement achieved. It is important to remember that the available

Table 4.7 Possible blocking combinations for files 1 and 2 in the example given above.

	Possible blocking combinations						
File 1	1	2	3	4	5	6	7
File 2	6	5	5	4	3	2	1
Inter-block gaps, files 1 + 2	105 000	56 000	39 334	32 500	30 000	31 667	44 286
Inter-block gaps, file 3	3 000	3 000	3 000	3 000	3 000	3 000	3 000
Total IBGs	108 000	59 000	42 334	35 500	33 000	34 667	47 286

92 Design of computer data files

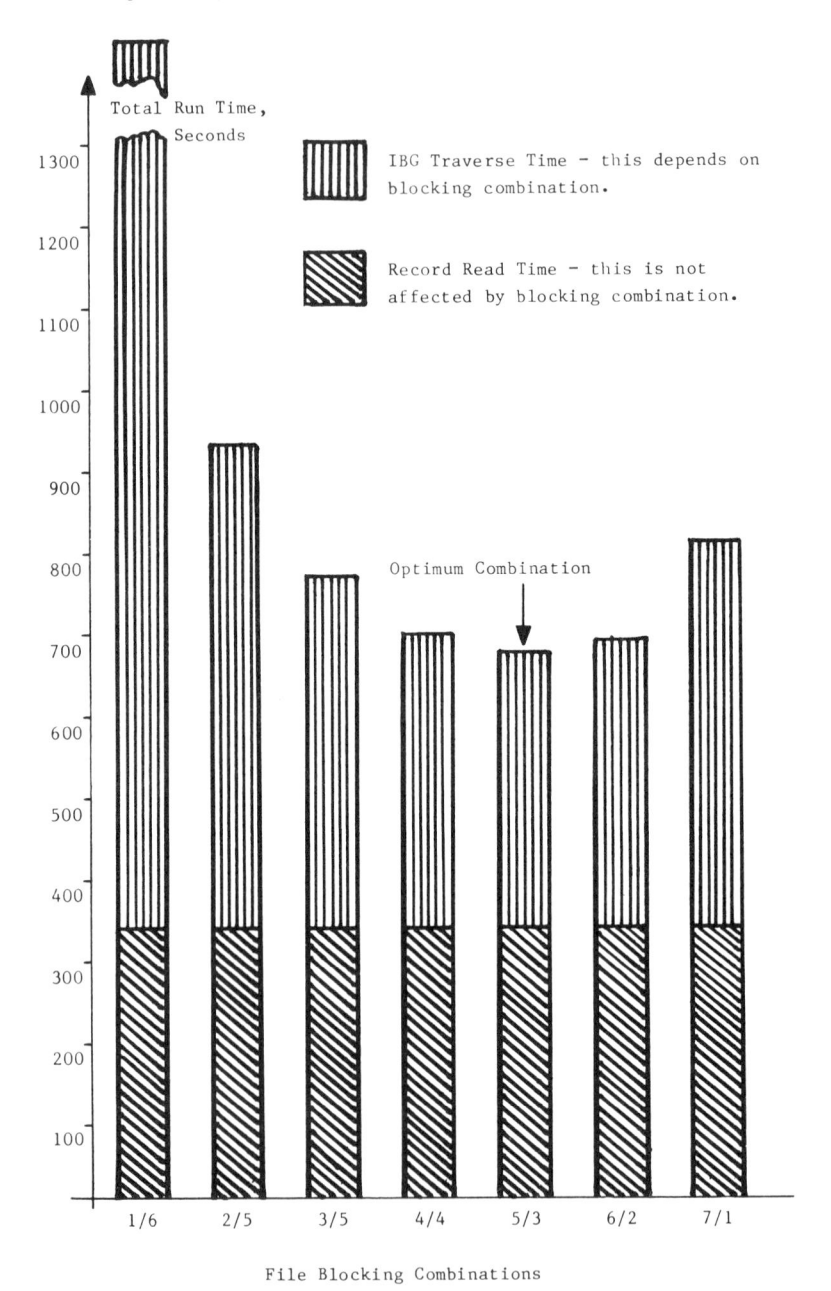

Fig. 4.7 Effect of blocking combination on run time.

space s is only a resource; the optimal solution quite often does not use all of s, but this does not matter as the intention is to minimize the total IBG traverse time.

This method of solution 'by inspection' can usually be employed when there are only two files with large records. However, the calculations can be tedious when s is large, as is usually the case in modern systems. For this reason it is useful to apply Water's method[7] to this example:

$$\sum_{i=1}^{3} (R_i C_i)^{\frac{1}{2}} = (100\,000 \times 250)^{\frac{1}{2}} + (30\,000 \times 300)^{\frac{1}{2}} + (30\,000 \times 25)^{\frac{1}{2}}$$

$$= 8866.02$$

therefore $B_1 = (2500/8866.02) \times (100\,000/250)^{\frac{1}{2}}$
$= 5.6395$

$B_2 = (2500/8866.02) \times (30\,000/300)^{\frac{1}{2}}$
$= 2.81975$

and $B_3 = (2500/8866.02) \times (3000/25)^{\frac{1}{2}}$
$= 9.767$

If it were possible to use these blocking factors as they stood, the total number of IBGs would be reduced to 31 443. This is a useful figure to calculate, as it allows any integer result to be compared with it. This has two advantages: the first, that any lower result indicates a calculation error; the second, that any figure very close to this implies it is not worth searching further for an optimal solution.

Truncation gives a result of 38 333 IBGs, which is far from optimal. The process of reaching the optimum is as follows: after truncation there is space—425 character positions—for either one extra record in file 1 blocks, or one extra record in file 2 blocks. Any remaining space can only be allocated to file 3. Both solutions should be checked, but a drop from 2.82 to 2 is much more in percentage terms than a drop from 5.64 to 5, so it is not surprising that the (5,3,14) solution proves to be optimal. The (6,2,16) solution gives rise to 33 542 IBGs, against the optimal 32 143.

More complex problems cannot easily be tackled by inspection, and equation (4.6) is used as a starting point. If the solution is entirely integer, no further work is necessary; generally, a short examination of integer solutions near to the theoretical optimum will provide the practical optimum. When s is large, there are a number of solutions close to the best possible, as will become clear to a reader who calculates results for question 11 on page 104. An example is given below.

A program inputs master data records on tape, updates a proportion of them using input card-images on tape, outputs the updated master file on tape, and produces transaction records on tape for later printing. Assume the following figures:

Available storage space   5000 bytes
Master input file   (1)   30 000 records of 200 bytes
Master output file   (2)   30 000 records of 200 bytes
Update file   (3)   3 000 records of 80 bytes
Print file   (4)   3 000 records of 120 bytes

Carrying out the calculations as defined by equation (4.6):

$$\sum_{i=1}^{4}(R_iC_i)^{\frac{1}{2}} = 2(30\ 000 \times 200)^{\frac{1}{2}} + (80 \times 3000)^{\frac{1}{2}} + (120 \times 3000)^{\frac{1}{2}}$$

$$= 5988.88$$

$$B_1 = B_2 = (5000/5988.88) \times (30\ 000/200)^{\frac{1}{2}}$$
$$= 10.225$$

$$B_3 = (5000/5988.88) \times (3000/80)^{\frac{1}{2}}$$
$$= 5.112$$

$$B_4 = (5000/5988.88) \times (3000/120)^{\frac{1}{2}}$$
$$= 4.174$$

Use of these non-integer values for B_i gives a number of IBGs of 7174 as the theoretical minimum. Truncation produces a value of 7350, and leaves exactly 120 byte positions free. This would allow one additional record per block for file 3 or file 4. It is clear that file 4 should be blocked in fives, both because more has been truncated from the theoretical value and because it has more impact on a 3000-record file to go from 4 to 5—a 25 per cent increase—than from 5 to 6—a 20 per cent increase. Calculation confirms that the ((10,10),5,5) format reduces IBGs to 7200, while the ((10,10),6,4) format produces a figure of 7250. The double brackets are used to indicate files that require the same blocking factor.

This procedure needs to be modified to take account of double or multiple buffered files.

2 Multi-buffered files

In this case the space allocated to a file will be increased in steps of D records, where D buffers are used for the file. C_i in equation (4.6) is replaced by D_iC_i, giving the relationship:

$$B_i = S\frac{(R_i/D_iC_i)^{\frac{1}{2}}}{\sum_{i=1}^{n}(R_iD_iC_i)^{\frac{1}{2}}} \qquad (4.7)$$

Using this modified equation to handle the situation in which file 1 of the example on page ** is double buffered while files 2 and 3 remain single buffered, the theoretical optimum solution is as follows:

$B_1 = 3.233$ (250 character records, double buffered);
$B_2 = 2.286$ (300 character records);
$B_3 = 7.918$ (25 character records).

This optimal solution gives a count of 47 849 IBGs.

In reaching the best integer solution, the first move is to truncate B_1 and B_2 while increasing B_3 to 8. The solution ((3,3),2,8) gives rise to 52 083 IBGs, and leaves 200 character storage spaces free. These spaces can only be allocated to file 3, and the solution ((3,3),2,16) yields a figure of 50 209 IBGs. This is the optimum integer solution (the alternative of blocking file 2 in threes, giving a solution of ((3,3),3,4) reduces the total IBGs to 50 834). If all files are double, treble, . . . n times buffered, S can be replaced by S/n in equation (4.6) rather than using the modified expression given in equation (4.7).

3 Different inter-block traverse times

To take account of the use of tape units with differing IBG times, equation (4.6) has to be modified to include the terms $R_i T_i$ in place of R_i:

$$B_i = S \frac{(R_i T_i / D_i C_i)^{\frac{1}{2}}}{\sum_{i=1}^{n} (R_i D_i C_i T_i)^{\frac{1}{2}}} \tag{4.8}$$

Using the same example once more, but on this occasion with single buffers for all files, a 10 ms IBG traverse time for files 1 and 3, and a 2 ms IBG traverse time for file 2, equation (4.8) gives the theoretical optimum solution:

$B_1 = 6.94$
$B_2 = 1.55$
$B_3 = 12.02$

If it were possible to implement these blocking factors, the total time taken up by IBG traverses would be 207.8 seconds. Truncation of the theoretical block sizes gives a total time of 251.7 seconds; two other combinations that use all available space seem worth investigating. They are:

(7, 1, 18), which gives a figure of 221.6 seconds; and
(6, 2, 16), which yields the *integer* optimum of 218.1 seconds.

4.6 General tape blocking considerations

The equations (4.5)–(4.8) above are used to give a starting point for further calculation; in the unusual circumstance that all the theoretically optimal blocking factors are integers, this is the end of the search. In most cases a check on the integer solutions nearest to the optimal solution will provide an integer optimum without difficulty. The limitations imposed by other programs using these files will then have to be checked and may lead to a sub-optimal solution being adopted for this particular program. This is examined, and examples of the calculations involved are given, in reference[10].

Variable-length records on magnetic tape are not so easily handled as fixed-length. Montgomery[11] has pointed out that, however carefully fixed-length records are handled, variable-length records minimize tape passing time; this is accepted in the industry, and many tape files are blocked in variable-length format for this reason. However, as Graham and Sprott showed[12], the fact that I-O areas are not filled by most variable-length blocks means that fixed-length blocks are *potentially* more efficient. In making blocking decisions it is usually best to use *buffer* size in the calculations; the slight over-estimate of average block size this leads to tends to apply to all such files, and so has a tendency to correct itself. Although transaction records are usually of fixed format they tend to have fewer, smaller records than master files, and barely affect this tendency.

4.7 General blocking considerations for magnetic disk and other track-oriented devices

These devices do not have a single equivalent of the IBG on tape. Very high speed processing can be achieved during operations such as copy disk or initialize disk, for which processing times are minimal, because the only hold-up is due to the very small gaps between records. However, if sequentially processed files are single-buffered the time available for processing each record will be very short. Only highly synchronized and rapid operations such as *copy disk* or *initialize disk* can be carried out in this time. The gap available is shown in Fig. 4.8.

An IBM 3380 only takes about 0.065 ms to traverse this gap. If both completion of record transfer and the necessary processing cannot be carried out in this time, a full revolution of the disk will have to elapse before the next sequential record is available. Methods of designing files so that the number of lost revolutions is minimized are discussed in later chapters.

The inter-block gap that applies to disk devices can thus in a sense be regarded as either very small or relatively large. This rather simplified picture is affected by a series of other factors:

1 *Hit rate*
Unlike tapes, non-hit records or blocks on disk can be skipped, and each skipped record provides extra time in which processing of a previous block can be completed before a subsequent block is required.

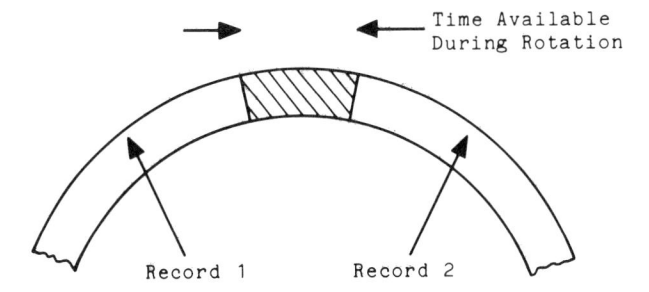

Fig. 4.8 The time taken by the read–write head to traverse the gap between records is available for processing.

Table 4.8 Timing data for IBM disk drives.

Device type	Seek times (ms) Minimum	Average	Maximum	Rotation times (ms) Full	Average (latency)
IBM 3330	10	30	55	16.67	8.33
IBM 3340	10	25	50	20.24	10.12
IBM 3350	10	25	50	16.67	8.33
IBM 3370	5	20	40	20.24	10.12
IBM 3375	4	19	38	20.24	10.12
IBM 3380	3	16	30	16.67	8.33

2 Head movement and rotational delay

When files are processed directly, the position of the next record to be processed is not predictable. A head movement may be necessary, which would cause a delay of the order shown in Table 4.8.

Even if no head movement is necessary, on average the required record will be half a disk revolution away when the CPU initiates a seek to retrieve it. This will lead to an average delay of between 8 and 10 ms, as is shown in Table 4.8.

Head movement and rotational delay are very important in all file handling, but have a particularly marked effect on direct file timing. This is discussed in Chapter 6.

3 Double/multiple buffering

The timing of sequentially processed files can be altered by the use of buffers; this is reviewed in the final section of this chapter as part of the general treatment of buffers.

The many factors involved in direct-access file processing mean that neither equations (4.5)–(4.8) nor derivatives of them can be used in the general case. In fact, as was explained earlier, low hit-rate disk files may benefit from *low* blocking factors. However, sequential files that have a 100 per cent hit rate can be handled in this way; depending on the processing time, the IBG traverse time will be very low or 1, 2, . . . *n* revolutions. The very exceptional case in which every second, third, . . . *n*th record is processed can also be treated in this way, adjusting the IBG time to take account of the extra records skipped.

A second case in which calculations can be carried out, based on a 'standard' IBG time, is the writing of records to disk followed by a check comparison of the record that has just been written. This is often omitted nowadays due to the reliability of modern disks. When it is carried out—often because the data is of crucial importance—an additional wait time of a full revolution per record written is added to timings. The check comparison itself is carried out very rapidly, so after the check it can be assumed that the next record to be processed can be read without further delay.

Various other situations that arise in handling records on disk are discussed in the appropriate parts of the book; there is no single technique that applies overall in handling track-oriented devices.

4.8 Use of buffers

In early computers the central processor would stop operating when data was transferred from an input-output device to main storage, or the reverse. Later, with asynchronous operation of CPU and I-O units, overlap became possible. In order to exploit this, buffers of two main sorts are now provided.

The first type is a *hardware buffer*. This is usually located in a device control unit, and is very widely employed for the slower devices such as card or paper tape readers and printers. ICL also provides this sort of buffer for tape and disk drives attached to 1900 series processors since the size of block the user can opt for is limited. Manufacturers who do not limit the user's choice of block size for fast devices have not in the past provided a large buffer as it would not be possible to decide on the size of buffer needed to hold a record; as a result a buffer able to hold a few characters of data is usually provided, and the channel is dedicated to this one device while data is being transferred in order to avoid loss of information. Recently, however, IBM has introduced the 3480 tape, which includes a 512 Kbyte buffer that can be used to accept data as it becomes available, and pass it on when the CPU is free to handle it.

The second type of buffer is a *software buffer* which is an area in main storage set aside by the user program for input-output operations, or provided by the operating system from a *buffer pool* for the same purpose. Buffer pools are used to reduce the amount of main storage allocated to buffers by sharing buffer space between a number of different files.

Both types of buffer are intended to allow the central processor and I-O devices to operate independently and overlap their operations. A hardware buffer is filled at device speeds and when full its contents are transferred at channel speeds to the CPU, where individual cycles are 'stolen' to transfer data into the software buffer. This process is known as *cycle stealing*, and is discussed in more detail elsewhere[13]. Choice of the number of software buffers is important, and is reviewed below.

A single software buffer

When a device is provided with a hardware buffer of full physical record size there is seldom any benefit in the program allocating more than one software buffer in main storage. The device is effectively double-buffered as records can be transferred from the hardware buffer to main storage very rapidly, leaving the device free to read the next record while the central processor de-blocks and processes the physical record. Thus calculations on block size need not take account of multiple buffers.

Disks and tapes are typically provided with very small hardware buffers, and data is transferred to the CPU in groups of characters requiring a single write operation into main storage. When this applies the programmer will have to decide whether a single software buffer is sufficient or whether multiple buffers would be of benefit. If multiple buffers are used, this may reduce the maximum size of block possible and so increase the number of IBGs on tape or record seeks on disk. This has been discussed above. On the other hand it will allow overlap of input-output operations with processing, and is a useful tool in achieving a balanced run of the sort described in Chapter 3 and discussed further in reference[14].

If a single buffer is provided, the following steps are involved in reading and processing a block of records:

1. A record read request is issued.
2. The record is read into main storage; this consists of either starting a tape drive or seeking a disk record, and the actual transfer process.
3. The identification of the first, second, . . . nth record in the block and the placing of its address in a pointer field—the locate mode of de-blocking—or the physical transfer of the record to a work area—the move mode of de-blocking.
4. Record processing until the block is exhausted.

Step 1 of the sequence will be very rapid unless the device is already in use. This is not likely in the case of a tape drive but may well occur when a disk is required. Step 2 will be likely to take 10–50 ms and may take even longer. During this period the CPU has not carried out any useful work on the data. Only when transfer is complete can de-blocking take place; during de-blocking and processing no input-output can occur and a situation similar to that shown in Fig. 4.9(a) exists.

100 Design of computer data files

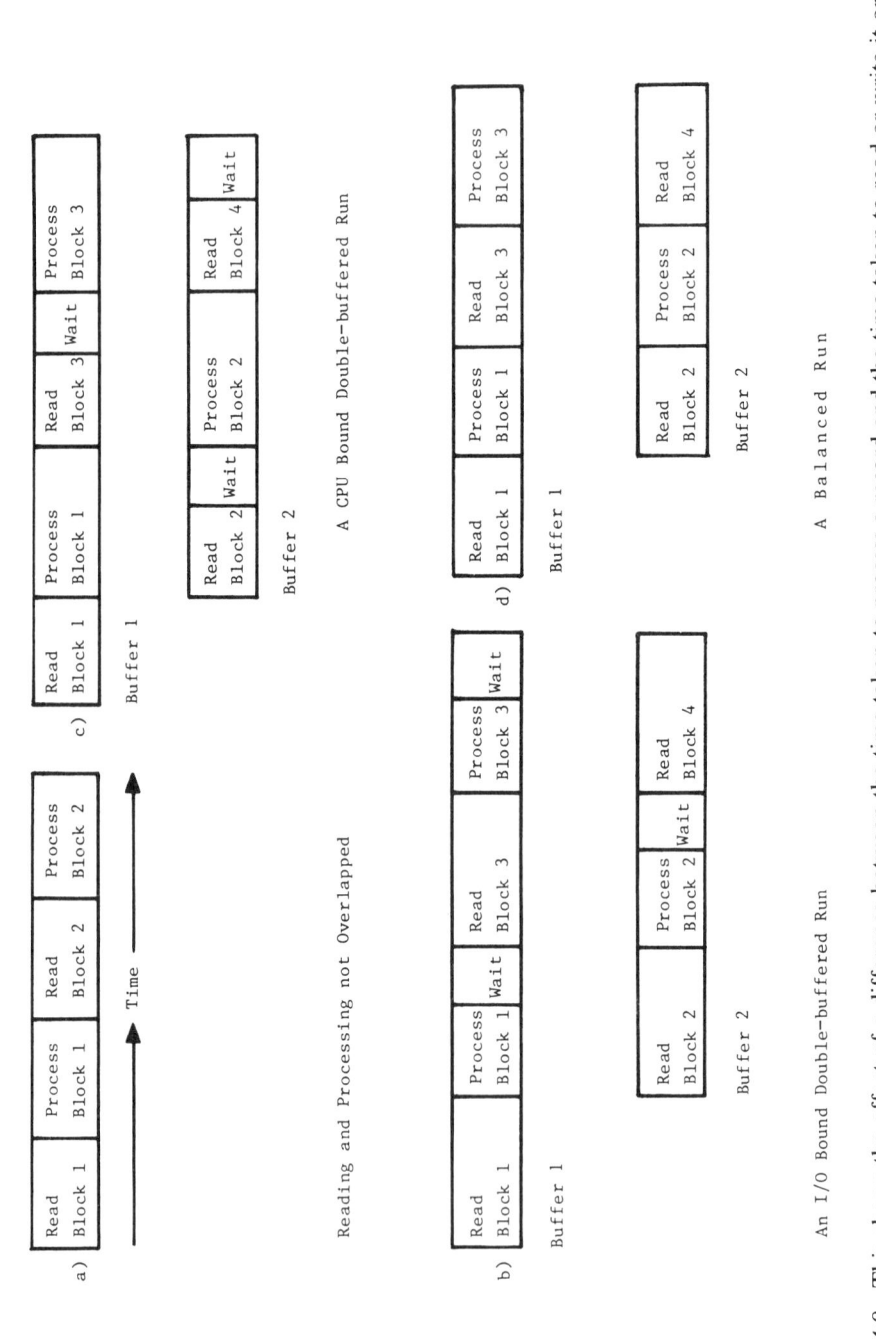

Fig. 4.9 This shows the effect of a difference between the time taken to process a record and the time taken to read or write it on the minimum time required to complete processing on it. Note that even when a run is balanced the read or write time still includes gap traverse or disk seek times, so there is still potential for improvement. (a) Reading and processing not overlapped. (b) An I-O-bound double-buffered run. (c) A CPU-bound double-buffered run. (d) A balanced run.

Double software buffers

The use of two buffers allows the second record or block of records to be transferred into main storage while the first is being processed. For tape files the situation will be as shown in Fig. 4.9(b), (c) or (d) depending on the balance of CPU and I-O time. The longer of the two times now becomes the major hold-up, as discussed in Chapter 3 (see p. 63), and the overall run time can be shortened by as much as 50 per cent. In the case of disk files only the special examples mentioned above will be as predictable as tape. Generally, the I-O time for a disk file will vary and some records may cause an I-O bound condition to occur, while others will appear to be process bound. The average I-O time will still give an overall indication, but it will not be as clear-cut as for tape files and is analysed further in later chapters.

Multiple software buffers

It is sometimes beneficial to provide more than two buffers. This can happen for a number of reasons; one is that manufacturer's software can use further main storage to advantage. This applies in certain operations to do with handling overflow records in IBM's ISAM and VSAM files, for example. The problem here is that the user may not be told when extra buffer space can be useful; for that reason, such situations are highlighted at the appropriate points in this book.

A second case is that in which the processing time of hit records is *greater* than record transfer time. When this applies, Hanson and Revell[15] have shown that triple buffers can improve performance in the following circumstances:

1 *100% hit rate*
Disk files can benefit, as extra buffers hold a 'reservoir' of records that can be processed while the disk rotates, and before the next group of records is read in. With double buffers, only the contents of these two blocks can be processed on a single disk rotation; with three buffers, three blocks can be processed per revolution, and so on. This technique is useful when it is not possible to use large blocks on the disk, or they do not fit well.

Tape files cannot benefit, as there is no loss of time equivalent to a full disk rotation to be exploited.

2 *Lower hit rates*
Both disk and tape files can benefit here, particularly if the file has areas of high and low hit rate, rather than a consistent hit rate. An example of this is given in the next chapter, on page 112. When gas or electricity meters are read, or local advertising campaigns launched, the effects on data files are likely to be the creation of high and low activity groups of records. When this is coupled with a longer processing time than record read/transfer time,

multiple buffers can provide a reservoir to allow processing to continue in high I-O groups, and I-O to continue in high processing groups.

The program or file designer has to bear in mind that, if space in main storage is limited, each additional buffer will mean a smaller blocking factor. When there is adequate space for more buffers, but block size cannot be increased—which might apply if the block size is determined by the limitations of a different program—a third buffer is worth a trial. In IBM OS/VS for example, a program can be modified temporarily to use three buffers by adding the sub-parameter DCB = BUFNO = 3. This does not involve a re-compilation of the program, and if this entry is omitted from a later run the program automatically returns to its original state.

In the more general case in which increased numbers of buffers mean smaller data blocks on the file storage device, it is pointless to create extra IBGs or seeks by employing multiple buffers. Double buffering will be the usual aim of the file designer.

Conclusion

This chapter has brought together a great deal of information on blocking and buffering that is not generally taken into account in the file design process. It takes only a little more time to calculate the optimum blocking factor to be used for a file rather than to make a guess at it. The benefits that can be obtained by design rather than guesswork are so marked that some manufacturers have provided optimizing routines to block and handle records without intervention by the user. However, it is more efficient if the user matches blocking and buffering decisions to the rest of the program design, rather than allowing a sub-optimization to be carried out on these values alone by manufacturers' software.

References

Many manufacturers' manuals have been used in the preparation of this chapter, but only specific references are cited here.

1. *Introduction to IBM Direct Access Storage Devices*, by Marilyn Bohl, SRA, 1981.
2. *IBM 3830 Storage Control—3330 Disk Storage Reference Manual*, GA 26-1592.
3. *ICL 1900 Series Direct Access Training Manual*, Technical Publication 4107, ICL.
4. 'Flexibility of block-length for magnetic files', by J. Inglis and E. G. Dee, *Computer Journal*, Vol. 16, No. 4, April 1973, pp. 303–307.
5. 'Hit ratios', by S. J. Waters, *Computer Journal*, Vol. 19, No. 1, January 1976, pp. 21–24.

6. *Basic File Design*, by Owen Hanson, IPC Business Press, 1978.
7. 'Blocking sequentially processed magnetic files', by S. J. Waters, *Computer Journal*, Vol. 14, No. 2, February 1972, pp. 109–112.
8. 'Choice of block sizes for magnetic tape files', by B. J. Edwards, *Computer Journal*, Vol. 20, No. 1, January 1977, pp. 10–14.
9. 'Optimization of tape operations', by E. S. Walker, *Software Age*, Vol. 4, August/September 1970, pp. 16–17.
10. *Essentials of Computer Data Files*, by Owen Hanson, Pitman, 1985.
11. 'Designing magnetic tape files for variable-length records', by Tony Y. Montgomery, *Management Informatics*, Vol. 3, 1974, No. 6, pp. 271–276.
12. 'Processing magnetic tape files with variable blocks', by J. W. Graham and D. A. Sprott, *CACM*, Vol. 4, No. 11, 1961, pp. 555–557.
13. *Digital Computer Fundamentals*, 4th Edition, by Thomas C. Bartee, McGraw-Hill, 1977, pp. 458 et seq.
14. *Systems Programming: Concepts of Operating and Data Base Systems*, by David K. Hsaio, Addison-Wesley, 1975, pp. 51 et seq.
15. 'Applications of multi-buffered input-output', by Owen Hanson and Normal Revell, *Proc. 1st Pan Pacific Computer Conf.*, Melbourne, Sept. 1985, Vol. 2, pp. 1617–1623.

Revision questions

1 Why are records blocked on magnetic tape? Your answer should consider data transfer rate and tape capacity.

2 Why are records blocked on magnetic disk? Illustrate your answer with examples showing cases for which it is useful to block records and for which it is not.

3 Compare the blocking of records on disk and tape, giving reasons for any differences that you mention.

4 Describe the formats used to store data on disk and explain their influence on blocking techniques.

5 What factors limit the maximum size of block the designer can provide for a given file?

6 Explain the significance of block activity in deciding on blocking factors for disk and tape files.

7 Give the binomial and Poisson expressions for the block activity of a block containing q records and with an average number of hits per block of t. What is the reason that the Poisson expression is more generally applicable?

104 Design of computer data files

8 Estimate the block activity of the following:

70 record blocks, average record hit-rate 0.02;
27 record blocks, average record hit-rate 0.03;
175 record blocks, average record hit-rate 0.006;
763 record blocks, average record hit-rate 0.0014.

9 How is the impact of blocking affected by the update pattern?

10 What factors should the designer consider in minimizing the effect of inter-block gaps?

11 Determine the optimum blocking factors for a tape run, given 37 500 storage positions available and the following file details (SB = single buffered, DB = double buffered, TB = treble-buffered). All blocking factors given must be integer.

(a) File 1   100 000 records of 357 characters, SB
     File 2   45 000 records of 407 characters, SB
     File 3   45 000 records of 50 characters, SB.

(b) File 1   248 000 records of 850 characters, DB
     File 2   248 000 records of 850 characters, DB
     File 3   33 000 records of 80 characters, SB
     File 4   33 000 records of 120 characters, SB
     File 5   7 500 records of 30 characters, SB.

(c) File 1   1 580 000 records of 780 characters, DB
     File 2   1 580 000 records of 780 characters, DB
     File 3   75 000 records of 65 characters, TB
     File 4   75 000 records of 120 characters, SB.

(d) File 1   1 240 000 records of 565 characters, DB and with IBG times of 3.0 ms;
     File 2   1 240 000 records of 565 characters, DB and with IBG times of 8.0 ms;
     File 3   250 000 records of 80 characters, SB and with IBG times of 3.0 ms;
     File 4   250 000 records of 120 characters, SB and with IBG times of 8.0 ms.

(e) File 1   1 240 000 records of 565 characters, DB and with IBG times of 8.0 ms;
     File 2   1 240 000 records of 565 characters, SB and with IBG times of 2.0 ms;
     File 3   250 000 records of 120 characters, DB and with IBG times of 5.0 ms;
     File 4   250 000 records of 80 characters, SB and with IBG times of 3.0 ms.

12 Explain why disk files cannot usually be treated in the same way as tape files in order to minimize the effect of gaps between the data blocks.

13 What types of buffer are used for slow devices such as card readers? Are the same types used for disks or tapes?

14 Trace the sequence of steps involved in reading and processing a block of records using single buffers. How does this change if double buffers are provided?

15 When are multiple buffers of benefit in handling disk files? What are their drawbacks?

16 Summarize the considerations involved in blocking records on magnetic tape.

17 Can multiple buffers be of benefit for 100 per cent hit rate tape files? Explain your answer carefully.

18 Discuss the reasons for blocking records on magnetic disk storage, making clear when it *is* beneficial, when it is *not*, and the precautions required to ensure optimum data storage.

5 Sequential file organization

5.1 Introduction

This chapter examines the way in which sequential files—those in which records are stored in ascending or descending key order—are organized and processed. In Chapter 1 it was made clear that the term 'serial' is used for files containing records stored in no particular key order; the distinction between sequential and serial files is re-emphasized here for clarity. Serial files are used for temporary or historical data storage, and will not be discussed further.

In the early days of data processing, the only backing storage available was magnetic tape. Most of the systems implemented at that time were based on previous manual systems with files that were usually arranged in sequential order, although reference to them was frequently direct—by physically leafing through pages or folders. This led naturally to the development of systems that required sequentially oriented file design and processing.

The development of RAMAC by IBM, followed by the 1311 disk storage drive on 1400 series computers, gave the designer the opportunity to develop effective direct access files. However, a great deal of the data processed today is still held and handled in sequential files. The first reason is that security is relatively simply ensured in sequentially organized systems. The second is that, for a run in which a high proportion of blocks is hit, other file organization techniques are less efficient, in the sense that they cannot handle so many updates per unit time. (Even fairly low hit rate files can sometimes be efficiently handled by batching the input and increasing the hit rate. That is discussed below.) Finally, humans find a sequential printout easy to handle; a large telephone directory can be searched directly very quickly, by estimating the likely position of the desired record, and adjusting as a result of the records actually found.

When a file is to be sequentially organized, the designer has a choice between holding it on disk or tape. For that reason the choice between tape and direct access devices is discussed in this chapter; the choice between sequential and other file organizations, however, is left to Chapter 9.

5.2 Batching

It was pointed out in Chapter 1 that updates for sequential files are batched to provide a higher hit rate when the file is updated. The increased time between update runs that results from accumulating larger batches was also pointed out. The longer wait for output that the user will experience due to this should be carefully considered by the run designer to ensure that it is acceptable. If it is, the dramatic improvement in update time achieved by batching can be estimated from the following analysis:

In updating a single record in a sequential tape file, half the file will have to be searched on average before the required record, or the block containing it if records are blocked, is found. Let:

T be the time required to search the whole file;
t be the time required to locate and process a single block;
p be the time required to process a single block.

Then, on average:

$$t = \frac{T}{2} + p \tag{5.1}$$

If n blocks are to be updated, and assuming that n is less than the total number of blocks in the file;

$$t = \frac{T(1 - \frac{1}{2}^n)}{n} + p \tag{5.2}$$

When n represents all the blocks in the file:

$$t = \frac{T}{n} + p \tag{5.3}$$

For practical purposes the error in using equation (5.3) is very small for values of n over ten, and can be ignored for n equals twenty, so a comparison of equations (5.1) and (5.3) is valid in most cases. T is usually of the order of minutes, while p will be measured in milliseconds. This is a difference of three orders of magnitude. Hence equation (5.1) will conservatively reduce to:

$$t = \frac{1000p}{2} + p \tag{5.4}$$

and equation (5.3) will reduce to approximately:

$$t = \frac{1000p}{n} + p \tag{5.5}$$

T will consist of at least n (start-stop time + block-read time) so that the minimum value of 1000 p/n will be of the order of 2–10 milliseconds. Thus, as a rough estimate, batching can reduce the average time to locate and process records to about 1/500th of the average time for a single record. In any particular case the actual values of processing, start-stop and block-read times can be used to give a more precise figure.

The basis of this analysis is that record or block location and reading time are greater than processing time. If the reverse is true and *processing* is the limiting factor, batching will give much reduced benefits. Even so, a case in which no improvement is achieved by batching will usually be better handled using a different file organization technique rather than by updating records held in a sequential file in some random sequence. Further details are given in Chapter 9 (see p. 300).

Records and blocks have been used interchangeably in this discussion. Generally, rather fewer blocks will be hit than records because two or more records in a single block may be updated. However, as there are considerably fewer blocks than records the overall effect will be an increase in the proportion of the file that has to be read on magnetic disk. This is the significance of block activity, which was discussed in the last chapter. As all tape records always have to be read, this does not affect the processing of tape files.

5.3 Sorting

When a batch of update records has been prepared, it has to be sorted into the same key sequence as the master file before the update process can be carried out, in order to obtain the benefits of batching demonstrated by equations (5.1)–(5.5). If the input records are not sorted the update run will be a random update, with relatively long searches for each required record. Sorting will itself take a significant time and, even though this is usually far less than the time that would be lost by updating in a random sequence, the file designer will wish to minimize it. Estimates of the proportion of commercial data processing time taken up by sorting are as high as 40 per cent[1], much of it due to the I–O operations involved, so it is important to design the system in such a way as to reduce sort times.

Although the techniques used in sorting can affect the speed of the sort, most file designers will not consider changing the software themselves. Those interested in the designing of sort programs should consult books on programming techniques[2]. The options generally available to the designer are to alter the format of the records to be sorted or the storage medium on which the sort is carried out. The next step, if necessary, is to try sorts provided by software houses, such as Syncsort or CAsort.

Record format

Keeping key lengths short improves sort times. When the file is sorted in complete record form the effect is marginal, in that the size of the file—and hence the amount of I–O—is reduced only slightly. If the keys are sorted separately from the data records, with a small data field that gives a reference to the position of the records on a storage device, the volume of data to be sorted can be reduced considerably by reducing key size. When the keys have been sorted into order, the records are read in that order on to a new sorted file, using the address field of the auxiliary file records.

Storage medium

When a small file containing data such as tables of item costs, descriptions or values is to be sorted there may be space to hold it in main storage. If this is possible a very fast sort can be achieved; sometimes only a part of the file can be sorted in main storage, but this allows the file to be sorted into a small number of sorted sections and so is still often worthwhile. A description of the application of this technique applied to summary files is given elsewhere[3]. Bradley[4] gives a further description of it on a more general level, using PL/I sort procedures.

Relatively small files may still be too large to handle in main storage, or no space may be available. In this case the fastest direct access storage available should be used as a sort medium, because direct access devices are generally far more efficient than magnetic tapes for this purpose, and the use of multiple direct access devices does not improve sort speeds unless the file is large. This contrasts with tapes, for which as many separate units as possible should be allocated to a single sort even if the file is relatively small. The more tape units allocated to a sort, the more rapid it will be.

The options open to the file or system designer will depend on the sort software and the range of hardware available. These should be examined to decide which of the points discussed above can be implemented in any given case.

If a file is to be stored sequentially, both batching and sorting must be thought of as part of its processing cycle. This will apply whatever storage medium is used to hold the file. The next decision the designer will have to make is what storage medium to use.

5.4 Choice of storage medium

Generally, sequential files are stored on magnetic tape. There are a number of reasons for this. They include the following:

1   Direct access devices perform relatively poorly for high hit rate files, due to the need for additional rotations when hit records are close together. This is examined later in the chapter (see p. 137).
2   Disk storage is more expensive both on-line and off-line than tape because disk packs, drives and control units are relatively costly. Mass

storage devices are cheaper per byte than disk, and avoid the need for manual intervention, but they start at a relatively high-volume high-cost threshold, as do large-volume fixed disks such as the 3380.

3   Tape provides built-in security copies during processing as a matter of course. The reliability and cost of a disk ensure that it is less often used in a 'tape-like' fashion, providing a new master file on each run. Instead, records are often updated in place on the same disk. The duplication of files that is adopted due to tape's inherent unreliability becomes an advantage in some respects.

4   There is still a shortage of direct access capability in some installations, which leads to the use of tape for sequential applications.

These considerations have ensured that magnetic tape has remained the predominant medium for sequential files. However, there are a number of specific situations in which direct access devices, and usually disk, are more suitable. These are discussed later.

5.5 Optimizing magnetic tape file handling

Because of the difficulty, lack of precision and time involved in back-spacing and overwriting records on tape, a new master file is created on each run. The process of updating is shown in Fig. 5.1.

This only applies to updating, however: when a sequential tape file is only being referenced and no new data is being written into the file or deleted from it, a new master file will not be created. The principles of updating are discussed by Dwyer[5], who also provides an update program written in COBOL for sequential files and relates the process to the updating of direct files. Levy[6] uses abstract data types to illustrate the underlying structure of

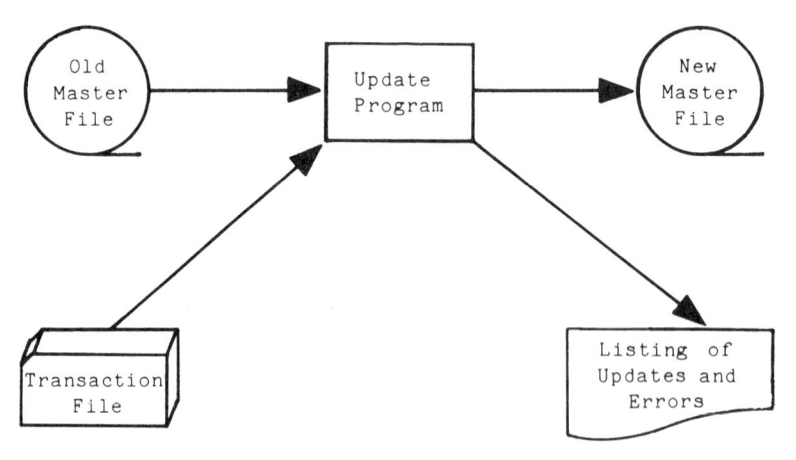

Fig. 5.1   A sequential tape file is updated as shown above. The transaction file may be held on any convenient medium, and nowadays is often on disk or tape. The error listing may not be output at this stage.

updating, and provides modular update code.

The logic of updating is shown in Fig. 5.2. As it is possible for the run to end either with an unchanged master record being written out on to the new master file, or with an update record that adds or deletes a master record, tests have to be made on both the old master file and the update file at the end of the run. A technique for handling this using program switches has been described[7]. It may or may not be possible for a single master record to have multiple updates, and both alternatives are shown in Fig. 5.2.

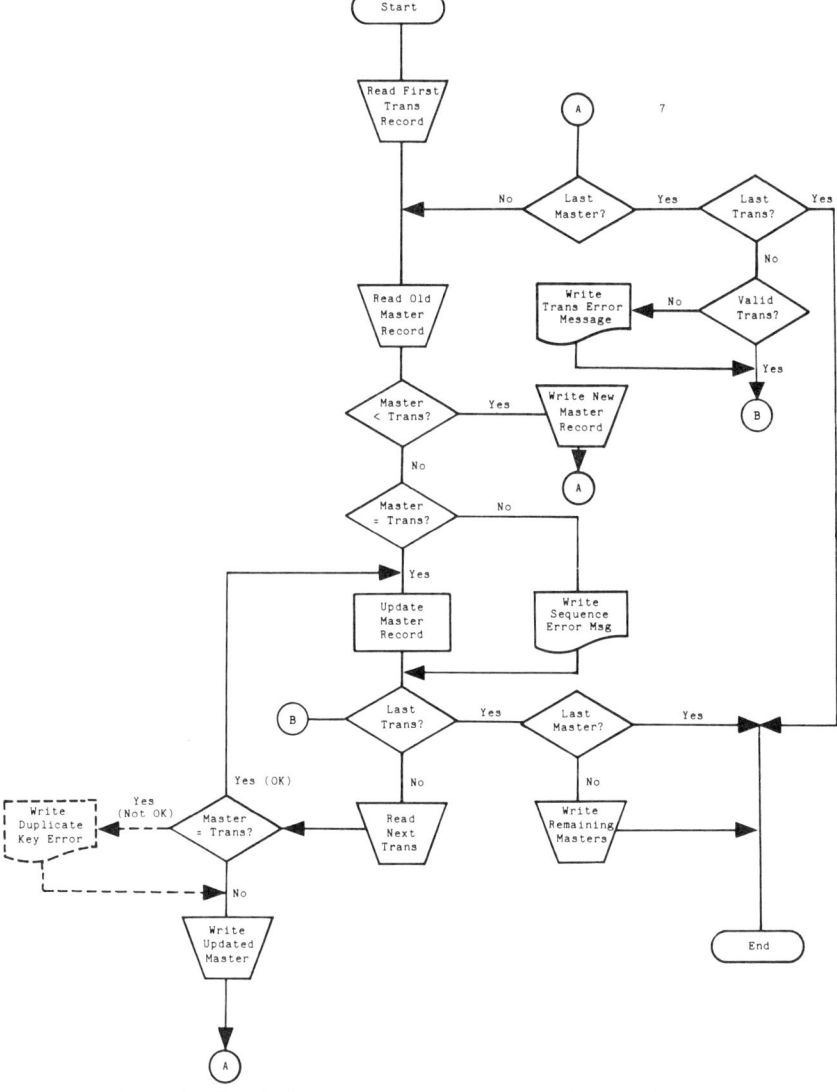

Fig. 5.2 The logic of updating a sequential tape file. Label checking and other tests have not been shown here. 'Master' and 'Trans.' each stand both for the records and their keys. If duplicate updates for a master record are possible the 'Yes OK' route will be taken; if they are not the 'Yes, not OK' route is taken.

112 Design of computer data files

Whether the user is updating a magnetic tape file or only referring to it, all the records in the file up to and including the desired record have to be read. In general, any run will involve reading every record in the file, so the designer will not be able to reduce the time taken up by reading data records. However, blocking and analysis of the file update pattern offer opportunities to improve processing efficiency.

Blocking

Blocking as many records as possible together to make large blocks will reduce the number of inter-block gaps to be traversed, and save time. This was discussed in detail in Chapter 4 under Competing Files (see p. 89). Fig. 4.7 shows the very marked improvement in run time that can be achieved, and the designer should never omit the step in design required to optimize blocking factors.

Update pattern

If the hit rate for a master file is high, sequential processing on tape is efficient. If it is low—and by this is meant less than 50 per cent of blocks are hit—many blocks are being read for no purpose. One way to raise the hit rate is to increase the time between runs, and so increase the number of records to be referenced. This makes the run more efficient, but at the expense of service to the user. The designer will have to decide whether this is a valid option.

Batching relies on increasing the hit rate of the whole file. When service considerations preclude less frequent runs, the next factor to examine is the pattern of updates or references to the file. A number of patterns occur frequently; they are examined below.

1 *Random updates*
If there is no predictable pattern or if update patterns vary from run to run, it is not possible to improve the handling of a sequential tape file. The designer should consider transferring the file on to a direct access device and skip-sequentially processing it (probably after reducing the blocking factor). The break-even point for this is discussed under Disk versus Tape—The Effect of Hit Rate later in the chapter (see p. 123).

2 *Grouped updates*
In many cases, as for example meter readings in public utility files or new customers after a campaign in a specific area, updates to a file will naturally show a grouping or pattern. When this is consistent and predictable it can be used to increase the hit rate of the file by processing the densely-hit parts frequently and the sparsely-hit parts less often.

The basis of this improvement is to divide or *section* the file, creating a number of mini-files. In the case of bills for gas, electricity or some other commodity that is invoiced quarterly, the file might be split into thirteen single-week sections. Readings for the current week would be used to update the appropriate section daily, while all the other sections would only be updated at the end of the week. As all the other sections would only have 'exception' readings for cases in which the meter had not been read on the initial call, this should not lead to unacceptable delays.

The improvement in tape passing-time can be dramatic. An example examined in *Basic File Design*[6], in which customer records were handled by sectioning the file into thirteen parts, gave a reduction of tape passing-time from two hours 37 minutes a week to just over 41 minutes. The reasons for such an improvement can be seen by examining a further case, in which insurance records are stored on an IBM 3420-8; the details are as follows:

> An insurance file, with 2 600 000 records of average size 500 bytes, was handled in alphabetic order. Daily runs to generate annual premium payment reminders took an average of just less than 24 minutes in tape passing-time alone, and as the file required ten reels of tape the operating overhead was considerable. Block size was a maximum of 5000 bytes; a larger block size would only have reduced tape usage and passing time by a relatively small amount—the number of tapes, for instance, could only have been reduced to eight; to achieve this, block size would have had to be increased to 17 500 bytes.
>
> The file was reorganized into renewal date order, and the reminders were generated from weekly sections of the file. Each minifile could be held on any convenient tape of at least 500 feet in length, and daily tape passing time was reduced to around 30 seconds, with no extra handling time due to additional tape mounts. It is worth noting that even use of a 3480 tape drive, with its automatic cassette handling and stacking device, would not have avoided handling time or reduced passing-time to anything like the extent that the redesign achieved.

Suitable cases for sectioning can thus offer considerable benefits; the process of file handling involved is shown in Fig. 5.3(a) and (b).

3 *Mixed updates*
When there is a pattern, but the 'background' random load of updates is also significant, it becomes a matter of judgement whether sectioning the file will be of benefit or whether it would be better to transfer the file on to a direct access device. It is often possible to divide the file into 'random' and 'grouped' update sections and handle them differently, which in effect creates two new files. When hit rates are high this is usually preferable to transfer of the file to a different medium.

4 *Regularly spaced updates*
A case that sometimes arises is that updates are regularly spaced, i.e. that

114 Design of computer data files

records $1, 1+n, 1+2n, 1+3n, \ldots$ are updated on one run while $2, 2+n, 2+n, 2+3n, \ldots$ are updated on another. If both the gap between updated records (n) and the starting record (1 on the first run, 2 on the second, and so on) are consistent and predictable, the file should be divided into n sections. An alternative, if the processing time for each record is precisely suited to disk processing without loss of revolutions, is to hold the file on disk. The conditions for this are shown in Fig. 5.4 and discussed later in the chapter.

This last part of the section on tape files has suggested a number of cases for which the designer might transfer the file to disk. It would be wrong to leave sequential tape files without pointing out that most sequential files are rightly stored on magnetic tape. There are, however, some other situations in which direct access devices are of benefit. For this reason they are examined in the next section.

FRIDAY OF WEEK 1

Master file
Sections 2-13

Section 1

Updates for
Section 1
Day 5

Updates for
Sections 2-13,
Days 1-5

Invoices, etc.
Whole file

Updated Master
Sections 1, 3-13

Section 2

(a)

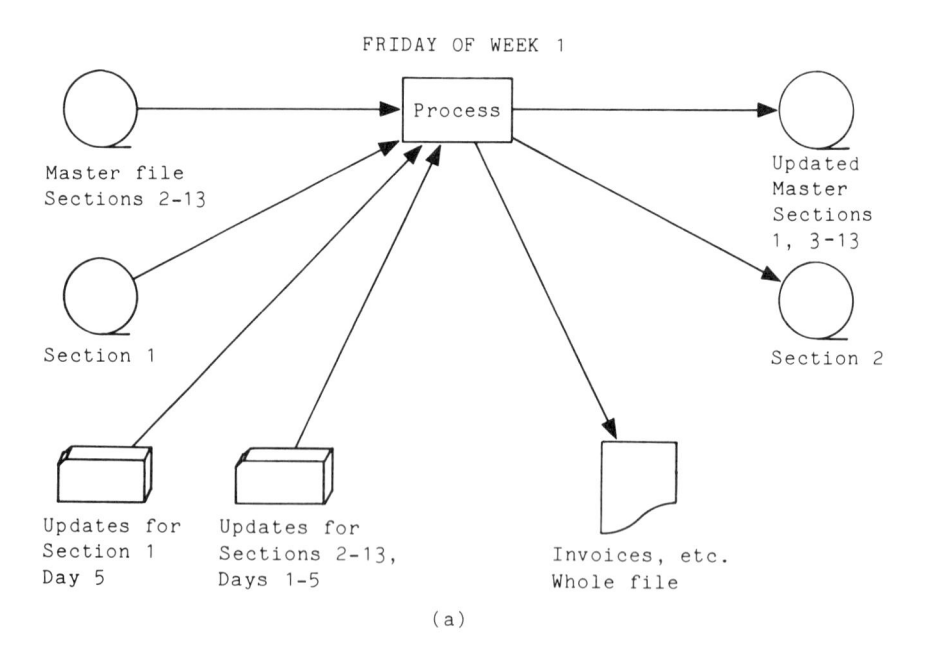

Fig. 5.3 Updating a sectioned file. The active section of the file is processed daily, and a new active section is selected weekly. This corresponds to a 13-week cycle with daily updates available, but this technique can be used for any time period and any number of sections. (a) The process on Friday of Week 1: Section 1 is recombined with the main file, while Section 2 is selected out. (b) Processing during Week 2.

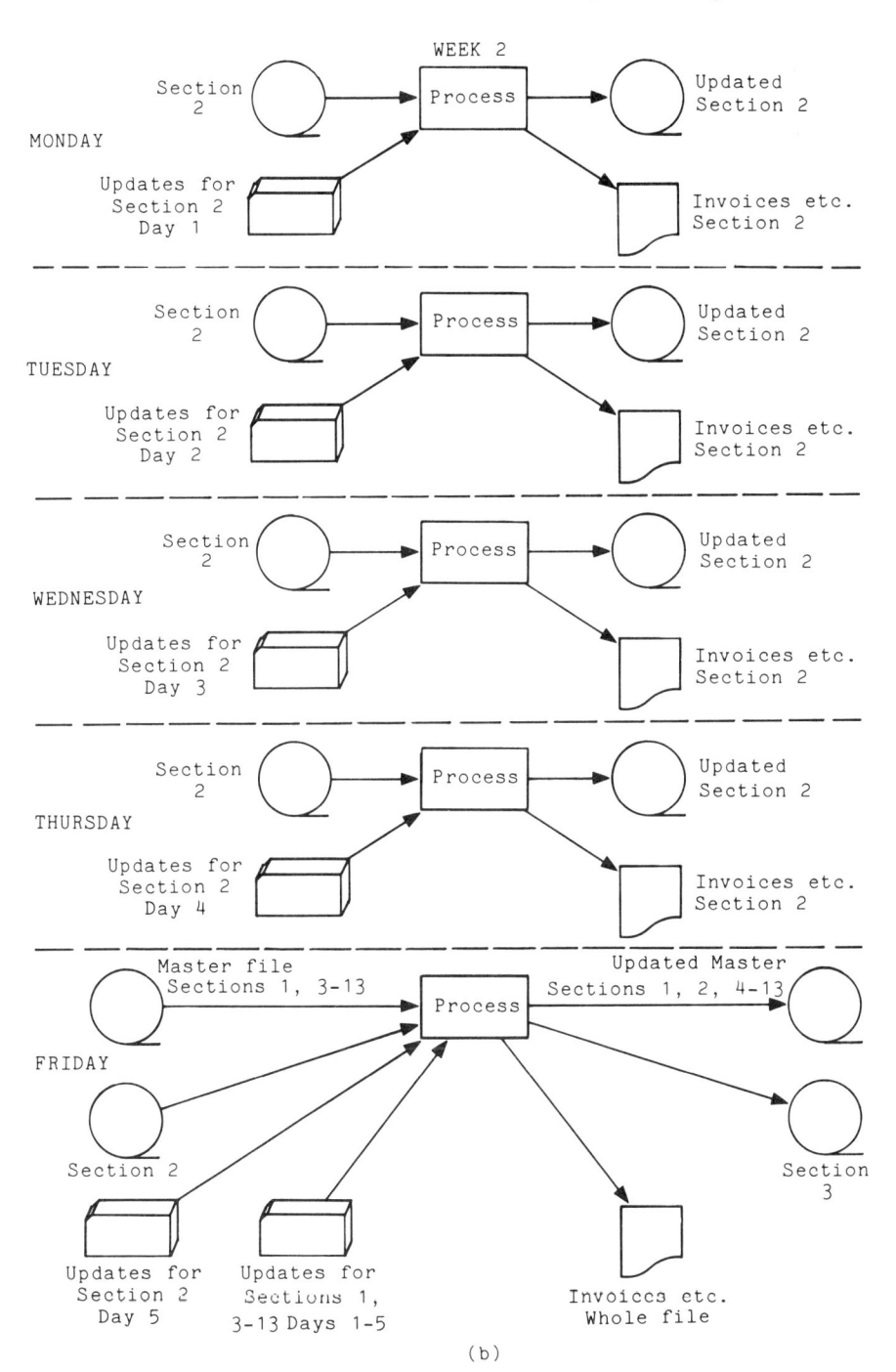

Sequential file organization **115**

MONDAY
- Section 2 → Process (WEEK 2) → Updated Section 2
- Updates for Section 2 Day 1 → Process
- Process → Invoices etc. Section 2

TUESDAY
- Section 2 → Process → Updated Section 2
- Updates for Section 2 Day 2 → Process
- Process → Invoices etc. Section 2

WEDNESDAY
- Section 2 → Process → Updated Section 2
- Updates for Section 2 Day 3 → Process
- Process → Invoices etc. Section 2

THURSDAY
- Section 2 → Process → Updated Section 2
- Updates for Section 2 Day 4 → Process
- Process → Invoices etc. Section 2

FRIDAY
- Master file Sections 1, 3-13 → Process → Updated Master Sections 1, 2, 4-13
- Section 2 → Process
- Updates for Section 2 Day 5 → Process
- Updates for Sections 1, 3-13 Days 1-5 → Process
- Process → Invoices etc. Whole file
- Process → Section 3

(b)

116 Design of computer data files

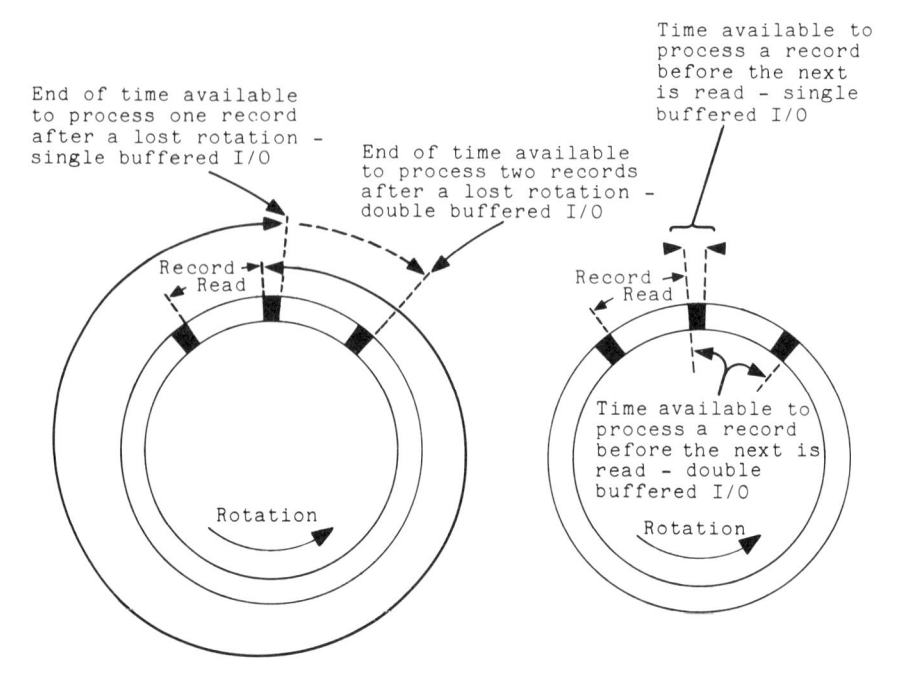

Fig. 5.4 The time available for processing during record rotation. If processing time is not close to these limits, maximum transfer speed will not usually be achieved.

5.6 Sequential files on direct access devices

Direct access devices are generally used either to meet some specific application requirements or because of some property of the device. A number of important cases are discussed below.

Low block activity

When the appropriate block size has been determined, as described in Chapter 4 (see p. 96), it may turn out that block activity is low. In this case, skip-sequential processing is the obvious method of access as it allows unwanted blocks to be ignored. The choice will be either between a sequential and an indexed sequential file, for which guidelines are given in Chapter 9, or between tape and disk storage of a sequential file. The main question to be answered by the file designer will be the point at which skip-sequential processing on disk is more efficient than sequential processing on tape. This is examined later in this chapter (see p. 123).

High transfer rate or very low error rates

For either of these a direct access file is often preferable. Disks and drums easily outperform any tape but the 3480 on transfer rate—although processing time or the ability of the computer itself to handle data may be limiting factors—and so they are suitable for these requirements. For example, apart from the 3480 tape drive the highest transfer rate is 1 250 000 bytes per second—well below the data transfer rates of disks such as the IBM 3380—3 000 000 bytes per second at maximum. Fixed head disks or semiconductor memories that simulate disk operation may be even faster. Even though these tapes are quoted as having transfer rates of up to 1 250 000 bytes per second, the actual transfer rate does not reach one million bytes per second until block sizes are almost 10 000 bytes. It is often neither practical nor efficient to use blocks of this size. For this reason, and also because it is impossible to locate the start of a desired file on disk very rapidly, direct access storage is ideally suited to high transfer rate applications. The limitation is that any processing should either be negligible, or require just less than 1, 2, . . . n revolutions plus one record traverse time if I–O is single-buffered, and two records traverse time if it is double-buffered. These situations are shown in Fig. 5.4.

These conditions are rather unusual, but such operations as reading disk into main storage or copying one disk to another can achieve maximum transfer rates; processing that takes just less time than one revolution is usually a matter of coincidence rather than planning, although the concept is used in certain file organizations and software enhancement packages (see Chapter 7).

A similar situation is the requirement for error-free processing. Disks are usually more reliable than tapes, although the same is not true of all direct access devices. For this reason it is occasionally decided to store a file on disk just because it gives a high probability of error-free running. Any reader who feels that tapes do not suffer from errors should observe operations closely. Back-spacing and re-tries are frequent on most tapes and even after 100 tries to read data a significant number of failures occur. However, the precautions that can be taken to improve tape reliability have been discussed in Chapter 2 (see p. 51), and some users can achieve very impressive results by applying them.

Small files

For security and control reasons it is not desirable to have more than one file on a tape reel. If several files are stored on a single reel, all of them are available even though authorization has been given only for one file to be processed. The chance of a reel being mislaid is increased if it is constantly out of the tape library. In addition, files have to be spaced through if multi-files are stored on a reel, and continual mounting and dismounting may be caused if small files are stored singly on tape reels. By contrast, multi-files stored on a single disk-pack can be located very quickly and do not cause continual mount-dismounts. For this reason, small files are often stored on direct access devices.

Frequently sorted files

Files that frequently need to be sorted into a different order may be stored on disk to facilitate the sorting process and avoid the need for constant transfers between disk and tape.

Whichever of these reasons leads to the use of direct access devices to hold sequential files, a number of processing modes are made available when a file is held on them. These alternatives are described below. They include the only important requirement that has not yet been discussed, that of occasional direct accesses to a sequentially organized file.

Access methods available

1 *Sequential*
Normal sequential processing is unusual unless one of the cases described above applies. This is because it is wasteful if the hit rate is low, and the skip-sequential mode would usually be preferred. If the hit rate is high, tape processing would usually be chosen.

2 *Skip-sequential*
As the block hit rate of the file gets lower, this alternative becomes more attractive. It will often be advantageous to *reduce* the block size when skip-sequential processing, in order to lower the block hit rate and so skip inactive records. Methods of calculating the effects of reducing block size were given in Chapter 4 (see p. 83).

In order to be able to pick up only the required records or blocks, the key must be separate from the body of the record. This format is not provided in some file organization systems, e.g. ICL 1900 series software. In IBM MVS it is directly available, while IBM DOS-VSE systems require the file to be created and processed using direct file organization macros. Details of the separate key format were given in Chapter 3 (see p. 57). The conditions in which a sequential file would be skip-processed, rather than turning to an indexed sequential file, are discussed in Chapter 9 (see p. 300).

3 *Direct access*
There are a number of ways in which a sequentially organized file can be referenced directly:

(*a*) FULL SEARCH   In principle the file could be searched from the start, reading in and examining every record until the required record was found; this is the only available technique on magnetic tape unless the record number in the file is known. On disk this method is only used if the file is serially organized, as a number of more efficient methods are available if the file is sequentially organized. A variant of this technique, in which a list is *self-organizing*—that is, the most used records, or the most recently used records, are stored at the front—is most often applied in searching lists in main storage. However, it can occasionally be helpful on disk or tape. Methods of organizing such lists, and their efficiency under various conditions, are reviewed in reference[9].

(*b*) SKIP SEARCH   If records have been stored with separate keys, the device can scan keys at rotation speed and read in only the desired record. This depends on the format being available and is generally used only to search a small area—a cylinder or track—after the area containing the record has been determined in some other way. For a full search of a file it would be very inefficient as an average length search would require half the file to be scanned before the record was found. The self-organizing type of list should also be considered here[9].

(*c*) BINARY SEARCH   Because it is possible to reach any part of a disk rapidly, it becomes practical to use a binary or logarithmic search technique, in which the middle record of the file is examined first, followed by the middle of the top or bottom half of the file depending on whether the key being sought was higher or lower than the middle key; the sequence continues until the desired key is found. This has been fully described elsewhere[10, 11, 12], and only the timing implications will be examined here. Once more the separate key format is helpful although, at the expense of reading and examining a limited number of records, the embedded key format can also be handled in this way.

For devices with up to 256 (2^8) cylinders (seek areas in ICL terminology), a maximum of eight head movements will be required. Ten head movements will allow for up to 1024 (2^{10}) cylinders, and very few disk devices require more than this—for example, the 3375 has 959, the 3380 885. As these head movements are not 'average' in size, but reduce with each probe, the total time involved is not unreasonable—on an IBM 3330, 200 milliseconds is a fair estimate. The next step will be a search of the cylinder containing the record, which may involve up to five full disk revolutions. This is followed by a search of the track containing the record. The cylinder search may take around 100 milliseconds, giving a total time—again for a 3330—of around 300 milliseconds. These times will be markedly increased if the embedded key format is being used, as records will have to be read into main storage to check whether their key is higher, lower or equal to the required key. The progress of a binary search is shown in Fig. 5.5.

The sequence shown in Fig. 5.5 required eleven separate head movements, even though the second of them was to a cylinder only one away from the cylinder that holds the record. Note that the last two probes are

120 Design of computer data files

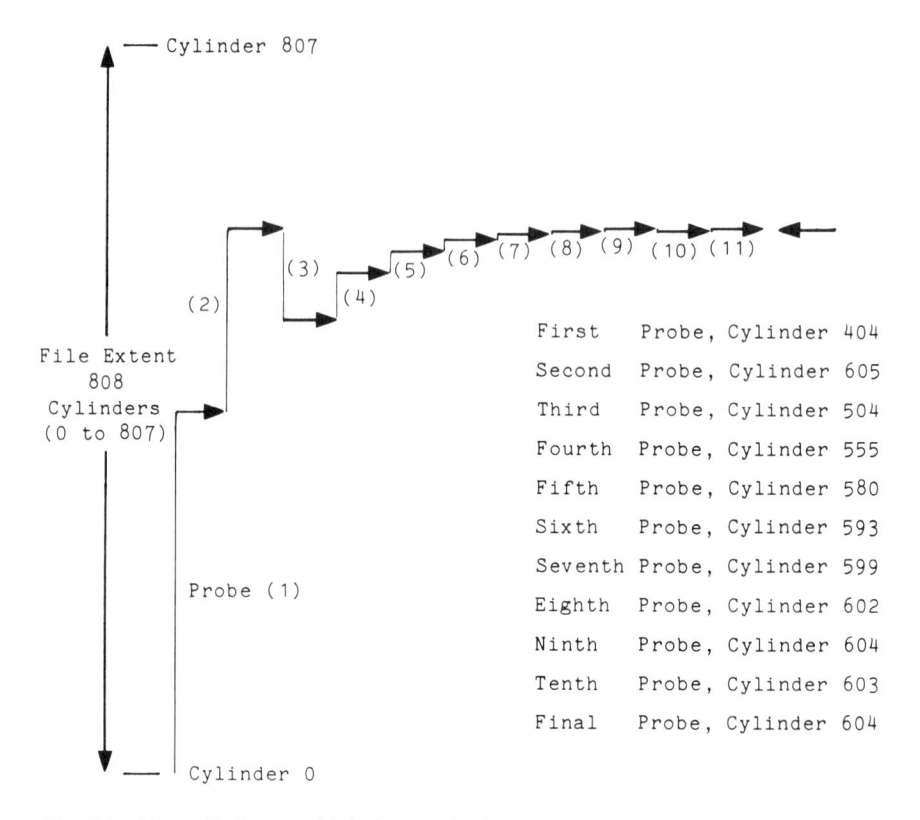

```
         ── Cylinder 807
```

```
                                    (7)  (8)  (9) (10) (11)
                          (5) (6)
                  (3)
                      (4)
             (2)
                              First    Probe, Cylinder 404
File Extent
    808                       Second   Probe, Cylinder 605
 Cylinders                    Third    Probe, Cylinder 504
 (0 to 807)
                              Fourth   Probe, Cylinder 555
                              Fifth    Probe, Cylinder 580
                              Sixth    Probe, Cylinder 593
                              Seventh  Probe, Cylinder 599
         Probe (1)            Eighth   Probe, Cylinder 602
                              Ninth    Probe, Cylinder 604
                              Tenth    Probe, Cylinder 603
                              Final    Probe, Cylinder 604

         ── Cylinder 0
```

Fig. 5.5 The cylinder on which the required record is stored is located by a series of decreasing head movements. Note that only a few of these movements require long head-traverses. Note also how many probes are required after the near-miss on probe two. The tenth and final probes may not be required; see text for discussion.

necessary unless the desired record happens to be the *first* on the cylinder, if the search examines the first record of each cylinder, or the *last* if the search examines the last record. This is a consequence of the rigid binary nature of the search process, which takes no account of the nearness of a key's value to that of the required key. All the decisions taken during the search are based on a crude comparison of the examined key with the required key to decide which is the higher; this is a waste of useful data and it results in loss of time in most cases. In order to exploit the value of the two keys involved in each comparison, a modified form of binary search has been developed[13]. In most cases this will reduce the time used in the search by a significant amount. The technique is described below.

(*d*) INTERPOLATION OR STATISTICAL BINARY SEARCH   If record keys are either randomly or fairly evenly distributed throughout the file, a rough arithmetic calculation of the expected position of the required record can speed the search process. In the example shown in Fig. 5.5, the second probe was close to the required cylinder and yet it took nine more probes to locate it. A statistical search does far better than this in most cases. The technique will fall down only if there is a considerable bias due to the component parts of the key—for example, where one area code represents a very densely populated area, while others represent sparsely populated areas and hence cover far fewer records. The presence of small groups in which keys are densely packed will not affect the method so long as they are themselves randomly distributed in a much larger file.

The principle of statistical searching is that the record keys are assumed to be evenly spread across cylinders, in order to get a starting value for the search. Each actual comparison is used to refine the search further by comparing the key *found* to that *calculated*. Without this precaution, a binary statistical search can take *longer* than a conventional binary chop. So long as this check is made at every step, statistical searching usually provides marked benefits, although the margin grows less as the key sequence diverges from random. This is particularly the case when the sequence is asymmetric, as pointed out above. If the sequence is absolutely even—no gaps in the keys, so that every cylinder has the same key range—statistical searching will be very efficient indeed, but in this case the file is likely to be organized as a self-indexing file, which is discussed in the next chapter (see page 145). Most other non-random sequences are a hindrance rather than a help.

The starting value for a statistical search is calculated as follows. Let:

KEY_{start} be the first key in the file;
KEY_{end} be the last key in the file;
KEY_{search} be the required key;
KEY_{found} be the highest key on an examined cylinder;
CYL_{start} be the first cylinder used by the file;
CYL_{search} be the next cylinder to be examined by the program;
m be the number of contiguous cylinders that contain the file.

Then the average key increment per cylinder is

$$\frac{(KEY_{end} - KEY_{start})}{m} \tag{5.6}$$

The first cylinder examined will be calculated on the assumption that the same key increment occurs on each cylinder. It is given by:

$$CYL_{search} = CYL_{start} + \frac{m(KEY_{search} - KEY_{start})}{(KEY_{end} - KEY_{start})} \tag{5.7}$$

The value of CYL_{search} obtained from equation (5.7) is truncated if cylinders are numbered from zero and rounded up to the next integer if cylinders are numbered from 1. The highest and lowest keys on the cylinder are inspected, and if this shows that the required record is on the cylinder the search continues on the track of the cylinder indicated by the original calculation.

If the required record is not on the cylinder, the search is continued by substituting the value of CYL_{search} from equation (5.7) in the right-hand side of the relationship:

$$CYL_{search} = CYL_{start} + \frac{(CYL_{search} - CYL_{start})(KEY_{search} - KEY_{start})}{(KEY_{found} - KEY_{start})} \quad (5.8)$$

This relationship is used recursively until the required cylinder is located. The process is straightforward for most key sequences, but a number of precautions are required to ensure that unusual key sequences do not cause problems. These are examined below.

1 *Biassed key sequences* If more than half of the range of a key sequence is held on a single cylinder, statistical searching can take considerably longer than a binary chop. A count of steps should be held, and when it reaches the expected number for a binary search the statistical basis of the search should be abandoned. More details are given in the original paper[13].

2 *Large gaps in key sequences* When keys are made up of a set of parts that represent country, area, function, product type, etc., the sequence may consist of small groups of 'used' keys separated by very large gaps. This can lead to endless looping of the search, and sometimes to references outside the file area. The latter problem can be avoided by holding maximum and minimum values for search cylinder number; the former can be limited by ensuring that each new search cylinder is *higher* than any previous one at the low end of the search, and *lower* than any previous one at the high end. It is usually best to switch to a normal binary search as soon as the statistical search leads to forced values, as this is an indication of incipient looping.

These are unusual situations. The number of head movements in a statistical search is usually cut to three or four, all but the first of which are short. For the IBM 3330 quoted earlier a saving of about 100 milliseconds per record can usually be achieved, as shown in[13].

The final two techniques described are very useful for occasional searches of a sequential file when the overwhelming body of file processing is sequential and an indexed sequential file is not appropriate. They do not compete with either indexed-sequentially or directly organized files for direct applications, as the latter are about four times faster.

Apart from the cases discussed above, sequential files will usually be stored on magnetic tape. The only situation that requires in-depth analysis is that of low block activity, which is examined below.

5.7 Disk versus tape—the effect of hit rate

A number of general points need to be made with respect to these two alternative media for sequential file storage. The first is that additions and deletions are not usually as easy on direct access devices. Because a new tape master file is created on each run, records can be added or deleted without any problem. By comparison, if records are to be added to a sequential disk file that is to be updated in place, gaps have to be left for insertions or a separate overflow area has to be provided for additions. Deletions would involve closing up the gaps left, so the usual solution is to set an indicator in deleted records and physically remove them during the next file reorganization.

ICL does allow the user both to provide gaps and to handle overflows in its 1900 series software, but most manufacturers see this as a complication of what is fundamentally a straightforward technique, and reserve these facilities for their indexed files.

The second point is that tape provides security automatically, while a deliberate plan to achieve it is required for sequential disk files. This is reviewed in Chapter 10 (see p. 331).

The third applies to both media. It is that most of the discussion in this chapter has been about *run* timing, while in fact the designer has to consider batching, sorting and running as a single timing entity. The overall process is illustrated in *Essentials of Computer Data Files*[14], and Fig. 5.6 is taken from it. In addition there are circumstances in which the program, once available, should be used to carry out as much processing of as many files as possible. The concepts and techniques involved in multi-master file processing, to exploit this opportunity, are discussed by Montgomery[15].

These points are important and may lead to a decision based on convenience. The crucial factors in choosing between tape and disk on the basis of processing speed are record hit-rate, blocking factor, the mode of reference and the processing time per record. The first two have been discussed in some detail in Chapter 4 (see p. 83) and the treatment of them here will be based on that discussion. The others have not yet been examined.

If a record is located and read into main storage for reference, but not altered and so not written back on to disk, timing calculations need only consider the times taken to locate the record, to read it into main storage and then process it. If the record is to be written back on to disk, at least a single revolution will elapse before the record or block is once more in a position to be accessed. This will have to be added to timing calculations. If the user decides to carry out a *read-after-write check* to ensure that the data has been correctly written, a further revolution will be required for each record or block. Hence the timings on disk will depend on whether the operations to be carried out are:

124 Design of computer data files

READ or WRITE only;
READ followed by WRITE;
WRITE followed by CHECK;
READ followed by WRITE followed by CHECK;

Magnetic tape operations are a great deal simpler, in that records are read from one tape and written to another, and read-after-write checks are carried out without loss of time. This simplifies the calculations, and it is convenient to examine the case of magnetic tape first.

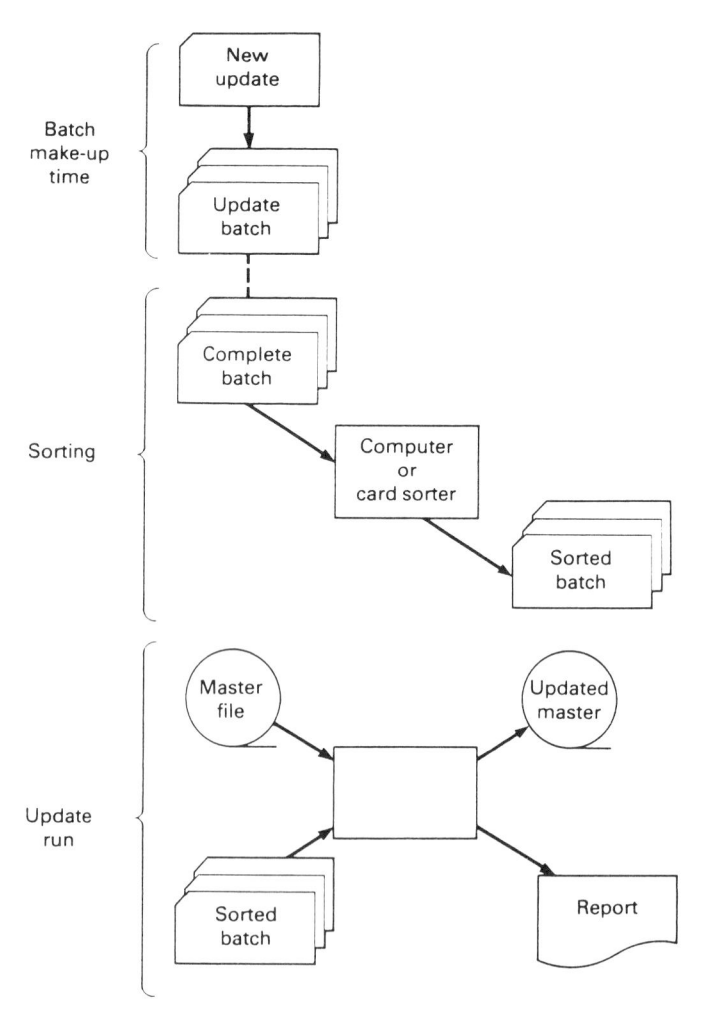

Fig. 5.6 Preparing for a sequential update run. Sorting may be carried out off-line using a card sorter, or on-line using the computer, in which case output would be onto magnetic tape.

Table 5.1

Block size	Effective transfer rate (kbytes/second)	Time to read one record, including IBG (milliseconds)
Single record	60	10.67
Blocks of 4 records	108	5.87
Blocks of 16 records	137	4.67
Infinite	150	4.27

For reasons that were explained in Chapter 4 (see p. 95), tape records will be blocked whenever possible. Disk records, on the other hand, may well not be. To take account of this difference, a record size has been chosen that allows reasonable disk efficiency in unblocked form. The record size used below is 640 bytes, with a key length (included in the 640) of eight bytes. The tape characteristics chosen are as follows:

150 kbytes per second transfer rate;
1600 bytes per inch packing density;
6.4 millisecond start-stop time;
0.6 inch inter-block gap (IBG).

These characteristics lead to the figures given in Table 5.1 for the block sizes shown.

The tape run being considered is assumed to be double-buffered, so there is no question of lost time due to longer start-stop periods than the minimum, unless the run becomes process-bound. Hit rate is only a factor when processing time becomes relatively long as every record has to be read whatever the activity of the file, so that input-output time imposes a lower limit on the handling time of each record.

The time required to read a single record (not a block) has been plotted against the processing time per record in Fig. 5.7. Each set of lines corresponds to a given hit rate, and they show that the rate-determining process is input-output until the processing time, including any blocking-deblocking and other housekeeping, equals the input-output time. From then on the run will be process-bound. In practice this point is often not reached, and the run remains I–O bound.

A tape with a higher data transfer rate would lead to the horizontal lines occurring at lower positions on Fig. 5.7 and intersecting the diagonal 100 per cent hit rate line earlier. There would be no change in overall shape of the diagrams.

Fig. 5.7 was derived as follows: in determining the time required to

126 Design of computer data files

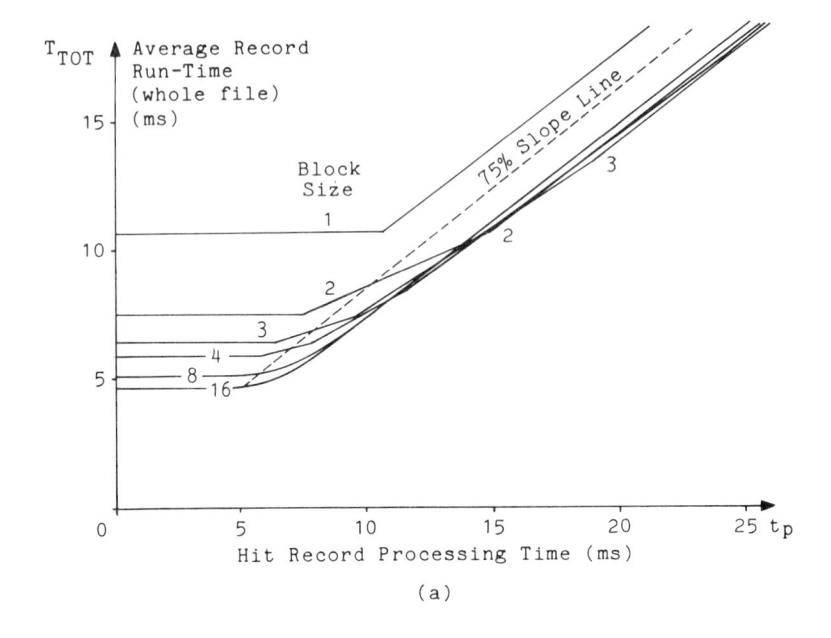

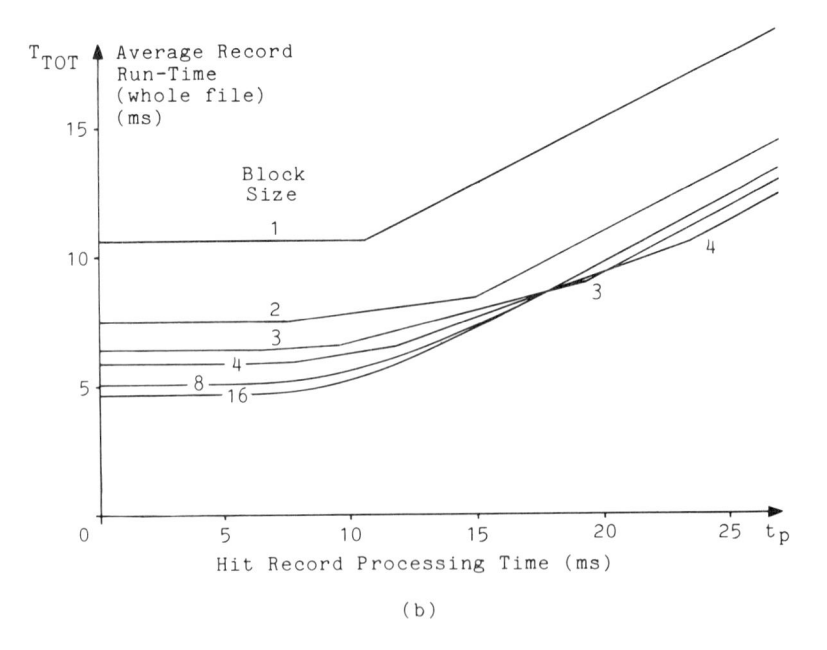

Fig. 5.7 Relationship between overall time to process a record (T_{TOT}) and the time required to process it (t_p). (a) 75 per cent hit rate. (b) 50 per cent hit rate. (c) 25 per cent hit rate. (d) 10 per cent hit rate.

Sequential file organization 127

(c)

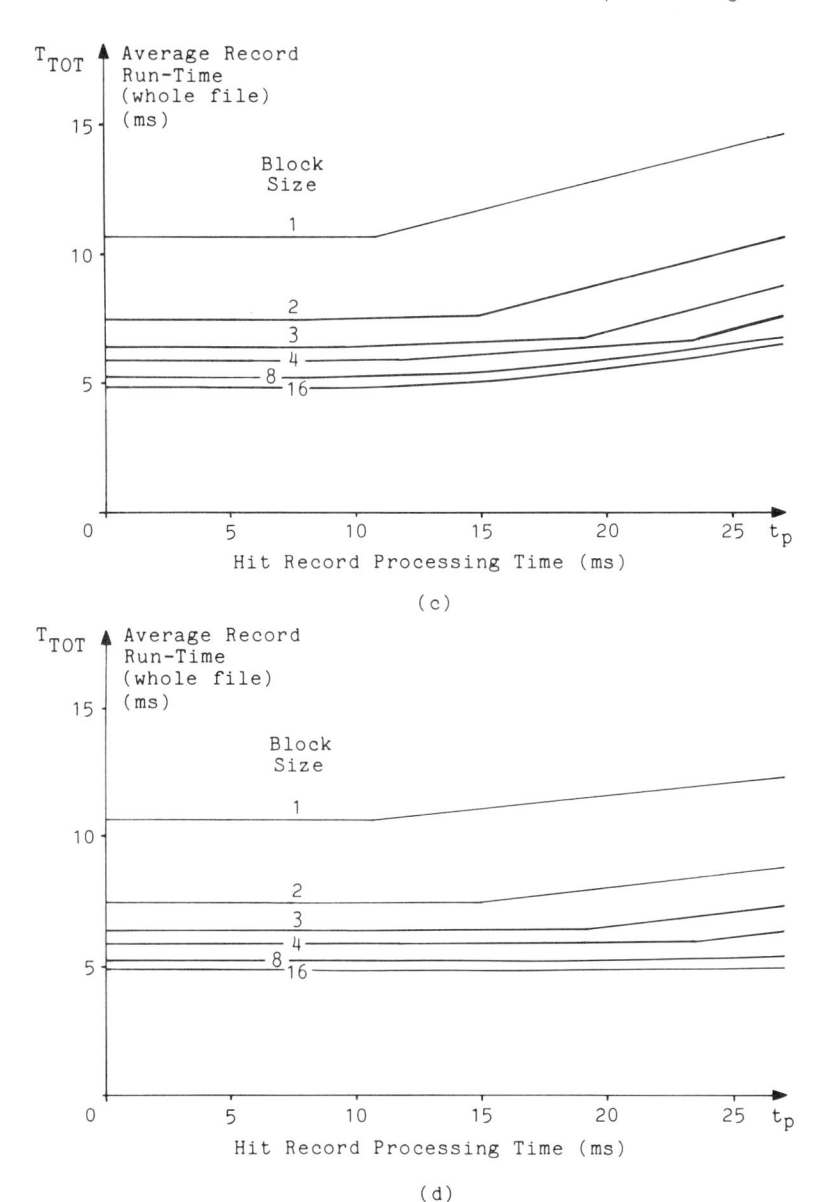

(d)

process unblocked records a comparison has to be made between the I–O time involved in reading a record and the time required to process it. If a proportion r of the records in the file is hit, $(1-r)$ will not be processed and will contribute I–O time only to the total run time. The hit records will contribute I–O time only, up to the point at which the time to read the record (including the IBG) is equal to the time required to process it. Hit records will thus contribute either an I–O time or a processing time, whichever is the larger, to the overall run time.

To analyse this relationship, let:

T_{TOT} be the overall time required to process a record;
t_{IO} be the time required to read it, including the IBG;
t_p be the time required to process it, including housekeeping.

Then, while $t_{IO} \geq t_p$

$$T_{TOT} = t_{IO} \tag{5.9}$$

and when $t_{IO} < t_p$

$$T_{TOT} = rt_p + (1 - r) t_{IO} \tag{5.10}$$

Fig. 5.7 plots the relationship between T_{TOT} and t_p for a number of hit rates.

T_{TOT} runs parallel to the t_p axis with a slope of zero until $t_{IO} = t_p$.

From that point on, the slope of the line will be r. The slope of the line is thus equal to the hit proportion of the file.

Blocked records are not so straightforward. The transfer of four record blocks into main storage will require one IBG time plus the record read time for four records. This will take a total of 23.48 ms for the case considered here. If hits are randomly distributed throughout the file the number of records processed in a block will be a matter of chance, and the probabilities of hitting one, two, three or four records per block are as shown in Table 5.2. The figures are given as cumulative percentages.

This table is derived from the binomial distribution. It shows that, for a 75 per cent hit rate, 31.6 per cent of blocks will contain four hit records, and will thus be process-bound for process times exceeding 5.87 ms. When process times reach 7.83 ms, blocks containing three hit records will become process-bound; 73.8 per cent of blocks will now be process, rather than I–O bound. When process times reach 11.74 ms, blocks containing two hit records switch from the I–O to the process-bound state, and the remainder will switch at a process time of 23.48 ms. From this point the slope of the resulting line is equivalent to that for single record blocks of the same hit rate.

Table 5.3 gives the probabilities that 1,2,3, . . . 16 records will be hit in a sixteen-record block for a number of hit rates. Extensive tables of this sort are not necessary for every possible case, as the required values are directly available in published binomial probability tables. However, a non-random distribution would require knowledge of the actual probabilities.

The curves for blocks of sixteen records have been calculated in the same way as those for four record blocks given above, using the probabilities in Table 5.3 and the break-even times from Table 5.4. It is worth noting that for larger block sizes the slope increases more rapidly than for smaller blocks.

Sequential file organization 129

Table 5.2 These figures show the cumulative percentage of four record blocks that will have the given number of records hit.

Number of records hit	Hit rate (%)								
	75	50	25	15	10	7	5	3	2
4	31.6	6.3	0.4	0.1	0.0	0.0	0.0	0.0	0.0
3	73.8	31.2	5.1	1.2	0.4	0.0	0.0	0.0	0.0
2	94.9	68.8	26.2	11.0	5.2	2.8	1.4	0.5	0.2
1	99.6	93.8	68.4	47.8	34.4	25.1	18.5	11.5	7.8

Table 5.3 The figures presented here are cumulative, and show the probability of blocks holding at least the number of records stated being updated. Block size is sixteen records.

Number of records hit	Hit rate (%)					
	75	50	25	15	10	5
16	0.010					
15	0.063					
14	0.197	0.002				
13	0.405	0.011				
12	0.630	0.038				
11	0.810	0.105				
10	0.920	0.227	0.001			
9	0.973	0.402	0.006			
8	0.993	0.598	0.027	0.001		
7	0.999	0.773	0.080	0.006	0.001	
6	1.000	0.895	0.190	0.024	0.003	
5		0.962	0.370	0.079	0.017	0.001
4		0.989	0.595	0.210	0.068	0.007
3		0.998	0.803	0.439	0.211	0.043
2		1.000	0.937	0.716	0.485	0.189
1			0.990	0.926	0.815	0.560
0			1.000	1.000	1.000	1.000

Table 5.4 These break-even times show the I–O time available to process records with the given number of hits per block. For example, a tape block containing six hit records will remain I–O bound until processing times reach 12.44 ms. A 3330 block in which six records are hit will cause a lost revolution if processing times exceed 2.79 ms.

Hits per block	16	15	14	13	12	11	10	9	8	7	6	5	4	3	2	1
Tape (ms)	4.67	4.97	5.33	5.74	6.22	6.79	7.47	8.30	9.30	10.66	12.44	14.93	18.67	24.88	37.33	74.66
3330 (ms)	1.04	1.11	1.19	1.29	1.39	1.52	1.67	1.86	2.09	2.39	2.79	3.34	4.18	5.57	8.36	16.71

130 Design of computer data files

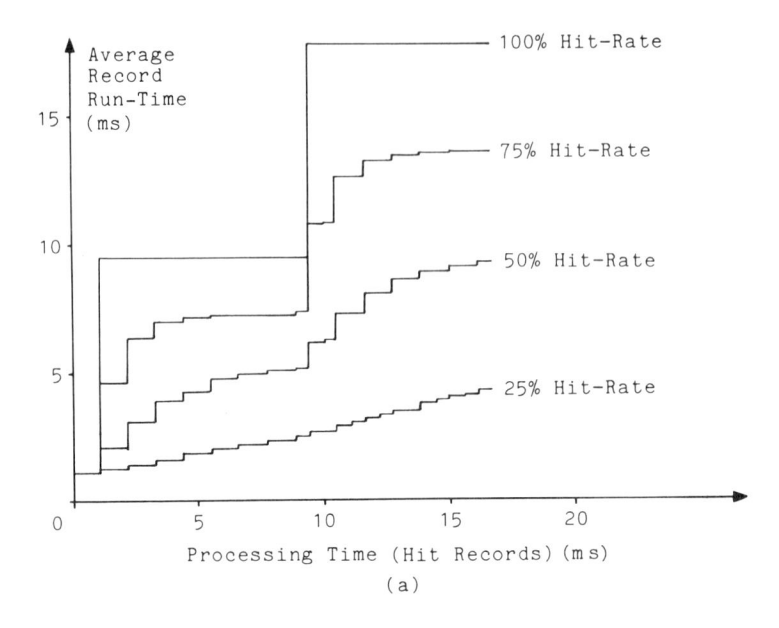

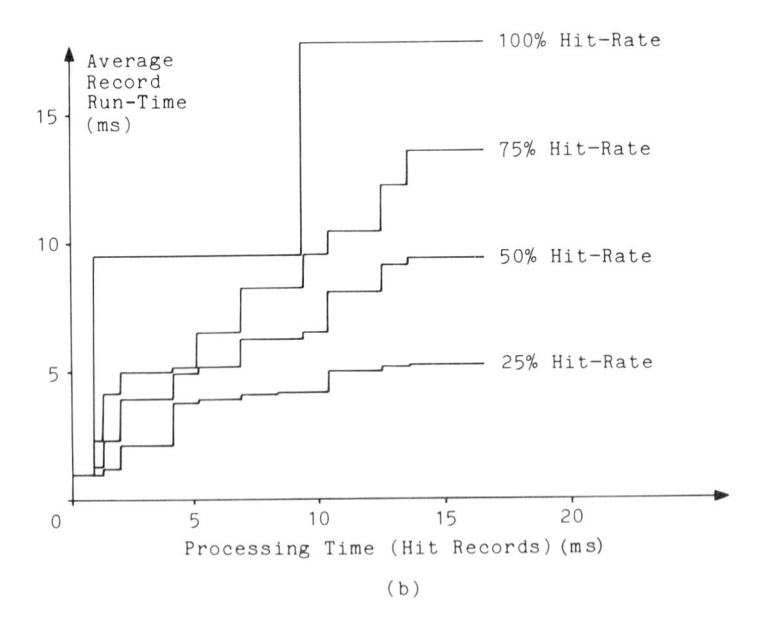

Fig. 5.8 Effect of hit rate on an IBM 3330. (a) Single-record blocks. (b) Four-record blocks. (c) Sixteen-record blocks. (d) Comparison of read, process, write and check, and read and write back.

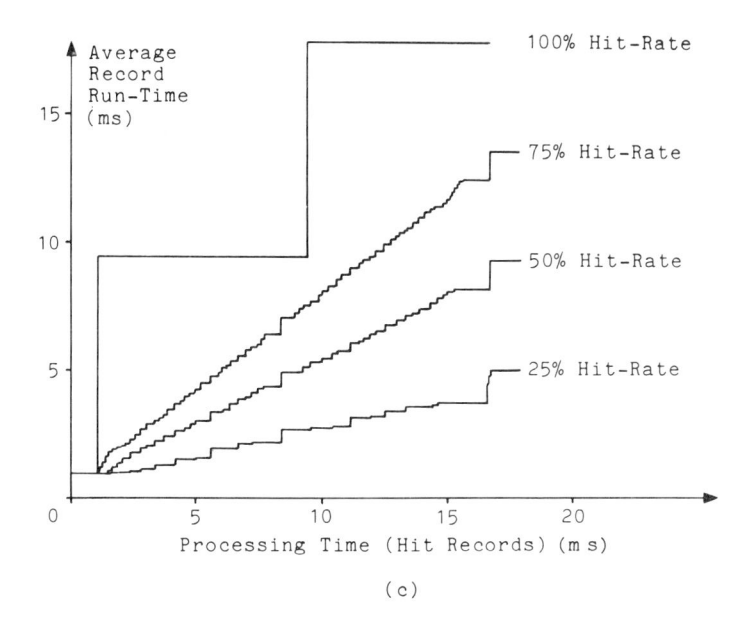

Sequential file organization **131**

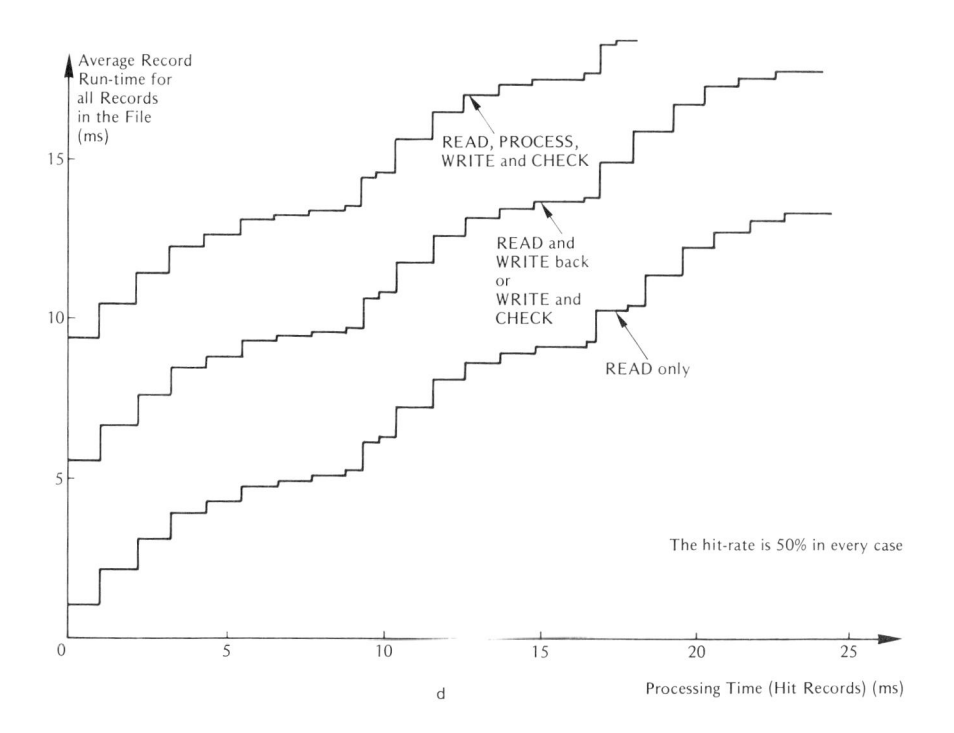

(c)

The hit-rate is 50% in every case

d

132 Design of computer data files

The 75 per cent and 50 per cent hit-rate lines for several block sizes shown in Fig. 5.7(a) and (b) intersect while those for lower hit rates do not. Details of the curves for various hit-rates and block sizes are given by the author in the paper[16] on which this discussion is based.

In order to make a comparison between magnetic tape and disk, equivalent figures are required. The most likely disk device available for the file designer today, which would be compared with this sort of tape for file storage purposes, is an IBM 3330 or its equivalent, e.g. ICL EDS 100. This has therefore been used to provide curves for comparison in Fig. 5.8. However, the 3330 is intrinsically much faster than the tape quoted, and in order to give a comparison that matches devices of similar speeds, curves for

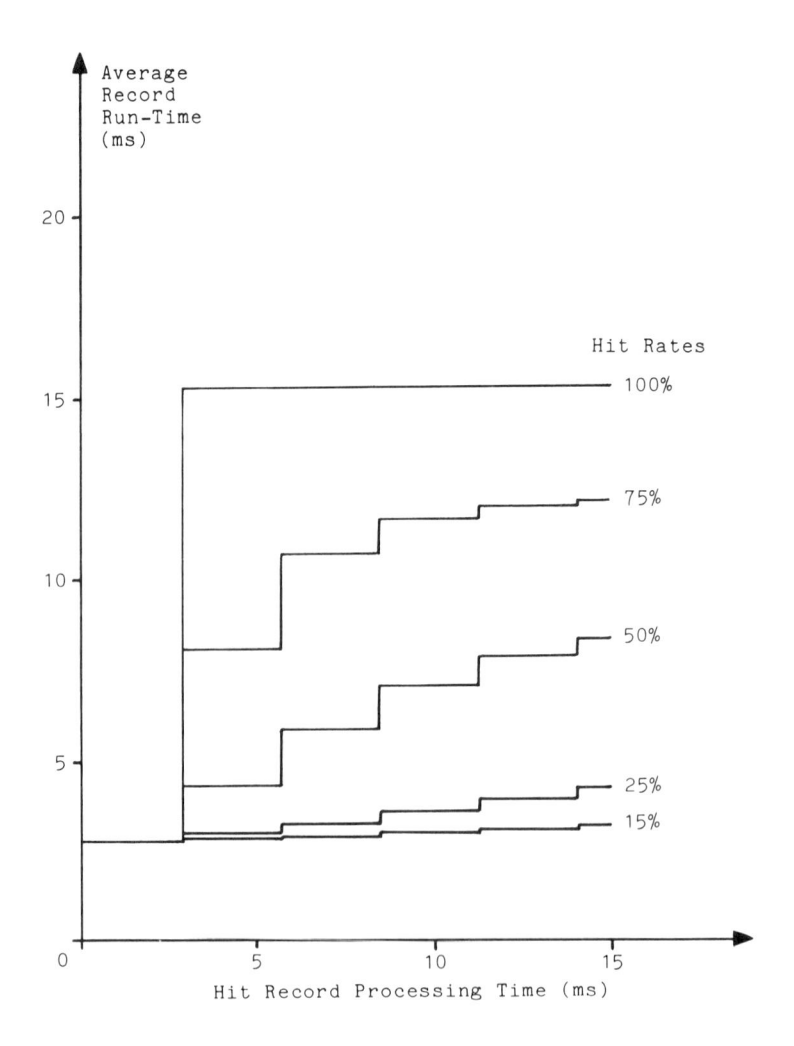

Fig. 5.9 Double-buffered records on an IBM 2314 or an ICL EDS 30.

the 2314 are shown in Fig. 5.9 and the 2311 in Fig. 5.10. Blocked records have been considered only for the 3330. Characteristics of these disks are given in Tables 5.5 and 5.6.

The same considerations—the hit rate, record processing time and number of records hit per block—apply to disk as to tape processing. However, loss of time is due to lost revolutions when processing is not completed by a certain point rather than the switch from I–O to processing at a given time. This leads to the step-like shape of the curves shown in Figs. 5.8, 5.9 and 5.10, while their precise form depends on the proportion of blocks that cause lost revolutions. These curves have been derived using the probabilities

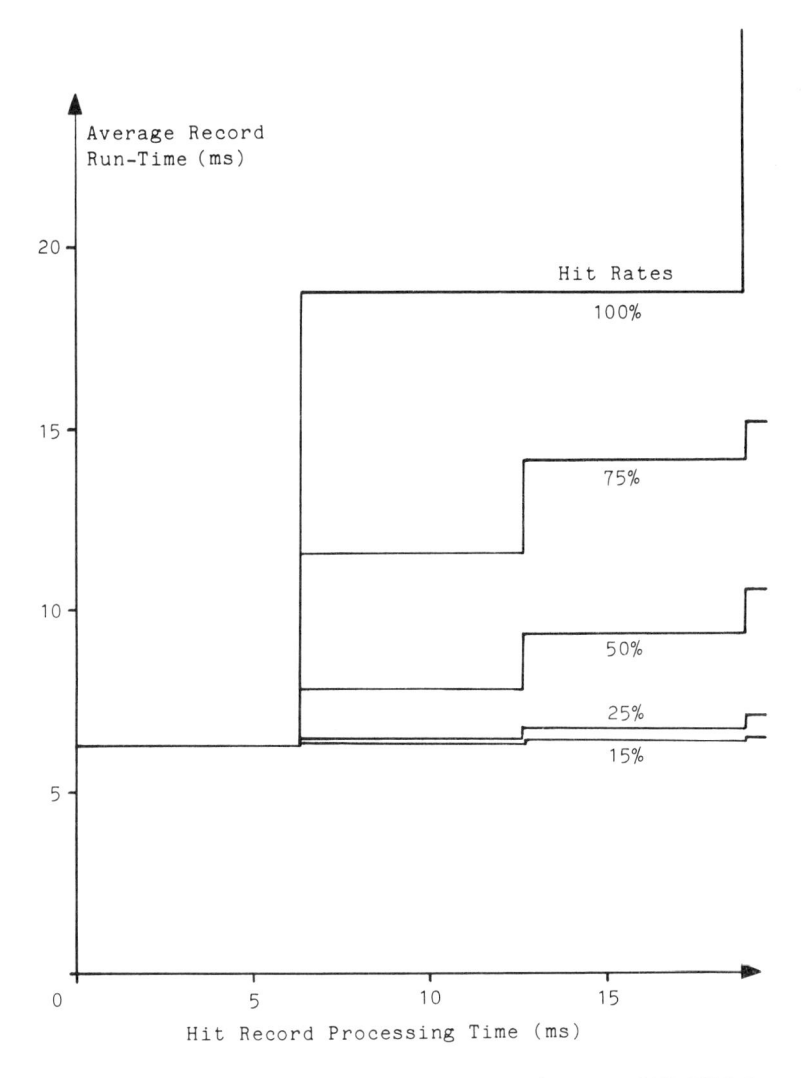

Fig. 5.10 Double-buffered records on an IBM 2311 or an ICL EDS 8.

Table 5.5 Records that can be stored per track in the formats used to illustrate device speed comparisons.

Disk device	Records per track		Transfer time per record (ms)	Limit to save one revolution (ms)
	CKD format	Embedded format		
3330	15	16	1.04	1.11
2314	9	9	2.78	2.93
2311	4	5	6.25	6.39

Table 5.6 The figures tabulated give the times in milliseconds at which the block switches from an I–O to a process-bound condition.

Records processed	Break-even time, I–O versus processing (ms)			
	Tape	3330	2314	2311
4	5.87	1.06	2.82	6.29
3	7.83	1.41	3.76	8.38
2	11.74	2.12	5.64	12.57
1	23.48	4.23	11.27	25.14

given in Tables 5.2 and 5.3, and the break-even times given in Tables 5.4 and 5.6. Work on an ICL EDS 60[17], similar in characteristics to a 2314 with double the cylinders, confirmed the general shape of these curves, but losses due to inefficient software led to greater delays than those shown (i.e. all curves were displaced upwards).

The column headed 'Limit to save one revolution' in Table 5.5 shows the length of time that elapses—when records are double-buffered—between the completion of one record (or block) read and the start of the next. It is the sum of the time taken to traverse one record and the gaps between two records. The relationship between the time required to transfer one record and the limit to save one revolution is shown in Fig. 5.11.

As was explained earlier, the CKD format is that in which record keys are stored separately from the data, while embedded format is the case where key and data are stored as a single entity. For the 2314 the same number of records can be held in both formats, while the 3330 and 2311 each lose one record in capacity per track when the key format is used. However, as the separate key allows the skipping of single records or blocks without reference to the CPU or the use of data channels, this format is usually used in such a case.

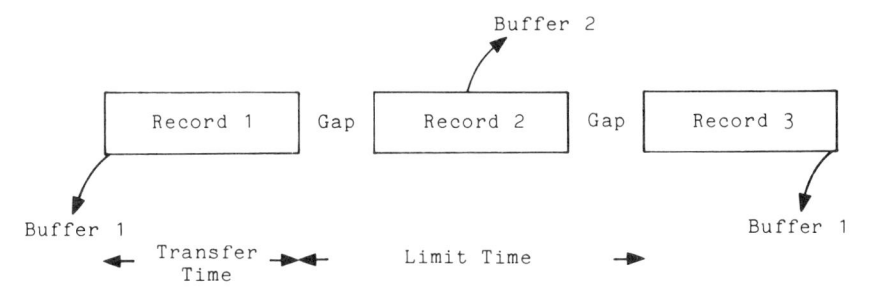

```
                              Buffer 2
                                ↗
  ┌──────────┐      ┌──────────┐      ┌──────────┐
  │ Record 1 │ Gap  │ Record 2 │ Gap  │ Record 3 │
  └──────────┘      └──────────┘      └──────────┘
   ↓                                               ↓
Buffer 1                                        Buffer 1
       ←─ Transfer ─→←──── Limit Time ────→
            Time
```

Fig. 5.11 The relationship between the time required to transfer a disk record to or from secondary storage and the time available to process a disk record (including housekeeping time). The transfer time is 1.07 milliseconds for *single* records of 640 bytes on an IBM 3330. The limit time is 1.11 milliseconds for *single* records of 640 bytes on an IBM 3330.

The break-even times given in Tables 5.4 and 5.6 were calculated on the basis of dividing the overall block I-O time by 16, 15, 14, . . . or 4, 3, 2, . . . to give maximum processing times per record for differing numbers of hit records per block. For processing times that exceed a given break-even time, those blocks affected will contribute at least a further half revolution to the average time. This operates as follows.

When records are stored singly and the hit rate is 100 per cent, the conditions shown in Fig. 5.11 apply. For a 3330 disk this means that data will be transferred at full disk-transfer rates for processing times of less than 1.11 ms per record. When this processing time is exceeded, average I-O times per record will go up to 9.41 ms. This is because the first pair of records have to be processed before the *fourth* record is read in (the first record will be processed well before the third record is read into buffer 1; the rate-determining step will be buffer 2 as this is processed after buffer 1). This is shown in Fig. 5.12.

This leads to an immediate jump in run time per record from 1.04 ms to 9.41 ms at a processing time of 1.11 ms. There is no further change in record run time until processing times of 9.41 ms per record or more increase the record run time to 17.74 ms due to the loss of two revolutions for each pair of records. This gives the characteristic stepped appearance to the relationship between average record run time and processing time shown in Figs. 5.8, 5.9 and 5.10.

Values for hit rates less than 100 per cent have been calculated on the basis of hit blocks only leading to loss of revolutions. Proportions of blocks hit depend on the blocking factor, hit rate and processing times given in Tables 5.2 and 5.6.

Figs. 5.8(a) to (c) show the effect of only *referring* to a record on a 3330. Although the curves are stepped, they have a tendency towards a straight line of the same slope as the hit rate, which is most marked for low hit rates and large numbers of records per block. Fig. 5.8(d) shows the very strongly

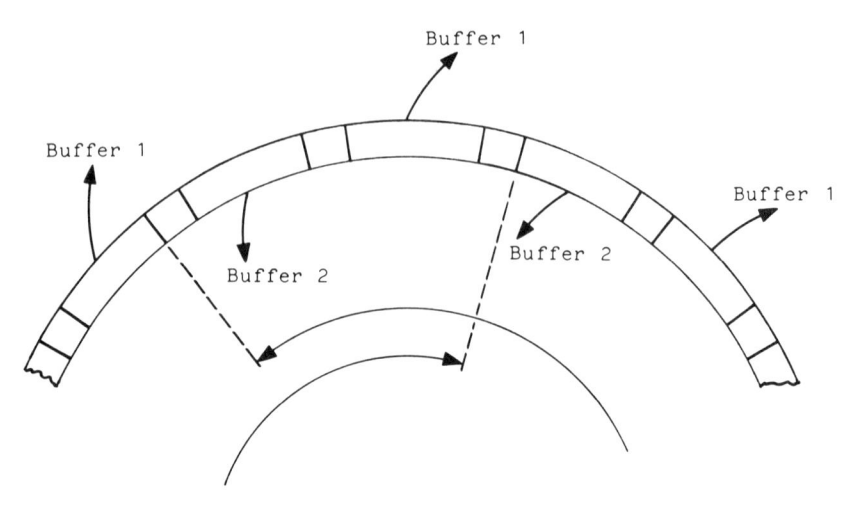

Fig. 5.12 The time available to process two records after a full revolution of the disk has been lost.

stepped form of the curves for the cases of reading and writing back, and reading, writing and checking the written information. For comparison the curves for the same hit rate—50 per cent—but reference only, have been added to the diagram.

The curves for the 2314 and 2311, for reference only rather than the cases in which revolutions have to be lost, are given in Figs. 5.9 and 5.10. These have been prepared using the figures in Tables 5.7 and 5.8. They apply only to individual double-buffered records, and are based on the situation shown in Fig. 5.11.

When three records in succession are hit, the time available for processing the first is that shown in Fig. 5.11. When the first or second hit record is followed by a non-hit record, the time available for processing the first record is increased by one record transfer time. If there are two gaps it is increased by two record transfer times and so on. Tables 5.7 and 5.8 were compiled using the probabilities of $1, 2, \ldots n$ record gaps between processed records given in Appendix 2.

Table 5.9 shows how the average run time for *all* the records in a sequential disk file stored on a 3330 depends on the type of reference required (reference only, read and write back, write and check or read, write and check), on the processing time per hit record, and on hit rate.

Comparison and extrapolation from the data presented in Tables 5.3 to 5.9 and Figs. 5.7 to 5.12 leads to the tabulated sets of break-even processing times (for hit records) given in Table 5.10. In general, disk will be preferred for processing times *less* than the break-even point, and tape for longer processing times. This data applies to *read* or *write* only.

Table 5.7 A double-buffered 2314. Figures tabulated show the average record run time for the given hit rates. Processing times apply only to hit records. The probability of consecutive records being hit was taken from the Tables in Appendix 2.

Processing time, hit records only	Hit rate (%)			
	75	50	25	15
2.93	8.06	4.34	2.98	2.82
5.71	10.69	5.91	3.27	2.89
8.49	11.68	7.08	3.60	2.99
11.27	12.01	7.86	3.93	3.09
14.05	12.11	8.35	4.24	3.20

Table 5.8 A double-buffered 2311. Figures tabulated show the average record run time for the given hit rates. Processing times apply only to hit records. The probability of consecutive records being hit was taken from the Tables in Appendix 2.

Processing time, hit records only	Hit rate (%)			
	75	50	25	15
6.39	11.53	7.81	6.45	6.29
12.64	14.17	9.38	6.74	6.36
18.89	15.15	10.55	7.07	6.46

For the cases of *read, process, write and check*, and of *read, process and write back*, tape and disk can conveniently be compared diagrammatically. The curves in Fig. 5.13 show the approximate break-even points between the two on the basis of average record processing time.

In summary, when records are to be read and written back, a 2311 would only outperform a magnetic tape of the type specified here for low hit rates, and if the records were blocked in twos at most. A 2314 is faster than magnetic tape for a wider range of blocking factors and hit rates, but for very large tape blocks it will only be preferred for hit rates of 15 per cent or less (read, process and write back) and 7 per cent or less (read, process, write and check). A 3330, which is in any case much faster in terms of transfer speed, outperforms the magnetic tape over a wide range of hit rates and block sizes. Disks such as the 3350 or 3380 have an even greater advantage over slow tapes, and the 3380 retains it in comparison with a 3420-8, but a 3480 is likely to handle sequential files more efficiently than any disk device unless the hit rate is below 10 per cent or the processing time is very short.

Table 5.9 The figures tabulated under the various hit rate percentages show the average run time for *all* the records in a sequential file on a 3330 disk drive, when processing times of hit records are within the ranges given. I–O is double buffered.

Type of reference required	Comment	Processing time of hit records (ms)	Hit rate % 100	75	50	25	15	10
READ, PROCESS, WRITE amended record and then CHECK it is correctly written.	Two revolutions must be lost, as separate revolutions are required for READ → WRITE and WRITE → CHECK.	NIL to 8.33 8.34 to 16.67 16.68 to 25.00	17.7 26.1 34.4	13.6 19.9 26.1	9.4 13.6 17.8	5.3 7.4 9.4	3.5 4.9 6.1	2.7 3.6 4.4
READ, PROCESS, WRITE amended record but do not check it.	One revolution must be lost, as it is required between the READ and the WRITE	NIL to 8.33 8.34 to 16.67 16.68 to 25.00	9.4 17.7 26.1	7.4 13.6 19.9	5.4 9.5 13.6	3.2 5.3 7.4	2.4 3.5 4.9	1.9 2.7 3.6
WRITE record to disk and then CHECK that it is correctly written.	One revolution must be lost, between the WRITE and the CHECK	NIL to 8.33 8.34 to 16.67 16.68 to 25.00	9.4 17.7 26.1		Not applicable except if the write is selective. Usually a write involves a 100% hit rate, eg when creating a file.
READ or WRITE only.	Revolutions are only lost if processing of *one* record is not complete before the *next* record to be processed comes under the read/write heads.	This depends on individual record processing times, rather than rotation time.		See the appropriate times in Figs. 5.8a,b,c; Figs. 5.9 and 5.10 can be used to give equivalent data, but for the 2311 and 2314 rather than the 3330.

Sequential file organization 139

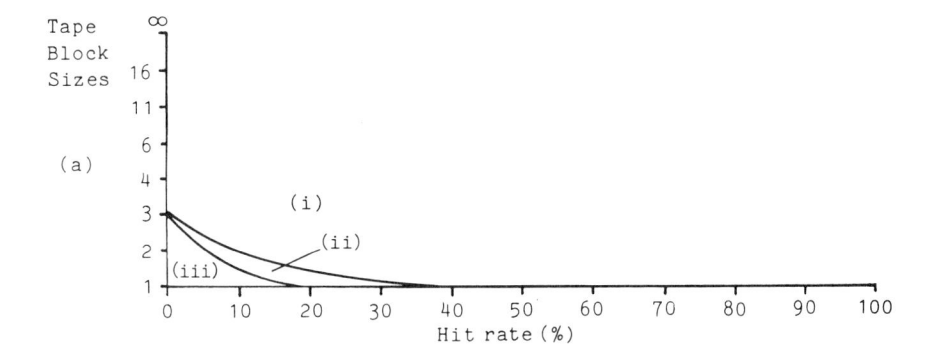

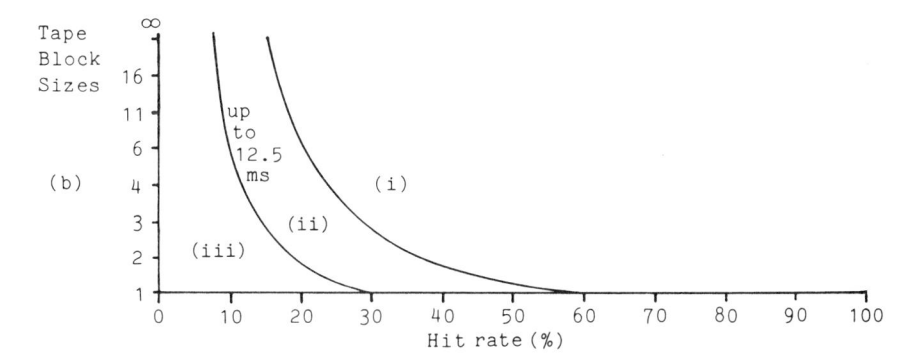

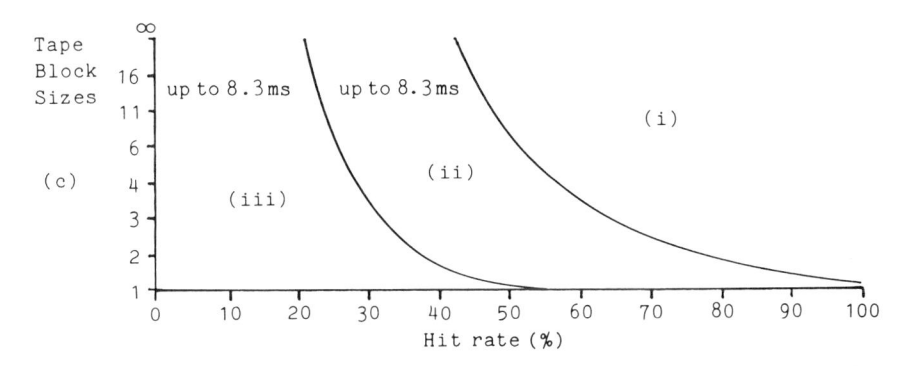

Fig. 5.13 Summary of break-even conditions between disk and tape for various tape block sizes and disk reference types. In the area above a curve, the tape sequential run times for the hit rates and blocking factors given will be shorter than those on disk.
(i) Tape run times shorter than READ and WRITE BACK.
(ii) Disk run times shorter for READ, PROCESS up to the limit shown and WRITE BACK.
(iii) Disk run times shorter for READ, PROCESS up to the limit shown WRITE and CHECK.

Diagram (a) shows the 2311, (b) the 2314, (c) the 3330, each compared with the same tape.

140 Design of computer data files

Table 5.10 The figures tabulated show the hit-record processing times in milliseconds for which the average record processing time on disk is faster than that on tape. These figures are a summary of the values taken from many curves such as Figs. 5.7, 5.8, 5.9 and 5.10.

Disk type	Disk block size	Hit rate	\multicolumn{7}{c}{Tape block size}
			1	2	3	4	6	11	16	infinite
3330	1	100	0 to 9.4	0 to 1.1	0 to 1.1	0 to 1.1	0 to 1.1	0 to 1.1	0 to 1.1	0 to 1.1
		75	0 to 9.4	0 to 9.4	0 to 3.3	0 to 2.2	0 to 2.2	0 to 2.2	0 to 2.2	0 to 1.1
		50	always	0 to 12.7	0 to 10.5	0 to 9.4	0 to 9.4	0 to 6.7	0 to 5.6	0 to 5.6
		25	always	always	always	always	always	always	always	always
		15	always	always	always	always	always	always	always	always
	4	100	0 to 9.4	0 to 1.1	0 to 1.1	0 to 1.1	0 to 1.1	0 to 1.1	0 to 1.1	0 to 1.1
		75	always	0 to 6.9	0 to 6.9	0 to 5.3	0 to 5.3	0 to 2.2	0 to 2.2	0 to 2.2
		50	always	0 to 12.5	0 to 10.4	0 to 6.9	0 to 6.9	0 to 4.3	0 to 4.3	0 to 4.3
		25	always	always	always	always	always	0 to 12.5	0 to 10.4	0 to 10.4
		15	always	always	always	always	always	always	always	always
	16	100	0 to 9.4	0 to 1.1	0 to 1.1	0 to 1.1	0 to 1.1	0 to 1.1	0 to 1.1	0 to 1.1
		75	always	0 to 11.5	0 to 8.4	0 to 7.6	0 to 6.7	0 to 6.1	0 to 5.6	0 to 5.0
		50	always	always	0 to 15.0	0 to 14.0	0 to 12.0	0 to 9.5	0 to 8.4	0 to 8.4
		25	always	always	always	always	always	always	always	0 to 17.7
		15	always	always	always	always	always	always	always	always
2314	1	100	0 to 2.9	0 to 2.9	0 to 2.9	0 to 2.9	0 to 2.9	0 to 2.9	0 to 2.9	0 to 2.9
		75	0 to 5.9	0 to 2.9	0 to 2.9	0 to 2.9	0 to 2.9	0 to 2.9	0 to 2.9	0 to 2.9
		50	always	0 to 14.0	0 to 8.5	0 to 5.7	0 to 5.7	0 to 5.7	0 to 5.7	0 to 5.7
		25	always	always	always	always	always	always	always	always
		15	always	always	always	always	always	always	always	always
2311	1	100	0 to 6.3	0 to 6.3	0 to 6.3	never	never	never	never	never
		75	0 to 6.3	0 to 6.3	0 to 6.3	never	never	never	never	never
		50	always	0 to 6.3	0 to 6.3	never	never	never	never	never
		25	always	always	0 to 12.5	never	never	never	never	never
		15	always	always	always	never	never	never	never	never

Conclusion

The case that has just been reviewed is limited to the actual devices concerned, and some other case might yield different results depending on the timing and other data associated with the devices in use. However, it is possible to draw some general conclusions. For reference only, the intrinsic speed of disk devices and the fact that no lost revolutions are incurred due to writing back operations means that tape is no longer so attractive as a storage medium. The figures for this case are given in Table 5.10, and it is clear that disk is preferable in many cases. Only the 2311 cannot compete with tape, and then only for blocks of four or more records.

When records have to be written back to disk, the situation is different. Unless hit rates are low, there will be no timing advantage in using disk and the usual situation applies, in that disk will only be used if one of the special situations reviewed on pages 116 to 122 exists. However, if a mass storage device is used to store data its cost is much nearer to that of storage on tape. Once the minimum storage requirement that justifies a mass storage device is reached, its use will eliminate the need for tape mounts, dismounts and library handling. This can lead to very useful savings in staff, space and security.

References

1. *Basic Training in Systems Analysis*, edited by Daniels and Yeates, Pitman, 1976.
2. *The Art of Computer Programming: Volume 3 Sorting and Searching*, by Donald Knuth, Addison-Wesley, 1973.
3. *Design of Sequential File Systems*, by Thomas R. Gildersleeve, Wiley, 1971.
4. *File and Database Techniques*, by James Bradley, Holt-Saunders, 1982.
5. 'One more time—how to update a master file', by Barry Dwyer, *CACM*, Vol. 24, No. 1, January 1981, pp. 3–8.
6. 'Modularity and the sequential file update problem', by Michael R. Levy, *CACM*, Vol. 25, No. 6, June 1982, pp. 362–370.
7. *DOS/VS Data Management Guide*, IBM Manual GC33-5372-3, pp. 149–52.
8. *Basic File Design*, by Owen Hanson, IPC Business Press, 1978.
9. 'Self-organizing linear search', by James H. Hester and Daniel S. Hirschberg, *ACM Computing Surveys*, Vol. 17, No. 3, Sept. 1985, pp. 295–311.
10. *Introduction to IBM Direct Access Storage Devices and Organization Methods*, IBM Manual No. GC20-1649-10, February 1978.
11. *The Art of Computer Programming: Volume 1 Fundamental Algorithms*, by Donald Knuth, Addison-Wesley, 1975.
12. 'Searching in a dynamic memory with fast sequential access', by Om Vicas and V. Rajamaran, *CACM*, Vol. 25, No. 7, July 1982, pp. 479–483.

13. 'Statistical searching of sequential disk files', by Owen Hanson, *CUBS Working Paper No. 15*, available from the Librarian, The City University Business School, London.
14. *Essentials of Computer Data Files*, by Owen Hanson, Pitman, 1985.
15. 'A discussion on a multi-master sequentially organized file maintenance system', by A. Y. Montgomery, *Australian Computer Journal*, Vol. 6, No. 3, November 1974, pp. 129–140.
16. 'The choice between magnetic tape and magnetic disk for sequential file processing', by O. J. Hanson, *Proc. 6th Internationaler Kongress Datenverarbeitung im Europaeischen Raum*, Vienna, March 1980, Vol. 1, pp. 89–122.
17. *Performance Evaluation of ICL Disk EDS 60 using Sequential File Organization*, MSc thesis by Suleman Ansari, available from the Librarian, The City University Business School, London.

Revision questions

1 Explain why updates to a sequentially organized file may be batched, illustrating your answer by using appropriate figures for overall run time, input-output and processing times. What are the considerations the system designer will bear in mind in deciding on the size of a batch?

2 What is the significance of sorting in estimating the time taken to process a master file sequentially?

3 How can record formats and the secondary storage device on which a sort takes place affect the time the sort requires?

4 Why are sequential files generally stored on magnetic tape?

5 Explain the overall process of updating a sequential file, making clear the decisions you would take on additions, deletions and updates to existing records.

6 Blocking and update pattern can be used to optimize the run time of a sequential tape file. Develop the equations to predict their influence, and show their effect in a number of possible cases.

7 What are the reasons for storing a sequential file on magnetic disk? List and explain the most important cases you know of.

8 Compare the various types of access available to a sequential disk file. When would you expect a statistical binary search to be of use?

9 What are the elements of timing involved in the processing of a sequential file on tape? How does this compare with the timing of such a file on disk? How does the mode of access affect the relative timings of the two media?

10 Draw a typical set of curves for the minimum overall processing time required by disk and tape files, comparing them with each other.

11 Discuss the effect of hit rate on the decision as to which medium is to be used to store a sequential file.

6 Direct file organization

6.1 Introduction

Records can be retrieved directly from files that have been organized in many ways. In this chapter we shall be dealing with files that have been designed to make direct record retrieval as easy and rapid as possible. These are known as *directly organized files*. It is possible to process the records in a directly organized file either directly, using the keys in any desired order, or serially, taking the records in the order they are stored and ignoring their keys.

Both direct and serial processing of directly organized files are dealt with in this chapter. Direct processing of files organized sequentially or using the indexed sequential technique is covered in the chapters devoted to those types of organization.

Records are often processed in a random order. A bank cannot predict which of its customers wish to withdraw or deposit money on any given day; a travel firm cannot control which of its package tours will be booked at a particular time. Customers arrive as a result of their own decisions, and not in an order dictated by the travel agent or bank. As these transactions are not predictable they present a processing problem. When an immediate response is not required, the transactions can be collected into batches, sorted into a key sequence that matches the appropriate master file, and processed sequentially. However, if the customer is waiting for an immediate answer, there is no time for this. The record has to be checked at once—to see if a booking is available, for example—and this means that the file has to be referenced without preparatory sorting or processing.

As the records are processed in a sequence that cannot be predetermined, we are faced with the problem that we know the key or control number of the record but have no indication of its location in storage. It would be possible to search through the file until the record was located, but this technique, and the more refined methods available for searching sequential files in which there is no direct relationship between the record key and its storage location, are too slow for the needs of most enquiry systems. We must look for a way of establishing a relationship between the *key* of the record and its *address*, and using this relationship to retrieve the record rapidly.

The relationship can take several forms. First, it can be an index of every record position in the file; modifications of this method lead to *indexed sequential files*, and are dealt with in Chapter 7. Second, each record can be stored at an address that is directly related to its key, e.g. at the address which is the same as the key (record 20 in address 20 and so on). This type of file is known as a *self-indexing* or *self-addressing file*. If it is not possible to find a relationship of this sort, some other method of assigning addresses to keys has to be found. Usually, a suitable algorithm is used to convert keys to addresses; the file is then described as a *randomized file*, and the algorithm used is called a *randomizing algorithm*. The process is often also described as *hashing*.

The application of these methods of assigning storage positions to records is discussed in detail in this chapter, and reference tables are provided to aid the file designer. This is followed by sections on optimizing the performance of direct files, and on the practical steps that can be taken to maximize the efficiency of these files in operation.

6.2 Self-indexing

Continuous key sequences

If record keys are numeric and there are not many gaps in the sequence, it is often possible to allocate a storage position based directly on the key. In the simplest case, records with keys such as 00 000 to 99 999 could be allocated to any contiguous set of 100 000 storage positions. Some direct access devices have available storage areas starting from 00 000 or 00 001, and addressed by a simple number. When devices of this type are available, the storing of records with a continuous set of keys is straightforward. However, the conversion from a numeric user-address to a device address in terms of cylinders and records is carried out by the manufacturer's software, and thus involves an overhead of both primary storage space and CPU time.

If locations with the same addresses as the record keys are available, then each record is stored in the appropriate position, and a record can be retrieved by the use of the relationship:

Location address = Key

If a contiguous area of storage is available elsewhere, or if the keys are continuous but start at a figure outside the range of the storage addresses available, an addition or subtraction will be needed. In this case:

Location address = Key ± β

where β is a constant.

For example, if 20 000 records with keys 40 000 000→40 019 999 are to be stored in locations 18 646→38 645, then:

Location address = Key − 39 981 354

146 Design of computer data files

An additional factor arises when keys do not go up in ones, but in twos, threes, fives, tens or some other increment. In this case, to allow for the increment not being unity, the relationship becomes:

$$\text{Location address} = (\text{Key}/\alpha) \pm \beta$$

where α and β are constants.

An example of this might be keys 00 003, 00 006, 00 009, 00 012, etc., to be stored in positions 00 352, 00 353, ... Then:

$$\text{Location address} = (\text{Key}/3) + 351$$

As explained in Chapter 2, many disks have a discontinuous or complex address format. An example of this is the IBM disk range, in which the basic form of disk address is CCHHR, where:

CC is a two-character cylinder number;
HH is a two-character head number;
R is a one-character record number.

R starts from record 1 on each track, as record 0 is a control record.

Because there is no record 0, the nearest that can be obained to a continuous set of numbers will be:

CC	HH	R
0	0	1→9
0	1	1→9
0	2	1→9
.	.	.
.	.	.
.	.	.
1	0	1→9

Thus addresses:

0	1	0
0	2	0
.	.	.
.	.	.
.	.	.
1	0	0
1	1	0
.	.	.

are missing. Such a near-continuous set of numbers can only be obtained if nine records are stored per track, and this will usually not be the best number of records for the file under consideration. Normally we shall have sets of addresses of the form:

Direct file organization

CC	HH	R
0	0	1→n
0	1	1→n
0	2	1→n
.	.	.
.	.	.
0	9 (2311)	.
0	11 (3340, 3370, 3375)	.
0	14 (3380)	.
0	18 (3330)	.
0	19 (2314)	.
0	29 (3350)	1→n
.	.	.
.	.	.
1	0	1→n

As calculations in main storage take very little time, it is well worthwhile converting the key values into this form by means of an algorithm. For example: a file is to be stored on a 3380 disk, fourteen records per track, starting at cylinder 23. The record keys are continuous starting from 14 836; the position of a record with the key 15 302 would be calculated as follows:

15 302 − 14 836 = 466

i.e. this is the 467th record in the file:

$$\frac{467}{14} = 33 + 5$$

This means that it will be stored as the fifth record on the thirty-fourth track of the file. As there are fifteen tracks per cylinder on the 3380, this means that the record address will be cylinder 25, track 3 (the fourth track on the cylinder because IBM use track numbers starting from 0), record 5. The full address will be

24.03.05

The general formula here is that, with:

a starting cylinder of C;
a starting key of K_0;
a record key of K, and
n records stored per track on a 3380, then:

$$\text{Cylinder number} = C + \frac{(K - K_0 + 1)}{15n}$$

where we consider only the integer part of the division. If the remainder is R:

$$\text{Head number} = \frac{R}{n}$$

where we consider only the integer part of the division. Let the remainder be R'; then:

$$\text{Record number} = R'$$

This calculation may look cumbersome, but it takes very little time and provides record storage positions very effectively. Integer arithmetic should be used, to avoid the problems of approximate answers. If necessary, considerably more complex calculations are justified because of the speed of internal storage operations, and because use of such a calculation allows the unbroken key sequence to be exploited. Manufacturers usually provide *relative record addressing* which carries out these calculations for the user.

Broken key sequences

Inherently continuous sequences Although the key sequence in a new file is often continuous, gaps will usually soon occur. Customers turn elsewhere or go out of business, old product numbers are replaced by new, and so on. The advantage of being able to store such a file on a direct access device in addresses which are directly related to the key then has to be balanced against the waste of space involved. A self-indexing file can be referenced sequentially by normal sequential processing, and directly using a single seek because of the relations between key and storage address. No other file organization can achieve this, so it is worth accepting a fairly low packing density to retain the file in this form. If direct access capacity is a limitation, a loss of 15–20 per cent of space will still compare well with other file organizations (see Chapter 7 and the calculations of packing density for randomly organized direct files later in this chapter). Where access time is the vital criterion and direct access storage is abundant, a packing density of as little as 50 per cent is justifiable for a file accessed both directly and sequentially. Where maximum direct access throughput is essential, even lower packing densities may be accepted (see the average space used by randomized files to compare, p. 310). Unused storage positions should be filled with dummy records, so that they can be recognized at once.

In setting up a file with a number of dummy records, these dummies will be filled with a character such as & or * that will be tested for during serial processing. The problem should not arise during direct processing, as every valid key has a corresponding record. If it does, then an error will be indicated. However, the test for a dummy must be carried out during direct processing to guard against an invalid key being processed (see Fig. 6.1).

This technique is only directly applicable to fixed-length records. It can be applied to variable-length records by padding or the use of fixed-length

Direct file organization 149

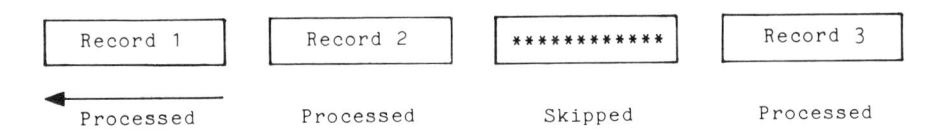

```
┌──────────┐   ┌──────────┐   ┌──────────────┐   ┌──────────┐
│ Record 1 │   │ Record 2 │   │ ************ │   │ Record 3 │
└──────────┘   └──────────┘   └──────────────┘   └──────────┘
◄─────────
 Processed     Processed         Skipped          Processed
```

Fig. 6.1 Sequential processing of a file with dummy records.

buckets for variable records, as discussed previously. In the latter case addressing will probably only point to a bucket number, and in searching the bucket for a particular record using the direct technique it will no longer be an error to detect a dummy record, but part of the search.

Naturally broken sequences Record keys often do not start as an unbroken sequence. In a simple case, we might have the following key set:

001, 002, 003, 004, 005, 006, 007, 008, 009,
101, 102,   104, 105,   107, 108, 109,
204, 205, 206, 207, 208, 209, 210, 211,
350, 351, 352, 353, 354, 355, 356, 357, 358, 359.

These thirty-four records need only 34 storage positions, but if they were stored in self-indexing form they would take up 359 storage positions, and there would be five gaps of 91, 1, 1, 94 and 138 positions respectively. These gaps can be eliminated by a sequence of tests of the type shown below:

```
        IF Key ≤ 009 THEN
            Address = Key
   ELSE IF Key ≤ 102 THEN
            Address = Key − 91
   ELSE IF Key ≤ 105 THEN
            Address = Key − 92
   ELSE IF Key ≤ 109 THEN
            Address = Key − 93
   ELSE IF Key ≤ 211 THEN
            Address = Key − 187
   ELSE IF Key ≤ 359 THEN
            Address = Key − 325
   ELSE PERFORM ERROR-ROUTINE
```

The gaps are eliminated as shown in Fig. 6.2.

150 Design of computer data files

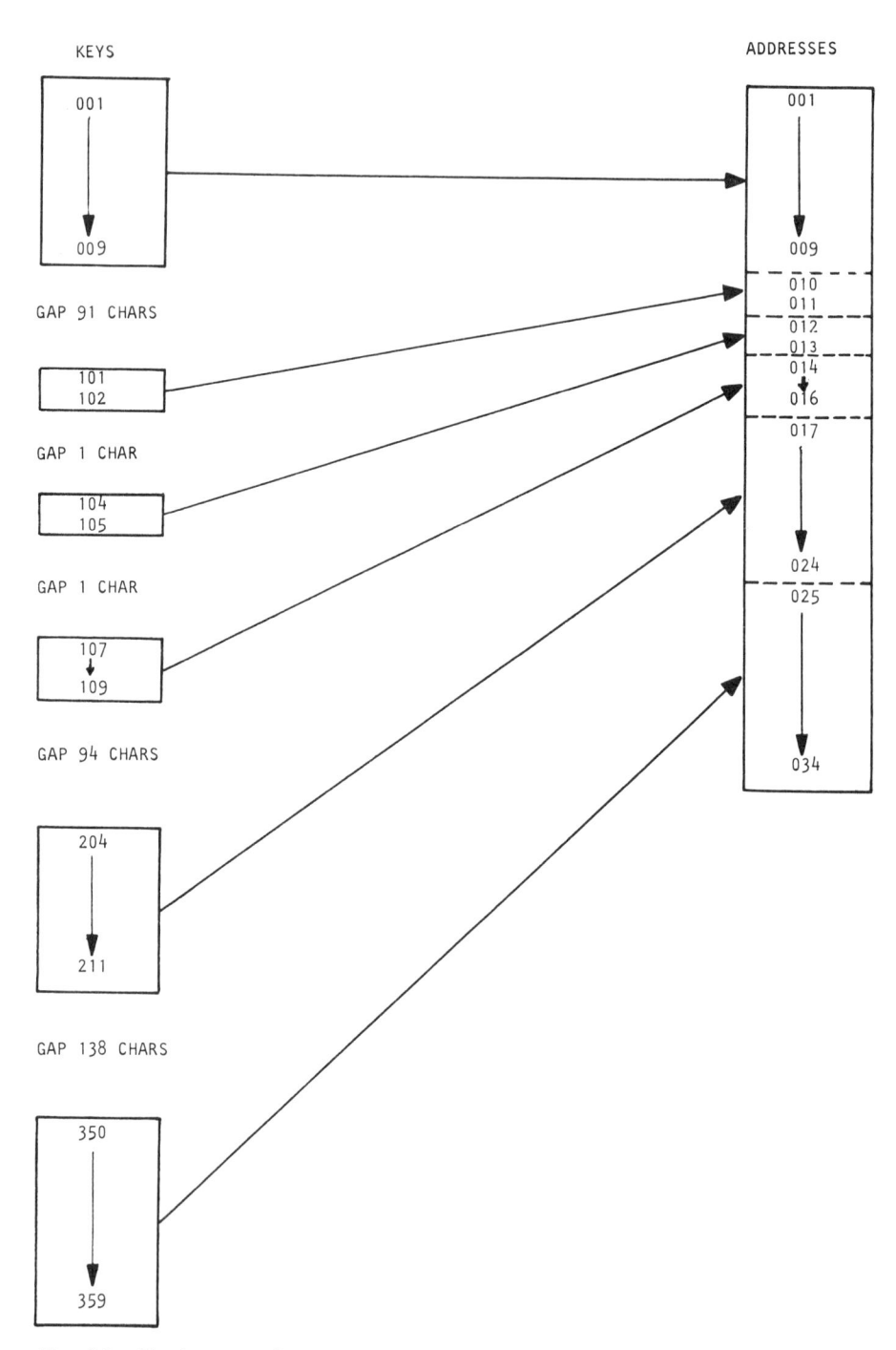

Fig. 6.2 Closing up a key sequence with gaps, to provide a continuous set of addresses.

Typically, keys form broken sequences because they contain separate items of information. For example, a product code used as a key may contain sections for such fields as:

category;	(CAT)	C	digits
factory;	(FAC)	FF	digits
product type;	(PROD)	PP	digits
number of products in type.		NNN	digits

There may be room left for additions to the number of products, product types, factories, categories, etc. This can lead to a series of continuous keys with gaps left in it at intervals. This can be converted into a continuous sequence of keys so long as the various constants involved in the key are known. For example, if the category can take the values 1 to 7, the factory number can be 01 to 11, the product type can be 01 to 37, and the number of products in the type can range from 001 to 999, with 147 being the largest required at present (the number varies with type), then we might have the following runs of continuous numbers made up of the digits representing the category, factory, product type and number of products:

C F F P P N N N → C F F P P N N N
1 0 1 0 1 0 0 1 → 1 0 1 0 1 1 4 7
1 0 1 0 2 0 0 1 → 1 0 1 0 2 1 3 6
1 0 1 0 3 0 0 1 → 1 0 1 0 3 0 8 4
. .
. .
. .
7 1 1 3 7 0 0 1 → 7 1 1 3 7 1 1 8

These runs of continuous numbers have to be turned into a single sequence, starting from 1. There are 2849 runs of numbers; as given above the most in one run is 147, and the least shown is 84. One way of combining these runs into a single sequence is shown in Fig. 6.3.

This process requires a table of 2849 entries, each showing the cumulative total of records up to the start of that set. To ensure that all the product types for a given category and factory are kept together, the following algorithm is used:

Search value = ((CAT − 1) × 37 × 11) + ((FAC − 1) × 37) + PROD

This arranges for every product type for category 1 and factory 1 to come first, and every factory in category 1 to precede those in category 2. If this routine is written in a programming language such as PL/1, Algol or Fortran, the calculation is not necessary; the subscript facility can be used, and the table entries referenced as TABLE (CAT, FAC, PROD). In the example shown in Fig. 6.3, the entry required would be TABLE (1, 1, 3).

152 Design of computer data files

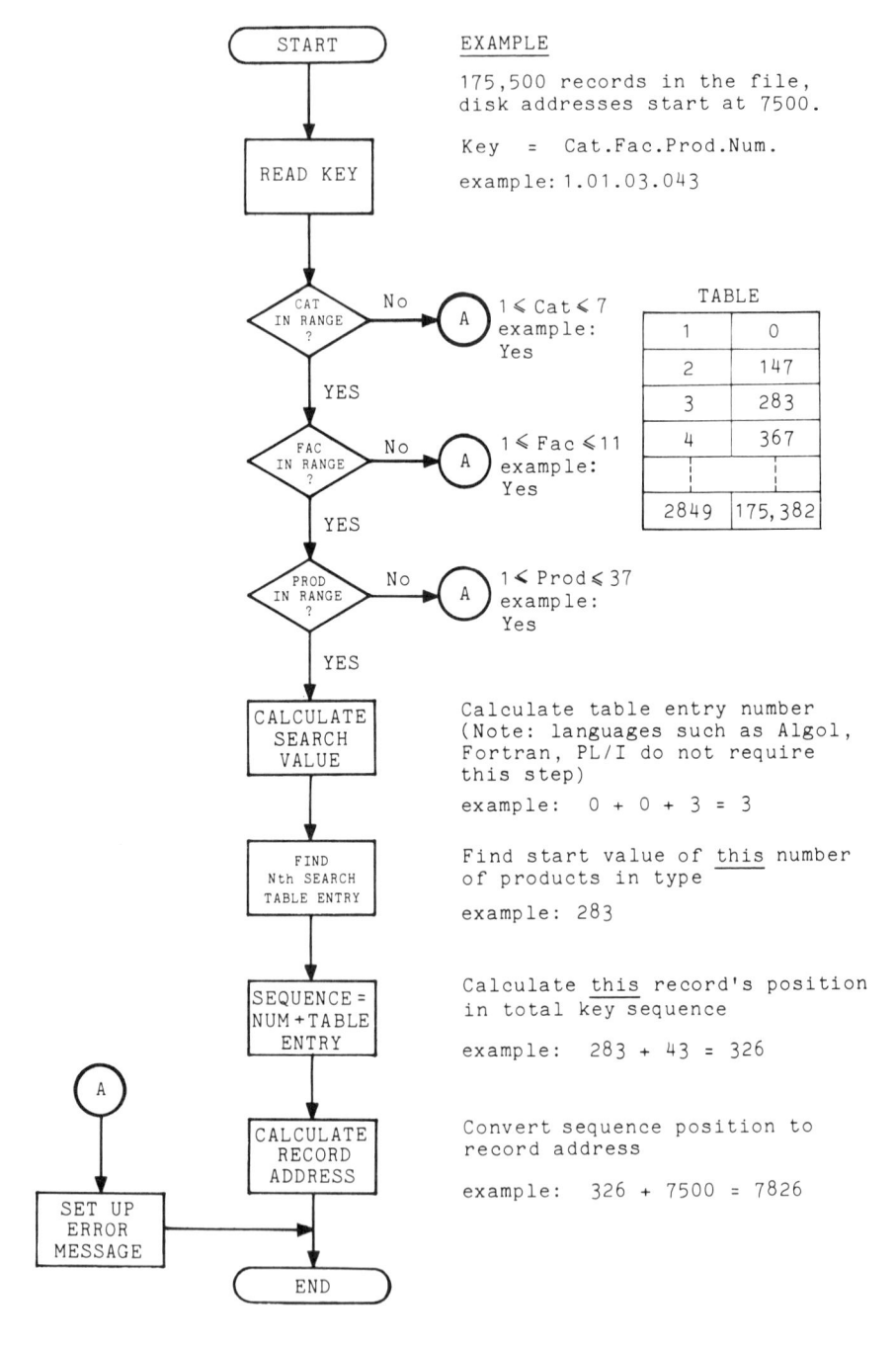

```
                    ┌─────────┐
                    │  START  │
                    └────┬────┘
                         │
                    ┌────▼────┐
                    │READ KEY │
                    └────┬────┘
                         │
                    ╱CAT╲   No
                   ╱ IN  ╲──────▶(A)
                   ╲RANGE╱
                    ╲ ? ╱
                     ╲ ╱
                    YES│
                    ╱FAC╲   No
                   ╱ IN  ╲──────▶(A)
                   ╲RANGE╱
                    ╲ ? ╱
                     ╲ ╱
                    YES│
                   ╱PROD╲   No
                   ╱ IN  ╲──────▶(A)
                   ╲RANGE╱
                    ╲ ? ╱
                     ╲ ╱
                    YES│
                ┌────▼────┐
                │CALCULATE│
                │ SEARCH  │
                │  VALUE  │
                └────┬────┘
                ┌────▼────┐
                │  FIND   │
                │Nth SEARCH│
                │TABLE ENTRY│
                └────┬────┘
                ┌────▼────┐
                │SEQUENCE=│
                │NUM+TABLE│
                │  ENTRY  │
                └────┬────┘
   (A)          ┌────▼────┐
    │           │CALCULATE│
    ▼           │ RECORD  │
 ┌──────┐       │ADDRESS  │
 │SET UP│       └────┬────┘
 │ERROR │────────────┤
 │MESSAGE│       ┌────▼────┐
 └──────┘       │   END   │
                └─────────┘
```

EXAMPLE

175,500 records in the file, disk addresses start at 7500.

Key = Cat.Fac.Prod.Num.

example: 1.01.03.043

$1 \leqslant$ Cat $\leqslant 7$
example: Yes

$1 \leqslant$ Fac $\leqslant 11$
example: Yes

$1 \leqslant$ Prod $\leqslant 37$
example: Yes

TABLE

1	0
2	147
3	283
4	367
⋮	⋮
2849	175,382

Calculate table entry number (Note: languages such as Algol, Fortran, PL/I do not require this step)

example: 0 + 0 + 3 = 3

Find start value of <u>this</u> number of products in type

example: 283

Calculate <u>this</u> record's position in total key sequence

example: 283 + 43 = 326

Convert sequence position to record address

example: 326 + 7500 = 7826

Fig. 6.3 One method of combining sets of continuous numbers into a single sequence.

This example requires a large table; if there is not room in primary storage for such a table it is not possible to handle the file as a self-indexing file, and a different method of addressing must be used. It is almost always a lack of storage space, or the fact that the file is dynamic and so cannot be loaded in a single operation, that prevents self-indexing, and not the time taken to carry out the calculations.

Before leaving the subject of self-indexing, it is worth mentioning *perfect hash functions*. These generally refer to finding a self-indexing function for tables in main storage; Jaeschke[1] has developed a method originally proposed by Cichelli[2], and he has shown that, however complicated the key sequence is, a self-indexing function can be found for up to 40 keys so that they fit exactly into a table with the same number of storage positions. For larger tables—up to about 1000 keys—a more approximate but less time-consuming method due to Sprugnoli[3] can be used. The small size of these 'files' make such techniques applicable only to main storage tables; in that sphere, they are very useful.

6.3 Algorithmic addressing

The keys used for many data files are not suited to any practical self-indexing transformation, so other methods of establishing a relationship between record keys and storage addresses have been developed. What is needed is a transformation—usually called an algorithm—that can be carried out on a key to yield a storage address. Naturally, it must always yield the same address from the same key. Any such transformation will involve the compression of a diffuse key set, containing many gaps, into a much smaller range of addresses; if this is not the case, the file should be self-indexed. Whatever the size and complexity of the key, the factors that control the transformation are the same. They are:

1 *The number of addresses to be generated.* This will depend on the number of records if each record is to have its own address. If groups of records are to be stored in buckets, it will be related to the number of buckets required.

2 *The direct access space required* and, in some cases, *its distribution*. It is desirable to have a single file area, both for efficient file processing and for simplicity, but this is not always possible. At all events the user will have to estimate the amount of direct access storage space the file needs, and this will affect the algorithm used. A number of techniques are available to handle files that have dynamic space requirements, and these are discussed later.

3 *The direct access starting address.* It will not be enough to produce a set of generated addresses corresponding to the number of record storage positions required. They will also have to start from the specified starting address on the device, and must all lie within the allocated range. The process will be as shown in Fig. 6.4.

154 Design of computer data files

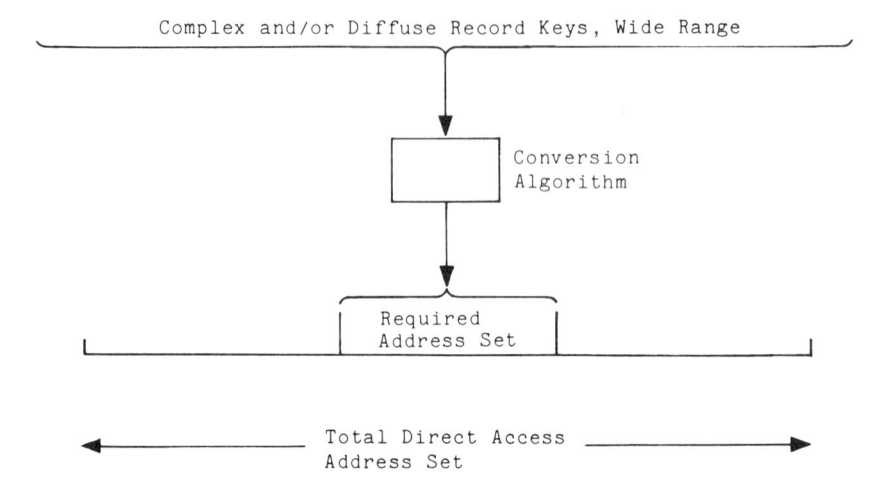

Fig. 6.4 Use of a conversion algorithm to produce the correct storage address.

Assume that n records are to be stored, and N addresses are available for record storage. Transformation of keys into addresses by an algorithm will produce r addresses.

The relationship between r, n and N is:

$$r < n < N$$

Ideally just one key would be associated with each address and every address available would be used. In this case $r = n = N$. In practice neither condition is likely to be met. The factors determining how closely the ideal case can be approached are examined in the following sections.

How synonyms occur

Sometimes two or more record keys are transformed by an algorithm into the same address. The first record to be allocated that address can be stored there, and is described as the *home record*. Any subsequent record to be allocated to that address has to be stored elsewhere. It is called a *synonym*, and will overflow from its natural home address because that is already full. The situation is modified when records are stored in buckets holding several records, but synonyms still occur. This is examined later (see p. 173). As a synonym is not held at the address the program has computed, a further search is needed to find it. This leads to loss of time, and synonyms are the reason that algorithmically addressed files give a slower response than self-indexing files; home records are retrieved just as quickly. Much of the rest of this chapter shows how to minimize the number of synonyms, and to reduce the effect of those that remain.

It might seem that a suitable algorithm could be found which would not generate synonyms. This is very unlikely. In some cases the algorithm will spread the addresses evenly over the allocated storage area, and in the ideal case will have an equal probability of generating any address within that area; in other cases the existing key order can be used to improve the efficiency of record storage. In either case some addresses will be generated more than once, while others will not be generated at all. A different set of keys will produce a different set of synonyms, and of unused record spaces. Statistically, however, the chance of avoiding synonyms altogether is vanishingly small. Heising[4] has pointed out that if n records are randomized into N addresses, there are N^n possible record distributions, only $N!/(N-n)!$ of which allocate no more than one record to any address. If 4000 records are stored in 5000 addresses then only one algorithm in every $10^{12\,000}$ will achieve this, which rules out a search for a perfect randomizing algorithm on a trial-and-error basis.

This can be seen in a qualitative way by considering the party game in which participants guess how many people would need to be asked their birthdays, on average, to find two with birthdays on the same day. Many people will answer 365 (or 366!). Some will answer 365/2 or 183 for safety. Few will guess that a group of twenty-three will, on average, contain two people with birthdays on the same day. This is followed by experimental proof, to general surprise. As twenty-three birthdays spread at random over 365 addresses can cause duplication, it is not surprising that no randomizing algorithm can avoid synonyms when packing thousands of records into a set of addresses that is only 10–20 per cent greater than the number of records!

When records are randomly distributed among the available addresses, the probability of 0, 1, 2, ..., x records being allocated to any given address that can hold a single record can be calculated as follows:

Let the number of records be defined as n and the total address locations as N. This corresponds with the symbols used in equation (6.1). When records are randomized to N locations the probability of any particular address being generated due to the transformation of a single key is $1/N$. As a result of n records being allocated, the probability of a given location having been allocated x records is given by the terms of the binomial expression:

$$\left(\left(1 - \frac{1}{N}\right) + \frac{1}{N}\right)^n$$

Thus

$$p(x) = \frac{n!(1/N)^x(1 - 1/N)^{n-x}}{x!(n-x)!} \qquad (6.2)$$

This expression is precise. However, it has the disadvantage that it is not general, but has to be calculated separately for every n and N.

When n and N are very much larger than 1, which applies in any normal data file, the Poisson distribution may be used as an approximation to the binomial. The derivation of this is given in statistics textbooks[5] and practical examples of its application, and an assessment of the closeness of the approximation, are given later in this chapter (see p. 169).

The advantage of using the Poisson distribution is that $p(x)$ now depends on the value of the ratio (n/N). This represents the packing density of the file, and is much more general than n or N used independently, as all files with the same packing density give the same results irrespective of the value of N and n.

From the Poisson distribution:

$$p(x) = \frac{(n/N)^x \, e^{-(n/N)}}{x!} \qquad (6.3)$$

By evaluating the above expression for x and setting $x = 0,1,2,3 \ldots$ we can obtain the corresponding probabilities that a given address will have:

No record assigned to it $(x = 0)$:   Let this be $p(0)$;
One record assigned to it $(x = 1)$:   Let this be $p(1)$;
Two records assigned to it $(x = 2)$:   Let this be $p(2)$;

and so on. Where a file area contains N addresses we can expect:

$Np(0)$ non-assigned addresses (these may later be filled by synonyms);

$Np(1)$ singly assigned addresses;

$\sum_{x=2}^{\infty} Np(x)$ addresses with one or more synonyms.

In theory we could provide just sufficient space in the file for all the records. This would certainly simplify equation (6.3) to yield:

$$p(x) = \frac{1}{e.x!} \qquad (6.4)$$

but it is clear intuitively that we cannot completely fill the file, as the last available storage position would on average be half the file area away from the last record's computed address. We shall look at ways of choosing a more suitable packing density in more detail later (see p. 172).

6.4 Methods of randomizing

Whenever an algorithm is used to store a direct file, the implication is that self-indexing is not practical. This usually means that the keys of the file are too diffuse to store directly, and the key range has to be compressed by using an algorithm. There are two possibilities: either to exploit the existing key order—if that is possible—or to completely destroy that order, and to allocate keys to addresses as randomly as possible. Both of these options are examined below.

Order-preserving algorithms

1 *Using the low order part of a key*
Where a key is a long number, consisting perhaps of ten digits, but we only have 8000 records and hence need only to allocate 10 000 storage positions, we could use the last four digits of the key as a storage address. This is suspect because keys may always end in 2, 5, or some other specific number, or always be divisible by 2, 5 or some such constant. There might also be a departmental or other code in the centre of the key, and we might obtain all the records in three areas starting with numbers such as 03, 05 or 07 if the choice of storage address is unfortunate. This is analysed further elsewhere[6]. This technique can, however, give very good results if the low order digits of the key are consecutive integers with few gaps.

2 *Using middle or upper order parts of a key*
The same considerations dictate against the use of either of these as storage addresses. It may not be obvious that order exists in the key sequence, yet it may be present and damaging.

3 *End folding*
A ten-digit key such as 1 234 567 890 may be reduced to 'fit' 50 000 storage positions by carrying out the steps:

a) 12 | 34567 | 890
b)   34567
      12890

      47457

c) Number greater than 50 000?
d) YES: subtract 50 000 (repeat until NO).
e) NO: number = address.

This method is fairly effective. It destroys the original key pattern more completely than operations **1** and **2** above, but retains the ability to separate keys that are part of consecutive runs. This can lead to results that improve on perfect randomization, but it depends on the key sequence and is not reliable (see Buchholz[6] and Lum et al.[7] for further details).

4 *Division by a non-prime*
If we divide a large key by an appropriate number—probably dictated by the

file storage area—and use the remainder as an address, this will provide a precise method of fitting addresses to available storage. For example, if we have 98 000 positions of storage in which to store the records, from 50 001 to 148 000, we could carry out the following calculation:

Key = 0 1 2 3 4 5 6 7 8 9
Key/98 000 = 1259, remainder 34 789
34 789 + 50 001 = 84 790

The record address is 84 790. This process looks effective, but the last three digits of the key are unchanged by the division. It turns out that any number divided by 98 000 will give a remainder with the last three digits unchanged, as 98 000 itself is divisible by 1000. This means that the last part of the original key pattern remains: if this includes a code of, say, 05 then randomization will be incomplete. For that reason a divisor should be chosen that is not itself divisible by 2, 3, 5, 10 or any of their simple multiples. In our example the divisor is divisible by 1000, which leads to three unchanged digits. Buchholz[6] has shown that non-prime *odd* numbers can give very good results, but are not reliable unless they have no divisors less than about 19. This choice is also discussed by Lum et al.[7]

5 Division by a prime

The logical extension of avoiding multiples of 2, 3, 5, 10, etc., is to use a large prime number. This usually leads to removal of the effect of any repeating pattern such as a 2, 5 or 0 in the last digit because every digit in the number divided is involved in the division, and so may be altered. However, sequences of keys differing by one will yield remainders differing by one. So long as two key sequences do not produce overlapping remainders this can achieve results considerably better than true randomization. The process is as follows:

a) Decide on a packing density for the file. If *n* records are to be stored in *N* addresses, this packing density (α) will be

$$\alpha = \frac{n}{N} \quad \therefore \quad N = \frac{n}{\alpha}$$

Let *n* be 85 000. A suitable α might be 85 per cent (this is discussed in more detail later). In our example this would mean that

(85 000 × 100)/85 = 100 000

storage positions would be required for the file.

b) Select a prime near to 100 000—say 99 991—and divide. The remainders of this division will lie in the range 0–99 990. If the storage area does not start at 0, then a simple addition will convert this figure to the address range required.

c) The number of synonyms resulting from this process should be compared with those to be expected from perfect randomization; see p. 166 for methods of doing this. If the results are similar to or better than those predicted theoretically, the transformation is satisfactory. If not, a different prime number should be selected and the process repeated.

In selecting a prime number, primes of the form $kB^m \pm 1$ should be avoided, where B is the number base and k a small integer. This is because the binomial expansion of $(B^m \pm 1)^{-1}$ shows that the remainder will contain superposed m digit groups of the original key. This tendency remains for small integer values of k, reducing as k increases in size. Thus primes such as 4999, 7001, 79 999, etc., are best not used for decimal keys.

A table of prime numbers, selected so that they are not too near to a factor of ten, and close enough in value to allow any packing density to be selected within half of a percent, is given in Appendix 4. Decimal keys should be retained in decimal form; alpha or alphanumeric keys are best handled in binary.

Some prime numbers can usually be found that give a good transformation—in fact it is the high probability that any suitable prime chosen will do so, allied to the ease with which this technique can be used to fit any number of records into precisely the required storage space, that makes this such a convenient method. However, if a number of primes have failed, it may be sensible to consider complete randomization.

6 *Order-preserving algorithms in general*

A large number of order-preserving algorithms were examined by Amble and Knuth[8], showing how they compared for completion of successful and unsuccessful searches for records. Many of these are suitable only for table searching in main storage, but the principles are of interest to direct file designers. Ouksel[9] presented a method in which parts of the original key such as area code, factory number and part type can be retained by the use of bit tables. Garg and Gotlieb[10] have developed a method that is related to interpolation searching, and in which the algorithm is based on an analysis of the key sequence, rather than on a presupposition such as the effectiveness of any particular procedure—say mid-square or division. Order-preserving algorithms are still being developed, but the success of division shows that order-preserving algorithms are an important resource to the file designer.

Genuinely randomizing algorithms

1 *Square the key and select a part*

This depends on squaring the whole or part of the key, and taking a number of digits from the centre of the resulting value. An example might be:

```
Key     = 9 1 5   0 0 0   3 1 7
Square  = 8 3 7   2 2 5   5 7 5   3 5 5   1 0 0   4 8 9
Address = 5 7 5   3 5 5
```

This gives a potential range of addresses between 000 000 and 999 999. The records can be compressed into some other range such as 250 000 by repetitive subtraction of 250 000, and the method usually gives very good randomization. It is often not convenient to square a large integer so a selected part of the key may be squared instead. This technique is not always as effective as division, but does achieve a nearly random distribution, and so is useful when it is not possible to exploit any existing order in the key sequence.

2 Selecting digits from different parts of the key
Sometimes, rather than selecting a single part of the key, several areas are used. This may operate as follows:

```
Key     = 0   1 2 3   4 5 6   7 8 9
Address = 2 3   6 7 8
```

This would normally be expected to produce results rather worse than the mid-square method, but it has proved to be very effective on occasions (see p. 169 for further discussion).

3 Quadratic and quadratic quotient hashing
These two techniques, due to Maurer[11] (quadratic hashing) and Bell[12] (quadratic quotient hashing), can be used to eliminate *primary* and *secondary clustering* of keys after division. Primary clustering results from runs of keys, in that they will be allocated to adjacent storage positions after division; this is dispersed by quadratic hashing, in which the final storage position of the record depends on a function of the remainder from the original division, summed with a function of the *square* of the remainder. This does separate members of a run of keys, but it fails to separate two or more records that randomize to a particular storage position. Bell termed this 'secondary clustering' and showed that, by using both the quotient and the remainder from the original division, it was possible to eliminate it.

These two techniques are primarily intended for use in table searching in main storage, and are only incidentally usable for direct files; it is worth noting that they are intended to eliminate the order-preserving properties of division, while using division as a convenient randomizing algorithm.

Examples of randomizing algorithms in practice

Although small files cannot be used to analyse the way in which randomization techniques perform, they are useful to demonstrate the essential features of these techniques. The ways in which division, mid-square and end-folding operate are illustrated below.

1 Division

Assume that a 'mini-file' of seventeen records is to be stored as a direct file, and that the file is to be 85 per cent packed. The file will therefore require twenty storage positions. Seventeen random numbers in the range 000 to 200 (representing the record keys) can be selected by choosing the first numbers within the required range occurring in a random number table. They are in the following order: 059, 035, 078, 136, 171, 148, 005, 135, 010, 196, 057, 187, 110, 100, 030, 127, 197.

These numbers are divided by 19, to give remainders in the range 0 to 18. This leaves the twentieth position of the storage area as an 'overflow', since no record will randomize to it. In effect, the key range 000–200 is cut into 19 digit sections, and the remainders that result from the division in each section are superposed on each other to provide the record addresses. The records in the same section cannot randomize to the same address, so that synonyms arise by records in different sections having the same remainder.

The result of this operation, for the keys given above, is shown in Fig. 6.5(a).

As a result of dividing by 19 there will be five synonyms—02, 02, 05, 15 and 16. This is 5/17 or 32.4 per cent of the total, and compares with an 'expected' value of 32.63 per cent. This is sheer chance, but suggests a good average result from the use of the algorithm!

This set of keys is intended to be random and so has no order to preserve. If a key includes fields to indicate district, stock classification or the like, runs of keys will occur in the key sequence. Division will avoid keys in the same run clashing, and causing synonyms. Seventeen records are to be stored as an 85 per cent packed direct file. Consider the key set:

010, 011, 012, 013,
020, 021,
082, 083, 084,
141, 142, 143,
169, 170, 171, 172, 173.

The remainders after the division by 19 are shown in Fig. 6.5(b).

The very good performance of division reported in some cases (Lum, Yuen and Dodd[7], Severance and Duhne[13]), and relatively poor performance in others (Kaimann[14]), is likely to have been the result of few or many clashes of this kind. Because there are fewer *runs* of keys than separate keys, the results of division are likely to be more variable than those of genuine randomization. However, division has a fundamental advantage, which is the reason for its good performance: no two records in any single section into which the key sequence is 'cut' by division can interfere with any other in the same section, because no two different numbers can have both the same quotient *and* the same remainder. Effectively, this means that if the file has been 'cut' into m sections, the effective packing density of the file—from the point of view of records *colliding* and causing synonyms—is:

$(m - 1)/m$ of the actual packing density.

162 Design of computer data files

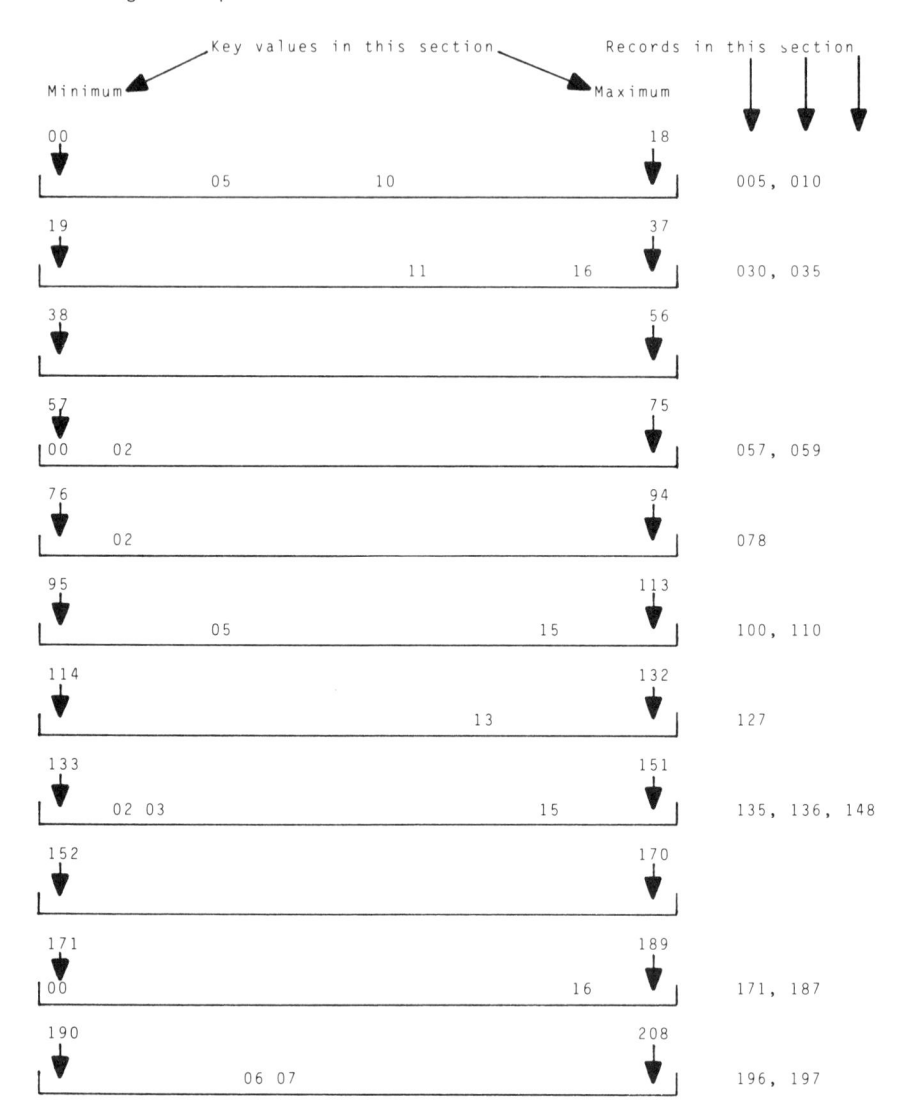

Fig. 6.5(a) The remainders after division by 19 are shown—as values between 0 and 18—in each of the eleven separate sections into which the key sequence has been 'cut', to fit it into nineteen addresses.

Direct file organization **163**

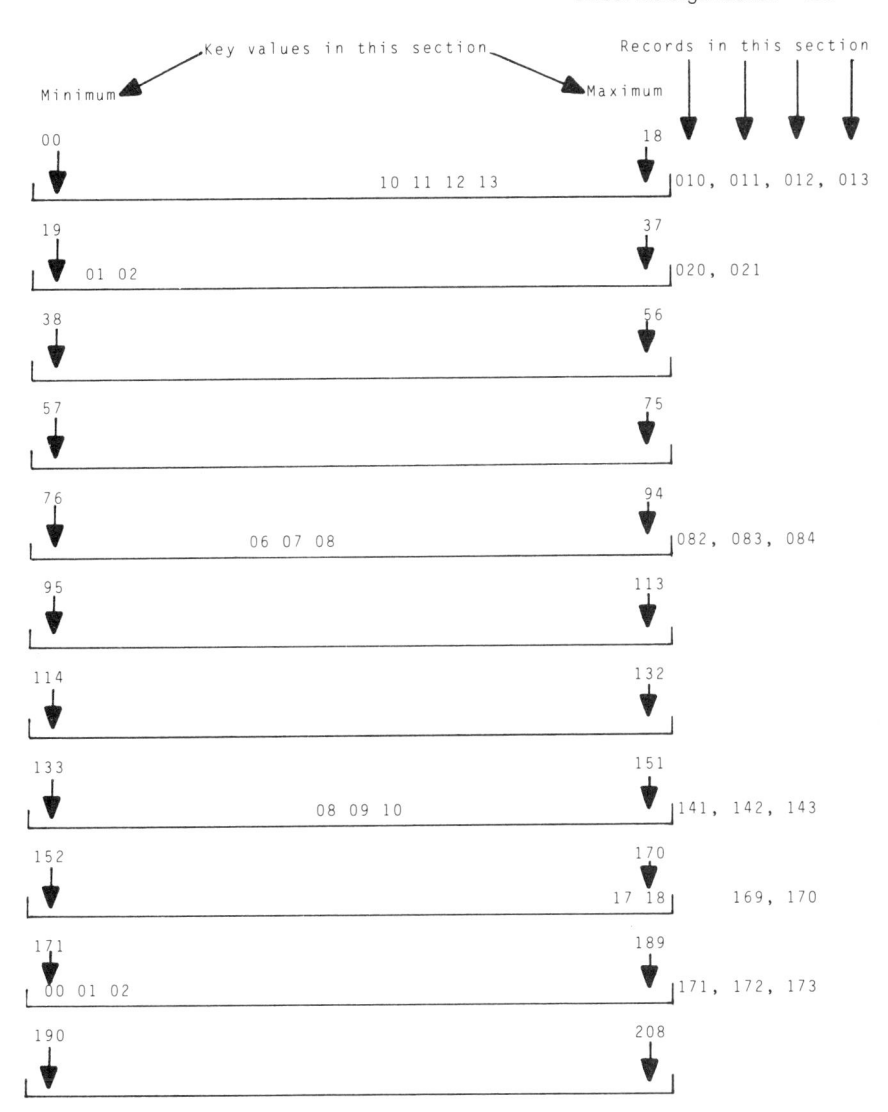

```
                    Key values in this section        Records in this section
        Minimum                        Maximum
        00                              18
         ▼                               ▼
        └────────────── 10 11 12 13 ─────┴── 010, 011, 012, 013
        19                              37
         ▼      01 02                    ▼
        └────────────────────────────────┴── 020, 021
        38                              56
         ▼                               ▼
        └────────────────────────────────┘
        57                              75
         ▼                               ▼
        └────────────────────────────────┘
        76                              94
         ▼          06 07 08             ▼
        └────────────────────────────────┴── 082, 083, 084
        95                              113
         ▼                               ▼
        └────────────────────────────────┘
        114                             132
         ▼                               ▼
        └────────────────────────────────┘
        133                             151
         ▼          08 09 10             ▼
        └────────────────────────────────┴── 141, 142, 143
        152                             170
         ▼                               ▼
        └──────────────────── 17 18 ─────┴── 169, 170
        171                             189
         ▼  00 01 02                     ▼
        └────────────────────────────────┴── 171, 172, 173
        190                             208
         ▼                               ▼
        └────────────────────────────────┘
```

Fig. 6.5(b) Note that synonyms arise where runs of keys clash, but that no two keys in any single run can cause synonyms, as no run can contain more records than the total number of addresses available.

164 Design of computer data files

2 Mid-square

In this case we square the whole key and take a centre part of it to allocate the records to buckets. In order to fit the result of selecting two decimal digits (a maximum value of 99) into a range of twenty storage positions, 20 is subtracted repetitively from the two digits until the result is less than 20.

KEY	SQUARE	CENTRE	FIT-FACTOR	ADDRESS
005	00025	02	00	02
010	00100	10	00	10
030	00900	90	$- 4 \times 20$	10
035	01225	22	$- 1 \times 20$	02
057	03249	24	$- 1 \times 20$	04
059	03481	48	$- 2 \times 20$	08
078	06084	08	00	08
100	10000	00	00	00
110	12100	10	00	10
127	16129	12	00	12
135	18225	22	$- 1 \times 20$	02
136	18496	49	$- 2 \times 20$	09
148	21904	90	$- 4 \times 20$	10
171	29241	24	$- 1 \times 20$	04
187	34969	96	$- 4 \times 20$	16
196	38416	41	$- 2 \times 20$	01
197	38809	80	$- 4 \times 20$	00

This process gives eight synonyms (00, 02, 02, 04, 08, 10, 10, 10). It is rather unexpected that most of the values obtained are even. This is not a general result, and shows that this algorithm, which gives 8/17 or 47 per cent of synonyms, does not suit this key set. The reader might like to check that, if the second and third digits are used instead of the third and fourth, there will be seven synonyms instead of eight (00, 01, 01, 04, 09, 12, 12). However, this is still not a good result.

Applying the same algorithm to the other key set, the results are shown at the top of the next page.

This gives a reasonable result in terms of synonyms: six out of seventeen, or 35 per cent. The reader may care to confirm that, if the third and fourth digits are selected instead, there will be eight synonyms.

3 End-folding

Usually we would be satisfied with the results of one or other of the first two techniques. Out of interest, we will try one other method on these key sets—end-folding. This involves 'folding' one part of the key under the rest and adding. If the value we get is more than 19, we will subtract 20 repetitively until it is brought into the range 0 to 19. For example:

KEY	SQUARE	CENTRE	FIT-FACTOR	ADDRESS
010	00100	01	00	01
011	00121	01	00	01
012	00144	01	00	01
013	00169	01	00	01
020	00400	04	00	04
021	00441	04	00	04
082	06724	67	-3×20	07
083	06889	68	-3×20	08
084	07056	70	-3×20	10
141	19881	98	-4×20	18
142	20164	01	00	01
143	20449	04	00	04
169	28561	85	-4×20	05
170	28900	89	-4×20	09
171	29241	92	-4×20	12
172	29584	95	-4×20	15
173	29929	99	-4×20	19

005 gives 00 + 5, address is 05
059 gives 05 + 9, address is 14

Using the 'random' set of keys, this gives the following addresses:

KEY	FOLDED RESULT	FIT-FACTOR	ADDRESS
005	05	0	05
010	01	0	01
030	03	0	03
035	08	0	08
057	12	0	12
059	14	0	14
078	15	0	15
100	10	0	10
110	11	0	11
127	19	0	19
135	18	0	18
136	19	0	19
148	22	-1×20	02
171	18	0	18
187	25	-1×20	05
196	25	-1×20	05
197	26	-1×20	06

Interestingly, this creates only *four* synonyms, and is thus a very effective algorithm.

With the five runs of keys, the resulting addresses are:

KEY	FOLDED RESULT	FIT-FACTOR	ADDRESS
010	01	0	01
011	02	0	02
012	03	0	03
013	04	0	04
020	02	0	02
021	03	0	03
082	10	0	10
083	11	0	11
084	12	0	12
141	15	0	15
142	16	0	16
143	17	0	17
170	17	0	17
171	18	0	18
172	19	0	19
173	20	-1×20	00

Here, the number of synonyms is three. In general, end-folding does not achieve such good results, but this illustrates how—with a very small 'file' and key size—results can be variable. In this case, due to the form of key and the end-folding digits chosen, end-folding is acting very similarly to an order-preserving algorithm.

6.5 Testing for successful randomization

After an algorithm has been selected, it is wise to ensure that it will be successful before using it in a program. A reasonable guide will be if it produces results near to or better than those predicted by equation (6.3). The algorithm and the file keys have to be analysed, which can be done either by writing an analysis program and inputting the keys, transforming them into addresses and recording the numbers of synonyms, or by using a standard analysis program. This is obtainable from manufacturers or from many bureaux, and will give numbers of synonyms, their distribution and comparisons with the 'ideal' randomized distribution.

Kaimann[14] has carried out a series of randomizing experiments, based on a file of 48 950 records. These were randomized to 100 000 storage positions. We shall examine the results of his experiments and compare them with the results that we would expect if the records were perfectly randomized. In order to decide this we shall calculate the expected probability that an

Direct file organization **167**

address will contain no record, one record only, one synonym (two records allocated to one address), two synonyms and so on. It was stated earlier that the Poisson distribution was a satisfactory approximation to the binomial in a case such as this; to test this assertion both equation (6.2) and equation (6.3) have been used to calculate the expected 'perfectly randomized' results.

Using equation (6.2) derived from the binomial theorem, the probability that an address will have x records allocated to it is:

$$p(x) = \frac{n!(1/N)^x(1 - 1/N)^{n-x}}{x!(n - x)!}$$

Now:

$$\frac{n!}{(n - x)!} = \frac{n(n - 1)(n - 2) \cdots (3)(2)(1)}{(n - x)(n - x - 1) \cdots (3)(2)(1)}$$
$$= n(n - 1)(n - 2) \cdots (n - x + 1)$$

Thus

$$p(x) = \frac{n(n - 1) \cdots (n - x + 1)}{x!}(1/N)^x(1 - 1/N)^{n-x} \qquad (6.5)$$

This looks formidable, and the probabilities for higher values of x are complicated to calculate. However, an iterative method of calculation can be developed from equation (6.2) as follows:

$$p(0) = \frac{n!}{0!n!}(1/N)^0(1 - 1/N)^n$$
$$= 1 \times 1 \times (1 - 1/N)^n$$
$$= ((N - 1)/N)^n \qquad (6.6)$$

$$\frac{p(x)}{p(x - 1)} = \frac{n(n - 1) \cdots (n - x + 1)(x - 1)!(1/N)^x(1 - 1/N)^{n-x}}{n(n - 1) \cdots (n - x + 2)(x!)(1/N)^{x-1}(1 - 1/N)^{n-x+1}}$$
$$= \frac{(n - x + 1)(1/N)}{x(N - 1)/N}$$
$$= \frac{(n - x + 1)}{(N - 1)x}$$

$$\therefore p(x) = \frac{(n - x + 1)}{(N - 1)x}p(x - 1) \qquad (6.7)$$

Using equations (6.6) and (6.7) we can calculate a starting value, $p(0)$, and a factor by which this and each succeeding value is to be multiplied to yield the next value. This is

$$\frac{(n - x + 1)}{(N - 1)x}$$

This binomial figure is relatively easy to calculate, but the Poisson values derived from equation (6.3) are a great deal simpler, in particular the starting value $p(0)$. Equation (6.3) stated that:

$$p(x) = \frac{(n/N)^x e^{-(n/N)}}{x!}$$

From this:

$$p(0) = \frac{(n/N)^0 e^{-(n/N)}}{0!}$$
$$= e^{-(n/N)} \qquad (6.8)$$

Dividing the probabilities for x and $(x - 1)$:

$$\frac{p(x)}{p(x-1)} = \frac{(n/N)^x e^{-(n/N)} (x-1)!}{x!(n/N)^{x-1} e^{-(n/N)}}$$
$$= (n/Nx)$$
$$\therefore p(x) = (n/Nx)p(x-1) \qquad (6.9)$$

As the Poisson calculations also provide general rather than specific figures, it would be preferable to use them if there is no reason to reject the results. Using equations (6.9) and (6.10) the required Poisson values can be calculated very rapidly; they are particularly suited to a pocket calculator, as the starting value can be calculated and then modified by multiplying the contents of the calculator by the packing density and dividing by the next value of 'x': 1 when the calculator holds $p(0)$, 2 when it holds $p(1)$ and so on.

The values obtained for binary and Poisson probabilities are shown in Table 6.1 for the case where a file of 48 950 records is randomized to 100 000 storage positions. It is clear from the table that the correspondence between binomial and Poisson values is very close. For a file of this size, no value has been altered materially due to the simplification of using Poisson values. In any real case a variation of several hundred from the predicted value would be expected due to chance alone, while predictions based on the two methods do not differ by as much as one record in any file examined by the author. For this reason the simpler and more general Poisson calculations are used from now on in this book.

One of the most comprehensive studies of the results of randomization trials that has been reported was due to Kaimann[14]. The values tabulated

Direct file organization   **169**

Table 6.1 Binary and Poisson probabilities calculated for a file of 48 950 records randomized to 100 000 storage positions

Probability p(x)	Binomial value	Poisson value	Number of home records
p(0)	0.612 931 283 8	0.612 932 784 0	nil (only synonyms)
p(1)	0.300 032 863 8	0.300 030 597 8	30 003
p(2)	0.073 432 277 5	0.073 432 488 8	7 343
p(3)	0.011 981 330 2	0.011 981 734 4	1 198
p(4)	0.001 466 140 0	0.001 466 264 7	147
p(5)	0.000 143 524 8	0.000 143 547 3	14
p(6)	0.000 014 049 7	0.000 011 711 0	1
p(7)	0.000 001 375 3	0.000 000 818 9	0.1

here give us a measure of comparison for Kaimann's experimental results. Fig. 6.6 shows the theoretical curve for the values of $p(0)$ to $p(7)$, taken from Table 6.1, plotted against equivalent curves for the following techniques:

1 The remainder after division by 100 000, i.e. the last digits of the nine-digit key.
2 The five high-order digits of the key used directly as an address.
3 The middle five digits of the square of the key.
4 Five of the six junior digits, discarding the thousands digit and combining the rest.
5 Five of the digits from the nine-digit key, two from the first five and three from the next four, e.g. for 987 654 321:
   987 65 4 321
       65   321
   the address is 65321.
6 The remainder after division of the key by the largest prime under 100 000 (99 991).

Table 6.2 shows the number of *addresses* that have been allocated the stated number of records per address (up to seven), and the percentage of the total number of records in the file that was successfully allocated by each of the six algorithms used by Kaimann.

The very wide differences between the results achieved by different randomizaton techniques are shown in Table 6.2 and Fig. 6.7. However, none of the results given here indicate randomization that is fully successful. It is interesting that a fairly ad-hoc method of transformation (Test 5) is in most respects more successful than division by a prime number. This suggests that by chance some underlying order in the key sequence has affected randomization. However, the number of long synonym chains is less after division by a prime than by this digit selection. A further search for a successful algorithm—probably for a more suitable prime—is indicated in

170 Design of computer data files

Table 6.2 Figures shown in 'Test' columns give the numbers of addresses to which the number of records stated in the left-hand column is allocated by each randomization method.

No of records per address	Test 1	Test 2	Test 3	Test 4	Test 5	Test 6
0	90 004	99 585	73 372	86 086	64 529	65 217
1	6 480	5	16 649	5 093	25 562	24 075
2	1 004	4	4 490	1 891	7 361	8 014
3	537	1	2 219	1 417	1 822	2 095
4	248	0	1 405	1 218	512	464
5	291	1	985	1 089	151	107
6	144	3	520	924	46	27
7	137	0	277	719	15	2
% of records allocated addresses	30.13	0.08	96.81	69.50	99.97	100.00

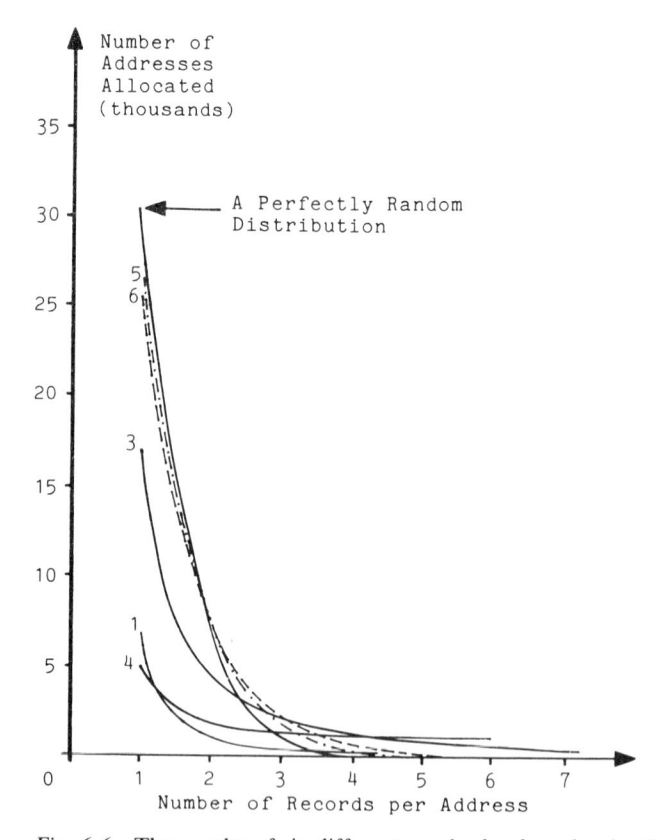

Fig. 6.6 The results of six different methods of randomization compared with the theoretically predicted results. Details of these methods are given in the text.

a case like this. As the key range, nine digits, is potentially 10 000 times the address range, 100 000, even division can only be expected to equal or very marginally improve on perfect randomization.

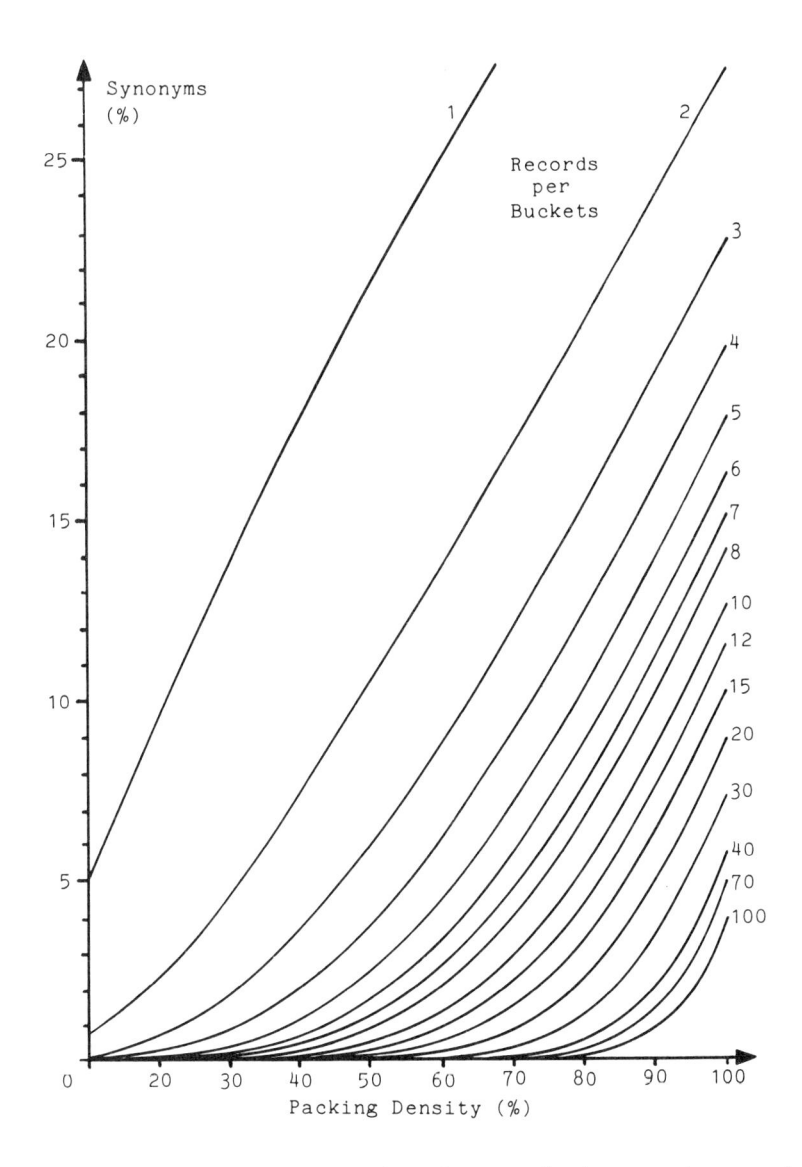

Fig. 6.7 Expected percentage of overflow records when records are randomized to buckets.

6.6 Minimizing the effect of synonyms

Now that the inevitability of synonyms occurring has been made clear, we must consider how to deal with them. This can best be described in a series of steps:

1 Ensure that the number of synonyms is at a minimum. This can be achieved by the selection of a suitable bucket size, packing density, randomizing algorithm and record-loading technique.
2 Use an efficient method of storing and retrieving the synonyms generated.
3 Arrange that the most frequently referenced records are in the home positions.
4 Reorganize the file at intervals—unless a randomization technique that allocates space as it is required has been used.

Each of these measures is examined in detail below.

Minimizing the number of synonyms

Packing density and bucket size

If we decide to store each record in a storage position able to hold only one record, even a perfectly random distribution will give a high proportion of synonyms. Table 6.3 has been calculated using equation (6.6.).

The table is built up by calculating $p(0)$, and hence the probability that any given address would not have a home record allocated to it. Multiplying this by 100 and subtracting the result from 100 per cent, we obtain the percentage of addresses that will contain home records. This is shown in the second row. Subtraction of this figure from the total of all the records as a percentage of the addresses, i.e. from the packing density, gives the number of synonyms as a percentage of the addresses. This figure is expressed as a percentage of the records in the bottom row.

For 30 per cent packing the calculation is as follows:

$p(0) = 0.74082$

$\therefore$ 74.082 per cent of addresses have no home record allocated.

$\therefore$ $(100 - 74.082)$ per cent $= 25.918$ per cent of addresses have one or more home records allocated.

$\therefore$ $(30 - 25.918)$ per cent $= 4.082$ per cent of the *addresses* hold synonyms, as the records not stored in their home addresses must be stored somewhere else.

$\therefore$ $4.082 \times 100/30$ per cent $= 13.61$ per cent of the *records* are stored as synonyms.

A glance at the percentages of synonyms shows that even when the file is

Direct file organization 173

Table 6.3 The effect of packing density on the percentage of records that become synonyms, for single record buckets.

	Packing density (n/N) (%)								
	10	20	30	40	50	60	70	80	90	100
p(0)	0.905	0.819	0.741	0.670	0.607	0.549	0.497	0.449	0.407	0.368
Home records as % of addresses	09.52	18.13	25.92	32.97	39.35	45.12	50.34	55.07	59.34	63.21
Synonyms as % of addresses	0.484	1.873	4.082	7.032	10.65	14.88	19.66	24.93	30.66	36.79
Synonyms as % of records	4.84	9.37	13.61	17.58	21.31	24.80	28.08	31.17	34.06	36.79

only 20 per cent packed, almost 10 per cent of the file will be stored as synonyms. When we wish to retrieve a synonym, the algorithm will give an 'incorrect' address. Whatever method of storing synonyms is used, time will be lost as a result. Some way must be found to reduce the number of synonyms, in order to increase the efficiency of direct retrieval.

If buckets large enough to hold several records are used, we can expect that these buckets will be more evenly filled than individual records fill single addresses; this can be examined using the Poisson distribution.

Equation (6.3) for randomization to individual addresses is:

$$p(x) = \frac{(n/N)^x e^{-(n/N)}}{x!}$$

Let the number of buckets be B; then during a single address calculation each bucket location has a probability of being generated of $(1/B)$, and a probability $(1 - 1/B)$ that it will not be generated. Assuming the number of buckets is large, the Poisson distribution can once more be used as an approximation to the binomial distribution. Then:

$$p(x) = \frac{(n/B)^x e^{-(n/B)}}{x!} \qquad (6.10)$$

Note that the value (n/B) will now usually exceed unity, and that the packing density of the file will depend on how many records can be stored in each bucket. To calculate $p(0)$ substitute (n/B) for (n/N) in equation (6.8):

$$p(0) = e^{-(n/B)} \qquad (6.11)$$

and also, modifying equation (6.9):

$$p(x) = \frac{n}{Bx} p(x - 1) \qquad (6.12)$$

The percentage of records that will be stored as synonyms, for any given bucket size and packing density, can be derived as follows (the full explanation of the calculations is given in reference 15):

Let the packing density be P and the number of records per bucket be r. The percentage of synonyms to be expected for any given case, assuming that record allocation to addresses is entirely random and that synonyms are only stored *after* all home records, is as follows:

Define the total file storage capacity as 1. The sum of the probabilities for space to which records have *not* been allocated, P_{EMPTY}, is:

$$P_{\text{EMPTY}} = p(0) + (r-1)p(1)/r + (r-2)p(2)/r \ldots + p(r-1)/r \tag{6.13}$$

The rest of the total file area must therefore hold *home* records, i.e.

$$(1 - P_{\text{EMPTY}}) \tag{6.14}$$

(*Note*: The proportion of the file area that contains home records is calculated indirectly rather than directly, because the sum of home record probabilities is made up of an infinite series, while that of the empty positions is finite, as is clear from equation (6.13).)

As the packing density is α, a proportion α of the total file area will hold records when the loading process is complete. The probability of a record becoming a synonym is therefore given by subtracting the proportion of the file area occupied by home records from the total proportion of the file area taken up by the file, that is α.

$$P_{\text{SYNONYMS}} = (\alpha + P_{\text{EMPTY}} - 1) \tag{6.15}$$

The user will normally wish to express this as a percentage of the records loaded, which is:

$$\text{SYNONYM \%} = \frac{100(\alpha + P_{\text{EMPTY}} - 1)}{\alpha} \tag{6.16}$$

The value of P_{SYNONYMS} can be calculated using an iterative procedure by combining the expressions given in equations (6.13) and (6.15):

$$P_{\text{SYNONYMS}} = \alpha + p(0) + \frac{(r-1)p(1)}{r} + \frac{(r-2)p(2)}{r} \ldots + \frac{p(r-1)}{r} - 1$$

$$= \alpha + e^{-\alpha r} + \frac{(r-1)}{r} e^{-\alpha r} \cdot \frac{\alpha r}{1} + \frac{(r-2)}{r} e^{-\alpha r} \frac{\alpha r \cdot \alpha r}{1 \cdot 2} \ldots$$

$$+ \frac{(r-n)}{r} e^{-\alpha r} \frac{(\alpha r)^n}{n!} \ldots + \frac{(r-r+1)}{r} e^{-\alpha r} \frac{(\alpha r)^{r-1}}{(r-1)!} - 1$$

$$= \alpha + \frac{e^{-\alpha r}}{r} \left\{ r + (r-1)\alpha r + (r-2)\frac{(\alpha r)^2}{2!} \cdots \right.$$
$$\left. + (r-n)\frac{(\alpha r)^n}{n!} \cdots + \frac{(\alpha r)^{r-1}}{(r-1)!} \right\} - 1$$

This expression can be summed iteratively, as the first term within the brace has the value $e^{-\alpha r}$. Let this be I_1. Then each successive term is obtained by using the relationship:

$$I_n = \frac{(r-n)\alpha r}{(r-n+1)n} I_{n-1} \qquad (6.17)$$

Table 6.4 shows the expected percentage of overflow records when records are randomized to buckets containing from one to 600 records. The table shows figures down to 0.01 per cent of synonyms, and Fig. 6.7 is useful for extrapolation between values, and understanding the overall relationship between bucket size and packing density.

From the table and figure, it is clear that far fewer records will be displaced if we randomize to a multi-record bucket rather than to an individual record position. For example, with a file that is only 50 per cent packed, we must expect 21.31 per cent of the records not to be stored in their home record positions if we randomize to a specific address. Using buckets capable of holding only two records will improve this figure to 10.36 per cent. If we use buckets of eight records at a time, less than 1 per cent of the records will be synonyms, and this is reduced to 0.1 per cent for buckets of fifteen records.

Hence it is clear that, if records are randomized to individual storage positions or to small buckets, many records will become synonyms. Unless the records are stored singly there is no corresponding improvement in speed of finding the desired record, because the access comb will reach the track at a point decided by chance, and there will be an average delay of at least half a revolution before the start of the record is reached.

The advantage of single records is that they can be stored in CKD format—with separate keys—and the track can be scanned for a particular record without having to read unwanted records into main storage. Multiple record buckets cannot be handled in this way, as groups of records that randomize to the same bucket do not generally have anything else in common, so that the whole bucket has to be searched to see if the desired record is in it. So, although there is clearly an argument for using buckets that are as large as possible, over-large buckets will mean that an extended search through the bucket will be required to locate the desired record.

Since there are advantages both in storing records singly and in using large buckets, one solution is to randomize to a track but to store records singly in CKD format. This is particularly useful when manufacturers' software is available (as for example SEARCH ON KEY for IBM computers) to carry out the search automatically. Although a number of writers[13,14] suggest that

176 Design of computer data files

Table 6.4 The figures tabulated show synonyms as a percentage of the records loaded.

Records per bucket	\multicolumn{20}{c}{Packing density α}
	0.05	0.10	0.15	0.20	0.25	0.30	0.35	0.40	0.45	0.50	0.55	0.60	0.65	0.70	0.75	0.80	0.85	0.90	0.95	1.00
---	---	---	---	---	---	---	---	---	---	---	---	---	---	---	---	---	---	---	---	---
1	2.46	4.84	7.14	9.37	11.52	13.61	15.63	17.58	19.47	21.31	23.08	24.80	26.47	28.08	29.65	31.17	32.64	34.06	35.45	36.79
2	0.16	0.60	1.29	2.19	3.27	4.49	5.83	7.27	8.78	10.36	11.99	13.65	15.34	17.03	18.73	20.43	22.11	23.79	25.44	27.07
3	0.01	0.09	0.29	0.63	1.13	1.80	2.63	3.61	4.73	5.99	7.35	8.82	10.37	11.99	13.66	15.37	17.11	18.87	20.64	22.40
4		0.02	0.07	0.20	0.44	0.80	1.30	1.96	2.78	3.76	4.88	6.15	7.54	9.05	10.65	12.33	14.07	15.86	17.69	19.54
5			0.02	0.07	0.18	0.37	0.68	1.12	1.72	2.48	3.40	4.49	5.73	7.12	8.63	10.26	11.98	13.78	15.64	17.55
6			0.01	0.02	0.08	0.18	0.37	0.67	1.10	1.69	2.45	3.38	4.48	5.75	7.18	8.75	10.44	12.24	14.12	16.06
7				0.01	0.03	0.09	0.21	0.41	0.72	1.18	1.80	2.60	3.58	4.74	6.09	7.60	9.25	11.04	12.93	14.90
8					0.02	0.05	0.12	0.25	0.49	0.84	1.35	2.03	2.90	3.97	5.23	6.68	8.30	10.07	11.96	13.96
9					0.01	0.02	0.07	0.16	0.33	0.61	1.02	1.61	2.38	3.36	4.55	5.94	7.52	9.27	11.16	13.18
10						0.01	0.04	0.10	0.23	0.44	0.79	1.29	1.98	2.88	3.99	5.32	6.86	8.59	10.48	12.51
11						0.01	0.02	0.07	0.16	0.33	0.61	1.04	1.66	2.48	3.53	4.80	6.30	8.01	9.90	11.94
12							0.01	0.04	0.11	0.24	0.48	0.85	1.40	2.15	3.14	4.36	5.82	7.51	9.39	11.44
14							0.01	0.02	0.06	0.18	0.30	0.57	1.01	1.65	2.52	3.64	5.03	6.70	8.54	10.60
16								0.01	0.03	0.10	0.19	0.39	0.74	1.28	2.05	3.09	4.41	6.00	7.85	9.92
18									0.02	0.06	0.12	0.28	0.55	1.01	1.70	2.65	3.90	5.45	7.28	9.36
20									0.01	0.04	0.08	0.20	0.42	0.81	1.42	2.30	3.48	4.99	6.80	8.88
25										0.01	0.03	0.09	0.22	0.48	0.93	1.65	2.70	4.10	5.86	7.95
30											0.01	0.04	0.12	0.29	0.64	1.23	2.16	3.47	5.18	7.26
35												0.02	0.06	0.18	0.45	0.94	1.76	2.98	4.64	6.73
40												0.01	0.04	0.12	0.32	0.73	1.46	2.60	4.22	6.30
50													0.01	0.05	0.17	0.46	1.04	2.05	3.57	5.63
60														0.02	0.09	0.30	0.76	1.65	3.10	5.14
75														0.01	0.04	0.16	0.50	1.25	2.59	4.60
100															0.01	0.07	0.27	0.83	2.02	3.99
150															0.01	0.01	0.09	0.43	1.37	3.26
200																	0.03	0.24	1.01	2.82
250																	0.01	0.14	0.78	2.52
300																	0.01	0.09	0.62	2.30
400																		0.04	0.42	1.99
500																		0.02	0.30	1.78
600																		0.01	0.22	1.63

More detailed data, covering packing densities for intermediate values and up to 580% packing, is given in Appendix 5.

Direct file organization 177

a full-track bucket is always too large, they are talking of a bucket that has to be transferred as a whole into and out of main storage. The solution suggested above allows the very low synonym levels of a multi-record bucket—in this case a track—to be combined with the CKD format of individually stored records, which makes it possible to search the whole track and retrieve only the desired record. As very few records will not be on their home tracks, this procedure is extremely efficient.

Fig. 6.8 shows how increased bucket size delays the onset of synonym occurrence in a well randomized file.

The curves show divergence from the relationship $r = n$ (for n records stored individually), $r = n/10$ (for records stored in buckets with a capacity of

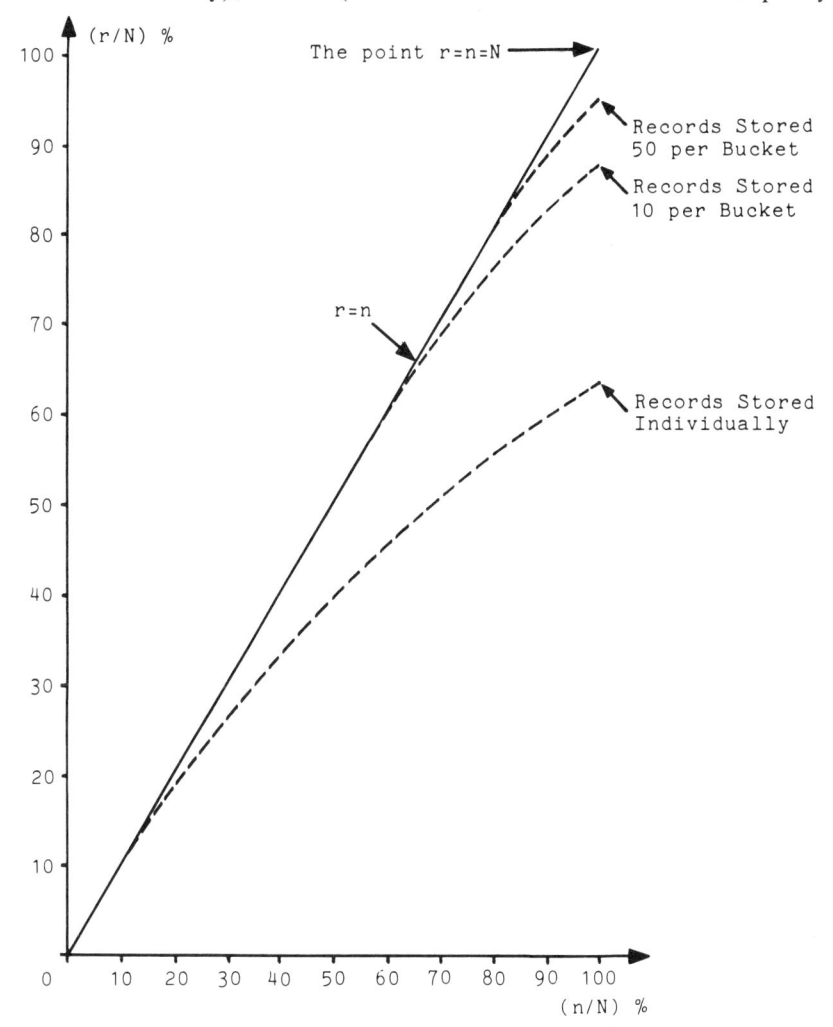

Fig. 6.8 Divergence from the simple relationship that r (the number of different addresses generated) = n (the number of records allocated) as packing density increases.

ten records), and $r = n/50$ (for buckets with a fifty-record capacity). They thus show the number of synonyms created, assuming a perfect randomizing algorithm, for various packing factors. Randomizing to buckets with a capacity of ten records markedly decreases the number of synonyms, and there is a further decrease if buckets with a capacity of fifty records are used.

Appendix 5 provides extended synonym tables and curves for more precise work in this field. In general, the file designer will choose a bucket size and packing density that reduce the percentage of synonyms to an acceptable level, bearing in mind the increased retrieval times large bucket size can cause. As is made clear below, bucket size may also affect the algorithm chosen.

Randomizing algorithm

In choosing an algorithm, the file designer will aim to minimize the number of synonyms. The key type and format should be assessed, to decide on the occurrence and frequency of runs of keys. The range of key values, divided by the number of addresses to be generated (the calculation is shown on page 161), will indicate the potential improvement, over and above the synonym percentages predicted by the Poisson distribution, that can be aimed for. Practical trials will indicate the success of any algorithms the designer selects, and this step in file design should never be omitted.

For general guidance on choice of algorithm, the author[16] has compared the number of accesses observed by Lum et al.[7] in practical trials with the theoretically predicted number, for buckets holding five, ten, twenty and fifty records. The results of this comparison are shown in Fig. 6.9.

As can be seen from the figure, for buckets holding five records division is not as effective as mid-square (which closely approximates the 'theoretical' figures) for packing densities above 0.7. For buckets holding ten records, division is superior up to a packing density of about 0.85, while for larger bucket sizes division is more efficient at all packing densities.

In general, the success of a randomizing method is partly dependent on the technique used to store synonyms, and this will be discussed further in a later section of the chapter (see p. 184). However, it is fair to say that division is usually the most efficient technique if synonyms are to be handled by chaining or tagging, but that if they are to be stored using the consecutive spill technique, bucket size and packing density should also be considered before a decision on randomizing method is made.

Before leaving randomizing algorithms, it should be made clear that the treatment of them here is based on the assumption that the file size, once created, can only be altered when the file is reorganized. Records can be added of course, but this will increase the packing density.

There is a great deal of interest at present in developing hashing algorithms for files that may vary in size. This is usually termed *dynamic hashing*; a particularly useful review of these techniques is given by Sachs-Davies et al.[17], describing both *extendible hashing*, in which a set of buckets

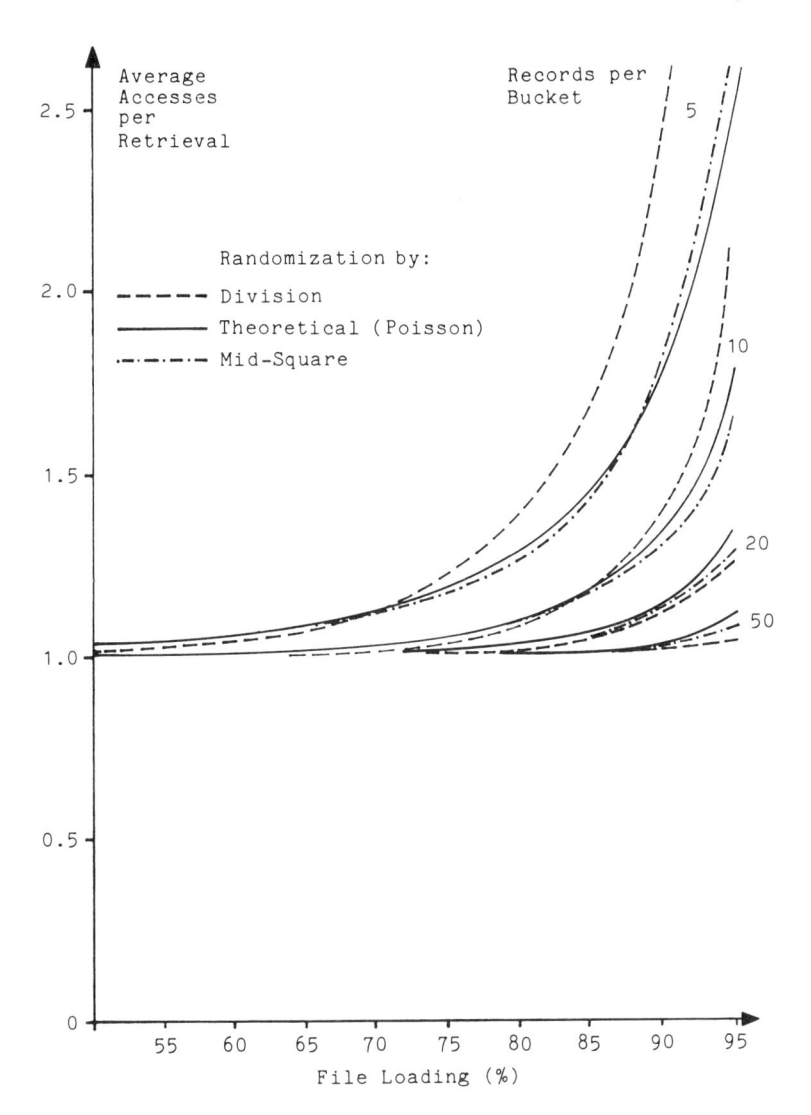

Fig. 6.9 Comparison of the effects of randomization techniques, bucket size and packing density on direct file accesses.

is referenced via a directory, and *linear hashing*, which is genuinely a direct technique in that there is no directory. Both of these methods suffer from oscillations in performance associated with their mode of action, and neither performs as well as 'static' randomization methods.

A form of extendible hashing that does not suffer from oscillations and is claimed to outperform most indexing methods, was reported by Lomet[18]. He named the method *bounded index exponential hashing*; it is not strictly a direct technique, and suffers from the drawback that the file packing density is generally low, but offers many advantages for files which can grow at a rate that cannot be accommodated in a static system.

Designers looking for examples of how to code randomizing algorithms should consult Snader[19], who gives examples of various functions coded in Fortran, Basic and Pascal; Morris[20], who gives Fortran code both for chaining and hashing; and Johnson and Cooper[21], who provide comprehensive coded examples in COBOL.

File loading

When a direct file is loaded for the first time, we may have little or no information about the individual records that make it up. However, it is still possible to keep the number of synonyms to a minimum. Records will be read into primary storage, their keys will be transformed by the algorithm being used, and if the address the algorithm produces is free they will be stored in that address on the direct access device. When a record turns out to be a synonym, there are two alternatives: these are to store the synonym at once, in which case the process is called a *one-pass load*, or to load it in two passes, which is called a *two-pass load*. A one-pass load will result in the creation of unnecessary synonyms, as shown in Fig. 6.10.

To avoid the creation of extra synonyms, the file has to be loaded in two passes. On the first pass, all the home records are loaded, but synonyms are not. On the second pass, all the synonyms are loaded. This process maximizes the number of home records in the file, and so maximizes the number of records that can be retrieved without further searching.

All the calculations carried out so far have assumed that it is possible to allocate any number of records to a given address. This is implied in the calculations, as no allowance has been made to store the synonyms that arise in other free addresses. Instead, the number of synonyms has been calculated, but they have then been ignored by the mathematics, and so have not interfered with the 'storage' of other records. This is precisely the process that occurs during a two-pass load, as the synonyms are stored on the second pass.

Although the calculations available in the literature have very largely assumed that direct files are loaded using two passes, there are a number of cases in which a one-pass load occurs in practice. These are:

1. If a simple one-pass load is used for the file.
2. Whenever records are added to an existing file, as both home and synonym records from the original load have already been stored; in this case the probability of an addition that is a potential home record being prevented from taking up its home position by a synonym that was loaded earlier is high.
3. In databases that offer the CALC option—as each record is loaded when it is added to the database, whether it is a home or synonym.

To estimate the number of synonyms that occur during creation of a direct

Direct file organization   **181**

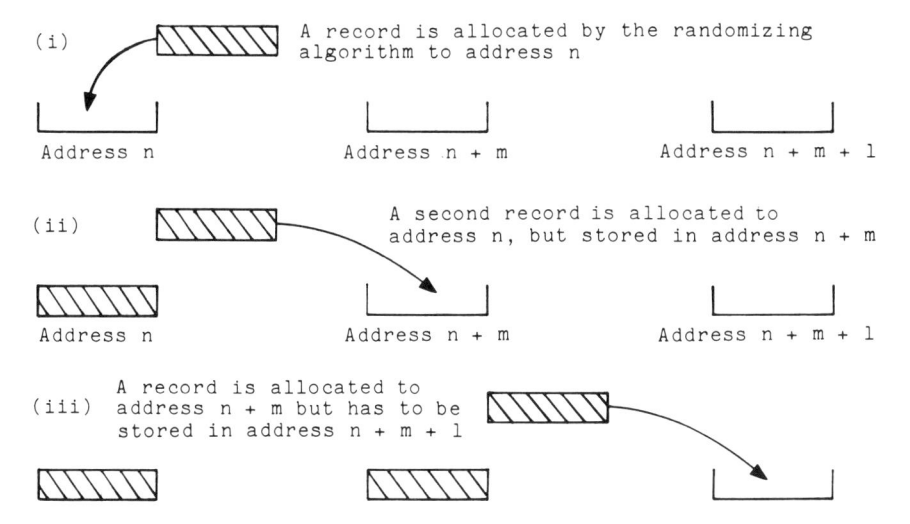

(i) A record is allocated by the randomizing algorithm to address n

Address n   Address n + m   Address n + m + 1

(ii) A second record is allocated to address n, but stored in address n + m

Address n   Address n + m   Address n + m + 1

(iii) A record is allocated to address n + m but has to be stored in address n + m + 1

Fig. 6.10 (a) Record stored at home address *n*. (b) As the home address *n* is full, the synonym is stored in position $(n+m)$ according to some previously arranged system. (c) A 'home' record arrives for address $(n+m)$, but it is already full. The record now becomes an unnecessary synonym, adding to the time taken to retrieve records.

file using a one-pass load, let us examine the result of storing *n* records at random in *N* addresses, on the assumption that each record has to be stored at once and each address can hold only one record.

The first record will be stored in its calculated address.

The second record has a probability of $1/N$ of becoming a synonym.

The *n*th record has a probability $(n-1)/N$ of becoming a synonym.

Summing this series of probabilities, and dividing by the number of records loaded, we obtain:

$$P_{\text{SYNONYMS}} = \frac{(1/N) + (2/N) + \ldots + (n-1)/N}{n}$$

$$= \frac{n(n-1)/2N}{n}$$

$$= \frac{(n-1)}{2N}$$

$$= \frac{\alpha}{2} - \frac{1}{2N} \qquad (6.18)$$

where $\alpha = (n/N)$, and represents the packing density as before.

For files of more than a few hundred records, $1/2N$ can be ignored. Thus the proportion of records stored as synonyms will be roughly equivalent to half the packing density in a file created using a single-pass load, and with single record buckets.

Design of computer data files

Table 6.5 The values tabulated show the predicted percentages of synonyms that will be created as a result of loading a direct file in a single pass, using an algorithm that converts record keys to addresses in a truly random manner.

Bucket Size	5	10	15	20	25	30	35	40	45	50	55	60	65	70	75	80	85	90	95	100
1	2.50	5.00	7.50	10.00	12.50	15.00	17.50	20.00	22.50	25.00	27.50	30.00	32.50	35.00	37.50	40.00	42.50	45.00	47.50	50.00
2	0.16	0.61	1.31	2.25	3.39	4.72	6.22	7.88	9.69	11.63	13.71	15.92	18.24	20.67	23.22	25.87	28.62	31.48	34.43	37.50
3	0.01	0.10	0.29	0.64	1.15	1.85	2.73	3.80	5.07	6.52	8.16	9.99	12.01	14.20	16.58	19.14	21.89	24.81	27.93	31.25
4		0.02	0.07	0.21	0.44	0.81	1.33	2.04	2.92	4.01	5.30	6.82	8.55	10.51	12.70	15.12	17.79	20.70	23.88	27.34
5			0.02	0.07	0.18	0.38	0.69	1.15	1.78	2.60	3.63	4.89	6.39	8.13	10.14	12.42	14.99	17.86	21.06	24.61
6			0.01	0.02	0.08	0.18	0.37	0.68	1.13	1.76	2.58	3.63	4.93	6.49	8.33	10.48	12.95	15.76	18.95	22.56
7				0.01	0.03	0.09	0.21	0.41	0.74	1.22	1.88	2.76	3.89	5.29	6.98	9.00	11.37	14.12	17.29	20.95
8					0.01	0.05	0.12	0.26	0.49	0.86	1.40	2.15	3.12	4.39	5.94	7.85	10.12	12.82	15.96	19.64
9					0.01	0.02	0.07	0.16	0.33	0.62	1.06	1.69	2.55	3.68	5.12	6.92	9.10	11.73	14.84	18.55
10						0.01	0.04	0.10	0.23	0.45	0.81	1.34	2.10	3.13	4.46	6.16	8.25	10.82	13.90	17.62
11						0.01	0.02	0.07	0.16	0.33	0.62	1.08	1.74	2.68	3.91	5.52	7.54	10.05	13.09	16.82
12							0.01	0.04	0.12	0.25	0.48	0.88	1.45	2.31	3.44	4.98	6.90	9.37	12.34	16.12
14								0.02	0.06	0.14	0.30	0.59	1.04	1.75	2.72	4.11	5.90	8.26	11.20	14.95
16								0.01	0.03	0.08	0.19	0.40	0.94	1.35	2.25	3.46	5.10	7.37	10.25	14.00
18									0.01	0.05	0.12	0.28	0.56	1.06	1.85	2.94	4.55	6.65	9.45	13.21
20									0.01	0.03	0.08	0.20	0.42	0.84	1.55	2.53	4.05	6.05	8.75	12.55
25										0.01	0.03	0.09	0.22	0.49	0.96	1.79	3.05	4.91	7.05	11.24
30											0.01	0.04	0.12	0.30	0.65	1.32	2.45	4.10	6.55	10.28
35												0.02	0.07	0.19	0.46	1.00	1.95	3.49	5.85	9.51
40												0.01	0.04	0.12	0.32	0.77	1.59	3.02	5.30	8.91
45													0.02	0.08	0.23	0.60	1.31	2.65	4.87	8.40
50													0.01	0.05	0.17	0.48	1.12	2.34	4.42	7.98
60														0.02	0.09	0.30	0.81	1.86	3.82	7.28
70														0.01	0.05	0.20	0.60	1.52	3.34	6.75
80														0.01	0.03	0.14	0.46	1.26	2.97	6.31
90															0.02	0.09	0.36	1.06	2.66	5.96
100															0.01	0.07	0.28	0.91	2.41	5.65
150																0.01	0.09	0.45	1.60	4.63
200																	0.04	0.25	1.20	4.01

Packing Density

Direct file organization   183

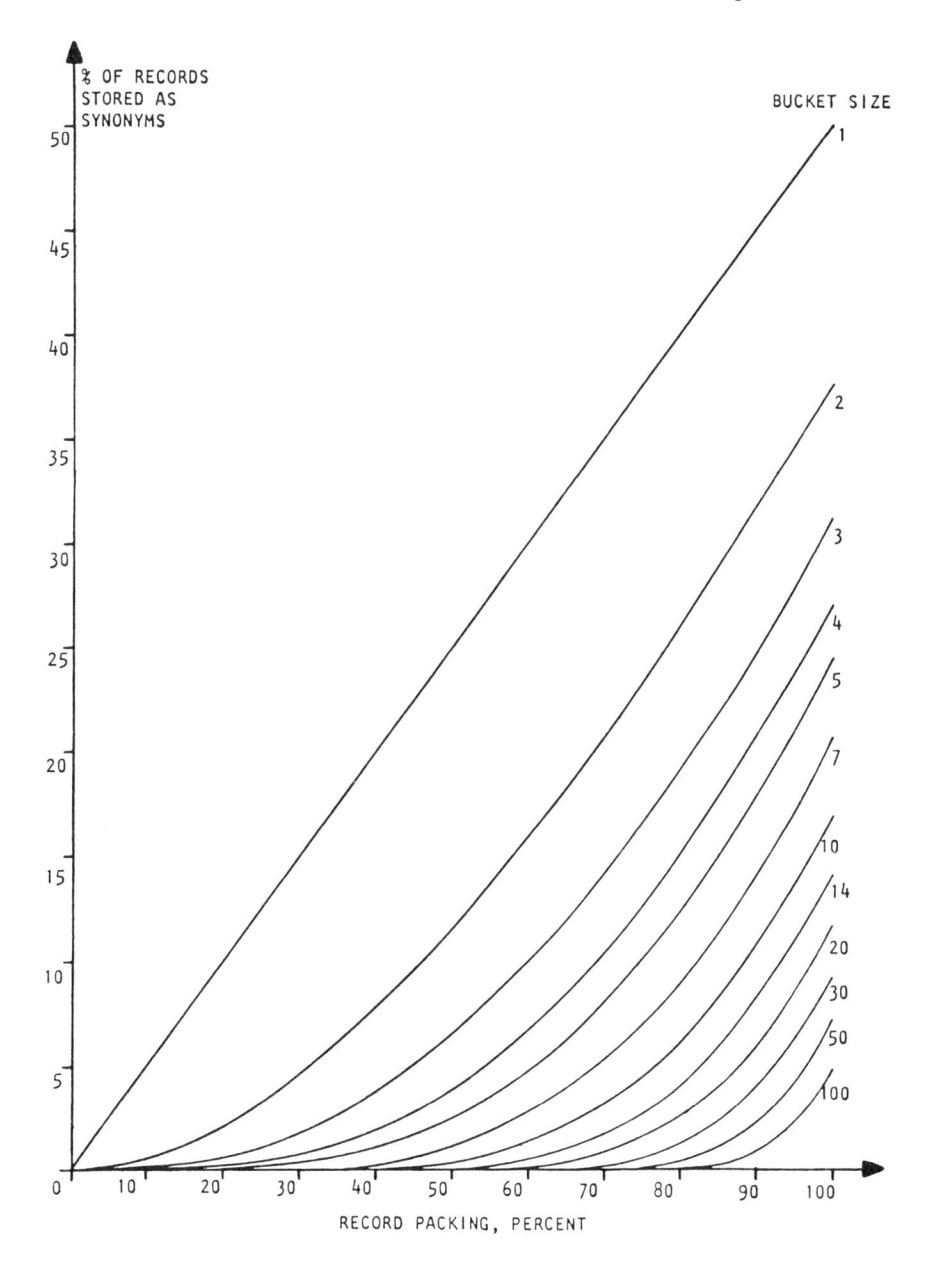

Fig. 6.11 The relationship between bucket size, percentage packing and the resulting synonym percentage after a one-pass load of a direct file. (A one-pass load is shown by the thicker line.)

The author has developed an iterative method of calculating the synonym percentages that would be expected as a result of loading buckets of various capacities to a range of packing densities[22]. These results have been confirmed using simulation techniques[23, 24], and are given in Table 6.5; they should be compared with Table 6.4. The divergence between the two loading techniques depends on packing density, and for single record buckets it is almost 10 per cent—one record in ten—for an 85 per cent packed file. Although the difference is less marked for multiple record buckets, it is still significant.

To provide quick reference for the file designer the data in Table 6.5 has been plotted in Fig. 6.11.

As the penalty that a one-pass load imposes in terms of extra synonyms is very quickly understood when it is shown visually, Fig. 6.12 compares the results of one-pass and two-pass loads for a number of bucket sizes.

Storing and retrieving synonyms

When a record cannot be placed in its home position, it must be stored at an address that can be located quickly. There are three widely used methods of doing this and we shall look at each in turn, assessing their advantages and drawbacks.

1 Consecutive spill (also called **progressive overflow**)
The simplest method of storage is to place a synonym in the first vacant record position following its home address. (This applies in just the same way if records are being randomized to multiple records buckets. The record is stored in the first bucket with available space following the original home bucket.) This method of storage, in which there is no link or pointer to the synonym from its home bucket, is called *consecutive spill* or *progressive overflow*. Record retrieval takes place as follows.

1 Seek the home address.
2 Check whether the records or records in the home address have the required key.
3 If not, search the rest of the track. If the record is not found on the track, search the rest of the cylinder. Note that, if the key that has been requested is not present on the file, the unsuccessful search length is potentially limited only by the size of the file.

Very few records will not find a place anywhere on the cylinder. Take for example a file that is 90 per cent packed, and can hold 250 records per cylinder. In this case the cylinder can be treated as a very large bucket. From Table 6.4, 99.86 per cent of records will be stored in their home cylinder and only 0.14 per cent will overflow on to another cylinder. As the packing density is usually lower than this and the number of records per cylinder greater, overflow from a cylinder is not usually a problem. It is shown in

Direct file organization **185**

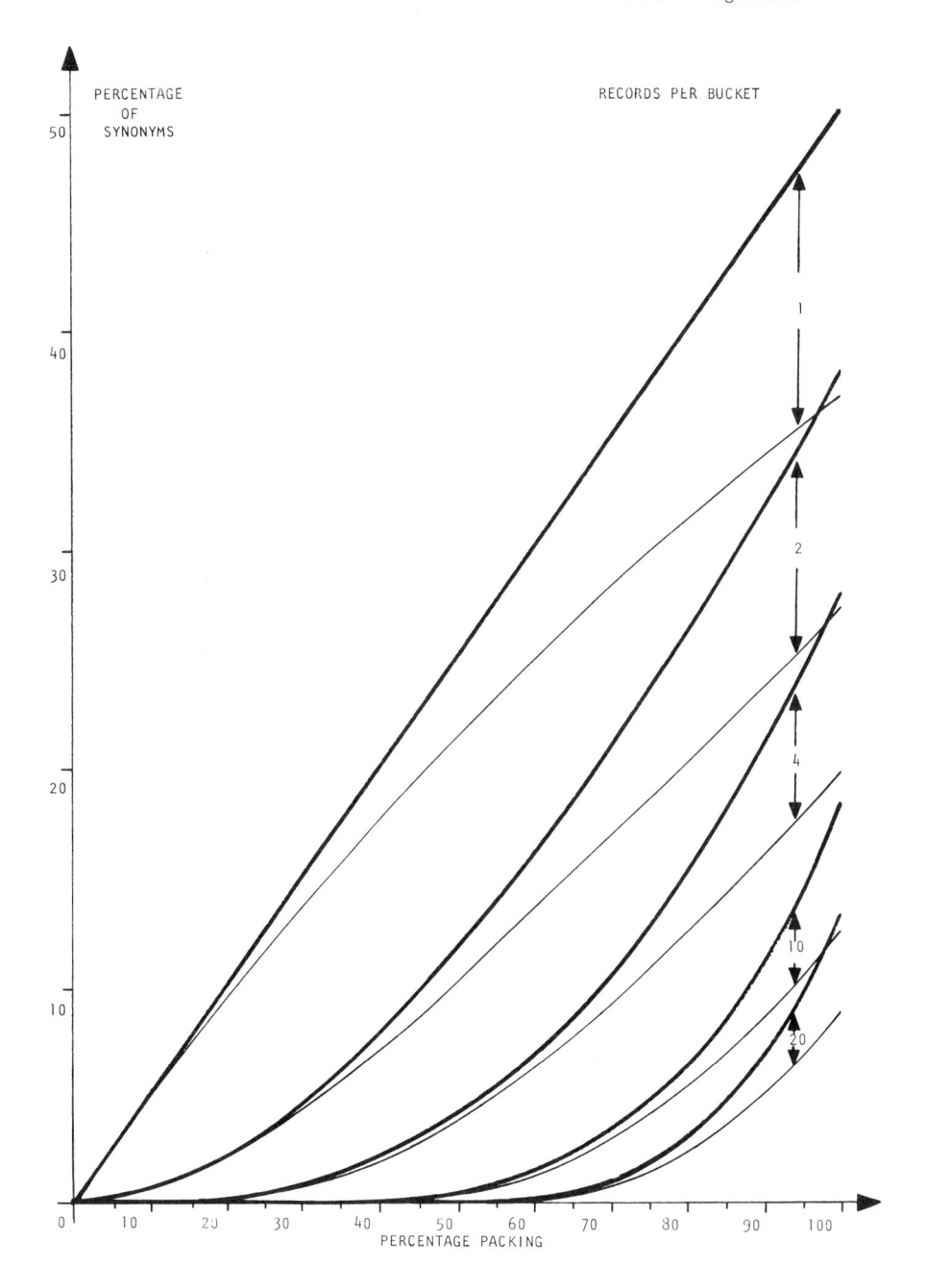

Fig. 6.12 The relationship between bucket size, percentage packing and the resulting synonym percentage after a one-pass load of a direct file. (A one-pass load is shown by the thicker line.)

Appendix 7 that, for a cylinder holding one hundred records and with other conditions as given above, the average retrieval time for *all* the records in the file will be $0.78R$, where R is the rotation time of the device. This compares with $0.5R$ for a self-indexing file.

A potential drawback of consecutive spill is that, while this method of handling synonyms can be effective in some circumstances to retrieve records that *are* held in a file, it is not a good method of dealing with records that are *not* in the file. As there is no way of knowing how many synonyms exist for any given home address, an unsuccessful search might require half the file to be scanned on average. The usual way to limit this search commitment is to place a synonym in any free position on its home cylinder, and in an independent area if no free space can be found in the cylinder. A second method is to note the longest search required to find a free storage position when synonyms are stored, and to limit searches to this length during retrieval.

2 Chaining

The second method generally available for synonym handling is to chain together all the records that randomize to the same address. A chain takes the form shown in Fig. 6.13. The home record storage area holds the address of the first synonym. This holds the address of the second synonym, and so on. A null link indicates the end of the chain.

If it is found that the home record is not the one required, the link address is used. This points to the second record that randomized to the home address. The chain is followed until the desired record is located or the end of the chain is reached. It eliminates the need to search the file sequentially.

The calculations involved in assessing the effect of chaining synonyms are complicated. For that reason they are given in detail in Appendix 6, The Effect of Synonym Storage Techniques on Search Times. Only the conclusions are discussed here.

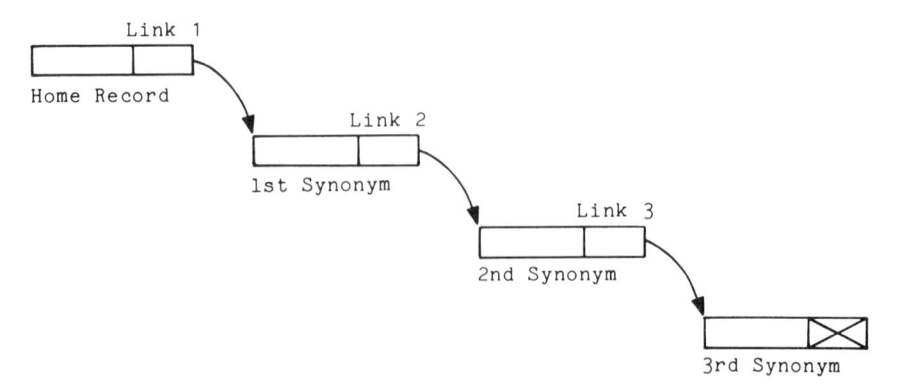

Fig. 6.13 Diagrammatic representation of chaining.

Direct file organization

Records randomized to individual record positions, with 90 per cent packing and ten record positions per track, give the following figures:

Number of records allocated per storage address	Percentage of records allocated
one	40.66 (all homes)
two	36.59 (18.3 home)
three	16.47 (5.49 home)
four	4.94 (1.24 home)
five	1.11 (0.22 home)
six	0.20 (0.03 home)

This shows that about one record in every 500 (0.2 per cent) will be part of a chain of six records. Of these, one-sixth (0.03 per cent) will be home records and an equal number will be first, second, third, fourth and fifth synonyms. At this packing density the average search time for a given record is $0.732R$, where R is the device rotation time.

When records are randomized to larger buckets—in this case we will examine ten record buckets—this will cause fairly long chains. Fig. 6.14 shows the pattern of record allocation for 80 per cent and 90 per cent packing. Buckets can hold ten records only, and any further records 'allocated' to a bucket will become part of a synonym chain.

Fig. 6.14 shows that quite long chains must be expected. For 90 per cent packing, just more than one bucket in every 200 (0.53 per cent) will have a chain of eight or more synonyms. A more detailed analysis shows the following:

Number of synonyms allocated per bucket	Percentage of buckets having this number of synonyms	Percentage of the file represented by these synonyms
one	9.7	1.08
two	7.3	1.62
three	5.0	1.68
four	3.2	1.44
five	1.9	1.07
six	1.1	0.73
seven	0.6	0.45
eight	0.3	0.26
nine or more	0.2	0.26

As 91.4 per cent of records will be located in their home buckets, the advantage of having relatively few synonyms outweighs the disadvantage of there being some long chains. The average search time for 90 per cent packed records stored in ten record buckets is $0.654R$. This figure is a great

188 Design of computer data files

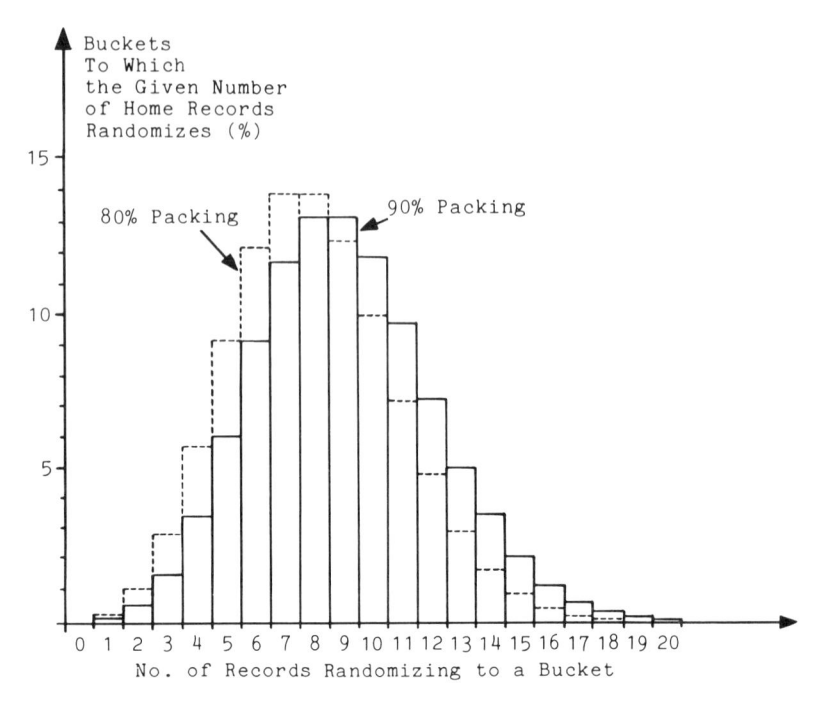

Fig. 6.14 Randomization to buckets that can contain ten records.

deal better than that for the consecutive spill method of handling overflows, and even chained records randomized to individual addresses show an advantage over consecutive spill.

A price has to be paid, however. To provide the links, an extra field has to be added to the home bucket or home record, and an extra field to each synonym. This effectively reduces the file packing, and may also cause fixed lengths to become variable in length. The last point could be put right, wasting more space, by adding a potential link field to every record. This might then be used when necessary, but be left empty in other cases. If the problem of providing space for link fields can be suitably handled, this method can offer considerable savings.

3 Tagging

One difficulty when processing linked records is that, if a record in the centre of a chain is inadvertently overwritten, the end of the chain is 'lost'. This can occur when adding records to the file. The third method of handling synonyms avoids this. It is called *tagging*. The technique used is to tag each synonym individually from the home address. Each tag will have to hold at least the information:

| KEY | ADDRESS |

This will mean that the few home addresses or home buckets which have large numbers of synonyms will have to allocate a lot of space for these tags. An example of the situation where there are five synonyms for a home record is shown in Fig. 6.15.

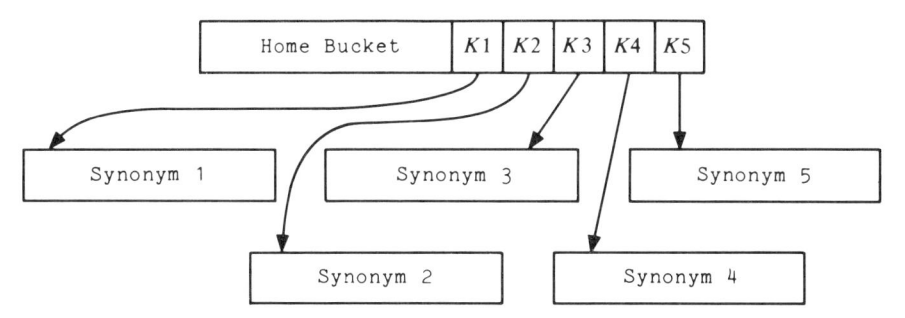

Fig. 6.15 Diagrammatic representation of tagging. $K1$ to $K5$ represent the keys of the five synonyms.

The tag system uses a little less space than the chaining system, as there is no need for a terminal 'link' field at the end of the chain. However, all the extra space is required in the home records. This can make planning and file creation difficult. If these problems can be overcome, it offers two advantages that chained overflow record handling does not. Firstly, the file organization is more robust, as the accidental overwriting of a record only affects that record itself and not other members of a chain. Secondly, it is never necessary to carry out more than two searches to locate a record. These are:

1. Search home record—if record not found pick up address from tag;
2. Search the address shown in the tag.

Using the example of a 90 per cent packed file with single-track buckets that can hold ten records: from Table 6.4, 91.4 per cent of records are located on their home tracks. Thus 8.6 per cent of records will require a full revolution of the home track, then a pick-up of the address required from a tag, then an average of $R/2$ while the record is located. The overall time required for the search will be:

$$\left(91.4 \times \frac{R}{2}\right) + \left(8.6 \times \frac{3R}{2}\right) = 0.586R \text{ per record on average}$$

If the records are stored on a 25-track cylinder, Table 6.4 indicates that 0.14 per cent of records will overflow from the cylinder, i.e. will not be held in a 250-record bucket. Although the tags will point to the required record addresses directly, accessing or retrieving these synonyms requires a head movement of at least one cylinder. Assume that the time to move from one cylinder to the next is the same as the rotation time of the device, which applies for some disk devices. This will mean an increase in the average access time of $0.0014R$. Thus the total average access time is:

$$(0.586 + 0.0014)R = 0.5874R$$

Comparing the techniques in practice

It might appear that chaining or tagging would always be preferable to the simpler system of storing records in the next available position. In practice they do not always turn out so much better, for a number of reasons. These include the following:

1. When records are stored in the next available position (i.e. using consecutive spill), no extra space is required for chain or tag fields.
2. Manufacturers' software is usually available for a SEARCH ON KEY operation throughout a whole cylinder. The search for a required record can start on the home track and continue until the record is located. There need be no holdup due to consecutive spill storage, however short. By comparison, following a chain or tag involves reading the link field, finding the key in it, picking up the address and searching for it. This will be carried out at primary storage speeds, but will still take time, often due to lost device revolutions. A home track and a track holding synonyms will appear as shown in Fig. 6.16.

Examining chained records first, tracks with spare space for the storage of synonyms often have room for a number of records, as is clear from Fig. 6.14. Tracks that have overflowed during the original file load will not have any synonyms from other tracks present on them, which explains the likely track formats shown in Fig. 6.16. In some cases members of the chain may directly follow each other on a track holding synonyms. This could cause the loss of a whole revolution for each member of the chain, because the processing of the link field might take long enough to miss the start of the next record. This would happen as shown in Fig. 6.17.

The tagged records case is straightforward. The tag is picked up at the end of a track and the synonym will also, on average, be at or near the end of a track, not in the middle. For this reason the time required to pick up the tagged record may be rather more than $R/2$. This depends on the manufacturers' software. Sometimes the start of a track has to be sensed before processing of the data stored on it can begin. This will lead to delays. In some systems, tag or chain link fields are stored at the start of a track, which will reduce delays caused for this reason.

Lum et al.[7] investigated the performance of a number of large files, and the author has analysed their results further[16]. Fig. 6.18 shows a plot of Lum

Direct file organization **191**

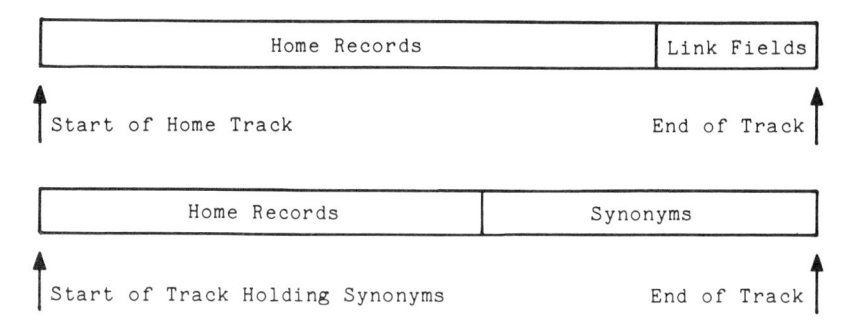

```
┌─────────────────────────────────┬──────────────┐
│         Home Records            │ Link Fields  │
└─────────────────────────────────┴──────────────┘
↑                                                ↑
Start of Home Track                    End of Track

┌─────────────────────────────┬──────────────────┐
│        Home Records         │     Synonyms     │
└─────────────────────────────┴──────────────────┘
↑                                                ↑
Start of Track Holding Synonyms        End of Track
```

Fig. 6.16 Possible situations on tracks holding home records only, and those holding both home and synonym records.

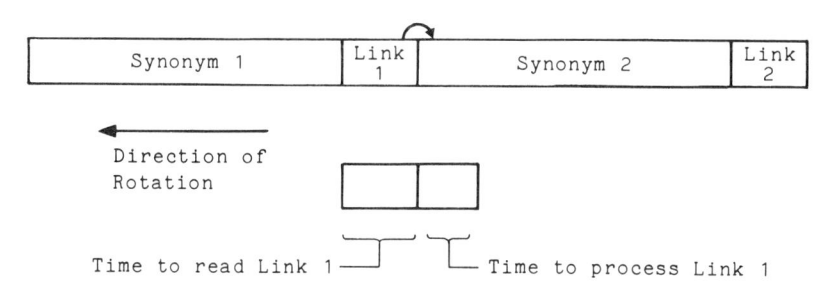

```
┌──────────────┬──────┬──────────────┬──────┐
│  Synonym 1   │ Link │  Synonym 2   │ Link │
│              │  1   │              │  2   │
└──────────────┴──────┴──────────────┴──────┘

     ←───────────
     Direction of
     Rotation

     Time to read Link 1 ──┘  └── Time to process Link 1

Synonym 2 is just missed due to link processing
```

Fig. 6.17 Processing chained records. Synonym 2 is just missed due to link processing, so one full revolution is lost. This can be avoided by careful handling of synonyms, but adds complexity to the processing.

et al.'s figures on the basis of average accesses per retrieval; it appears from the curves that consecutive spill is only useful for larger bucket sizes, but the figures are misleading, as the chained overflow was to a separate file area, necessitating head movement. Table 6.6 shows the very different results obtained when the actual time required for each retrieval, including head movements, is used to calculate break-even points, rather than average accesses per retrieval.

Although most of the work reported in the literature has examined chaining to a separate overflow area[6, 7, 25], this is not the most effective way of using chaining. If records are stored in the next available position in the prime data area—the consecutive spill method—but a link field is provided from the home record or from the last synonym, this avoids unnecessary head movements and cuts down the search time required for the consecutive spill techniques. Table 6.7 compares the additional times added to an average record seek due to consecutive spill (for files using mid-square and division randomizing techniques), chained overflow in a separate area and chained overflow in the prime data area.

Table 6.6 Results entered in this table are packing densities. The break-even column based on average numbers of accesses shows the packing densities above which chained overflow in a separate area appears to be more efficient than consecutive spill, if actual timings are not taken into account[7]. The actual times column presents the break-even points if actual head movement and rotation times are used[16]. The results were obtained with 240-character records on IBM 3330 disk drives.

Records per bucket	Break-even (average numbers of accesses)	Break-even (actual timings)
1	Below 0.5	0.80–0.85
2	Below 0.5	0.85
5	0.6	0.85–0.90
10	0.8	0.90–0.95
20	0.9	0.90–0.95
50	0.96	Above 0.95

The results tabulated here show that, for low packing densities, the most effective technique is generally chained overflow. At higher packing densities a separate overflow area may be useful for small bucket sizes, while chained overflow in the prime data area remains best for large bucket sizes.

Choosing an overflow technique

Tagging is superior to chaining whenever it is feasible (see Appendix 6 for an analysis). Very large numbers of synonyms for even a few home addresses can make it impractical, however. The distribution of records produced by a given algorithm should be checked to see that this will not occur. If it is unavoidable, chaining should be employed (assuming, of course, that the packing density is too high, and bucket size too small, to make consecutive spill attractive).

In general, consecutive spill should be considered for low packing densities and/or very large bucket sizes. In the intermediate range of these factors, chaining or tagging records stored in the prime file area is the most efficient solution, while at packing densities in excess of unity a separate overflow area will be required. Although many writers recommend it, it is seldom worth using such a separate overflow area when the packing density is below unity. The packing density referred to here is measured in terms of the total number of records, both in the prime and overflow areas, divided by the prime data storage capacity only.

Reducing the effect of synonyms on access times

The analysis of the last section has shown that synonyms will slow up direct access to records on average. The average figure means little in this case,

Direct file organization **193**

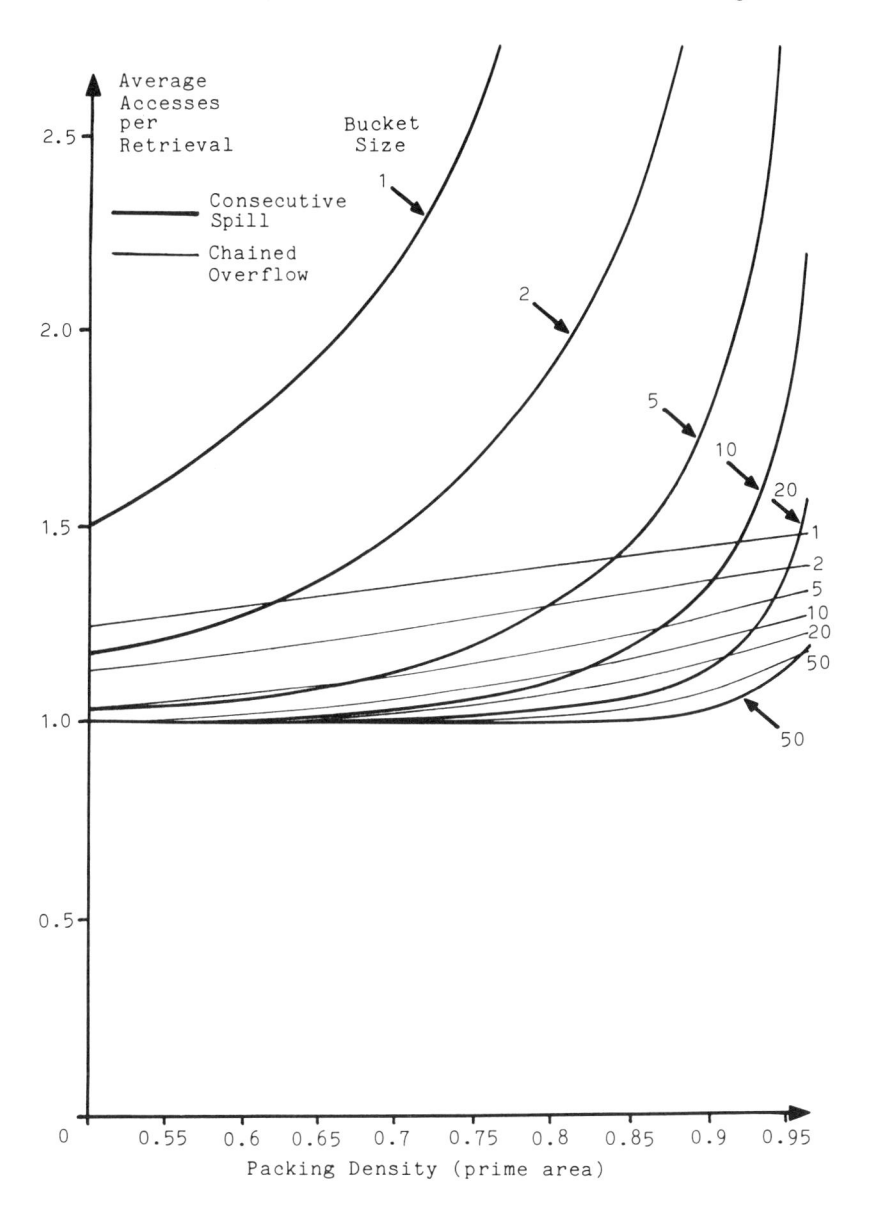

Fig. 6.18 Comparison of consecutive spill and chained overflow techniques.

Table 6.7 The figures tabulated show the average increases in seek time per access added to the retrieval time, as a result of using consecutive spill (for mid-square and division) or chained overflow (in prime area and separate area) in order to store synonyms. These increases are quoted in milliseconds and refer to 240-character records stored on an IBM 3330 disk drive. To obtain the overall average seek time, 38.3 ms must be added to each of these.

Packing density	Records per bucket	Mid-square	Division	Chained overflow separate area	Chained overflow prime area
0.75	1	4.87	3.45	5.67	3.43
	2	1.27	3.74	3.48	1.87
	5	0.74	1.08	2.01	0.54
	10	0.40	0.27	1.28	0.14
	20	0.33	0.17	0.55	0.09
	50	—	—	—	—
0.80	1	6.82	5.07	6.22	5.01
	2	2.86	6.10	4.76	3.05
	5	1.00	1.15	2.38	0.58
	10	0.67	0.53	1.46	0.27
	20	0.33	0.50	0.73	0.25
	50	—	—	0.18	—
0.85	1	11.59	6.83	7.50	6.68
	2	4.82	8.83	5.86	4.42
	5	1.63	5.34	3.66	2.67
	10	1.20	1.40	4.58	0.70
	20	1.17	1.34	5.31	0.67
	50	0.33	0.33	0.37	0.17
0.90	1	14.55	11.92	6.95	11.51
	2	8.81	6.04	5.49	3.02
	5	3.01	3.49	4.39	1.75
	10	1.96	2.14	2.93	1.07
	20	1.84	1.34	1.65	0.67
	50	1.00	0.33	0.55	0.17
0.95	1	20.34	13.80	7.50	13.09
	2	15.59	15.59	6.22	7.80
	5	7.13	12.88	4.58	6.44
	10	4.48	8.82	3.66	4.41
	20	4.84	4.18	3.11	2.09
	50	2.67	1.00	1.46	0.50

however. Access to home records only requires a single seek and search, just as in self-indexing files. This is increased for any synonym by at least half a revolution of the device. There are at least as many home records as synonyms in all circumstances (Table 6.5 shows that, even with 100 per cent packing and randomizing to individual record positions, 50 per cent of records are home records; with a two-pass load 63 per cent are home records). If all records are accessed equally frequently, the effect of any synonyms will be directly proportional to the figures in Table 6.4. However, this is a very unusual state of affairs. Normally, some records are accessed more frequently than others, and this tendency can be used to decrease average access time. The potential improvement in performance and ways of achieving that improvement after a two-pass load are discussed below.

Patterns of record access

A rule-of-thumb often used for updating is that '20 per cent of the records give rise to 80 per cent of the transactions'. It is certainly true that, in most applications, some records are processed far more frequently than others, and a number of commonly occurring distributions of update frequency are examined below.

1 *The 80/20 arrangement.* Assume that 20 per cent of the records are equally frequently accessed and give rise to 80 per cent of the total transactions. The remaining 80 per cent of the records are also equal in update frequency, but account in total for only 20 per cent of transactions.
2 *A smooth curve of accesses* in which some records are updated more regularly than others. The case shown in Fig. 6.20 is taken as an example of a very frequently met distribution (it is probable that the original 80/20 rule-of-thumb is based on a similar curve).
3 *A random distribution.* In this case a few records are updated very frequently, a few very seldom, and most records are updated more or less an average amount; the distribution is shown in Fig. 6.21.

This is not meant to be a comprehensive list of possible situations; the intention is to show how to tackle any distribution that occurs in practice. A limitation must be mentioned here. It is not possible to improve on equal access synonym handling in two cases. The first is when all records are equally likely to be accessed, i.e. there is no difference in access frequency to exploit. The second is when there is no permanent pattern. If a record that is updated or accessed frequently in one time period is likely not to be referenced at all in the next, any analysis breaks down and the equal access assumption is the best guide for design decisions. Usually there will be some random variation of this sort superposed on a relatively constant overall pattern. In examining the effect of the patterns defined above, random influences will be ignored.

Each of the three cases will be examined for 90 per cent packed files, randomized to individual record positions and to a bucket that can hold ten records.

1 The 80/20 case When 20 per cent of the records generate 80 per cent of the accesses to a file, and the file is loaded in a random order, the percentage of accesses to synonyms will be the same as the percentage of synonyms; if the file is 90 per cent packed and randomized to individual record storage positions, accesses to synonyms will be 34.063 per cent of all accesses.

If the 20 per cent of records that are most accessed are loaded first, the situation is quite different. As the file will be 90 per cent packed when it is fully loaded, 20 per cent of the records will occupy 18 per cent of the available storage addresses. This 'mini' file will have 8.483 per cent of synonyms, so that the 80 per cent of accesses made to these records will be split in the proportion of 91.517 home accesses to 8.483 synonym accesses.

When the whole file has been loaded, it will contain 34.063 per cent of synonyms. However, as the first fifth of the file (20 per cent) only contained 8.483 per cent of synonyms, the four-fifths of the file loaded later must have a higher average number of synonyms than 34.063 to bring the overall average to that figure. Let that higher number be y. Then:

$$(0.2 \times 8.483) + (0.8 \times y) = 1.0 \times 34.063$$
$$y = 40.458$$

Hence, the four fifths of the file loaded later contains 40.458 per cent of synonyms, and 59.542 per cent of home records; the 20 per cent of all accesses to the file that are to these records will therefore be split in this proportion. The total accesses to home and synonym records will thus be as follows:

	Home accesses	*Synonym accesses*
First 20% of records	91.517 × 0.8	8.483 × 0.8
Last 80% of records	59.542 × 0.2	40.458 × 0.2
Total accesses to records	85.122	14.878

By loading in access frequency order, the accesses to synonym records—and these are the records that slow up the average retrieval times of the file—have been cut from 34.063 per cent to 14.878 per cent. This reduces the effect of the synonyms to a figure that could have been achieved by choosing an initial packing density of just over 33 per cent for the file—but this file is 90 per cent packed.

Fig. 6.19 shows the improvement that can be achieved in 80/20 type files—those in which 80 per cent of the accesses are to 20 per cent of the records—for buckets holding one, two, three and four records over a wide range of

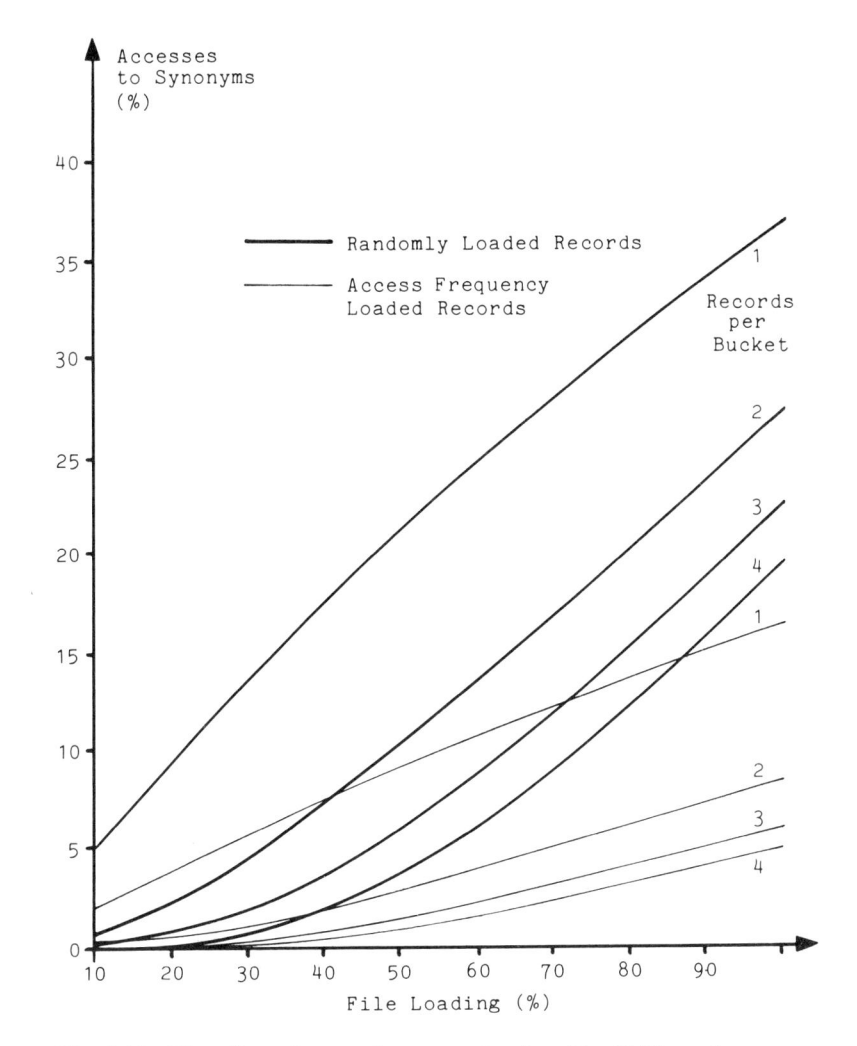

Fig. 6.19 The effect of access frequency loading (the 80/20 case).

packing densities, and Table 6.8 provides figures for a number of bucket sizes and packing densities.

These curves and figures apply only to the 80/20 case. A general expression to assess the potential improvement that *access frequency loading* can provide for any case in which A per cent of records account for B per cent of accesses is derived below. It should be made clear both that $(A+B)$ does not need to add up to 100—it is an unfortunate chance that the 80/20 or 90/10 'rules' are so well known—and that access frequency loading will only be of benefit when A is less than B. If A were greater than B, meaning that the *less* active records were loaded first, file access times would be poorer than those of randomly loaded files!

Table 6.8 The figures tabulated give the percentage of access that will be to synonyms after files with the bucket sizes shown are loaded in access frequency order. The calculations were carried out on the basis of the first 20 per cent of the records accounting for 80 per cent of all access.

Bucket size	\multicolumn{11}{c}{Packing density (%)}										
	50	55	60	65	70	75	80	85	90	95	100
1	8.95	9.75	10.53	11.29	12.03	12.77	13.48	14.19	14.88	15.56	16.22
2	3.04	3.54	4.05	4.58	5.11	5.65	6.20	6.75	7.30	7.86	8.41
3	1.57	1.93	2.32	2.74	3.18	3.63	4.10	4.58	5.08	5.57	6.08
4	0.95	1.24	1.56	1.92	2.30	2.72	3.15	3.60	4.07	4.55	5.04
5	0.62	0.85	1.13	1.44	1.79	2.17	2.58	3.02	3.48	3.95	4.44
10	0.11	0.20	0.32	0.49	0.72	1.00	1.33	1.72	2.15	2.62	3.13

The following symbols will be used in the derivation:

A is used for the per cent of records loaded first.
B is used for the per cent of accesses made to A (in total).
α is used for packing density.
r is used for bucket capacity.
S is used for synonym per cent.

Suffices of S are equations that will be evaluated in any given case to give a packing density, followed by r to indicate bucket size, so that the correct synonym percentage can be calculated or looked up.

The percentage of synonyms when A per cent of the file has been loaded is

$$S_{(A\alpha/100)r}$$

As these records have given rise to B per cent of accesses, the percentage of references to synonyms from these records will be

$$S_{(A\alpha/100)r} \times B/100 \qquad (6.19)$$

After the remaining records have been loaded, the percentage of synonyms in the whole file will be $S_{\alpha r}$. Of these:

$$\frac{AS_{(A\alpha/100)r}}{100}$$

had been loaded previously so:

$$S_{ar} - \frac{AS_{(A\alpha/100)r}}{100}$$

have arisen from $(100 - A)$ per cent of the records, and the percentage of synonyms in these later records is:

$$\left(S_{ar} - \frac{AS_{(A\alpha/100)r}}{100}\right) \frac{100}{(100 - A)}$$

These records will give rise to $(100 - B)$ per cent of the total accesses to the file. Thus the percentage of references to synonyms from these later loaded records will be:

$$\left(S_{ar} - \frac{AS_{(A\alpha/100)r}}{100}\right) \frac{100}{(100 - A)} \frac{(100 - B)}{100}$$

This simplifies to:

$$\left(S_{ar} - \frac{AS_{(A\alpha/100)r}}{100}\right) \frac{(100 - B)}{(100 - A)} \qquad (6.20)$$

Combining equations (6.19) and (6.20), the total accesses to synonyms will now be:

$$S_{ar}\left(\frac{100 - B}{100 - A}\right) + S_{(A\alpha/100)r}\left(\frac{B - A}{100 - A}\right) \qquad (6.21)$$

For the case in which $A = B$ this equation simplifies to S_{ar}, as would be expected.

As $S_{(A\alpha/100)r} \to 0$, which is approximately true for large values of r, the value of equation (6.20) tends to

$$S_{ar}\left(\frac{100 - B}{100 - A}\right) \qquad (6.22)$$

This compares with the value S_{ar} if records are stored in random order. Division of equation (6.22) by S_{ar} to show the improvement expected after access frequency loading, yields $(100 - B)/(100 - A)$, i.e. the general equation of which the value $\frac{1}{4}$ for the 80/20 case is an example.

When A per cent of records that give rise to B per cent of accesses is loaded first, the improvement obtained tends to $(100 - B)/(100 - A)$ as $S_{(A\alpha/100)r} \to 0$.

Table 6.8 shows the percentage of accesses to synonyms to be expected for various bucket sizes, in the 80/20 case.

Many situations cannot be handled on the basis of 'A per cent of records give rise to B per cent of accesses'. For this reason two other common situations are analysed here.

200 Design of computer data files

2 A smooth access curve Fig. 6.20 shows a histogram of records divided into nine groups of equal numbers. The most active group accounts for 43 per cent of accesses, the least active for 1 per cent. It is no longer enough to divide the records into two groups, and the analysis has been carried out on the nine separate groups of records responsible for 10 per cent, 20 per cent, 30 per cent . . ., 90 per cent packing.

As the calculations required in this case are complex, they have been set out in Appendix 8. The results show that a 90 per cent packed file of this type loaded in access frequency order into single record buckets will achieve a

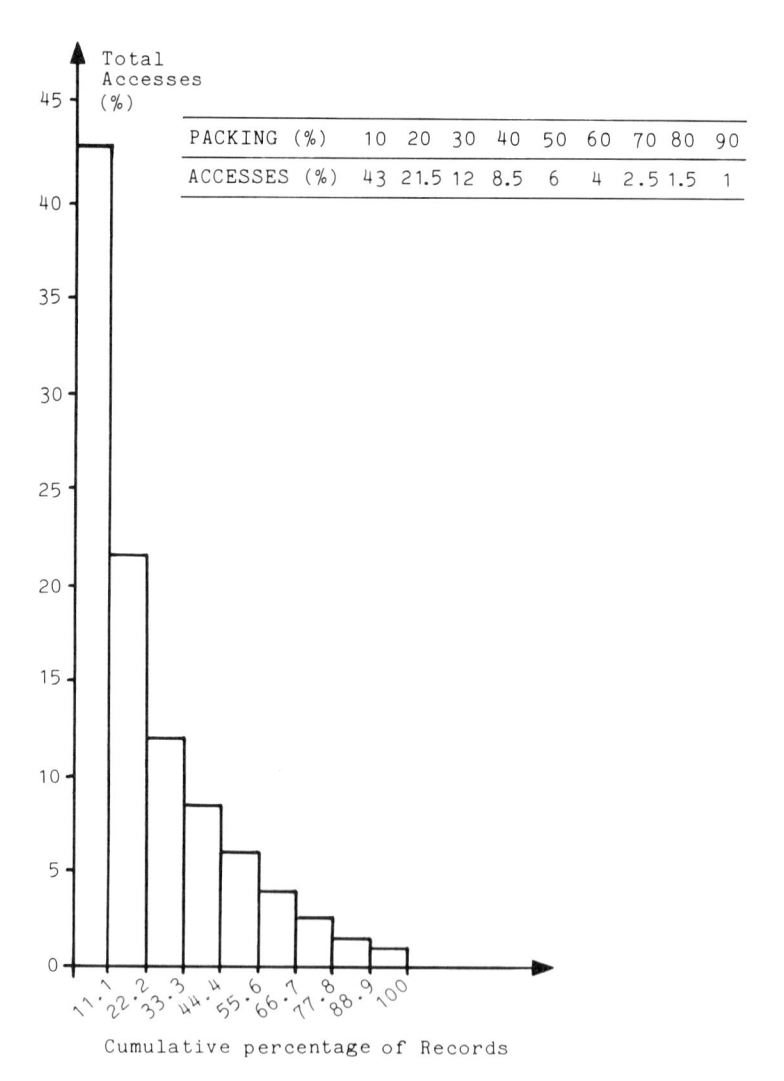

PACKING (%)	10	20	30	40	50	60	70	80	90
ACCESSES (%)	43	21.5	12	8.5	6	4	2.5	1.5	1

Fig. 6.20 A smooth curve of accesses, in which some records are updated more regularly than others.

Direct file organization **201**

reduction from 34.06 down to 16.63 per cent references to synonyms. If instead the file is loaded into ten-record buckets, the reduction is from 8.59 per cent down to 1.36 per cent.

3 A random distribution If the records are very variable in their number of accesses, but this variation is distributed about a mean value, a curve such as that in Fig. 6.21 occurs.

There is an average number of accesses during a specified period of about sixty-five. However, a small group of records have been accessed over 120 times, and another small group less than ten times. To analyse this, the

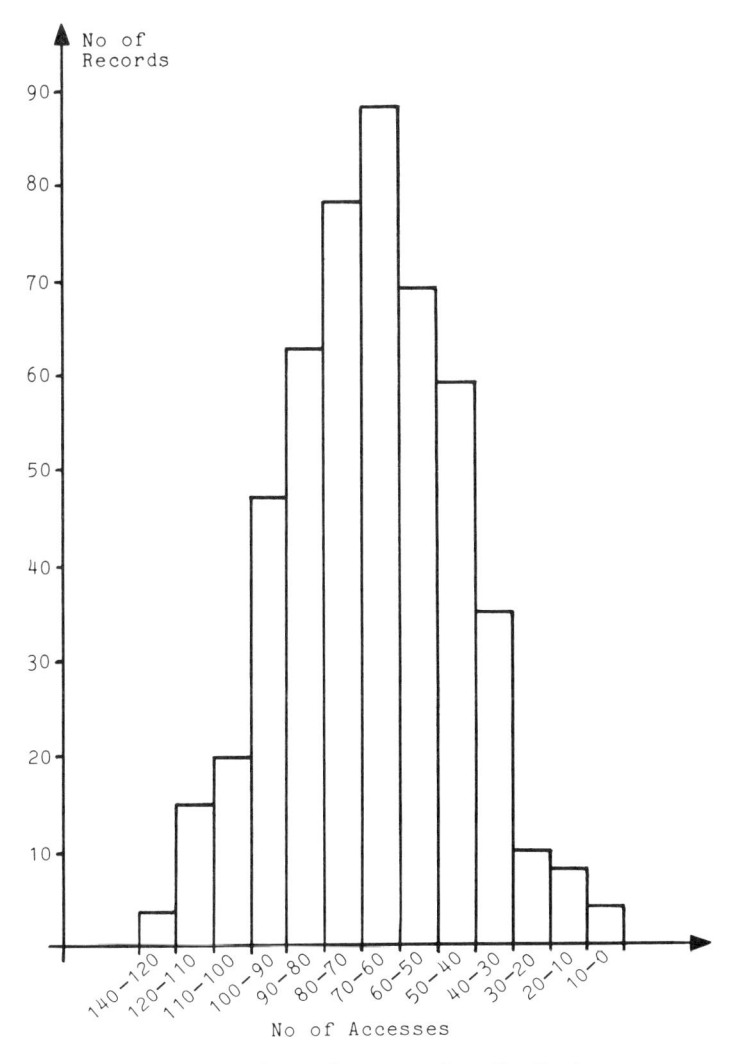

Fig. 6.21 Updating of records on a random distribution.

frequency curve in Fig. 6.22 (case 3) is constructed relating the percentage of accesses to the file to the percentage of records loaded at any cumulative percentage of records loaded, using the methods shown in Appendix 8.

From the case 3 curve we can decide on the percentage of accesses corresponding to the 10–90 per cent packing points, i.e. 11.1 per cent, 22.2 per cent, . . . of records. This can be used to calculate the required information; it turns out that the improvements that can be achieved by access frequency loading are to reduce accesses to synonyms from 34.06 per cent to 28.4 per cent for single–record buckets, and from 8.59 per cent to 4.90 per cent for ten-record buckets.

Assessment of possible improvement
The cumulative frequency curves for all three cases analysed earlier are shown in Fig. 6.22. The more to the left of and above the dashed straight line a curve is, the more potential exists for improvement. This can be seen by comparing the three cases discussed above with each other, and with the data for the 90/10 case, that has been included for comparison.

If in doubt as to the possible use of this technique, the user should collect enough data to plot a curve of this type. A visual check will indicate whether improvement can be expected, and will give some indication of its magnitude. In general terms, however, if there is a consistent access frequency pattern, this type of load will be of benefit. Even in the third case analysed above, the use of an access frequency load is equivalent to reducing the packing density of the file by nearly 20 per cent, or doubling the bucket size. This improvement can be achieved by collecting and using access data as explained on page 399.

Additions to access frequency loaded files
Additions to a file set up by loading in access frequency order will have a disproportionate effect on file access time; this is because they will be of at least average activity and often more, as new records tend to be very active, but are loaded into a densely packed file. A high proportion of them will be synonyms—if the file is 85 per cent packed, for example, 17 in every 20 would be expected to be synonyms—and this will lead to rapid deterioration of the file access speed.

The key figure here is the number of *seeks per access*. This will rise markedly as additions are made, and should be monitored frequently. The deterioration to be expected has been analysed by the author[15], and results for the 80/20 case are given here. Tables 6.9(a) and (b) shows the result of access frequency loading up to 20 per cent, 30 per cent, 40 per cent, 50 pcr cent, 60 per cent, 70 per cent, 80 per cent and 90 per cent packing, followed by additions of records of average activity until the file is 100 per cent loaded. The results are tabulated for ten-record buckets and single-record positions, and the rapid deterioration in both cases is very clear.

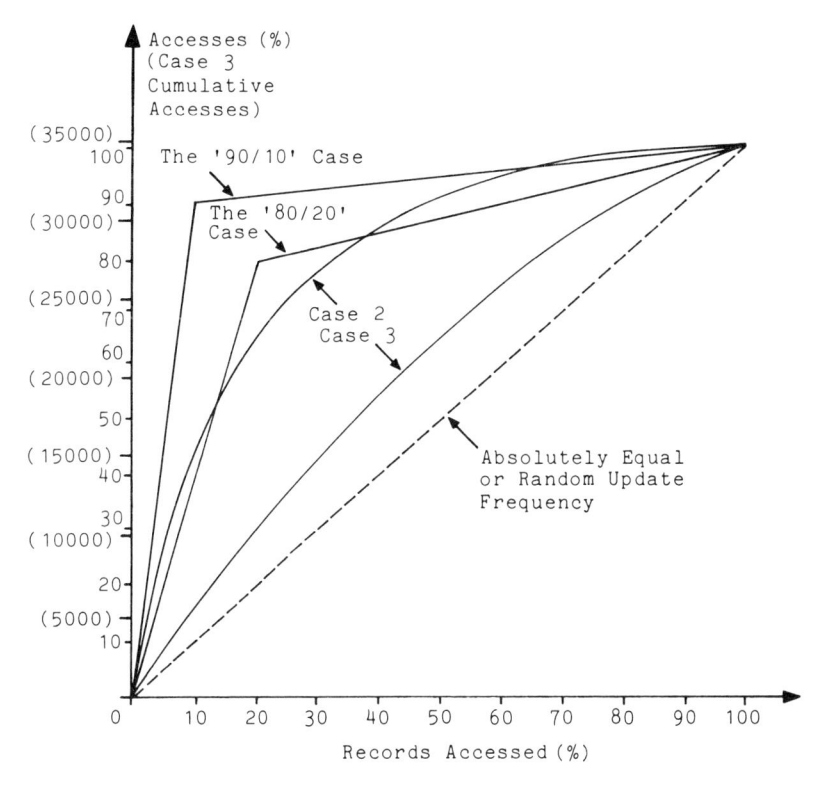

Fig. 6.22 Percentage of accesses to percentage of records for various cases.

Table 6.9(a) The result of adding records of average activity to 80/20 files that have previously been access-frequency loaded.

Random load from	\multicolumn{17}{c}{80/20, Single-record buckets}
	20	25	30	35	40	45	50	55	60	65	70	75	80	85	90	95	100
20	3.82	7.08	9.91	12.46	14.81	17.01	19.09	21.07	22.95	24.76	26.50	28.17	29.78	31.33	32.83	34.28	35.68
30		5.61	8.77	11.58	14.14	16.51	18.72	20.80	22.78	24.66	26.45	28.17	29.81	31.40	32.92	34.39
40			7.32	10.35	13.10	15.62	17.96	20.16	22.22	24.18	26.04	27.81	29.50	31.13	32.68
50				8.95	11.85	14.51	16.96	19.26	21.41	23.44	25.37	27.20	28.94	30.61
55					9.75	12.58	15.19	17.66	19.87	22.00	24.01	25.92	27.73	29.46
60						10.53	13.29	15.85	18.23	20.46	22.56	24.55	26.43	28.22
65							11.29	13.99	16.49	18.83	21.03	23.10	25.06	26.92
70								12.03	14.67	17.12	19.42	21.58	23.62	25.55
75									12.77	15.34	17.74	20.00	22.12	24.13
80										13.48	15.99	18.34	20.55	22.64
85											14.19	16.64	18.94	21.11
90												14.88	17.27	19.52
95													15.56	17.90
Fully access-frequency loaded														16.22

Table 6.9(b) The result of adding records of average activity to 80/20 files that have previously been access-frequency loaded.

Random load from	\multicolumn{15}{c}{80/20, Ten-record buckets}
	30	35	40	45	50	55	60	65	70	75	80	85	90	95	100
30	0.00	0.03	0.09	0.22	0.44	0.78	1.28	1.97	2.87	3.99	5.32	6.86	8.59	10.48	12.51
40			0.03	0.16	0.39	0.73	1.24	1.93	2.83	3.95	5.29	6.83	8.56	10.45	12.48
50					0.11	0.48	1.01	1.72	2.64	3.77	5.11	6.67	8.41	10.31	12.34
55						0.20	0.75	1.48	2.41	3.56	4.92	6.48	8.23	10.14	12.19
60							0.32	1.08	2.05	3.22	4.60	6.18	7.95	9.87	11.93
65								0.49	1.49	2.70	4.11	5.72	7.52	9.47	11.54
70									0.72	1.98	3.44	5.09	6.91	8.90	11.00
75										1.00	2.52	4.22	6.10	8.12	10.27
80											1.33	3.10	5.04	7.12	9.32
85												1.72	3.73	5.88	8.14
90													2.15	4.38	6.71
95														2.62	5.04
Fully access-frequency loaded															3.13

206 Design of computer data files

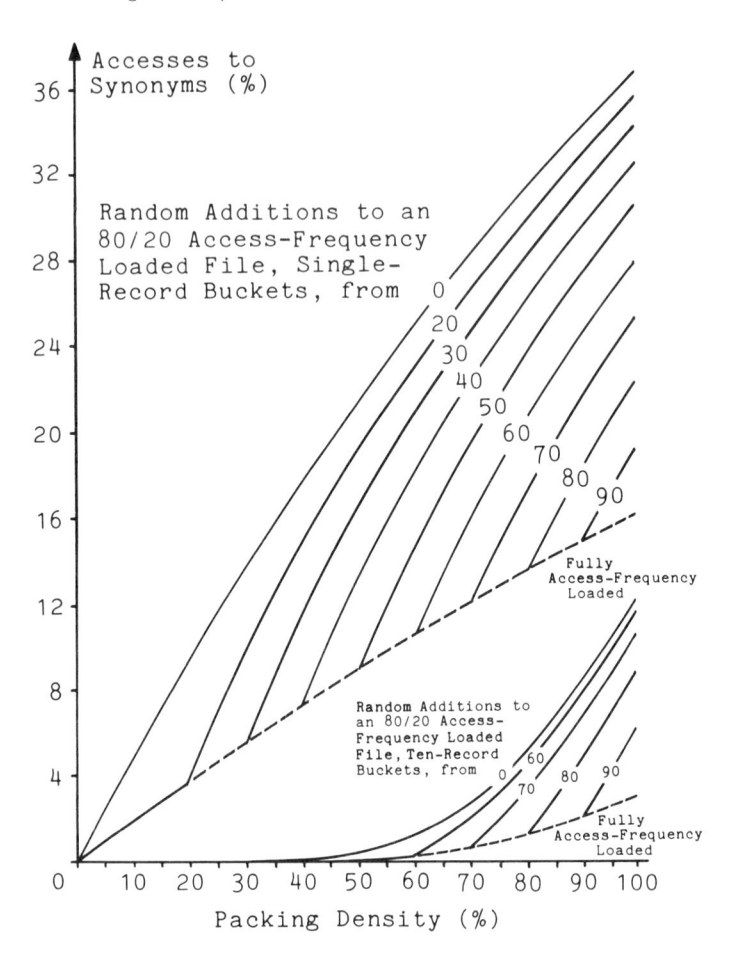

Fig. 6.23 The effect of bucket size and the packing density from which random additions are made on the performance of access frequency loaded files.

Fig. 6.23 shows the results of additions of average access frequency to an access frequency loaded file. The dashed curves trace the results of a full access frequency load to 100 per cent packing, while the unbroken curves show the effect of adding records of average activity from the packing densities set into each curve. In reality, as pointed out above, these curves are likely to represent a 'best' case, as additions to a file are usually new customers, products, personnel, etc. and tend to be highly active, while they also have a high probability of being synonyms.

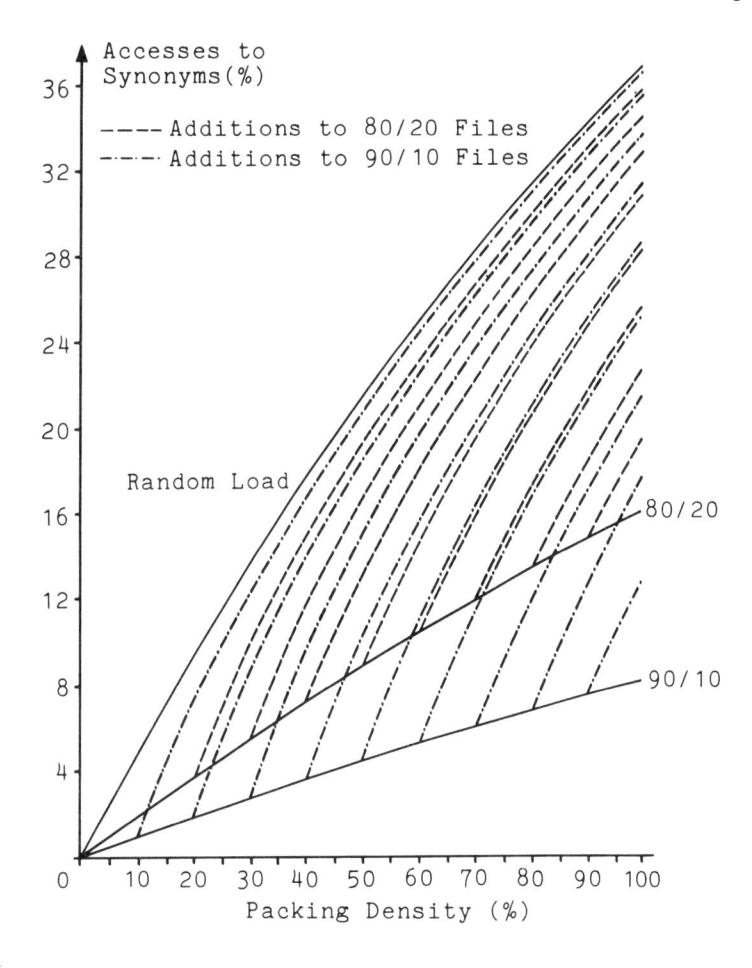

Fig. 6.24 The effect of making random additions to access frequency loaded files with differing degrees of asymmetry in their access frequency distributions.

Fig. 6.24 superposes the deterioration of access frequency loaded 90/10 files as a result of loading additional records in random order, on to an 80/20 file loaded in the same way. The dashed and dotted curves do not intersect, which makes it clear that the rate of deterioration caused by adding records of average activity to an access frequency loaded file is only dependent on the starting point of the random load, and not on the particular file access situation, such as 90/10, 85/25, etc.

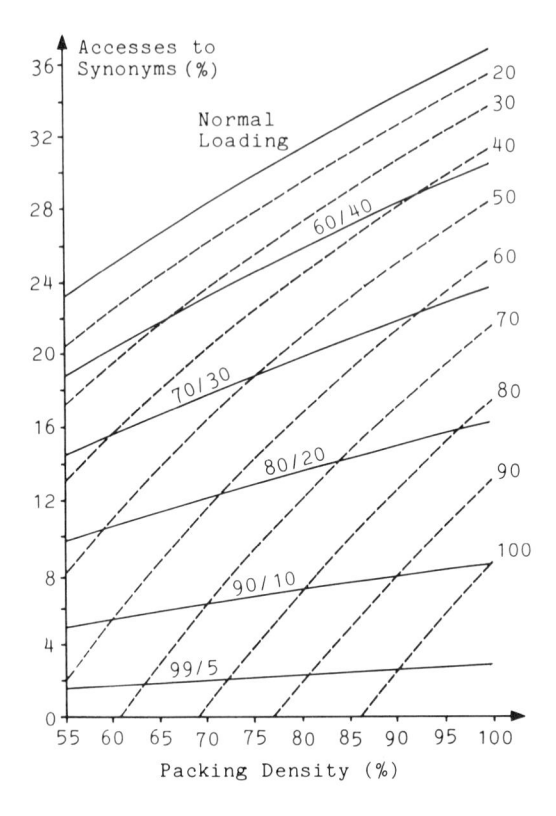

Fig. 6.25 Single-record buckets.

The situation has been explored in detail by the author[15], and Figs 6.25 and 6.26 are taken from that paper. They provide the file designer with reference charts for buckets of size one and ten records, and can be used to predict the rates of deterioration of any access frequency loaded file using the given bucket sizes. The unbroken curves show the improvements due to loading files with asymmetries in access frequency of 60/40, 70/30, 80/20, 90/10 and, for single-record buckets, 99/5. These are provided for convenience, but the designer can use the charts from *any* point, and the slope of the broken lines indicates the rate of deterioration to be expected. Similar curves for buckets holding 2, 3, 4 and 5 records are given in Appendix 1.

The figures against the broken lines correspond to the packing percentages from which a 90/10 case file has received random additions. The broken curve shows the percentages of access to synonyms as more random additions are made, demonstrating how rapid the degradation is.

In this section we have seen that it is usually possible to reduce the number of accesses to synonyms by loading first the records most frequently accessed. In cases where a small number of records is accessed very

Direct file organization 209

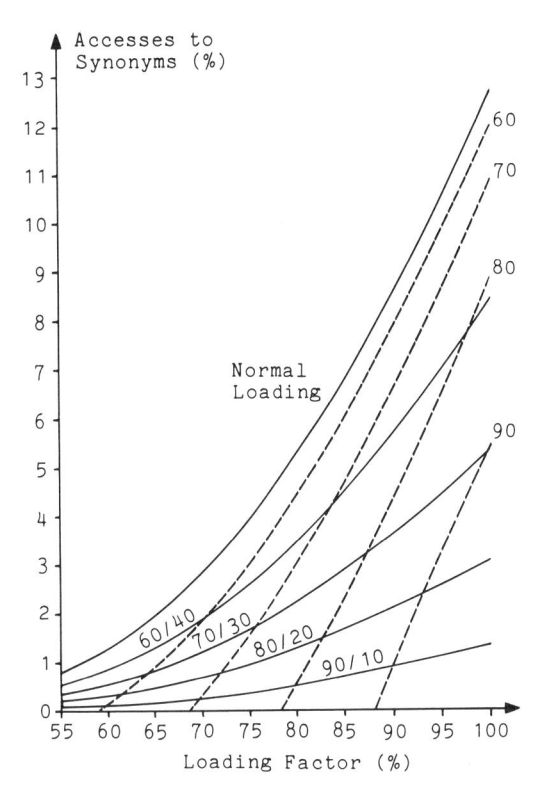

Fig. 6.26 Ten-record buckets.

frequently, the saving is marked, and may even be dramatic. When a file is first set up it may not be possible to load in most frequently accessed order. The savings that can be made usually justify the collection of statistics during the life of the file, and some ways of arranging this are described in the next section.

6.7 Practical considerations in setting up direct files

Preparing a device for a direct file

Self-indexed files will need little or no prior formatting of the direct access device on which they are to be stored. It is essential to ensure that every storage position has been initialized, or at least to remove any data remaining from previous uses of the device. In every other respect the file load will be a normal—and sequential—operation, except that some positions may be left vacant to retain the address/key relationship.

When files are randomly organized using an algorithm, the device must first be initialized to remove all prior data. If this were not done, data from previous files might still be present in addresses to which records were not allocated. If the records are to be stored in full track buckets, no formatting is required as the track address is available at all times. However, if the records are to be stored in individual address positions, the addresses and record storage positions have to be created before the file is loaded. This applies both for single-record positions and for buckets that are only part of a track in size.

Some manufacturers provide pre-formatted buckets of various sizes on a track. In this case the user only needs to specify the bucket size required from the alternatives provided, as the formatting and addressing have already been carried out by the manufacturer. However, it is then often necessary to read a whole bucket into primary storage at a time; it is not possible to search the bucket and read in only the required record, but this does not apply if a device such as ICL's CAFS-ISP is available to speed up the search. Some manufacturers provide a capacity record at the start of a track, used to indicate whether space remains on the track during loading. If this is not provided, the user will need to set up an equivalent record.

The load process will be:

1 Decide on the bucket size required.
2 Initialize the file area on the direct access device.
3 Pre-format the file area by setting up dummy records of individual record or bucket size, to provide all the addresses within the range that the address algorithm can generate.
4 Load the file.

File statistics

In order to get the best possible performance from a direct file, information is required. Run times will give an indication that reorganization is due; access data will allow more efficient processing; service times will indicate the effect of user demand or the need for file reorganization; a log of the number of sequential processing runs required may point to the use of ancillary files or a different file organization technique. We shall look at each of these in turn.

Run times

The basic criterion for the need to reorganize a direct file is that the number of seeks per access has risen appreciably. When a direct file is being processed on its own, the run times for the file will point to this. A predetermined figure should be set, and when this is reached the file should be reorganized. This situation may come about in several ways. First, the file may be growing. If new records are added faster than old records are deleted, the packing of the file will get higher; as we saw earlier in the chapter, this will cause more synonyms. Second, the randomizing algorithm may be becoming less useful due to some pattern in new record keys. Third, many of the new records will have become synonyms; if they are relatively frequently accessed this may cause a marked increase in run times. Van der Pool[30] described what he called the 'ageing' process in direct files, pointing out that performance degrades over time due to additions, even if the packing density does not change.

Usually a direct file will be one of a number of files being processed at any time. In this case the manufacturer's operating system may be used to keep track of the file run-time. It is helpful to keep a count of references to home and synonym records. This can be held in main storage during processing and be printed out on the log or stored in a file label area at the end of the run. A figure for the ratio of seeks required per access should be specified on the basis of the design criteria used, and the file should be reorganized when this figure is exceeded.

Access data

It was shown on page 195 that knowing how frequently a record is accessed can lead to reduced seek times. Usually we do not have this information when a file is set up. There are two ways in which it can be provided for in later reorganizations of the file. The first is to have a count field in each record, and increment it each time the record is accessed. This has the advantage that records can be sorted into descending count order for loading during reorganization.

When records are being updated during the run, and so have to be written back on to the device after they have been read into main storage, this method involves no loss of time. However, if records are only being referred to, the position is different. A half-revolution would be lost for every record, just to update the count field. In this case a second method of gathering access data is preferable. It is to set up an ancillary file with the records in sequential key order and each record consisting only of a count field. This file will be very small and, if indexed, it will usually match the access speed of a larger direct file because it can be held on a single cylinder of disk, with its index in main storage.

When the master file is to be reorganized, this ancillary file will be sorted into descending count order, and the records are read from the old direct file and loaded on to the new in this order. The resulting master file will be in access frequency order.

Access data is only useful when records remain relatively constant in their activity. This often happens, as large customers will always remain more 'active' than small customers, and some lines of stock are consistently required more frequently than others. In other cases it is not true; for example, a flight will be available in an airline booking system long before it takes place. At first, bookings will be few, then they will increase, and after the flight date the record will vanish. Statistics of overall popularity of flights will help in planning, but the profile of interest in any one flight will vary with time.

However, some flights will naturally be more likely to be accessed than others. A Boeing 747 flight between London and New York will always be a candidate for a home position. A DC9 or BAC 111 cannot hold so many passengers and would tend to be loaded later. Naturally, if a small aircraft is overbooked consistently, it might rate early loading. In that case, it would also be likely to merit a larger aircraft.

In some cases no clear pattern emerges. Then it may not be possible to load records in any predetermined order, and lower packing densities and changes in bucket size or type of algorithm may be needed to give an acceptable performance.

Service times
The access times considered in this chapter have been simply the time taken to position the device access mechanism to read or write a selected record. In practice this is not complete, since two additional times need to be considered in order to obtain the true picture.

The first of these is the *data transfer time*. This depends mainly on the size of the record and the operating speeds of the direct access device in question. For example if the records took up half a track on a device with a rotation time of 25 ms (2400 rpm) then the data transfer would take about 12.5 ms.

The second is the time taken from the moment a record is requested by the program to the time when accessing and transfer takes place, known as *wait time* or *queue time*. This may be zero, though in multi-programming or multi-tasking it is likely to be finite. For example, if the direct file were being used by an on-line system there could be several concurrent terminal tasks at any one time using the file, and queues would then develop. Indeed, some operating systems are geared to handling queues by offering the user a choice of queuing algorithm.

If the accesses on a file are completely random, it is often sensible to sort the accesses into cylinder address sequence and minimize individual seek times. Input or output requests to a file are queued by the operating system and then sorted into sequence before any operations commence. Updating of a direct file by sorting a batch of update records into their physical order *after* using the algorithm, and so avoiding the typical random sequence of seeks, can provide rapid 'sequential' batch updating. This has been discussed by Nijssen[26].

Type of processing
Some files may be predominantly processed directly, but occasionally be processed sequentially. If a file is self-indexed, this presents no problem. If it has been randomized, then the process has to be reversed. A list of keys in sequential order is fed into the program and the keys are transformed into addresses in the usual way. Every synonym will need to be accessed, so no benefit will be derived from the order in which the records were loaded.

This may mean that a file which operates well under normal conditions, i.e. many home records being accessed but few synonyms, may take a relatively long time to process sequentially. In such a case it can pay to set up an ancillary file when the file is loaded. This will be a sequential or indexed-sequential file, in key order, with the actual device address of each record as the data. This actual address will be identical with the key as transformed by the algorithm for home records, but will be different for synonyms, as the ancillary file used will allow *all* the records to be reached in a single seek, as if the file were self-indexed.

The use of such a file will eliminate extra searching for synonyms and may save a fair bit of time. It will need to be updated whenever the direct file is updated if the file is very volatile, and this may require the two files to be on-line together. If there are relatively few additions it may be updated in batch mode later. This latter case will favour the use of a sequential magnetic tape file. The former will tend to require an indexed sequential file on a direct access device.

Additions and deletions

Precautions have to be taken to avoid the possibility of excessively long search times or of failure to retrieve records held in a direct file. When a file has been newly loaded, a search for any record will allow it to be retrieved whether it is a home or a synonym record. Additions or deletions can change this situation. An addition may not be able to take up its home address, because it is already occupied by a synonym from some other address. Deletion of a home record may mean that, even though the home position is now free, a number of other records that originally randomized to that address are held as synonyms. Either of these cases may give the appearance that no home record exists for this address, and this situation will thus cause a 'no record found' error to be given, even though the desired record *is* in the file.

Thus, if the consecutive-spill method of handling synonyms has been used, a search may still be necessary even if no home record is detected when the home position is searched. The precautions that should be taken to avoid this situation were set out in the section on consecutive spill, page 186. If the chaining method is used, the lack of a home record will lead to the inability to retrieve any record further along the chain. Only the tagging method of handling synonyms is unaffected.

To avoid these problems, addition and deletion algorithms will have to ensure that at least *one* home record remains in any bucket to which *any* records randomize. When a record is added, this will involve storing it in its home address unless a home record is already in that address; a synonym from some other address would have to be moved to make way for it. When a home record is deleted, any synonym that is stored elsewhere, or the first if there are more than one, should be placed in the home address to take the place of the original home record. This is particularly important if records are handled by chaining.

This system, which is discussed in detail by Montgomery and Wallace[27], leads to a fairly high number of accesses required to retrieve records from a *well-aged file*, i.e. one that has had a large number of additions or deletions since it was last loaded. A stricter file housekeeping discipline, requiring that every home record possible is stored in home addresses, was analysed theoretically by Johnson[28]. This requires that when a record is added to the file it is stored in its home bucket if *any* record that is a synonym is at present in the home bucket, and that if space becomes available in a bucket, any synonym that randomizes to the bucket in which space is now available is moved into the home bucket.

The predictions made by Johnson[28] were tested by simulation studies[27], which showed that even for a 100 per cent packed file, if the discipline he recommended is adhered to, the average number of accesses can be kept down to 1.5 per retrieval, and for larger bucket sizes this is reduced to around 1.25. Despite the extra work involved in moving records about to ensure that all possible records are held in their home addresses, compared with the less restrictive requirement of at least one home record discussed earlier, this stricter file housekeeping pays off when retrievals outnumber additions and deletions. This is the usual case, but if it turns out that a particular file is very volatile the less restrictive system should be used.

The most appropriate bucket size

The optimum bucket size to minimize the time taken by operations carried out on a file depends on the nature of the operation. When retrievals and updating predominate, which is the usual situation, the optimum bucket size[27] is as small as possible. This means a single sector for sector-oriented devices, or one record per bucket in systems that allow the user to choose any bucket size within the capacity of the device. This does not invalidate the earlier comment that a full-track bucket is advantageous, so long as records are *randomized* to a full track but *stored* in single-record format on the track.

If additions and deletions are more numerous than retrievals and updates, it turns out that the larger the proportion of additions, the larger the bucket size that provides the minimum number of accesses per reference to the file[29]. This is a result of the very much larger number of accesses required to find spare space for an addition, in comparison with those required to locate a record already in the file. (This only applies for files that are relatively fully loaded; a 50 per cent packed file would require approximately equal numbers of accesses for addition and reference.) However, even if additions make up most of the processing carried out on the file, it appears that bucket sizes small in comparison with a full track give optimal results. The full-track bucket, but single-record storage, remains a good option in this case.

Conclusion

Direct files have been used less than might be expected in data processing. There is certainly a security problem, in that arranging for security and integrity of data is more complex by comparison with sequential files and this, coupled with their poor performance for sequential applications, makes it obvious why they are not used if a sequential file is appropriate. It is equally true that they are not as suitable for a truly mixed sequential-direct application as indexed sequential files. However, for enquiry systems with no sequential requirement, or when that requirement is minimal, a well-designed direct file will outperform a well-designed indexed-sequential file, often very substantially.

The probable reason that indexed sequential files are so often used when direct files would perform better is the ready availability of software. Direct files require extensive design work, because every file and every algorithm will differ slightly from every other. This means that manufacturers' software can only provide the more basic requirements such as GET and PUT macros and record-formatting software. Randomizing algorithms are sometimes provided, but it is generally wise for the user to allocate and test them for each file on an individual basis. This chapter has shown the steps that can be taken to ensure that a direct file is optimized, and if the file designer follows the rules laid down here, good results should be obtained in almost any situation. The choice between indexed sequential and direct files is examined in Chapter 9, and security of direct files in Chapter 10.

References

1. 'Reciprocal hashing: a method for generating minimal perfect hashing functions', by G. Jaeschke, *CACM*, Vol. 24, No. 12, December 1981, pp. 829–833.
2. 'Minimal perfect hash functions made simple', by R. J. Cichelli, *CACM*, Vol. 23, No. 1, January 1980, pp. 17–19.
3. 'Perfect hashing functions; a single probe retrieval method for static sets', by R. Sprugnoli, *CACM*, Vol. 20, No. 11, November 1977, pp. 841–850.
4. 'Note on random addressing techniques', by W. P. Heising, *IBM Systems Journal*, June 1963, pp. 112–116.
5. *A First Course in Mathematical Statistics*, by C. E. Weatherburn, Cambridge University Press, 1952.
6. 'File organization and addressing', by Werner Buchholz, *IBM Systems Journal*, June 1963, pp. 86–111.
7. 'Key to address transform techniques: a fundamental performance study on large existing formatted files', by V. Y. Lum, P. S. T. Yuen and M. Dodd, *CACM*, April 1971, pp. 228–239.
8. 'Ordered hash tables', by O. Amble and D. E. Knuth, *Computer Journal*, Vol. 17, No. 2, May 1974, pp. 135–142.

9. *Order-preserving Dynamic Hashing Schemes for Associative Searching in Data Base Systems*, by Mohamed Ouksel, University Microfilms International, Ann Arbor, Michigan, USA, 1985.
10. 'Order-preserving key transformations', by A. K. Garg and C. C. Gotlieb, *ACM Trans. on Database Systems*, Vol. 11, No. 2, June 1986, pp. 213–234.
11. 'An improved hash code for scatter storage', by W. D. Maurer, *CACM*, Vol. 11, No. 1, January 1968, pp. 35–44.
12. 'The quadratic quotient method: a hash code eliminating secondary clustering', by James R. Bell, *CACM*, Vol. 13, No. 2, February 1970, pp. 107–109.
13. 'A practitioners guide to addressing algorithms', by D. Severance and R. Duhne, *CACM*, Vol. 19, No. 6, June 1976, pp. 314–326.
14. *Structured Information Files*, by R. A. Kaimann, Melville, 1973.
15. *Improving the Efficiency of Randomly Organized Files by Loading in Access Frequency Order*, by O. J. Hanson, City University Business School, Working Paper No. 7, obtainable from the Librarian, The City University, London.
16. 'Handling overflows in direct files', by O. J. Hanson, *Proc. 8th Australian Computer Conference*, Camberra, 1978, Vol. 2, pp. 668–680.
17. 'Dynamic hashing schemes—a review of recent developments', by R. Sacks-Davis, G. Gupta and K. Ramamohanarao, *Proc. 1st Pan-Pacific Computer Conference*, Melbourne, September 1985, Vol. 1, pp. 203–215.
18. 'Bounded index exponential hashing', by David B. Lomet, *ACM Trans. on Database Systems*, Vol. 8, No. 1, March 1983, pp. 136–165.
19. 'Look it up faster with hashing', by Jon C. Snader, *Byte*, January 1987, Vol. 12, No. 1, pp. 129–144.
20. 'Scatter storage techniques', by Robert Morris, *CACM*, Vol. 11, No. 1, January 1968, pp. 38–44.
21. *File Techniques for Data Base Organization in Cobol*, by L. F. Johnson and R. H. Cooper, 2nd edn., Prentice Hall International, 1986.
22. 'The effect of one-pass loading on direct files', by Owen Hanson, *Proc. 11th Australian Computer Conference*, Sydney, November 1984, pp. 213–222.
23. *An Evaluation of the Various Parameters Affecting the Design of Direct Access Files*, by M. Yaffe, MSc Dissertation, 1982, available from the Librarian, The City University, London.
24. *One- and Two-Pass Loading of Direct Files*, by R. Cardoz, MSc. Dissertation, 1984, available from the Librarian, The City University, London.
25. 'Optimum storage allocation for initial loading of a file', by J. A. van der Pool, *IBM J. Res. Develop.*, November 1972, pp. 579–586.
26. 'Index sequential versus random', by G. M. Nijssen, *IAG Journal*, Vol. 5, No. 3, 1971, pp. 29–37.
27. 'Evaluation and design of random access files', by A. Y. Montgomery and C. S. Wallace, *Proc. 5th Australian Computer Conference*, Brisbane, 1972.
28. 'An indirect chaining method for addressing on secondary keys', by

L. R. Johnson, *CACM*, Vol. 14, No. 5, May 1961, pp. 218–222.
29. 'Algorithms and performance evaluation of a new type of random access file organisation', by A. Y. Montgomery, *Australian Computer Journal*, Vol. 6, No. 1, March 1974.
30. 'Optimum storage allocation for a file in steady state', by J. A. van der Pool, *IBM J. Res. Develop.*, January 1973, pp. 27–38.

Revision questions

1 What is meant by self-indexing files? Explain the advantages and drawbacks of organizing a file in this way, illustrating your answer with appropriate figures.

2 What relationships between key and address allow a self-indexing file to be created?

3 Explain the functions of a randomizing algorithm. How do synonyms arise? Can they be avoided in a randomized file?

4 What methods of randomizing are you aware of? Describe and discuss each method you name.

5 Calculate the number of synonyms expected when

      15 records are randomized to 180 addresses
      150 records are randomized to 180 addresses
      1500 records are randomized to 1800 addresses
      15 000 records are randomized to 18 000 addresses.

Use (a) the binomal theorem, (b) the Poisson distribution, (c) a one-pass load. Comment on the results you obtain.

6 Discuss the difference between one-pass and two-pass loading. Derive equations for the synonyms created in each case for single-record buckets.

7 What methods of storing synonyms are in common use? Describe how they operate, and explain their advantages and disadvantages. When would you use each method?

8 What is meant by access frequency loading? Explain how and why it improves some files but not others. Outline the data required to apply it, and the way that data can be obtained.

9 Compare the benefits of random and access frequency loading in a file that is 93 per cent packed, fourteen records to a bucket, and for which 21 per

cent of the records account for 82 per cent of the accesses. How does the file degrade as a result of continued random additions to 100 per cent loading?

10 Describe the way in which a file area is prepared to receive a direct file. How does this compare with the precautions needed for other file organizations?

11 Use the keys given on [page 165 of the Chapter] to test the effectiveness of using the remainder after division as a randomizing algorithm; divide by 37, 41, 43, and 101, and comment on the results you obtain.

12 Explain why you might expect division to perform better than a 'perfect' randomizing algorithm, and by how much. How is this affected by the ratio of key range to address range?

13 Why do you think that direct file organization is less used than some other file organization techniques? When would you strongly recommend it?

7 Indexed sequential files

7.1 Introduction

Sequential processing of data files makes up a large proportion of data processing. However, there is often a need to refer to sequential files just to answer one or relatively few enquiries. Such a need could be met by processing the whole file sequentially and looking for the records required, but this would be very inefficient. If the file is large the query may take some time to answer; meanwhile the computer is occupied processing unwanted records rather than doing useful work.

A second technique that greatly improves the speed of searching a sequential file is to use a logarithmic search. This method has been described in Chapter 5 on sequential files (see p. 119). It is very useful for a few enquiries but cannot handle a large number, as a series of storage device movements is involved in each search. Although technically possible on magnetic tape, logarithmic searches are too slow to be economic, so they are normally only considered for direct access devices. When the number of enquiries gets too large for a logarithmic search, or even some form of interpolation search, an indexing technique can be used to retrieve records more quickly.

The simplest form of index is one that holds the address of every record. This is called *full indexing* and provides a very rapid means of locating any given record. If the main file is large this index too will be large and there will be problems due to its size. For this reason one or more indexes may be used in a hierarchy, with the lowest-level index pointing to records while higher-level indices point to the index next below them. Because of the way in which direct access devices operate, it is not normally necessary or desirable for the lowest-level index to point to every record. Usually one record per track (IBM) or bucket (ICL) has an entry in the index. This is sometimes called *partial indexing*.

A sequential data file that is indexed is called an *indexed sequential file*. The facilities provided by this type of file usually include:

1. Rapid direct retrieval of records by the use of indexes;
2. Addition of records and subsequent sequential processing of them by the provision of overflow areas;

3 Deletion of records;
4 Statistics on the state of the file, giving warning when reorganization is necessary.

Properly used, such a file provides an excellent compromise between the extremes of sequential processing with very rare enquiries that is best handled by sequential files, and direct processing with very infrequent sequential processing, for which direct files are most suitable. It is not as efficient as either in their own fields, but performs very much better than they can in a situation where a significant enquiry facility is necessary and where the data is frequently processed sequentially. The precautions needed to ensure that such a file performs satisfactorily are discussed in the main body of this chapter.

7.2 File structure

An indexed sequential file generally has the following components.

1 A *data storage area*: this may include some unused space to allow for additions embedded in the data. It may also incorporate the lowest-level index elements.
2 A *separate index* or *indexes*: any enquiry will reference this index first; it will direct the enquiry to the part of the data file in which the desired record is stored.
3 An *optional separate overflow area*: the decision as to whether such an overflow area is required, and how best to allow for it, is considered later in this chapter.

These parts of the file are interrelated as shown in Fig. 7.1.

7.3 Indexes

General principles of indexing

It was stated above that full indexing—knowing the position of a record on a track—is seldom useful, because it does not usually speed up the search for that record. The read-write head reaches any track at a time which is 'random' in the sense that it is not possible to tell which part of the track will be reached first. This means that, even if a given address is known, it will be reached no more quickly than if only the track on which the record is stored is known. This may not always hold good. It is a result of the physical make-up of present access devices. The main case in which full indexing is useful is that in which individual records take up a whole track (in IBM terminology) or sufficient buckets or sectors (eight, fifteen or twenty-five in ICL 2900 series terms, depending on the disk in question) to fill a track completely.

Indexed sequential files 221

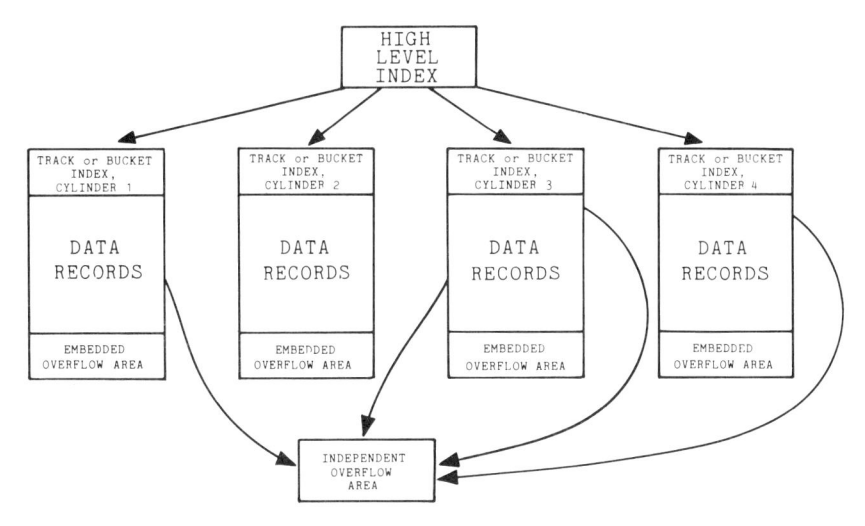

Fig. 7.1 Interrelationships between various parts of an indexed sequential file.

The search time can be overlapped by using rotational position sensing, however (see Chapter 2), and in this case the 'wasted' time can be used by some other operation or program. In this case, knowing the address of the individual record may be useful.

As most of the considerations discussed below do not depend on whether indexing is full or partial, the reader should assume from now on that partial indexing is being discussed. Exceptions will be pointed out as they arise.

All the common direct access devices, whether disk, semiconductor 'disk' or mass storage device, have a track concept that is important in deciding on the best arrangement of indexes. It is not possible to control the part of an index track that is read first. This means that, on average, half a revolution of the device is necessary before the desired entry is found. If the software writers arranged that the start of the track has to be detected before the search begins, this becomes a full revolution; this is made up of half a track to locate the start, and half a track for the search. When the desired entry is *not* on that track, these search figures become a full revolution and one-and-a-half revolutions respectively before it is clear that the record is not on the track, and the search must continue on a further track.

In designing a hierarchy of indexes, these figures are very useful. The following calculations assume that indexes are stored on a direct access device.

Let I_1 and I_2 both be higher-level indexes, and of these let index I_1 be the higher-level index, pointing to index I_2. Then the time to locate an address in I_2 will be:

(SEARCH I_1 + SEARCH I_2)

I_1 will only be created when it is quicker to search I_1 and then the track to

222 Design of computer data files

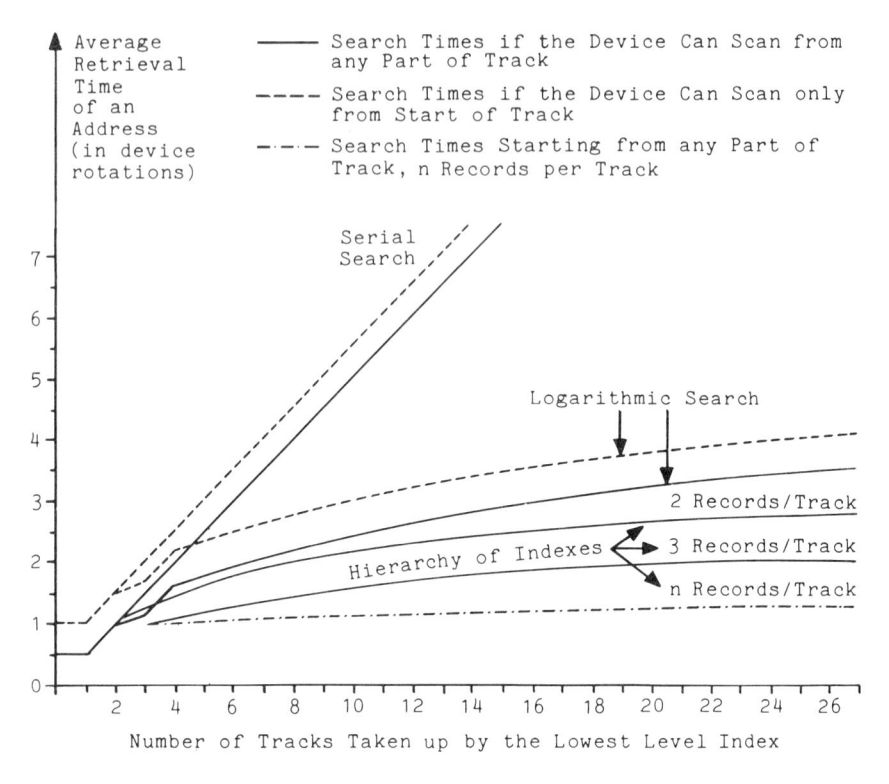

Fig. 7.2 The effect of index searching technique on the time required to find the track of the lowest-level index that has to be searched for a particular record.

which it points in I_2, than to carry out an average length search of I_2. Assume first that I_2 is one track or less in extent. In this case a search will take $R/2$ on average, when the time of rotation of the device is R. Each additional track will add a further $R/2$ to this. In the case where the start of the first index track searched has to be located before the search begins, a single-track index will require an average search time of R, but each additional track will again only add $R/2$. Total sequential search times for these cases are shown in Fig. 7.2.

When a higher-level index is first added, it can be expected to be less than one track in size. A search will therefore take the minimum time shown in Fig. 7.2. The higher-level index will point directly to the required track of the lower-level index, so this will also require the minimum search time. The break-even point is therefore two tracks if there is no requirement to seek the start of the track, or three tracks if there is. This shows that as soon as some part of a further track (over and above two or three respectively) is necessary for I_2, a higher-level index I_1 should be created. This process is repeated each time the highest-level index existing at that time requires a third or fourth track to be added.

The above discussion is based on a sequential search for index I_2. An alternative is to search using the logarithmic technique. This is not significant for less than three tracks, as it is effectively the same as a sequential search for one or two tracks. In the three-track case it is possible to search the *centre* track first. This must be a complete search to ensure that if the desired record is on the track it is found. If the record is not on the centre track the first or last track will be searched, depending on a comparison of the key being looked for with the highest key on the track. This will take R (or $3R/2$ if the start of the track has to be detected first) for the centre track, and $R/2$ for the other track searched.

There is a 1/3 chance that the desired record is on the centre track, and this brings the average search time to $(7/6)R$ (or $(10/6)R$ where the track start has to be located). These figures are similar to those for sequential searching, although the lower one is slightly better.

The logarithmic technique is not normally used because it requires an extra search for every power-of-two increase in the number of records, while a higher-level index only needs to be built when an index has reached three or four tracks in size. This means that an extra search will be added only for every additional $(2n+1)$ or $(3n+1)$ records, where n is the number of records per track. This can never be inferior to a logarithmic search (as n cannot be less than one) and is usually far superior. The effect is shown in Fig. 7.2 for several values of n. A number of types of index are in common use, and three of the most important are reviewed below.

Types of index

Balanced tree indexing Indexes are said to be of order e when there are e records per index entry, and of height h, where there are h levels of the index. A *tree index* is one in which the top level of the index, which is the one consulted first in a search for a record, points to lower levels of the index. This top level of the tree is often described as the *root index* of the tree, while the lower-level index items are equivalent to the branches of the tree, and the records are often called *leaves* or *nodes*. A *balanced tree* is one in which any record can be retrieved in a number of steps s or $s-1$, that is the path length to the record varies by no more than one step.

The balanced tree index shown in Fig. 7.3(a) is made up of a series of index levels, each pointing to the level below it. The records and the index entries are grouped into twos, so $e = 2$ and this is described as a tree of order 2 and height 4.

When a record is added it is necessary to use an overflow area, as the data areas are already full. The added records have to be indexed, which requires a second index entry for each 'track' of the data file. By track here, is meant e records. The arrangement of the file after a number of additions is shown in Fig. 7.3(b). This type of index is used in the Indexed Sequential Access Method (ISAM) that has been available on IBM mainframe computer

224 Design of computer data files

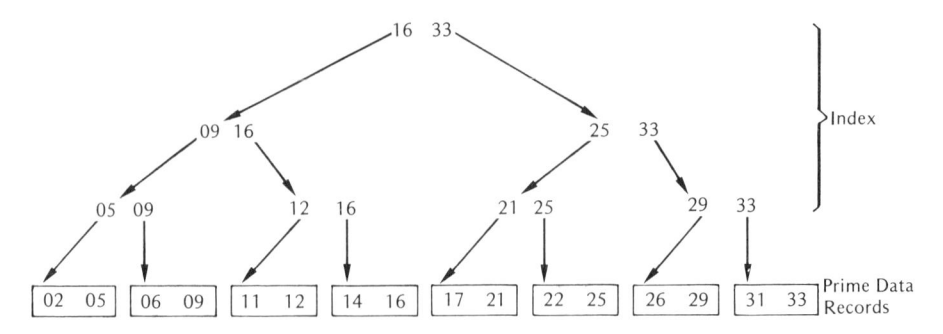

Fig. 7.3(a) A balanced tree file and index in the newly loaded state.

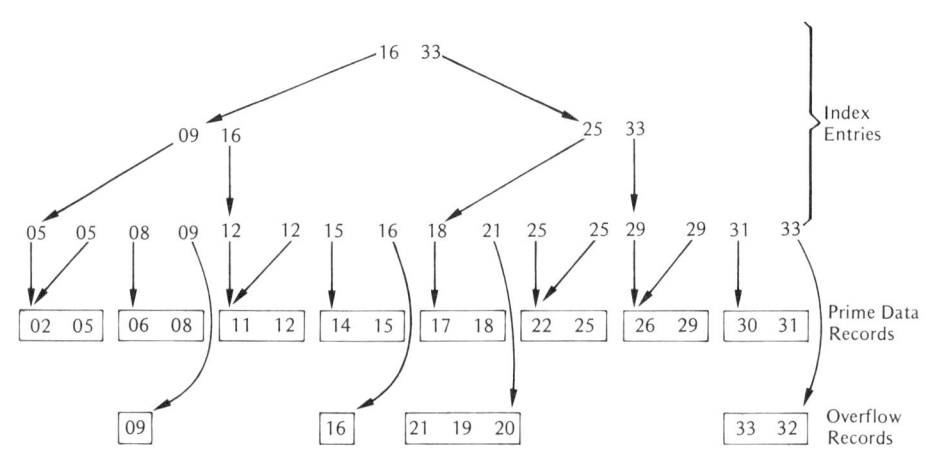

Fig. 7.3(b) A balanced tree file after the addition of records with the keys 08, 15, 18, 19, 20, 30 and 32.

systems since the late sixties, and is now available on some microcomputers.

The balanced tree index allows for deletions without difficulty, because records are tagged but not removed, so that no data manipulation is required. In some systems, tagged records are removed if they are pushed into overflow; this depends on decisions taken by the software writers. However, allowing for additions by providing areas that are *logically* extensions of the prime data tracks, rather than just physically, has made it necessary to double the size of the lowest-level index, with separate entries for records on the prime data and overflow tracks.

Direct-link balanced trees A second indexing technique, that treats additions as part of the prime data track, is the direct-link balanced tree. This method of indexing was used on the IBM 1400 series computers—the control sequential method—and is at present in use with ICL's 2900 series.

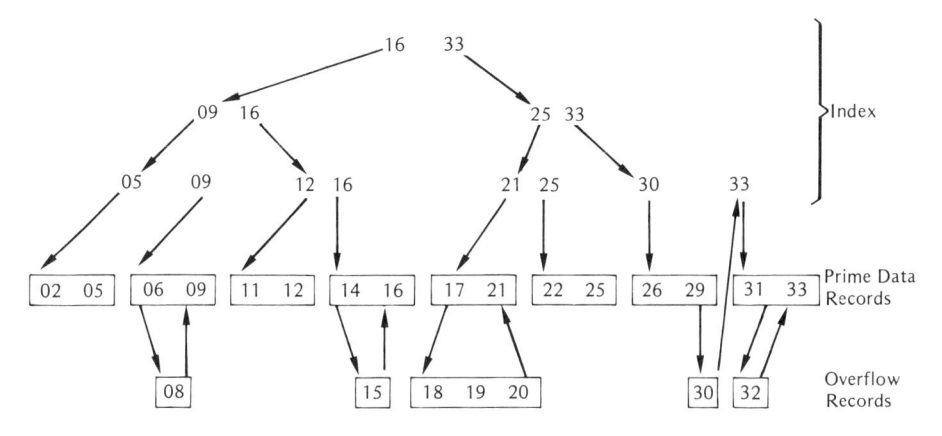

Fig. 7.4

A direct-link balanced tree index would also look just as in Fig. 7.3(a) before additions. However, after additions it would appear as in Fig. 7.4.

This technique is most effective for very volatile files, as the additions change the keys in indexes but do not cause alteration of prime data tracks. This means that additions are made quickly, but sequential retrievals suffer. McDonnell and Montgomery[1] have shown that this technique is as good as the other balanced tree method for direct retrieval. Both methods suffer from the problem that performance of the file degrades as additions are made, and in consequence they both require that the file should be reorganized at regular intervals. In order to combat this problem, a number of other indexing methods have been developed.

B-trees Bayer, McCreight and Kaufman[2] proposed the B-tree. In this type of index, there are always more pointers than index items: $P = I + 1$. The order of the B-tree is said to be one more than the maximum number of keys per index block. A modified form of B-tree is used in IBM's VSAM files, to be discussed later in the chapter. Indirectly, B-trees are also used in IBM's DB/2 relational database system.

Using the same data as before, a B-tree has been set up. Here, $e = 2$, so the order is 3. This is very low, and would never be used in practice, but it allows an example to be shown in a compact diagram. The minimum number of keys per block has to be $e/2$, which in this case is one (1). The keys given in the index entries do not have to be actual keys. Usually, they are intermediate values to allow for later additions.

Fig. 7.5(a) shows the same set of keys as in Fig. 7.3(a), but stored in a B-tree. Note that they are now in groups of 1 or 2.

The number of index levels here is the same as in Fig. 7.3(a)—that is, the height is again 4—but there is much more room for additions. The way in which additions are handled is shown in Fig. 7.5(b); the same additions have

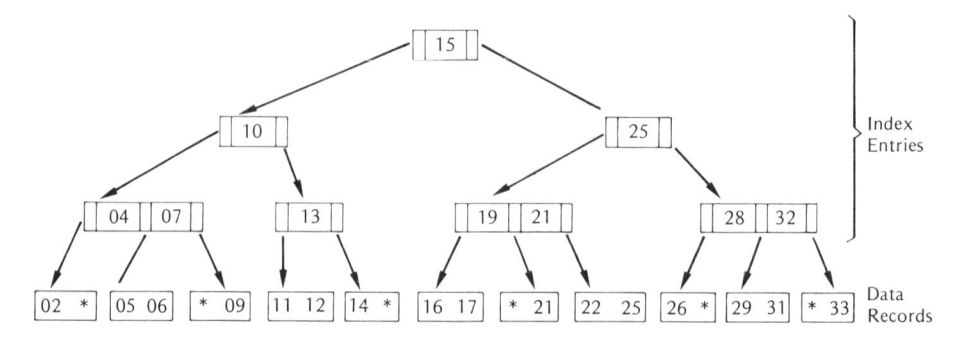

Fig. 7.5(a) A B-tree using the same data as in Fig. 7.3(a), showing a possible arrangement of key and index data. The asterisks show where there is room for a further record without altering the file structure.

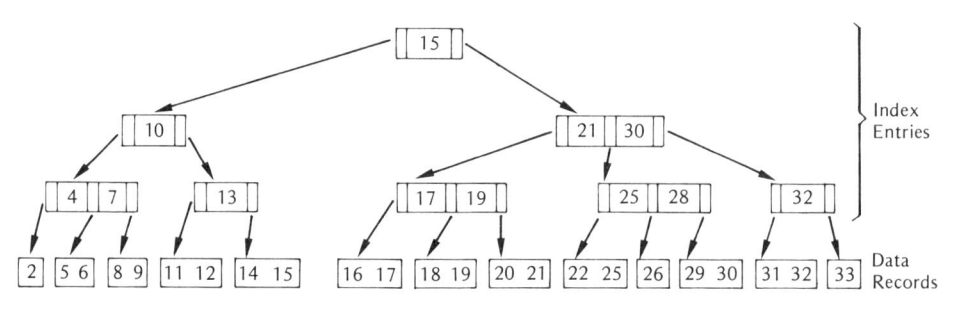

Fig. 7.5(b) The B-tree structure shown in Fig. 7.5(a), after the addition of records 8, 15, 18, 19, 20, 30, 32.

been made, but have resulted in index and data block splitting, so that no records are in 'overflow'. This prime data/index structure can continue to propagate itself as needed. However, it takes much longer to add records that cause splitting, so the addition versus update-only figures are very important in assessing the efficiency of a B-tree. A volatile file with relatively little processing might be better handled by a balanced tree index. VSAM uses a modified form of B-tree, so that the number of keys and pointers is the same, and index entries are greater than or equal to the keys pointed to rather than taking some intermediate value.

The additions to this B-tree have had no effect on the index entries on the left-hand side of the tree, but have led to several changes to the right-hand index entries. In order to examine this further, let us look at another case. Fig. 7.6 shows an example of a B-tree of order 5. In this case the maximum number of keys per block is four (e), and the minimum is 2 ($e/2$). Note that the top level index may have as few as one.

Indexed sequential files 227

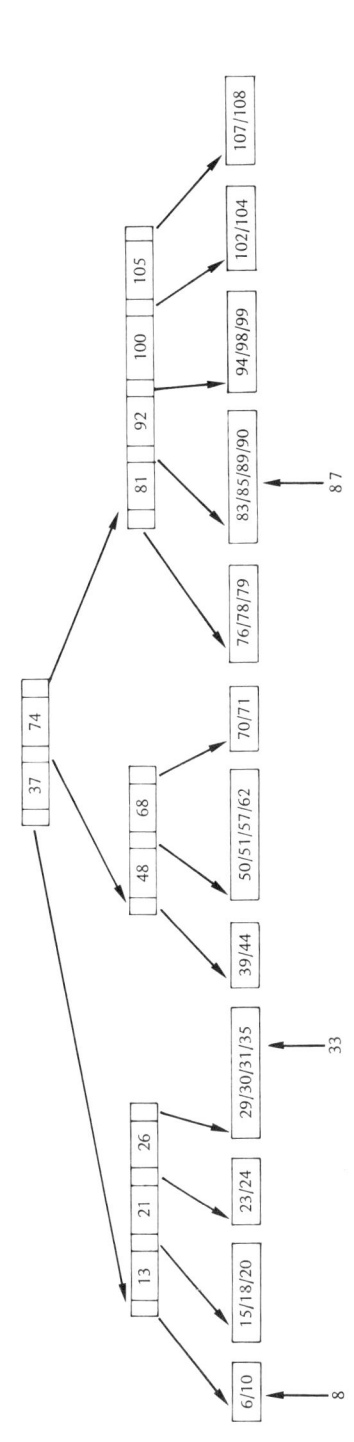

Fig. 7.6(a) Example of a B-tree of order 5. In this case the maximum number of keys per block is four (*e*), and the minimum is 2 (*e*/2). The top level index may have as few as one. Records to be added are shown on the bottom line.

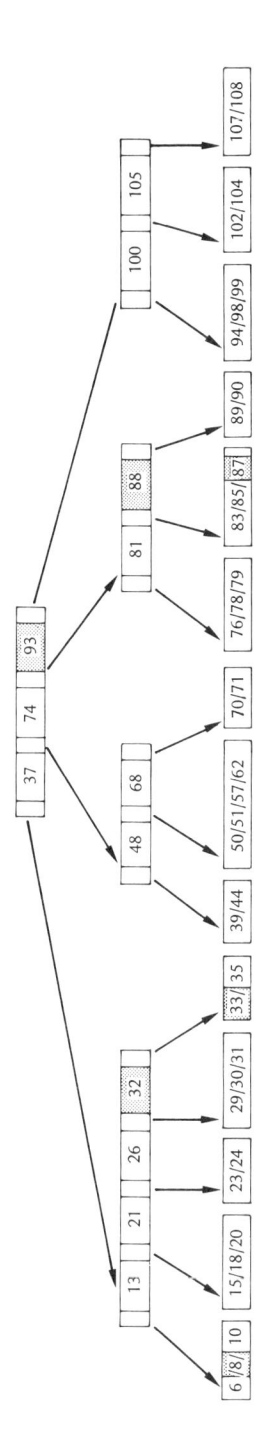

Fig. 7.6(b) The result of adding records with keys of value 8, 33 and 87. Note the many changes to indexes (three), number of data groups (from 12 to 14) and content of data groups imposed by just three added records.

228 Design of computer data files

Choice of index technique It is clear that the changes to the indexes caused by even a very few additions mean a great deal of reading and writing of data into the index areas on disk. This is a definite weakness of the B-tree. It is counterbalanced by the ability of the structure to accept very large numbers of additions—given sufficient space, the structure can grow in an unlimited fashion. We therefore have a choice between index types that is affected by the use to which the file is put. In Table 7.1 the three methods are compared, scoring 1 for the best of the three, 2 for the second, and 3 for the worst.

Table 7.1 A comparison of some frequently used indexing methods. Despite the scores, the balanced tree index with two index entries for each group of records is often a good compromise.

Index type	High volatility	High sequential access	High direct access	High growth
B-tree	3	1	1	1
Balanced tree (two indexes)	2	2	2=	2
Balanced tree (one index)	1	3	2=	3

Bradley[3] has discussed index design and optimization in some detail. Montgomery[4] describes the *n*ary tree method of indexing, and compares it with hashing of keys (discussed later in the chapter, see p. 230). Rathmann[5], in a paper particularly concerned with optical disks, compares the balanced tree method with the *trie index* technique, as did Severance[6]. A trie index is particularly useful when keys are of varying sizes, and the path of a search at any point of the tree depends on a part of the key rather than its full value. As most available file organization techniques use the methods discussed earlier, rather than *n*ary trees or trie indexes, they will not be discussed further here, but a full description of tries is given by Knuth[7].

Index position

The start of any direct search, and the first step in any sequential run, is a search of the higher-level indexes. The process, for direct reference, is as follows:

    Seek the highest-level index   (an average head movement)
    Search the high-level indexes   (a variable search time)
    Seek the data cylinder   (an average head movement)
    Search the low-level index   (a single track search time)
    Search the prime data track   (a single track search time)
    Search the overflow area   (a variable search time).

As this is time-consuming, particularly in the case of direct reference, the file designer will aim to minimize it. The first high-level index set up by the software is called the *cylinder index* in ISAM files, or the *seek area index* in some ICL 2900 series systems. This index has an entry for each data cylinder of the file indicating the highest key on the cylinder. Ideally, the file designer will aim to reduce the time taken to reference this index; however, when it exceeds a certain threshold value described earlier, a *master index*, which has one entry for each track of the cylinder index, can be created to reduce the total search time as described above. IBM systems usually provide the software to create up to five higher-level indexes automatically in this way if the user specifies MSTIND = YES. If two or more higher-level indexes exist, each of them may be handled using a different one of the techniques described below aimed at reducing index search time, depending on their size.

1 To hold all or part of the index in main storage
This will avoid the need for a head movement to the index and can yield very marked savings. If the entire index is in main storage, the correct cylinder to search is located in well under a millisecond. This compares with head movement times that are usually orders of magnitude greater, and the direct access throughput is often roughly doubled if this technique is used[1].

Unless the file is small or main storage is very large, the cylinder index size may exceed the space available for it. In this case IBM software allows the user to store an exact sub-multiple of the index in main storage, i.e. one half, one third, etc. When this applies, the *average* seek time will be reduced to a half, two thirds, etc., of average head movement time, as the information will be available in main storage—so saving a seek—in an equivalent proportion of cases.

If, because of the size of the cylinder index, only a higher-level index than the cylinder index can be held in main storage, a 20–50 per cent improvement over the performance of the file when the master index is stored on disk can still be achieved[1,8].

2 To hold the higher-level indexes on fast devices
Head movement times for fixed-head disks or semiconductor 'disks' are much shorter on average than those of standard disks. It is very good practice to store high-level indexes on these devices, so that every direct reference is reduced by the difference in timing. When the device is dedicated to this file the benefits can be very marked, since the index cylinder on the fast device is available without head movement at all times; if IBM 3340, 3350 or similar devices that offer some fixed-head capacity are available, these indexes can be held in the fixed-head area.

If the file is held on a mass storage device, location of higher-level indexes on a disk will make a very significant contribution to reducing run times.

3 *Storage on a separate device*
If no faster device is available it is often beneficial to use a separate device of the same sort. This can be most effective if this device can be dedicated to the file, but is still useful in normal multi-programming; there is certain to be constant arm movement if the file and its high-level indexes are stored on the same device, while this is less likely if they are on separate devices.

4 *Positioning on a device that also holds the data*
When no separate device is available, the optimal position for the cylinder index should be determined. This has been investigated in great detail elsewhere[9,10], and the guidelines may be summarized as follows:

a) If nothing is known about the distribution of hits in the file, the cylinder index should be placed in the centre of the file area. In a multi-pack file this will be the *centre* of one of the packs that is completely dedicated to the file.

b) If, in a multi-pack file, the only information about hits is the relative number per pack or area, the index should be placed in the centre of the pack or area with the *lowest* hit density.

c) If the hit density across a file area or areas is known, the index should be placed in the centre of the *highest* peak of hits on the *least* active pack used by the file.

The objective of these guidelines is to place the cylinder index on the file cylinder that is of lowest possible activity, in such a position that the majority of head movements away from the index will be short. This allows movement back to the index to be rapid.

Past practice has often been to allocate the cylinder index to a cylinder preceding or following the file area. This is never the best solution; as pointed out above, the centre of the file is the logical position if nothing is known about hit pattern.

Fig. 7.7 summarizes the rules for placement of the cylinder index if it is to be situated in the main file area.

Alternative indexing techniques

There have been a number of suggestions for alternatives to the lowest-level index of indexed sequential files. Ghosh and Senko[11] put forward an interpolation search in place of the track or lowest-level index, and showed that for normal key distributions it would improve the direct retrieval performance of IS files. In addition, this measure gives a potentially better packing density than conventional indexing techniques.

Mullin[12] suggested the use of hashing, rather than indexing, for the lowest-level index. As he makes clear, this is only of benefit when the *average* number of records that has overflowed from a track is two or more. This limits the possible uses of such a technique to very active files that the user does not wish to reorganize frequently.

Indexed sequential files 231

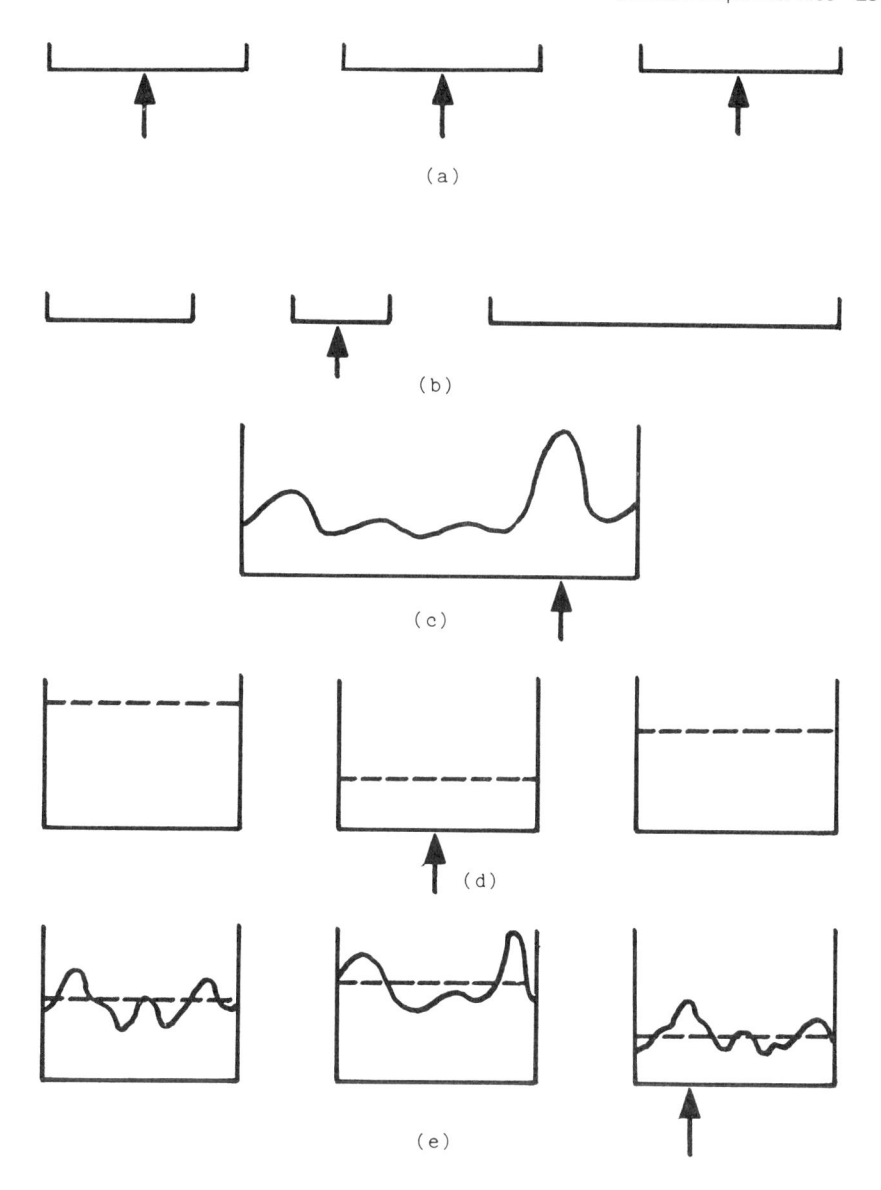

Fig. 7.7 Each area shown is on a separate unit. The vertical scale shows activity, the horizontal shows the quantity, or extent, of each storage area. Arrows point to optimum cylinder index positions. (a) Equal-sized file areas on separate units; cylinder index at centre of any one. (b) Unequal-sized file areas on separate units; cylinder index at centre of smallest area. (c) Activity pattern known; cylinder index at centre of peak. (d) Activity known, no details; cylinder index at centre of least-active area. (e) Activity pattern known; cylinder index at centre of peak in lowest-activity area.

7.4 Additions

Most indexed sequential file software allows for additions to be made to the file without reorganizing it. The provision of space for additions is an optional feature. If no additions are expected, it is not necessary to leave space for that purpose. When additions are expected, two techniques are used to store those additions so that they are available for both sequential and direct access. The first is *embedded overflow*. In this case, space is left unused in the main data area when the file is created, and additions are located on the same cylinder (IBM) or seek area (ICL) that they would have occupied if they had been part of the file when it was created. In this way the record can be found when necessary without movement of the access heads. Although this allows fast retrieval of records, it can lead to very low packing density of data because there may be many additions in one area and few in others. To allow for many additions to every cylinder, when only one cylinder has a large number of additions, is wasteful of space. This is discussed in more detail below.

The second commonly used technique is to provide an *independent* or *global overflow* area which is used to store records added to any part of the file. This is a very efficient way of handling additions, because all the available space can be used before there is any need to provide extra overflow space. However, it means that references to added records will require movement of the access heads, which wastes a great deal of time.

As one overflow technique saves time but wastes space, while the other saves space but is slow, many users choose a compromise. A reasonably-sized embedded overflow area is provided on each cylinder, while a small independent overflow area is used to store additions that overflow from their home cylinder. Variations in numbers of additions from one cylinder to another are to be expected. This method ensures that the file designer is not forced to provide very large embedded overflow areas on every cylinder, when only a few cylinders require them.

The distribution of additions to a file guides the designer in allocating overflow areas. Before the appropriate decision can be made, the pattern of additions to the file has to be determined. Sometimes this can be predicted or measured, but on other occasions there may be no prior information for the designer to work on. A number of typical cases are discussed below.

No additions expected This can arise when, for example, a file contains records of policyholders under a policy no longer offered. The number of policyholders cannot grow, and in this case the designer would not allocate any overflow areas. This provides a file that is well packed; however, if conditions change later the file needs to be respecified.

Equal numbers of additions to each area This is a very unusual case. The designer must know that additions *will* be equal. It might arise if one additional record were added to each group of consecutive records; for example, a group of stores might begin to open on a Saturday, and require an extra record for each store to record transactions. The superficially similar case in which there is an equal *probability* of additions to any area is covered below. If the designer is satisfied that equal additions to every cylinder are going to occur, then it is possible to provide only embedded overflow areas. This will allow rapid retrieval from the file as no extra head movements will be caused by additions.

The designer has to decide on the size of the embedded overflow areas. Very often, if it is known that additions will be made precisely evenly throughout the file, it will also be known when they will be made. An example would be when an extra record is added for each project in a company every day. If this information is not available the designer will have to estimate it. The intention will be to plan how frequently the file will require reorganization to merge additions and remove deleted records. After this has been done several times, the actual frequency of reorganization can be compared with that expected, and the future reorganization schedule will be based on the results.

All additions concentrated in a few areas This can occur when, for example, recruitment campaigns for customers have taken place in a limited area, or a competitor has gone out of business. In these cases, if customer numbers are based on areas, additions will be in groups. It is unusual for this to be the normal form of additions. If the designer is faced with it, the requirement for embedded overflow areas will be minimal or nil; the main provision must be a large independent overflow area. As this will lead to slow retrieval of added records, more frequent reorganization will be required than in any other case. If the times at which additions are expected can be predicted, it may be wise to hold additions in an ancillary file until each 'burst' of activity is over and then to reorganize the main file to include them.

Additions equally probable anywhere This is both the most usual case and the assumption the designer should work on if no information is available. It is not the same as equal numbers of additions to each area, since there will naturally be variations from cylinder to cylinder in the number of additions just because those additions are random. The Poisson distribution used to predict synonym behaviour in direct files is the appropriate mathematical tool to use here (note that if the number of embedded overflow areas is small the binomial distribution should be used instead).

Assume that l records are to be added to S embedded overflow areas. Then the probability $p(x)$ that x records will be added to a given embedded overflow area is given by the expression:

$$p(x) = \frac{(l/S)^x e^{-(l/S)}}{x!} \qquad (7.1)$$

An overflow area will be able to hold some number of records n. The probability that this area will be able to hold all the records added to it will thus be:

$$\sum_{x=0}^{n} p(x) \qquad (7.2)$$

To demonstrate what this means in practice, assume that, on average, four records are to be added to each embedded overflow area, and that these overflow areas can hold a maximum of five records.

From equation (7.1), the percentage of embedded overflow areas that will have 0, 1, ... n additions is given in Table 7.2.

These figures are plotted in Fig. 7.8, where the shaded section shows the percentage of areas from which at least one record will overflow into the independent overflow area. This turns out to be about 21.5 per cent of embedded overflow *areas*. The percentage of added *records* that cannot be held in these embedded overflow areas is about 10.26 per cent. This difference is due to the fact that only one-sixth of the records added to the 'six additions' figure will overflow, two-sevenths of the 'seven additions', three-eighths of the 'eight additions', and so on.

Table 7.3 shows the percentage of all additions that will be held in independent overflow for various combinations of embedded overflow area size and number of additions. This has similar values to those given in Table 6.4. The reason is that the addition of records to direct access files is mathematically similar to the random addition of records to overflow areas. The derivations given here are due to the author and were published in the first edition, but Larson[13] has also carried out similar work independently.

Cases of equal numbers of additions to each area and all additions concentrated in a few areas are depicted schematically in Fig. 7.9. This shows files with a twenty-cylinder prime data area, and a two-cylinder independent overflow area. Each prime data cylinder contains ten tracks. A track can hold up to five records. One track in each cylinder is set aside as an embedded overflow area. The files have each had eighty records added. The assumptions made are:

a) equal numbers of additions have been made to every cylinder;
b) additions of twenty, twenty-four and thirty-six records have been made to cylinders five, ten and fifteen.
c) additions have been made as they occur, in an entirely chance sequence.

As this is a small file, it is useful to check how accurately the Poisson distribution approximates to the more strictly accurate binomial distribution. Using equations (6.6)–(6.9), the figures obtained are shown in Table 7.4. The correspondence between the two sets of figures appears to be good. A check on this using the chi-squared significance test (see Moroney[14] or any standard statistical text for further details) shows that there is no significant

Indexed sequential files   235

Table 7.2 The percentage of embedded overflow areas that will have the given number of additions.

No. of additions	0	1	2	3	4	5	6	7	8
Poisson (%)	1.83	7.33	14.65	19.54	19.54	15.63	10.42	5.95	2.98

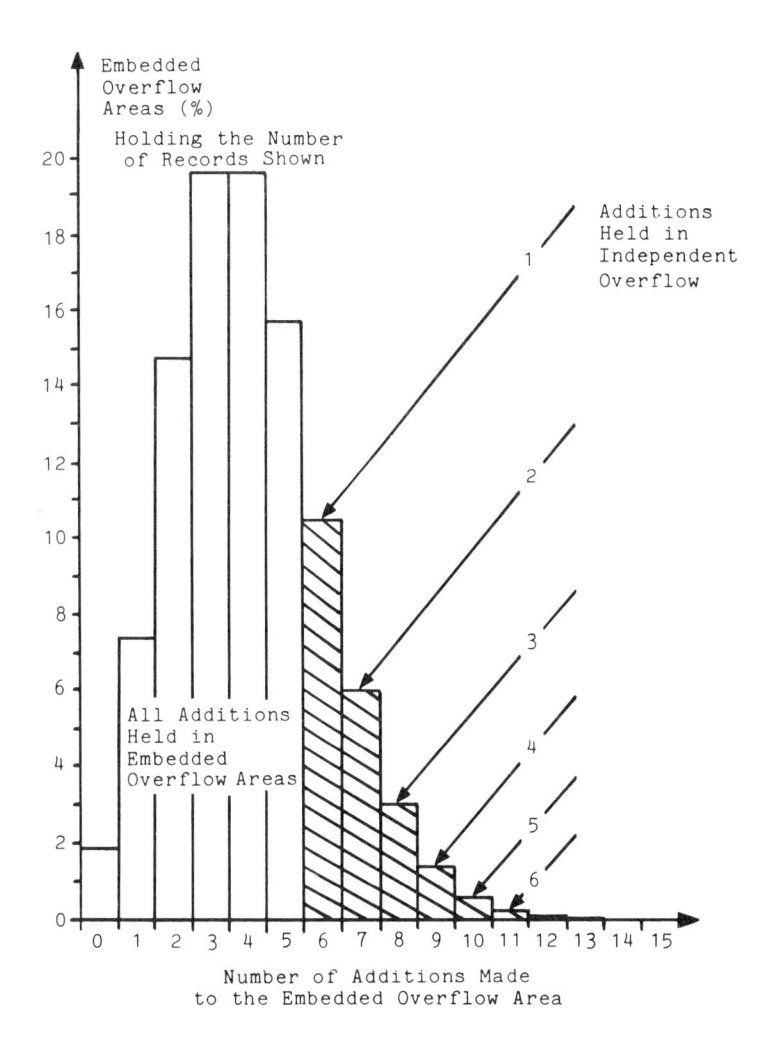

No. of additions	9	10	11	12	13	14	15	16	17
Poisson (%)	1.32	0.52	0.19	0.06	0.02	0.006	0.002	0.0004	0.0001

Fig. 7.8 The percentage of embedded overflow areas that will have 0, 1, ... *n* additions.

Table 7.3 Figures tabulated show records stored in independent overflow as a percentage of all the records added, i.e. held in overflow areas that are either embedded or independent.

Maximum number of records per embedded overflow area	\multicolumn{10}{c}{Additions as a percentage of the total embedded overflow area available}
	10	20	30	40	50	60	70	80	90	100
1	4.84	9.37	13.61	17.58	21.31	24.80	28.08	31.17	34.06	36.79
2	0.60	2.19	4.48	7.27	10.36	13.65	17.03	20.43	23.79	27.07
3	0.09	0.63	1.80	3.61	5.99	8.82	11.99	15.37	18.87	22.40
4	0.02	0.20	0.79	1.96	3.76	6.15	9.05	12.32	15.86	19.54
5		0.07	0.37	1.12	2.48	4.49	7.11	10.26	13.78	17.55
6		0.02	0.18	0.67	1.69	3.38	5.75	8.75	12.24	16.06
7		0.01	0.09	0.41	1.18	2.60	4.74	7.60	11.04	14.90
8			0.05	0.25	0.84	2.03	3.97	6.68	10.07	13.96
9			0.02	0.16	0.61	1.61	3.36	5.94	9.27	13.18
10			0.01	0.10	0.44	1.29	2.88	5.32	8.59	12.51
11			0.01	0.07	0.33	1.04	2.48	4.80	8.01	11.94
12				0.04	0.24	0.85	2.15	4.36	7.51	11.44
14				0.02	0.14	0.57	1.65	3.64	6.67	10.60
16				0.01	0.08	0.39	1.28	3.09	6.00	9.92
18					0.05	0.28	1.01	2.65	5.45	9.36
20					0.03	0.20	0.81	2.30	4.99	8.88
25					0.01	0.09	0.48	1.65	4.10	7.95
30						0.04	0.29	1.23	3.47	7.26
35						0.02	0.18	0.94	2.98	6.73
40						0.01	0.12	0.73	2.60	6.29
50							0.05	0.45	2.04	5.63
60							0.02	0.30	1.65	5.14
70							0.01	0.20	1.37	4.76
80								0.01	0.13	1.14	4.46
90									0.09	0.97	4.20
100									0.06	0.83	3.99

Indexed sequential files 237

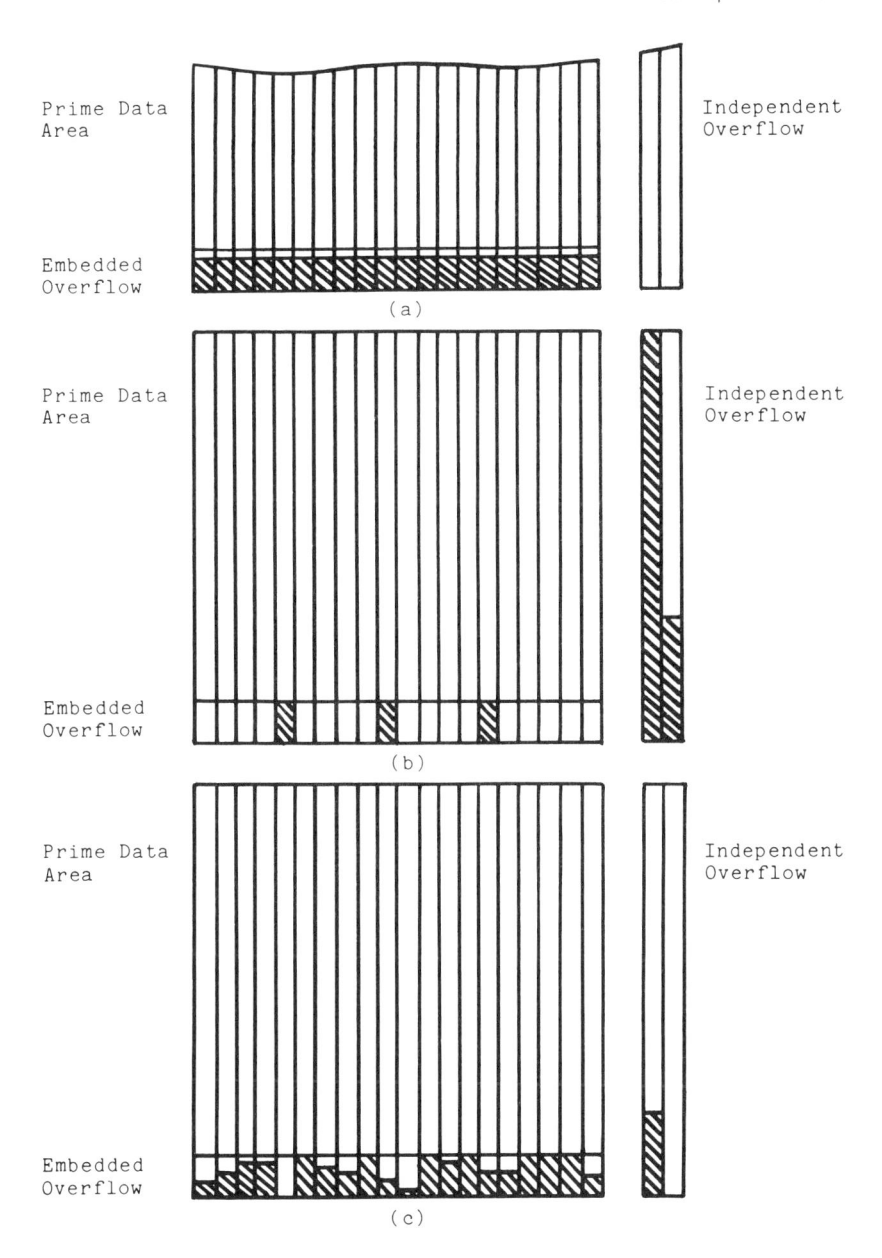

Fig. 7.9 Diagrammatic representation of additions to a file. (a) Equal numbers of additions to each area. (b) All additions concentrated in a few areas. (c) Additions equally probable anywhere.

Table 7.4 Comparison of Poisson and binomial distribution for additions to a small file.

Number of additions	0	1	2	3	4	5	6	7	8
Poisson (%)	1.83	7.33	14.65	19.54	19.54	15.63	10.42	5.95	2.98
Binomial (%)	1.65	6.95	14.45	19.78	20.04	16.03	10.55	5.87	2.82

Number of additions	9	10	11	12	13	14	15	16	17
Poisson (%)	1.32	0.52	0.19	0.06	0.02	0.006	0.002	0.0004	0.000 09
Binomial (%)	1.19	0.44	0.15	0.05	0.01	0.003	0.001	0.0002	0.000 03

difference between the two. This means that any real set of figures obtained by adding records to a file would be expected, due to normal random variations, to show larger discrepancies from the calculated figures. Thus the Poisson distribution can safely be used instead of the binomial for files of this size.

These three examples show the wide range of conditions that will have to be handled in providing for additions. Whenever possible, the file designer will have data available on the pattern of additions to a given file. When no data is provided, or if the only information available is an average number of additions, it should be assumed that additions are equally probable anywhere. As experience is gained in using the file, any original assumptions about additions should be checked. Manufacturers' software often provides information about overflow areas that can assist in this; the use of this information is discussed in a later section.

7.5 Addition techniques

The way in which additions to an indexed file are made can affect both sequential and direct access to the file. There are two commonly used techniques. In the first the record that is added is *inserted* into its correct position in the file, and the record at the end of the track to which it was added drops off into overflow. In the second, the added record is placed in overflow, *linked* from the record before it in sequence, and back to the record following it.

Record insertion

The principle is as shown in Fig. 7.10. The advantage of this technique is that, in subsequent processing, the whole prime data track can be handled

Indexed sequential files   **239**

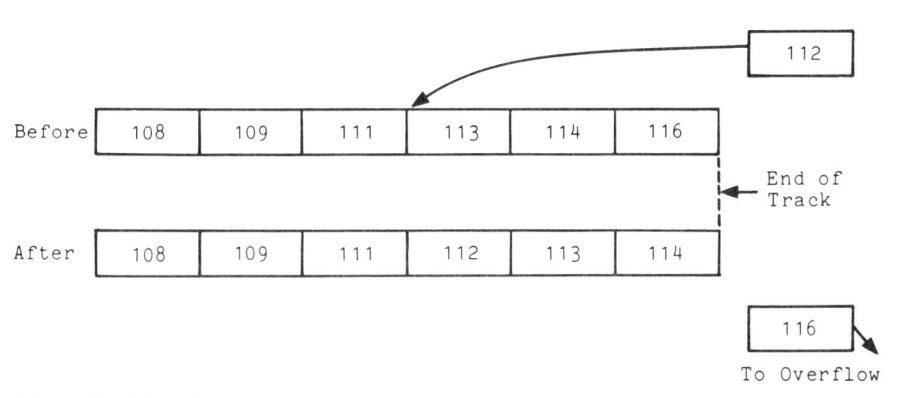

```
Before  | 108 | 109 | 111 | 113 | 114 | 116 |
                                              ← End of Track
After   | 108 | 109 | 111 | 112 | 113 | 114 |

                                    [112]
                                    [116] → To Overflow
```

Fig. 7.10 The principle of record insertion.

sequentially by the software, and overflow records are picked up only when the prime track has been processed. The disadvantage is that, on average, half the records on the track need to be shunted up (in this example records 113, 114 and 116 have been moved), and the overflow area will also require updating. Both of these functions can be carried out quickly and efficiently in main storage, and it is important to use the manufacturers' software and allocate space to allow this to happen. If half the records on a track have to be moved one at a time, and a device revolution is required for each movement, additions can take a great deal of time. This would be the situation if the programmer had not allocated sufficient working storage to the file.

The IBM indexed sequential file management system ISAM works on the insertion principle. The cylinder index, a track index and a data cylinder are shown in Fig. 7.11(a) as they are set up. The file consists of four cylinders, 00–03, and cylinder 01 is illustrated. Each cylinder index entry gives the address of the cylinder it refers to, and the highest key on the cylinder. In the case shown this is 341. *This will remain the highest key on the cylinder.* If a record with the key 342 is added, it will be stored on the first track of cylinder 02. The same principle applies to the highest key on any track; as the highest key on track 06 was 298 when the file was created, a record with the key 299 belongs logically to track 07, whether it is stored on that track already or has not yet been added.

The form of balanced tree index used in ISAM operates as follows. There are two track index entries for each track. The functions of these entries are given in Fig. 7.12. The normal entry links the highest key *at present* on the prime data track with the address of the track. It allows a program to check what records are at present physically on that track. The overflow entry links the highest key on the *logical* track, which comprises both the prime (physical) and overflow parts of it, and the address of the first record in the chain of overflow records for that track. A program can check from this what

240 Design of computer data files

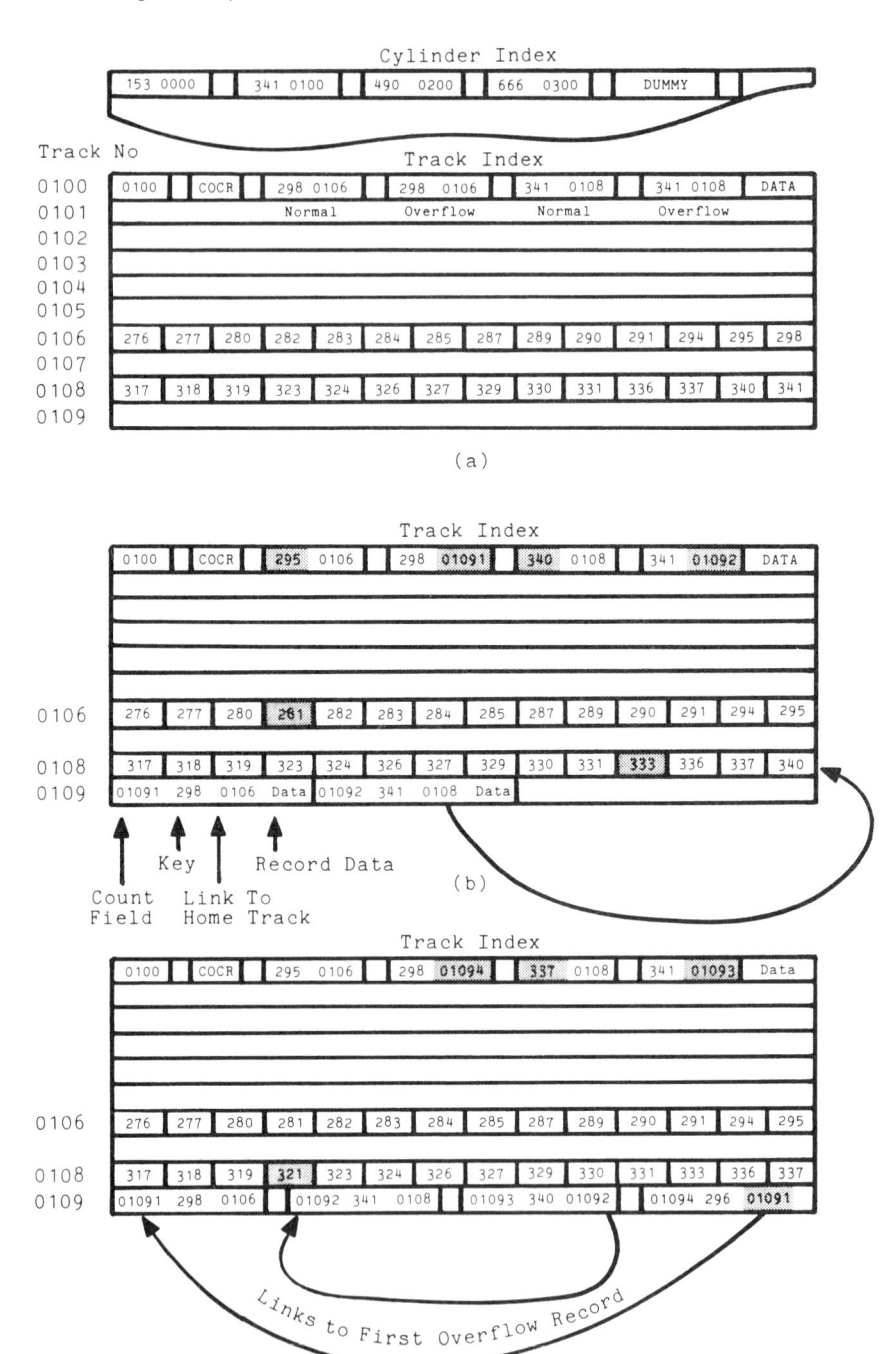

Fig. 7.11 Additions and changes to index and link entries in IBM's ISAM system. (a) A cylinder index, track index and data cylinder as they are set up. (b) After inserting records with the keys 281 and 333. (c) After inserting records with keys 321 and 296. COCR = cylinder overflow control record.

Indexed sequential files 241

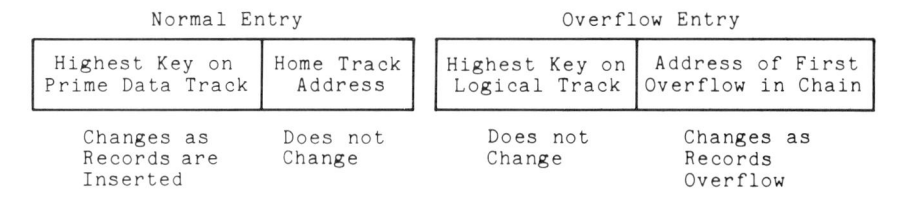

Normal Entry		Overflow Entry	
Highest Key on Prime Data Track	Home Track Address	Highest Key on Logical Track	Address of First Overflow in Chain
Changes as Records are Inserted	Does not Change	Does not Change	Changes as Records Overflow

Fig. 7.12 The function of the track index in IBM's ISAM system.

records are at present logically on that track. 'Logical' here means those records that are processed as if they were on the track.

The effect of additions on processing times is discussed under the sections on sequential and direct access to indexed sequential files (see pp. 251 and 261). The way in which additions occur, and the changes to index and link entries, are shown in Fig. 7.11.

The field shown as COCR in the track index stands for *cylinder overflow control record*. This is used to store information about the address of the last overflow record on the cylinder, the number of bytes of overflow space still remaining and additional data required if the file contains variable-length records.

When records are added to a file organized in this way, there is an advantage to be gained by planning the additions procedure. Additions should be sorted into descending order. As the last record added is the first in the overflow chain, it is helpful if this physical order is also the logical order of the record keys. Coyle[8] has pointed out that significant savings can be made in ISAM file timings by using this technique.

Record linking

This method operates as shown in Fig. 7.13. The advantage of the method is that records on the prime data track do not have to be moved; a link field has to be inserted in record 111, however. The disadvantage for sequential

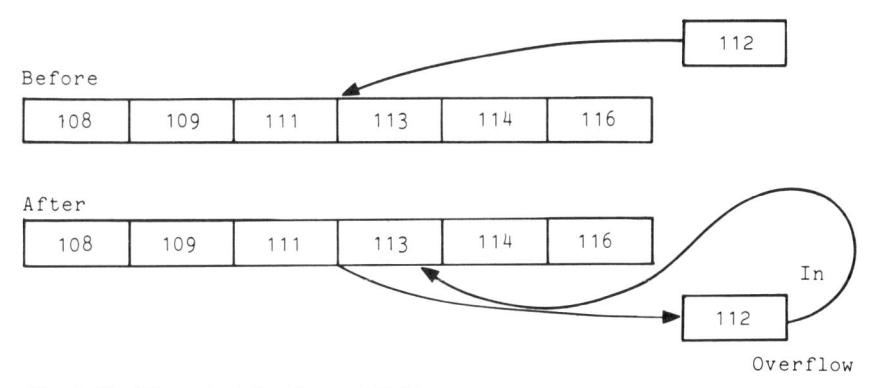

Fig. 7.13 The principle of record linking.

242 Design of computer data files

processing is that there will be several rotations during the processing of a track with overflow. For direct processing the track index does not make it clear which records are in overflow and which in the prime data area; this prevents the *first* overflow record being retrieved as quickly as is achieved in the two-entry index system—at least while it is the only overflow record. However, the index itself takes up less space.

IBM's control sequential file organization, used with the 1400 series computers, added link fields to the records shown above as 111 and 112. This was the organization that preceded the indexed sequential file management system. The smaller machines in ICL's 2900 series provide an eleven-bit link field that points back to the home bucket if the record is stored in overflow. This field is present in all records, whether they are in overflow or in a home bucket. However, it is only used if the record is in overflow. Otherwise all the bits are set to zero. If a record is stored in overflow, a *tag* is placed in the home bucket, pointing to the overflow storage position. This is made up of a twenty-four-bit field containing the overflow address plus control information, followed by the record key, which can be up to sixty-four characters in length. The details are shown in Fig. 7.14.

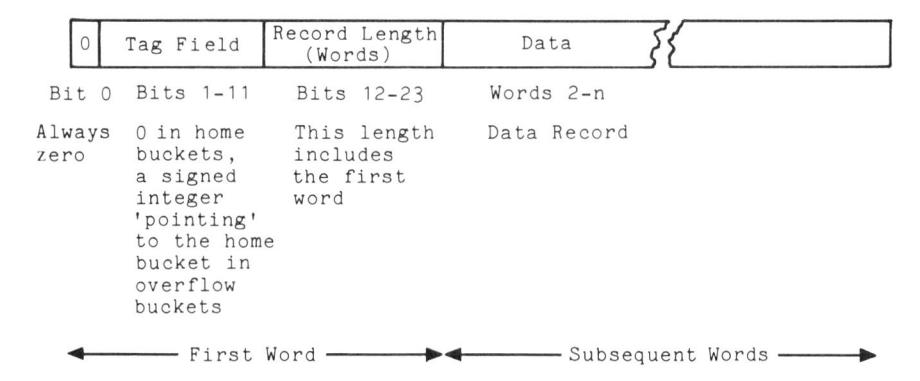

0	Tag Field	Record Length (Words)	Data
Bit 0	Bits 1-11	Bits 12-23	Words 2-n
Always zero	0 in home buckets, a signed integer 'pointing' to the home bucket in overflow buckets	This length includes the first word	Data Record

◄──── First Word ────►◄──── Subsequent Words ────►

Fig. 7.14 A record stored in overflow in the ICL 2900 series format.

It is usually somewhat easier to insert link fields to handle overflow—particularly when they are already available in the records—than to move up all the records on a track to accommodate a record in its correct sequence. However, the extra speed of processing will repay the time taken to move these records if the file is frequently processed sequentially. If the file is mainly processed directly, the link method may be more efficient. In most cases, however, the user will have no choice in the matter. It is usually a case of accepting the method used by the manufacturer whose software is being employed.

Addition techniques compared in practice

Montgomery and Hubbard[15] have compared the performance after additions of IBM's ISAM and ICL's 1900 series indexed sequential software, the files being held on a 2314 and its ICL equivalent, an EDS 30.

They looked at:

1. random retrieval;
2. random insertion;
3. sequential processing;

for buckets holding two, six and fourteen records.

Random processing Random retrieval gave very variable results for ICL files. Buckets containing two and six 500-character records required retrieval times of 60–70 ms per record, while for fourteen-record buckets this increased to 120–140 ms. IBM files, on the other hand, yielded retrieval times of 75–95 ms and the effect of bucket capacity was small. The fraction of the file in overflow did not markedly affect performance until it reached 30 per cent of the total file; the only exception was the ICL fourteen-record bucket file, which began to perform worse as soon as additions were made.

Random insertions were found to be variable in their effect on timing. IBM files performed better the *larger* the bucket capacity, while ICL files performed better the *smaller* the bucket capacity; very roughly, the six-record buckets were equivalent, while IBM two-record buckets performed as badly as the ICL fourteen-record buckets. The ICL two-record buckets required about 130 ms per insertion, and the IBM files showed little variation due to the fraction of the file in overflow, but ICL files improved as additions were made, up to 10 per cent, and degraded after this.

Sequential processing The sequential retrieval times for both file structures were identical before additions, but IBM files outperformed ICL in every case after additions. This was most marked for large bucket sizes; IBM fourteen-record bucket files gave average retrieval times increased from 40 ms to 55 ms as a result of 40 per cent of the file being stored in overflow. Average retrieval times for ICL files, however, increased from 40 ms to 150 ms due to the same number of additions.

Comment on these comparisons These findings are generally in accord with the considerations on the two types of balanced tree discussed earlier. However, it should be noted that additions to IBM files did not take a great deal longer than to ICL files, while random *retrievals* from IBM files were not markedly more rapid. The authors point out[15] that record size is an important factor which was not varied in the work quoted, and it would not be safe to draw far-reaching conclusions from a limited investigation of this sort. Further work may clarify the differences between these two methods of handling overflow records over a wider range of conditions.

7.6 Data format

Individual records

Manufacturers' software usually provides for two formats, as discussed in Chapter 3 (see p. 57). Because it is necessary for indexed sequential software to build indexes, insert records, etc., the keys of records must be available to the software. For this reason the separate count, key and data format is usually required, i.e.

| Count | Gap | Key | Gap | Data |

The software that handles index building and additions can operate on the keys separately, while the size of the gap between key and data allows the data record to be transferred into main storage if it turns out to be the required record after examination of the key by the control unit. A SEARCH ON KEY, for example, will compare every record key with the search key value, but will only read in the data record or records that satisfy the search conditions. These are generally:

KEY EQUAL
KEY HIGH OR EQUAL
KEY LOW OR EQUAL

In the case of unblocked records, the most likely condition would be KEY EQUAL, as a particular record would be searched for.

It is usual for the file to be arranged in ascending key sequence, and for the file creation software to expect input to the file to be *physically* in this order (on initial creation) or *logically* in this order (when a file with overflow records is reorganized). In principle, a file could be arranged in descending order, but most manufacturers' software checks that the order is ascending and, if it is not, halts until the input order is corrected.

Blocked records

Searching for a record in blocked format is complicated by the fact that only one key can be placed in front of the block. This is usually the key of the last record in the block, as is shown in Fig. 7.15.

In the example shown in Fig. 7.15(a), record 112 is in the second block. If we were searching for this record, a comparison with the 'key' of the first block would be low, and of the second, high. Thus a HIGH OR EQUAL comparison condition will be used to search a blocked file looking for a given record. In this case the whole block will have to be moved into main storage, and the desired record will be retrieved by the use of a de-blocking algorithm. If the ISAM method is in use, the effect of adding a new record to

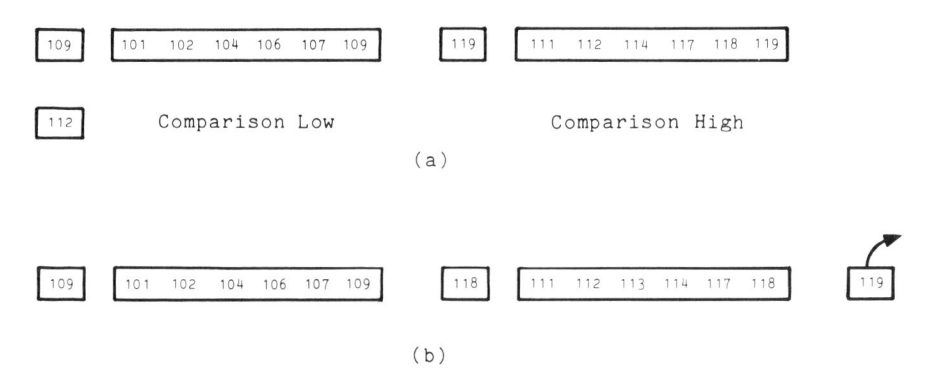

```
  ┌───┐   ┌───────────────────────┐     ┌───┐   ┌───────────────────────┐
  │109│   │101  102  104  106  107  109│     │119│   │111  112  114  117  118  119│
  └───┘   └───────────────────────┘     └───┘   └───────────────────────┘

  ┌───┐
  │112│            Comparison Low                     Comparison High
  └───┘
                                    (a)


  ┌───┐   ┌───────────────────────┐     ┌───┐   ┌────────────────────────────┐     ┌───┐
  │109│   │101  102  104  106  107  109│     │118│   │111  112  113  114  117  118│     │119│
  └───┘   └───────────────────────┘     └───┘   └────────────────────────────┘     └───┘
                                    (b)
```

Fig. 7.15 (a) Blocked records showing the separate key format. (b) New arrangement after addition of the record with key 113.

a block of records is to cause the block to be re-built, incorporating the new record and pushing the last record of the last block on the track off into overflow. If record 113 were an addition to the file in Fig. 7.15(a), the new structure would be as in Fig. 7.15(b). Record 119 goes into the next block, if that is on this track, or otherwise into overflow. Note that overflow records arise singly, however the prime data area is formatted, and that they are usually stored singly in indexed sequential files (but see discussion of VSAM on p. 266).

The process described is that used in IBM systems. ICL does not provide a separate key format in its 2900 series buckets. Instead, home records are located using the bucket index and overflow records via the home bucket and a tag.

Variable-length records

In many cases variable-length records are not provided for by manufacturers' software. It is possible to pad out all records to the length of the largest and handle them as fixed-length. This wastes space, but the user will not be able to avoid such a shortcoming in manufacturers' software by any other technique.

Often the solution is to move to a different *operating system*. The smaller IBM operating systems do not support variable-length records for indexed sequential files, but the larger ones do. There are obvious additional tasks to be carried out, such as de-blocking, overflow calculations and efficient packing of the file storage areas that make this limitation understandable. Even if an installation finds it convenient to use one of the smaller operating systems for much of its work, it may be possible to switch to an operating system that provides the extra facility to handle variable-length records, just for those files that need it.

Overflow records

It was mentioned above that overflow records arise singly. In addition, an embedded overflow area will usually contain varying numbers of records from several tracks. This leads to overflow records usually being stored in unblocked format, even if the records in the prime data area are blocked. There is some advantage in treating the whole embedded overflow area as a single large blocked record, and manufacturers' software often does transfer the whole track into main storage when an addition is to be made; this allows for the addition itself, creation of link fields, changes of index, etc. However, handling the whole track as a single block would prevent rapid transfer of individual records from the embedded overflow area during direct access reference, which is the reason this method is often not adopted (but see the section on software packages, p. 264).

Key size

On a 3330, the space taken up by the track index will be at least 57 per cent of track zero if all but one track of the device is allocated to data storage (the remaining track is assumed to be reserved for overflow records). If keys are greater than 155 bytes in length, the track index will exceed one full track in extent, and maximum length keys of 256 bytes will cause the cylinder index to take up as much as 28 per cent of the second track on the cylinder as well. Equivalent figures for the 3350 are even higher: the minimum track index size for a full cylinder file with no embedded overflow areas is 85 per cent of track zero, while maximum key sizes could expand this to almost one and two-thirds of a track. The influence of key size is shown in Fig. 7.16.

7.7 File packing

The prime data area of an indexed sequential file is less densely packed than the data area of a sequential file. There are three reasons for this. They are as follows:

1 The records or blocks of records take up more space, because they are in the CKD format with separate keys. The effect of this depends on record or block size, but can be calculated using the methods given in Chapter 4 on blocking and buffering (see p. 75). (Note that in some cases sequential files also use this format. This point would then not apply.)

2 The track index will take up part or all of the first track on each cylinder. The system-defined parts of this are standard in size, but the record key length depends on the user. A typical value might be eight bytes, leading to an index size of rather more than half a track (the number of entries in the index depends on the number of tracks or buckets, while the size of the track depends on the device). If the user decided on very large keys—and IBM

Indexed sequential files 247

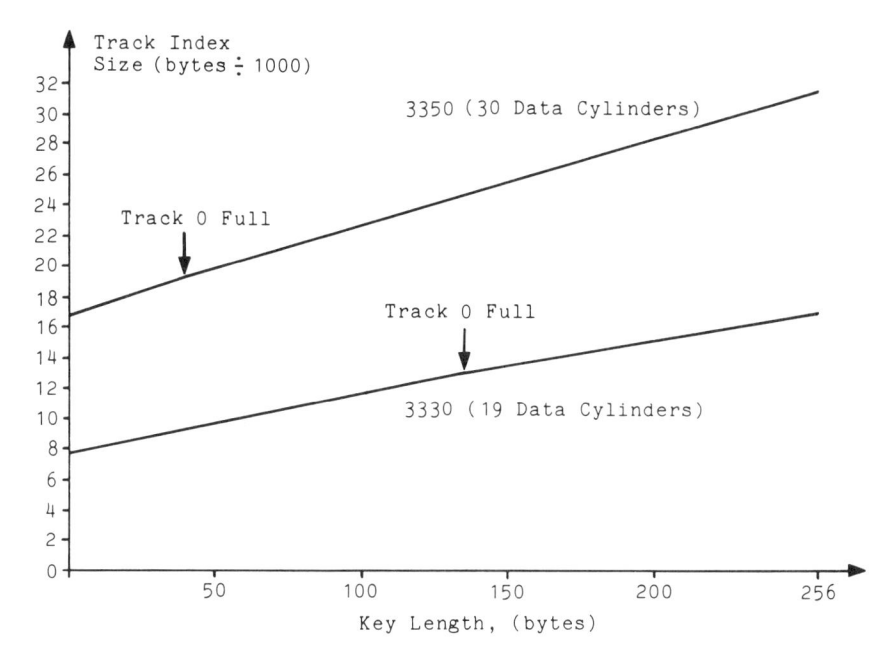

Fig. 7.16 The effect of key size on the space taken up by the track index on an IBM 3330 or 3350 that has no space reserved for overflow records, and so requires index entries for every track.

allows up to 256 bytes, for example—the track index might take up more than a single track. This is one reason to choose a fairly short key for indexed sequential use. A further reason is the size of the higher indexes; they, too, will be very much affected by the key size.

3 If embedded or cylinder overflow areas are provided they will take up one or more tracks of every cylinder. The file designer will try to keep these areas as small as possible to produce a well-packed file. However, the considerations given earlier on overflow area size and the need to allow for a relatively long period between reorganizations will guide the designer to a reasonable compromise. If a great deal of direct on-line storage is available, the balance will be tilted towards a larger provision of overflow space. If direct on-line storage is limited, it may be worth accepting more frequent reorganizations as the price for cutting down overflow space. ICL 2900 series software allows the user to specify the packing of home buckets that is desired when the file is created. This can be used to replace or supplement a cylinder overflow area; it is a form of *distributed free space* that is more evenly available through the file than a cylinder overflow area.

These three points will lead in most cases to something between 80 per cent and 90 per cent of the space in the prime data cylinders being used to store records. The best that can be achieved is 95–98 per cent packing if keys are small and no overflow is expected. There are, however, two further file structural areas that may reduce data packing.

4 The cylinder index and any higher-level indexes: it is unlikely that any but the largest files will require more than one cylinder for these indexes, although a complete cylinder has often to be set aside for them, as is required by some manufacturers' software. If this applies, small indexed sequential files bear a heavy burden compared with larger files. The probable penalty in packing density for a large file is of the order of 0.5 to 1 per cent, while for small files it can be very much more—50 per cent in the most extreme case, when the file takes up only one data cylinder.

5 The independent overflow area uses additional space, although in most cases this will not be excessive as the increase in time caused by continual head movements to the independent overflow area from the prime data area and back will soon show up in run times. The usual loss in packing density is again of the order of 0.5 per cent to 1 per cent, but as with the high-level indexes, there will be a proportionately heavy overhead for small files if the software requires a complete cylinder to be used for independent overflow.

Apart from the points discussed above, which are due to the structure of the file, two more considerations will influence the space required by the file.

6 Blocking of records: the demand for records in CKD format is more wasteful the smaller the record size. One way to use direct access storage more efficiently is to block effectively. This will depend on space being available to handle larger blocks in main storage; it was considered in more detail in Chapter 4 (see p. 75).

7 The use of variable-length records is sometimes unavoidable, but always leads to waste. It may appear as padding to a fixed size due to software limitations or it may be wasted space at the end of tracks and overflow areas because the record that should have gone there was too large. To this must be added the extra time and space demanded in main storage for relatively complex blocking–deblocking routines. The designer of an indexed sequential file will try to avoid using variable-length records; when they are necessary the discussion in Chapter 3 (see p. 67) should be helpful.

Coyle[8] has shown that it pays to leave some distributed free space within a file. As pointed out above, ICL allows the user to specify the packing density in buckets, but IBM does not. Dummy records can be provided to take the place of this space, by placing them where additions are expected, or in a pre-determined pattern throughout the file. This solution (used by Coyle) led to marked improvement in ISAM file performance. The packing density is not usually critical, but the additional space used does have an effect on file timing, which will be examined later.

Indexed sequential files can be processed either sequentially or directly. As handling of the file is very different in these two cases, we shall examine them separately.

7.8 Sequential processing

The user may wish to start at the beginning of the file, or at any other point. using IBM terminology, the SETL macro can be employed to indicate a starting point in the file and the ESETL macro to set a finishing point. When the processing program issues a GET macro the routine shown in Fig. 7.17 is initiated. The user is not directly aware of the steps shown but they will result in both 'housekeeping' processing time and input-output operations. The

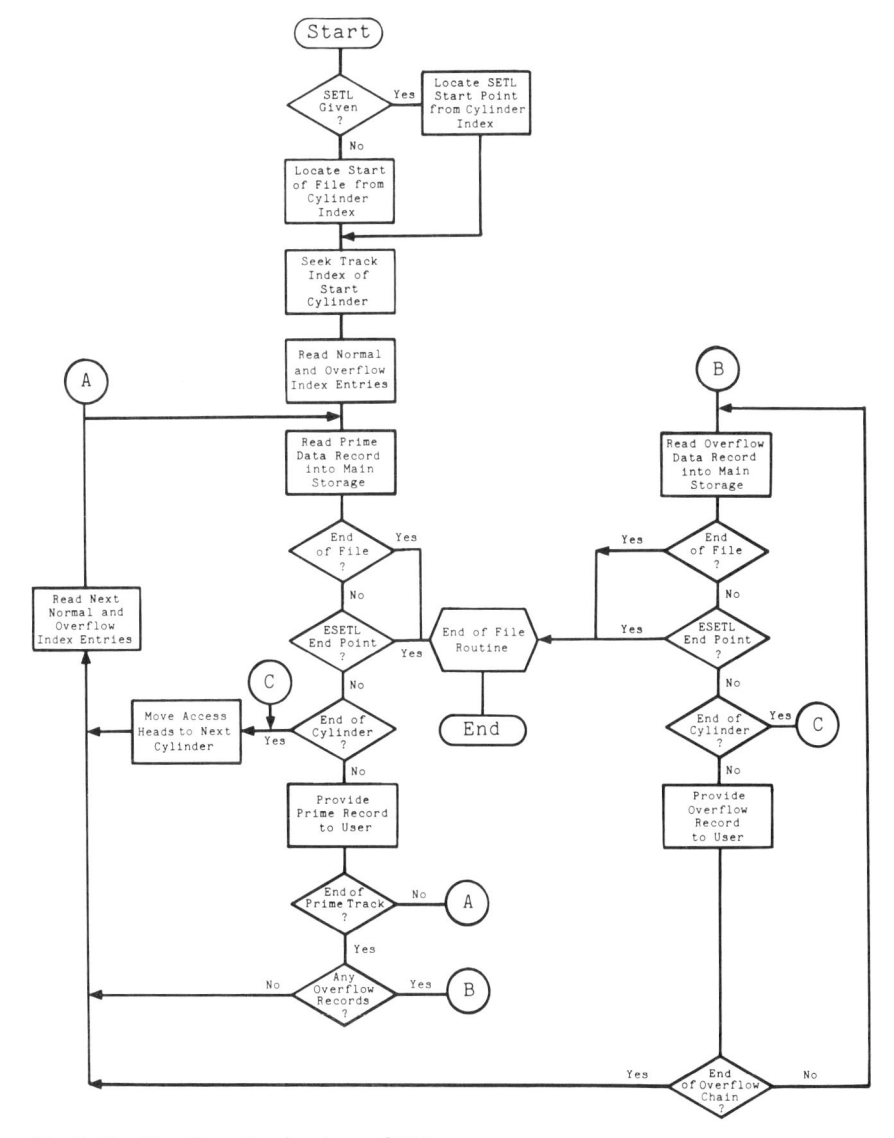

Fig. 7.17 Routine after issuing a GET macro.

sequence has been simplified for convenience, but it shows the essential stages in sequential retrieval. We shall refer to it in examining the various operations that can be carried out sequentially.

Retrieval before additions

All records will be in their correct places and the file will be physically as well as logically in sequence. The cylinder index (and any higher indexes) will only be referenced once at the start of the run. Head movement to the first data cylinder will be dependent on the size and position of the file. All further head movements will be from the current cylinder to the next and so will be of minimum duration—3 to 10 ms for modern disks. For semiconductor 'disks' or fixed-head disks all that is involved is electronic switching, which takes negligible time. The length of a sequential retrieval run will be slower than an equivalent run using a sequentially organized file for the following reasons:

1 *Reference to the cylinder index and any higher indexes*
This is not likely to take longer than 100 ms and average times are much lower, e.g. 30 ms average head movement for the IBM 3330, 25 ms for the 3350 and 16 ms for the 3380, followed by a search of the index. Thus the addition to a given run time will not be significant.

2 *Reference to the track index*
There will be a rotational delay of half a revolution on average before the required track index entries are found. This will be repeated for every track on the cylinder, so it will cause a sizeable addition to run times.

3 *Increased file size*
The track index will take up part of the first track of each cylinder. Overflow areas, even if empty, will take additional space. This will mean that the data requires more direct access storage space than a sequential file. Timing will be increased by:

   a) extra cylinder-to-cylinder head movements;
   b) an increased number of data tracks, each of which will require index entries and so will add to the time required for rotational delays described in 2 above.

As we are examining the case of sequential retrieval before additions, the items given above do not include overflow retrieval. However, there is more housekeeping activity in handling an indexed sequential file than the corresponding sequentially organized file. This will add to CPU usage, and the greater software module size will mean that more space is required in main storage.

The two file organizations are fully compared in Chapter 8 (see p. 300).

The effect of additions

We shall examine random additions to a file; as the principles involved do not change if the additions are grouped or regular in pattern, the methods used can be adapted to suit those cases. Table 7.5 shows the percentage of tracks with 0,1,2, . . . additional records as a result of additions made randomly to a file. These figures only hold accurately for large files—100 or more tracks in extent—although they will act as a guide even for very small files. Fig. 7.18 displays the results pictorially. Note that Table 7.5 only applies to the given number of records per track while Fig. 7.18 is more general.

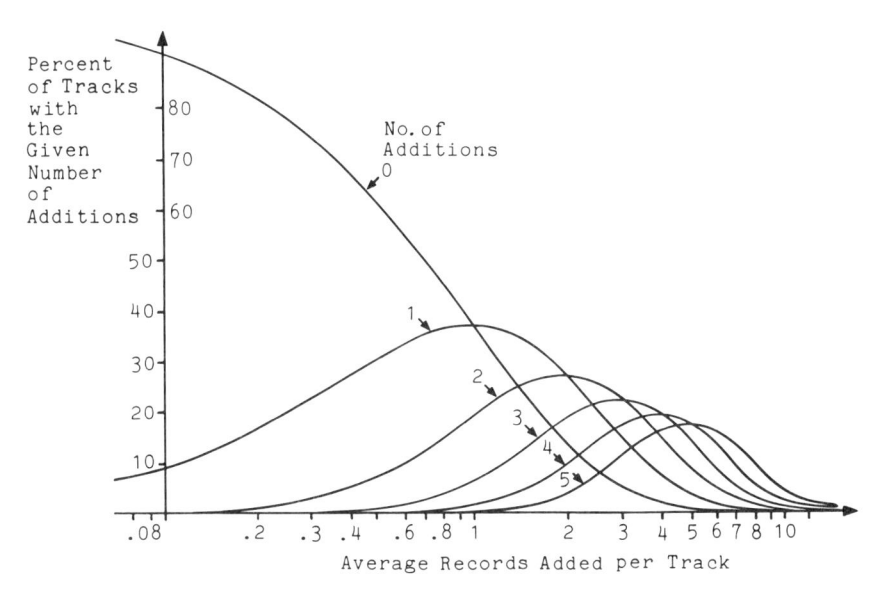

Fig. 7.18 The curves show the percentage of tracks with the given number of records added.

The impact of additions depends on the additions technique used.

1 Record insertion

This is the standard balanced tree type of index, described on page 223. If a single record has been inserted, the last record logically on the track will now be held in overflow. The average wait before this is located would be half a revolution if the whole overflow track were full. Usually this is not the case so the average wait will be less than half a revolution. For timing purposes it is best to assume a wait of half a revolution, bearing in mind that this is usually an overestimate.

The duration of this wait may often lead to the overflow record being processed more rapidly than prime data track records because processing

252 Design of computer data files

Table 7.5 The figures show the percentage of tracks with the given number of records added.

	Percentage additions	\multicolumn{13}{c}{Number of records added to the track}
		0	1	2	3	4	5	6	7	8	9	10	11	12
1 Record per track	20	81.87	16.37	1.64	0.11	0.01								
	40	67.03	26.81	5.36	0.72	0.07	0.01							
12 Records per track	20	9.07	21.77	26.13	20.90	12.54	6.02	2.41	0.83	0.22	0.05	0.01		
	40	0.82	3.95	9.48	15.17	18.20	17.47	13.98	9.59	5.75	3.07	1.47	0.64	0.26
14 Records per track	20	6.08	17.03	23.84	22.25	15.57	8.72	4.07	1.63	0.57	0.18	0.05	0.01	
	40	0.37	2.07	5.80	10.82	15.15	16.97	15.84	12.67	8.87	5.52	3.09	1.57	0.73

time will often be low enough to allow this record to be processed as soon as it is located. Records on the prime data track, as has been explained earlier, may each cause a full revolution to be lost if they cannot be processed during the time the inter-record gap is traversed.

When there are two or more overflow records on a track, the first overflow record in logical sequence, i.e. the last to go into overflow, will require half a revolution on average to locate it. This is usually an underestimate as the first logical overflow record is always the last from that track physically and tends to be located near the end of the overflow track.

Each later overflow record will require nearly a full revolution. Fig. 7.19 shows the situation on an overflow track.

In this case an overflow chain of three records has been established from the prime track. The logical and physical sequence of these records is inverted, and the wait-time spiral (WAIT 1 + WAIT 2 + WAIT 3) shows that it will take more than two revolutions of the disk to access the three records. WAIT 1 cannot be overlapped, except with separate functions of this or some other program. WAIT 2 and WAIT 3 will be overlapped with the

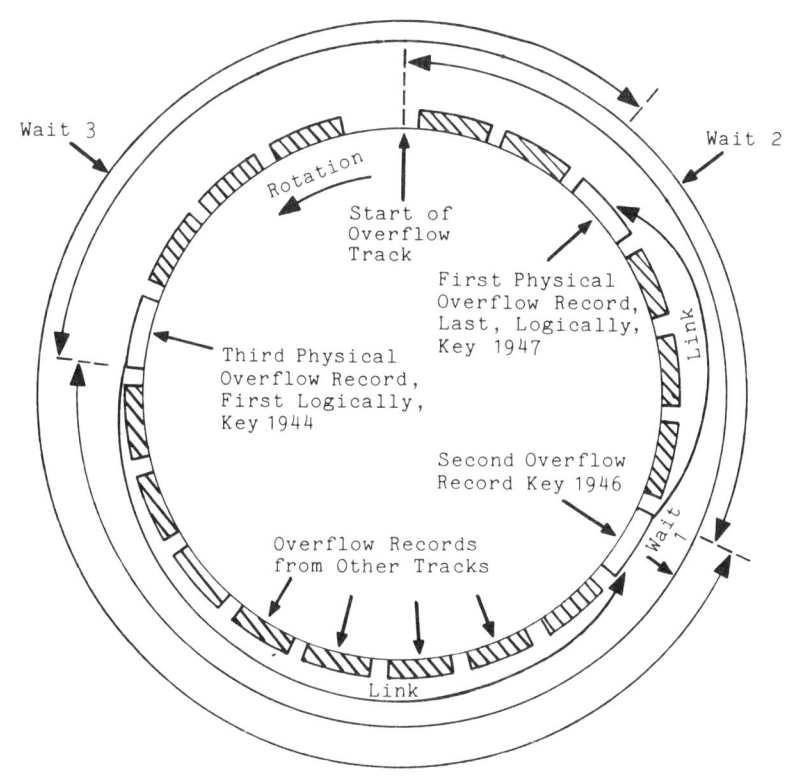

Fig. 7.19 Record insertion—the situation on an overflow track. Wait 1: this time elapses while the software seeks the first logical overflow record. Wait 2: during this time the first logical overflow record is processed and the second is searched for. Wait 3: the second logical overflow record is processed and the third is searched for.

processing of records 1 and 2, while the processing time for record 3 has to be added to the minimum delay of the three WAITS. The estimate of three revolutions for three overflow records will thus be fairly accurate in this case. As n overflow records will require $(n-1)$ full revolutions, to which the seek and processing times for the last record have to be added, this estimate will get more accurate the more records there are in the overflow chain. These timings will hold so long as wait times exceed processing times, which is often true. When this does not hold, additional full revolutions will be added to the total time because the next record to be processed will be missed, and a further revolution or revolutions will be required before it is available once more.

2 Record linking

This technique is used in the direct-link balanced tree. If the overflow record is held on the same cylinder as the prime data there will be an average wait of half a revolution to refer to the overflow record. If processing time is negligible there will be an additional half a revolution to return to the next prime track record, and the total time to locate and process the overflow record will be precisely one revolution. The longer the overflow record processing time, the more frequently will this not be completed before the next prime-track record is available. This will mean that an additional revolution is lost, so the total time incurred per overflow record will exceed one revolution on average. The range of processing times that will allow processing to be completed in a single revolution is shown in Fig. 7.20. Note that, as the time available to process the prime record increases, that available to process the overflow record decreases proportionally.

If the minimum figure—a loss of one revolution per overflow record—is assumed as an average, it will certainly not be an overestimate. For long processing times this will be too low a figure, but it will then be part of run times markedly higher as a result of overall long processing times and it is probable that overflow records will not cause much extra delay.

3 Comparison of the two techniques

Experimental and simulation work carried out by Montgomery and his co-workers[1,15] has shown that the sequential retrieval time for records increases as more of the file is held in overflow. This is less marked for smaller numbers of records per block and some trials have shown an improvement for blocks of only two records. McDonnell and Montgomery[1] found that higher overflow percentages than 10–25 per cent led to increased retrieval times for all block sizes.

Random insertions to balanced tree files that use two index entries per track took rather less time as the overflow percentage in the file built up. This was more marked for larger blocks than smaller ones. In comparison, the time required to make random insertions to direct-linked balanced tree files did not change with overflow percentage. This is to be expected, bearing in mind the way in which insertion is handled.

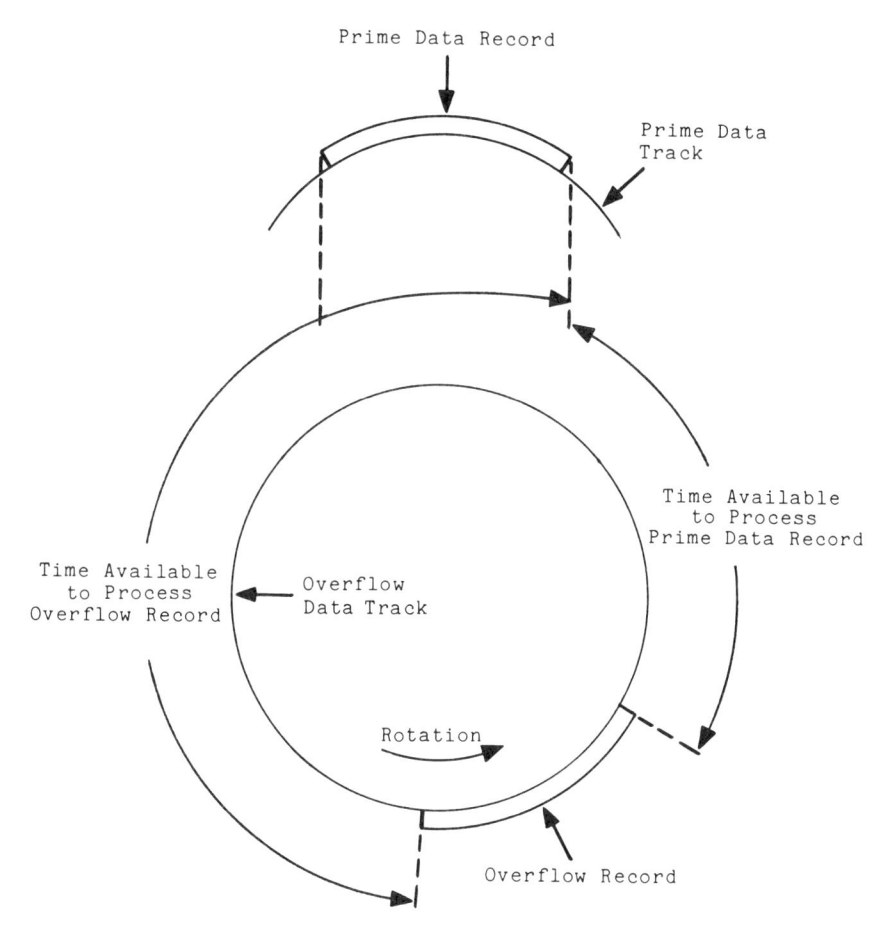

Fig. 7.20 If both prime data record and overflow record can be processed while the disk rotates, only one rotation is lost. Depending on the relative position of the two records, the time available for each record to be processed will vary, but the total will be nearly one revolution.

The effect of hit rate

One of the great strengths of indexed sequential files is that skip-sequential processing is made easy. When the hit rate—the percentage of records that has to be processed—is low, records, whole tracks and even cylinders may be skipped without reading them if they are not required. Although a sequential file using a record storage format in which keys are separate from data can also skip records, every key has to be checked so every track has to be traversed, whether any records on it are required or not. An indexed file can allow more marked savings to be made, as only the index entries need to be read, and these show which tracks and cylinders can be skipped.

The effect of hit rate depends also on the pattern of hits. Analysis of this is mathematically similar to that of patterns of overflow record occurrences, and the following cases will be considered:

1. random;
2. even;
3. grouped;
4. grouped superposed on random.

1 Random update pattern
When hit rates are low, the probability that two adjacent records will *both* require updating is also low. This implies that there is a good chance the processing of the first record will be complete by the time that the second record is located, so that skip-sequential processing will provide benefits. Whether such benefits are available depends both on average hit rate and on processing time.

The results of a series of experiments have shown that the pattern obtained is very similar to those given for sequential disk files in Fig. 5.8(d). Thus the relationship between hit rate and overall run time is roughly equivalent to hit rate, but stepped in characteristic disk fashion. As hit rate reduces, more and more benefit is obtained from skip-sequential processing. This is examined in detail in Chapter 9, pages 300–307.

2 Even update pattern
When every second, third, . . . nth record is updated, conditions are ideal for rapid skip-sequential runs. A constant period is available during seeks to process the records already in main storage, and if every record requires the same processing time this will lead to very predictable run timings. These will increase stepwise in that, up to some limiting time, processing will be entirely overlapped with seeking. Beyond this threshold processing time there will be a loss of one revolution for every one, two, . . . b records, depending on the number of I–O buffers, b, that is in use.

A precisely even update pattern is not usual, so the designer is unlikely to be able to rely on such an occurrence in deciding on file timings. However, in the few cases where it does occur, this type of update pattern makes timing calculations relatively easy.

3 Grouped updates
This pattern occurs frequently due to factors such as the way in which meter readings for, say, electricity supply are made from house to house, i.e. not at random, or the effects of localized advertising campaigns on a larger file in which many unaffected records are stored.

The effect of grouped updates is to cause parts of the file to require few, if any, updates so records are being skipped, and other areas in which all—or most—records are updated, and thus there will be lost revolutions because processing times exceed inter-record gap times. If skip-sequential processing is correctly used, whole areas of the file can be skipped, producing an improvement in run time similar to that achieved by sectioning a sequential file on magnetic tape (see Chapter 5 for details, p. 112). In group update areas, if every record in the group has to be processed there will be extra revolutions for every record, every second record, ... every bth record, depending on buffering arrangements, where b is the number of buffers as before. For all normal record updating a loss of this magnitude can be expected, but it would not apply if the processing involved is trivial because then the records can be processed at reading—that is, rotation—speeds.

In summary, the areas in which there are few updates can be skipped very quickly. Grouped update areas will take an overall time related to individual record processing time, buffer arrangement, update density, i.e. hit rate, and device rotation time. Although this is complex to analyse, the average times are easily checked in any given case. The file designer can measure the results of applying groups of updates to the file and make timing estimates based on the results of these tests.

4 Grouped updates with additional random updates

This case also often occurs in practice due to the results of cases such as grouped meter readings from customers who were at home when the meter reader called, combined with customers' own readings carried out because they were out when the meter reader called, and a number of special checks that are carried out at a different time.

Timings can be handled by considering the two separate situations and combining their effects. The skip-sequential processing of sparsely updated file areas cannot now be regarded as straightforward. Every cylinder, and quite probably most tracks, will have one or more records that require updating. However, the likelihood is that processing and seeking will be entirely overlapped so this will not hold up the overall run very seriously.

In the grouped update areas there will be little or no effect, as the hit rate is already high. Additional transactions from the 'background' random distribution will only make it more unlikely that seeking and processing can be overlapped. This will reduce the variability of timings due to chance variations in overlap, and so make it possible to calculate run timings more accurately.

The effect of blocking

The blocking of records in general has been dealt with in Chapter 4 (see pp. 71–98). The main significance of blocking here is that, even if a low percentage of *records* is hit in a run, blocking them together will increase this figure. Again, the increase is not directly proportional to the blocking factor. The results of any given blocking factor on hit rate can be calculated from Table 4.5 and Fig. 4.6. For example, if a file has an individual record hit rate

Table 7.6 Results of varying the blocking factor for a file with an individual hit rate of 1 per cent, the hits being randomly distributed.

Blocking factor	Percentage of records that must be read (as at least one record in the block is hit)
1	1
3	3
10	9.5
30	26.0
100	63.2
300	95
1000	100

of 1 per cent and the hits are randomly distributed, the results of varying the blocking factor are as shown in Table 7.6.

The reason for the need to read more records is that as the blocks get larger there is an ever-increasing likelihood of at least one update being required from amongst the records in the block. Concentration of updates in a particular area—case 3 above—reduces the number of blocks that have to be read and in the most extreme case, where all or none of the records in a block require updating, the percentage of records that need to be read would not change due to blocking.

At the other extreme, very even updating patterns would mean that most blocks or even every block required to be read and such a pattern would therefore make skip-sequential processing pointless.

The main impact of blocking on the speed of skip-sequential processing is usually counter-productive, although it often achieves more in space-saving and rapid data transfer than is lost in increased block activity. Blocking will not usually increase the probability of having to read data from a given track, except insofar as it allows more records to be stored on that track. It will, however, mean that a larger quantity of data has to be transferred into main storage for each update operation, even if only one record in the block is required. Overall, a larger blocking factor will not markedly change the balance of choice between skip-sequential processing of sequentially and indexed sequentially organized files.

7.9 Direct processing

The overall set of operations that take place when an indexed sequential file is directly processed is shown in Fig. 7.21. This sequence occurs whenever a reference is made to the file, and it is helpful to examine each stage of the process:

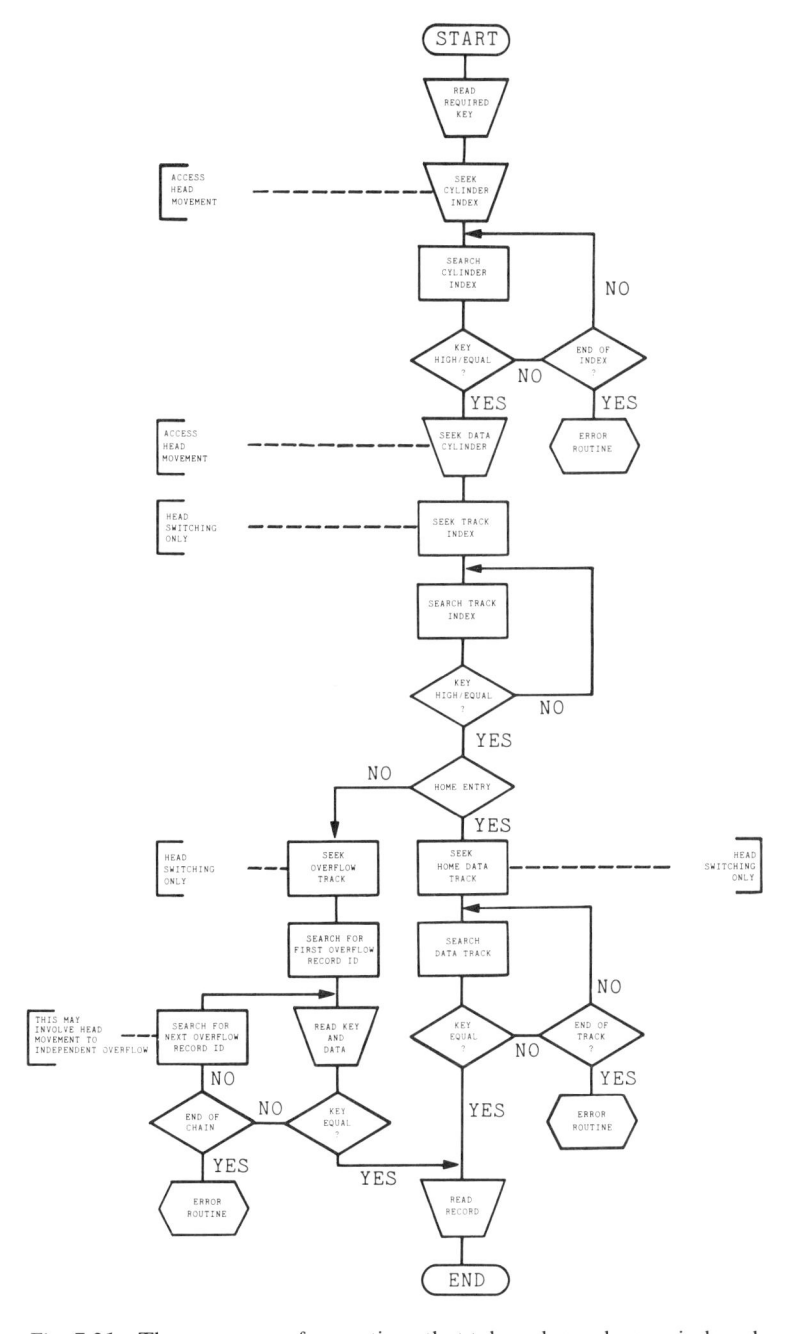

Fig. 7.21 The sequence of operations that takes place when an indexed sequential file is directly processed.

Reference to the cylinder and higher-level indexes This will involve a head movement in most cases. If the file is small, the cylinder index may be partly or entirely held in main storage, as explained earlier in this chapter (see p. 228). Otherwise it should be stored on the most rapidly accessible device available.

Reference to the track index This will take between three-quarters of a revolution and a full revolution as the start of the index will need to be located before it can be searched. This will take $R/2$ on average, followed by half the index—which is usually slightly over half a track in extent—before the required entry is located.

Reference to the appropriate data track The timing here depends on whether the record in question is stored on a prime or an overflow track.

1 *Prime track storage*
If the record required is available on the prime data track it should be located, on average, in half a revolution. When the start of the track has to be detected, this will be modified; the track index start will have been found—taking a time $R/2$—and the index entry will have been located, read and processed during a single revolution (in most cases). Thus the overall time to read the track index and locate the data record will be:

$R/2$ (to seek start of index track)
$+ R$ (to read and process index entry and seek start of data track)
$+ R/2$ (to locate data record)
$= 2R$

These calculations will apply to files in which all the data records are held in sequence on the prime data track, as for example in IBM systems. Retrieval of records in files handled using linked overflow will not be so straightforward. Depending on the software and the linkages provided it is probable that overflow records will have to be retrieved and checked as they are encountered. This will add at least one revolution for every overflow record and will mean that the time to locate a data record, after the data track has been located, will be:

$$\frac{R(m + 1)}{2}$$

where there is an average of m overflow records per track.

The additional times caused by linkage handling can be avoided if the link held on the prime data track contains the record key, and if the software can detect whether the required record is in overflow quickly enough to avoid missing the start of the next record.

2 Storage on an overflow track
The effects here can be analysed in three stages. They are:

a) first overflow records from a track;
b) further overflow records from tracks on a cylinder stored in the cylinder overflow area;
c) records stored in an independent overflow area on some other cylinder.

First overflow records do not add any additional time if the index has two entries per track, and if the index items point to the first record in the overflow chain. The software will recognize the key concerned, and the prime data track will be bypassed. In the linked overflow case, however, each overflow represents a break in the search. Thus the link would be expected to occur on average after $R/2$, and the overflow record would also take an average of $R/2$ to locate (or R if the start of the overflow track has to be found before the record search can begin). Depending on the software, further overflow records may take no additional time—if it is not necessary to follow all chains—or the *average* time per overflow record may be $nR/2$, where there are n overflow records per track and every overflow chain has to be followed during a record search.

Overflow records other than the first will cause a time lapse of at least $(n-1)R$ (see page 254 for details).

Overflow records held on a separate cylinder will require a head movement to the overflow cylinder. An estimate of their number is given in Table 7.3 for the case where additions are random. There will be little difference between embedded (that is, on the cylinder) and independent overflow methods when additions are random, and independent overflow will prove to be very wasteful of time. As explained earlier, it is therefore important to avoid the use of independent overflow areas except as a safety precaution; the one exception to this is when updates are grouped in a few areas.

The effect of overflow records on the average seek times for directly processed records has been investigated by Montgomery and Hubbard[15] and the author[16]. This work has shown the gradual deterioration of performance as random additions are made to a file, and the marked acceleration of this process as records are allocated to independent overflow.

Factors involved in design

1 Blocking
Unlike its impact on sequential retrieval, the result of blocking on direct retrieval is not marked. The record search process is not usually lengthened at all, so only the increased data transfer time needs to be considered. This is generally of the order of a millisecond or so at most.

262 Design of computer data files

2 Batching and sorting input

Sequential processing of an indexed sequential file avoids many access head movements and minimizes those that are unavoidable. As an example, if there are 200 enquiries made to a file and the file is stored on a disk with 200 cylinders, a completely random distribution of these enquiries would lead to:

126 cylinders with one or more active records in them;
74 inactive cylinders.

Handling these enquiries directly would involve 200 average head movements, about 200 × 30 ms for a 3330, giving a total of 6 seconds.

By comparison, batching and sorting the enquiries would lead to 126 head movements, most of which would be an absolute minimum of 10 ms and none of which would be much longer than 15 ms. In addition, about seventy-four cylinders could be skipped so there would be around 126 × 10 ms required for head movements. This gives a time of about 1.3 seconds for head movements, rather less than a quarter of the earlier figure. The difference grows as numbers increase; with anything over 1000 enquiries *all* the cylinders would be likely to be referenced, thus giving a time of 20 × 10 ms or 2 seconds for the batched and sorted input, and 2000 × 30 ms or 60 seconds for the unsorted input.

These figures do not allow for two important aspects of the situation. The first is that sorting itself takes time. This is relatively short, but there is also an operating time involved, and for safety a one-minute or five-minute overhead has been added to the actual sort times given in Fig. 7.22. These

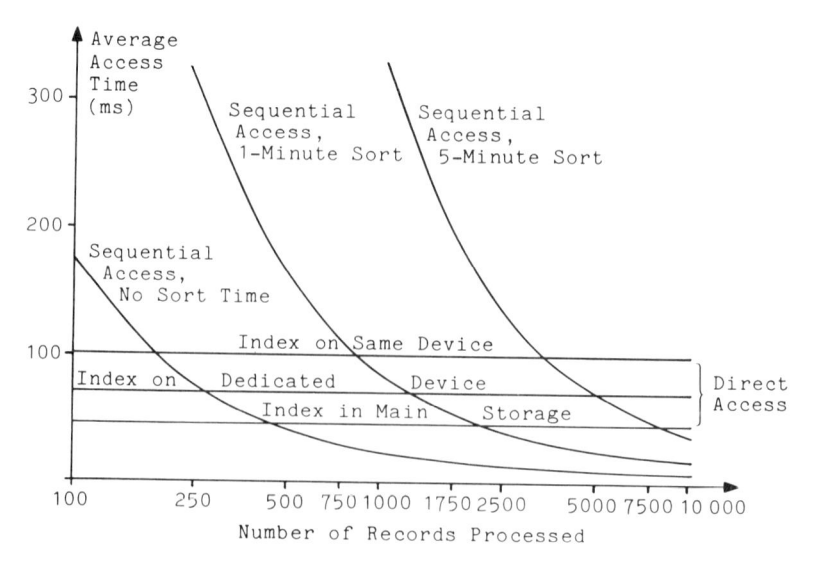

Fig. 7.22 Comparison of batching and sorting times with direct reference for a file that requires a whole 2314 disk.

compare batching and sorting times with direct reference, for a file that takes up the whole of a 2314 disk[16].

The second consideration is that batching implies holding up the first enquiries to be received. For a true enquiry such a delay is probably not possible, but in cases where the input is directly processed for convenience alone it should always be considered. In the many instances where updates arise in a 'batch' mode, as for example incoming mail, there is seldom any good reason to process directly, as the overall level of service will be improved by batching and sorting. The few quickly-processed updates that are handled first, if direct processing is adopted, are more than counter-balanced by the shorter overall run time and thus better average service performance achieved by batching and sorting.

The file designer will find it worthwhile to examine every direct processing application of an indexed sequential file critically. When batches are large, overall throughput will be much improved if any runs can be converted to batched and sorted operations. The break-even points between the two modes of processing can be seen clearly in Fig. 7.22; for numbers of records for which a sequential curve is above each straight line that represents the time required to process a record directly, direct processing is faster. After the curve is below any given line, batches of that size or greater should be processed by batching and sorting when that is possible.

7.10 The impact of software on indexed sequential files

Manufacturers' software

Generally, manufacturers provide software to format, load, update and reference indexed sequential files. Statistics on the number of embedded overflow areas that are full, how much space remains in the independent overflow area, how many non-first overflow records are being directly referenced, etc., are usually available. These are of considerable assistance to the file designer, and should be examined at the end of each run, at least while operating data for a file is still limited.

The options available to the user will also allow definition of blocking factor, overflow technique and size of overflow areas. As all of these may have default options, it is important that the designer should make positive decisions about them and ensure that the file does reflect the design intended for it.

Some other helpful features may be available but not made clear. For example, handling of overflow is facilitated in IBM systems if the designer allocates sufficient buffer space (usually this means defining more than two I-O buffers).

A number of manufacturers provide a *filestore* facility that handles the storage of data files in a way that uses backing storage efficiently but does not allow the user any opportunity to optimize file performance. Although ease of use is important, this approach to file design is not desirable unless the manufacturer's software also optimizes[7], which is seldom possible.

On occasions manufacturers' software is not highly efficient for a given application, and software houses have taken advantage of this to provide alternative packages. The shortcomings focussed on by alternative suppliers are usually these:

1 Large user keys increase index size;
2 Records are unblocked in the overflow areas, which wastes space;
3 Separate software modules are required to handle direct and sequential retrieval, using a great deal of space in main storage;
4 Overflow records add markedly to run times;
5 When high hit rate files are processed, many revolutions are lost due to processing not being complete when the next record is located.

Some of the software that is available to exploit these conditions is discussed below.

Software packages

The COMTEN AMIGOS software allows the user to replace two separate IBM modules, one for sequential and the other for direct reference to an indexed sequential file, by a single module that requires less space and performs the same functions; this is particularly helpful if a single run updates sequentially but allows enquiries during the runs. On the other hand, the dual-function module is larger than either of the single-function modules it replaces, so it offers no benefit for single-function runs.

The AMIGOS package includes two other functions that improve space utilization and processing speed. As a standard, each track is divided into just THREE data blocks, so arranged that they are read in the order 1,3,2 as shown in Fig. 7.23. This allows a reasonable time for processing, and results in fewer lost revolutions than is normally possible. However, it doubles the minimum run time, and so will not help in some cases. The second change is that records are also blocked in overflow. Although this will mean a slightly increased retrieval time (of the order of 5–8 ms depending on the device) it is claimed that the space saving more than offsets this overhead.

Universal Software Inc. offer a PSAM package that achieves improvement by splitting additions between blocks in the prime data area—i.e. providing distributed free space—rather than defining separate overflow areas. This provides more rapid access to established files, and less-frequent reorganizations. Freshly reorganized files are identical in performance, whether organized using PSAM or IBM's ISAM. It is also claimed to reduce space usage.

Examples like these make it appear that the performance of manufacturers' software can always be bettered. Coyle[8] showed that it was possible to improve the speed of an ISAM file by more than four times by using the

Indexed sequential files   **265**

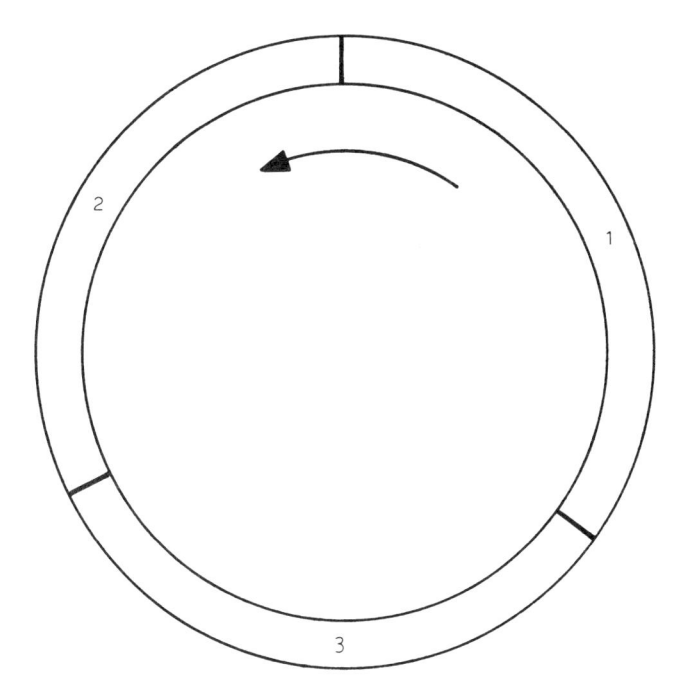

Fig. 7.23 Design of data blocks in the COMTEN AMIGOS software package. All three blocks can be read in two rotations so long as processing can be carried out during rotation. Note that the *minimum* processing time for a track is now two revolutions.

```
8000 Trs./Hr ◄── Original Throughput
        New records added in descending order
        'Dummy' records to handle future additions

12000 Trans./Hour

        Addition of a master index

16000 Trans./Hour

        Master index held in main storage

22000 Transactions/Hour

        Cylinder index held in main storage

28000 Transactions/Hour

        Binary search of in-core tables replaces
        manufacturers routine
                                            ◄── Optimized
33000 Transactions/Hour                         Throughput
```

Fig. 7.24 Improvements in the speed of an IBM ISAM file due to a series of optimizing steps[8].

optimization options available in IBM's software. The steps he took are shown in Fig. 7.24. In the case he quotes it was decided not to use alternative software, and other users should ensure that they have already exhausted the possibilities of improving the performance of their present software before they turn to other sources.

The manufacturers have incorporated some of the ideas introduced by software houses into their own offerings, and the facilities provided by IBM's VSAM illustrate this process. VSAM is of interest to us, partly because the indexing technique used, which has been described in detail by Wagner[17], is a modified B-tree.

IBM's VSAM (Virtual Sequential Access Method)

This file organization technique is a development of ISAM that incorporates many of the concepts used in the software obtainable from independent suppliers. The method is only available for use with virtual storage systems, and offers access to records in three ways. These are:

1 Reference by record key;
2 Reference by address relative to the start of the file using the *relative byte address* (RBA for short);
3 Reference by relative record number (fixed-length records only).

Of these, 1 (referring to the record by its key) can be compared to ISAM in operation, so the similarities and differences are examined here. A key-sequenced file or *data set* is created, with its associated indexes, as a *cluster*. For our purposes the cluster is an indexed file.

Data storage is divided into *control intervals* which are continuous areas of storage of a size that is not necessarily related to the physical make-up of the device on which the data is stored. This is shown in Fig. 7.25. A control interval is the unit of data moved between virtual and backing storage. In a sense it is equivalent to a track in an ISAM file, in that there is one index entry per control interval.

A group of control intervals makes up a *control area*. The whole of a control area is referenced by the entries in a single index record, and in a sense this is equivalent to a cylinder in ISAM terms. The index relates key values to the relative byte address locations of the data record.

Indexes are arranged as follows. All the higher indexes are collectively called the *index set*, and they are divided into index records containing a number of pointers. One of these pointers indicates the next index record at *this* level, and is used to move sequentially through the file. The other pointers indicate the location of a number of index records at a lower level. The lowest level of index records makes up the *sequence set*, and in this case the pointers are to control intervals; the total number of control intervals indexed by one index record makes up a control area. The structure of a key-sequenced VSAM file is shown Fig. 7.26.

Indexed sequential files **267**

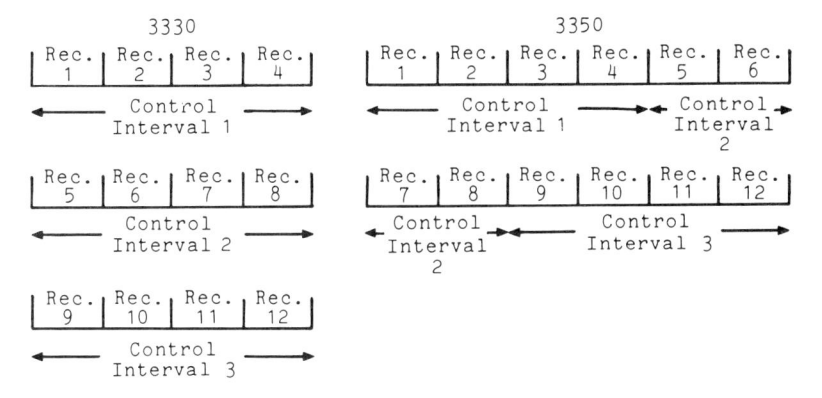

```
            3330                              3350
| Rec.| Rec.| Rec.| Rec.|     | Rec.| Rec.| Rec.| Rec.| Rec.| Rec.|
|  1  |  2  |  3  |  4  |     |  1  |  2  |  3  |  4  |  5  |  6  |
◄─────Control──────►         ◄─────Control──────►◄────Control────►
      Interval 1                   Interval 1         Interval
                                                          2
| Rec.| Rec.| Rec.| Rec.|     | Rec.| Rec.| Rec.| Rec.| Rec.| Rec.|
|  5  |  6  |  7  |  8  |     |  7  |  8  |  9  | 10  | 11  | 12  |
◄─────Control──────►         ◄──Control──►◄──────Control──────►
      Interval 2                Interval          Interval 3
                                    2
| Rec.| Rec.| Rec.| Rec.|
|  9  | 10  | 11  | 12  |
◄─────Control──────►
      Interval 3
```

Fig. 7.25 IBM's VSAM file organization technique. Control intervals are usually best adjusted to the size of a track. However, clusters can be transferred to other devices without redefinition; this is shown here for the IBM 3330 and the result of transferring data to the 3350 with its greater capacity.

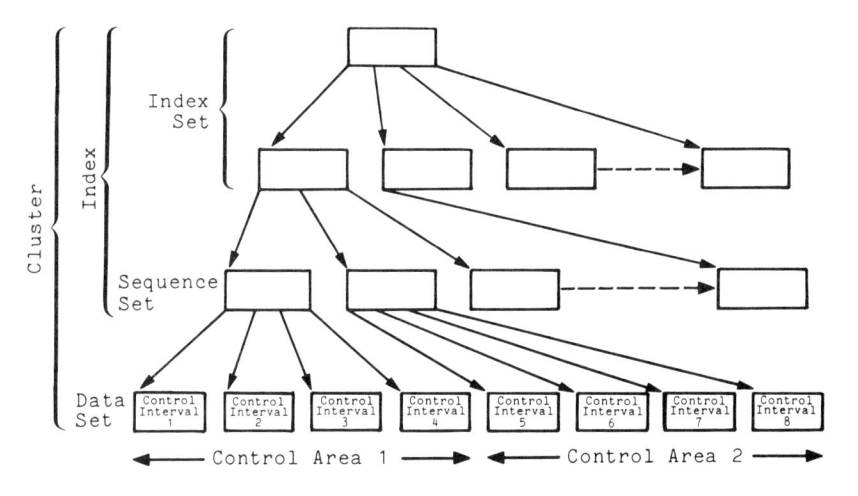

Fig. 7.26 The make-up of a key-sequenced VSAM file or cluster.

Additions to the file are catered for by the provision of *distributed free space*. This can be allocated by allowing a number of control intervals to remain entirely empty, by leaving space at the end of every control interval that contains data records, or by a combination of both techniques. As all the space available in a control area is allocated when the file is set up, VSAM provides the equivalent of a cylinder overflow area in ISAM and a proportion of free space in data storage areas, just as was done in ICL 1900 series software. Records added to a file are blocked in the same way as the original data and not unblocked as in ISAM. VSAM does not leave deleted records in the data area, as does ISAM. Instead, the area occupied by the record or part of a record that has been deleted is added to the distributed free space available. Within the control interval the remaining records are moved towards the start of the control interval, which requires their RBAs to be altered and avoids fragmentation of the free space in the control interval.

When records are inserted, the RBAs of any following records will be increased as a result of their movement in the control interval. If there is not sufficient space for the inserted records in the control interval, a *control interval split* takes place under VSAM control. This uses any free control intervals in the control area rather than the free space in other control intervals containing data. The consequence of this is that the records may not be physically in sequence after a control interval split, although they will be handled in sequence by the indexes.

If there is insufficient room in the control area to handle all additions, a *control area split* takes place under VSAM control. Approximately half the control intervals in the old control area are moved to the new control area, which is made available either as a result of decisions taken when the file was defined or by extending the file as required. The new control area is likely to be physically remote from the original site of the data. Although VSAM will handle it sequentially, the situation is similar to that of providing an independent overflow area in ISAM and should be avoided whenever possible. Splits in control intervals and control areas are shown in Fig. 7.27.

VSAM provides the possibility of holding *alternate indexes*, so the user can reference a file using a number of different keys. The index set defined first is known as the prime index, to distinguish it from the alternate indexes. Alternate indexes are updated when records are added or deleted, if UPGRADE is specified in the alternate index definition. Alternate keys can be duplicated, unlike primary keys, so that a department code could be an alternate key and allow searches to be carried out to select personnel from a particular department. Keys in all VSAM indexes are compressed, only the distinguishing parts of the keys being stored, in order to reduce the size of index entries. These facilities make VSAM more similar to database software than most of the file organization techniques that have been examined so far—in fact, many of the database systems available for mini- and micro-computers provide only this multiple index facility. VSAM itself is used to handle the tables in IBM's DB2 relational database software.

VSAM can be optimized by careful design, applying the same principles that have been described earlier. The designer should look at the following factors:

1 The relation of data areas and index position to the physical characteristics of the device. The portability of a VSAM file from one device to another, and from operation under one OS/VS system to another, or from DOS/VS to OS/VS is helpful, as it allows for rapid conversion when different

Indexed sequential files **269**

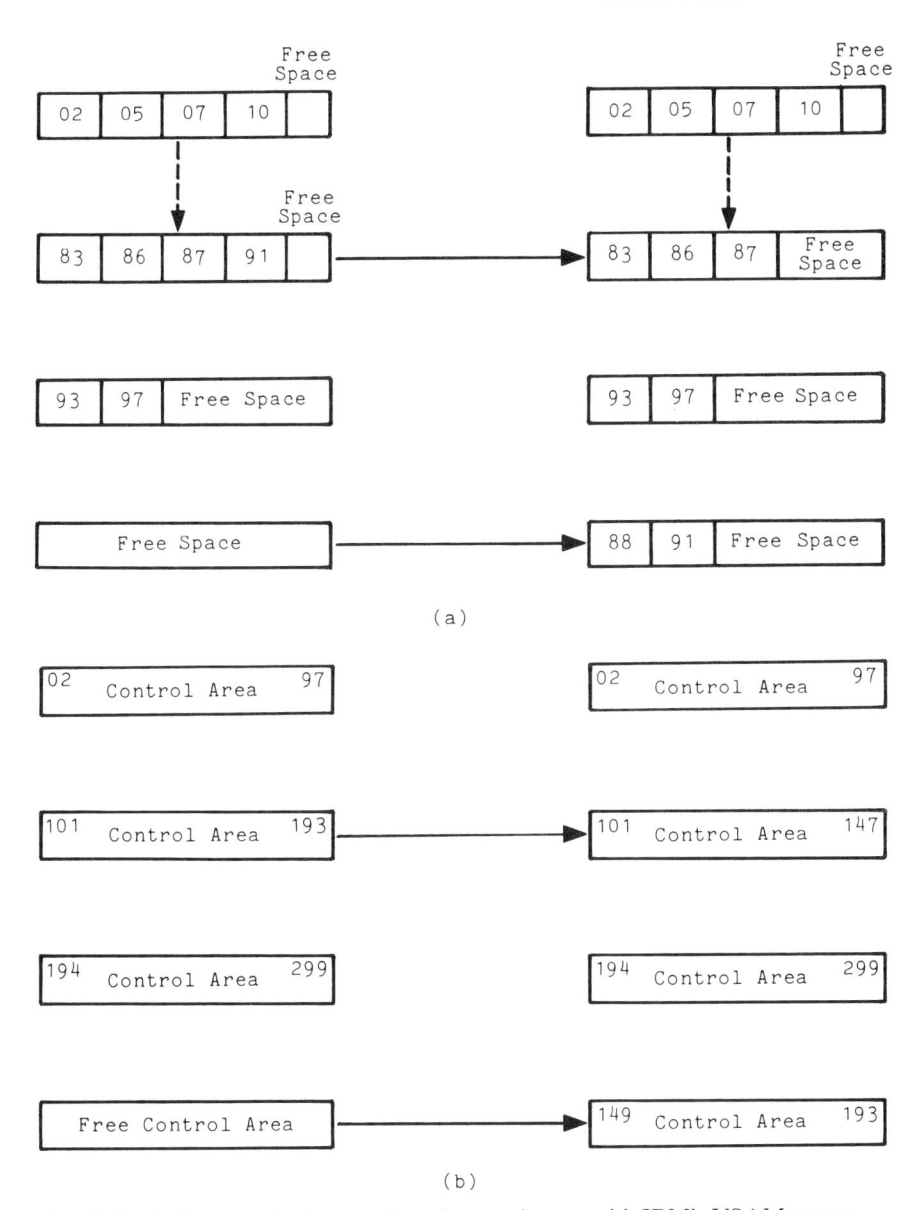

Fig. 7.27 Splits in control intervals and control areas with IBM's VSAM system.

(a) The addition of record 88 causes the free control interval at the end of the control area to be brought into use. Note that the records are no longer physically in sequential order. If no free control interval is available a control area split occurs.

(b) If a record is added to a control area, and there is neither sufficient free space in the appropriate control interval nor a free control interval in that control area, a new free control area is used to split the control area to which the record has been added. About half the records in the original control area are transferred. In this case a record has been added to the second control area and, as there is no room for it, a control area split has occurred.

disks are installed. However, for optimum performance the size of control intervals and control areas should be so arranged that a sequence set record will be stored on the same cylinder as the control area it indexes. This means that movement from, say, a 3330 to a 3350 will require the definition of new control area sizes unless the number of control areas on a cylinder is already $2n$ on the 3330. There will then be $3n$ control areas per cylinder on the 3350 and no loss of performance will result from the transfer. The way the conversion operates is shown in Figure 7.25.

2   The size and number of the buffers provided by the user for VSAM directly determines the number of higher index records held in virtual storage (as against backing storage). Hence, buffers should be both as large as possible and related in size to index record size.

3   Distribution of free space—the ability to define empty control intervals where they are required—means that careful planning with a knowledge of the likely distribution of additions will reduce the need for control area splits, and possibly of control interval splits. This will improve performance. Further details of VSAM are available in IBM publications[18,19].

4   The size of blocks used to hold data. Although the user may imagine that any block size will be acceptable, VSAM only uses blocks of size $512b$ or $2048b$, where b can take any value in the range 1–16; this means that VSAM will round up any intermediate value to the next available block size, so wasting the difference between the two values. Choice of block size is therefore important if wasted space is to be avoided.

Conclusion

Wright[20] has described both ISAM and VSAM files as applied to bubble memory, taking account of the particular design requirements imposed by bubble memory. He also provides a very detailed description of the medium. Jalics[21] has compared the performance of IBM's ISAM on a PC AT, a 370/158 and a 3081; contrary to expectations, the micro comes very well out of this trial, due to its use of an improved balanced tree index structure.

Indexed files are easily created as a result of the provision of software by manufacturers. Improvements are offered by many software houses; the designer will generally find that it pays to explore all possible optimization techniques for the manufacturers' software before examining alternatives. In some cases, however, the design philosophy of another supplier will meet the user's needs more precisely. A full examination of the application will lead to an informed choice, and optimum performance.

References

1. 'The design of indexed sequential files', by K. J. McDonnell and A. Y. Montgomery, *Australian Computer Journal*, Vol. 5, No. 3, November 1973, pp. 115–126.
2. 'Organization and maintenance of large ordered indices', R. Bayer and E. McCreight, *Acta Informatica*, Vol. 1, No. 3, 1972, pp. 173–189.
3. *File and Database Techniques*, by James Bradley, Holt-Saunders, 1982, pp. 134–137.
4. *Evaluation and Design of Tree-Structured Files*, by A. Y. Montgomery.
5. *Dynamic Data Structures on Optical Disks*, by Peter Rathmann, IEEE, 1984, CH-20, 31–3 84, pp. 175–180.
6. 'Identifier search mechanisms: a survey and generalized model', by Dennis G. Severance, *ACM Computing Surveys*, Vol. 6, No. 3, September 1984, pp. 175–194.
7. *The Art of Computer Programming, Vol. 3 Searching and Sorting*, by D. E. Knuth, Addison-Wesley, 1973, pp. 517–525.
8. 'Hidden speed of ISAM', by F. T. Coyle, *Datamation*, 15 June 1971, pp. 48–49.
9. 'A file organization evaluation model (FOREM)', by V. Y. Lum et al., *Proc. IFIP Congress*, 1968, Vol. 1, pp. 514–519.
10. *File Design Handbook—Final Report*, by V. Y. Lum et al., IBM Research, San Jose, California, F 30602-69, November 1969.
11. 'File organization: on the selection of random access index points for sequential files', by S. P. Ghosh and M. E. Senko, *JACM*, Vol. 16, No. 4, October 1969, pp. 569–579.
12. 'An improved index sequential access method using hashed overflow', by James K. Mullin, *CACM*, Vol. 15, No. 5, May 1972, pp. 301–307.
13. 'Analysis of index-sequential files with overflow chaining', by Per-Ake Larson, *ACM Trans. on Database Systems*, Vol. 6, No. 4, December 1981, pp. 671–680.
14. *Facts from Figures*, by M. J. Moroney, Pelican.
15. 'Quantitative file evaluation and design', by A. Y. Montgomery and D. Hubbard, *Proc. 8th Australian Computer Conference*, 1978, Vol. 3, pp. 1242–1265.
16. 'Direct or indexed sequential? A file designer's guide', by Owen Hanson, *Proc. 6th New Zealand Computer Conference*, Auckland, August 1978, Vol. 1, pp. 517–533.
17. 'Indexing design considerations', by R. E. Wagner, *IBM Systems Journal*, 1973, No. 4, pp. 351–367.
18. *Introduction to IBM Direct-Access Storage Devices and Organization Methods*, IBM Manual No. GC 20-1649-10.
19. *OS/VS1 and VS2 Access Method Services*, IBM Manuals Nos. GC26-3840, and GC26-3841.
20. 'Some file structure considerations pertaining to magnetic bubble memory', by William E. Wright, *The Computer Journal*, Vol. 26, No. 1, 1983, pp. 43–51.
21. 'COBOL on a PC: a new perspective on a language and its performance', by Paul J. Jalics, *CACM*, Vol. 30, No. 2, February 1987, pp. 142–154.

Revision questions

1 Describe the main areas of an indexed sequential file. Indicate which of them are essential and which are used only when required.

2 Why is a hierarchy of indexes used in IS files rather than a single large index? What effect does the size of the record key have on index size?

3 Explain the effect of index positioning on file performance and set out the rules for positioning in various circumstances.

4 What overflow areas are provided in these files? Explain and justify the options you would take up in the case of: even additions; random additions; grouped additions; no additions.

5 How are records inserted into IS files? Describe and comment on two or more techniques, and the way they affect:

a) record addition;
b) subsequent record retrieval.

6 Explain how blocking of records affects skip-sequential processing.

7 Outline the sequence of events during direct retrieval of a record from an IS file. Give times for each step, and hence or otherwise comment on methods of optimizing direct retrieval.

8 How would you decide whether input to a file should be processed directly or batched and sorted? Give worked examples to justify your conclusions.

9 Why do some software houses offer 'improved' indexed sequential file organization software? How valid are their claims?

10 Describe IBM's VSAM software, explaining how it operates and how it can be optimized.

11 What is a balanced tree? Describe two versions of balanced tree indexing and their associated files, commenting on the strengths and weaknesses of each method.

12 Describe a B-tree. Explain the advantages this type of tree has over balanced trees, and compare and contrast their performance over as full a range of applications as possible.

8 File organization for multiple-key processing

8.1 Introduction

Much of data processing involves retrieving records that refer to a given customer, stock item or member of staff. In each of these cases a single key is all that is required to reference the record. However, in retrieving documents from a database holding the contents of a library, or when a request is based on meeting several different criteria, the situation is quite different. There are no longer any single 'keys' that uniquely define the document or documents wanted by the user. Generally, a combination of words or phrases is used as *descriptors* that can be combined to select the desired record. For example, a business in the United States may wish to assign an engineer to work in Japan for some months. The personnel file might be examined to list all the employees who meet the following criteria:

Speaks Japanese AND Graduate Engineer AND Single

The personnel department would make the final choice, from the list produced by this enquiry. If the resulting list were too large, further descriptors could be added to reduce it. If it were too small, the 'single' restriction might be removed; if the whole family also needed to be sent to Japan this would add to the assignment costs, which might be an acceptable price to pay in order to send the right person.

Multiple-key applications present different problems from those associated with the single-key files discussed so far. For smaller files, magnetic tape is the obvious storage medium—an example is the International Food Information Service described by Larbey[1]. Small files that demand multiple-key handling are usually stored on magnetic tape and processed sequentially. A file arranged as in Fig. 8.1 has considerable advantages for the retrieval of records that meet some request based on a number of separate criteria which are often called *record attributes* or *descriptors*.

| DATA 1 | D1 D2 D3 D4 | DATA 2 | D3 D5 D6 | DATA 3 | D1 D6 D7 | DATA 4 | D8 D9 D10 |

◄──── RECORD 1 ────►◄──── RECORD 2 ────►◄──── RECORD 3 ────►◄──── RECORD 4 ────►

Fig. 8.1

Each record (such as a title, a summary or a full text) is characterized by the descriptors D1, D2, etc. Records 1 and 2 have a common descriptor D3, records 2 and 3 share D6, while records 1 and 3 have D1 in common. Record 4 has no shared descriptors with the other three records, although it may have with later records.

The file organization techniques used for multiple-key processing are discussed in this chapter, but chained and tree structures used in database systems are not.

8.2 File types

Two main file types are used in multiple-key retrieval. These are serial, which was described briefly above, and inverted. There are variations of each technique, and they are considered below.

Serial files

The straightforward method of handling the examination of multiple keys is to hold all the keys in the record, as in Fig. 8.1. A further example of this is shown in Table 8.1; each personnel record holds a number of fields, any one of which may be used as a key.

A specific request might require a count of all the grade 2 employees in the systems department. This could be answered by scanning the whole file record by record, examining each to see whether it met the specified requirements. After all the records have been scanned a list of two names—Mason and Vince—would be provided.

In the case of a personnel file, the list is likely to be sorted into an order that depends on some major key—in this case, usually alphabetic order or personnel number. If the file were made up of documents, books or papers the overall classification would probably be based on subject, and the order within subject might well be accession date. In these library databases the major key is often an accession number. In either case, the order does not affect the amount of searching to be done and in this sense the file is serial, although it will probably be in sequential order with respect to the major key.

This type of file has to be scanned completely before a single query can be answered. Each record is examined in turn, and its descriptors are compared with those of the search request (which might be like that for a graduate engineer with other attributes shown above). Because only one record is examined at a time, it is possible to test the descriptors against very complex Boolean conditions, expressed in terms of the descriptors desired by the user, to obtain a match. The work areas required in main storage are relatively small as only one record is being examined at any one time. However, as the data file increases in size, the time taken to search through

Table 8.1 Part of a personnel file shown in sequential order.

Master file key	Name	Sex	Grade	Department	Branch	Languages spoken
18	Brown	M	1	Systems	South	—
23	Collins	M	3	Prog	North	—
35	Duncan	F	2	Prog	North	French
41	Farrar	M	5	Admin	Central	—
42	Jablonski	F	4	Operations	North	—
47	Kellman	F	3	Systems	North	German, Polish
59	Lawrence	M	3	Prog	Central	—
83	Mason	F	2	Systems	South	—
94	Norris	M	1	Operations	South	—
101	Oliver	F	1	Operations	Central	French, German
110	Ordinale	F	4	Systems	South	—
115	Stewart	F	3	Prog	North	—
122	Taylor	M	1	Operations	Central	French, German, Italian
128	Vince	F	2	Systems	South	—
133	Westcott	M	1	Prog	South	Italian

the data increases in proportion. At between 20 000 and 60 000 records, the search time becomes so slow that it no longer allows a reasonable number of requests to be handled in a working day. The point at which this happens depends on a number of factors such as complexity of requests in terms of Boolean conditions, speed of access of the medium in use, and size of data file.

A number of steps can be taken to speed up processing, each depending on some different method of handling the search. The first of these is the bit-pattern index, in which all the alternative descriptors for each record are given values of 1 if the attribute is present and 0 if it is not. The data in Table 8.1 has been organized into bit-pattern format in Table 8.2.

In cases such as that of a personnel file, for which the number of attributes is relatively low and the same for each record, a bit-pattern index can be a compact way of storing information about the file. However, it is not very useful for a bibliographic file in which there may be thousands of potential attributes for each record, only a very few of which are non-zero. The storage of this sort of data causes the difficulty that the compact format is counterbalanced by the redundant information.

Bit-pattern indexes will be examined in more detail later; however, in some circumstances a more rapid reference technique than that provided by a serial file is required. For this purpose, inverted files have been developed.

Inverted files

When records are to be selected on the basis of the state of one or more attributes, a serial search concentrates on the *records*, examining each in turn to see if it meets the specified conditions of the search. In fact, what is known from these specified conditions is the *attributes* required. A search of the records having a given attribute, to see which of them also has a second, third, . . . etc. in the required list, will eliminate all the records that are not wanted. This is achieved by inverting the file, i.e. by providing lists of records or record references possessing each one of the various attributes in turn. The resulting set of lists—which are, in effect, indexes—is shown in Fig. 8.2 for the same records in a data file that have already been shown in Fig. 8.1.

A further example is shown in Table 8.3, which is an inverted version of the data set out in Tables 8.1 and 8.2. Given that a male in the operations department is required who is able to speak Italian, the male list is scanned first. This provides seven records. When the operations condition is added, only records 94 and 122 meet the double condition. Adding the need to speak Italian eliminates record 94, leaving only a single employee from this small part of the personnel file, with personnel number 122, who meets all the three conditions.

D1	ADDRESS OF RECORD 1	ADDRESS OF RECORD 3
D2	ADDRESS OF RECORD 1	
D3	ADDRESS OF RECORD 1	ADDRESS OF RECORD 2
D4	ADDRESS OF RECORD 1	
D5	ADDRESS OF RECORD 2	
D6	ADDRESS OF RECORD 2	ADDRESS OF RECORD 3
D7	ADDRESS OF RECORD 3	
D8	ADDRESS OF RECORD 4	
D9	ADDRESS OF RECORD 4	
D10	ADDRESS OF RECORD 4	

Fig. 8.2 The data shown in Fig. 8.1, but now arranged in inverted form. The main index is of descriptors, and each has a reference for every record to which the descriptor applies.

Table 8.2 A bit-pattern index of the personnel file entries shown in Table 8.1.

Name		Brown	Collins	Duncan	Farrar	Jablonski	Kellman	Lawrence	Mason	Norris	Oliver	Ordinale	Stewart	Taylor	Vince	Westcott
Master file key		18	23	35	41	42	47	59	83	94	101	110	115	122	128	133
Sex	M	1	1	0	1	0	0	1	0	1	0	0	0	1	0	1
	F	0	0	1	0	1	1	0	1	0	1	1	1	0	1	0
Grade	1	1	0	0	0	0	0	0	0	1	1	0	0	1	0	1
	2	0	0	1	0	0	0	0	1	0	0	0	0	0	1	0
	3	0	1	0	0	0	1	1	0	0	0	0	1	0	0	0
	4	0	0	0	0	1	0	0	0	0	0	1	0	0	0	0
	5	0	0	0	1	0	0	0	0	0	0	0	0	0	0	0
Department	Systems	1	0	0	0	0	1	0	1	0	0	1	0	0	1	0
	Prog	0	1	1	0	0	0	1	0	0	0	0	1	0	0	1
	Admin	0	0	0	1	0	0	0	0	0	0	0	0	0	0	0
	Operations	0	0	0	0	1	0	0	0	1	1	0	0	1	0	0
Branch	South	1	0	0	0	0	0	0	1	1	0	1	0	0	1	1
	North	0	1	1	0	1	1	0	0	0	1	0	1	0	0	0
	Central	0	0	0	1	0	0	1	0	0	0	0	0	1	0	0
Language	French	0	0	1	0	0	0	0	0	0	1	0	0	1	0	0
	German	0	0	0	0	0	1	0	0	0	1	0	0	1	0	0
	Polish	0	0	0	0	0	1	0	0	0	0	0	0	0	0	1
	Italian	0	0	0	0	1	0	0	0	0	0	0	0	1	0	1

File organization for multiple-key processing

Table 8.3 The personnel file shown in Table 8.1 might be inverted to give this set of attribute indexes. Note that the first four attributes are exclusive, in that every record will have one and only one attribute. The language class is different in two respects; no person has to be able to speak a foreign language, but some can speak several rather than one only.

Class	Attribute	Master file keys
Sex	M	18, 23, 41, 59, 94, 122, 133
	F	35, 42, 47, 83, 101, 110, 115, 128
Grade	1	18, 94, 101, 122, 133
	2	35, 83, 128
	3	23, 47, 59, 115
	4	42, 110
	5	41
Department	Systems	18, 47, 83, 110, 128
	Prog	23, 35, 59, 115, 133
	Admin	41,
	Operations	42, 94, 101, 122
Branch	South	18, 83, 94, 110, 128, 133
	North	23, 35, 42, 47, 115
	Central	41, 59, 101, 122
Languages spoken	French	35, 101, 122
	German	47, 101, 122
	Polish	47
	Italian	122, 133

A file in which all the attributes are inverted, i.e. have indexes provided so that a direct search can be made on any attribute, is known as *fully inverted*. A file in which only a number of selected attributes have indexes provided is known as *partially inverted*.

In the case of a fully inverted file the designer has the option of holding very little information in the master file itself, and assembling records from their constituent parts as they are referenced. In practice many designers prefer to hold the complete record in the master file, as this avoids the problem of assembling information about attributes possessed by the record but not specifically referenced in the request. To take the example of record 122, grade and branch were not included in the request for a male from operations department who can speak Italian. This information would not be automatically collected from the request, but is essential in order to describe the person fully, and the retrieval process has to ensure that it is provided.

A master file record in a partially inverted file will always be required to hold at least the data on fields that are not inverted. The most usual arrangement is to have inverted lists of each descriptor, with a list of the major record keys and addresses or, if each record has a separate address, addresses only, for each of the records to which that descriptor applies. The master file contains the complete record. Keeping the index record size down is helpful because if the inverted indexes are small they can be held in main storage, and so cut search times down to a minimum.

Inverted files should not be confused with the alternate indexes available in many indexed file systems such as VSAM or ICL's 2900 series equivalent. Each such index can be used to give limited partial inversion, i.e. of one descriptor at a time, but they are generally provided and employed to allow the file to be accessed in ways other than by the major key, rather than to carry out an elimination of master file records not meeting some search criterion. An example would be to use department code as an alternate key to provide personnel listings by department from a personnel file arranged in some other order, such as alphabetic.

When an inverted organization is employed, a number of limitations may follow. First, the file may not be able to support such complicated search conditions as a serial file, because the size of work area required to process a request is now much larger; instead of dealing with one record at a time, the system now deals with all relevant records at once. This speeds request handling but greatly increases the work area size needed, particularly if a very widely used descriptor is the first to be cited in the retrieval request.

Second, addition of records to the file is no longer a matter of adding to the end of the file. Each descriptor record throughout the file that applies to this new record has to be updated, so the process is relatively slow. Third, the space requirements for such a file are considerably greater than those for a serial file. Spiegel and Miller[2] investigated IBM's STAIRS/AQUARIUS system (Storage and Information Retrieval System/A Query and Retrieval Interactive Utility System). The system uses four main files: a dictionary, a text data set, a text index data set, and an inverted file of all descriptors used in the database. These files are indexed by the use of BDAM (Basic Direct Access Method) and in a typical database of just over 2 Gbytes, which they found was the average size of those they examined, the number of characters in the files comprising the database was as follows:

TEXT	864 000 000
TEXT INDEX	83 000 000
INVERTED	781 000 000
DICTIONARY	442 000 000

It is clear that the basic text file has been increased by around 150 per cent in order to provide the retrieval capabilities offered by the package. This is typical, and should be borne in mind before abandoning single-key reference, which usually involves an overhead of only 5–20 per cent in providing the facilities offered by indexed sequential or direct organizations.

The system described by Spiegel and Miller could handle up to one thousand queries per hour, but many of them were relatively straightforward. Larbey[1] described a tape-based system in which the text file contained a maximum of 1400 items, each of 4300 characters or less—six megabytes at most. This system provided SDI (Selective Dissemination of Information) on current data only to eighty scientists who used a set of thirty-eight separate query profiles. Each profile was made up of a combination of descriptors and Boolean conditions, and averaged twenty-six distinct search terms. Production of the complete SDI output took 12 minutes, or just under 200 queries an hour.

A further file storage technique is sometimes useful in handling information retrieval applications. This is the *multilist*.

Multilist files

In this type of file there are the same sets of indexes as are required for an inverted file. However, in this case only the *first* reference to any descriptor appears in an index, while all further linkages are made from record to record (rather as in a chain of synonyms in a direct file). The arrangement of the same data that has been shown in Figs. 8.1 and 8.2, but now held as a multilist, is shown in Fig. 8.3.

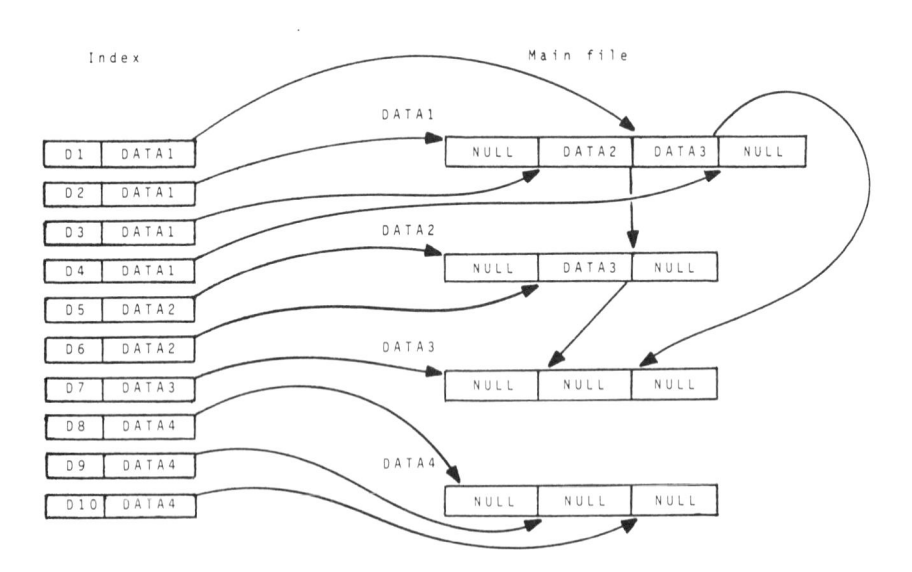

Fig. 8.3 The same data used in Figs. 8.1 and 8.2, showing how it might be arranged in a multilist. Each list has only *one* index entry, which is the start of the list.

Cardenas[3] compared inverted files with multilists, showing that their space requirements are usually very similar, and that the speed of access provided by each file organization is dependent on the structure of the data. In particular, multilists provide rapid access when the file has many different descriptors that apply to only a few records, as in this case each chain will be short. Cardenas also commented that '. . . the manner in which secondary indexes or dictionaries and associated lists are managed, may have underestimated impacts.' Much of this book is aimed at ensuring that file designers know how to minimize the impact of such indexes or dictionaries on space used and time wasted in file processing.

McDonell[4] provided a useful analysis of what is involved in addition, deletion or modification of records, so far as the maintenance and use of associative key lists is concerned; he defined an associative key list as 'a list for each indexed key which joins together all the main file records containing that key'. He also compared multilists with inverted files, and showed that inverted files have an advantage when the indexes have to be altered frequently. As the performance of the two is relatively similar and inverted files are more widely used in their own right, most of this chapter deals with serial and inverted files.

8.3 Record reference

For small numbers of records, serial files have significant advantages. The first is that, because each record is dealt with singly, the main storage work area space requirements are very low. This allows relatively complex Boolean conditions to be built up and tested, such as: in the programming department AND able to speak French BUT NOT if in grade 3 UNLESS from North branch. In the example in Table 8.1 the only person corresponding to this request is Duncan. In this case the BUT NOT condition was not fulfilled, but would in any case have been overridden by the UNLESS.

This example is not in itself very complex. However, it indicates how very complicated multiple conditions can be built up in the creation of user profiles for information retrieval systems. This is because in searching a very large library collection it is essential to attempt to ensure that the user gets just those references that are required. A profile that provides far too many irrelevant references is of little use; such lists normally find their way into a wastepaper basket because the user sees that they are full of irrelevant material and is not prepared to search through them hoping to find some relevant references. On the other hand a profile that fails to provide the user with required material is equally useless, however brief it may be. This second problem is more dangerous than the first because the user may not realize that information is missing.

Information retrieval systems include the concepts of *relevance*—the proportion of retrieved material that is relevant—and *recall*—the proportion of relevant material that is retrieved. These are dealt with in some detail elsewhere[5,6,7], but the reader who wishes to study the matter in depth should consult specialist references[8].

As the numbers of records increase, the problem of waiting for a reply to a query until the whole of a serial file has been searched increases in proportion, and eventually this delay becomes unacceptable. As mentioned earlier, one possible answer is to use a bit-pattern index of the sort shown in Table 8.2. When the number of attributes is low, this allows very economical storage of the data about a particular record. A single bit represents each possible attribute. If it is set to one, the record in question has this attribute. If it is set to zero, the record does not.

Searching such an index is very rapid. For simple cases an equal compare is all that is needed. However, this means that *every* attribute has to be specified. In an earlier example it was shown that a large proportion of requests only require *some* attributes to be present or absent. In these cases a Boolean AND condition can be set up. For instance, a request for a male in operations department who can speak Italian can be tested by comparing each of the bit-pattern index entries in Table 8.3 against a mask of:

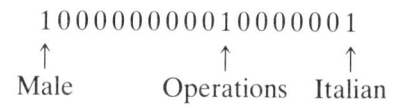

1 0 0 0 0 0 0 0 0 0 1 0 0 0 0 0 0 1
↑   ↑   ↑
Male   Operations   Italian

The Boolean condition will be an AND, which will only return a true indication if all these bits are on.

A bit-pattern index can extend the use of serial files when the number of attributes is limited, but a break-even point will occur somewhere between 20 000 and 100 000 records, depending on record size, number of possible attributes and the complexity of Boolean conditions required. In bibliographic applications the number of possible attributes may be many thousands. In this case the only possible solution when retrieval times become too long is to turn to an inverted file or a multilist. An inverted file is the usual choice, but when there are many attributes, each of which is used by relatively few records, it will be worth considering multilist files.

It was pointed out earlier that one difficulty in using inverted files is the need to deal with all the records possessing a given attribute at the same time, so that a great deal of working space is required in main storage. This is reduced if there are many possible attributes because each attribute index list will tend to be shorter. Thus, the more suitable the application is for bit-pattern index handling (small numbers of possible attributes), the less suitable it is for inverted file handling.

The number of nested Boolean conditions that can be handled by an inverted file is generally less than the number a serial file can handle. In addition, the conditions OUT OF, specifying any n conditions out of a larger number, and BETWEEN, setting upper and lower limits to the value of an attribute, are difficult to achieve[9]. These conditions can be very useful in setting up a user search profile, which is one reason that information retrieval systems often use a serial file for new accessions, which are matched against user profiles intended to inform users of the latest accessions in their subject field. This is linked to a complete file of the bibliographic collection held in inverted form. All the records in the serial file are transferred to the inverted file at intervals, generally when the size of the serial file is beginning to make reference to it relatively slow. The reasons for keeping down the number of updates to an inverted file are discussed below, and the form of a dual serial–inverted file system is shown in Fig. 8.4. Such a system has been discussed further by the author[10].

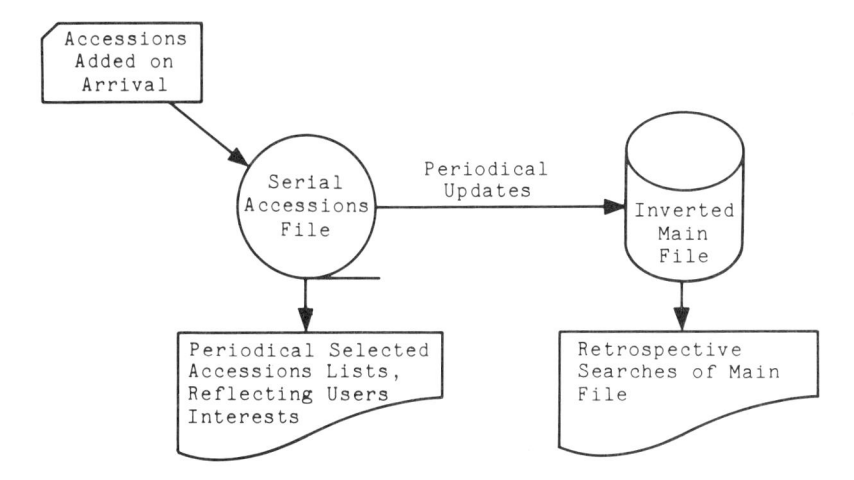

Fig. 8.4 Accessions are added to the serial tape file, which is used to prepare accessions lists tailored to the needs of each user. At intervals determined by the number of accessions and the number of potential attributes, the serial file is used as input to the main file. Searches of the main file are carried out as and when required.

8.4 Additions and alterations

Serial files can handle additions without difficulty. In very simple cases the new record is added to the end of the file. Even if the master file is held in a sorted order there will be no particular difficulty, as these files are usually stored on magnetic tapes. All that is required is to create a new file, although this can be time-consuming.

Inverted files require quite different treatment. Ideally, the indexes should be held in main storage. They will certainly need to be on a direct access device. Addition of a new record will mean that a number of indexes will have to be updated, one for each attribute possessed by the new record. Thus, even if space is left within and at the end of each index, updating will involve the shifting and shuffling of a number of records or the use of pointers and links to the new records.

The contrast between these two is a further reason for the popularity of dual systems. It is easier to handle the file in serial form until sufficient new records are available to justify the time and effort involved in an update of the inverted file.

8.5 Storage requirements

Serial files can be held in one coherent file. This is very convenient for the user as it requires the minimum of handling. An inverted file, however, has to be held in a number of related indexes, and is thus far more 'bitty'. In addition, the typical overhead of indexes and related files leads to a final size of about two and a half times the size of the corresponding serial file. However, there can very occasionally be a space-saving in the use of an inverted file as is shown in the discussion below, due to Revell[11].

Suppose a file contains N fixed-length records and each record is comprised of a key of k characters and n data items of average size a characters. If this file is fully inverted, the resultant file will contain as many records as there are unique descriptor values—say V. The inverted file will be made up of variable-length records. For each descriptor value, the rest of the record will be a list of the keys of the original file records which possess that specific value.

If the average number of keys in the inverted file records is A then:

$$A \times V = N \times n \tag{8.1}$$

since the total number of terms in both the original and inverted files must be equal.

The size of the original file is:

$$N \times (k + na) \text{ characters}$$

and the size of the inverted file is:

$$V \times [a + k(nN/V)] \text{ characters}$$

It is therefore advantageous, purely from a size point of view, to use an inverted file when:

$$V\left(a + \frac{nNk}{V}\right) \leq N(k + na)$$

or

$$\frac{k}{a} \leq \frac{(n - V/N)}{(n - 1)} \tag{8.2}$$

For applications of size such that $V/N \ll n$, equation (8.1) approximates to:

$$\frac{k}{a} \leq \frac{n}{n - 1} \tag{8.3}$$

Additionally, if n is large the expression simplifies further to:

$$\frac{k}{a} \leq 1 \tag{8.4}$$

Thus, the decision as to whether a file takes up more space in serial or inverted form depends on the ratio of the size of the key and the data items. Note that this is of limited use as it implies that the data is held *only* in the index or in the main file. The more usual arrangement is that the inverted indexes are an *addition* to the main file, as explained earlier. For this reason it is not often possible to achieve a reduction in space requirement by using an inverted file.

Conclusion

Serial or inverted files specifically designed for the retrieval of records on the basis of the values of multiple keys are a useful tool for the file designer. Generally the file itself, and the associated processing programs, will have to be written by the user if high standards of optimization are required. However, the alternate index facility of VSAM and similar software can sometimes be used to build the indexes required.

Salton[12,13] has reviewed the methods of handling information retrieval, while a number of authors have described specific techniques that offer advantages in particular situations. Ramamohanarao et al.[14] described a mixed hashing/descriptor-based method of retrieval; Nievergelt et al.[15] presented a 'grid' file that performs particularly well when the number of search attributes is ten or less, and offers a high data storage utilization, good growth characteristics and efficient processing of range queries; Stanfill and Kahle[16] explain the principles of a parallel free-text search on a particular parallel computer, and claim a retrieval speed of 2–3 minutes for Boolean queries of 25 and 20 000 terms respectively when the database in question takes up 15 Gbytes of storage space. Their method of searching does not depend on pre-determined descriptors.

Many database systems use the inverted technique, and the convenience of having the software provided by such systems will often outweigh its relative inefficiency. 'Tuning' of the database software may also be possible using manufacturer-supplied options to achieve results more in line with those attainable by programs written in-house. In order to obtain optimum results, however, there is no substitute for a carefully user-designed and written system.

References

1. 'Inclusion of International Food Information Service's Magnetic Tapes as a Data-Base of the Unilever Research SDI System', by D. W. Larbey, text of a paper given to IFIS at the Institut fuer Dokumentationswesen, Frankfurt, 7th Sept., 1972. Available in microfiche only from IFIS.
2. 'Evaluation of a large-scale data retrieval system—STAIRS/AQUARIUS', by M. G. Spiegel and C. M. Miller, *Proc. Computer Performance Evaluation Conf.*, London, 1978, pp. 189–208.
3. 'Evaluation and selection of file organization—a model and system', by Alfonso F. Cardenas, *CACM*, Vol. 16, No. 9, September 1973, pp. 540–548.
4. 'The design of associative key lists (secondary indices)', by Ken J. McDonell, *Australian Computer Journal*, Vol. 8, No. 1, March 1976, pp. 13–18.
5. *Basic File Design*, by Owen Hanson, IPC Electrical and Electronic Press, 1978, Chapter 5.
6. *Basic Training in Systems Analysis*, edited by Alan Daniels and Donald Yeates, Pitman, 1976, Appendix A.
7. *Datenorganisation*, by Hartmut Wedekind, Walter de Gruyter, 1975, Chapter 5.3.
8. *Concept Organization for Information Retrieval*, by Sunan Datta, PhD Thesis, obtainable from the City University Library, St. John's St, London EC1, UK.
9. *Systemanalyse*, by Hartmut Wedekind, Carl Hanser Verlag, 1976, Chapter 4, Section 6.5.2.
10. 'Problems in the design of large databases', by O. J. Hanson, *Cybernetics and Systems '86*, edited by Robert Trappl, D. Reidel Publishing Co., Dordrecht, Holland, 1986, pp. 473–480.
11. Private communication from Norman Revell, of the Centre for Business Systems Analysis, The City University, London.
12. 'Advanced information retrieval methods', by G. Salton, *Proc. 1st Pan-Pacific Computer Conference*, Melbourne, September 1985, Vol. 1, pp. 118–133.
13. 'Another look at automatic text-retrieval systems', by G. Salton, *CACM*, Vol. 29, No. 7, July 1986, pp. 648–656.
14. 'Partial-match retrieval using hashing and descriptors', by K. Ramamohanarao, John W. Lloyd and James A. Thom, *ACM Trans. on Database Systems*, Vol. 8, No. 4, December 1983, pp. 552–576.
15. 'The grid file: an adaptable, symmetric multikey file structure', by J. Nievergelt, H. Hinterberger and K. C. Sevcik, *ACM Trans. on Database Systems*, Vol. 9, No. 1, March 1984, pp. 38–71.

16. 'Parallel free-text search on the Connection Machine system', by Craig Stanfill and Brewster Kahle, *CACM*, Vol. 29, No. 12, December 1986, pp. 1229–1239.

Revision questions

1 Give an example of an application that might require multiple-key processing.

2 What are the main file types used in multiple-key retrieval? Describe the make-up of each type and use the same set of data to show the different data structures required in each file type.

3 Use your own data to show how records are retrieved from each of the types of file you have described.

4 When would a bit-pattern index be useful and when not? Explain and justify your answer.

5 When would you use a serial file for information retrieval? At what point would you switch to an inverted file? Explain the factors that influence this break-even point.

6 What are the advantages and drawbacks of inverted files? When might you be forced to use an inverted file, even if it is not very efficient?

7 How and why would a dual system including both inverted and serial files be used?

8 Describe a multilist file. When might such a file be preferred to an inverted file for multiple-key processing?

9 Discuss the space requirements of serial, inverted and multilist files, making clear the assumptions on which you are working.

10 Show how software that allows alternate indexes to be created can be used to set up an inverted file system

9 Choice of file organization

9.1 Introduction

In previous chapters the main file organization techniques have been discussed and methods of optimizing their performance have been examined. Usually this is the principal aim of the file designer, but sometimes the first question is which file organization technique to employ. The present chapter looks at this choice, and where necessary at the related question of which storage medium to use.

The most important element in deciding on the type of file is the reference facility required by the user; however, it is by no means the only factor that the file designer needs to know. In making a choice, the following points will be considered:

Reference facility
Type of access required
Hit rate
Size
Life expectancy
Growth
Volatility
Run integration
Data integrity and backup

Each of these is examined in turn below

The main emphasis in the choice of file organization techniques given here is on those organizations that have been examined in the last four chapters. This does not mean that more complex data storage techniques are unimportant. Generally, in addition to using some or all of the indexing, self-indexing or randomizing methods called for by the conventional file organization techniques, database software will use one or more additional ways of retrieving data. These include the provision of alternate indexes, as in VSAM and many database packages at present available for use on microcomputers, inversion of data (either fully or partially), which is often desirable when data is to be retrieved on the basis of some combination of keys, or the use of chaining or linking of records for the production of reports such as Bills of Material.

9.2 Reference facility required

The key word here, as has been indicated elsewhere in the book, is 'required'. An enquiry system will typically expect a response in seconds at most, even allowing for queuing of enquiries. A batch system based on sequential files will usually provide output daily or weekly, and more than two runs per day for a particular application is very unusual.

Based on this alone one might expect every system to operate in real time, providing very rapid response. In reality, the cost of processing large numbers of transactions directly, coupled with the fact that it is often not necessary, leads to most files being processed sequentially. The cost mentioned here is that many more transactions can be processed in batch than in real-time mode in a given time, so real-time processing is relatively inefficient. The relation of costs per transaction to hit-rate is shown in general terms in Fig. 9.1.

For swift direct reference to data, all the data has to be online. This may occasionally present a problem, due to the large volume of disk storage required. However, the IBM 3850 Mass Storage Facility, the CDC 38500, the Braegen 7110 Automated Tape Library and the Masstore M860 provide direct access storage capacities in the range 16 Gbytes to 1400 Gbytes of storage that is accessible in 5 to 30 seconds, so these devices provide an ideal

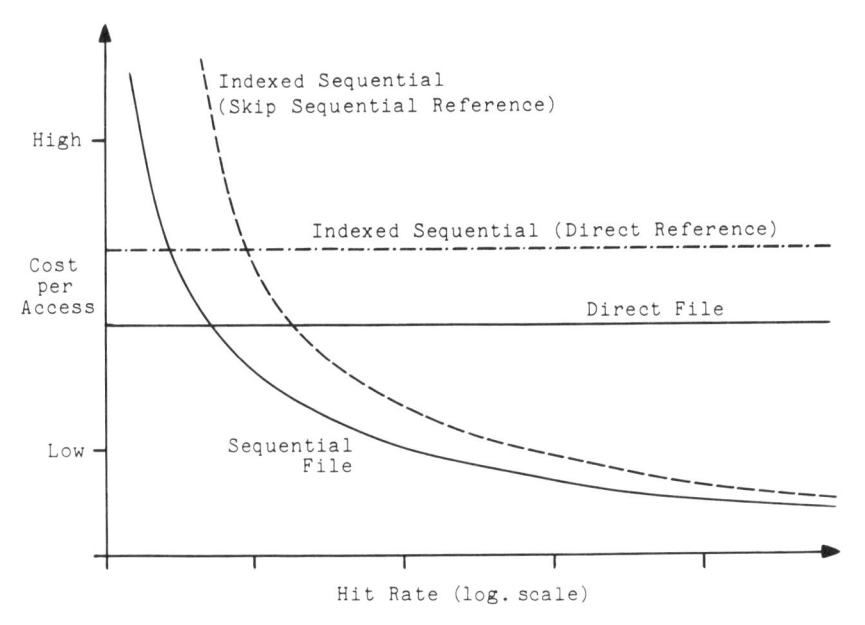

Fig. 9.1 The relationship of cost per access to hit rate for the main file organization techniques. The shape of the curves and position of the break-even points depends on the actual parameters of each case, but the relative position of the curves is generally as shown.

292 Design of computer data files

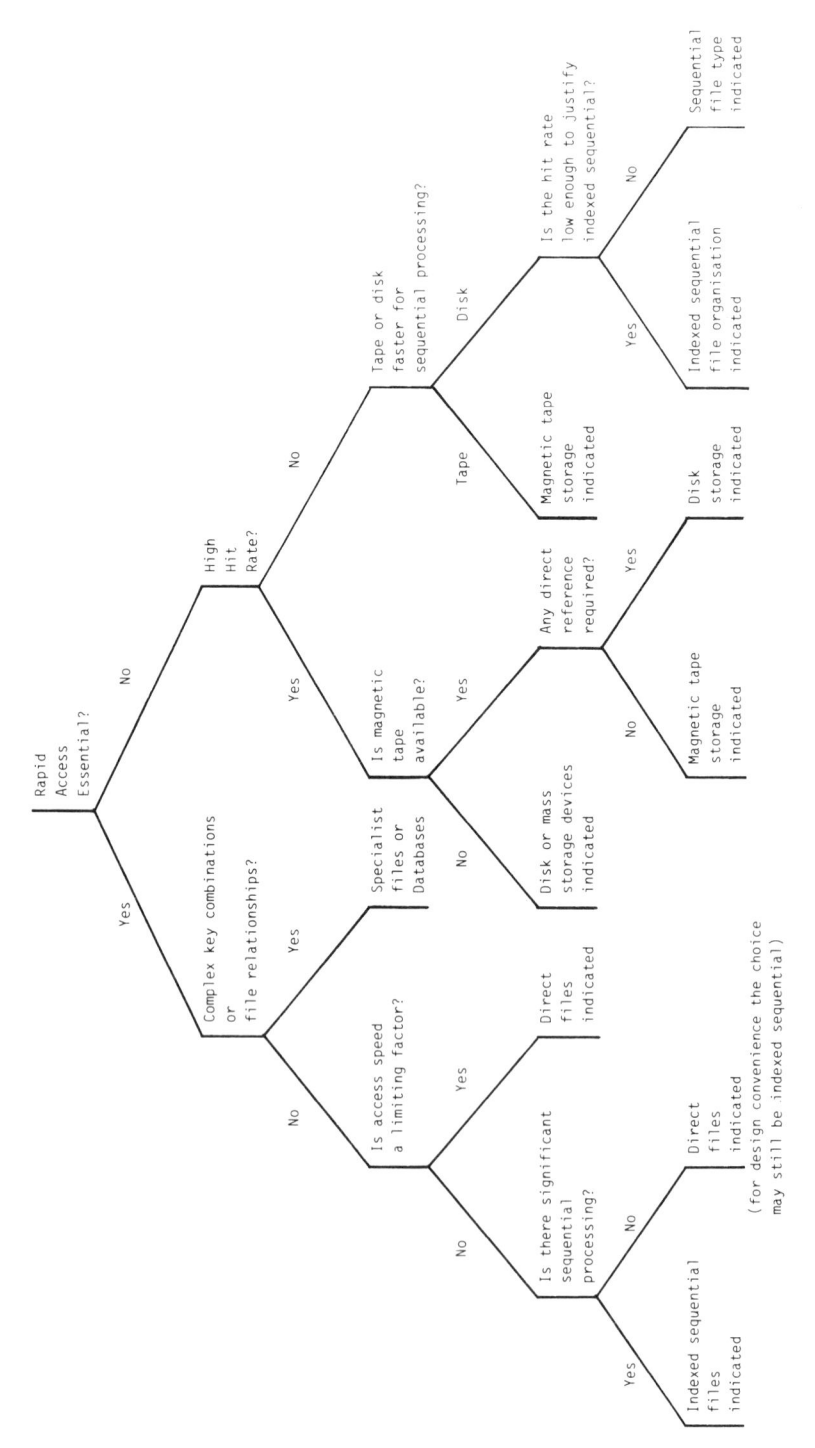

Fig. 9.2 This diagram gives a top-down view of the process of selecting the most suitable file organization for a given application.

Choice of file organization   289

9.2 Reference facility required

The key word here, as has been indicated elsewhere in the book, is 'required'. An enquiry system will typically expect a response in seconds at most, even allowing for queuing of enquiries. A batch system based on sequential files will usually provide output daily or weekly, and more than two runs per day for a particular application is very unusual.

Based on this alone one might expect every system to operate in real time, providing very rapid response. In reality, the cost of processing large numbers of transactions directly, coupled with the fact that it is often not necessary, leads to most files being processed sequentially. The cost mentioned here is that many more transactions can be processed in batch than in real-time mode in a given time, so real-time processing is relatively inefficient. The relation of costs per transaction to hit-rate is shown in general terms in Fig. 9.1.

For swift direct reference to data, all the data has to be online. This may occasionally present a problem, due to the large volume of disk storage required. However, the IBM 3850 Mass Storage Facility, the CDC 38500, the Braegen 7110 Automated Tape Library and the Masstore M860 provide direct access storage capacities in the range 16 Gbytes to 1400 Gbytes of storage that is accessible in 5 to 30 seconds, so these devices provide an ideal

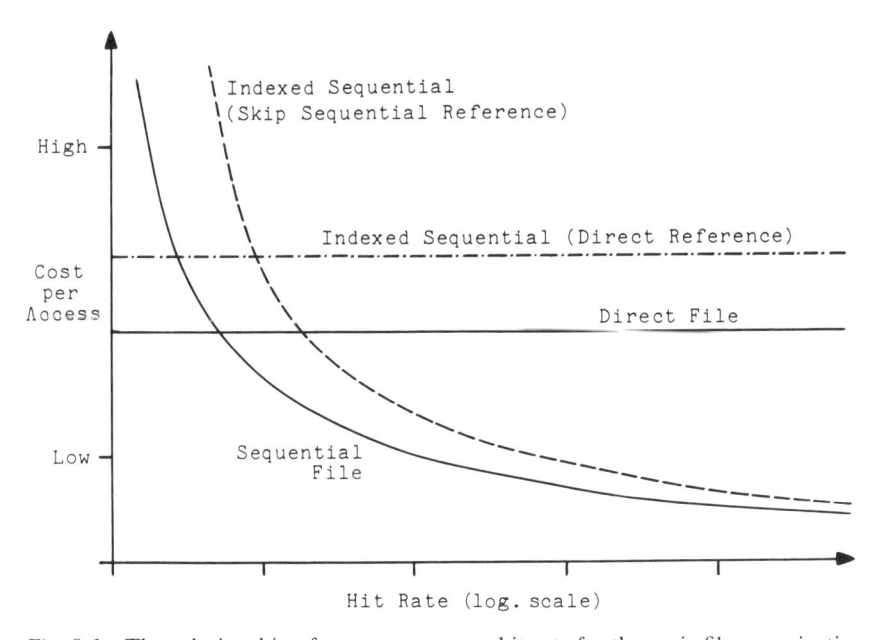

Fig. 9.1   The relationship of cost per access to hit rate for the main file organization techniques. The shape of the curves and position of the break-even points depends on the actual parameters of each case, but the relative position of the curves is generally as shown.

cheap medium to hold files that have a relatively infrequent direct access requirement. Insurance data fits this definition, but booking systems do not. The more successful an insurance application is, the less it is referenced—the less claims the better. A booking system will be more successful, the more references there are—the more bookings the better. Thus, large booking systems will generally require IBM 3380 disks or their equivalent rather than mass storage devices.

9.3 Type of access required

Sequential Although this has been discussed for a number of specific cases above, it is worth summarizing the rules here. For sequential access only, the obvious choice of storage medium is tape. However, as the hit-rate reduces, at some point skip sequential processing on disk becomes more efficient. This is because all records stored on magnetic tape have to be read, whether they are required or not, while on disk inactive records can be skipped. The file organization to be used has to be sequential while the storage medium is tape, but can be either sequential or indexed sequential when the file is held on disk. As hit rates fall even lower, indexed sequential begins to outperform skip sequential due to the ability of this type of file to skip complete tracks and cylinders that contain no active records. Note that the separate key format for record storage has to be available if a sequential disk file is to be skip-sequentially processed. These choices are examined in detail in papers by the author[1,2].

Direct Direct processing has to be on a direct access device, and the only question—so far as media is concerned—is whether the throughput is low enough to allow the use of the relatively cheap, slow mass storage devices. If it is, the cost can be very low. If not, disk or—for page data sets or reference tables—semiconductor 'disks' such as the STC 4325 or Intel Fast 3805 must be used. These devices can be accessed about seven times faster than a fixed-head disk and fifty times faster than a 3380. For processing that is direct only, a directly organized file will be at least 10 per cent faster than an indexed-sequential file, and roughly twice as fast if the Cylinder Index of the indexed sequential file is too large to be held in main storage. More complex database software is very much slower than this, so it should only be used if there is a need for multiple indexing, linked records, multiple-key reference or some other facility offered by the software that cannot be provided by simpler methods.

Mixed processing This generally implies direct access devices and an indexed sequential file organization. If the *sequential* element of the processing requirements is low, there may be an argument for using a direct file, and also holding an ancillary file giving actual rather than algorithmically calculated addresses in sequential key order to allow for rapid sequential processing. If the *direct* element in the processing requirements is low, it may be possible to meet it by a binary or statistical binary ('interpolation') search of a sequential file. Both of these options are unusual, and the presumption should be that an indexed sequential file is suitable unless there is good reason to opt for one of the other file organizations.

Multiple keys   As pointed out in Chapter 8, although a great deal of data processing depends on retrieval or recognition of records by the use of a single key, in retrieving documents from a database holding the contents of a library, the situation is quite different. There are no longer any single 'keys' that uniquely define the document or documents wanted by the user. Generally, a combination of words or phrases will be used as descriptors that can be used to select data items that may meet the user's needs. As this is a different requirement from those that apply to the other file organization techniques, there is seldom any possible confusion between the need for one of the methods described earlier and a file organization that is suited to multiple-key processing.

9.4 Hit rate

As pointed out in Chapter 1, most update files have a 100 per cent hit rate. Master files, on the other hand, vary widely. A payroll file will usually show at least a 90 per cent hit rate on monthly runs and a relatively high hit rate weekly, while the payments received for an insurance customer file that is updated weekly will only represent changes to around 2 per cent of the records; if claims only are being processed, the hit rate should be much lower still.

Because sequential organization is very suitable for high hit rate files, update files are usually organized sequentially. The alternative, for master files that can be referenced directly, is to use a serial update file in the order that the updates arise. This is usually only considered for cases in which the update records represent only a low percentage of the master file. Problems in the choice of a suitable file organization are almost always caused by master files, rather than update files.

If the hit pattern is bunched it may be possible to section the data (as described in Chapter 5, page 112), so that the active part of the data is updated, while the passive data is not. This is a very effective technique, so long as there is no requirement for direct access to the data. A good example of a file that would perform very well in sectioned form, but for the need for direct access, is an insurance file. Policy renewal dates, retirement dates, benefit payment dates are all predictable, and could be handled by arranging the data in date order. Only the records to be processed on any given day would need to be accessed, which would cut the run time on any given day to

292 Design of computer data files

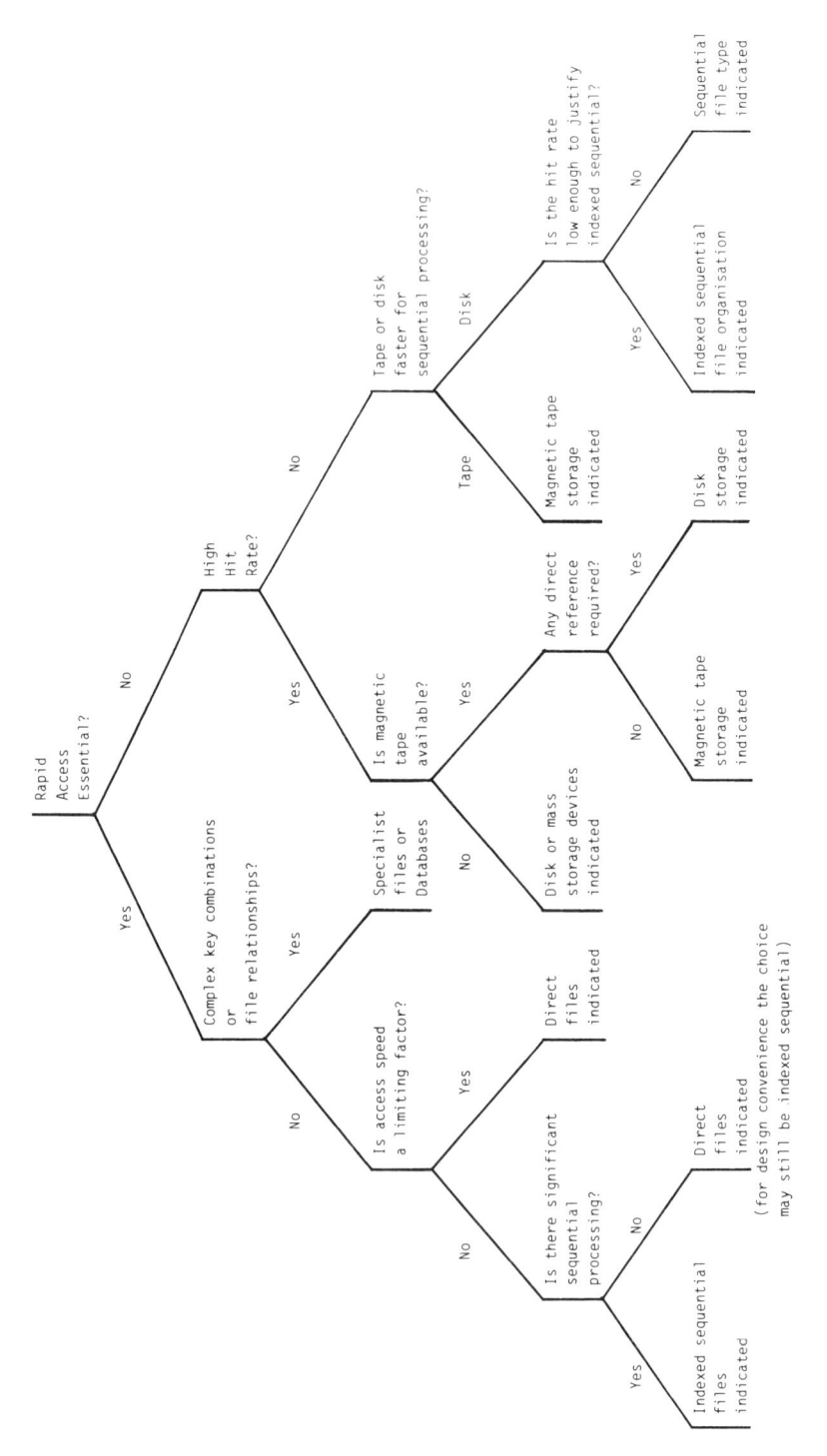

Fig. 9.2 This diagram gives a top-down view of the process of selecting the most suitable file organization for a given application.

about one 250th of the total file. Unfortunately, direct accesses to the data as a result of accidents, deaths and the like may occur anywhere within the full extent of the file, and this has led to most of these databases being held in indexed sequential form.

Two other types of file may need to be considered. The first is a reference file—tables, schedules, price lists, etc. This is usually organized so that it can be directly referenced, although very occasionally it may need to be handled sequentially. This will depend on the other records to be processed during the run being so arranged that all the items requiring a given reference record can be processed as a group. The second is a historical file, and this is almost always sequentially organized. The fact that a file is 'historical' implies that data will not be required urgently, so there is little need for more expensive forms of organization.

In assessing the impact of a given hit rate on master file design, it is seldom sufficient to have data on the average hit rate over a period, and the standard deviation from that average. In addition, it is essential to know whether the updates occur in a predictable pattern, and the designer should be aware of any seasonal or cyclical variations to be expected.

The combined effects of type of access required and hit rate are summarized in Fig. 9.2. This is a decision tree that gives guidance to the designer on choice of storage medium and the appropriate file organization for the application.

9.5 The effect of size on design

The first point to make is that, if a file is small, the effects of poor design will not be so marked as they would have been if the file had been large. However, there are good reasons for holding small data files on magnetic disk. First, it is usual to hold only one file on a magnetic tape. This is because all but the first file would have to be accessed by spacing along the tape until the desired file was found, which involves considerable waste of time. An average time might be 25–30 seconds, while the wait could be as long as three minutes in an extreme case—e.g. a Sperry-Univac Uniservo 12 with a rewind time of three minutes—for data at the far end of the tape. Second, if many files are held on a single tape, they are *all* available to the operator as soon as the tape has been issued, even though authorization has only been given for the use of *one*. Disk, on the other hand, is well suited to the handling of small files because its VTOC (volume table of contents) allows immediate control of access to any file, and provides a first defence against unauthorized reference to files other than that intended.

There is one further factor that makes the choice of disk for small files very suitable. Knight[3] pointed out in an internal report to his employers that, unless it was possible to pre-load a tape, the time required to load it in his installation was 74 seconds. It turned out that only 28 per cent of job steps in the installation used tape, but that these job steps accounted for 64 per cent of all processing time (including allocation time). As a graphic demonstration of what this meant to the installation, he pointed out that the time lost in tape mounting was equivalent to turning off both computers for two hours out of every 24. Just to make matters worse, he observed that pre-mounting of tapes only saved time when the operators did not have to delay any other operation in order to carry out the pre-mount.

His main recommendations were:

- Move small data sets to disk, adding disk capacity as required.
- Introduce self-loading tape drives.
- Maintain redundancy in tape drives, to allow for pre-mounting and backup.
- Plan the physical positioning of tape drives so as to minimize the distance travelled by operators.

Implementation of these points led to much improved performance.

At the other extreme, files can often be so large that it is not practical to store them on magnetic tape. Table 9.1, taken from a recent paper by the author[4], shows the tape passing times required for sequential files of varying sizes stored on an IBM 3420 model 8; this takes no account of the time required for processing, and is made up of the time required to read the data, and the time lost due to traversing IBGs (inter-block gaps). The limits on minimum data (25 Mbytes), maximum data (1024 Gbytes), minimum number of records (150 thousand) and maximum number of records (64 million) have been chosen to cover the range from large commercial databases to national insurance files in countries such as Germany, France and the United Kingdom. For a full discussion of the considerations involved in optimizing tape operations, see Chapter 4.

As the time required to update the whole file increases, so the system designer's options are reduced. Of course, if the hit rate is very high—as would apply for a payroll, for example—there is no way to avoid long run times. In fact, a high hit-rate file is almost always best held on magnetic tape[1]. However, whenever the hit rate is relatively low, the designer will consider transferring the file to direct-access storage. This was, earlier, often magnetic card storage such as IBM's Data Cell or NCR's CRAM. The British national insurance records were held on CRAM for many years, because their volume was too large to be held on disk. The capacity of modern disks is now so great—1260 Mbytes per unit of a 3380, for example—that magnetic card devices have virtually disappeared, and their successor mass storage devices are less widely used than might have been expected.

It was pointed out in Chapter 7 (see p. 229) that, when direct reference is made to an IS file, the cylinder index should be held in main storage whenever possible. In terms of access speed this is highly advantageous, but

Table 9.1 The figures tabulated show the time required to read the total quantity of data given in the left-hand column, when it is held in the number of records shown at the top of each column. Values in **bold** type show minutes and seconds, while those in normal type represent hours and minutes. Processing is not included in the times tabulated, and they are therefore minima, not averages.

	\multicolumn{10}{c}{Number of records}
Total data	150 K	300 K	500 K	1 M	2 M	4 M	8 M	16 M	32 M	64 M
25 Mb	**4.05**	**7.50**	**12.50**	**25.20**	**50.20**	1.40	3.20	6.40		
50 Mb	**4.25**	**8.10**	**13.10**	**25.40**	**50.40**	1.41	3.21	6.41	13.21	
125 Mb	**5.25**	**9.10**	**14.10**	**26.40**	**51.40**	1.42	3.22	6.42	13.22	26.42
250 Mb	**7.05**	**10.50**	**15.50**	**28.20**	**53.20**	1.43	3.23	6.43	13.23	26.43
500 Mb	**10.25**	**14.10**	**19.10**	**31.40**	**56.40**	1.47	3.27	6.47	13.27	26.47
1 Gb	**17.05**	**20.50**	**25.50**	**38.20**	1.03	1.53	3.33	6.53	13.33	26.53
2 Gb	**30.25**	**34.10**	**39.10**	**51.40**	1.17	2.07	3.47	7.07	13.47	27.07
4 Gb	**57.05**	1.01	1.06	1.18	1.43	2.33	4.13	7.33	14.13	27.33
8 Gb	1.50	1.54	1.59	2.12	2.37	3.27	5.07	8.27	15.07	28.27
16 Gb	3.37	3.41	3.46	3.58	4.23	5.13	6.53	10.13	16.53	30.13
32 Gb	7.12	7.16	7.21	7.34	7.59	8.49	10.29	13.49	20.29	33.49
64 Gb	14.17	14.21	14.26	14.38	15.03	15.53	17.33	20.53	27.33	40.53
128 Gb	28.30	28.34	28.39	28.52	29.17	30.07	31.47	35.07	41.47	55.07
256 Gb	56.57	57.01	57.06	57.18	57.43	58.33	60.13	63.33	70.13	83.33
512 Gb	113.50	113.54	113.59	114.12	114.37	115.27	117.07	120.27	127.07	140.27
1024 Gb	227.37	227.41	227.46	227.58	228.23	229.13	230.53	234.13	240.53	254.13

it sometimes has to be ruled out because of lack of main storage space. Very small files can be held on fixed-head disks to improve performance, but again the decision is one of storage availability against speed. These situations illustrate the costs involved in some design decisions. If main storage has to be upgraded or a new semiconductor 'disk' drive obtained in order to accommodate a file, the cost of improved performance can easily be measured. However, the enhanced storage facilities are available for other purposes as well, and the cost should be considered with that in mind.

9.6 Expected life

When a file is set up, the feasibility—and indeed the desirability—of designing it with great care depends very much on its likely lifespan. A short-lived file is unlikely to repay a great deal of design work. In addition, by the time data have been collected to check whether the original decisions taken were correct, the file will no longer be active. For these reasons a file with a short life-expectancy is best designed for convenience rather than for optimal performance.

9.7 Growth

In designing a file that will be in operation for some time, allowance should be made for growth. This can occur either as a result of increased record size or due to additional records, or both. Hence the designer must allow for possible future additional processing, as well as further records.

Growth has two aspects. Additions will apparently increase file size unless deletions are removed, but this is not true growth; only *real* increases in file size should be catered for, and the illusion of growth created by actual additions but tagged deletions—i.e. records that have been logically but not physically removed from the file—should be ignored. Of course, the file will have to be given sufficient room to accommodate these additions, but the extra space provided will depend on the time between reorganizations. After reorganization the file should return approximately to its previous size.

Magnetic tape files do not suffer from this problem as they never need to hold deleted records, and the same applies to sequential disk files that are not updated in place, but handled by creating a new copy of the file on each run. Overflow space to be provided in other cases has been discussed in the appropriate chapters.

9.8 Volatility

As pointed out above, additions and deletions can cause apparent changes in size. However, highly volatile files also suffer from the problem that analyses of hit pattern and frequency rapidly become out of date. For this reason direct files—in which any hit pattern is partially or entirely destroyed—tend to give more consistent results than sequential or indexed files. They do, however, suffer from a progressive degradation from the synonym percentages produced by a two-pass load to the higher percentages produced by a one-pass load. Access-frequency-loaded direct files are more sensitive to changes in the record population due to volatility than any other type, because of their reliance on data that relates to a particular set of records, and their rapid deterioration as additions are made.

As the processing involved in adding records to an inverted file is considerable, this organization technique becomes less attractive if the record is not likely to remain active for long. In this case the serially organized information retrieval file remains appropriate for larger numbers of records than would normally be considered acceptable.

In summary, all files held on direct access devices are adversely affected by volatility. One solution is to carry out processing in a tape-like fashion, producing a new file on each run. If this is not acceptable—and for many applications it is not—a price has to be paid that is made up of extra space and periodic reorganizations. The greater *one* of these is, the less the other needs to be. In the case of a direct file, the designer may decide to 'pay' in extra processing time instead by arranging that deleted records are physically removed during processing. Many types of file, such as VSAM, are claimed to need little or no reorganization—but they perform far better if they *are* reorganized at regular intervals.

9.9 Run integration

In Chapter 1 (p. 15) it was shown that direct processing allowed a number of runs to be consolidated into a single run. This depends on the ability of direct or indexed sequential files to handle transactions in any order and so to reference at the same time several files organized in different key sequences and with different techniques. This can offer a simplification of run design, but there are a number of dangers involved.

The first is the relative complexity of the program required. This will demand more thorough testing and maintenance and involve longer development than is the case for simpler file runs. The program will also be more likely to fail due to undetected errors, as the testing conditions are more complex.

The second is that of possible problems in interaction between files. A run can be planned so easily that logical errors such as the lack of matching of transactions can occur[5]. To avoid this the system will probably require either temporary files or a large main storage work area, both of which complicate the run and increase its cost. The discipline imposed by designing a series of separate runs will avoid this type of situation; multi-file runs will always require both careful run design and programs that have been designed to avoid problems.

If these precautions are taken, an integrated run can lead to substantial savings in overall run timing. Databases or direct files, in which records can be obtained in any order, make an integrated run easier to plan and control, but may reduce its efficiency.

9.10 Data integrity and backup

Sequential tape files are very easily provided with recovery facilities in case of loss of data. All direct access files are more vulnerable if records are updated in place, although the devices themselves are inherently more error-free. Integrity thus has to be built into a file quite deliberately; in order of difficulty, sequential is the easiest, indexed next, and direct the most difficult. The specialist file organizations also present difficulties. The more complex a file structure is, the more vulnerable it is to error and the more difficult is the process of reconstruction. Against this must be set the comprehensive automatic recovery routines built into software such as databases or IBM's CICS (Customer Information Control System).

298 Design of computer data files

Table 9.2 The table gives a general rating of each file organization technique, showing 6 as best and 1 as worst, for the factors given in the left-hand column. For detailed information, the text should be consulted.

FACTOR OF CHOICE			FILE ORGANIZATION USED				
			Sequential	Direct	Indexed sequential	Inverted	Database/complex
Storage requirements			6	4/5 (depending on load technique)	4/5 (influenced by overflow requirement)	3	1
Access Speed	Access using keys	In serial order	6	1 (unless in algorithm-determined order)	4/6 (depending on hit-rate)	1 (except if in main file order)	4 (depending on the application)
		In enquiry order	1	6	5	4	3
	Access based on the values of multiple attributes		1	1	1/4 (depending on whether alternate indexes provided)	6	3

Choice of file organization 299

		1 (disk) 6 (tape)	5 (additions) 3/4 deletions	5 (can be poor if hits are clustered)	4 (if well designed)	5 (depends on the precise software)
Effect of additions or deletions	Ease of alteration					
	In serial order	1/6 (as above)	2	5/6 (affected by hit rate)	4	4/5
	In random order	1	6	4/5 (better if index in main storage)	5	3/4
Effect of hit rate (sequential access only)	Low	2 (tape) 5 (disk)	3/4	4/6 (the lower the better)	3/4	4/5
	Medium	4 (tape) 4/5 (disk)	2/3	3/5 (as above)	2/3	2/4
	High	6 (tape) 3/4 (disk)	1/2	2/3	1/2	1/3

If data integrity is the principal consideration in the design of a file, precautions can be provided by adding to the cost and in these circumstances it is no longer true that direct access files are at a disadvantage. Both security and data integrity are dealt with in Chapter 10 (p. 318).

9.11 Analysis of the criteria

When the file designer has decided what criteria to apply, the next step is to determine an appropriate file design. If this is obvious, optimization of the file organization required can be carried out using the guidelines given in the relevant chapter; in some cases simulation programs exist or can be modified to apply[6,7,8,9,10], which simplifies the task. Table 9.2 summarizes the relative merits of a number of file organizations in many of the cases looked at above. A further useful table is given in[11].

9.12 Run timings

When factors such as security or mode of reference to the file are not of vital importance, the decision between file organizations is usually based on the time a run will take. This time may be expressed either as the average time for a single transaction or as the total run time. When large numbers of records have to be updated and batching is practicable, the choice will be between sequential and indexed sequential files. This is examined below, and guidelines on the effect of hit rate and blocking factor have been provided so that the file designer can make an informed choice.

When the number of updates is relatively few and the hit rate is low, the choice will be between direct and indexed sequential files. Here again the designer can calculate the benefits of the two file types precisely, rather than relying on a rule of thumb or a hunch about the situation. This too is discussed below.

9.13 Sequential versus indexed sequential

In Chapter 7 (p. 250) it was pointed out that, for sequential processing, indexed sequential files usually take longer to process than sequential files for these reasons:

- reference to the cylinder index and higher indexes
- increased file size
- longer housekeeping processing times.

To put into perspective the difference in timing between the sequential retrieval of *all* the records in a sequential file and those same records in an

Table 9.3 Comparison of run timings for sequential and indexed sequential files. t_{min} = minimum time cylinder-to-cylinder; m = cylinders required for the sequential file; m' = cylinders for the indexed file, where $m' = (ml/(l-3/2))^*$; n = number of records in file; l = tracks per cylinder; R = rotation time; C = integer/2 (*see* text for explanation).

Elements of timing	Type of file	
	Sequential	Indexed sequential
Higher index references	Nil	1–100 ms
Seek to start	10–60 ms	10–60 ms
Seeking track index entries (read adds ~5%)	Nil	$m'\dfrac{(l-1)R}{2}$
Minimum record read time	mlR†	$m'lR$†
Probable record read time	minimum + CnR	CnR
Cylinder-to-cylinder time	$(m-1)t_{min}$	$(m'-1)t_{min}$

* The figure of 3/2 represents one track for embedded overflow and half a track for the track index.
† Assuming both are in the *same* format, i.e. CKD with key separate.

indexed sequential file, general figures have been compared in Table 9.3 taken from the author's work elsewhere[2]. The *minimum record read* figures are calculated on the assumption that records can be processed as quickly as they are read, i.e. that processing can be completed while the device is traversing the gap between one record and the next. This is seldom possible. The more likely situation is that one or more revolutions will be 'lost' between reading successive blocks, because processing of one record or block is not completed until the start of the next has already been passed. Some direct access software only permits one read per revolution[12]. The probable record read figures shown are based on the number of blocks and the time for a full track rotation. The constant multiplier C would be 1 or 2 or 3, etc., for individual blocks processed using a single buffer, while double buffering would reduce it to 1/2 or 2/2 or 3/2, etc., and a larger number of buffers would reduce the figures further. However, it is normally more useful to increase block size than to provide more input buffers than two or three, as was discussed in Chapter 4 (p. 101).

Table 9.4 gives results for the comparison of a file held in sequential and in indexed sequential form on an IBM 2314 disk[13]. From these figures it is clear that the main increase in run time when the file is held in indexed form is due to seeking and reading track index entries. The file timings are increased by about 25 seconds as a result of being held as an indexed sequential file with the consequent need to read index entries. This is more than a 50 per cent increase in the special case when processing is very rapid and no revolutions are lost. In the more normal case that there is a loss of revolutions due to

Table 9.4 40 000 records of 200-character length held on an IBM 2314 ($m = 100$, $m' = 109$, $l = 20$, $R = 0.025$).

Elements of timing	Type of file	
	Sequential	Indexed sequential
Higher index references	—	100 ms
Seek to start of file	60 ms	60 ms
Seeking track index entries	—	24.5 s
Minimum record read times	50 s	50 s
Probable record read times	550 s or 1050 s etc.	550 s or 1050 s etc.
Cylinder-to-cylinder time	2.47 s	2.7 s
Total times	52.5 s + 500C s	77.4 s + 500C s
Difference	~25 s	

processing, the difference in timing is less than 3 per cent. As some manufacturers' software arranges that only one record is processed per track revolution[12], this is a significant limitation of potential performance.

Table 9.5 shows the effect of using a faster removable disk drive (a 3330) for file storage. In this case the difference between the two file organizations is about 16.5 seconds, which is just more than 53 per cent if all records can be processed without loss of revolutions, but just over 3 per cent once more if revolutions are lost during processing. This pattern is maintained for larger files[2].

A newly-loaded indexed sequential file is thus only a little less efficient than a sequential file for sequential retrieval, even for 100 per cent hit rate. Additions will if anything be more damaging to a sequential file, although this depends on the methods used to handle new records. The result is that after additions even a 100 per cent hit file can sometimes be updated more

Table 9.5 57 000 records of 240-character length held on an IBM 3330 ($m = 100$, $m' = 109$, $l = 19$, $R = 0.0167$).

Elements of timing	Type of file	
	Sequential	Indexed sequential
Higher index references	—	60 ms
Seek to start of file	30 ms	30 ms
Seeking track index entries	—	16.3 s
Minimum record read time	30 s	30 s
Probable record read times	506 s or 981 s, etc.	506 s or 981 s, etc.
Cylinder to cylinder time	1 s	1.1 s
Total times	31 s + 476C s	47.5 s + 476C s
Difference	~16.5 s	

rapidly if it is organized as an indexed sequential file rather than a sequential file.

As the hit rate reduces from 100 per cent, more and more records do not need to be processed. If the records are held in the separate key format, skipping them provides more time to process the records that precede them without losing revolutions. Indexed sequential files usually allow this. ICL's 1900 series hardware prevents it, however, as do systems, such as IBM's 3370, that employ disks in the sector mode of operating. We shall first look at the case where *both* file organizations use the separate key format and then that in which only the indexed sequential file uses it.

1 Separate key format in both files

When both files use the separate key format, the indexed sequential file can benefit as compared to the sequential file only by the skipping of whole tracks or cylinders. In order to calculate when this will apply, we procede as follows:

The indexed sequential file software will always have to locate the first index entry on a cylinder, which will require an average of half a revolution. Further index entries can be scanned at rotation speeds if tracks are skipped, but half a revolution will be required to pick up the next index item after any record has been referenced. If n tracks have to be referenced on a cylinder, there will be a total loss of time due to index references of:

$$\frac{R}{2} \text{ (first index entry)} + \frac{nR}{2} \text{ (further index entries)} \tag{9.1}$$

Every skipped track, on the other hand, will represent a saving of a full revolution in comparison with the sequential scanning of the track that is required if the file is sequentially organized. If there are C data tracks per cylinder and n tracks are referenced, then $(C-n)$ tracks are skipped.

To determine the break-even point in input-output terms between skip sequential processing of indexed sequential files, and skip sequentially processed sequential disk files, set the loss and gain of time equal. Then:

$$R(C - n) = \frac{R(n + 1)}{2}$$
$$2(C - n) = n + 1$$
$$n = \frac{(2C - 1)}{3} \tag{9.2}$$

The probability of being able to skip a full track, when the update pattern is random, is given in Table 9.6. These figures show that either a low hit rate or a small number of blocks per track, or both, will be necessary for sufficient entire tracks to be skipped to make up the loss of time caused by the reading of index items during indexed sequential processing.

304 Design of computer data files

Table 9.6 Figures tabulated show the break-even record hit rate (%) between sequential and indexed-sequential files, assuming that the hit pattern is random, and the disk has twenty tracks per cylinder ($C = 20$). For example, a file that has four records per track should be organized as sequential if the hit rate is over 23.1 per cent, but indexed-sequential if it is below.

Track capacity (blocks)	1	2	3	4	5	7	10	15	20	25	35	40	50	70	100
1	65.0	40.8	29.5	23.1	18.9	13.9	10.0	6.8	5.1	4.1	3.0	2.6	2.1	1.5	1.0
2	40.8	23.1	16.1	12.3	10.0	7.2	5.1	3.4	2.6	2.1	1.5	1.3	1.0	0.8	0.5
3	29.5	16.1	11.0	8.4	6.8	4.9	3.4	2.3	1.7	1.4	1.0	0.9	0.7	0.5	
4	23.1	12.3	8.4	6.4	5.1	3.7	2.6	1.7	1.3	1.0	0.8	0.7	0.5		
5	18.9	10.0	6.8	5.1	4.1	3.0	2.1	1.4	1.0	0.8	0.6	0.5			
6	16.1	8.4	5.7	4.3	3.4	2.6	1.7	1.2	0.9	0.7	0.5				
7	13.9	7.2	4.9	3.7	3.0	2.1	1.5	1.0	0.8	0.6					
8	12.3	6.4	4.3	3.2	2.6	1.9	1.3	0.9	0.7	0.5					
9	11.0	5.7	3.8	2.9	2.3	1.7	1.2	0.8	0.6						
10	10.0	5.1	3.4	2.6	2.1	1.5	1.0	0.7	0.5						
12	8.4	4.3	2.9	2.2	1.7	1.2	0.9	0.6							
14	7.2	3.7	2.5	1.9	1.5	1.1	0.8	0.5							
16	6.4	3.2	2.2	1.6	1.3	0.9	0.7								
18	5.7	2.9	1.9	1.5	1.2	0.8	0.6								
20	5.1	2.6	1.7	1.3	1.0	0.8	0.5								
23	4.5	2.3	1.5	1.1	0.9	0.6									
26	4.0	2.0	1.3	1.0	0.8	0.6									
30	3.4	1.7	1.2	0.9	0.7	0.5									
35	3.0	1.5	1.0	0.8	0.6										
40	2.6	1.3	0.9	0.7	0.5										
45	2.3	1.2	0.8	0.6											
50	2.1	1.0	0.7	0.5											
60	1.7	0.9	0.6												
70	1.5	0.8	0.5												
80	1.3	0.7													
90	1.2	0.6													
100	1.0	0.5													
200	0.5														

Typical values for C are ten, nineteen, twenty and thirty data tracks per cylinder. These yield break-even points of 37 per cent, 35.1 per cent, 35 per cent and 34.4 per cent of tracks not referred to. This means that, if higher percentages of tracks than these can be skipped, the file designer should recommend an indexed sequential file; otherwise a sequential file with separate keys will perform better, at least so far as input-output times are concerned.

The percentage of tracks not requiring reference depends on the record hit rate and the number of records per track. For convenience, Table 9.6 gives break-even points for a number of different combinations of block size and number of records per block. However, if there are m records per block, r blocks per track, and the probability that any single record will be hit is p, then the probability $\text{PROB}_{\text{SKIP}}$ that a given record will *not* be hit, and can thus be skipped, is:

$$\text{PROB}_{\text{SKIP}} = (1 - p) \tag{9.3}$$

The probability that a complete block will not be hit is:

$$\text{PROB}_{\text{SKIP}} = (1 - p)^m \tag{9.4}$$

and the probability that no record on the track will be hit is:

$$\text{PROB}_{\text{SKIP}} = (1 - p)^{mr} \tag{9.5}$$

Given a normal-sized file, it is justifiable to use equation (9.5) as a guide to the proportion of tracks that can be skipped. From equation (9.2) the break-even point will be about $\text{PROB}_{\text{SKIP}} = 0.35$ for nineteen- and twenty-track disks. Thus, for any given m and r, the break-even hit rate p can be determined as follows:

$$(1 - p)^{mr} = 0.35$$
$$(1 - p) = (0.35)^{1/mr}$$
$$p = 1 - (0.35)^{1/mr} \tag{9.6}$$

Break-even hit rates calculated in this way are given in Table 9.6 and plotted as curves in Fig. 9.3. For devices with slightly different $\text{PROB}_{\text{SKIP}}$ figures the results will be only approximately true, but the overall relationship will be as shown.

If a known hit pattern exists, the file designer should use it rather than make the assumption that it is random; the percentage of tracks that must be skipped to break-even does not change, but most non-random patterns increase the number of skipped tracks because references are more concentrated. This favours the use of indexed sequential files for higher hit rates than given here. There is one exception; the very unusual distribution in which updates occur at intervals of every n records will cause a sequential file with separate keys to be more suitable than an indexed file at all hit rates for which there is at least a single update per track.

In cases for which no entry is given in Table 9.6, a fairly accurate rule is that any given combination of records per track and record hit rate will lead to 35 per cent of tracks being skipped if references are random and the following condition holds:

$$pmr < 1.04 \tag{9.7}$$

This equation does not apply for small numbers of records per track, but values for such cases are given in the table.

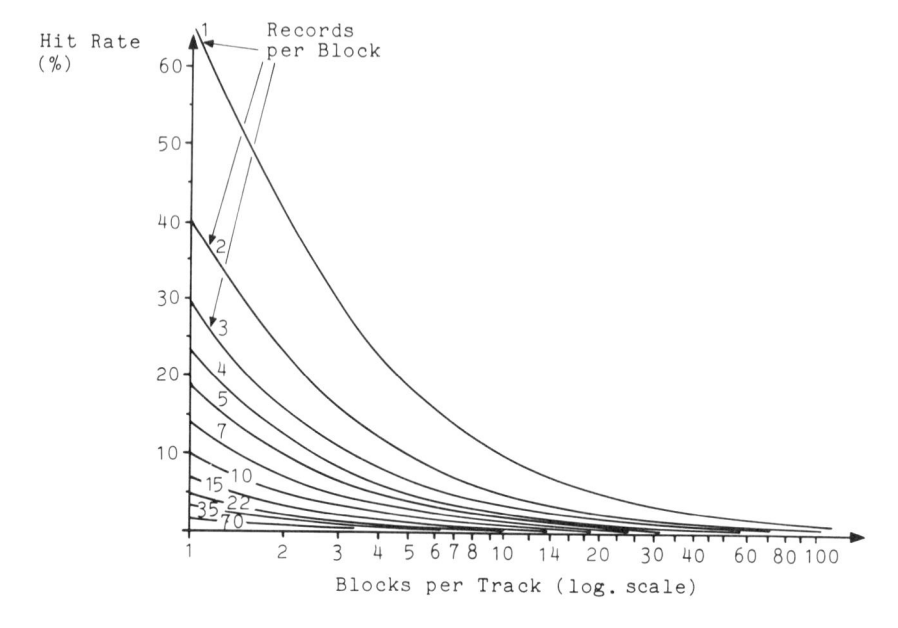

Fig. 9.3 These curves show the approximate break-even points between sequential files with separate key format and indexed sequential files. Hit rates *above* a given curve indicate sequential files, while those *below* are more rapidly processed using the indexed sequential file organization.

2 Sequential file with embedded keys

When each record or block of records in the sequential file has to be read into main storage to decide whether it is required, while the records in the indexed sequential file can be scanned on disk, the conditions for break-even between the two files change.

1 *Single-buffered files*

In this case the sequential file will miss a revolution after every block has been read while the block is examined to see whether any record in it requires processing. This will, of course, allow a full revolution in which the record or records that are hit can be processed.

The indexed sequential file, on the other hand, will lose one revolution per track due to index references and one revolution per block each time the *next* hit block follows the previous one immediately. This is because there will not generally be time to process a block before the start of the next block has passed the read-write heads. When *no* block on a track requires updating, the indexed sequential file will gain one revolution as the index reference will show that the track can be skipped. Thus, if there are B blocks in the file, n blocks per track, r records per block, and if q is the block activity (see Chapter 4, pp. 83–89, for a discussion of block activity), the conditions for a break-even between sequential and indexed sequential processing in terms of lost revolutions will be that:

Sequential revolutions lost = Indexed sequential revolutions lost

$$B = \frac{B}{n} + Bq^2 - \left(\frac{B}{n}\right)(1-q)^n$$

Rearranged, this expression becomes:

$$B + \left(\frac{B}{n}\right)(1-q)^n = \frac{B}{n} + Bq^2$$

Dividing by B gives:

$$1 + \left(\frac{1}{n}\right)(1-q)^n = \frac{1}{n} + q^2 \tag{9.8}$$

Substituting $q' = (1-q)$:

$$1 + \frac{q'^n}{n} = \frac{1}{n} + (1-q')^2$$

This expression simplifies to:

$$q'^n - nq'^2 + 2nq' - 1 = 0 \tag{9.9}$$

Solving for q' for each value of n and reversing the substitution provides the figures given in Table 9.7 for the break-even points for various numbers of blocks per track. Note that the block activity, while related to record hit rate, is not the same in value. The relationship was dealt with in Chapter 4 (see p. 88).

The break-even block activities have been plotted against the number of blocks per track in Fig. 9.4. This shows only the *potential* advantage of using indexed sequential files. Much of this advantage is lost in given implementations; for example, ICL's 1900 series software is limited to processing one record per revolution [12], and so can gain only by the skipping of whole tracks. In this case the potential situation reduces to that shown in Fig. 9.3.

The file designer will have to decide on the precise situation after investigating the way in which the software under consideration operates.

2 Double-buffered files

It is usually possible to check whether any record in a block requires processing during the time taken to read the next block into another buffer. Lost revolutions in the sequential file only occur when one or more records in a block are processed and the combined record identification and processing times exceed a single-block read time. The same situation applies to indexed files, so the difference between the two file organizations is more closely modelled by the curves in Fig. 9.3 rather than Fig. 9.4.

Table 9.7 Break-even points for various numbers of blocks per track for single-buffered sequential and indexed-sequential files.

Blocks per track (n)	Break-even block activity (%)
1	61.8
2	75.0
3	81.8
4	86.6
5	89.4
6	91.3
7	92.6
8	93.54
9	94.28
10	94.87
12	95.74
14	96.36
16	96.82
18	97.18
20	97.47
23	97.80
26	98.06
30	98.32
35	98.56
40	98.74
45	98.88
50	98.99
60	99.16
70	99.28
80	99.37
90	99.44
100	99.50
150	99.67
200	99.75

9.14 Indexed sequential versus direct

The applicability of these two file types overlaps mainly where there is some direct and some sequential requirement, although indexed sequential files are often used for enquiry-only systems because the software is available without the need for extensive user programming. We shall look first at the need for space.

Choice of file organization 309

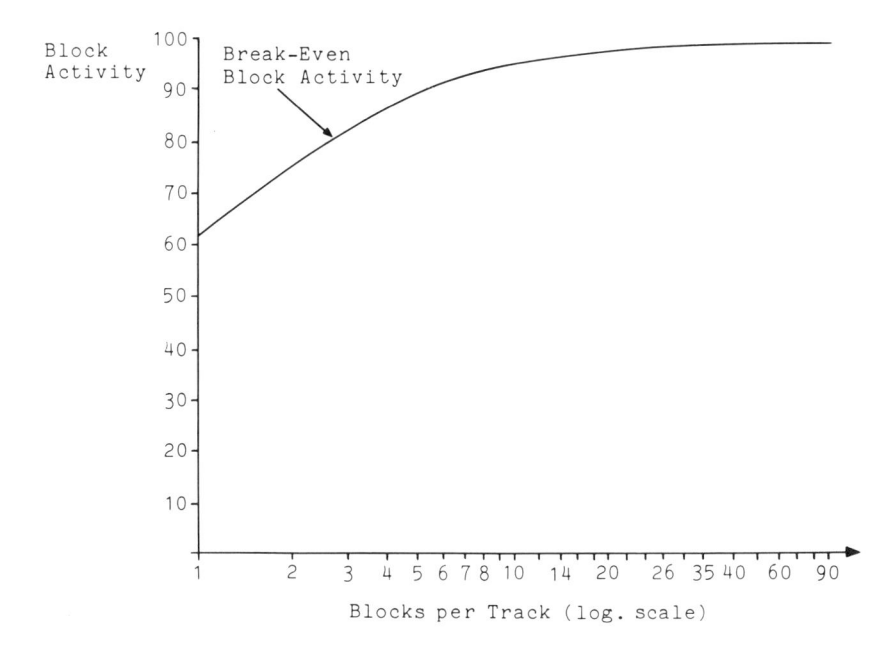

Fig. 9.4 Below the curve indexed sequential files are *potentially* faster than sequential files with embedded keys. *Actual* comparisons will depend on the way in which any given software is written.

Indexed sequential files will take up a disk extent that depends on the record key size, which affects index size as discussed in Chapter 7 (p. 246), any blocking factor and the overflow arrangements. Direct file space requirements are dependent on record format, bucket size and packing density, and as higher packing densities can be used if access frequency loading has been employed, this too will affect the space needed.

A comparison was made for a 400 000 record file on a 3330, where record size was eighty characters, including a six-character key[14]. The results are shown in Table 9.8.

It is clear that there is no marked difference between the two file organizations except when records are stored singly. Even in this case an access-frequency loaded file is comparable with an indexed file in its space requirements, and in general terms storage space is not a determining factor between the two file organizations. Once more the decision becomes a question of file timings.

Direct reference only

The time required to reference an indexed sequential file directly will be made up of the following steps:

Table 9.8 Comparison of the space requirements of various file types using an IBM 3330. The record size is eighty characters, of which six are taken up by the key. For direct files the predicted synonym percentages are also tabulated.

File type				Block or bucket size			
		One record	Five records	Ten records	Twenty-five (twenty-four*) records	Fifty-three (fifty-two*) records	Full track
Sequential	Tracks required	6558	3810	2858	2667	2516	2470
	Cylinders required	**346**	**201**	**151**	**141**	**133**	**130**
Direct, random loaded	Key format	Separate	Embedded	Embedded	Embedded	Embedded	Embedded
	Packing (%)	75	80	85	90	90	95
	Synonyms (%)	29.65	15.37	6.86	4.10	2.05	1.27
	Tracks required	11112	4762		2963	2796	2600
	Cylinders required	**585**	**251**	**177**	**156**	**148**	**137**
Direct, access frequency loaded	Key format	Separate	Embedded	Embedded	Embedded	Embedded	Embedded
	Packing (%)	90	95	95	95	95	95
	% synonyms referred to	15.2	5.6	2.6	1.25	0.87	0.32
	Tracks required	9260	4011	3009	2808	2649	2600
	Cylinders required	**488**	**212**	**159**	**148**	**140**	**137**
Indexed-sequential with overflow areas	Tracks required	8334	4598	3077	2778*	2565*	2470
	Cylinders required	**479**	**265**	**178**	**161***	**149***	**144**
Indexed-sequential without overflow areas	Tracks required	8334	4598	3077	2778*	2565*	2470
	Cylinders required	**453**	**251**	**169**	**153***	**141***	**136**

*The indexed sequential file organization technique requires a separate key record format; twenty-five and fifty-three record blocks would be very wasteful of space. For this reason smaller block sizes have been used, which provide a more complete utilization of disk space.

Step 1   Head movement to the higher-level indexes
Step 2   Search of the higher-level indexes
Step 3   Head movement to the data cylinder
Step 4   Search of the track index
Step 5   Search of the data track
Step 6   A possible search of the overflow track or separate area.

If the cylinder index is held in main storage the first two of these steps can be ignored, as they will be very rapid. This case, and also that of a typical time penalty—an average head movement plus one and a half revolutions of the disk to search the cylinder index—will be used in calculation. If the cylinder index exceeds three tracks—and hence the average search time exceeds 3/2 revolutions—a higher-level index which acts as a track index to the cylinder index will generally be provided, and thus 3/2 revolutions can be taken as a typical value.

Step 3 will be taken to be an average head movement, while steps 4 and 5 will each be assumed to require half a disk revolution. This will hold true for all prime data track records and for first overflow records from tracks organized using IBM or IBM-compatible software; if a significant number of records are non-first overflows, the timings given here will be too low. However, they provide a useful basis for comparison.

For a 3330 the figures will be:

Step 1   30 ms
Step 2   25.1 ms
Step 3   30 ms
Step 4   8.4 ms
Step 5   8.4 ms.

Thus the time required to reach a record, as an absolute optimum, will be:

102 ms if the cylinder index is held on the same disk;
 72 ms if it is held on a separate, dedicated 3330;
 47 ms if the cylinder index is in main storage.

These times will be reduced in some cases, e.g. with a small file, but generally they will be optimistic, as software overheads and non-first overflow records slow up record retrieval.

For direct access files, access to a home record in a direct file involves only the calculation of its storage address from its key, which is carried out at processing speed, followed by a single head movement and a single track search. For a file taking up the whole of a 3330 disk pack, this would require:

Head movement   30 ms
Track search   8.4 ms.

Allowing 0.6 ms for calculation of the address, this gives a total of 39 ms.
Synonyms require more time to locate because the home record is reached

first; when it has been retrieved and found not to be the required record, a further search is necessary. For this reason the file designer aims to minimize the number of synonyms occurring and to reduce the impact to those that cannot be avoided. This has been discussed in Chapter 6 (see pp. 172–209). After the precautions discussed there have been taken, a well-designed file should not show an average additional time due to synonyms of more than 0.2 revolutions per record retrieved, and usually far less. This leaves the direct file access at less than 43 ms, still some way better than the fastest possible indexed sequential retrieval.

A direct file that does not outperform an indexed file should be redesigned. In general, direct files are very much faster than indexed files, not least because they have a much smaller software overhead, and it is unusual to be able to hold a cylinder index in main storage in order to speed up the direct operation of an indexed file. Semiconductor disks may affect this, however, now that their capacity has reached 768 Mbytes (p. 47), as may the expanded main storage options on recent mainframes such as the 3090 model 600E, with up to one gigabyte of extended memory.

Curves representing the access speeds quoted here are given in Fig. 9.5 for comparison with each other and with batched and sorted operations.

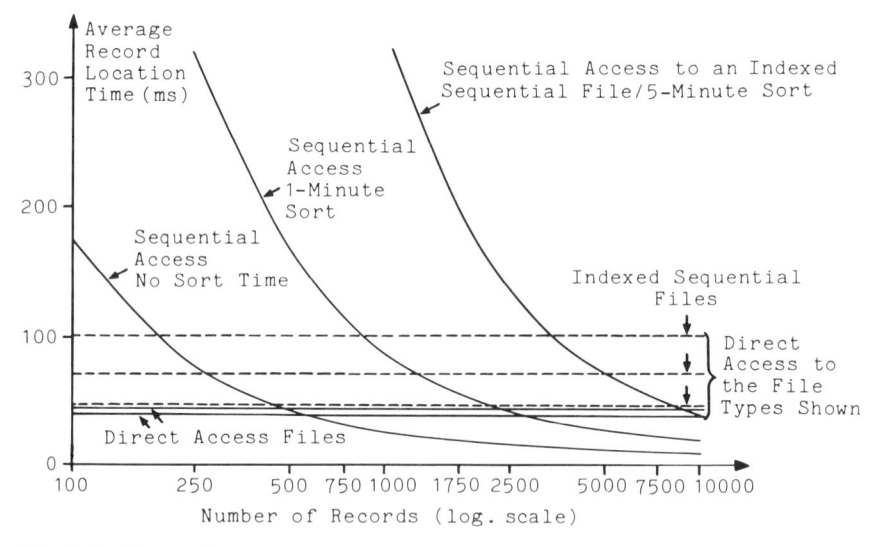

Fig. 9.5 Comparison of break-even points for indexed sequential files and direct access files.

Sequential reference

When updates or enquiries to a direct or an indexed sequential file can be batched, it may be more efficient to update them in a sequential order. Two factors will decide this. First, if the updates are naturally batched as occurs with mail deliveries, very fast service times are impossible for the whole batch and average service times will often be faster if updates are sorted into order. Second, overall throughput may be increased by batching and sorting input that arrives over a period, rather than handling it as it arrives.

The file designer will take these considerations into account in deciding on the form of processing required. While much of this depends on individual circumstances, it is possible to decide which mode of processing will offer the most rapid overall throughput of a batch.

1 *Indexed sequential files*
In reading an indexed file sequentially, there will be a number of factors to be considered:

1. Head movement to the start of the file;
2. Track index entries have to be read for each track in the file;
3. Cylinder-to-cylinder transitions take place at the end of each cylinder.

Taking the case of the 400 000-record file held on a 3330 that was mentioned earlier, and assuming ten-record blocks, the 'overhead' costs of referencing an indexed sequential file would be:

30 ms to start of file;
177×10 ms cylinder-to-cylinder transitions;
3077×8.4 ms track index references.

This gives a total of 27.65 seconds; if some tracks are not hit, this figure will be an over-estimate. There will be an additional 8.4 ms rotational delay for each record referenced, and this is used to give figures for the average retrieval time of various numbers of records that have been batched for retrieval rather than processed without batching and sorting.

The batch sizes involved in this sort of comparison will be likely to be relatively low, as high hit rate files that can be handled sequentially almost certainly will be. For this reason the actual sorting of a batch of records will be relatively rapid. However, the set-up time for a sort involves other operations, and sort times of 1 and 5 minutes have been added to the figures to give a realistic comparison. These figures are given in Table 9.9, taken from [14].

2 *Direct files*
These too can be updated 'sequentially', as was pointed out by Nijssen[15]. The principle in this case is to run the keys of the updates against the randomizing algorithm to provide home addresses. The update records are then sorted into ascending home address order and applied to the file in this order.

By comparison with indexed sequential files, direct 'sequential' access will involve a head movement to the start of the file, minimum head

Table 9.9 Figures tabulated show the average time in milliseconds required to locate a single record. Direct access minimum—38.4 ms; Direct access average—43.0 ms; Indexed-sequential minimum—46.7 ms; Indexed-sequential, cylinder, index on separate device—71.1 ms; Indexed-sequential, cylinder, index on same device—101.7 ms.

Number of records	Indexed sequential files, sequentially accessed			Direct files, 'sequentially' accessed		
	No sort time allowed for	1-minute sort	5-minute sort	No sort time allowed for	1-minute sort	5-minute sort
100	175.9	776.4	3176.4	59.1	651.1	3051.1
250	75.4	315.4	1275.4	29.1	269.6	1229.6
500	41.9	161.9	641.9	19.8	139.8	619.8
750	30.7	110.7	430.7	16.5	96.5	416.5
1 000	25.2	85.2	325.1	14.1	74.1	314.1
1 750	18.0	52.3	189.4	12.8	47.1	184.2
2 500	15.1	39.1	135.1	12.0	36.0	132.0
5 000	11.8	23.8	71.8	11.0	23.0	71.0
7 500	10.6	18.6	49.3	10.6	18.6	50.6
10 000	10.1	16.1	40.1	10.5	16.5	40.5

movements from cylinder to cylinder, and the loss of half a revolution on average for each record or block referenced. Time will be saved because there are no index references and this means that, for small batch numbers, direct files will outperform indexed sequential files.

The figures tabulated for direct files in Table 9.9 are calculated on the basis of

30 ms for an average head movement
$+ (48.8 \times 10)$ ms for minimum head movements
$+ n \times (8.4 + 1.6)$ ms

where n represents the number of records in the batch, and allowing the extra 1.6 ms per record as a figure to cover synonym retrieval.

On the assumptions made here, direct files will allow more rapid batch updating when batches contain less than 7500 records. Every case will depend on the precise conditions that apply; 'sorts' for direct files may well be more time-consuming than those for indexed sequential files. On the other hand, direct files use more efficient coding than is typical of indexed sequential software supplied by manufacturers, so these two factors may well cancel out. Note that this method can only be used for update or reference, and not for sequential reports.

Overall choice

The details given above indicate that for very small batches there is no point in batching and sorting. Depending on the time required to set up and carry out a sort and the conditions governing index placement or direct file design, at some given batch size there will be a time advantage in batching rather than processing updates as they arrive. Fig. 9.5 gives a good starting point in deciding on this break-even point. The particular software in use will influence the exact value of this point but not the nature of the general relationship.

Conclusion

In most cases choice between the available file organizations is relatively clear-cut. The criteria on which a choice will be based and the factors that may influence that choice were set out and discussed at the start of the chapter.

The main areas of uncertainty concern the choices between sequential and indexed sequential files when hit rates are relatively low, and between indexed sequential and direct files for direct updating or reference. A number of technical reasons for choice between these file organizations have been presented and explored. This does not rule out other reasons that may be important in any given case, such as programming expertise, installation standards, etc. However, it does provide the file designer with a number of tools that can be applied to produce a rational choice in most situations.

References

1. 'The choice between magnetic tape and magnetic disk for sequential file processing', by O. J. Hanson, *Proc. 6th Internationaler Kongress fuer Datenverarbeitung im Europaeischen Raum*, Vienna, March 1980, Vol. I, pp. 89–122.
2. 'Choosing between sequentially and indexed-sequentially organized files for sequential processing', by Owen Hanson, *Proc. 6th New Zealand Computer Conference*, Auckland, 1978, Vol. 2, pp. 136–155.
3. *The Use of Magnetic Tape Drives at The Royal Bank of Scotland*, 1976, by A. J. Knight, Royal Bank of Scotland Internal Report.
4. 'Problems in the design of large databases', by Owen Hanson, in *Cybernetics and Systems '86*, edited by Robert Trappl, publ. by D. Reidel Publishing Co., Dordrecht, Holland, 1986, pp. 473–480.
5. 'A discussion on a multi-master sequentially organized file maintenance system', by A. Y. Montgomery, *Australian Computer Journal*, Vol. 6, No. 3, November 1974, pp. 129–140.
6. 'Quantitative file evaluation and design', by A. Y. Montgomery and D. Hubbard, *Proc. 8th Australian Computer Conference*, Canberra 1978, Vol. 3, pp. 1241–1266.
7. 'Computer aids to the design of efficient file structures', by A. Y.

Montgomery, *Computers in Education*, edited by O. Lecarme and R. Lewis, North Holland Publishing Co., 1975, pp. 547–553.
8. *Simulation Studies of File Structures*, by C. S. Wallace, 17 pp., supplied by Professor A. Y. Montgomery, Royal Melbourne Institute of Technology, Victoria, Australia.
9. *Quantitative Timing Analysis and Verification for File Organization Modeling*, by V. Y. Lum, E. Senko, H. Ling and J. H. Barlow, IBM Research Paper RJ1024, May 3rd, 1972, 12 pp.
10. 'Performance evaluation of file organizations through modelling', by Dennis G. Severance and Alan G. Merten, *Proc. ACM Annual Conference*, Boston 1972, pp. 1061–1072.
11. *Essentials of Computer Data Files*, by Owen Hanson, Pitman, 1985.
12. 'Modelling of indexed sequential files: monitoring disk transfers', by Eva Huzan, *Computer Journal*, Vol. 22, No. 1, Feb. 1979, pp. 22–27.
13. *Performance Evaluation of ICL Disc EDS 60 Using Sequential File Organization*, by S. P. Ansari, MSc thesis in The City University, London, 1982.
14. 'Direct or indexed sequential? A file designer's guide', by Owen Hanson, *Proc. 6th New Zealand Computer Conference*, Auckland, 1978, Vol. 1, pp. 517–533.
15. 'Index sequential versus random', by G. M. Nijssen, *IAG Journal*, Vol. 5, No. 3, 1971, pp. 29–37.

Revision questions

1   What criteria would you apply to decide which file organization should be used in any given case?

2   What factors would you examine or estimate to modify the criteria of choice you have applied? Explain the influence of these factors on choice.

3   Discuss the differences in run timing between sequential and indexed sequential files. Estimate the differences on an IBM 3350. How do hit rates and additions affect these timings?

4   Calculate break-even timings between sequential and indexed sequential files as a function of hit rate and records per block. Distinguish between records stored in separate key format and those stored in embedded key format.

5   Compare the space requirements of sequential, indexed sequential and direct files on an IBM 3350. State and justify any assumptions that you make.

6   Explain the steps involved in the direct retrieval of records from direct and indexed sequential files. Estimate retrieval times for the IBM 3350 and

3380 disk drives, both with some indexes in main storage and when all indexes have to be held on direct access devices.

7 When would you batch and sort input to an indexed sequential file? Use reasonable figures for timing calculations and explain how large a batch is needed in various circumstances to persuade you to do so.

8 When would you batch and sort input to a direct file? Explain the process, the reasoning involved and the benefits to be expected.

9 Set out the steps you would follow in choosing between direct and indexed sequential files in any given case.

10 Accuracy, integrity and security

10.1 Introduction

In this closing chapter a number of vital matters will be considered. The *accuracy of data*, i.e. the data in the file being correct on entry to the system, is obviously crucial to the operation of any file, and the information management system it is part of. Although the accuracy of data usually depends on actions taken before it enters a file, the precautions that can be taken to ensure its accuracy are important enough to be described here; these measures also affect the design of files based on such data.

The *integrity of data* already in the system, i.e. that data should not be altered or lost except as a result of valid processing, depends on the operation of hardware and software. The appropriate techniques to optimize integrity are discussed below, showing how file organizations affect the situation.

Security, i.e. the *protection of data* from unauthorized reference, copying or alteration, is generally a matter of cost. File design, systems design and operating systems parameters provide the tools for the technical side of this; they will be considered, but it should not be forgotten that in the last resort security depends on people and the measures they are prepared to pay for.

The reader may be surprised to note that no mention is made of *privacy* in the title of this chapter. This is because, although computers are tools that allow privacy to be breached, the decisions affecting privacy are social in nature rather than relating to data processing. The considerations are mentioned and references are given at the end of the chapter. In any case, the Data Protection Acts now in force in many countries differ widely from each other, and the professional file designer will have to ensure that the requirements of a particular country are met by files to be used in that country.

As has been made clear, direct access storage is not fundamentally more prone to problems of loss or corruption of data than is tape; if anything, the reverse is true, as explained in Chapter 2. However, the fact that records stored on these devices are generally updated in place rather than copied does impose additional demands on the design of files using them. This will be made clear in the following pages.

10.2 Accuracy and integrity during processing

In general terms it is possible to apply controls of some sort, aimed at ensuring that all the data required for a run is correct, at four stages. These are pre-input, input, processing and output. Many of the same considerations apply to both batch and on-line systems; a section specifically on on-line topics is given later in the chapter (p. 343).

Pre-input controls

Data generated within an organization may often be entered directly onto forms which are later used as punching documents. Orders or other externally generated data are often more variable in format; in this case it is usual to transcribe the data onto standard forms[1].

In either case, in batch systems a given number of forms will be sent to the data preparation department. This provides two possibilities for checking: the first is that all orders, requests, etc., should be entered on some sort of register, while the second is that a count of the forms sent to data preparation should be made. Preferably, both these measures should be taken and a check should be made that they agree in number of entries.

In data preparation, data will be entered using VDUs (visual display units), tape cassettes or floppy disk, or, very occasionally now, cards. Some form of validation, by physical or visual verification, should be applied here. Once more, a count of records prepared should equal the number of forms that entered the system. Any discrepancy, such as that due to incorrectly filled in or unreadable forms, should be noted and explained.

Entry by the data originator, or entry through an enquiry system, may avoid most of these hazards as the system responses will lead to correction of the data on-line.

Input controls

On input to the system in order to create or update a master file, data will require extensive validation. It is at this stage that the accuracy of input, and hence the integrity of master files, can be most effectively ensured.

For batch processing a separate validation run is desirable, as this allows the results of validation to be checked and errors to be corrected before input to the file. When this is not possible, the first phase of processing will consist of validation only. Either an incorrect record will be rejected individually and re-input on a later run, or the complete batch will be rejected.

Whatever technique is used, it is important that *all* validation checks should be carried out before a record or batch is rejected. Failure to ensure this may lead to a second rejection due to errors that had not been tested for on the first run, and batches could be seriously delayed due to rejections on several separate runs.

Validation is generally carried out on characters, fields, batches, and control fields such as record keys. Requirements vary, but most systems will use some or all of the following:

1 Character checks
These are usually carried out on a complete field at a time, but may also apply to gaps between fields. Note that VDU entry will usually have pre-set fields, so no gaps exist unless they have been planned.

(a) Testing for blanks There may be a blank separator between fields, or a field may be blank on input to allow for late usage. Comparison with a constant of the required size can be used here. Note that blank is usually taken to be an alphabetic character and may lead to problems in a numeric field. Input from a VDU with pre-specified fields will avoid this problem.

(b) Testing for numeric Each character defined as numeric should be tested, but leading zeros have to be punched in every position so tested. A position that can optionally be either blank or a digit can be tested only for alphanumeric characters. If it turns out that some digit positions are alphabetic, this may be due to inadvertently using the shift key, to an incorrect field content or position. In any case it will require attention.

(c) Testing for sign Signs may be positively punched or assumed. It is sensible to ensure that signs actually are present in cases where they are expected to be punched. A check on the correctness of a sign is sometimes useful. EBCDIC (Expanded Binary Coded Decimal Interchange Code) zoned decimal fields output from a previous computer run will contain C or D in the leftmost position of the field, which can cause problems if this position is checked for numeric characters. It should be compared with C or D instead, or both if either sign is acceptable.

(d) Testing for alphabetic Fields intended to be alphabetic *only* can be tested for this. However, note that an address or even a name—O'Reilly for example, because it contains an apostrophe—may include numeric or special characters and is thus not alphabetic. Codes are the most likely groups of characters to be purely alphabetic.

(e) Testing for special characters On occasions it may be convenient that a code, separator or header character should be a special character. The appropriate constant is then set up and compared with the character position in question.

2 Field controls
These are the most wide-ranging set of tests, and they can often pinpoint errors of logic and lack of consistency in the data, in addition to incorrect data.

(*a*) *Sequence tests*   Keys may be required to be in a given order for further processing. Records out of sequence, or the batch itself, might then be rejected. Multiple records can be checked; if several records are required to make up a given transaction, the presence and sequence of the records can be checked before they are processed.

(*b*) *Limit check*   Upper and lower limits may be set on a field. For instance we may write:

> IF   HOURS WORKED IS NUMERIC
>   AND HOURS-WORKED <80
>   AND HOURS-WORKED >ZERO
>   PERFORM NORMAL PROCESSING
> ELSE
>   PERFORM HW-ERROR-ROUTINE.

This example[2] demonstrates that the limits set are within the *possible* limits of 0 and 168 and are reasonable figures. Any exception merits examination; note that 365, while apparently a reasonable limit for the number of days in the year, will lead to problems in leap years, and ensure that 'reasonable' figures *are* reasonable!

In the same way, a percentage limit representing increase and/or decrease from an earlier value can be set to call for manual intervention in cases such as a bill or a payment that is *half* or *twice* the expected value.

In all cases it is wise to set a limit that corresponds to the absolute maximum possible. This might be 168 hours in a week, 366 days in a year, or the maximum payment possible in a month—not usually £99, £9999, etc.! This is what is usually meant by 'limit' checking. The earlier examples are often described as 'reasonableness' checks.

(*c*) *Completeness checking*   The presence of every field in the record should be confirmed. In the case of records with variable numbers of fields, every mandatory field should be checked and its size confirmed.

(*d*) *Date checking*   Dates are held in various forms, e.g. YYDDD, MMDDYY, DDMMYY. Some systems achieve a three-digit date by using additional characters. The validation program should check the presence of the date in correct form, and ensure that the limits of earliest and latest dates acceptable to the system have not been exceeded. If the earliest date acceptable is not long ago, care should be taken to avoid rejecting re-entries that have been corrected.

(*e*) *Consistency*   A number of fields may be related, so that it is possible to check them with respect to each other. For example, input of a credit amount might mean that one field was blank while the other held the amount. Input of a debit might require an amount in the other field. Hence the two fields could be checked together.

The same principle can be used to check age and birth date, part number and description, discount given with customer class, etc. This can be a very effective technique to ensure the validity of a record.

(f) Check digit usage   Most errors in numeric fields are due to:

1. Transcription, in which the wrong digit is written, e.g. 1237 for 1234;
2. Transposition, in which two digits swap places, e.g. 1324 for 1234;
3. Double transposition, in which two digits that are not adjacent swap places, e.g. 4231 for 1234;
4. Random, in which a selection of the above errors occurs, e.g. 0214, 3914 or 2124.

All the first three types of error can be detected by adding an appropriate check digit. The objective of a check digit is to provide extensive self-checking facilities in the number. This it does by weighting each position of the original number differently and using a prime number modulus for calculation, so that changes in position of *two* digits will be detected. If larger number of digits are in error the sum of the changes in weighting may add up to the modulus, which would make the error undetectable. The method operates as follows:

Take a number, say 1234. Multiply each digit, starting from the right, by 2, 3, 4, . . . 11, 2, 3, 4, . . .:

```
      1   2   3   4
     ×5  ×4  ×3  ×2
   =  5   8   9   8
```

Add these sums:

$5 + 8 + 9 + 8 = 30$

Divide by 11 to give

2, remainder 8

Subtract 8 from the modulus to give the number required to make up the sum to a multiple of the modulus:

$11 - 8 = 3$

This provides a check digit of 3.

The full number is now stored as 12343. The sum of

$(1 \times 5) + (2 \times 4) + (3 \times 3) + (4 \times 2) + (3 \times 1) = 33$

which is divisible by 11. The number is therefore assumed to be valid, as there is no remainder when it is divided by the modulus (11).

All single- or double-digit errors will be detected so long as the modulus is a prime and larger than the number of digits in the number being checked. This is because the error introduced will be the product of the difference between the numbers and the difference between their positions, i.e. their *weights*. This cannot be the modulus or a multiple of it because neither of the terms making up the product is as large as the modulus, which is a prime. Thus, using our earlier examples of errors, and assuming that in each case the number was intended to be 1234 with a check digit of 3, we will obtain:

12373 gives
$(1 \times 5) + (2 \times 4) + (3 \times 3) + (7 \times 2) + (3 \times 1) = 39$
13243 gives
$(1 \times 5) + (3 \times 4) + (2 \times 3) + (4 \times 2) + (3 \times 1) = 34$
42313 gives
$(4 \times 5) + (2 \times 4) + (3 \times 3) + (1 \times 2) + (3 \times 1) = 42$
21243 gives
$(2 \times 5) + (1 \times 4) + (2 \times 3) + (4 \times 2) + (3 \times 1) = 31$

None of these is divisible by 11, and so each is immediately shown to be in error. However, the other two 'random' errors lead to a different result:

02143 gives
$(0 \times 5) + (2 \times 4) + (1 \times 3) + (4 \times 2) + (3 \times 1) = 22$
39143 gives
$(3 \times 5) + (9 \times 4) + (1 \times 3) + (4 \times 2) + (3 \times 1) = 55$

Both of these would appear to be correct; they were deliberately intended to seem so. With modulus n, it must be expected that there will be a probability of $1/n$ that random errors will lead to numbers that appear to be correct. Thus the effectiveness of check digits will depend on the rate of occurrence of random errors and the size of the modulus. IBM[3] claim a 97 per cent detection rate for transposition and transcription errors using modulus 11 checking. Daniels and Yeates[4] predict 100 per cent detection for these errors and 90.9 per cent for random errors. They quote a case in which only five errors were undetected out of 1000 actual errors (this figure itself was 1 per cent of the total data entries).

Check digits are usually calculated by computer and lists of correct numbers are made available to clerical staff. They are usually used for keys, codes and similar fixed numbers. It is seldom practical to provide them for fields such as cash input unless the card punch, terminal or other input device will do the calculation automatically.

Even if a field does self-check, this does not prove that the quantity held is valid. It may represent a discontinued stock line or a staff member who has left.

(g) *Code existence*   Codes can be checked against a table to ensure that they are valid and current. Processing should take account of the need to enter new codes from time to time, so an override routine is required with space to store the new codes in any tables used.

(h) *Code range checking*   If the number of valid codes is too great to allow table checking to be used, some sort of check to ensure validity is still necessary. A composite code may be checked in parts, using separate tables to cut down the many combinations possible.

(i) *Handling errors*   Many errors will lead to record or batch rejection. However, some 'errors' can be ignored; in a statistical survey the loss of one value on height, salary, age, etc., is not significant. While the same cannot be done with an electricity reading, lack of a meter reading can be 'corrected' by substituting an estimate. When the meter is next read this will correct itself.

Fields not yet available, such as new stock numbers, can be provided with an obviously invalid number for processing and corrected at a later date. This technique can also be used to update master files with data that becomes valid only at a later date.

Fields that appear to be in error may have been entered backwards, or in inverted order. It is sometimes worth trying out various combinations of reading and interpretation of fields in error. However, it is usually better to ensure that such occurrences are few and to withhold them for later manual analysis.

3 Batch controls

A batch control record is generally included either as the first or the last record in a batch. It will be prepared last, but may then be entered first. The control record will contain fields such as batch number, record count, and any control or cash totals. Generally, a batch will be rejected if any records are in error; if the reduced batch is processed the batch control record will have to be modified. The contents of the record may include the following.

(a) *Batch record count*   The actual number of records read must equal this number. Discrepancies must be accounted for before the batch is accepted. If other fields balance, this number may itself have been wrongly punched.

(b) *Batch number*   If each record has a batch number on it, the two should correspond. Any that do not should be examined to see if it is a punching error or if records from another batch have been inserted by mistake.

(c) *Batch control totals*   These should include all cash, count and other important totals. The total of the same fields on the detail records should equal the total held in the batch control record. If it does not, the difference must be investigated. Such totals may be directly comparable with cash takings from a till, for example.

(*d*) *Batch hash totals* A key or control field in each record can be summed to give an overall total. This is not meaningful in itself but shows up addition or removal of records very clearly.

If the sum of all the fields is unreasonably large, carries can be ignored. This has the disadvantage that it is less easy to pinpoint *which* record is missing or added, but it is just as sensitive in indicating an error as the complete sum. 'Hash' implies that the total has no intrinsic meaning.

The procedure for handling rejections during editing depends on whether records or batches are rejected. If batches are handled as a whole, a single procedure will apply. However, if individual records in error are extracted and later re-entered the process is more complicated. Batch control records have to be adjusted, part orders may be handled, and the re-entered records may require different handling from original entries. If cash payment records are delayed, no reminder or demand for payment should be sent out while the record is pending.

Processing controls

During the run itself it is essential to retain the tight control over the accuracy and integrity of data that was established by validation. Although the operation of CPUs and backing storage generally involves both error correction and warnings to the user when uncorrectable errors have occurred, it is wise to check constantly. The steps that can be taken include control checks on updates and periodic checks on the whole file. In this section the precautions taken to ensure correctness of data and processing are described; methods of reconstructing files after data has been lost or corrupted are given later.

1 Control fields When it is not possible to find a master file record to match an input record, the reason is usually that this is an addition. If it is not it will be either an incorrect control field or an update for a record that has not yet been added to the master file. The cause should be determined and the record re-input at an appropriate time if that is necessary. The correct sequence of additions, updates and deletions is discussed by Dwyer[5].

2 Arithmetic operations All the calculations carried out during processing should be duplicated by using two different calculation paths. For example, individual calculations can be checked by taking all payments, subtracting all additional bills, and confirming that the balance is the difference between them. Particularly in the case of disk storage, in which the record will be changed, it is important to check the accuracy of the calculation before writing the new record.

Addition or subtraction can be checked by carrying out the calculation:

$$FLDA + FLDB + FLDC = RESULT$$

and then re-calculating:

$$RESULT - FLDA - FLDB - FLDC = 0$$

In carrying this out, the effect of rounding should be considered and a minimum error should be acceptable rather than precisely zero.

Multiplication can be carried out using the formats $A \times B$ and $B \times A$. Alternatively it may be possible to obtain or calculate A or B from other sources, which would be preferable.

Division is often checked on the basis that:

$$DIVIDEND - DIVISOR = QUOTIENT + REMAINDER$$

and to confirm the accuracy of the division:

$$DIVIDEND = (QUOTIENT \times DIVISOR) + REMAINDER$$

3 Data file balance Direct access files will only occasionally require every record to be updated; usually only a part of the file is involved. This means that errors can build up in the apparently inactive part of the file without attention being drawn to them by incorrect output. By the time these errors are detected, considerable corruption of the file may have occurred. To avoid this problem trial balances of the entire file should be taken at intervals.

In order to be able to do this, overall figures for the file should be kept and updated from run to run. When a trial balance is taken this set of figures will be compared with what is actually found. The trial balance procedure should be linked to the periodic recording of data for reconstruction in case of need. This is described later.

Output controls

There are two main problems in controlling output. One is that it does not necessarily correspond with input; the other is that of sheer volume.

If the output is to be tied to input, account has to be taken of rejected records, orders not met due to lack of stock, back orders activated by a new order, and other similar considerations.

Physical control of forms can be provided by pre-numbered forms, but it causes difficulty in changing paper, repeating unsatisfactory work, and similar situations. However, if this is overcome—as it has to be in the case of cheques, cash orders, etc.—a basis will have been established for ensuring that the expected number of output documents has been produced.

A sensitive method of detecting trends that may be endangering operations is to carry out statistical analyses of the occurrence of given output. The size of pay packets and the distribution of overtime figures are examples of values that can be analysed in this way. The subject of output controls has been examined in detail by Alwyn Jones[6], and readers interested in extending their knowledge in this area should consult his work.

Output is the only indication the user has of how the computer system operates. It is very important for the system designers, one of whom will be the file designer, to ensure that user's views are considered. User satisfaction should be the prime aim here, so long as this allows an acceptable level of security and integrity.

The precautions discussed so far have concentrated on ensuring that input or output *data* is accurate and that it remains correct during file processing. Master files can be destroyed or corrupted by correct data meant for a different file, so it is equally important to ensure that *files* are kept under close physical and logical control.

10.3 Physical file security

File storage

In the case of installations that use a *filestore* facility which provides automatic file copying, as in ICL's 1900 series, or when a mass storage system is in use, all files may be held on tapes or cassettes and the user may not know precisely where a given file is stored. So long as no manual intervention is required, e.g. to store tapes, these systems will provide a very convenient and relatively secure file storage arrangement. However, it should be noted that ICL systems usually allow for *exofiles*, i.e. files which are handled outside the system to avoid the time involved in making copies for filestore; even allowing for the speed of modern backing storage devices, security in this sense can be costly in time, and thus money.

In most installations there will be a need to mount and dismount both tapes and disks manually. In these circumstances the system should allow for checks that the *correct* tape or disk has been mounted and that it has been issued to an *authorized* person. The precautions that can be taken come under four headings, that are examined below:

1 Library storage If the installation is large enough, a librarian should be put in charge of tapes and disks. The functions of the librarian will be as follows.

Newly arrived disks or tapes have electronic labels used by the manufacturers in testing and may still contain residual test data. They have to be initialized, which at least involves writing new electronic labels on each volume. Details of these will be given later; a unique serial number will be allocated by the librarian, who should also ensure that the storage medium is cleared of all previous data.

After initialization the disks or tapes will be added to the store of *scratch storage* available to users on demand, and a note of the serial number and user's name should be made. As soon as a master file is written onto tape or disk it can only be issued to authorized users at and for specified times, to avoid putting the information on the file at unnecessary risk. The principle remains the same for fixed disks, although they cannot of course be 'issued' in the physical sense.

A log of the location and users of all storage media allows loss of information to be pinpointed and so both reduced and quickly traced; it also often reduces the usage of given storage devices because it is always obvious what disks and tapes are available for use.

Smaller installations may have to assign the job of librarian to a chief programmer, operations manager or other person. This is not so desirable because it permits two functions to be carried out by one person, but it is still far better than allowing free use of storage media and unrestricted access to files.

A mass storage device may remove the need for separate librarians, location logs, etc., and can contribute markedly to installation security and efficiency. The system has to provide the same data and control as any alternative system, however, if it is to be successful.

2 Physical labels As was explained earlier, tapes generally only contain one master file. A sticky label with the name of the file on it is stuck to the tape reel and is read by librarian and user before issue.

Disks may contain many files. Where practicable, the same technique is used as with tapes. If this is not possible, a list of files on the disk should be consulted before issue or authorization of disk usage. The use of physical labels will prevent most cases of mistakenly using the wrong file; deliberate misuse is dealt with later.

3 Device safeguards Tape drives will not write on a tape unless a *write protect ring* is present—the mnemonic is 'no ring, no write'. All rings should be removed from incoming tapes, so that they can only be written to when a ring has been issued and the issue logged.

Disk drives usually have an *enable write switch* or its equivalent, which carries out the same function but is more easily reversed. It is also harder to trace. However, use of these precautions should reduce genuinely mistaken overwriting of files to a minimum.

4 Electronic labels Magnetic tapes will have a header label at the start of the tape, identifying the tape itself. Each file will have a header label at its start to identify the file, to give details of when it was created and how long it remains current. In most cases there will also be a *generation number* to show which version of a given file it is. The arrangement is shown in Fig.

Accuracy, integrity and security 329

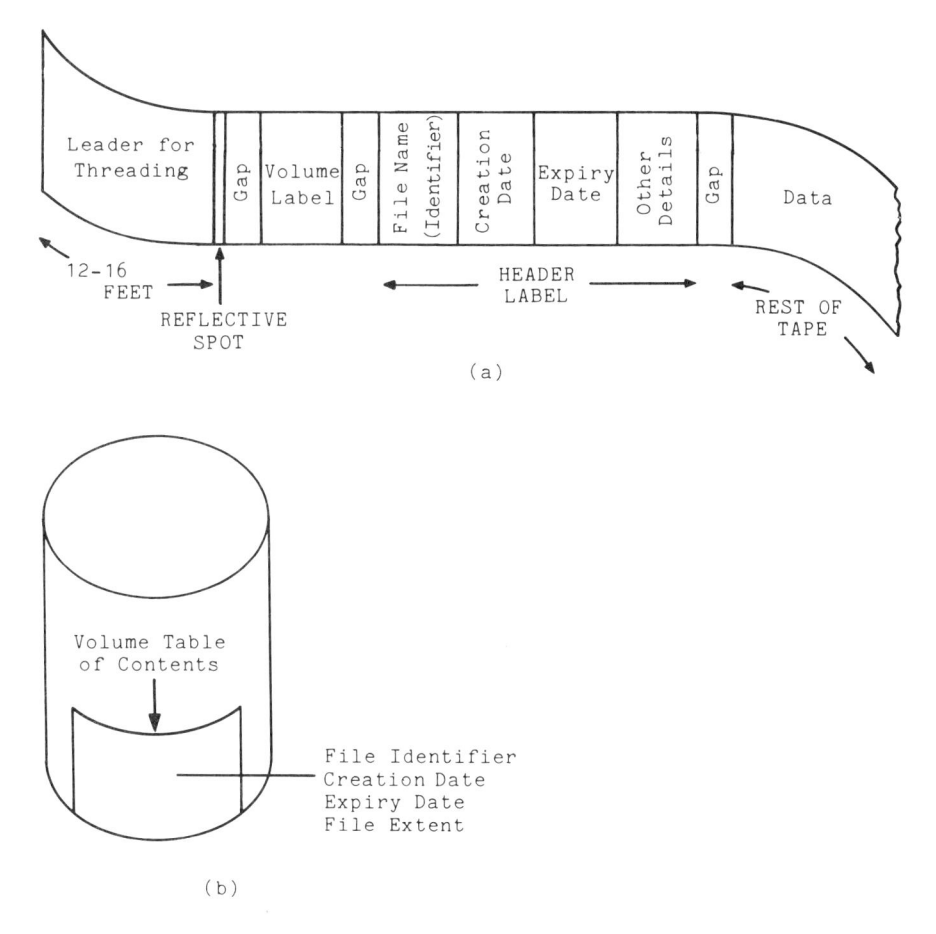

Fig. 10.1 Electronic labels. (a) The data at the start of a tape will be arranged somewhat as shown. (b) The volume table of contents is usually fixed in position.

10.1. Label arrangement and usage is complicated and for further details users should consult the appropriate manufacturers' manuals.

Magnetic disks hold all label information in a specified area. IBM systems call this the VTOC, or Volume Table Of Contents. In ICL systems it is the FIA, or File Information Area. In addition to the information required for tapes, the area of disk on which the file is stored is also recorded to allow control of reading and writing.

When a file is opened, the information held on the electronic label is compared with that provided by the program that wishes to use the file. The program will include label information read into a specified part of the system—usually disk—on input, but is not used until the OPEN command is given. At that time the following checks will be carried out:

330 Design of computer data files

To READ a file, the correct file name and generation number have to be given. To WRITE a file, the important consideration is whether the previous file's expiry date has passed. If it has, writing is permissible. If not, it is not. In the case of a disk, the area made available is only that which is specified in the VTOC, and READ or WRITE commands for part of the disk outside this area are not allowed by the operating system. The process of label checking is shown in Fig. 10.2.

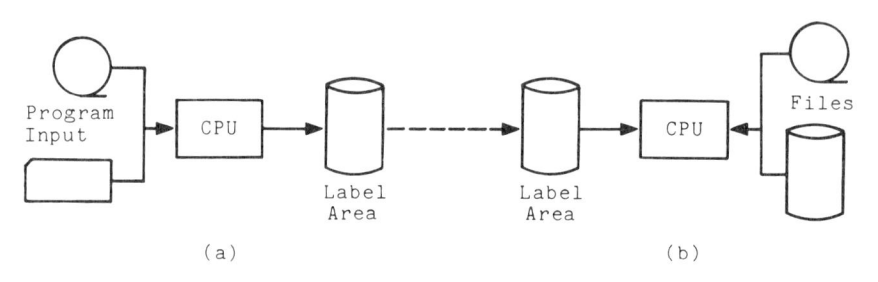

Fig. 10.2 Label checking. (a) Label information provided by the program is stored by the operating system in the label area of the system's disk when the program is input. It is not used yet. (b) When a file is opened, the information in the disk VTOC or the tape label is compared with that provided by the program and now stored in the label area.

All the precautions described so far are aimed at avoiding potential problems. Generally, some of these potential problems will have been overlooked in the planning and execution of the precautions; even if no such cause for loss or corruption of data remains, difficulties may occur due to physical failure of power supply, CPU, backing storage devices or some similar cause. In addition, many financial transactions require that auditors can trace the progress of the processing sequence for any given record—that is, an *audit trail* has to be provided.

For both these reasons it has to be possible to recreate files and data after a failure. The techniques used in the case of on-line processing are different from those applied to batch operations, so they will be examined separately.

10.4 Recovery in batch systems

When data is lost during file processing it is generally possible to re-submit the data at once. When a file is corrupted by data that is erroneous, when a device becomes unreadable due to damage or failure, or when power to the system fails, the position is different. The file has to be created in some earlier form and then brought back to the state it was in at the time of failure by updating with the same data as before.

Magnetic tape files

If a failure of the new master file occurs during a run, the present state can be reached once more by starting the run again. However, if the old master file is destroyed or corrupted, this procedure is not possible. To re-create the file it is necessary to go back to the previous run and to re-create the present old master file as the previous new master file. The procedure is shown in Fig. 10.3.

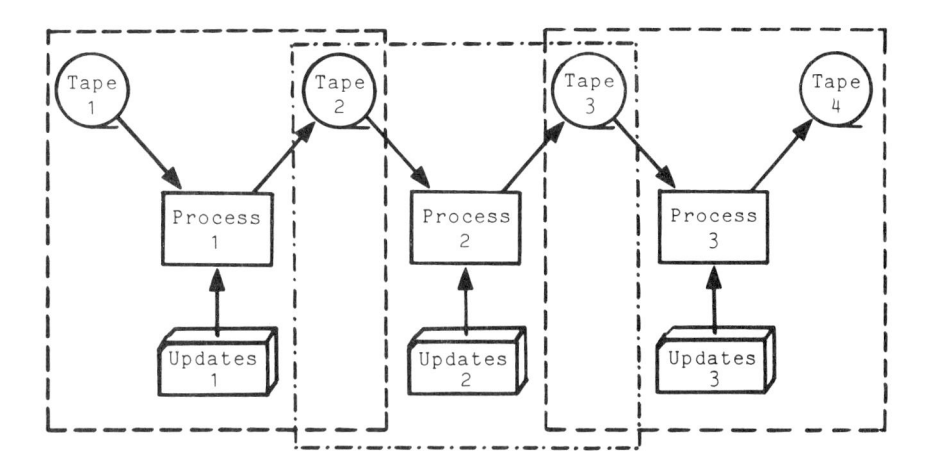

Fig. 10.3 Tape security. The updating of tape files calls for the re-writing of the file on a new tape reel. As each run is completed without error the old tape and the updates are retained. If tape 2 is subsequently corrupted, tape 1 and update 1 can be used to re-create tape 2. The minimum number of tapes required is three and this is referred to as the grandfather–father–son method. If only the minimum three tapes are in use, tape 4 would in fact be tape 1.

This is known as the *grandfather–father–son* technique, based on a minimum of three tape generations required to provide backup. In most cases more generations than this will be held to guard against further failures. Banks keep up to twenty generations, and some defence files may hold as many as fifty. Before starting the re-run, the first precaution should be to copy the old master file and update records that are to be used in the re-run, preferably on a different tape drive.

The simplicity of this form of processing, based on the sequential processing and re-creation of files on each run, makes it attractive. However, direct and indexed sequential files cannot generally be handled in this way. In some cases, sequential disk files are treated as if they were tapes, with separate disk areas for input and output, but usually they too are updated in place. This means that the old record is lost.

Disk files

When a file is seriously corrupted, a complete re-creation cycle is required. This is achieved by *dumping* the disk to tape at intervals. By retaining all the updates from that time until the next dump, it is always possible to restore the state of the file. This is shown in Fig. 10.4. In a sense this is a 'super' GFS (grandfather–father–son) technique, in that a number of runs may take place between each dump and a number of 'generations' of dump-update cycles can be held.

If the volume of transactions is very low, it is not efficient to have to dump a largely unchanged file at regular intervals. An alternative procedure is to write the keys of all updated and added records to tape during the day so that they can be dumped at the end of the run. This dump, and others since the last full dump, are used to re-create the file after a failure. To avoid unnecessary duplication keys are only referenced *once*. This can be achieved by tagging the records referenced or by scanning the list of keys and eliminating duplications. If tagging is used, each tag must be removed after the record is dumped.

To ensure that the file has not been corrupted in some way, for instance by alteration of a record that has been missed out of the selective dump procedure, it is wise to take a trial balance at intervals. Preferably this should be just before the next full file dump. Overall hash and control totals should have been included in the file label when it was created. At the end of each run these should be altered to reflect the new state of the records that have been updated, added or deleted. On the trial balance run, the actual overall totals should be calculated once more and compared with those on the file label. If they balance, all processing has been accounted for. If they do not, further investigation will be needed to locate the problem.

Much of this checking is provided automatically by database software, which will reduce the incidence of errors in the system.

Long runs—disk or tape

If a run takes hours or even days to complete, it is often not practical to re-start it from the beginning. Sometimes there is not even time to re-run the job before some other deadline is passed, say in production planning.

In order to avoid the need to start again from the beginning, the technique of taking *checkpoints* has been evolved. At intervals the files, main storage, CPU registers, etc., are dumped to tape giving all the data required to start the run from that point. After a failure it is possible to go back to the last checkpoint rather than the start of the run, and thus to restore the situation more rapidly.

The checkpoint facility is provided by most manufacturers, and can be programmed by the user when it has not been made available. However, checkpoints are generally only useful in two cases:

Accuracy, integrity and security **333**

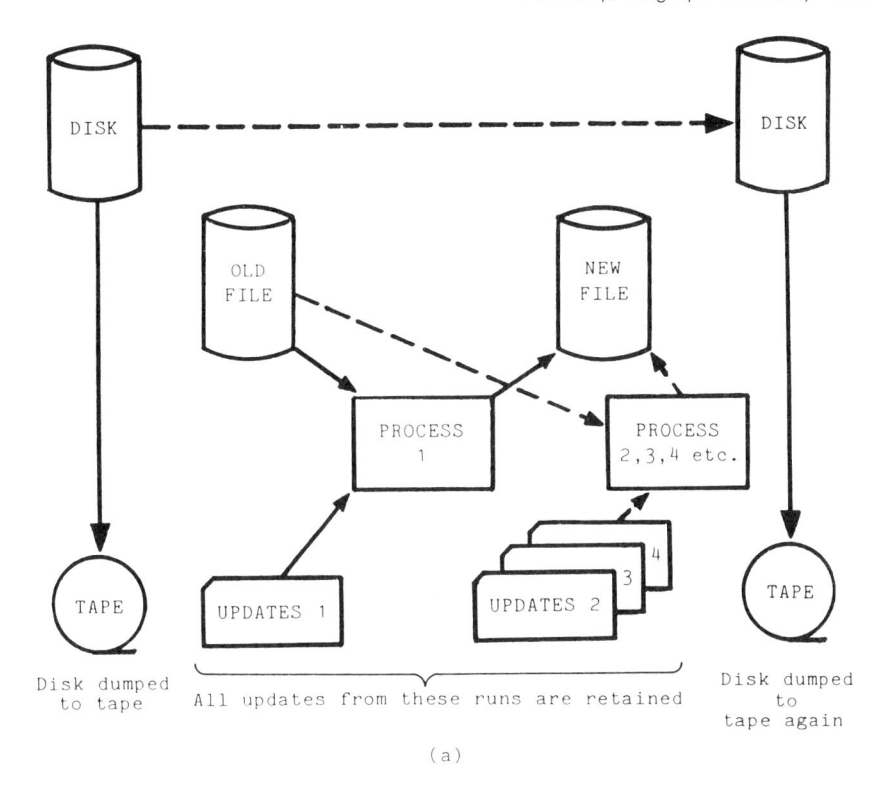

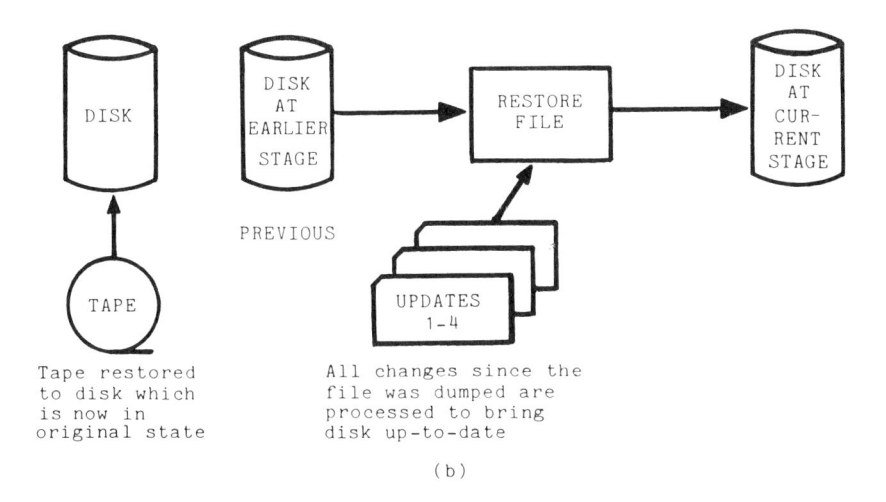

Fig. 10.4 (a) As a security precaution disk files are dumped to tape at intervals. When the disk is dumped to tape again, the updates since the first dump, and the tapes used for it, can be released. (b) The procedure that is followed after a failure.

1 To save time in the *overall* sense, that is when the *average* run time is reduced by the use of checkpoints.
2 To meet some deadline, even after one or more failures. In this case the average run time may be greater than it would have been without checkpoints, due to the time they take to record, but the *maximum* run time after one or more failures will fall within the required limits. Some examples are shown in Fig. 10.5.

Note that a successful run is lengthened by the addition of checkpoints, while a failed run is shortened. See the theoretical discussion on page 337 for the meaning of the symbols used.

A saving in overall time will only be possible if the run is inherently unreliable, as can happen when equipment is old, or amendments are made frequently to programs. This was pointed out by Bloomer[15]. In some countries power failures are very frequent at certain times of year due to electric storms, and this also can lead to a reduction in average run time as a result of the use of checkpoints. The optimum number of checkpoints required to minimize average run time has been investigated by a number of authors (Young[7], Chandy, *et al.*[8], Chandy[9] and Gelenbe[10]).

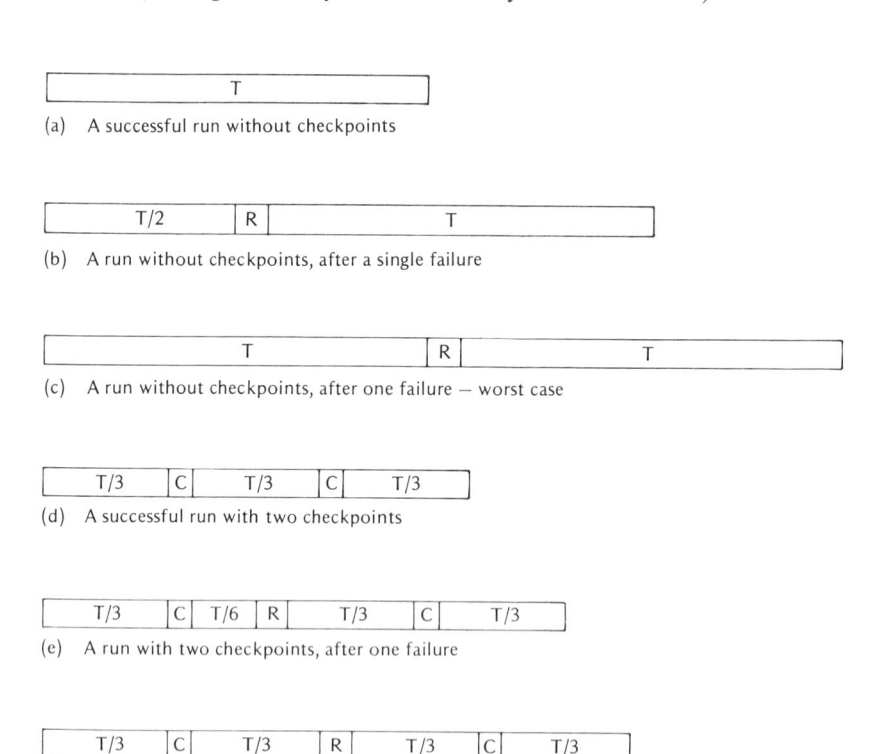

T

(a) A successful run without checkpoints

T/2	R	T

(b) A run without checkpoints, after a single failure

T	R	T

(c) A run without checkpoints, after one failure — worst case

T/3	C	T/3	C	T/3

(d) A successful run with two checkpoints

T/3	C	T/6	R	T/3	C	T/3

(e) A run with two checkpoints, after one failure

T/3	C	T/3	R	T/3	C	T/3

(f) A run with two checkpoints, after one failure — worst case

Fig. 10.5

The requirement to meet a deadline is a much more generally applicable situation—for example, when a production schedule, if it is to be useful, has to be prepared by Monday morning, or in process control applications for which time limits are extremely tight. The models developed to calculate optimum checkpoint intervals have been modified to take account of this situation by the author[11], and the treatment presented here is taken from that paper.

Intuitively it is clear that the longer a run takes, the more likely it is that a failure will occur. The more unreliable a machine, specific I–O units or the power supply may be, the greater the probability of failure. Against these must be set the cost of taking checkpoints. One or more I–O units will be required, although some systems arrange for checkpoints to be written as separate records on a specified tape that can also hold a data file. If direct access devices are used to record information, then one or more direct access units will not be available for processing, at least at the time when checkpoints are taken.

The total run time will inevitably be increased by anything from a few seconds to a few minutes for each checkpoint taken. This will set an absolute limit if lack of time is the reason for having checkpoints, and sufficient time must also be allowed for the recovery procedure. In the general case of taking checkpoints to save *overall* time, there will clearly be a break-even point beyond which further checkpoints will not be justified.

Applicability of checkpoints

Checkpoints can be used to minimize recovery time after failures due to operator error, program failure or error, data error, hardware or system failure. After an alteration to a program, failures are often immediate; in this case checkpoints will not offer any advantage.

Checkpoints can be *dynamic*, i.e. taken at a time appropriate to optimize run time, or *static*, i.e. taken at fixed intervals. Although dynamic checkpoints may be superior in the performance sense, it is convenient for users of a database to know beforehand when they will not get rapid service. For this reason, database applications generally use static checkpoints. Batch runs can more easily allow for dynamic checkpoints, but it is still simpler operationally to arrange for static checkpoints, and this has been the basis of the present discussion. Routines are available for calculating the optimum positions for checkpoints in the dynamic environment, and this subject has been examined by Chandy *et al.*[8]. In an operational situation, the requirement is generally for a reasonably accurate solution at once, rather than a perfect solution later.

Practical points in taking checkpoints

In order to allow for a restart from the checkpoint, the system will record information on:

- The present program state (in IBM systems, by retaining the PSW, the program status word).
- The contents of main storage.
- The contents of registers.
- Device positioning information.
- Checkpoint control information to allow restart.

Tape systems, and sequential disk files that are not updated in place, present little problem. After a failure the system is restarted from the last checkpoint, and the present state is reached once more after all the subsequent updates have been re-processed. It is convenient to arrange for a checkpoint at the end of each reel or volume, to avoid the need to remount tapes or disks. Specific points are as follows:

1 *Tape files.* All that is needed is a note of the records being processed. Tapes will be back-spaced and positioned at the appropriate place, and from then on the old master records and changes will be used to create the new master file; records written since the checkpoint will be overwritten. Unless reel changes are necessary, back-spacing of tapes is all that is involved. To ensure that reel changes can be detected, the checkpoint routine should include a print-out of all the units and tapes in use when the checkpoint was taken.

2 *Direct-access files.* These present a more serious problem, and are often not catered for by commercial checkpointing routines. As records are updated in place, the original records no longer exist to be updated once more. Instead, the exact state of all files at the time of the checkpoint has to be recreated. To do this, the checkpoint routine has to include writing of the present files to tape or to direct access devices. It will generally be necessary to provide a log or audit trail of altered records, as well as taking a dump of the complete file at intervals.

If the files are stored on magnetic tape during checkpointing they will have to be restored by loading them from the tape back onto the direct access device. This will take some minutes; for example, dumping a 3380 disk to tape takes 5 minutes, and two full 6250 bpi tapes are required to hold the dump. If the files are stored on a direct access device they will be in a usable form at once; however, the available direct access storage will be reduced by the number of drives required to hold the files. This may not always be practicable, and is a heavy price to pay for security.

3 The details of main storage and CPU registers, etc., are written to tape. This takes a few seconds.

Each run is likely to have a characteristic restart time, depending on the number and type of files being processed, and the size of main storage. Although restart times will vary within a run, depending on the need to remount tapes and discs, the number of units in use when failure occurs, etc., these variations will still be related to an average, 'characteristic' time.

This would be likely to be markedly different from the characteristic time for some other updating run, and hence the restart time for a given run is treated as a constant here.

It is usually possible to choose to take checkpoints:

after n records have been processed;
after a given time period has elapsed;
at end of volume;
due to an operator decision.

However, the options offered will depend on the software available.

Many checkpoint options can be decided on when the system is generated. When a checkpoint is taken, most files will be OPEN, but IBM's VSAM files have to be CLOSED. Certain languages, e.g. COBOL, will require particular set-up requirements. This discussion does not set out to deal with these matters in detail, but further information is usually available from manufacturers.

Analysis of checkpoint models

Young[7] and Chandy[9] have based their analysis of checkpoints on the frequently used value of mean time between failures. This is a suitable measure for hardware reliability, but it is seldom the most useful figure for software reliability. Littlewood[12] points out that it may be totally useless in some circumstances, and is generally limited in that it gives no indication of failure distribution.

The criterion used here is more often available, and has previously been used in Chambers and Hanson[1]; that is, the probability of failure during a single run. While it is standard practice to record failures of any given program, this will only be directly related to mean time between failures for the system overall, if the system is dedicated to a single program. This may well be appropriate in very large database processing applications of the sort discussed by Chandy[9]. However, it does not represent a typical batch or job shop installation, nor a mixed online/batch environment.

Some of the conclusions reached, and the expressions derived for optima, are similar to those previously reported, but are expressed in terms of probability of failure rather than mean time to failure. The expression given for the optimum number of checkpoints when there is a limit on individual run times—which often applies for applications such as payroll or production control in which the output has to be available by some specified time—appears to be unique. As this is a frequent situation, it is useful to take account of it in planning the number and position of checkpoints in a run.

Let
the run time of a program, without failures or checkpoints, be T,
the probability of failure be p,
the time required to take a checkpoint be C,
the number of checkpoints be n

338 Design of computer data files

(n_{OPT} = the optimum value of n, n_{MAX} = the maximum value of n), the time required to restart the run be R, the ratio of *actual* update activity during normal processing to *maximum* update activity during restoration of file status be k.

Model 1 *Minimum overall time per run*
Using this nomenclature, the time a successful run containing checkpoints takes to complete will be:

$$T + nC \qquad (10.1)$$

The provision of n checkpoints will divide the run into $(n + 1)$ segments, so on average a failure will lead to the addition of

$$\frac{kT}{2(n+1)} + R$$

to this time as on average the failure will occur half-way through the segment. In a batch run this will usually be $[T/2(n+1)]+R$, because restoration of the files to their previous state can only occur at the same rate as the original updating. In a database application there may be periods during which there are no updates, so the term will be $kT/2(n+1)$. However, in a proportion of cases there will be further failures during restarted runs, and to take account of these, and the overall probability of failure, the time added to the run has to be multiplied by $p/(1-p)$. The derivation of this is given in Hanson[11].

The total additional time on average is thus:

$$\left(\frac{kT}{2(n+1)} + R\right)\left(\frac{p}{1-p}\right) \qquad (10.2)$$

The average time a run takes is:

$$T + \left(\frac{kT}{2(n+1)} + R\right)\left(\frac{p}{1-p}\right) + nC \qquad (10.3)$$

Denoting the average run time by T_{AVG}, then

$$T_{AVG} = T + \left(\frac{kT}{2(n+1)} + R\right)\left(\frac{p}{1-p}\right) + nC \qquad (10.4)$$

In order to find the optimum number of checkpoints, the partial derivative of T_{AVG} with respect to n is set equal to zero. Thus,

$$-\left(\frac{kT}{2(n_{OPT}+1)^2}\right)\left(\frac{p}{1-p}\right) + C = 0 \qquad (10.5)$$

This leads to the expression:

Accuracy, integrity and security **339**

$$n_{OPT} = \left(\frac{pkT}{2C(1-p)} \right)^{1/2} - 1 \tag{10.6}$$

Using this expression, break-even checkpoint times have been calculated for the provision of various numbers of checkpoints during a one-hour run. The figures are given in Table 10.1.

The relationship of T_{AVG} with n_{OPT} is shown in Fig. 10.6. These curves

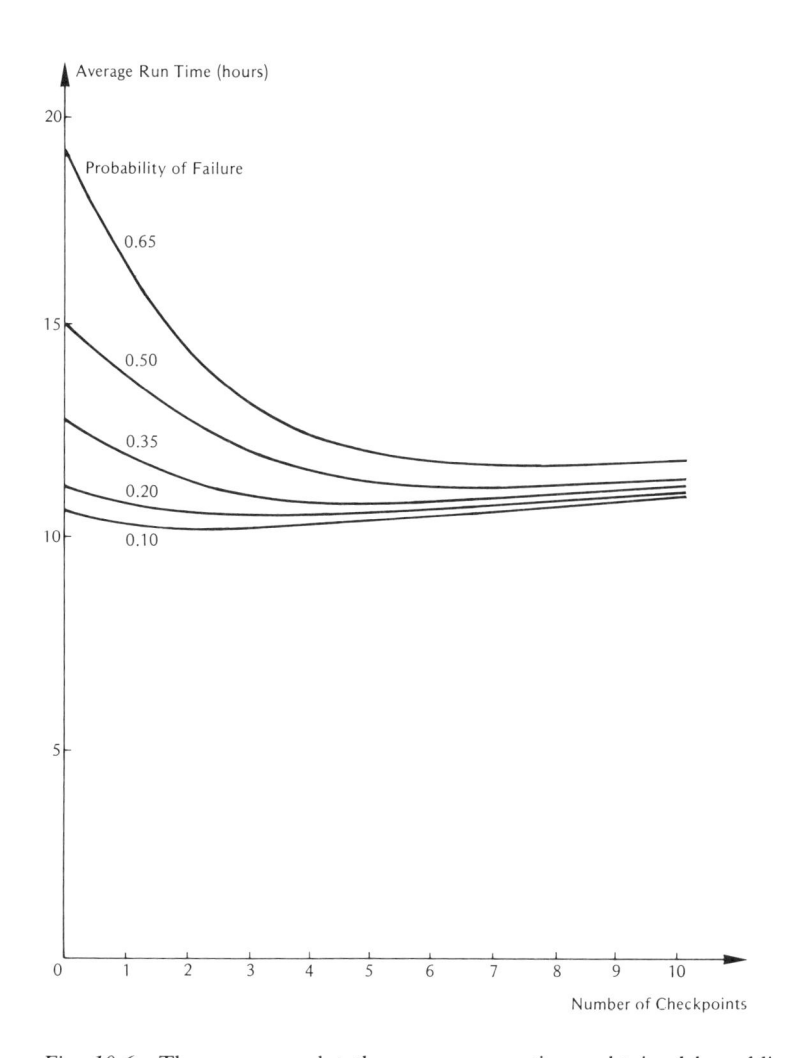

Fig. 10.6 These curves plot the average run times obtained by adding varying numbers of checkpoints, each taking six minutes, to a run that takes ten hours to complete without failures. Note that, as the probability of failure increases, the number of checkpoints required to minimize overall run time also increases.

340 Design of computer data files

Table 10.1 The figures tabulated show the break-even checkpoint time in seconds that will justify the provision of the number of checkpoints shown by minimising the overall run time. Longer times reduce the justification.

Number of checkpoints per hour	\multicolumn{10}{c}{Probability of failure during a single run}
	0.01	0.02	0.03	0.05	0.075	0.1	0.15	0.2	0.3	0.4	0.5
1	4.55	9.18	13.92	23.68	36.49	50.00	79.41	112.50	192.86	300.00	450.00
2	2.02	4.08	6.19	10.53	16.21	22.22	35.29	50.00	85.71	133.33	200.00
3	1.14	2.30	3.48	5.92	9.12	12.50	19.85	28.13	48.21	75.00	112.50
4	0.73	1.47	2.23	3.79	5.84	8.00	12.71	18.00	30.86	48.00	72.00
5	0.51	1.02	1.55	2.63	4.05	5.56	8.82	12.50	21.43	33.33	50.00
6	0.37	0.75	1.14	1.93	2.98	4.08	6.48	9.18	15.74	24.49	36.73
7	0.28	0.57	0.87	1.48	2.28	3.13	4.96	7.03	12.05	18.75	28.13
8	0.22	0.45	0.69	1.17	1.80	2.47	3.92	5.56	9.52	14.81	22.22
9	0.18	0.37	0.56	0.95	1.46	2.00	3.18	4.50	7.71	12.00	18.00
10	0.15	0.30	0.46	0.78	1.21	1.65	2.63	3.72	6.38	9.92	14.88
11	0.13	0.26	0.39	0.66	1.01	1.39	2.21	3.13	5.36	8.33	12.50
12	0.11	0.22	0.33	0.56	0.86	1.18	1.88	2.66	4.56	7.10	10.65
13		0.19	0.28	0.48	0.74	1.02	1.62	2.30	3.94	6.12	9.18
14		0.16	0.25	0.42	0.65	0.89	1.41	2.00	3.43	5.33	8.00
15		0.14	0.22	0.37	0.57	0.78	1.24	1.76	3.01	4.69	7.03
16		0.13	0.19	0.33	0.51	0.69	1.10	1.56	2.67	4.15	6.23

demonstrate the effect of the probability of failure on the average time for a run, but they are not very useful when deciding on the optimum number of checkpoints in general, as they give optima for only a few particular cases. Generally, (T/C) will be constant for any given application; exploiting this, Fig. 10.7 takes a number of typical examples of one hour runs and shows how the optimum number of checkpoints varies with checkpoint time and probability of failure. The figures on which these diagrams are based were

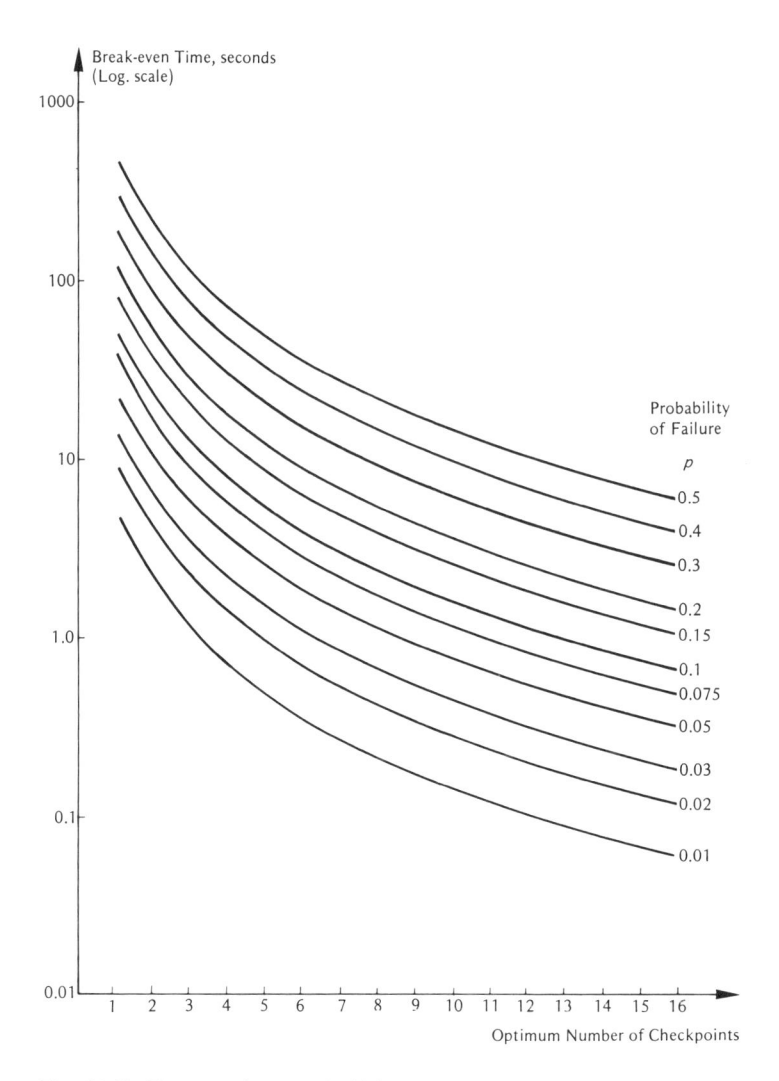

Fig. 10.7 For any given probability of failure during a one-hour run, the appropriate curve shows the relationship between the *time* required to take a checkpoint and the optimum number of checkpoints for the run.

calculated using equation (10.6), and are given in Table 10.1. Both diagrams are useful in demonstrating the relationships that exist between run time, checkpoint time and probability of failure, but Fig. 10.7 will usually be the better design tool.

Although all the figures given in Table 10.1 and the curves in Fig. 10.7 are based on a run time T of one hour, both the table and the figure can be adjusted for other run times, as (T/C) is the vital ratio here. For a half-hour run for example, the break-even checkpoint times will be halved, and for a three-hour run they will be trebled.

The most interesting point to come out of these figures is that, for runs of reasonable reliability, few if any checkpoints will be justified if disk dump/restore is involved. The increasing capacity of modern disks, and the speed with which programs are run, both militate against checkpoints being used to reduce the overall run time of jobs using disk files. However, tape-based jobs will often benefit from the use of checkpoints due to the inherent speed and simplicity of restarting them, and the same will apply to sequential disk files using two file areas rather than updating in place. Chandy et al.[8] have dealt with cases in which a cyclical activity pattern is observed in updating a database. While this is an important model, it applies to a dedicated system, and is not dealt with futher here.

Model 2 *Minimum elapsed time for a failed run*

The common case in which the run has to be completed by some deadline has not previously been examined. In this case, the aim is to complete the run in a limited time, even if failures occur at the end of the run or of any segment of the run. The time added due to failure is thus

$$\frac{kT}{(n+1)} + R$$

and the total time, T_{TOT}, is given by the expression

$$T_{\text{TOT}} = T + \left(\frac{kT}{n+1}\right) + R + nC \tag{10.7}$$

No allowance is made for the probability of failure in some runs, and hence of other successful runs, as the aim is to minimize the time taken by those runs that do fail. The probability of failure is now more accurately regarded as an indication of the proportion of runs that may fail at least once. In this model, partial differentiation with respect to n leads to the expression:

$$n_{\text{OPT}} = (kT/C)^{1/2} - 1 \tag{10.8}$$

In the more general case, the probability of m failures will be p^m; the longest time this can take will be:

$$T_{\text{TOT}} = T + \left(\frac{mkT}{n+1}\right) + mR + nC \tag{10.9}$$

Partial differentiation of this expression with respect to n leads to an optimum number of checkpoints to reduce this time to a minimum:

$$n_{\text{OPT}} = (mkT/C)^{1/2} - 1 \tag{10.10}$$

This expression leads to the figures given in Table 10.2.

The first thing that emerges from these figures is that it is far more valuable to insert checkpoints to guard against missing a deadline, even when these checkpoints take a considerable time to record, than to use them to attempt to reduce average run times. Of course, the overall time of all runs will be longer than it would be without checkpoints, but the benefit is reaped in reducing the time of runs that suffer one or more failures and thus in keeping within a deadline. However, very large numbers of checkpoints are not usually provided, and the run designer has to aim at integer numbers of checkpoints. The figures in Table 10.2 have been used to plot the relationship between checkpoint time and the optimum number of checkpoints required to minimize the run time after a failure or multiple failures in Fig. 10.8.

Because the run designer usually works in integer numbers of checkpoints, Table 10.3 has been drawn up to provide break-even times for a large number of possible checkpoints per hour, and various numbers of failures per hour. The relationship is plotted in Fig. 10.9.

It is clear that, for a run that takes an hour without failures, a single checkpoint is justified even if it takes up to 15 minutes to record, and two checkpoints if they take up to 6 minutes and 40 seconds each. Planning to minimize run time after multiple failures will justify even longer checkpoint times, although the probability of such failures, p^m, will have to be taken into account by the systems designer in planning for a given run.

10.5 Recovery in on-line systems

The most obvious difference between terminal systems and batch runs is that each individual transaction in an on-line system is unique. It is not part of a group, however typical it may be in processing requirements, but stands alone both in entry to the system and in handling of output.

Other ways in which on-line systems differ are that:

1 Files are available for reference or updating for longer periods than apply in most batch systems.
2 There are more operators, so that control of system operations is not centralized and is more difficult to ensure than in batch systems.

Table 10.2 Figures tabulated show the number of checkpoints that will reduce the time of a run to a minimum after the given number of failures, as a function of the time taken by checkpointing.

Checkpoint time (seconds)	\multicolumn{8}{c}{Number of failures allowed for}
	1	2	3	4	6	8	10	16
0.123	169	239	293	338	415	479	536	678
0.25	119	169	207	239	293	338	379	479
0.5	84	119	146	169	207	239	267	338
1	59	84	103	119	146	169	189	239
2	41	59	73	84	103	119	133	169
4	29	41	51	59	73	84	94	119
8	20	29	36	41	51	59	66	84
16	14	20	25	29	36	41	46	59
32	10	14	17	20	25	29	33	41
64	6.5	10	12	14	17	20	23	29
128	4.3	6.5	8.2	10	12	14	17	20
256	2.8	4.3	5.5	6.5	8.2	10	11	14
512	1.65	2.8	3.6	4.3	5.5	6.5	7.4	10
1 024	0.88	1.65	2.25	2.8	3.6	4.3	4.9	6.5
2 048	0.33	0.88	1.30	1.65	2.25	2.8	3.2	4.3
4 096			0.62	0.88	1.30	1.65	1.96	2.8
8 192					0.62	0.88	1.10	1.65
16 384							0.48	0.88

3 There are fewer separate stages of input, which is thus inherently less prone to chance error than the multi-stage input process for batch systems.

4 Because there are no discrete breaks in processing, transient or very infrequent errors may persist in an on-line system. Generally these have to be tolerated, and the system operated normally until the cause can be found and eliminated. It is not practical to shut down a system until all bugs have been removed.

As a result of these differences, there are a number of special problems that occur in on-line systems. They are discussed below.

Programmed controls

1 Transaction initiation The transaction itself should be acknowledged by the processing program, not the terminal or even the CPU. This means that the entry has reached the correct program and so eliminates a number of possible errors. If the response were from the hardware, the transaction

Accuracy, integrity and security **345**

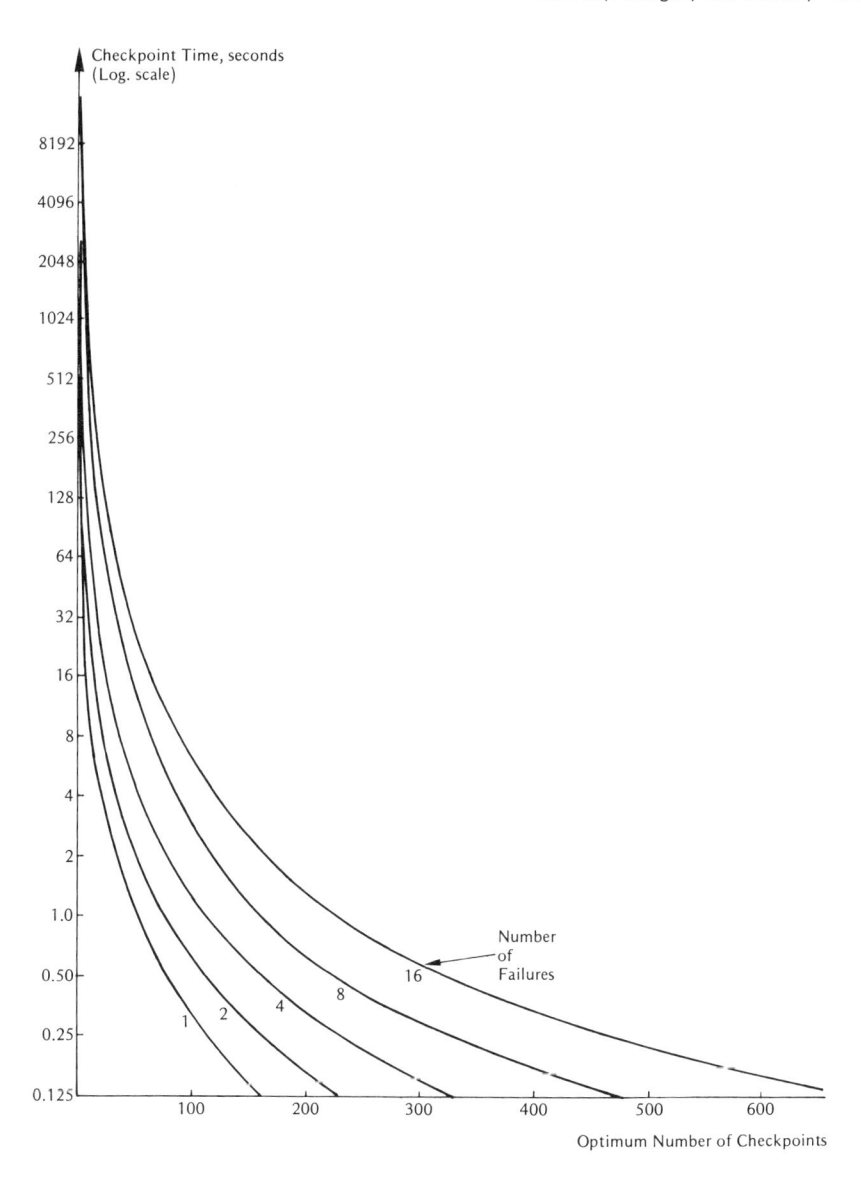

Fig. 10.8 The curves show the relationship between the time required to take a checkpoint, and the optimum number of checkpoints. As the optimum number of checkpoints is altered by the number of failures that is to be guarded against, there is a different curve for each number of failures considered.

Table 10.3 The figures tabulated are the break-even checkpoint times for a one-hour run without failures, to minimise the overall run time after the given number of failures.

Number of checkpoints per hour	\multicolumn{8}{c}{Number of failures allowed for}
	1	2	3	4	6	8	10	16
1	15.00	30.00	45.00	60.00	90.00	120.00	150.00	240.00
2	6.40	13.20	20.00	26.40	40.00	53.20	66.40	106.40
3	3.45	7.30	11.15	15.00	22.30	30.00	37.30	60.00
4	2.24	4.48	7.12	9.36	14.24	19.12	24.00	38.24
6	1.13	2.27	3.40	4.54	7.21	9.48	12.15	19.36
8	0.44	1.29	2.13	2.58	4.27	5.56	7.24	11.51
10	0.30	1.00	1.29	1.59	2.58	3.58	4.58	7.56
16	0.13	0.25	0.37	0.50	1.15	1.40	2.05	3.19
32	0.03	0.07	0.10	0.13	0.20	0.26	0.33	0.53
64	0.01	0.02	0.03	0.03	0.05	0.07	0.09	0.14
128			0.01	0.01	0.01	0.02	0.02	0.03
256							0.01	0.01

could be lost between terminal and program without the operator being aware of it.

Some systems use an input time-stamp by adding an entry time to the transaction data. However, this does not guarantee that the transaction is traceable, as differing priorities or availability of files may cause a later transaction to overtake an earlier one and be processed before it. Methods of following a given transaction in detail are discussed below under 'Outages'.

2 Control field checking After a transaction has been initiated, the operator should be *prompted* by the system to enter each item of data required. This implies that the program will provide the maximum meaningful information, and demand a minimum of operator input. Keys and codes essential for the establishment or recognition of a record should be formatted with check digits, which will operate as described earlier.

A further check, usually on the relevance of the control field provided, is for the system to give alphabetic confirmatory information based on the data entered. For example, a stock code entered could return an item description, so ensuring that the code does represent the desired item; a personnel number might return the name of the staff member concerned. When available, a voice response unit gives very definite checking, as people respond positively to item descriptions, names, etc., given in this way even when their attention may be wandering and a visual check might be ignored.

3 Validation checks The same standard checks described earlier should be carried out on entries to an on-line system. Only batch checks are omitted, and even these may be used in some cases (*see* under 'Bucket Processing', p. 351).

Accuracy, integrity and security **347**

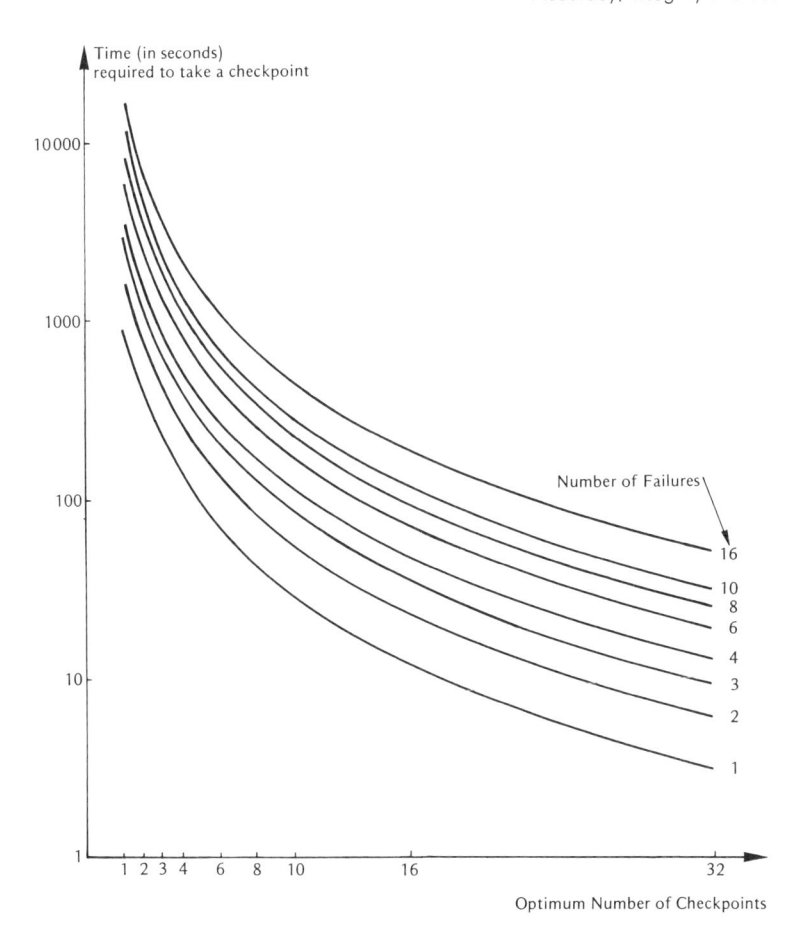

Fig. 10.9 These curves relate the optimum number of checkpoints required to minimize a particular run time after the given number of failures, with the time required to take a checkpoint. Note that, although the optima given are correct in guarding against failure at the *end* of a run, slightly different figures may be obtained if failures are assumed to occur in the middle of the run.

To use the figure, first select the time required to take a checkpoint on the y-axis. Then draw an imaginary line parallel to the x-axis, to intersect the curve of the number of failures for which you wish to minimize run time. Then draw an imaginary line from that point on the curve down to the x-axis. The value of the intercept on the x-axis is the optimum number of checkpoints.

Outages

When a failure occurs, any transaction at present in the system, i.e. acknowledged by the program, may or may not have been serviced. If this was a query, no harm is done; the user will make the request again if necessary, and the system is self-compensating. However, if the transaction was an update, an addition or a deletion, the situation is more complicated. The operator has to guard against two possibilities:

> *Case 1*: that the transaction is not serviced at all, because it appears to have been processed while in fact it has not been;
> *Case 2*: that the transaction is processed twice because it appeared that the first entry was a failure while in reality it was successful.

For additions or deletions the remedy is straightforward. When the system is in operation again, the user requests access to the record to ensure that a deletion has been made, or displays the record if the success of an addition is in doubt. The main problem is that of handling updates.

The original acknowledgement can remove one of the problems presented above but not both. If it is given by the program *before* updating, the outage may occur between the message and the update action. This leads to case 1. If the acknowledgement is given *after* updating, the outage may occur between the update and the message, producing case 2.

The solution here depends on the record contents. If these include a stock or cash balance for instance, this can be recorded away from the record in the same processing cycle that updates it with the transaction data. Often the information is put on a transaction log that allows every action taken by the program to be traced at a later stage. Otherwise, or in addition, the program can return the old figure to the operator before updating and the new one after it.

If no significant field of this sort can be selected the program or the operator can append a unique sequence number to each updated record in the same processing cycle that updates it. This means that the record contains an indication of the last update applied to it. Any previous sequence number will usually be removed or written to a log to save space.

Deadly embrace

When two or more transactions attempt to access the same two or more records at the same time, the system can be brought to a halt because each transaction is halted, waiting for the other to finish. Each has control of one record, and is queued for access to the other. Neither can continue, because they cannot release the record they control until they have processed it, using the record they are waiting for. A number of techniques can be used to resolve this problem. *Active locking*, in which a transaction has to specify which records and access paths it wishes to lock, and also has the responsibility of freeing them after use, is one technique. *Passive locking*, in which all records and access paths are automatically dedicated to a single transaction, does give full protection, but only at the expense of serious performance degradation in systems with large numbers of users. This subject, which is very important in database systems, is discussed in detail by Deen[13].

Transaction backout

When a transaction fails it may have left some files or databases correctly and successfully altered before the failure. Any changes to a file cannot be allowed to remain, since the overall operation was only partially successful. A case in point might be that a customer wishes to travel from Anchorage, Alaska to New York on one day, followed by a sector to London two days later, and on to Rome and Bombay after a further two days. Provisional bookings would be made on each sector in turn. If the London–Rome sector were not available on the desired date, this might force all the earlier bookings to be changed—and the provisional bookings would have to be reversed. The process of reversing all the successfully completed operations carried out up to the point of failure is known as *backout*.

The chain of alterations to files that may have been left in a large on-line system can be considerable. A user who is doing all the programming will have to ensure that no alteration is left unreversed; if the system (which will be described shortly) is adequately designed, this will be possible. Because of the complexity of such a system, many users will install a program such as IBM's CICS (Customer Information Control System) which will provide backout automatically. Database systems often carry out the same functions.

Page image posting

Virtual storage systems usually operate on the basis of swapping pages of data into and out of main storage when necessary. Pages that have been altered—for example, by the updating of a data record—are not written back to disk until this is required by the overall system operation. This means that a system failure can lead to the loss of data that the user believed to be safely stored on disk. Even a transaction log can be slightly out of date for this reason.

In order to ensure that important data is stored on disk, some systems offer the *forced write facility*, by which a given transaction is written to secondary storage at once. Other systems, particularly those that are UNIX-based, will use a periodical *flush command* that writes all the data at present held in the operating system buffers out to disk. Both of these alternatives, and especially the second, can cause serious deterioration of system performance.

In order to obtain both acceptable performance and a high level of security, some systems use the *page image posting* technique. Pages of data

350 Design of computer data files

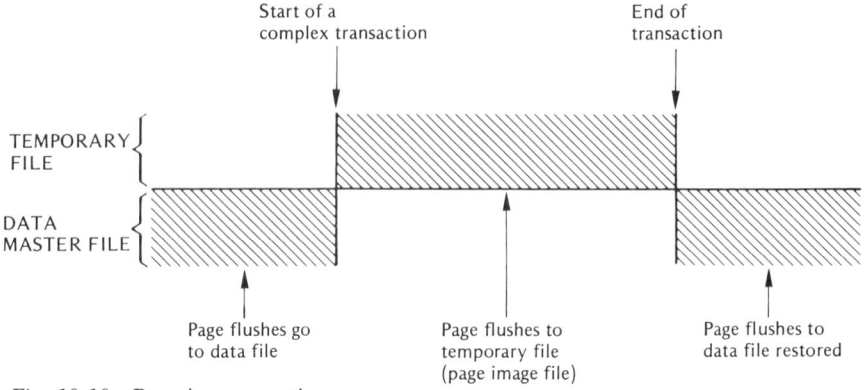

Fig. 10.10 Page image posting.

are written to a temporary file while the transaction is in process, and are only stored permanently when all parts of the transaction are complete. This solves both the backout problem discussed above, and the reduction of performance caused by constant updating of the master file. The process is shown in Fig. 10.10.

10.6 Run controls

Both for the ability to recreate files after failure, and to provide an audit trail, a record of transactions and data is necessary. Generally the information required is stored on magnetic tape, although printed output may supplement or replace tape in some cases.

Typically, this data takes the form of a number of journals or logs that record (i) input, (ii) transactions, and (iii) output. With the help of these logs all system operations can be traced. Dumping the master files to tape at intervals, so that a copy exists of the files at a time when they were correct, provides a form of 'checkpoint' facility. The old files can be updated with the transactions that have occurred since they were written, to produce an up-to-date file. In some cases the dumping may be to disks used just for backup rather than to hold the main file, which speeds up the recovery process.

When it is time to dump the master files, and if no failure has been detected, a trial balance can be taken to ensure that the logs do represent the actual changes since the last dump. This is done by comparing each record in the old file, plus the appropriate transactions, with the record in the current file. This should show up any undisclosed changes since the last check.

A useful additional control is to record the number of transactions entered from each terminal. At intervals this will be consolidated with the figures for all other terminals and compared with the number of entries on the transaction log. A discrepancy will indicate that there may have been unauthorized access to the system.

Accuracy, integrity and security 351

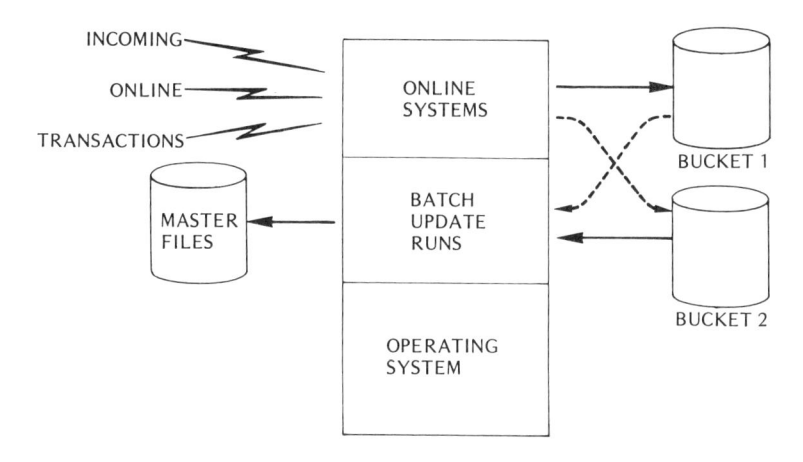

Fig. 10.11 The operation of the bucket system for updating an on-line data file in batch mode (for greater throughput).

10.7 Bucket processing

The precautions described above are expensive in terms of processing time. Bank networks in particular can reach the point where they cannot cope with the required transaction volume. One way of handling this is to collect—or batch—updates and apply them in a group. The set of updates is called a *bucket* to distinguish it from a batch in the usual sense. The method is shown in Fig. 10.11.

Banks generally choose to update the file at the end of a day's business; this means that the balance given to a customer on enquiry is generally the balance as at the end of yesterday's business, despite the impression that it is 'up to the minute'. If a whole day is too long to wait, a bucket system can be used in which a bucket of transactions is applied to the file when it becomes full, while a second bucket is made available to hold later transactions. When this is full the buckets are reversed and they continue to flip-flop while the system is in operation. In this case the bucket size represents a compromise: the smaller it is, the more nearly 'on-line' the enquiry system is; the larger it is, the greater the system capacity.

Bucket processing improves both security and throughput, but at the cost of genuinely real-time operation. Reference to the file does not guarantee up-to-date information, as some transactions may be pending in a bucket.

10.8 Duplicate facilities

Many systems have to be kept in operation if this is at all possible. To avoid

352 Design of computer data files

hardware failure having the effect of bringing the system to a halt, a number of units may be duplicated or even triplicated.

1 Central processors Two CPUs may be running at one time, but only one is actually handling the system input. If this fails, the other can be switched in with minimal loss of time. Some systems have a third CPU normally used to handle batch jobs, but available at very short notice if both the others fail; an example of this technique is the British Airways BABS booking system.

2 Files These are very commonly duplicated. In this case both sets are updated but only one is used to return messages to the originating terminal. This set-up will avoid problems due to equipment failure, but not due to incorrect data or logical errors. Holding further file copies on tape or disk, which was described earlier, can be used to deal with these errors at the cost of yet more hardware.

Duplication is costly, and the designer will think carefully before advising it. However, many on-line systems are so vital to the operations of their parent organization that most of them incorporate some duplication. This can be planned by making use of the mathematics of reliability theory to obtain the best possible value for money in terms of improved performance[16,17]. An overall on-line system might take the form shown in Fig. 10.12.

10.9 Complete system failure

If the system fails despite all the precautions described earlier, users have to have some way out. There are two types of overall failure. One is temporary, and might occur if the CPU were unusable for some time. The other is relatively permanent, as when fire, explosion or other disaster destroys an installation. As the two cases are rather different, we shall look at them separately.

Bypass procedures

When a computer system cannot be used as a result of a temporary breakdown, it is still essential to keep many applications in operation. This is particularly true of on-line systems, which is the reason for the provision of duplicate or triplicate units. Customers booking accommodation, requesting airline seats or wishing to use banking facilities must be dealt with, even if the system is down; however successful the security measures taken may be, such an eventuality must be planned for.

One preparatory measure is to provide lists of stock, seats, rooms or other appropriate information on a daily or weekly basis. Some such allocation was usually the basis of the manual system that preceded computer usage, so

Accuracy, integrity and security **353**

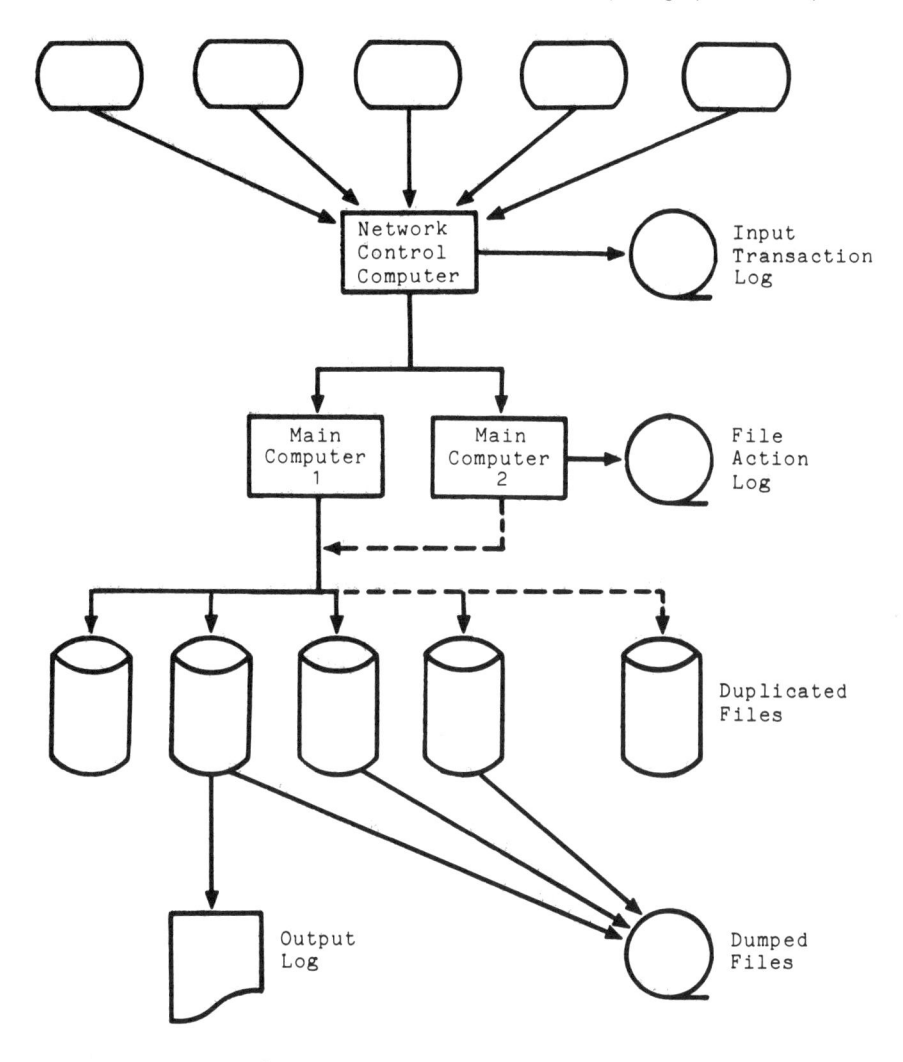

Fig. 10.12 An overall on-line system incorporating duplication. If output is remote a tape or disk record of all output should be held locally.

it may well be available. In batch systems, manual methods may be used to process important orders, updates, etc. This in itself is not difficult; the problem is control.

All manually handled transactions will have to be totalled, recorded and entered into the computer system as soon as it is available once more. This may mean a process of entry, checking successful entry, updating control totals, ensuring that all appropriate tags are set and so on.

Batch systems are not generally very sensitive to delay, so the need for bypass procedures is usually less than in on-line systems. However, at some stage a further operation will be held up if information is not available and at this stage the bypass procedure has to be initiated.

Catastrophic failure

After a disaster that puts an installation out of action for some time it is necessary to have an alternative means of operation. This will be dependent on the availability of:

1. an alternative machine;
2. duplicate programs;
3. duplicate files.

Large companies may well have identical installations in a number of different sites. This will allow complete back-up of one installation by another. Not only will the hardware be the same but the operating systems and other utility programs are likely to be identical. It is still necessary to have copies of programs, files and data available. These may be stored in a fire-proof safe in the computer room, but it is better to store them at a distance in a secure place.

Smaller companies will need to find users of the same or similar equipment nearby. The manufacturers can usually supply suitable contacts, but it should be remembered that in most cases back-up will be only partial. The installation with less hardware will only be able to run *some* of the programs required by the other partner, who is in consequence not entirely secure.

Conditions for a back-up operation should be practised, if only to ensure that the promised facilities are available. This precaution should ensure that, when the need arises, operations can continue with only a short break.

10.10 Security considerations

The only real security threat is posed by people. No system can be made entirely secure, as this would imply that no change could ever be made to the system. Hence the precautions that can be taken depend more on control than on hardware.

Physically, entry to terminal and computer rooms should be limited to those people authorized to enter. This rule should not be relaxed, and a register of persons entering should be kept. Only persons with the required identifying information should be able to enter. Controls of this sort will reduce the opportunity for fraud, tampering with files, illegal access, etc.

Electronically, a multi-level security system can be implemented. Users usually have to sign on, using a given customer number, before they gain access to a computer system. In order to acess certain files, or sensitive parts of a file, they may have to use one or more further passwords. This allows both logging of the entry and exclusion of people not in possession of the password. Some systems recognize the need to train staff by providing a special training log-in code, that causes the system to simulate the appropriate action on the files, while not in fact updating any records.

In a general sense, no operator should be allowed to program a system or vice versa. Shifts should be altered in personnel to avoid group frauds, and times of shifts should ensure that no shift is always able to run any given program. More details of these precautions are given in Chambers and Hanson[1], and the full field is covered in Martin[14].

Conclusion

The designer will achieve as much security, accuracy and integrity as a blend of thought and expense will procure. Since thought is a great deal cheaper and more cost effective than spending in quantity on equipment, files should be designed from the outset with security in mind. If this is done, the system will pose little problem in operation.

References

1. *Keeping Computers Under Control*, edited by Andrew Chambers and Owen Hanson, Gee & Co., 1975, Chapter 3.
2. *Program Design Course Notes*, by S. K. Folkes, The City University Centre for Business Systems Analysis, London.
3. *Introduction to IBM Direct Access Storage Devices and Organization Methods*, IBM Manual No. GC20-1649, pp. 11–17.
4. *Basic Training in Systems Analysis*, edited by Daniels and Yeates, Pitman, 1971, p. 93.
5. 'One more time—how to update a master file', by Barry Dwyer, *CACM*, Vol. 24, No. 1, January 1981, pp. 3–8.
6. *Keeping Computers Under Control*, edited by Andrew Chambers and Owen Hanson, Gee & Co., 1975, Chapter 7.
7. 'A first-order approximation to the optimum checkpoint interval', by John W. Young, *CACM*, Vol. 17, No. 9, September 1974, pp. 530–531.
8. 'Analytic models for rollback and recovery strategies in database systems', by K. M. Chandy *et al.*, *IEEE Transactions on Software Engineering*, Vol. SE1, No. 1, March 1975, pp. 100–110.
9. 'A survey of analytic models of rollback and recovery strategies', by K. M. Chandy, *Computer*, May 1975, pp. 40–47.
10. 'On the optimum checkpoint interval', by Errol Gelenbe, *JACM*, Vol. 26, No. 2, April 1979, pp. 259–270.
11. 'Checkpoints—when and how to use them', by Owen Hanson, *Proc. 9th Australian Computer Conference*, Hobart, Tasmania, 1982, Vol. 1, pp. 421–435.
12. *Software reliability measurement: some criticisms and suggestions*, by Bev Littlewood, internal paper, The City University, London.

13. *Principles and Practice of Database Systems*, by S. M. Dean, Macmillan, 1985.
14. *Security, Accuracy and Privacy in Computer Systems*, by James Martin, Prentice-Hall, 1973.
15. The Royal Air Force Pay System, private communication from A. Bloomer, 1975.
16. *Maintenance, Replacement and Reliability*, by A. K. S. Jardine, Pitman, 1973.
17. *Mathematical Models for the Study of the Reliability of Systems*, by A. Kaufmann, D. Grouchko and R. Cruon, Academic Press Inc., 1978.

Revision questions

1 Define accuracy, integrity and security of data.

2 What are the stages at which checks on the accuracy and integrity of data can be carried out in a batch system and an on-line system?

3 Describe the pre-input controls you feel should be applied to data.

4 What input controls do you know of? Describe their application.

5 Discuss the use of check digits in maintaining data integrity.

6 What are batch controls? When and how do they operate?

7 How can processing controls be applied to a data processing system?

8 What output controls are you aware of? Describe their application, and explain the problems posed by output controls.

9 Explain the concepts of physical file security, emphasizing the differences between disk and tape practice.

10 Explain the significance of *opening* a file for reading and writing, and make clear why there is a difference between them.

11 Describe the principles of file recovery after a failure that involves loss or corruption of data. How do tape and disk (updated in place) differ in their requirements?

12 When, why and how are checkpoints justified? Ensure that you make it clear what they cost and what they provide in return.

13 How do on-line systems differ from batch systems? What special problems does this cause?

14 Describe the meaning of *outages* and *transaction backout*. Ensure that you make the complexities of each situation clear.

15 What is *bucket processing*? Explain the advantages and drawbacks of the system. Why is it used?

16 Outline the components of a large on-line system, emphasizing the elements of the system designed to provide security.

17 What can be done to minimize the impact of a complete system failure?

18 Describe the precautions that can be taken to ensure the security of data in a system.

19 What is meant by the term 'deadly embrace'? Describe how this situation arises, and how it can be avoided.

20 When can a *page flush* be of use? Explain the advantages and disadvantages, and compare any alternatives to this technique.

Appendix 1 Curves plotting accesses to synonyms against packing density

These curves relate accesses to synonyms with bucket size, the asymmetry of record access pattern (90/10, 70/30, etc.), and the effect of a random load from an intermediate point.

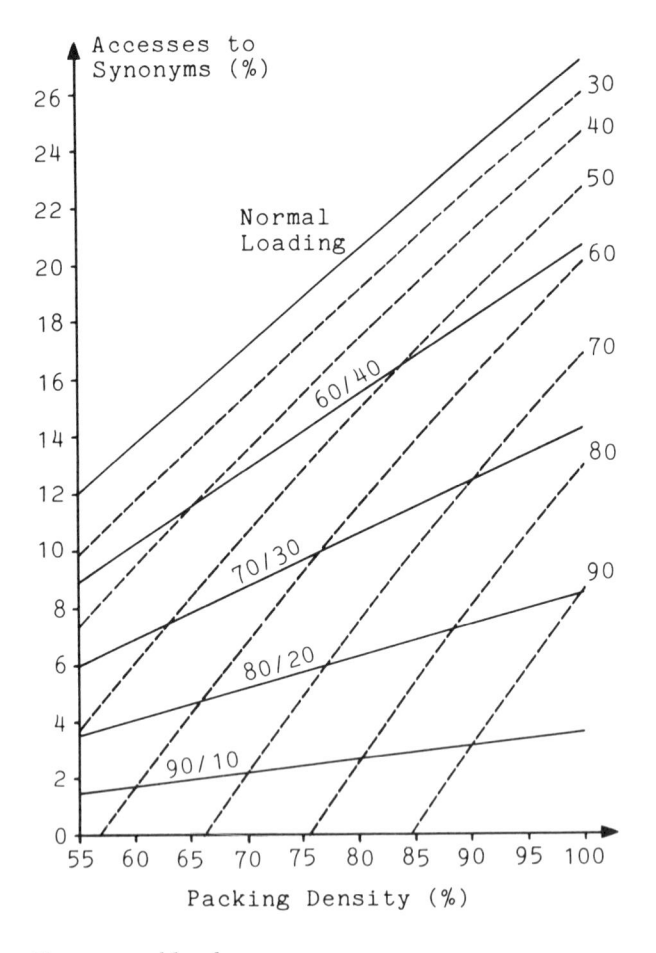

Two-record buckets

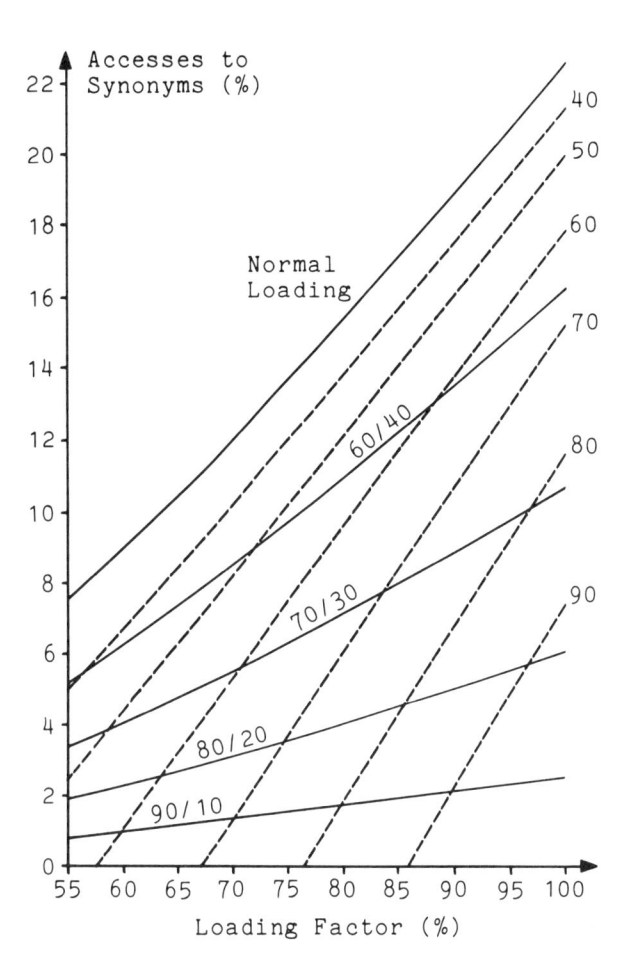

Three-record buckets

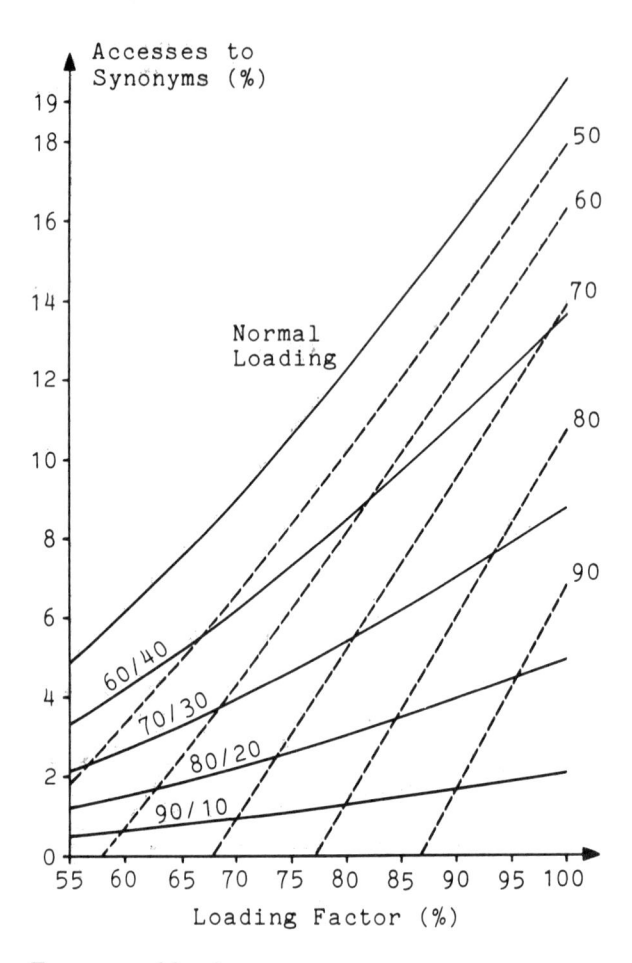

Four-record buckets

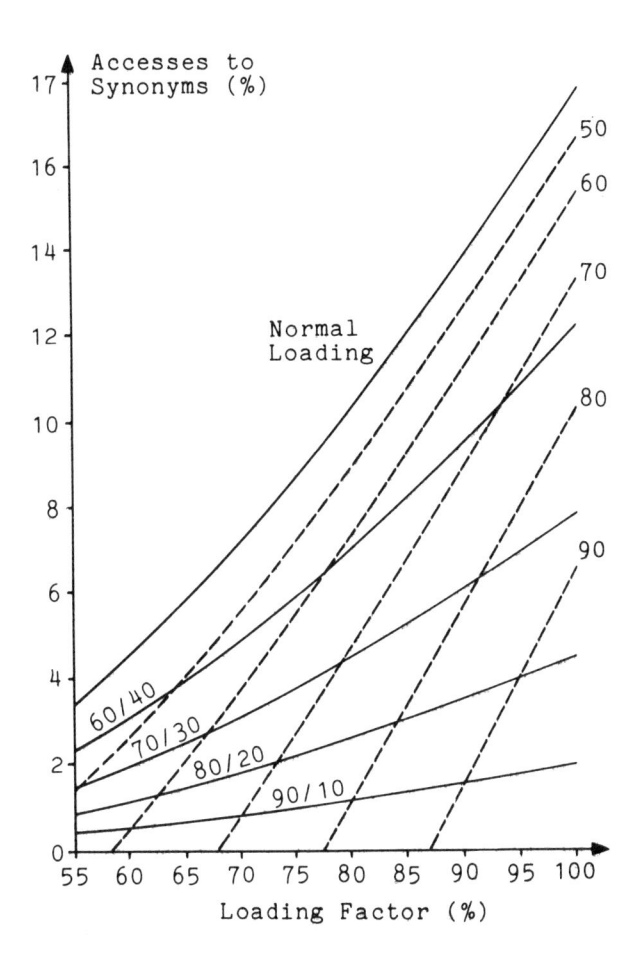

Five-record buckets

Appendix 2 **Hit record distribution on disk**

For a hit rate below 100 per cent some records on disk will not be hit. If records are being updated in place, this provides gaps between hit records. These allow more processing to be carried out between hit records, without losing a disk revolution, than would otherwise be possible.

In order to provide data to aid predictions on the pattern of these gaps, we shall examine both single- and double-buffered file processing on the premise that hits are randomly distributed throughout the file.

Single-buffered disk files

Let the hit rate be r, in the range 0–1. Then the hit rate per cent is:

$R = 100r$

The probability that a hit record will be followed by a second hit record is r, and the probability that a hit record will be followed by a non-hit record is $(1-r)$. When there is only a **single** record gap this implies that the **third** record is also hit, hence the probability of a single record gap is $r(1-r)$. It follows that the probability that there will be a gap of n records between hits is $r(1-r)^n$.

Table 1(a) presents the expected gap distributions for a number of hit rates, and Table 1(b) shows the percentage of *hit* records for which the gap is too short for processing to be completed. As this depends on the processing time, the Table gives figures for various times expressed in terms of record length. In any given case the time available for processing will be less than that shown due to software function usage, but the Table gives absolute maximum times and can be used as a guide. Once software overhead time is known it can be added to processing time and the composite time used to refer to the table.

The figures in Table 1(b) are, as stated above, only for hit records. This means that in the 50 per cent hit rate case 50 per cent of the *hit* records—which is 25 per cent of *all* the records in the file—will be followed by another hit record. Thus revolutions will be lost for 25 per cent of the records in the file if processing time lies between the very short gap time and the time to read a single record.

Table 1(a) The figures tabulated show the percentage of *processed* records that will be followed by groups of the size shown in the left-hand column.

Probability of records followed by a gap of	\multicolumn{20}{c}{Hit rate (%)}
	1	2	3	5	7	10	15	20	25	30	35	40	45	50	55	60	65	70	75	80	85	90	95
Zero	1	2	3	5	7	10	15	20	25	30	35	40	45	50	55	60	65	70	75	80	85	90	95
1	1	2	2.9	4.8	6.5	9	12.8	16	18.8	21	22.8	24	24.8	25	24.8	24	22.8	21	18.8	16	12.8	9	4.8
2	1	1.9	2.8	4.5	6.1	8.1	10.8	12.8	14.1	14.8	14.8	14.4	13.6	12.5	11.1	9.6	8.0	6.3	4.7	3.2	1.9	0.9	0.2
3	1	1.9	2.7	4.3	5.6	7.3	9.2	10.2	10.5	10.3	9.6	8.6	7.5	6.3	5.0	3.8	2.8	1.9	1.2	0.6	0.3		
4	1	1.8	2.7	4.1	5.2	6.6	7.8	8.2	7.9	7.2	6.2	5.2	4.1	3.1	2.3	1.5	1.0	0.6	0.3				
5	1	1.8	2.6	3.9	4.9	5.9	6.7	6.6	5.9	5.0	4.1	3.1	2.3	1.6	1.0	0.6	0.3						
6	0.9	1.8	2.5	3.7	4.5	5.3	5.7	5.2	4.4	3.5	2.6	1.9	1.2	0.8	0.5								
7	0.9	1.7	2.4	3.4	4.2	4.8	4.8	4.2	3.3	2.5	1.7	1.1	0.7										
8	0.9	1.7	2.4	3.3	3.9	4.3	4.1	3.4	2.5	1.7	1.1	0.7											
9	0.9	1.7	2.3	3.2	3.6	3.9	3.5	2.7	1.9	0.9	0.7												
10	0.9	1.6	2.2	3.0	3.4	3.5	3.0	2.1	1.4	0.6													
11	0.9	1.6	2.1	2.8	3.2	3.1	2.5	1.7	1.1														
12	0.9	1.6	2.1	2.7	2.9	2.8	2.1	1.4	0.8														
13	0.9	1.5	2.0	2.6	2.7	2.5	1.8	1.1															
14	0.9	1.5	2.0	2.4	2.5	2.3	1.5	0.9															
15	0.9	1.5	1.9	2.3	2.4	2.1	1.3																

364 Design of computer data files

Table 1(b) The figures tabulated show the percentage of records that will cause lost revolutions due to processing not being complete when the next record is located. 'GAP' refers to the gap between adjacent records, if any. 'PT' represents processing time.

	\multicolumn{19}{c}{Hit rate (%)}
	1	2	3	5	7	10	15	20	25	30	35	40	45	50	55	60	65	70	75	80	85	90	95
GAP<PT≤ RL	1	2	3	5	7	10	15	20	25	30	35	40	45	50	55	60	65	70	75	80	85	90	95
RL<PT≤ 2RL	2	4	5.9	9.8	13.5	19	27.8	36	43.8	51	57.8	64	69.8	75	79.8	84	87.8	91	93.8	96.0	97.8	99	99.8
2RL<PT≤ 3RL	3	5.9	8.7	14.3	19.6	27.1	38.6	48.8	57.8	65.7	72.5	78.4	83.4	87.5	90.9	93.6	95.7	97.3	98.4	99.2	99.7		
3RL<PT≤ 4RL	3.9	7.8	11.5	18.5	25.2	34.4	47.8	59.0	68.4	76.0	82.1	87.0	90.8	93.8	95.9	97.4	98.5	99.2	99.6				
4RL<PT≤ 5RL	4.9	9.6	14.1	22.6	30.4	41.0	55.6	67.2	76.3	83.2	88.4	92.2	95.0	96.9	98.2	99.0	99.5						
5RL<PT≤ 6RL	5.9	11.4	16.7	26.5	35.3	46.9	62.3	73.8	82.2	88.2	92.5	95.3	97.2	98.5	99.2								
6RL<PT≤ 7RL	6.8	13.2	19.2	30.2	39.8	52.2	67.9	79.0	86.7	91.8	95.1	97.2	98.5	99.2									
7RL<PT≤ 8RL	7.7	14.9	21.6	33.7	44.0	57.0	72.8	83.2	90.0	94.2	96.8	98.3	99.2										
8RL<PT≤ 9RL	8.6	16.6	24.0	37.0	48.0	61.3	76.8	86.6	92.5	96.0	97.9	99.0											
9RL<PT≤10RL	9.6	18.3	26.3	40.1	51.6	65.1	80.3	89.3	94.4	97.2	98.5												
10RL<PT≤11RL	10.5	19.9	28.5	43.1	55.0	68.6	83.3	91.4	95.8	98.0	99.1												
11RL<PT≤12RL	11.4	21.5	30.6	46.0	58.1	71.8	85.8	93.1	96.8	98.6													
12RL<PT≤13RL	12.2	23.1	32.7	48.7	61.1	74.6	87.9	94.5	97.6	99.0													
13RL<PT≤14RL	13.1	24.6	34.7	51.2	63.8	77.1	90.0	95.6	98.2														
14RL<PT≤15RL	14.0	26.1	36.7	53.7	66.3	79.4	91.6	96.5	98.7														

Double-buffered disk files

Using the same notation as before, the analysis is now as follows.

A record can be processed while any number of non-hit records, and just one hit record, are traversed. If it is still being processed when a second hit record comes under the read–write heads a full disk revolution will be lost.

The probability of various gaps between the **first** and **third** hit records is:

    single record gap   —   always ($=1$)

    double record gap   — $2r^2(1-r)$

(The records can be arranged with the non-hit in the first, second or third position, but only the first or second provide an extra record read time for processing.)

    treble record gap   — $3r^2(1-r)^2$

    n record gap   — $nr^2(1-r)^{n-1}$

These relationships have been used to calculate the size of the gap to be expected between first and third hit records for various hit ratios, and the results are presented in Tables 2(a) and (b).

The values given in Tables 1(a) and (b) and 2(a) and (b) have been used to provide data that is used in Chapter 5, and to analyze a number of file-choice situations in Chapter 9.

366 Design of computer data files

Table 2(a) Double buffered input–output. The figures show the percentage of processed, i.e. hit, records that will be followed by groups of the size shown in the left-hand column.

Probability of records followed by a gap of	\multicolumn{19}{c}{Hit rate (%)}																		
	1	2	3	5	7	10	15	20	25	30	35	40	45	50	55	60	65	70	75	80	85	90	95
1			0.1	0.3	0.5	1.0	2.3	4.0	6.3	9.0	12.3	16.0	20.3	25.0	30.3	36.0	42.3	49.0	56.3	64.0	72.3	81.0	90.3
2		0.1	0.2	0.5	0.9	1.8	3.8	6.4	9.4	12.6	15.9	19.2	22.3	25.0	27.2	28.8	29.6	29.4	28.1	25.6	21.7	16.2	9.0
3		0.1	0.3	0.7	1.3	2.4	4.9	7.7	10.5	13.2	15.5	17.3	18.4	18.8	18.4	17.3	15.5	13.2	10.5	7.7	4.9	2.4	0.7
4		0.2	0.3	0.9	1.6	2.9	5.5	8.2	10.5	12.3	13.5	13.8	13.5	12.5	11.0	9.2	7.2	5.3	3.5	2.0	1.0	0.3	
5		0.2	0.4	1.0	1.8	3.3	5.9	8.2	9.9	10.8	10.9	10.4	9.3	7.8	6.2	4.6	3.2	2.0	1.1	0.5			
6	0.1	0.2	0.5	1.2	2.0	3.5	6.0	7.9	8.9	9.1	8.5	7.5	6.1	4.7	3.3	2.2	1.3	0.7	0.3	0.1			
7	0.1	0.2	0.5	1.3	2.2	3.7	5.9	7.3	7.8	7.4	6.5	5.2	3.9	2.7	1.8	1.0	0.5	0.3	0.1				
8	0.1	0.3	0.6	1.4	2.4	3.8	5.8	6.7	6.7	5.9	4.8	3.6	2.4	1.6	0.9	0.5	0.2	0.1					
9	0.1	0.3	0.6	1.5	2.5	3.9	5.5	6.0	5.6	4.7	3.5	2.4	1.5	0.9	0.5	0.2	0.1						
10	0.1	0.3	0.7	1.6	2.6	3.9	5.2	5.4	4.7	3.6	2.5	1.6	0.9	0.5	0.2	0.1							
11	0.1	0.4	0.7	1.6	2.6	3.8	4.9	4.7	3.9	2.8	1.8	1.1	0.6	0.3	0.1								
12	0.1	0.4	0.8	1.7	2.6	3.8	4.5	4.1	3.2	2.1	1.3	0.7	0.3	0.1	0.1								
13	0.1	0.4	0.8	1.8	2.7	3.7	4.2	3.6	2.6	1.6	0.9	0.5	0.2	0.1									
14	0.1	0.4	0.8	1.8	2.7	3.6	3.8	3.1	2.1	1.2	0.6	0.3	0.1										
15	0.1	0.5	0.9	1.8	2.7	3.4	3.5	2.6	1.7	0.9	0.4	0.2	0.1										
16	0.1	0.5	0.9	1.9	2.6	3.3	3.1	2.3	1.3	0.7	0.3	0.1											

Table 2(b) Double buffered input–output. The figures tabulated show the percentage of records that will cause lost revolutions due to processing not being complete when the next record is located. 'PT' represents processing time.

Processing time per record	1	2	3	5	7	10	15	20	25	30	35	40	45	50	55	60	65	70	75	80	85	90	95
RL≤PT< 2RL			0.1	0.3	0.5	1.0	2.3	4.0	6.3	9.0	12.3	16.0	20.3	25.0	30.3	36.0	42.3	49.0	56.3	64.0	72.3	81.0	90.3
2RL≤PT< 3RL		0.1	0.3	0.8	1.4	2.8	6.1	10.4	15.7	21.6	28.2	35.2	42.6	50.0	57.5	64.8	71.9	78.4	84.4	89.6	94.0	97.2	99.3
3RL≤PT< 4RL	0.1	0.2	0.6	1.5	2.7	5.2	11.0	18.1	26.2	34.8	43.7	52.5	61.0	68.8	75.9	82.1	87.4	91.6	94.9	97.3	98.9	99.6	100
4RL≤PT< 5RL	0.1	0.4	0.9	2.4	4.3	8.1	16.5	26.3	36.7	47.1	57.2	66.3	74.5	81.3	86.9	91.3	94.6	96.9	98.4	99.3	99.9	99.9	
5RL≤PT< 6RL	0.1	0.6	1.3	3.4	6.1	11.4	22.4	34.5	46.6	57.9	68.1	76.7	83.8	89.1	93.1	95.9	97.8	98.9	99.5	99.8			
6RL≤PT< 7RL	0.2	0.8	1.8	4.6	8.1	14.9	28.4	42.4	55.5	67.0	76.6	84.2	89.9	93.8	96.4	98.1	99.1	99.6	99.8	99.9			
7RL≤PT< 8RL	0.3	1.0	2.3	5.9	10.3	18.6	34.3	49.7	63.3	74.4	83.1	89.4	93.8	96.5	98.2	99.1	99.6	99.9	99.9				
8RL≤PT< 9RL	0.3	1.3	2.9	7.3	12.7	22.4	40.1	56.4	70.0	80.3	87.9	93.0	96.2	98.1	99.1	99.6	99.8						
9RL≤PT<10RL	0.4	1.6	3.5	8.8	15.2	26.3	45.6	62.4	75.6	85.0	91.4	95.4	97.7	99.0	99.6	99.8	99.9						
10RL≤PT<11RL	0.5	2.0	4.2	10.4	17.8	30.2	50.8	67.8	80.3	88.6	93.9	97.0	98.6	99.5	99.8	99.9							
11RL≤PT<12RL	0.6	2.3	4.9	12.0	20.4	34.0	55.7	72.5	84.2	91.4	95.7	98.1	99.2	99.8	99.9								
12RL≤PT<13RL	0.7	2.7	5.7	13.7	23.0	37.8	60.2	76.6	87.4	93.5	97.0	98.8	99.5	99.9									
13RL≤PT<14RL	0.8	3.1	6.5	15.5	25.7	41.5	64.4	80.2	90.0	95.1	97.9	99.3	99.7										
14RL≤PT<15RL	1.0	3.5	7.3	17.3	28.4	45.1	68.2	83.3	92.1	96.3	98.5	99.6	99.8										
15RL≤PT<16RL	1.1	4.0	8.2	19.1	31.1	48.5	71.7	85.9	93.8	97.2	98.9	99.8	99.9										
16RL≤PT<17RL	1.2	4.5	9.1	22.0	33.7	51.8	74.8	88.2	95.1	97.9	99.2	99.9											

Hit rate (%)

Appendix 3 **Response time as a function of device utilization**

The response time t for random arrivals and randomly distributed service times in a single-server queuing situation is given by:

$$t = \frac{s}{1-\rho}$$

where s is the mean service time, i.e. the actual time the device is in use for a transaction, and ρ is the device utilization. For example, if a disk drive whose mean access time is 100 milliseconds is accessed five times a second, then the device utilization is given by the ratio:

$$\rho = \frac{\text{time in use}}{\text{time available}}$$

In this case

$$\rho = \frac{5 \times 100}{1000}$$
$$= 50\%$$

and

$$t = \frac{100}{1-0.5}$$
$$= 200 \text{ ms}$$

Appendix 4 **Useful prime numbers**

These prime numbers include all primes up to 10093, and primes that are near, but not too near, to convenient factors of ten thereafter. These later primes should not cause additional synonyms by reflecting patterns in key sequences. See text for explanation.

2	3	5	7	11	13	17	19	23	29	31	37
41	43	47	53	59	61	67	71	73	79	83	89
97	101	103	107	109	113	127	131	137	139	149	151
157	163	167	173	179	181	191	193	197	199	211	223
227	229	233	239	241	251	257	263	269	271	277	281
283	293	307	311	313	317	331	337	347	349	353	359
367	373	379	383	389	397	401	409	419	421	431	433
439	443	449	457	461	463	467	479	487	491	499	503
509	521	523	541	547	557	563	569	571	577	587	593
599	601	607	613	617	619	631	641	643	647	653	659
661	673	677	683	691	701	709	719	727	733	739	743
751	757	761	769	773	787	797	809	811	821	823	827
829	839	853	857	859	863	877	881	883	887	907	911
919	929	937	941	947	953	967	971	977	983	991	997
1009	1013	1021	1031	1033	1039	1049	1051	1061	1063	1069	1087
1091	1093	1097	1103	1109	1117	1123	1129	1151	1153	1163	1171
1181	1187	1193	1201	1213	1217	1223	1229	1231	1237	1249	1259
1277	1279	1283	1289	1291	1297	1301	1303	1307	1319	1321	1327
1361	1367	1373	1381	1399	1409	1423	1427	1429	1433	1439	1447
1451	1453	1459	1471	1481	1483	1487	1489	1493	1499	1511	1523
1531	1543	1549	1553	1559	1567	1571	1579	1583	1597	1601	1607
1609	1613	1619	1621	1627	1637	1657	1663	1667	1669	1693	1697
1699	1709	1721	1723	1733	1741	1747	1753	1759	1777	1783	1787
1789	1801	1811	1823	1831	1847	1861	1867	1871	1873	1877	1879
1889	1901	1907	1913	1931	1933	1949	1951	1973	1979	1987	1993
1997	1999	2003	2011	2017	2027	2029	2039	2053	2063	2069	2081
2083	2087	2089	2099	2111	2113	2129	2131	2137	2141	2143	2153
2161	2179	2203	2207	2213	2221	2237	2239	2243	2251	2267	2269
2273	2281	2287	2293	2297	2309	2311	2333	2339	2341	2347	2351
2357	2371	2377	2381	2383	2389	2393	2399	2411	2417	2423	2437
2441	2447	2459	2467	2473	2477	2503	2521	2531	2539	2543	2549
2551	2557	2579	2591	2593	2609	2617	2621	2633	2647	2657	2659
2663	2671	2677	2683	2687	2689	2693	2699	2707	2711	2713	2719
2729	2731	2741	2749	2753	2767	2777	2789	2791	2797	2801	2803
2819	2833	2837	2843	2851	2857	2861	2879	2887	2897	2903	2909
2917	2927	2939	2953	2957	2963	2969	2971	2999	3001	3011	3019
3023	3037	3041	3049	3061	3067	3079	3083	3089	3109	3119	3121
3137	3163	3167	3169	3181	3187	3191	3203	3209	3217	3221	3229
3251	3253	3257	3259	3271	3299	3301	3307	3313	3319	3323	3329
3331	3343	3347	3359	3361	3371	3373	3389	3391	3407	3413	3433
3449	3457	3461	3463	3467	3469	3491	3499	3511	3517	3527	3529
3533	3539	3541	3547	3557	3559	3571	3581	3583	3593	3607	3613
3617	3623	3631	3637	3643	3659	3671	3673	3677	3691	3697	3701
3709	3719	3727	3733	3739	3761	3767	3769	3779	3793	3797	3803
3821	3823	3833	3847	3851	3853	3863	3877	3881	3889	3907	3911
3917	3919	3923	3929	3931	3943	3947	3967	3989	4001	4003	4007
4013	4019	4021	4027	4049	4051	4057	4073	4079	4091	4093	4099
4111	4127	4129	4133	4139	4153	4157	4159	4177	4201	4211	4217
4219	4229	4231	4241	4243	4253	4259	4261	4271	4273	4283	4289
4297	4327	4337	4339	4349	4357	4363	4373	4391	4397	4409	4421
4423	4441	4447	4451	4457	4463	4481	4483	4493	4507	4513	4517
4519	4523	4547	4549	4561	4567	4583	4591	4597	4603	4621	4637
4639	4643	4649	4651	4657	4663	4673	4679	4691	4703	4721	4723
4729	4733	4751	4759	4783	4787	4789	4793	4799	4801	4813	4817
4831	4861	4871	4877	4889	4903	4909	4919	4931	4933	4937	4943
4951	4957	4967	4969	4973	4987	4993	4999	5003	5009	5011	5021
5023	5039	5051	5059	5077	5081	5087	5099	5101	5107	5113	5119
5147	5153	5167	5171	5179	5189	5197	5209	5227	5231	5233	5237
5261	5273	5279	5281	5297	5303	5309	5323	5333	5347	5351	5381
5387	5393	5399	5407	5413	5417	5419	5431	5437	5441	5443	5449
5471	5477	5479	5483	5501	5503	5507	5519	5521	5527	5531	5557
5563	5569	5573	5581	5591	5623	5639	5641	5647	5651	5653	5657
5659	5669	5683	5689	5693	5701	5711	5717	5737	5741	5743	5749
5779	5783	5791	5801	5807	5813	5821	5827	5839	5843	5849	5851
5857	5861	5867	5869	5879	5881	5897	5903	5923	5927	5939	5953
5981	5987	6007	6011	6029	6037	6043	6047	6053	6067	6073	6079
6089	6091	6101	6113	6121	6131	6133	6143	6151	6163	6173	6197
6199	6203	6211	6217	6221	6229	6247	6257	6263	6269	6271	6277
6287	6299	6301	6311	6317	6323	6329	6337	6343	6353	6359	6361
6367	6373	6379	6389	6397	6421	6427	6449	6451	6469	6473	6481
6491	6521	6529	6547	6551	6553	6563	6569	6571	6577	6581	6599
6607	6619	6637	6653	6659	6661	6673	6679	6689	6691	6701	6703
6709	6719	6733	6737	6761	6763	6779	6781	6791	6793	6803	6823
6827	6829	6833	6841	6857	6863	6869	6871	6883	6899	6907	6911
6917	6947	6949	6959	6961	6967	6971	6977	6983	6991	6997	7001
7013	7019	7027	7039	7043	7057	7069	7079	7103	7109	7121	7127
7129	7151	7159	7177	7187	7193	7207	7211	7213	7219	7229	7237
7243	7247	7253	7283	7297	7307	7309	7321	7331	7333	7349	7351
7369	7393	7411	7417	7433	7451	7457	7459	7477	7481	7487	7489
7499	7507	7517	7523	7529	7537	7541	7547	7549	7559	7561	7573

Design of computer data files

7577	7583	7589	7591	7603	7607	7621	7639	7643	7649	7669	7673
7681	7687	7691	7699	7703	7717	7723	7727	7741	7753	7757	7759
7789	7793	7817	7823	7829	7841	7853	7867	7873	7877	7879	7883
7901	7907	7919	7927	7933	7937	7949	7951	7963	7993	8009	8011
8017	8039	8053	8059	8069	8081	8087	8089	8093	8101	8111	8117
8123	8147	8161	8167	8171	8179	8191	8209	8219	8221	8231	8233
8237	8243	8263	8269	8273	8287	8291	8293	8297	8311	8317	8329
8353	8363	8369	8377	8387	8389	8419	8423	8429	8431	8443	8447
8461	8467	8501	8513	8521	8527	8537	8539	8543	8563	8573	8581
8597	8599	8609	8623	8627	8629	8641	8647	8663	8669	8677	8681
8689	8693	8699	8707	8713	8719	8731	8737	8741	8747	8753	8761
8779	8783	8803	8807	8819	8821	8831	8837	8839	8849	8861	8863
8867	8887	8893	8923	8929	8933	8941	8951	8963	8969	8971	8999
9001	9007	9011	9013	9029	9041	9043	9049	9059	9067	9091	9103
9109	9127	9133	9137	9151	9157	9161	9173	9181	9187	9199	9203
9209	9221	9227	9239	9241	9257	9277	9281	9283	9293	9311	9319
9323	9337	9341	9343	9349	9371	9377	9391	9397	9403	9413	9419
9421	9431	9433	9437	9439	9461	9463	9467	9473	9479	9491	9497
9511	9521	9533	9539	9547	9551	9587	9601	9613	9619	9623	9629
9631	9643	9649	9661	9677	9679	9689	9697	9719	9721	9733	9739
9743	9749	9767	9769	9781	9787	9791	9803	9811	9817	9829	9833
9839	9851	9857	9859	9871	9883	9887	9901	9907	9923	9929	9931
9941	9949	9967	9973	10007	10009	10037	10039	10061	10067	10093	10099
10141	10193	10289	10391	10487	10589	10691	10789	10891	10993	11093	11177
11287	11393	11491	11593	11689	11789	11887	11987	12073	12163	12289	12391
12491	12589	12689	12791	12893	12983	13093	13187	13291	13381	13487	13591
13693	13789	13883	13967	14087	14177	14293	14389	14489	14593	14683	14783
14891	14983	15091	15193	15289	15391	15493	15583	15683	15791	15889	15991
16091	16193	16273	16381	16493	16573	16693	16787	16889	16993	17093	17191
17293	17393	17491	17581	17683	17791	17891	17989	18089	18191	18289	18379
18493	18593	18691	18793	18869	18979	19087	19183	19289	19391	19489	19583
19687	19793	19891	19993	20089	20183	20287	20393	20483	20593	20693	20789
20887	20983	21089	21193	21283	21391	21493	21589	21683	21787	21893	21991
22093	22193	22291	22391	22483	22573	22691	22787	22877	22993	23087	23189
23293	23371	23473	23593	23689	23789	23893	23993	24091	24181	24281	24391
24481	24593	24691	24793	24889	24989	25087	25189	25261	25391	25471	25589
25693	25793	25889	25981	26083	26189	26293	26393	26489	26591	26693	26783
26983	26993	27091	27191	27283	27367	27487	27583	27691	27793	27893	27983
28087	28183	28289	28393	28493	28591	28687	28793	28879	28979	29077	29191
29287	29389	29483	29683	29783	29789	29881	29989	30091	30187	30293	30391
30493	30593	30689	30781	30893	30983	31091	31193	31277	31393	31489	31583
31687	31793	31891	31991	32089	32191	32261	32381	32491	32587	32693	32789
32887	32993	33091	33193	33289	33331	33493	33589	33679	33791	33893	33967
34061	34183	34283	34381	34487	34591	34693	34781	34883	34981	35089	35171
35291	35393	35491	35593	35677	35771	35879	35993	36083	36191	36293	36389
36493	36587	36691	36793	36887	36979	37087	37189	37277	37379	37493	37591
37693	37783	37889	37993	38083	38189	38287	38393	38461	38593	38693	38791
38891	38993	39089	39191	39293	39383	39461	39581	39679	39791	39887	39989
40093	40193	40289	40387	40493	40591	40693	40787	40883	40993	41081	41189
41281	41389	41491	41593	41687	41777	41893	41983	42089	42193	42293	42391
42491	42589	42689	42793	42863	42989	43093	43189	43291	43391	43487	43591
43691	43793	43891	43991	44089	44189	44293	44389	44491	44587	44687	44789
44893	44987	45083	45191	45293	45389	45491	45589	45691	45779	45893	45989
46093	46187	46279	46381	46489	46591	46691	46771	46889	46993	47093	47189
47293	47389	47491	47591	47681	47791	47881	47981	48091	48193	48281	48383
48491	48593	48679	48787	48889	48991	49081	49193	49279	49393	49481	49559
49681	49789	49891	49993	50093	50177	50291	50387	50461	50593	50683	50789
50893	50993	51071	51193	51287	51383	51487	51593	51691	51787	51893	51991
52081	52189	52291	52391	52489	52583	52691	52783	52889	52981	53093	53189
53281	53381	53479	53593	53693	53791	53891	53993	54091	54193	54293	54377
54493	54583	54679	54781	54881	54983	55079	55171	55291	55381	55487	55589
55691	55793	55889	55987	56093	56179	56269	56393	56489	56591	56687	56783
56893	56993	57089	57193	57287	57389	57493	57593	57689	57793	57881	57991
58073	58193	58271	58393	58481	58579	58693	58789	58889	58991	59093	59183
59281	59393	59473	59581	59693	59791	59887	59981	60091	60169	60293	60383
60493	60589	60689	60789	60889	60961	61091	61169	61291	61381	61493	61583
61687	61781	61879	61991	62081	62191	62273	62383	62483	62591	62687	62791
62873	62989	63079	63193	63281	63391	63493	63589	63691	63793	63863	63977
64091	64189	64283	64381	64489	64591	64693	64793	64891	64969	65089	65183
65293	65393	65479	65587	65687	65789	65881	65993	66089	66191	66293	66383
66491	66593	66683	66791	66889	66977	67079	67189	67289	67391	67493	67589
67679	67789	67891	67993	68087	68171	68281	68389	68491	68581	68687	68791
68891	68993	69073	69193	69263	69389	69493	69593	69691	69779	69877	69991
70079	70183	70289	70393	70489	70589	70687	70793	70891	70991	71089	71191
71293	71389	71483	71593	71693	71789	71887	71993	72091	72173	72287	72383
72493	72577	72689	72767	72893	72977	73091	73189	73291	73387	73483	73589
73693	73783	73883	73973	74093	74189	74293	74383	74489	74587	74687	74779
74891	74959	75083	75193	75289	75391	75479	75583	75689	75793	75883	75991
76091	76163	76289	76387	76493	76579	76679	76781	76883	76991	77093	77191
77291	77383	77491	77569	77669	77783	77893	77983	78079	78193	78283	78367
78487	78593	78691	78791	78893	78989	79087	79193	79283	79393	79493	79589
79693	79777	79889	79987	80077	80191	80287	80387	80491	80567	80687	80789
80863	80989	81083	81181	81293	81373	81463	81569	81689	81773	81883	81973

Appendix 4

```
82073   82193   82279   82393   82493   82591   82657   82793   82891   82981   83093   83177
83273   83389   83477   83591   83689   83791   83891   83987   84089   84191   84263   84391
84481   84589   84691   84793   84871   84991   85093   85193   85259   85381   85487   85577
85691   85793   85889   85991   86083   86183   86293   86389   86491   86587   86693   86783
86869   86993   87083   87187   87293   87383   87491   87589   87691   87793   87887   87991
88093   88177   88289   88379   88493   88591   88681   88793   88883   88993   89087   89189
89293   89393   89491   89591   89689   89783   89891   89989   90089   90191   90289   90379
90481   90583   90679   90793   90887   90989   91081   91193   91291   91393   91493   91591
91691   91781   91873   91969   92083   92189   92269   92387   92489   92593   92693   92791
92893   92993   93089   93187   93287   93383   93493   93581   93683   93787   93893   93983
94079   94169   94291   94379   94483   94583   94693   94793   94889   94993   95093   95191
95287   95393   95483   95581   95651   95791   95891   95989   96079   96181   96293   96377
96493   96589   96671   96787   96893   96989   97081   97187   97283   97387   97463   97583
97687   97789   97883   97987   98081   98179   98269   98389   98491   98573   98689   98779
98893   98993   99089   99191   99289   99391   99487   99581   99689   99793   99881   99991
100493  100987  101489  101987  102481  102983  103483  103993  104491  104987  105491  105983
106487  106993  107473  107981  108463  108991  109481  109987  110491  110989  111493  111977
112481  112979  113489  113989  114493  114973  115471  115987  116491  116993  117443  117991
118493  118973  119489  119993  120473  120977  121493  121993  122479  122971  123493  123989
124493  124991  125471  125963  126493  126989  127493  127979  128489  128993  129491  129971
130489  130987  131489  131969  132491  132989  133493  133993  134489  134989  135479  135979
136483  136993  137491  137993  138493  138977  139493  139991  140477  140989  141481  141991
142469  142993  143489  143981  144481  144983  145487  145991  146477  146989  147487  147977
148483  148991  149491  149993  150473  150991  151483  151969  152461  152993  153487  153991
154493  154991  155473  155921  156493  156979  157489  157991  158489  158993  159491  159979
160483  160981  161471  161983  162493  162989  163487  163993  164477  164987  165479  165983
166487  166987  167491  167987  168491  168991  169493  169991  170483  170971  171491  171947
172489  172993  173491  173993  174491  174991  175493  175993  176489  176989  177493  177979
178489  178987  179483  179989  180491  180959  181459  181981  182489  182981  183487  183979
184489  184993  185491  185993  186481  186959  187477  187987  188491  188983  189493  189989
190471  190979  191491  191977  192463  192991  193493  193991  194483  194989  195493  195991
196477  196993  197479  197971  198491  198977  199489  199967  200483  200989  201493  201979
202493  202987  203461  203989  204487  204991  205493  205993  206489  206993  207491  207973
208493  208993  209477  209987  210491  210967  211493  211979  212479  212987  213491  213989
214483  214993  215483  215983  216493  216991  217489  217981  218479  218993  219491  219983
220473  220973  221489  221989  222493  222983  223493  223969  224491  224993  225493  225989
226487  226991  227489  227993  228479  228989  229487  229981  230479  230977  231493  231967
232487  232987  233489  233993  234473  234991  235493  235979  236479  236993  237487  237977
238481  238991  239489  239977  240491  240967  241489  241993  242491  242989  243487  243989
244493  244957  245477  245989  246473  246979  247491  247993  248487  248993  249463  249989
250489  250993  251491  251983  252481  252983  253493  253993  254491  254993  255487  255989
256493  256981  257489  257993  258491  258991  259459  259993  260489  260987  261467  261983
262489  262981  263491  263983  264487  264991  265493  265987  266491  266993  267493  267961
268493  268993  269473  269987  270493  270973  271489  271981  272477  272989  273473  273979
274491  274993  275491  275987  276487  276973  277477  277993  278491  278981  279481  279991
280487  280979  281431  281993  282493  282991  283489  283979  284489  284989  285473  285983
286493  286987  287491  287977  288493  288991  289489  289987  290489  290993  291491  291983
292493  292993  293483  293989  294479  294991  295459  295993  296489  296987  297487  297991
298483  298993  299479  299993  300493  300977  301493  301993  302483  302989  303493  303983
304489  304981  305489  305971  306491  306991  307491  307969  308491  308989  309493  309989
310489  310987  311473  311981  312469  312989  313477  313993  314491  314989  315493  315977
316493  316991  317491  317987  318473  318991  319489  319993  320483  320953  321469  321991
322463  322969  323473  323987  324491  324991  325487  325993  326479  326993  327493  327983
328481  328981  329489  329993  330469  330981  331489  331973  332483  332993  333493  333989
334493  334993  335477  335957  336491  336989  337489  337973  338477  338993  339491  339991
340481  340979  341491  341993  342481  342989  343489  343963  344483  344987  345487  345989
346469  346963  347489  347993  348487  348991  349349  349981  350459  350989  351479  351991
352493  352991  353489  353963  354479  354983  355483  355969  356479  356989  357473  357989
358487  358993  359483  359987  360461  360993  361481  361993  362473  362989  363491  363989
364471  364993  365489  365983  366479  366983  367469  367957  368491  368957  369491  369991
370493  370949  371491  371981  372491  372979  373489  373987  374491  374993  375481  375983
376483  376969  377491  377981  378493  378977  379459  379993  380483  380983  381487  381991
382493  382979  383489  383987  384487  384973  385493  385991  386489  386993  387493  387977
388489  388991  389483  389989  390493  390983  391487  391983  392483  392983  393487  393983
394489  394993  395491  395971  396479  396983  397493  397981  398491  398989  399493  399989
400481  400963  401477  401993  402487  402991  403483  403993  404483  404983  405491  405991
406481  406993  407489  407993  408491  408979  409483  409993  410491  410983  411491  411991
412493  412987  413477  413981  414487  414991  415489  415993  416491  416989  417493  417983
418493  418993  419491  419959  420481  420977  421493  421987  422479  422987  423487  423991
424493  424967  425489  425989  426487  426973  427477  427993  428489  428977  429487  429991
430487  430987  431479  431993  432491  432989  433471  433981  434479  434989  435481  435983
436483  436993  437473  437977  438047  438091  438143  438169  438241  438287  438341  438391
438479  438989  439493  439991  440471  440989  441479  441971  441983  442289  443489  443987
444487  444979  445477  445969  446477  446983  447481  447991  448451  448993  449473  449989
450493  450991  451481  451987  452453  452989  453461  453993  454483  454991  455491  455993
456461  456991  457469  457987  458483  458993  459479  459961  460477  460991  461479  461983
462493  462983  463483  463993  464483  464993  465469  465989  466483  466957  467491  467977
468493  468983  469487  469993  470489  470993  471487  471959  472477  472993  473479  473979
474491  474983  475483  475991  476479  476989  477469  477991  478493  478991  479489  479971
480463  480989  481489  481963  482483  482971  483491  483991  484493  484987  485479  485963
486491  486991  487489  487979  488473  488993  489493  489989  490493  490993  491489  491983
492491  492979  493481  493993  494471  494987  495491  495983  496493  496963  497491  497993
498493  498989  499493  499979  500483  500977  501493  501971  502487  502973  503483  503989
```

Design of computer data files

Appendix 5 **Extended synonym table**

This Table, plus graphs, shows the synonym percentages in the home area when a separate overflow area is also used. Thus a percentage packing of 300 per cent implies that three times the number of records that can fit in the *home* area have been loaded to the file.

Records per bucket	1%	2%	3%	4%	5%	6%	7%	8%	9%	10%	11%	12%
1	0.498	0.993	1.485	1.974	2.459	2.941	3.420	3.895	4.368	4.837	5.304	5.767
2	0.007	0.026	0.058	0.103	0.159	0.226	0.305	0.394	0.494	0.604	0.724	0.853
3		0.001	0.003	0.007	0.013	0.022	0.034	0.050	0.070	0.094	0.123	0.157
4					0.001	0.002	0.004	0.007	0.011	0.016	0.023	0.032
5							0.001	0.001	0.002	0.003	0.005	0.007
6										0.001	0.001	0.002
7												
8												
9												
10												
11												
12												
13												
14												
15												
16												
17												
18												
19												
20												
25												
30												
35												
40												
45												
50												
55												
60												

374 Design of computer data files

Records per bucket	13%	14%	15%	16%	17%	18%	19%	20%	21%	22%	23%	24%	25%
1	6.227	6.684	7.139	7.590	8.038	8.483	8.926	9.365	9.802	10.236	10.667	11.095	11.520
2	0.991	1.138	1.294	1.458	1.630	1.810	1.997	2.192	2.394	2.602	2.817	3.038	3.265
3	0.196	0.241	0.291	0.347	0.409	0.477	0.552	0.632	0.720	0.813	0.914	1.020	1.134
4	0.043	0.057	0.073	0.092	0.114	0.140	0.169	0.202	0.240	0.281	0.328	0.379	0.435
5	0.010	0.014	0.019	0.026	0.034	0.044	0.055	0.069	0.085	0.104	0.125	0.149	0.177
6	0.003	0.004	0.005	0.008	0.011	0.014	0.019	0.024	0.031	0.040	0.050	0.061	0.075
7	0.001	0.001	0.002	0.002	0.003	0.005	0.007	0.009	0.012	0.016	0.020	0.026	0.033
8				0.001	0.001	0.002	0.002	0.003	0.005	0.006	0.009	0.011	0.015
9						0.001	0.001	0.001	0.002	0.003	0.004	0.005	0.007
10									0.001	0.001	0.002	0.002	0.003
11											0.001	0.001	0.001
12													0.001
13													
14													
15													
16													
17													
18													
19													
20													
25													
30													
35													
40													
45													
50													
55													
60													

Records per bucket	26%	27%	28%	29%	30%	31%	32%	33%	34%	35%	36%	37%
1	11.943	12.363	12.780	13.194	13.606	14.015	14.422	14.825	15.227	15.625	16.021	16.415
2	3.498	3.737	3.981	4.231	4.485	4.744	5.008	5.276	5.549	5.826	6.106	6.391
3	1.254	1.380	1.513	1.653	1.799	1.952	2.111	2.277	2.449	2.627	2.812	3.002
4	0.496	0.562	0.634	0.712	0.795	0.884	0.979	1.080	1.187	1.300	1.420	1.545
5	0.208	0.243	0.282	0.325	0.372	0.424	0.481	0.542	0.609	0.681	0.758	0.841
6	0.091	0.110	0.131	0.154	0.181	0.212	0.245	0.283	0.324	0.370	0.420	0.475
7	0.041	0.051	0.062	0.075	0.091	0.109	0.129	0.152	0.178	0.207	0.239	0.276
8	0.019	0.024	0.030	0.038	0.047	0.057	0.069	0.083	0.099	0.118	0.139	0.163
9	0.009	0.012	0.015	0.019	0.024	0.030	0.038	0.046	0.057	0.068	0.082	0.098
10	0.004	0.006	0.008	0.010	0.013	0.016	0.021	0.026	0.033	0.040	0.049	0.060
11	0.002	0.003	0.004	0.005	0.007	0.009	0.012	0.015	0.019	0.024	0.030	0.037
12	0.001	0.001	0.002	0.003	0.004	0.005	0.007	0.009	0.011	0.014	0.018	0.023
13		0.001	0.001	0.001	0.002	0.003	0.004	0.005	0.007	0.009	0.011	0.014
14			0.001	0.001	0.001	0.002	0.002	0.003	0.004	0.005	0.007	0.009
15					0.001	0.001	0.001	0.002	0.002	0.003	0.004	0.006
16							0.001	0.001	0.001	0.002	0.003	0.004
17								0.001	0.001	0.001	0.002	0.002
18									0.001	0.001	0.001	0.002
19											0.001	0.001
20												0.001
25												
30												
35												
40												
45												
50												
55												
60												

Appendix 5

Records per bucket	38%	39%	40%	41%	42%	43%	44%	45%	46%	47%	48%	49%	50%
1	16.806	17.194	17.580	17.963	18.344	18.723	19.099	19.473	19.844	20.213	20.580	20.944	21.306
2	6.679	6.970	7.265	7.563	7.864	8.168	8.474	8.784	9.095	9.409	9.725	10.044	10.364
3	3.198	3.401	3.609	3.823	4.042	4.267	4.498	4.733	4.974	5.220	5.471	5.727	5.987
4	1.678	1.816	1.961	2.112	2.270	2.434	2.604	2.780	2.963	3.153	3.348	3.549	3.757
5	0.929	1.024	1.124	1.231	1.344	1.463	1.588	1.720	1.859	2.004	2.155	2.313	2.478
6	0.534	0.599	0.669	0.744	0.825	0.911	1.004	1.102	1.207	1.318	1.435	1.559	1.690
7	0.316	0.360	0.408	0.462	0.519	0.582	0.651	0.724	0.804	0.889	0.980	1.077	1.181
8	0.190	0.221	0.254	0.292	0.334	0.380	0.430	0.485	0.545	0.611	0.682	0.758	0.841
9	0.117	0.137	0.161	0.188	0.218	0.251	0.289	0.330	0.376	0.426	0.481	0.542	0.607
10	0.072	0.087	0.103	0.122	0.144	0.168	0.196	0.227	0.262	0.301	0.344	0.391	0.444
11	0.045	0.055	0.067	0.080	0.096	0.114	0.135	0.158	0.185	0.215	0.248	0.286	0.327
12	0.029	0.036	0.044	0.053	0.065	0.078	0.093	0.111	0.131	0.154	0.181	0.210	0.244
13	0.018	0.023	0.029	0.036	0.044	0.054	0.065	0.078	0.094	0.112	0.132	0.156	0.183
14	0.012	0.015	0.019	0.024	0.030	0.037	0.046	0.056	0.068	0.082	0.098	0.116	0.138
15	0.008	0.010	0.013	0.016	0.021	0.026	0.032	0.040	0.049	0.060	0.072	0.087	0.104
16	0.005	0.007	0.009	0.011	0.014	0.018	0.023	0.029	0.036	0.044	0.054	0.066	0.079
17	0.003	0.004	0.006	0.008	0.010	0.013	0.016	0.021	0.026	0.033	0.040	0.050	0.061
18	0.002	0.003	0.004	0.005	0.007	0.009	0.012	0.015	0.019	0.024	0.030	0.038	0.047
19	0.001	0.002	0.003	0.004	0.005	0.006	0.008	0.011	0.014	0.018	0.023	0.029	0.036
20	0.001	0.001	0.002	0.002	0.003	0.005	0.006	0.008	0.010	0.013	0.017	0.022	0.028
25					0.001	0.001	0.001	0.002	0.002	0.003	0.004	0.006	0.008
30									0.001	0.001	0.001	0.002	0.002
35												0.001	0.001
40													
45													
50													
55													
60													

Records per bucket	51%	52%	53%	54%	55%	56%	57%	58%	59%	60%	61%	62%
1	21.666	22.023	22.378	22.731	23.082	23.430	23.776	24.120	24.462	24.802	25.139	25.475
2	10.686	11.010	11.335	11.662	11.991	12.321	12.652	12.984	13.317	13.652	13.987	14.323
3	6.252	6.521	6.794	7.072	7.354	7.640	7.929	8.223	8.520	8.820	9.123	9.430
4	3.971	4.190	4.416	4.647	4.884	5.126	5.374	5.627	5.886	6.150	6.418	6.692
5	2.649	2.827	3.012	3.203	3.401	3.606	3.816	4.034	4.257	4.487	4.724	4.966
6	1.828	1.972	2.123	2.281	2.446	2.618	2.797	2.983	3.176	3.376	3.583	3.797
7	1.291	1.408	1.532	1.662	1.800	1.945	2.097	2.256	2.422	2.596	2.778	2.966
8	0.929	1.024	1.125	1.233	1.348	1.470	1.599	1.736	1.879	2.031	2.189	2.356
9	0.678	0.755	0.839	0.928	1.024	1.127	1.237	1.353	1.478	1.609	1.748	1.895
10	0.501	0.564	0.632	0.706	0.787	0.873	0.967	1.067	1.174	1.289	1.411	1.541
11	0.374	0.425	0.481	0.543	0.610	0.683	0.763	0.849	0.942	1.042	1.149	1.264
12	0.281	0.323	0.369	0.420	0.477	0.539	0.606	0.680	0.761	0.848	0.942	1.044
13	0.213	0.247	0.285	0.328	0.375	0.427	0.485	0.549	0.619	0.695	0.778	0.868
14	0.162	0.190	0.221	0.257	0.297	0.341	0.391	0.445	0.506	0.573	0.646	0.725
15	0.124	0.147	0.173	0.203	0.236	0.274	0.316	0.363	0.416	0.474	0.538	0.609
16	0.096	0.114	0.136	0.160	0.189	0.221	0.257	0.297	0.343	0.394	0.451	0.514
17	0.074	0.089	0.107	0.128	0.151	0.178	0.209	0.245	0.284	0.329	0.379	0.435
18	0.057	0.070	0.085	0.102	0.122	0.145	0.171	0.202	0.236	0.276	0.320	0.369
19	0.045	0.055	0.067	0.081	0.098	0.118	0.141	0.167	0.197	0.231	0.270	0.314
20	0.035	0.043	0.053	0.065	0.080	0.096	0.116	0.139	0.165	0.195	0.229	0.269
25	0.010	0.014	0.018	0.023	0.029	0.036	0.046	0.057	0.070	0.086	0.104	0.126
30	0.003	0.005	0.006	0.008	0.011	0.014	0.019	0.024	0.031	0.039	0.050	0.062
35	0.001	0.002	0.002	0.003	0.004	0.006	0.008	0.011	0.014	0.019	0.024	0.031
40		0.001	0.001	0.001	0.002	0.002	0.003	0.005	0.007	0.009	0.012	0.016
45					0.001	0.001	0.002	0.002	0.003	0.004	0.006	0.009
50							0.001	0.001	0.001	0.002	0.003	0.005
55										0.001	0.002	0.002
60											0.001	0.001
65												0.001
70												
75												
80												
85												
90												
95												
100												
150												

Design of computer data files

Records per bucket	63%	64%	65%	66%	67%	68%	69%	70%	71%	72%	73%	74%	75%
1	25.808	26.139	26.469	26.796	27.121	27.444	27.765	28.084	28.401	28.716	29.029	29.340	29.649
2	14.660	14.997	15.335	15.673	16.012	16.351	16.691	17.031	17.371	17.711	18.051	18.390	18.730
3	9.740	10.053	10.369	10.687	11.008	11.332	11.658	11.986	12.316	12.649	12.983	13.319	13.657
4	6.971	7.254	7.542	7.834	8.131	8.432	8.737	9.046	9.358	9.675	9.995	10.318	10.645
5	5.214	5.469	5.729	5.995	6.267	6.544	6.827	7.115	7.408	7.706	8.009	8.317	8.630
6	4.018	4.246	4.480	4.721	4.969	5.224	5.485	5.752	6.026	6.305	6.591	6.883	7.180
7	3.163	3.366	3.577	3.796	4.022	4.255	4.496	4.743	4.998	5.260	5.529	5.805	6.087
8	2.530	2.712	2.902	3.100	3.306	3.520	3.741	3.971	4.208	4.453	4.706	4.966	5.234
9	2.050	2.213	2.384	2.564	2.751	2.947	3.151	3.363	3.584	3.813	4.050	4.296	4.550
10	1.679	1.825	1.979	2.141	2.312	2.491	2.679	2.876	3.081	3.296	3.519	3.750	3.991
11	1.386	1.517	1.656	1.803	1.959	2.123	2.297	2.479	2.670	2.870	3.080	3.299	3.527
12	1.153	1.270	1.395	1.529	1.671	1.822	1.982	2.151	2.329	2.516	2.713	2.920	3.136
13	0.965	1.070	1.183	1.304	1.434	1.573	1.720	1.877	2.043	2.218	2.403	2.598	2.803
14	0.812	0.906	1.008	1.119	1.237	1.364	1.500	1.645	1.800	1.964	2.139	2.323	2.517
15	0.687	0.771	0.863	0.964	1.072	1.189	1.314	1.449	1.593	1.747	1.911	2.085	2.269
16	0.583	0.659	0.742	0.833	0.932	1.040	1.156	1.281	1.415	1.560	1.714	1.878	2.053
17	0.497	0.565	0.640	0.723	0.814	0.913	1.020	1.136	1.262	1.397	1.542	1.697	1.863
18	0.425	0.486	0.554	0.630	0.713	0.804	0.903	1.011	1.128	1.255	1.391	1.538	1.696
19	0.364	0.419	0.481	0.550	0.626	0.709	0.801	0.902	1.011	1.130	1.259	1.398	1.548
20	0.313	0.363	0.419	0.481	0.551	0.628	0.713	0.806	0.909	1.020	1.142	1.273	1.415
25	0.152	0.182	0.216	0.256	0.301	0.352	0.410	0.476	0.549	0.630	0.721	0.821	0.932
30	0.077	0.095	0.116	0.141	0.171	0.205	0.245	0.291	0.344	0.404	0.472	0.549	0.636
35	0.040	0.051	0.064	0.081	0.100	0.123	0.151	0.184	0.222	0.266	0.318	0.377	0.445
40	0.021	0.028	0.036	0.047	0.060	0.076	0.095	0.118	0.146	0.179	0.218	0.264	0.317
45	0.012	0.016	0.021	0.028	0.036	0.047	0.061	0.077	0.098	0.122	0.152	0.188	0.230
50	0.006	0.009	0.012	0.017	0.022	0.030	0.039	0.051	0.066	0.085	0.107	0.135	0.169
55	0.004	0.005	0.007	0.010	0.014	0.019	0.026	0.034	0.045	0.059	0.077	0.098	0.125
60	0.002	0.003	0.004	0.006	0.009	0.012	0.017	0.023	0.031	0.042	0.055	0.072	0.093
65	0.001	0.002	0.003	0.004	0.006	0.008	0.011	0.016	0.022	0.030	0.040	0.053	0.070
70	0.001	0.001	0.002	0.002	0.004	0.005	0.008	0.011	0.015	0.021	0.029	0.040	0.053
75		0.001	0.001	0.001	0.002	0.003	0.005	0.007	0.011	0.015	0.021	0.030	0.040
80			0.001	0.001	0.001	0.002	0.003	0.005	0.008	0.011	0.016	0.022	0.031
85				0.001	0.001	0.002	0.002	0.004	0.005	0.008	0.012	0.017	0.024
90					0.001	0.001	0.002	0.003	0.004	0.006	0.009	0.013	0.018
95						0.001	0.001	0.002	0.003	0.004	0.006	0.010	0.014
100							0.001	0.001	0.002	0.003	0.005	0.007	0.011
150													0.001

Appendix 5

Records per bucket	76%	77%	78%	79%	80%	81%	82%	83%	84%	85%	86%	87%
1	29.956	30.261	30.565	30.866	31.166	31.464	31.760	32.054	32.346	32.637	39.926	33.213
2	19.070	19.410	19.749	20.088	20.427	20.765	21.103	21.440	21.777	22.113	22.449	22.784
3	13.997	14.338	14.680	15.024	15.369	15.716	16.063	16.412	16.761	17.111	17.462	17.813
4	10.975	11.308	11.644	11.983	12.325	12.669	13.015	13.364	13.715	14.068	14.423	14.780
5	8.947	9.268	9.594	9.924	10.258	10.595	10.937	11.281	11.630	11.981	12.336	12.693
6	7.484	7.792	8.106	8.426	8.750	9.079	9.413	9.752	10.095	10.443	10.794	11.150
7	6.376	6.672	6.974	7.282	7.596	7.916	8.242	8.574	8.911	9.253	9.600	9.953
8	5.509	5.792	6.081	6.378	6.682	6.993	7.310	7.634	7.964	8.301	8.643	8.991
9	4.812	5.082	5.360	5.646	5.939	6.241	6.549	6.865	7.188	7.519	7.856	8.199
10	4.240	4.498	4.765	5.040	5.323	5.615	5.915	6.223	6.539	6.863	7.194	7.533
11	3.764	4.010	4.266	4.530	4.804	5.087	5.378	5.678	5.987	6.304	6.630	6.963
12	3.361	3.597	3.842	4.096	4.360	4.634	4.917	5.210	5.511	5.822	6.142	6.470
13	3.018	3.242	3.477	3.722	3.977	4.242	4.517	4.802	5.097	5.401	5.715	6.038
14	2.721	2.936	3.161	3.397	3.643	3.900	4.167	4.444	4.732	5.030	5.338	5.656
15	2.464	2.669	2.885	3.112	3.350	3.598	3.857	4.128	4.409	4.701	5.003	5.316
16	2.238	2.435	2.642	2.860	3.090	3.330	3.582	3.846	4.120	4.406	4.703	5.011
17	2.040	2.228	2.426	2.637	2.858	3.091	3.336	3.593	3.861	4.141	4.432	4.735
18	1.864	2.044	2.235	2.437	2.651	2.877	3.115	3.365	3.627	3.901	4.187	4.485
19	1.708	1.880	2.063	2.258	2.465	2.684	2.915	3.158	3.414	3.682	3.963	4.256
20	1.568	1.733	1.909	2.096	2.296	2.508	2.733	2.970	3.220	3.483	3.759	4.047
25	1.053	1.185	1.329	1.485	1.654	1.836	2.031	2.240	2.463	2.700	2.952	3.218
30	0.732	0.839	0.958	1.088	1.231	1.388	1.558	1.743	1.942	2.156	2.386	2.632
35	0.522	0.609	0.707	0.816	0.938	1.073	1.222	1.386	1.565	1.759	1.970	2.197
40	0.379	0.450	0.531	0.624	0.728	0.845	0.975	1.121	1.281	1.458	1.651	1.862
45	0.280	0.338	0.405	0.483	0.572	0.674	0.789	0.918	1.062	1.223	1.401	1.597
50	0.209	0.256	0.313	0.378	0.455	0.543	0.645	0.760	0.890	1.037	1.200	1.382
55	0.157	0.197	0.244	0.299	0.365	0.442	0.531	0.634	0.752	0.886	1.037	1.206
60	0.120	0.152	0.191	0.239	0.295	0.362	0.441	0.533	0.640	0.762	0.901	1.059
65	0.092	0.118	0.151	0.192	0.240	0.299	0.369	0.451	0.548	0.660	0.788	0.935
70	0.070	0.093	0.120	0.155	0.197	0.248	0.310	0.384	0.471	0.574	0.693	0.830
75	0.055	0.073	0.096	0.125	0.162	0.207	0.262	0.328	0.408	0.502	0.612	0.740
80	0.042	0.058	0.077	0.102	0.134	0.173	0.222	0.282	0.354	0.440	0.542	0.662
85	0.033	0.046	0.062	0.084	0.111	0.146	0.189	0.243	0.308	0.387	0.482	0.594
90	0.026	0.036	0.050	0.069	0.092	0.123	0.162	0.210	0.269	0.342	0.430	0.535
95	0.020	0.029	0.041	0.057	0.077	0.104	0.138	0.182	0.236	0.303	0.385	0.483
100	0.016	0.023	0.033	0.047	0.065	0.088	0.119	0.158	0.208	0.269	0.345	0.437
150	0.002	0.003	0.005	0.008	0.012	0.019	0.029	0.043	0.063	0.091	0.128	0.177
200			0.001	0.001	0.003	0.005	0.008	0.013	0.022	0.034	0.053	0.080
250					0.001	0.001	0.002	0.004	0.008	0.014	0.024	0.039

378 Design of computer data files

Records per bucket	88%	89%	90%	91%	92%	93%	94%	95%	96%	97%	98%	99%	100%
1	33.498	33.782	34.063	34.343	34.622	34.898	35.173	35.446	35.718	35.988	36.256	36.523	36.788
2	23.119	23.452	23.785	24.117	24.449	24.779	25.109	25.438	25.766	26.092	26.418	26.743	27.067
3	18.165	18.517	18.870	19.223	19.577	19.930	20.284	20.637	20.991	21.345	21.698	22.051	22.404
4	15.139	15.499	15.860	16.224	16.588	16.953	17.320	17.688	18.056	18.425	18.795	19.166	19.537
5	13.053	13.416	13.782	14.150	14.520	14.892	15.267	15.643	16.021	16.400	16.781	17.163	17.547
6	11.509	11.873	12.239	12.609	12.982	13.358	13.737	14.119	14.503	14.890	15.279	15.670	16.062
7	10.310	10.672	11.038	11.408	11.782	12.160	12.542	12.928	13.316	13.708	14.103	14.500	14.900
8	9.345	9.704	10.069	10.439	10.813	11.192	11.575	11.963	12.355	12.751	13.150	13.553	13.959
9	8.549	8.905	9.268	9.636	10.010	10.389	10.773	11.162	11.556	11.955	12.358	12.765	13.176
10	7.879	8.232	8.591	8.957	9.330	9.709	10.093	10.848	10.879	11.280	11.686	12.096	12.511
11	7.305	7.654	8.011	8.375	8.746	9.124	9.508	9.899	10.296	10.698	11.106	11.519	11.938
12	6.807	7.153	7.506	7.868	8.237	8.614	8.997	9.388	9.786	10.190	10.600	11.015	11.437
13	6.371	6.712	7.063	7.421	7.789	8.164	8.547	8.938	9.336	9.740	10.152	10.570	10.994
14	5.984	6.322	6.669	7.025	7.390	7.764	8.146	8.536	8.934	9.340	9.753	10.173	10.599
15	5.640	5.973	6.317	6.670	7.033	7.405	7.786	8.175	8.573	8.980	9.394	9.815	10.244
16	5.330	5.659	5.999	6.350	6.710	7.080	7.460	7.849	8.247	8.654	9.069	9.491	9.922
17	5.049	5.375	5.712	6.059	6.417	6.785	7.164	7.552	7.950	8.357	8.772	9.196	9.628
18	4.795	5.116	5.449	5.794	6.149	6.516	6.893	7.280	7.678	8.085	8.501	8.926	9.360
19	4.562	4.880	5.209	5.551	5.904	6.268	6.644	7.030	7.427	7.834	8.251	8.677	9.112
20	4.348	4.662	4.988	5.327	5.678	6.040	6.414	6.800	7.196	7.603	8.020	8.447	8.884
25	3.498	3.794	4.103	4.427	4.766	5.118	5.484	5.864	6.257	6.663	7.081	7.511	7.952
30	2.894	3.172	3.466	3.776	4.102	4.444	4.803	5.176	5.565	5.968	6.386	6.818	7.263
35	2.441	2.703	2.983	3.280	3.595	3.927	4.277	4.644	5.029	5.430	5.847	6.279	6.727
40	2.090	2.338	2.603	2.888	3.192	3.515	3.857	4.218	4.598	4.996	5.412	5.845	6.295
45	1.811	2.044	2.297	2.570	2.863	3.177	3.512	3.867	4.242	4.637	5.051	5.484	5.936
50	1.583	1.804	2.045	2.307	2.590	2.895	3.222	3.571	3.942	4.334	4.745	5.180	5.633
55	1.394	1.603	1.833	2.085	2.359	2.656	2.976	3.319	3.685	4.073	4.484	4.917	5.371
60	1.236	1.434	1.654	1.896	2.161	2.449	2.762	3.100	3.461	3.847	4.256	4.688	5.143
65	1.102	1.290	1.499	1.732	1.988	2.270	2.576	2.908	3.265	3.647	4.055	4.486	4.942
70	0.987	1.165	1.365	1.589	1.838	2.111	2.411	2.738	3.090	3.470	3.875	4.306	4.763
75	0.888	1.057	1.248	1.464	1.704	1.971	2.265	2.586	2.934	3.311	3.714	4.145	4.601
80	0.801	0.962	1.145	1.353	1.586	1.846	2.133	2.449	2.794	3.167	3.569	3.999	4.456
85	0.726	0.878	1.054	1.254	1.480	1.733	2.015	2.326	2.666	3.037	3.437	3.866	4.323
90	0.659	0.804	0.972	1.165	1.384	1.631	1.907	2.214	2.550	2.918	3.316	3.744	4.201
95	0.600	0.738	0.899	1.085	1.298	1.539	1.809	2.111	2.444	2.808	3.204	3.632	4.089
100	0.547	0.679	0.833	1.013	1.219	1.454	1.720	2.017	2.346	2.707	3.102	3.528	3.986
150	0.241	0.323	0.426	0.553	0.708	0.894	1.115	1.371	1.667	2.003	2.379	2.797	3.256
200	0.118	0.170	0.241	0.333	0.452	0.601	0.786	1.011	1.278	1.592	1.953	2.362	2.820
250	0.062	0.096	0.144	0.212									

Appendix 5

Records per bucket	101%	102%	103%	104%	105%	106%	107%	108%	109%	110%	111%	112%
1	37.051	37.313	37.573	37.832	38.089	38.345	38.599	38.851	39.102	39.352	39.600	39.846
2	27.390	27.712	28.032	28.352	28.670	29.987	29.303	29.618	29.932	30.244	30.555	30.865
3	22.757	23.109	23.461	23.812	24.163	24.513	24.862	25.211	25.559	25.906	26.253	26.598
4	19.908	20.280	20.652	21.024	21.396	21.768	22.139	22.511	22.883	23.254	23.624	23.995
5	17.931	18.317	18.703	19.090	19.478	19.866	20.255	20.644	21.033	21.423	21.812	22.201
6	16.457	16.853	17.251	17.650	18.050	18.451	18.853	19.256	19.660	20.064	20.468	20.873
7	15.303	15.707	16.114	16.523	16.933	17.345	17.758	18.173	18.588	19.005	19.422	19.840
8	14.368	14.779	15.194	15.610	16.029	16.451	16.873	17.298	17.724	18.151	18.580	19.009
9	13.590	14.008	14.429	14.852	15.279	15.708	16.139	16.573	17.008	17.445	17.883	18.322
10	12.930	13.353	13.780	14.210	14.643	15.079	15.518	15.959	16.402	16.848	17.295	17.744
11	12.361	12.788	13.220	13.656	14.095	14.537	14.983	15.431	15.882	16.336	16.791	17.248
12	11.863	12.295	12.731	13.172	13.616	14.065	14.517	14.972	15.430	15.890	16.353	16.818
13	11.424	11.859	12.299	12.744	13.194	13.648	14.105	14.567	15.031	15.498	15.968	16.440
14	11.032	11.470	11.914	12.364	12.818	13.276	13.739	14.206	14.677	15.150	15.626	16.105
15	10.679	11.120	11.568	12.021	12.480	12.943	13.411	13.883	14.359	14.838	15.321	15.806
16	10.359	10.804	11.255	11.711	12.174	12.642	13.114	13.591	14.073	14.558	15.046	15.537
17	10.068	10.515	10.969	11.429	11.896	12.367	12.845	13.326	13.813	14.303	14.797	15.293
18	9.801	10.251	10.708	11.171	11.641	12.117	12.598	13.084	13.575	14.071	14.569	15.072
19	9.556	10.008	10.467	10.933	11.407	11.886	12.371	12.862	13.358	13.858	14.362	14.869
20	9.329	9.783	10.244	10.714	11.190	11.673	12.163	12.657	13.157	13.662	14.170	14.683
25	8.405	8.868	9.340	9.822	10.313	10.812	11.318	11.831	12.350	12.875	13.405	13.939
30	7.721	8.191	8.673	9.165	9.668	10.180	10.700	11.229	11.764	12.306	12.854	13.407
35	7.190	7.666	8.155	8.656	9.169	9.692	10.225	10.767	11.317	11.874	12.438	13.007
40	6.761	7.242	7.738	8.247	8.769	9.302	9.846	10.400	10.963	11.534	12.111	12.695
45	6.405	6.891	7.392	7.909	8.439	8.982	9.536	10.101	10.675	11.258	11.848	12.444
50	6.104	6.594	7.101	7.624	8.161	8.713	9.276	9.851	10.436	11.030	11.631	12.239
55	5.845	6.339	6.851	7.379	7.924	8.483	9.055	9.640	10.234	10.838	11.450	12.068
60	5.620	6.116	6.633	7.167	7.718	8.285	8.865	9.458	10.062	10.675	11.296	11.924
65	5.420	5.920	6.441	6.980	7.537	8.111	8.699	9.300	9.912	10.534	11.164	11.801
70	5.243	5.746	6.270	6.814	7.377	7.957	8.552	9.161	9.781	10.412	11.050	11.695
75	5.083	5.589	6.117	6.666	7.235	7.821	8.422	9.038	9.666	10.304	10.950	11.603
80	4.939	5.447	5.979	6.532	7.106	7.698	8.306	8.929	9.564	10.209	10.862	11.523
85	4.808	5.318	5.853	6.411	6.990	7.587	8.202	8.831	9.472	10.124	10.785	11.452
90	4.687	5.200	5.739	6.300	6.884	7.487	8.107	8.742	9.390	10.049	10.716	11.389
95	4.577	5.092	5.633	6.199	6.787	7.395	8.021	8.662	9.316	9.981	10.653	11.333
100	4.475	4.992	5.536	6.106	6.698	7.311	7.942	8.589	9.249	9.919	10.598	11.283
150	3.753	4.288	4.858	5.459	6.088	6.743	7.418	8.110	8.816	9.532	10.256	10.983
200	3.324	3.872	4.462	5.088	5.746	6.432	7.140	7.866	8.604	9.351	10.102	10.855

380 Design of computer data files

Records per bucket	113%	114%	115%	116%	117%	118%	119%	120%	121%	122%	123%	124%	125%
1	40.091	40.335	40.577	40.818	41.057	41.295	41.531	41.766	42.000	42.232	42.463	42.692	42.920
2	31.174	31.481	31.788	32.092	32.296	32.698	32.999	33.298	33.596	33.893	34.189	34.483	34.775
3	26.943	27.287	27.629	27.971	28.311	28.651	28.989	29.327	29.663	29.998	30.331	30.664	30.995
4	24.364	24.733	25.102	25.470	25.836	26.203	26.568	26.932	27.295	27.657	28.018	28.378	28.737
5	22.590	22.979	23.367	23.755	24.143	24.530	24.916	25.301	25.686	26.069	26.452	26.833	27.214
6	21.278	21.682	22.087	22.492	22.896	23.300	23.704	24.107	24.509	24.910	25.311	25.710	26.109
7	20.258	20.677	21.096	21.515	21.934	22.352	22.771	23.188	23.606	24.022	24.438	24.853	25.267
8	19.439	19.870	20.301	20.732	21.164	21.595	22.027	22.458	22.888	23.318	23.748	24.176	24.604
9	18.763	19.204	19.647	20.089	20.532	20.975	21.418	21.861	22.303	22.745	23.186	23.627	24.066
10	18.194	18.645	19.097	19.550	20.003	20.456	20.910	21.363	21.816	22.269	22.721	23.172	23.623
11	17.707	18.167	18.628	19.090	19.552	20.015	20.479	20.942	21.405	21.867	22.329	22.790	23.250
12	17.285	17.753	18.222	18.693	19.164	19.636	20.108	20.580	21.052	21.523	21.994	22.464	22.934
13	16.914	17.390	17.867	18.346	18.825	19.305	19.785	20.265	20.746	21.226	21.705	22.184	22.661
14	16.586	17.069	17.554	18.040	18.526	19.014	19.502	19.990	20.478	20.966	21.453	21.939	22.425
15	16.294	16.783	17.275	17.768	18.261	18.756	19.251	19.747	20.242	20.737	21.231	21.725	22.217
16	16.031	16.527	17.025	17.524	18.025	18.526	19.028	19.530	20.032	20.534	21.035	21.535	22.035
17	15.793	16.295	16.799	17.305	17.812	18.319	18.828	19.336	19.845	20.353	20.861	21.367	21.873
18	15.577	16.085	16.594	17.106	17.619	18.133	18.647	19.162	19.676	20.191	20.704	21.217	21.728
19	15.380	15.893	16.408	16.925	17.444	17.963	18.483	19.004	19.524	20.044	20.563	21.082	21.598
20	15.198	15.717	16.237	16.760	17.284	17.809	18.335	18.861	19.386	19.912	20.436	20.960	21.482
25	14.477	15.019	15.563	16.109	16.657	17.206	17.756	18.306	18.855	19.404	19.952	20.498	21.042
30	13.964	14.525	15.089	15.655	16.223	16.792	17.361	17.930	18.499	19.066	19.632	20.196	20.758
35	13.581	14.158	14.739	15.322	15.906	16.492	17.077	17.663	18.247	18.830	19.411	19.989	20.565
40	13.283	13.875	14.470	15.068	15.667	16.266	16.866	17.465	18.063	18.658	19.252	19.842	20.429
45	13.045	13.650	14.259	14.869	15.481	16.093	16.705	17.315	17.924	18.530	19.134	19.734	20.330
50	12.852	13.469	14.089	14.710	15.333	15.956	16.578	17.199	17.818	18.433	19.045	19.653	20.257
55	12.692	13.319	13.950	14.582	15.214	15.847	16.478	17.108	17.734	18.358	18.977	19.592	20.202
60	12.557	13.195	13.834	14.476	15.117	15.758	16.398	17.035	17.669	18.299	18.924	19.545	20.160
65	12.443	13.089	13.738	14.389	15.037	15.685	16.332	16.976	17.616	18.252	18.882	19.508	20.127
70	12.346	13.000	13.656	14.313	14.970	15.625	16.278	16.928	17.573	18.214	18.849	19.479	20.102
75	12.261	12.923	13.586	14.250	14.913	15.574	16.233	16.888	17.538	18.183	18.823	19.456	20.082
80	12.188	12.856	13.526	14.196	14.865	15.532	16.196	16.855	17.510	18.159	18.802	19.438	20.067
85	12.123	12.798	13.474	14.150	14.824	15.496	16.164	16.828	17.486	18.138	18.784	19.423	20.054
90	12.067	12.747	13.429	14.110	14.789	15.465	16.138	16.805	17.466	18.122	18.770	19.411	20.044
95	12.017	12.703	13.389	14.075	14.759	15.439	16.115	16.786	17.450	18.108	18.758	19.401	20.036
100	11.972	12.663	13.355	14.045	14.733	15.417	16.096	16.769	17.436	18.096	18.749	19.393	20.030
150	11.711	12.438	13.163	13.883	14.597	15.303	16.002	16.693	17.374	18.046	18.709	19.362	20.005
200	11.606	12.205											

Appendix 5

Records per bucket	126%	127%	128%	129%	130%	140%	150%	160%	170%	180%	190%	200%
1	43.147	43.373	43.597	43.819	44.041	46.185	48.207	50.119	51.923	53.628	55.240	56.767
2	35.067	35.356	35.645	35.932	36.218	38.996	41.631	44.124	46.477	48.695	50.783	52.747
3	31.324	31.653	31.980	32.305	32.630	35.791	38.795	41.635	44.309	46.818	49.167	51.363
4	29.094	29.451	29.805	30.159	30.511	33.948	37.217	40.300	43.192	45.892	48.407	50.744
5	27.593	27.971	28.348	28.723	29.097	32.751	36.223	39.489	42.540	45.375	48.002	50.429
6	26.506	26.902	27.297	27.691	28.083	31.915	35.550	38.959	42.130	45.064	47.769	50.257
7	25.680	26.092	26.502	26.911	27.319	31.301	35.071	38.595	41.860	44.868	47.628	50.158
8	25.030	25.455	25.879	26.302	26.723	30.834	34.718	38.337	41.676	44.739	47.540	50.099
9	24.505	24.942	25.378	25.813	26.246	30.470	34.451	38.148	41.546	44.653	47.484	50.063
10	24.072	24.520	24.967	25.412	25.856	30.180	34.246	38.007	41.454	44.593	47.447	
11	23.710	24.168	24.624	25.079	25.532	29.946	34.084	37.901	41.386	44.552	47.423	
12	23.402	23.869	24.334	24.798	25.260	29.753	33.956	37.819	41.337	44.523		
13	23.138	23.613	24.086	24.558	25.028	29.594	33.853	37.756	41.299	44.502		
14	22.909	23.391	23.872	24.351	24.829	29.461	33.769	37.707	41.272			
15	22.708	23.198	23.686	24.172	24.656	29.348	33.701	37.667	41.250			
16	22.532	23.029	23.523	24.015	24.506	29.252	33.644	37.636	41.234			
17	22.377	22.879	23.379	23.878	24.374	29.170	33.597	37.611	41.222			
18	22.238	22.746	23.252	23.756	24.257	29.100	33.558	37.591	41.212			
19	22.114	22.627	23.138	23.647	24.154	29.039	33.526	37.575	41.205			
20	22.002	22.521	23.037	23.551	24.062	28.987	33.498	37.562	41.199			
25	21.584	22.124	22.661	23.195	23.725	28.807	33.412	37.525	41.184			
30	21.317	21.873	22.426	22.974	23.519	28.710	33.373	37.510				
35	21.137	21.706	22.270	22.831	23.387	28.656	33.354					
40	21.011	21.590	22.164	22.734	23.298	28.624	33.344					
45	20.921	21.508	22.090	22.666	23.237	28.604	33.339					
50	20.855	21.449	22.037	22.618	23.194	28.592						
55	20.806	21.405	21.998	22.584	23.164	28.585						
60	20.769	21.372	21.969	22.559	23.142	28.580						
65	20.741	21.347	21.947	22.540	23.126	28.577						
70	20.719	21.329	21.931	22.526	23.114							
75	20.702	21.314	21.919	22.516	23.105							
80	20.689	21.303	21.909	22.508	23.098							
85	20.678	21.294	21.902	22.502	23.093							
90	20.670	21.287	21.896	22.497	23.090							
95	20.663	21.282	21.892	22.494	23.087							
100	20.658	21.277	21.888	22.491	23.085							
150	20.638	21.262	21.877	22.482	23.078							
Minimum possible value						28.571	33.333	37.500	41.176	44.444	47.368	50.000

Records per bucket	210%	220%	230%	240%	250%	260%	270%	280%	290%	300%	310%	320%	330%
1	58.212	59.582	60.881	62.113	63.283	64.395	65.452	66.458	67.415	68.326	69.195	70.024	70.815
2	54.595	56.331	57.964	59.499	60.943	62.302	63.582	64.788	65.924	66.997	68.010	68.968	69.874
3	53.414	55.328	57.115	58.783	60.340	61.796	63.158	64.433	65.629	66.751	67.806		
4	52.912	54.925	56.792	58.526	60.137	61.635	63.032						
5	52.671	54.740	56.653	58.421	60.058								
6	52.545	54.650	56.588										
7	52.477	54.603											
8	52.438												
9													
10													
11													
.													
.													
.													
95													
100													
150													
Minimum possible value	52.381	54.545	56.522	58.333	60.000	61.538	62.963	64.286	65.517	66.667	67.742	68.750	69.697

382 Design of computer data files

Records per bucket	340%	350%	360%	370%	380%	390%	400%	410%	420%	430%	440%	450%
1	71.570	72.291	72.981	73.641	74.273	74.878	75.458	76.014	76.548	77.060	77.552	78.025
2	70.732	71.546	72.318	73.051	73.747	74.410						
3												
4												
5												
6												
7												
8												
9												
10												
11												
.												
.												
.												
90												
95												
100												
Minimum possible value	70.588	71.429	72.222	72.973	73.684	74.359	75.000	75.610	76.190	76.744	77.273	77.778

Records per bucket	460%	470%	480%	490%	500%	510%	520%	530%	540%	550%	560%	570%	580%
1	78.479	78.917	79.338	79.744	80.135	80.512	80.875	81.226	81.565	81.892	82.209	82.515	82.811
2													
3													
4													
5													
6													
7													
8													
9													
10													
11													
.													
.													
.													
90													
95													
100													
Minimum possible value	78.261	78.723	79.167	79.592	80.000	80.392	80.769	81.132	81.481	81.818	82.143	82.456	82.759

Appendix 5 **383**

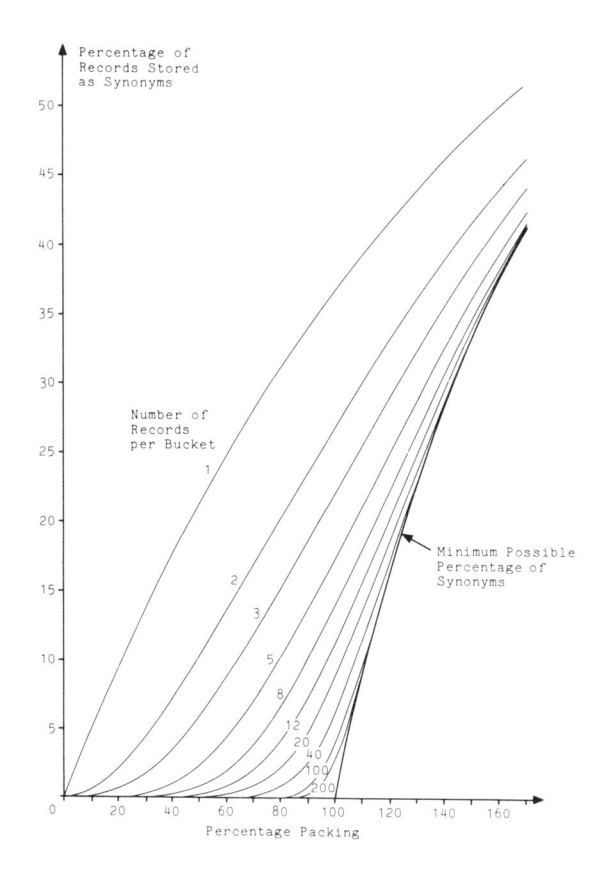

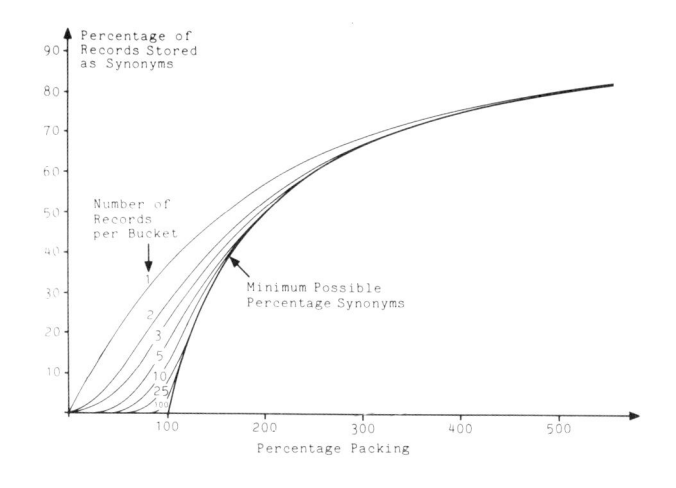

Appendix 6 The effect of chaining and tagging synonyms on search times

In Chapter 6 on direct access, Equation 6.9 states that $p(0) = e^{-(n/N)}$ and Equation 6.10 states that $p(x) = (n/Nx) \cdot p(x-1)$.

In these equations, $p(0)$ is the probability of *no* records being randomized to an address, and $p(x)$ is the probability of x records being allocated to an address. The number of records is defined as n, and the number of addresses as N.

The equations above are used to calculate the value of $p(x)$ from the value of an earlier term in the series. However, it is sometimes convenient to calculate $p(x)$ directly.

Now:

$$p(0) = e^{-(n/N)}$$
$$p(1) = (n/N)(1/1)e^{-(n/N)}$$
$$p(2) = (n/N)(1/2)p(1)$$
$$= (n/N)^2(1/1.2)e^{-(n/N)}$$

and by extrapolation:

$$p(x) = (n/N)^x(1/x!)e^{-(n/N)} \tag{VI.1}$$

These equations are used in the calculations below.

Chained synonyms

The first step in assessing the effect of chained synonyms is to determine the number of records randomized to particular addresses, whether of single records or of buckets. This can be done using the formulae for $p(1) \rightarrow p(z)$, where $p(z)$ is so small that the probability of as many records as z being randomized to a given address can be discounted. An example of this, for records randomized to individual addresses, and for 50 per cent packing, would be as follows:

$p(0) = 0.606\,5$ — 60.65 per cent of addresses are empty;
$p(1) = 0.303\,3$ — 30.33 per cent of addresses are allocated one record;

$p(2) = 0.0758$ — 7.58 per cent of addresses are allocated two records;

$p(3) = 0.0126$ — 1.26 per cent of addresses are allocated three records;

$p(4) = 0.0016$ — 0.16 per cent of addresses are allocated four records;

$p(5) = 0.0002$ — 0.02 per cent of addresses are allocated five records;

$p(6) = 0.000036$ — 0.004 per cent of addresses are allocated six records.

For timing purposes, anything less than 0.01 per cent of addresses can be ignored. In this case $z = 6$, and only six values are required, for $p(0)$ to $p(5)$.

Records randomized to individual addresses

The values of address percentages with $0, 1, 2 \cdots$ records allocated have been calculated for packing values of 50–100 per cent in steps of 10 per cent, and are shown in Table VI.1(a).

The percentage of the total records allocated to a particular set of single record addresses, e.g. those 'holding' three records, depends on a number of factors. Taking 50 per cent packing, if 30.33 per cent of addresses 'hold' one record, then this will represent 30.33×2 per cent of records. In general record percentage = address percentage $\times (N/n)$, as (n/N) is the packing factor. This holds for single address allocation.

However, if x records have been allocated to an address, then the number of records is the number of addresses, modified by the packing, and multiplied by x.

Thus the general relationship is:

$$Record\ \% = Address\ \% \times (Nx/n) \qquad (VI.2)$$

But;

$$p(x) = (n/Nx)p(x-1) \qquad (6.10)$$

And by definition of p and per cent:

$$Address\ \% = 100p(x) \qquad (VI.3)$$

Now:

$$\begin{aligned} Record\ \% &= Address\ \% \times (Nx/n) & \text{(from (VI.2))} \\ &= 100p(x)(Nx/n) & \text{(from (VI.3))} \\ &= 100(n/Nx)p(x-1)(Nx/n) & \text{(from (6.10))} \\ \therefore Record\ \% &= 100p(x-1) & \text{(VI.4)} \end{aligned}$$

From Equations (VI.3) and (VI.4) it is clear that the record percentage for z is the same as the address percentage for $(z-1)$. **This only applies for randomization to a single address position.**

The values of percentages of records allocated one, two, three or more to an address are given in Table VI.1(a). The reader will observe the relationship in the figures derived above. These record percentages show us how many records are involved in chains of one (no synonyms), two (one synonym) and so on.

The average retrieval time depends on the total number of home records, the total number of first synonyms, the total number of second synonyms and so on. A home record will be stored in every address to which **one or more** records have been allocated. A first synonym will be chained from every address to which **two or more** records were randomized, and so on. However, if x records were randomized to one position, only $(1/x)$, i.e. 1, of them will be a home record, $(1/x)$ will be a first synonym, etc. Thus the total number of home records will be the sum of

$$\frac{Record\ \%}{x}\ \text{for each value of } x = 100 \sum_{x=1}^{\infty} p(x-1)/x \qquad \text{(from (VI.4))}$$

Substituting for $p(x-1)$ (from Equation (VI.1)):

$$\frac{Record\ \%}{x}\ \text{for each value of } x = 100 \sum_{x=1}^{\infty} \frac{(n/N)^{x-1} e^{-(n/N)}}{x(x-1)!} \qquad \text{(VI-5)}$$

The first synonyms can be calculated by summing starting with $x = 2$, the second synonyms by summing with $x = 3$, and so on.

Values calculated in this way are shown in Table VI.1(b). As an example, in a 50 per cent packed file:

78.69 per cent of records are homes;
18.04 per cent of records are first synonyms;
2.88 per cent of records are second synonyms;
0.35 per cent of records are third synonyms;
0.03 per cent of records are fourth synonyms.

The proportion of records that could be expected to be involved in longer chains is negligible. However, this is for perfect randomization. An inefficient algorithm will generate many more long synonym chains (*see* the discussion on Kaimann's findings in Chapter 6, pp. 166–170).

With the figures for numbers of home records and synonyms in various positions in chains available, timings can now be calculated.

Home records will require half a device rotation on average. This figure would have to be raised to a complete rotation if manufacturers' software is in use that first seeks the start of the track—which takes half a

Appendix 6 **387**

Table VI.1 Chained records, ten per track stored singly

(a)

Records allocated per storage address	Packing (%)											
	50		60		70		80		90		100	
	REC. (%)	ADDR. (%)	REC. (%)	ADDR. (%)	REC. (%)	ADDR. (%)	REC. (%)	ADDR. (%)	REC. (%)	ADDR. (%)	REC. (%)	ADDR. (%)
None		60.65		54.88		49.66		44.93		40.66		36.79
1	60.65	30.33	54.88	32.92	49.66	34.76	44.98	35.95	40.66	36.59	36.79	36.79
2	30.33	07.58	32.92	9.88	34.76	12.17	35.95	14.38	36.59	16.47	36.79	18.39
3	7.58	01.26	9.88	1.98	12.17	2.84	14.38	3.83	16.47	4.94	18.39	6.13
4	1.26	00.16	1.98	0.30	2.84	0.50	3.83	0.77	4.94	1.11	6.13	1.53
5	0.16	00.02	0.30	0.04	0.50	0.07	0.77	0.12	1.11	0.20	1.53	0.31
6	0.02	—	0.04	—	0.07	0.01	0.12	0.02	0.20	0.03	0.31	0.05
7	—	—	—	—	0.01	—	0.02		0.03		0.05	0.01

(b)

	Packing (%)											
	50		60		70		80		90		100	
	REC. (%)	TIME (s)	REC. (%)	TIME (s)	REC. (%)	TIME (s)	REC. (%)	TIME (s)	REC. (%)	TIME (s)	REC. (%)	TIME (s)
Home	78.69	0.3935	75.20	0.3760	71.92	0.3598	68.83	0.3442	65.94	0.3297	63.21	0.3161
1st Synonym	18.04	0.1804	20.32	0.2032	22.26	0.2226	23.90	0.2390	25.28	0.2528	26.42	0.2642
2nd Synonym	2.88	0.0432	3.86	0.0579	4.88	0.0732	5.92	0.0888	6.98	0.1047	8.03	0.1204
3rd Synonym	0.35	0.0070	0.56	0.0112	0.82	0.0164	1.13	0.0226	1.49	0.0298	1.90	0.0380
4th Synonym	0.03	0.0008	0.06	0.0015	0.11	0.0028	0.17	0.0042	0.26	0.0065	0.36	0.0090
5th Synonym			0.01	0.0003	0.01	0.0003	0.02	0.0006	0.03	0.0009	0.06	0.0018
6th Synonym											0.01	0.0004
Search	0.625R		0.650R		0.675R		0.699R		0.724R		0.750R	
Head movement	—		—		—		+0.001R		+0.008R		+0.040R	
Total	0.625R		0.650R		0.675R		=0.700R		=0.732R		=0.790R	

revolution—and only then searches for the record, which will take a further half revolution. However, in this case it is often possible to write routines that bypass the software in question. In any case, the comparison of various situations is not invalidated, as the increase in times applies to all operations. Assuming the minimum times:

home records require $R/2$ (half a revolution);
first synonyms require $R/2 + R/2$ (half a revolution for each record);
second synonyms require $R/2 + R/2 + R/2$;
etc.

Using these figures, search times have been calculated, and are shown in Table VI.1(b). In addition, some synonyms may not find a place on the home cylinder and may require a head movement before they are retrieved. In this case it has been assumed that the records are stored 100 to the cylinder and that one head movement takes the same time as one device rotation. The figures can be adjusted for changes in cylinder size or head movement time, using Table 6.4 and altering the head movement times in Table VI.1(b).

Records randomized to buckets

The mathematical analysis of this is identical to that given above, except where stated. However, Equations (6.12) and (6.13) are used for the calculations.

Table VI.2(a) shows the percentage of buckets with $1, 2, 3 \cdots$ synonyms. This is shown visually in Fig. 6.15 for two cases. The Table does not include figures for buckets that have no synonyms; these can be calculated from Equations (6.12) and (6.13) if they are required.

For an individual value of x, the number of records randomizing to a bucket, the relation equivalent to Equation (VI.1) is:

$$p(x) = \frac{(n/B)^x e^{-(n/B)}}{x!} \qquad \text{(VI.6)}$$

As the derivation of Equation (VI.6) follows the lines of (VI.1), it is not given here.

The percentage of records randomized to buckets 'holding' one or more synonyms is given in Table VI.2(a). The relation between number of buckets to which records are randomized and the percentage of records is $(x-b)B/n$, so that

$$\text{Record } \% = ((x-b)B/n) \text{Bucket } \% \qquad \text{(VI.7)}$$

where b is the capacity of the bucket, and B the total number of buckets.

The percentage of records that are first, second $\cdots n$th synonyms follows the previous model. *All* the records from buckets with only one synonym, plus *half* the records from buckets with two synonyms, *one third* of those with three synonyms, etc., are summed to give the *first*

Table VI.2 Chained records blocked ten per track
(a)

No of synonyms	Packing (%)											
	50		60		70		80		90		100	
	Record	Bucket	Record	Bucket	Record	Bucket	Record	Bucket	Record	Bucket	Record	Bucket
1	0.164	0.82	0.375	2.25	0.646	4.52	0.903	7.22	1.078	9.70	1.137	11.37
2	0.136	0.34	0.377	1.13	0.754	2.64	1.203	4.81	1.618	7.28	1.896	9.48
3	0.078	0.13	0.260	0.52	0.609	1.42	1.110	2.96	1.680	5.04	2.187	7.29
4	0.032	0.04	0.147	0.22	0.406	0.71	0.845	1.69	1.440	3.24	2.084	5.21
5	0.01	0.01	0.075	0.09	0.236	0.33	0.563	0.90	1.071	1.94	1.735	3.47
6			0.030	0.03	0.129	0.15	0.338	0.45	0.726	1.09	1.302	2.17
7			0.012	0.01	0.040	0.04	0.184	0.21	0.451	0.58	0.896	1.28
8					0.023	0.02	0.090	0.09	0.258	0.29	0.568	0.71
9					0.013	0.01	0.045	0.04	0.14	0.14	0.333	0.37
10							0.025	0.02	0.067	0.06	0.190	0.19
11							0.014	0.01	0.037	0.03	0.099	0.09
12									0.013	0.01	0.048	0.04
13											0.026	0.02
14											0.014	0.01

The figures tabulated show percentages of records randomized to buckets that will have the given number of synonyms, and the percentage of buckets having that same number of synonyms. The calculations are based on a truly random loading.

Table VI.2 (Cont'd)
(b)

Record description	Packing (%)									
	50		60		70		80		90		100	
	REC. (%)	TIME (s)	REC. (%)	TIME (s)	REC. (%)	TIME (s)	REC. (%)	TIME (s)	REC. (%)	TIME (s)	REC. (%)	TIME (s)
Home	99.57	0.4979	98.71	0.4936	97.12	0.4856	94.68	0.4734	91.41	0.4571	87.49	0.4375
1st Synonym	0.268	0.0040	0.709	0.0106	1.406	0.0211	2.301	0.0345	3.266	0.0490	4.17	0.0626
2nd Synonym	0.104	0.0021	0.334	0.0067	0.760	0.0152	1.398	0.0280	2.188	0.0438	3.033	0.0607
3rd Synonym	0.036	0.0009	0.145	0.0036	0.383	0.0096	0.796	0.0199	1.379	0.0345	2.085	0.0521
4th Synonym	0.010	0.0003	0.058	0.0017	0.180	0.0054	0.426	0.0128	0.819	0.0246	1.356	0.0407
5th Synonym	0.002	0.0001	0.022	0.0008	0.079	0.0028	0.215	0.0075	0.459	0.0161	0.835	0.0292
6th Synonym			0.007	0.0003	0.032	0.0013	0.103	0.0041	0.244	0.0098	0.488	0.0195
7th Synonym			0.002	0.0001	0.010	0.0005	0.046	0.0021	0.123	0.0055	0.271	0.0122
8th Synonym					0.004	0.0002	0.020	0.0010	0.059	0.0030	0.143	0.0072
9th Synonym					0.001	0.0001	0.009	0.0005	0.027	0.0015	0.072	0.0040
10th Synonym							0.004	0.0002	0.011	0.0007	0.035	0.0021
11th Synonym							0.001	0.0001	0.004	0.0003	0.016	0.0010
12th Synonym									0.001	0.0001	0.007	0.0005
13th Synonym											0.003	0.0002
14th Synonym											0.001	0.0001
Search		0.505R		0.517R		0.542R		0.584R		0.646R		0.730R
Head movement		nil		nil		nil		+0.001R		+0.008R		+0.040R
Total		0.505R		0.517R		0.542R		0.585R		0.654R		0.770R

synonyms. This same sequence, less the first synonyms, is used for second synonyms and so on. The results are tabulated in Table VI.2(b). From Equations (VI.6) and (VI.7), the relationship for first synonym records will be:

$$\text{First synonym \%} = 100 \sum_{x=b+1}^{\infty} \frac{((n/B)^x)e^{-(n/B)}}{((x-b)x!)((x-b)B/n)} \quad \text{(VI.8)}$$

Using these figures the times required can be calculated. In Table VI.2(b) home records are shown as requiring $R/2$ search time. The first synonym link in a chain will normally only be read after a full rotation of the track has shown that the record is not stored on the home track. The first synonyms are assumed, therefore, to require $R + R/2$ search, second synonyms $R + R/2 + R/2$, etc. Again, the effect of software restrictions such as positioning of link fields, the need to seek the start of track marker before searching, etc., may alter the computed figures.

Tagged records

As no considerations of position in a chain occur for tagged records (*see* Chapter 6 for details), the calculations are relatively simple. Each synonym can be picked up directly from the link address. The timing considerations are thus:

1. search for home record;
2. if missing, pick up link address;
3. search for synonym.

Home records will on average require $R/2$ to locate them.

If the record is a synonym, it is assumed that the whole bucket will be searched before this is established. This means that, for blocked records, *every* synonym will require (1 bucket = 1 track):

   R (search home bucket);
   $+R/2$ (search overflow track).

In the case of unblocked records, the tag will be in the home record position, and thus only:

   $R/2$ (search home address);
   $+R/2$ (search overflow track);

will be required. The figures given in Table VI.3 reflect these assumptions.

In addition, it will be necessary to take account of head movement for some synonyms if the file packing density is 80 per cent or more. This again is shown in the values of Table VI.3.

While software and hardware conditions can affect these calculations, they give a basis for comparison. Figure 6.17 shows a comparison of the techniques.

392 Design of computer data files

Table VI.3 Tagged records, ten per track, stored singly.
(a)

Time factor	Packing (%)											
	50		60		70		80		90		100	
	REC. (%)	TIME (s)	REC. (%)	TIME (s)	REC. (%)	TIME (s)	REC. (%)	TIME (s)	REC. (%)	TIME (s)	REC. (%)	TIME (s)
Home	78.69	0.3935	75.20	0.3760	71.92	0.3596	68.83	0.3442	65.94	0.3297	63.21	0.3161
Synonyms	21.31	0.2131	24.80	0.2480	28.08	0.2808	31.17	0.3117	34.06	0.3406	36.79	0.3679
Head movement	—		—		—		0.06	0.0006	0.83	0.0083	3.99	0.0399
Total	0.607R		0.624R		0.640R		0.656R		0.679R		0.724R	

(b)
Tagged records, blocked ten per track.

Time factor	Packing (%)											
	50		60		70		80		90		100	
	REC. (%)	TIME (s)	REC. (%)	TIME (s)	REC. (%)	TIME (s)	REC. (%)	TIME (s)	REC. (%)	TIME (s)	REC. (%)	TIME (s)
Home	99.56	0.4978	98.71	0.4936	97.12	0.4856	94.68	0.4734	91.41	0.4571	87.49	0.4375
Synonyms	0.44	0.0066	1.29	0.0193	2.88	0.0432	5.32	0.0798	8.59	0.1288	12.51	0.1876
Head movement	Nil		Nil		Nil		0.06	0.0006	0.83	0.0083	3.99	0.0399
Total	0.504R		0.513R		0.529R		0.554R		0.594R		0.665R	

Appendix 7 A detailed example of the results of storing synonyms using consecutive spill

Very few records will not find a place anywhere on the cylinder. Take for example a file that is 90 per cent packed, and can hold 100 records per cylinder. In this case the cylinder can be treated as a very large bucket. From Table 6.4 (p. 176), 99.2 per cent of records will be stored in their home cylinder and only 0.8 per cent will overflow on to another cylinder. As the packing density is usually lower than this and the number of records per cylinder greater, overflow from a cylinder is not usually a problem.

The timing considerations for this method of synonym handling are as follows. If a file is 90 per cent packed, with ten records per track and ten tracks per cylinder, then from Table 6.4:

91.4 per cent of records will be on their home tracks;
3.6 per cent will be on the next track;
1.5 per cent will be two tracks displaced;
0.9 per cent will be three tracks displaced;
0.6 per cent will be four tracks displaced;
0.6 per cent will be five or six tracks displaced;
0.6 per cent will be seven, eight or nine tracks displaced;
0.8 per cent will be on another cylinder.

This set of figures is derived from Table 6.4 by treating the placing of synonyms as the placing of records in successively larger buckets (one, two, three, four tracks, etc.). In attempting to store an average of nine records per track on tracks that can contain up to ten records, 91.41 per cent of the records would be home records and 8.59 per cent synonyms.

To determine if there would be room on the *next* track, treat the two tracks as a single bucket. Table 6.4 shows that on average only 4.99 per cent of records will overflow from a bucket that can hold twenty records, and hence $(8.59 - 4.99) = 3.6$ per cent of records will find a storage position one bucket away from their home buckets.

Similarly only 3.47 per cent of records overflow from a bucket with a capacity of thirty records, so $(4.99 - 3.47) = 1.52$ per cent of records will find a storage position two buckets away.

The application of this reasoning to the ten tracks of a cylinder that can contain 100 records gives the figures listed above.

Table VII.1 presents the results of applying this method of calculation for packing densities of 50 per cent to 100 per cent.

It is assumed that a cylinder is treated as a whole. If a record will not fit on the last track in the cylinder it is attempted to store it in the first, second and so on in the same cylinder. A record is only stored elsewhere when there is no space anywhere in the cylinder. If a record is located on its home track, then half a revolution will be required on average to retrieve it. If it is not on its home track, the whole track will be searched before this is established; any record not on a track will require a full revolution to search the track: the overall time to retrieve all the records is:

$$91.4 \times \frac{R}{2} \text{ per cent home records}$$

$$+ \; 3.6 \times \frac{3R}{2} \text{ per cent one track displaced}$$

$$+ \; 1.5 \times \frac{5R}{2} \text{ per cent two tracks displaced}$$

$$+ \; 0.9 \times \frac{7R}{2} \text{ per cent three tracks displaced}$$

$$+ \; 0.6 \times \frac{9R}{2} \text{ per cent four tracks displaced}$$

$$+ \; 0.6 \times 6R \left(\text{i.e. } \frac{1}{2} \left(\frac{11R}{2} + \frac{13R}{2} \right) = 6R \right) \text{ per cent five or six tracks displaced}$$

$$+ \; 0.6 \times \frac{17R}{2} \text{ per cent seven, eight or nine tracks displaced}$$

$$+ \; 0.8 \times (1 \text{ head movement} + 10R) \text{ per cent}$$

$$= \; 0.774R + (0.008 \times 1 \text{ head movement})$$

In the case of a disk drive with a head movement from one track to the next of 25 milliseconds and a rotation time of 25 milliseconds the addition of all these factors gives an *average* search time for a record of 0.782×25 milliseconds with 90 per cent packing. This falls to 0.621×25 milliseconds for 80 per cent packing, and would be only 0.5×25 milliseconds if no records were displaced from their home tracks.

Fig. VII.1 shows average search times graphed for packing densities of 50–100 per cent. It should be remembered that files are not usually randomly distributed by an algorithm. This curve is a 'best possible' one; in practice results will usually be somewhat worse than this. If they are very much

Table VII.1 This table gives the values plotted in Fig. 6.13. The total average time is given in units of R, the device rotation time.

Location	50% packing		60% packing		70% packing		80% packing		90% packing		100% packing	
	%	Time (ms)	%	Time (ms)	%	Time (ms)	%	Time (ms)	%	Time (ms)	%	Time (ms)
Home	99.6	0.498	98.7	0.494	97.1	0.486	94.7	0.474	91.4	0.457	87.5	0.438
1 away	0.4	0.006	1.1	0.016	2.1	0.032	3.0	0.045	3.6	0.054	3.6	0.054
2 away			0.2	0.005	0.5	0.013	1.1	0.027	1.5	0.038	1.6	0.040
3 away					0.2	0.007	0.5	0.018	0.9	0.031	1.0	0.035
4 away					0.1	0.005	0.2	0.009	0.6	0.027	0.7	0.031
5/6 away							0.3	0.018	0.6	0.036	0.8	0.048
7/8/9 away							0.1	0.019	0.6	0.051	0.8	0.068
Overflow							0.1	0.011	0.8	0.088	4.0	0.440
Total time (average)		0.504R		0.515R		0.543R		0.621R		0.782R		1.154R

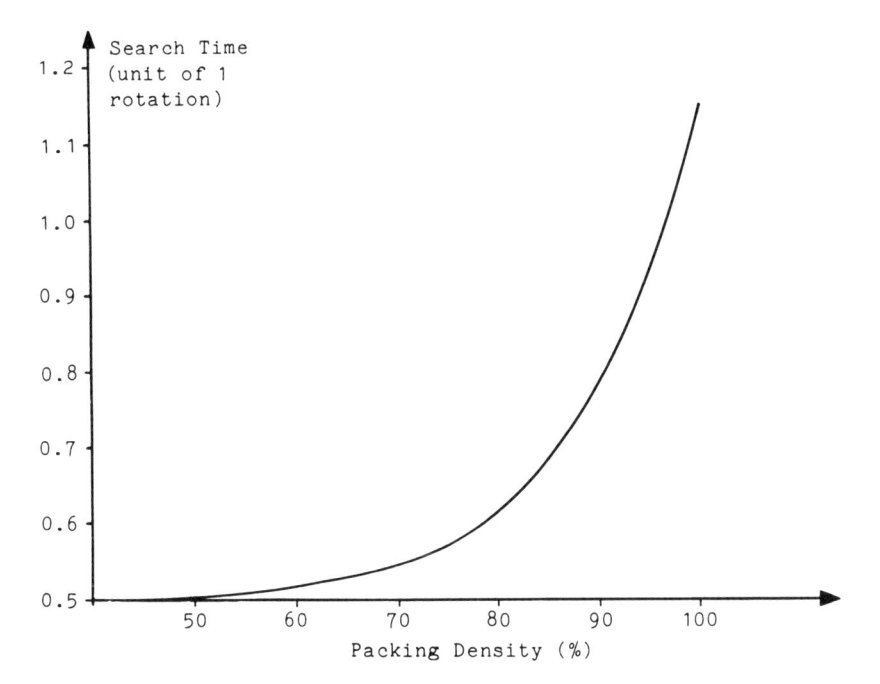

Fig. VII.1 The influence of packing density on search time. Home bucket = one track, ten records per track, ten tracks per cylinder.

worse, it indicates poor randomization and different algorithms should be considered.

It must be emphasized that the times shown are search times and not retrieval times. Record transfer has not been included in the values plotted.

396 Design of computer data files

Using the figures in Table 6.4 we can work out an equivalent set of figures for any bucket and cylinder size. Very long searches will be required for distant records. This suggests that better techniques may be available for storing synonyms than consecutive spill.

Table VIII.1 Records stored individually.

(a)

	% Packing									
	10	20	30	40	50	60	70	80	90	100
% of home records	95.16	90.63	86.39	82.42	78.69	75.20	71.92	68.83	65.94	63.21
% of synonyms	4.84	9.37	13.61	17.58	21.31	24.80	28.08	31.17	34.06	36.79
Cum. home addresses (%)	9.52	18.13	25.92	32.97	39.35	45.12	50.34	55.06	59.35	63.21
Cum. synonym addresses (%)	0.48	1.87	4.08	7.03	10.65	14.88	19.66	24.94	30.65	36.79
Partial homes (%)	95.2	86.1	77.9	70.5	63.8	57.7	52.2	47.2	42.9	38.6
Partial synonyms (%)	4.8	13.9	22.1	29.5	36.2	42.3	47.8	52.8	57.1	61.4

(b)

	% Packing								
	10	20	30	40	50	60	70	80	90
% of total accesses	43	21.5	12	8.5	6	4	2.5	1.5	1.0
% of accesses to synonyms	4.8	13.9	22.1	29.5	36.2	42.3	47.8	52.8	57.1
Contribution to total synonym accesses	2.06	2.99	2.65	2.51	2.17	1.69	1.20	0.79	0.57
Synonym accesses	16.63 per cent (compares with 34.06 per cent for random loading)								

(c)

	% packing								
	10	20	30	40	50	60	70	80	90
% of total accesses	17	14.5	14.0	13.0	12.0	10.0	8.5	6.5	4.5
% of accesses to synonyms	4.8	13.9	22.1	29.5	36.2	42.3	47.8	52.8	57.1
Contribution to total synonym accesses	0.81	2.02	3.09	3.84	4.34	4.23	4.06	3.43	2.57
Synonym accesses	28.4 per cent (compares with 34.06 per cent for random loading)								

Appendix 8 Handling smooth and random access curves

1 Handling a smooth access curve

Looking first at records stored in individual addresses, Table 6.4 gives figures for the expected percentage of synonyms, and home records are found by difference. These are both given in Table VIII.1(a) for 10 per cent to 100 per cent packing. The next line shows figures for cumulative home addresses in the file area (the figures are given as home *addresses* because they are always true for addresses, but only correspond to *record percentages* if the file is 100 per cent packed). They are calculated as follows.

Of the first 10 per cent of record storage positions filled 4.84 per cent are synonyms. Thus 0.484 per cent of the *total* set of addresses is now occupied by synonyms. Correspondingly, 95.16 per cent of the first 10 per cent of storage positions will hold home records (note that if the file is finally to be 90 per cent packed one ninth, or (100/9) per cent, of the *records* are now stored.).

When 20 per cent of the record storage positions are occupied, 9.37 per cent of these will hold synonyms. Therefore $9.37 \times 20/100$, or 1.87 per cent of the total set of addresses holds synonyms, and $20 - 1.87$ or 18.13 per cent holds home records.

The cumulative lines of the table are completed by carrying out this calculation up to 100 per cent packing for both home and synonym addresses.

In order to analyse the effect of loading in access frequency order the addresses are divided into ten groups. The proportion of home records to synonym records in each 10 per cent of addresses is required, and is calculated as follows.

The first 10 per cent of addresses consists of 9.52 per cent of home addresses and 0.48 per cent of synonyms. The second 10 per cent has a cumulative figure of 18.13 per cent home addresses and 1.87 per cent of synonyms. Therefore $18.13 - 9.52 = 8.61$ per cent of the addresses hold home records *from the second 10 per cent*, and similarly $1.87 - 0.48 = 1.39$ per cent of the addresses hold synonyms from this 10 per cent. The figures due to each 10 per cent of packing are shown in the last two lines of Table VIII.1(a) and are labelled 'partial' to distinguish them from the 'cumulative' figures that precede them.

398 Design of computer data files

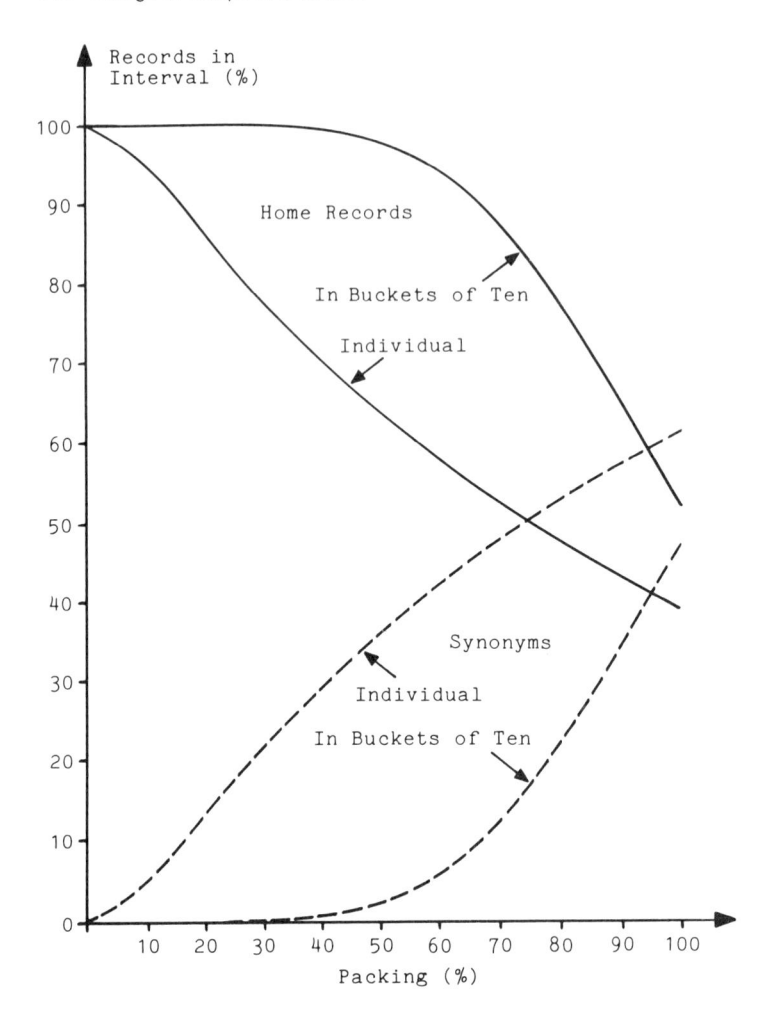

Fig. VIII.1 The percentage of records that is allocated to home and synonym addresses in the intervals 0–10%, 10–20%, etc.

These figures are plotted in Fig. VIII.1, which shows the effect of adding records to a file that is already created. For unblocked records new additions will give rise to more synonyms than home records for files packed to about 75 per cent. Of the records added to a file that take it from 90 per cent to 100 per cent packing, 61.4 per cent will be stored as synonyms and only 38.6 per cent as home records. The heavy penalty in synonyms that is incurred by adding records to a well-packed file is brought out in Fig. VIII.1, although it is not obvious from the figures in Table VIII.1.

This same data is used to calculate the effect of loading in access frequency order as follows. Taking a 90 per cent packed file, with accesses due to the nine equal groups of records given in Fig. 6.20, the first ninth of the records lead to 10 per cent packing. From Table VIII.1(a) synonyms will make up 4.8 per cent of the records. As this set of records causes 43 per cent of all accesses to the file, $43 \times 4.8/100 = 2.06$ per cent of all file accesses will be to synonyms in this set.

The second ninth of the records will lead to 20 per cent packing. This set contains 13.9 per cent of synonyms (see Table VIII.1(a)) and accounts for 21.5 per cent of all accesses. The contribution to all accesses to synonyms is thus $21.5 \times 13.9/100 = 2.99$ per cent. This process is carried out for each set of records, and the results are given in Table VIII.1(b). The overall figure for accesses to synonyms has been reduced from 34.06 per cent to 16.63 per cent by loading in access-frequency order. This is equivalent to a reduction in packing down to about 38 per cent, or to storing in buckets that hold three records.

The calculations for records stored ten to a bucket follow the same lines; the results are given in Tables VIII.2(a) and (b). The contribution to synonyms of each additional set of records is again shown in Fig. VIII.1. The very large number of synonyms created by additions to well-packed files should be noted. It turns out that access frequency loading reduces the percentage of references to synonyms from 8.59 per cent to 1.36 per cent. This is equivalent to reducing packing to 61 per cent if the same improvement were achieved by reducing packing density alone.

The user is often not faced with such a clear-cut choice, nor with such a conveniently divided group of records. The data on access frequencies might be as shown in Table VIII.3 where only a few records are accessed very frequently or very little. This situation is described below.

2 A random distribution

If the records are very variable in their number of accesses, but this variation is distributed about a mean value, a curve such as that in Fig. 6.21 might occur. There is an average number of accesses during some period (not specified) of about sixty-five. However, a small group of records have been accessed over 120 times, and another small group less than ten times. To analyse this, the frequency curve in Fig. 6.22 (case 3) is constructed relating the percentage of accesses to the percentage of records, as shown in Table VIII.3.

From the case (3) curve we can decide on the percentage of accesses corresponding to the 10–90 per cent packing points, i.e. 11.1 per cent, 22.2 per cent . . . records. This can be used to calculate the required information. If records are loaded strictly in access order, this will lead to the data shown in Table VIII.4.

These figures, read from the curve, are not very accurate. However, they give sufficient precision to estimate the likely saving.

Taking the case where records are randomized to individual addresses, the analysis follows as described for case (2). The results of the calculations

Table VIII.2 Records stored in ten-record buckets.

(a)

	% Packing									
	10	20	30	40	50	60	70	80	90	100
% of home records	100	100	99.99	99.90	99.56	98.71	97.12	94.68	91.41	87.49
% of synonyms	—	—	0.01	0.10	0.44	1.29	2.88	5.32	8.59	12.51
Cum. home addresses (%)	10	20	30	39.96	49.78	59.23	67.98	75.74	82.27	87.49
Cum. synonym addresses (%)	—	—	—	0.04	0.22	0.77	2.02	4.26	7.73	12.51
Partial homes (%)	100	100	99.97	99.6	98.2	94.5	87.5	77.6	65.3	52.2
Partial synonyms (%)	—	—	0.03	0.4	1.8	5.5	12.5	22.4	34.7	47.8

(b)

	% Packing								
	10	20	30	40	50	60	70	80	90
% of total accesses	43	21.5	12	8.5	6	4	2.5	1.5	1.0
% of accesses to synonyms	—	—	0.03	0.4	1.8	5.5	12.5	22.4	34.7
Contribution to total synonym accesses	—	—	0.004	0.03	0.11	0.22	0.31	0.34	0.35

Synonym accesses	1.36 per cent (compares with 8.59 per cent if loading is random)

(c)

	% Packing								
	10	20	30	40	50	60	70	80	90
% of total accesses	17	14.5	14.0	13.0	12.0	10.0	8.5	6.5	4.5
% of accesses to synonyms	—	—	0.03	0.4	1.8	5.5	12.5	22.4	34.7
Contribution to total synonym accesses	—	—	0.004	0.05	0.22	0.55	1.06	1.46	1.56

Synonym accesses	4.90 per cent (compares with 8.59 per cent if loading is random)

Table VIII.3 Percentage of accesses to percentage of records from Fig. 6.22 (case 3).

Avg. group accesses	130	115	105	95	85	75	65	55	45	35	25	15	5
No of records	4	15	20	47	63	78	88	69	59	35	10	8	4
Cumulative no	4	19	39	86	149	227	315	384	443	478	488	496	50
Cumulative percentage	0.75	3.8	7.8	17.2	29.8	45.4	63.0	76.8	88.6	95.6	97.6	99.2	100.0
No of accesses	520	1 725	2 100	4 465	5 355	6 630	5 720	3 795	2 655	1 225	250	120	20
Cumulative accesses	520	2 345	4 445	8 910	14 265	20 895	26 615	30 410	33 065	34 290	34 540	34 660	34
Cumulative percentage	1.5	6.8	12.8	25.7	41.1	60.3	76.7	87.7	95.3	98.9	99.6	99.9	100.0

Table VIII.4 Values of packing and partial per cent of accesses estimated from the curve on Fig. 6.22.

% packing	10	20	30	40	50	60	70	80	90
% of records	11.1	22.2	33.3	44.4	55.6	66.7	77.8	88.9	100
% of accesses	17	31.5	45.5	58.5	70.5	80.5	89.0	95.5	100
Partial % of accesses	17	14.5	14.0	13.0	12	10	8.5	6.5	4.5

are given in Table VIII.1(c). Loading in access-frequency order has reduced the access to synonyms from 34.06 per cent to 28.4 per cent. This is not dramatic, but it is still equivalent to a reduction in packing density from 90 per cent to 71 per cent.

Results for the calculations with records stored ten per bucket are given in Table VIII.2(c). Accesses to synonyms are reduced from 8.59 per cent to 4.9 per cent. This again is an acceptable improvement, equivalent to a reduction of about 9 per cent in packing density.

Additional questions

1. A magnetic tape run uses three files: an input master file, an output master file and an update file. 5000 storage positions are available for input-output areas. File and record sizes are:

    INPUT MASTER   100 000 records of 500 characters each.

    OUTPUT MASTER 100 000 records of 525 characters each.

    UPDATE FILE   20 000 records of 30 characters each.

Calculate the optimum blocking factors for each file.

2. Describe carefully the methods by which you would optimize the performance of an indexed sequential file and a direct file, for direct reference to records. Explain which you would use in an enquiry system, justifying your choice by giving appropriate timing estimates.

3. Compare and contrast the considerations that affect the blocking of records on magnetic disk and magnetic tape.
    In a tape run, there are 6000 bytes available for input-output areas. Only deletions are carried out on this run, so the time the run takes is limited by tape passing time. The files are made up as follows:

    Input file: 120 000 records of 80 bytes each

    Output file: 95 000 records of 80 bytes each

    Deletion file: 25 000 records of 80 bytes each

    The deletion file is single buffered, the other two are double buffered. What blocking factors would you recommend, and why? Give your supporting calculations in full.

4. What are the fundamental differences between the provision of security from accidental corruption of data in online, as against batch systems? Explain how these differences affect the types and number of checks that can be built into each system, and sketch typical approaches to the planning of such systems. Take care to cover the field thoroughly: you should not, however, take into account precautions against deliberate loss, access to or alteration of data.

5. What is the purpose of a randomizing algorithm? Describe several such algorithms, indicating how they work, when you would use them and when not. Relate this discussion to the likely or assumed distribution of keys in a file.

You have been asked to provide an algorithm for the following set of keys: 108, 205, 003, 358, 001, 103, 359, 104, 007, 210, 356, 106, 101, 005, 208, 353, 002, 206, 109, 008, 351, 207, 354, 004, 357, 107, 204, 009, 355, 102, 350, 209, 006, 211, 352, 105. Decide on an algorithm, try out its results, and make adjustments until you feel that your algorithm is satisfactory - and explain on what basis you decide that it is. Show all your working. Then show that the file can be stored in not more than 41 storage positions, and apply at least three different algorithms. Test how the results you obtain compare with those predicted theoretically.

6. Explain briefly the concept of a probability distribution, and give reasons why such a distribution should always sum to one. How does the Poisson distribution meet this criterion, and why is it useful in file design? Illustrate your answer by calculating the percentage of synonyms to be expected when 8 150 records are loaded into 10 000 buckets, each of which can hold only one record. You should assume that records have been loaded using a two-pass load.

7. Compare and contrast the problems of security in batch and online systems.

8. Explain carefully when you would use single, when double and when multiple buffers. How might this recommendation be affected by the manufacturer's hardware?

9. Compare and contrast the performance of magnetic disk and magnetic tape as secondary storage devices, paying particular attention to the influence of their physical characteristics on their uses. Illustrate your answer with examples that are realistic; you may quote any device that you know well, but your performance figures must be accurate.

10. The last twenty update runs to a particular file have involved the numbers of updates shown below:

2421, 2414, 2466, 2308, 2516, 2435, 2460, 2472, 2388, 2462, 2382, 2375, 2447, 2309, 2462, 2421, 2501, 2438, 2457, 2514.

The file contains 242 900 records, held in blocks holding five records each and stored twenty blocks to the track. You have been asked to choose between holding the file in sequential and in indexed sequential form. Set out the calculations you make, and the decisions you reach, in deciding on a file organization, and justify your choice fully. Would your decision be different if the hit rate were gradually increasing? If so, why?

11. Indexed sequential files are often poorly designed. Set out the steps you would take to optimize such a file, pointing out how and why each would improve file performance. Describe the 'weaknesses' of IS files that led to software houses offering their own 'improved' packages; comment on the likely success of such software.

An IS file is made up of 150,000 records, each of 275 bytes. You have been asked to specify the space needs of the file, pointing out where each part of the file is to be located. Distinguish between the cases in which additions are to be expected in a random fashion, and in which they will all be to five cylinders (equally distributed between them). Illustrate your answers with calculations based on 6% of additions to the file. You may assume the figures for the IBM 3350 disk given below. Records may be blocked if you decide it is helpful.

Bytes per Record		Records per Track	Bytes per Record		Records per Track	Bytes per Record		Records per Track
min.	max.		min.	max.		min.	max.	
9361	18987	1	474	503	25	119	125	49
6152	9360	2	447	473	26	111	118	50
4547	6151	3	421	446	27	104	110	51
3584	4546	4	397	420	28	97	103	52
2943	3583	5	375	396	29	90	96	53
2484	2942	6	355	374	30	84	89	54
2140	2483	7	335	354	31	77	83	55
1873	2139	8	317	334	32	71	76	56
1659	1872	9	300	316	33	65	70	57
1484	1658	10	284	299	34	60	64	58
1338	1483	11	268	283	35	54	59	59
1215	1337	12	254	267	36	49	53	60
1109	1214	13	240	253	37	44	48	61
1017	1108	14	227	239	38	39	43	62
937	1016	15	215	226	39	34	38	63
866	936	16	203	214	40	30	33	64
803	865	17	192	202	41	25	29	65
747	802	18	181	191	42	21	24	66
696	746	19	171	180	43	17	20	67
650	695	20	161	170	44	13	16	68
609	649	21	152	160	45	9	12	69
571	608	22	143	151	46	5	8	70
536	570	23	135	142	47	4	4	71
504	535	24	126	134	48			

406 Design of computer data files

12. Explain how you would approach the problem of updating a direct file that holds share values, before the working day begins; there is not time to set all the required values <u>directly</u>, but the file is not in sequential order. Explain carefully the process of providing backup copies to such a file, and of recovering from failure using this backup copy or copies.

13. Why and when would checkpoints be provided in a computer program? What data would be required in a tape run? How does this compare with a direct-access run? In a particular run that takes one hour, the probability of failure is 0.1. It takes one minute to record a checkpoint, and two minutes to restart the run. Would you recommend checkpoints, and if so, how many? You should support your recommendation with appropriate calculations.

14. A large direct file has been loaded to 87.5% packing density. What percentage of synonyms would you expect if the file had been perfectly randomly loaded? How could accesses to synonyms be reduced if eighty five percent of all accesses to the file were due to ten percent of the records? Support your answers using calculations based on the information given. What happens when records are later added to the file? Explain your statements carefully, and base them on appropriate calculations that use the one-pass and two-pass load models.

15. What is meant by the term 'block hit rate'? Given a record hit rate of r, derive an expression for the block hit rate of a block holding b records. Using this expression, or otherwise, explain the way in which the choice between disc and tape as storage media for sequential files depends on hit rate.

16. 'A sequential file is rightly held on magnetic tape'. Comment on this statement, making clear whether - and if so why - it applies.

17. In an insurance application, a file of 3 630 000 customer records is held on magnetic tape. On any given day an average of 10 000 records is updated, using details of premiums paid, and for each of these transactions a report line is stored on magnetic tape from which it is later printed. Customer records are 350 bytes in length, update records 20 bytes and print lines 80 bytes.

There are 6400 bytes available for use as input-output areas; how would you allocate this space to the three files? Assume that all the files are held on the same type of magnetic tape; you must show all your working.

What else might you recommend to reduce run time?

18. The data processing manager has asked you to decide whether a particular file should be organized in sequential or indexed sequential form. The last ten update runs have referenced the following percentages of records:

2.37, 3.84, 7.26, 4.87, 4.91, 6.31, 5.08, 5.55, 9.12, 6.09.

Due to space considerations, an indexed-sequential file would require records to be blocked in tens, which would take up a whole track. Sequential file records could be stored singly, eight per track. The track index takes up a whole track, and a further whole track per cylinder of an IS file is required for overflow areas. Each cylinder is made up of ten tracks.

Cylinder-to-cylinder transitions take 20 milliseconds. A track can be read in 16.667 milliseconds.

Answer the question by setting out in note form the stages in your investigation of which organization to use. Any figures you give should be justified by appropriate mathematical analysis, showing your working. Any assumptions that you make should be stated. Mention any additional information you would require, in order to have more confidence in your decision.

19. What is meant by the term 'checkpoint'? How may such a facility be organized? Explain the costs and benefits of using checkpoints, and indicate the basis on which you would decide whether they are justified in any given case.

A program that takes four hours to run turns out to fail on average once in every three runs. Each checkpoint takes ten minutes to record. Restarting the run from a checkpoint takes five minutes. How many checkpoints, if any, would you recommend? How would your answer be changed - if at all - if the output were required at latest 5 hours 20 minutes after the start of the run? State any assumptions that you make, and justify your answers with full calculations.

20. What do you understand by access frequency loading? Explain how it can be used to improve the performance of direct files, and when it cannot be used.

A file holding records in single record buckets has been access-frequency loaded to a packing density of 80%. If 90% of accesses are to 10% of records, what improvement will there be over conventional loading? Trace the effect of adding records at random to 90% and 100% packing.

21. Explain the precautions you would take while creating the file and during processing to ensure that an indexed-sequential file will handle direct references as rapidly as possible.

408 Design of computer data files

22. What information would you require before deciding on the type of organization that is appropriate for a file? When might the choice be difficult? Set out the considerations that would guide you in any case of difficulty.

23. Explain the difference between one- and two-pass loading of direct files, and illustrate your answer by making appropriate calculations for single record buckets. Why, when a two-pass load appears to be superior, do we need to know the results of a one-pass load?

24. Describe the principles involved in taking checkpoints during processing of disk and tape, explaining when and how you would use them. Illustrate your answer by giving realistic figures and calculations.

25. What do you understand by the term access-frequency loading? Explain how it can be used to improve the performance of direct files, and when it cannot be used.

   A file holding records singly has been access-frequency loaded to a packing density of 80%. if 90% of accesses are to 10% of records, what improvement will there be over conventional loading? Trace the effect of adding records at random to 90% and 100% packing. Use Appendix 5 to give the synonym percentages you require to carry out your calculations.

26. Calculate the expected number of synonyms when 8 350 records are allocated randomly to 10 000 storage positions; do this for both one-pass and two-pass loads, and compare their results.

27. What questions would you ask in deciding whether a file should be organized using the indexed-sequential or direct organisation techniques?
   Trace the process of deciding between these techniques in the following case: (Where possible, justify your choices numerically).

   Batches of 2,000 updates are received in the post daily, for a file that will take up 100 cylinders independent of the file organisation. Over this area of the device, the following figures apply:

   minimum head movement 10 milliseconds
   average head movement 30 milliseconds
   maximum head movement 55 milliseconds
   disk rotation time   16 2/3 milliseconds

   If the file is organized in IS form, one track per cylinder is set aside for overflow, and 3/4 of a track for the track index.

28. You have been asked to design a direct file that will be 86.5% packed, as there are 8 650 records to fit into 10 000 addressable buckets. Your manager wishes to know the following:

   a) How many synonyms will there be?

   b) What measures can you recommend to minimize their effect?

Produce a written report, including the calculations to back up your recommendations; these should be given where appropriate, and it should be stated when they are not, with reasons.

29. A particular file, holding customer account details on magnetic tape, is used in two separate runs. The first updates the customer account details, and is run daily. The second prints out selected account details, matching them against the previous month's selected records and adding a few more as requested by management. All files are on magnetic tape.

Calculate the blocking factors that will minimize tape passing time for the two runs.

Run 1:   File A;   3,500,000 records of 650 characters, double buffered.

        File B;   750,000 records of 30 characters, single buffered.

        File C;   750,000 records of 680 characters, single buffered.

        File D;   750,000 records of 120 characters, single buffered.

Space available for input/output is 31,750 characters.

Run 2:   File A;   3,500,000 records of 650 characters, double buffered.

        File E;   20,000 records of 730 characters, single buffered.

        File F;   5,000 records of 50 characters, single buffered.

        File G;   25,000 records of 120 characters, single buffered.

Space available for input/output is 9,500 characters.

All the tapes in the installation are IBM 3420.8's, with an instantaneous data transfer rate of 1.25 million characters per second, 6250 characters to the inch, an inter-block gap of 0.3 inches, and an IBG traverse time of 1.5 mS.

30. Describe the structure and mode of operation of an indexed sequential file, explaining carefully the considerations you would take into account in the design process.

A file of 17,500,000 records is to be stored in indexed sequential form. The records are 380 bytes in length, including keys. The hit rate is 2% on sequential runs, which are required daily. At all other times the file is online for enquiries.

The installation has 100 removable single density 3330 disks, that transfer data at 806 KB per second, have a single cylinder seek time of 10 mS, an average of 30 mS and a maximum of 55 mS. Rotation time is 16.67 mS.

16 spindles of 3380 disk storage have just been installed. These spindles each have 885 cylinders with a maximum capacity of 712 140 bytes per cylinder. These disks have an average head movement time of 16 mS, and a minimum of 6 mS. Data is transferred at 3 MB per second, and the rotation time is 16.67 mS.

Table 1 below shows the effect of blocking on the 3330, Table 2 on the 3380.

Decide on a design for your file, justifying your decision by appropriate calculations at each stage. Your answer can be in note form, but must show calculations, not just conclusions.

31 What are the reasons for taking checkpoints during a computer run? Compare the data required when checkpointing a tape run with that required if a direct file is being processed. If a certain job takes five hours, has a 20% probability of failure on any run, taking the checkpoint requires 2 minutes and the restart 5 minutes, how many checkpoints would you recommend? State all your assumptions and give appropriate mathematical working to support your conclusions.

32 Explain in detail how you would optimize the performance of an indexed sequential file. You may assume that the software available will allow you to control file design in detail. A tabular answer, setting out all the points you would consider, will be acceptable. However, all suggested actions must be justified by reasoned argument and suitable calculations.

33 Explain carefully when a sequential file should be stored on magnetic tape, and when on disk. While you need not quote figures for any particular device, you should show how the characteristics of disk and tape affect your decision.

34 Why and when are checkpoints useful in data file processing? Illustrate your answer by giving calculations for a run that lasts six hours without failures or checkpoints. A checkpoint will take 3 minutes, and the restart time after failure will be 5 minutes. State any assumptions you have made.

35 A certain batch computer run has been observed to take 10 hours of actual running time to complete. As it is run in multi-programming mode, the elapsed time before it is completed is variable, but is 15 hours on average, with a standard deviation of 1.25 hours. The results of the run are always required exactly 24 hours after the run commences - in elapsed time, not actual running time. Recommend an optimum number of checkpoints aimed at achieving the completion of the run before its results are required. A checkpoint takes 6 minutes to record, and restarting the run takes 10 minutes. You should explain your recommendations in detail, giving calculations to justify them wherever possible.

36 In an installation that has only magnetic tapes, the customer file is used in two separate processes, the first to create invoices, the second to prepare stock reports. Details of the files are as follows:

> Invoice run :

customer file :   150 000 records of 650 chars.

update file   :   3 500 records of 175 chars.

print file   :   3 500 records of 120 chars.

log file   :   3 500 records of 945 chars.

> stock report run:

customer file :   150 000 records of 650 chars.

stock file   :   830 000 records of 280 chars.

print file   :   550 000 records of 120 chars.

All files will be single buffered, and 32 000 positions of storage are available for file handling.

Recommend optimum integer blocking factors for every file in the two runs. Show all your working, and trace the way you came to your decision.

37 A sequential file is to be stored on an IBM 3350 disk, in separate key format. The hit-rate when the file is created is expected to be 1% increments over the next year. The size of a single record is 130 bytes, and the largest block size that can be accommodated in an input/output area is 1 300 bytes.

Explain, and justify by suitable calculations, the blocking factor you would choose for the file; if you would change it at any point, explain your decision. If it were possible, would you use an indexed-sequential file instead of sequential? See question 11 for the capacity of a 3350.

412 Design of computer data files

Records per Track	Bytes per Record Without Keys Min	Max	Bytes per Record With Keys Min	Max	Records per Track	Bytes per Record Without Keys Min	Max	Bytes per Record With Keys Min	Max
1	6448	13030	6392	12974	26	353	371	297	315
2	4254	6447	4198	6391	27	336	352	280	296
3	3157	4253	3101	4197	28	319	335	263	279
4	2499	3156	2443	3100	29	304	318	248	262
5	2060	2498	2004	2442	30	290	303	234	247
6	1746	2059	1690	2003	31	277	289	221	233
7	1511	1743	1455	1689	32	264	276	208	220
8	1328	1510	1272	1454	33	253	263	197	207
9	1182	1327	1126	1271	34	242	252	186	196
10	1062	1181	1006	1125	35	231	241	175	185
11	963	1061	907	1005	36	221	230	165	174
12	878	962	822	906	37	212	220	156	164
13	806	877	750	821	38	203	211	147	155
14	743	805	687	749	39	195	202	139	146
15	688	742	632	686	40	187	194	131	138
16	640	687	584	631	41	179	186	123	130
17	597	639	541	583	42	172	178	116	122
18	558	596	502	540	43	165	171	109	115
19	524	557	468	501	44	158	164	102	108
20	492	523	436	467	45	152	157	96	101
21	464	491	408	435	46	146	151	90	95
22	438	463	382	407	47	140	145	84	89
23	414	437	358	381	48	134	139	78	83
24	392	413	336	357	49	129	133	73	77
25	372	391	316	335	50	124	128	68	72

TABLE 1

Maximum and minimum lengths of the blocks that can be fitted on the track of a 3330 disk in separate and embedded key format are given in the table, related to the number of blocks per track. AS an example, if records are stored in the embedded key format, a 13,030 byte record will completely fill the track. Two records of 6,448 bytes would be just too large for the track, as the end of the second record would overwrite the start of the track; two 6,447 byte records would just fit on the track, with no waste space.

Equal Length Physical Records With Keys

KL & DL Bytes (Max)	Track Capacity Records	Track Capacity Bytes	KL & DL Bytes (Max)	Track Capacity Records	Track Capacity Bytes
47,240	1	47,240	963	28	27,104
23,240	2	46,490	904	29	26,216
15,240	3	45,720	840	30	25,200
11,240	4	44,960	808	31	25,048
8,840	5	44,200	744	32	23,808
7,240	6	43,440	712	33	23,496
6,120	7	42,840	680	34	23,120
5,256	8	42,048	616	35	21,560
4,584	9	41,256	584	36	21,024
4,040	10	40,400	552	37	20,424
3,624	11	39,864	520	38	19,760
3,240	12	38,880	488	39	19,032
2,952	13	33,376	456	40	18,240
2,696	14	37,744	424	41	17,384
2,440	15	36,600	392	42	16,464
2,248	16	36,968	360	43	15,840
2,088	17	36,496	328	45	14,760
1,928	18	34,704	296	46	13,616
1,768	19	33,502	264	48	12,672
1,640	20	32,800	232	49	11,368
1,544	21	32,424	200	51	10,200
1,448	22	31,856	168	53	8,904
1,352	23	31,096	136	55	7,480
1,256	24	30,144	104	57	5,928
1,160	25	29,000	72	59	4,248
1,096	26	28,406	40	62	2,480
1,032	27	27,864	8	65	520

TABLE 2

Records on a 3380 are incremented in a minimum of 32 byte blocks, so that the size of a record or block is rounded up to the next multiple of 32. The table shows the possible block sizes, number of records per block and total bytes per track available on a 3380.

Index

access comb (disk), 33
    — frequency loading, 195
    — — — , additions to AF files, 202
    — — — , improvement due to, 202
    — — — , diagram, 197
    — — — , random distribution, 201
    — — — , smooth access curve, 200
    — — — , the 80/20 case, 196
accessing of data files, 8
active locking, 348
activity ratio (see hit rate for discussion), 9
accuracy of data, 318
added (of records), 2
additions (of records), 2, 8
    — to IS files, 232
    — — — , bunched, 233
    — — — , sequential processing, 251
    — — — , equal numbers, 232
    — — — , — probability, 233
    — — — , none expected, 232
    — — — , techniques, 238
    — — — , — in practice, 243
    — — — , — of insertion, 238
    — — — , — — linking, 241
addressing of disk, 33
algorithm, randomizing or hashing, 145
algorithmic addressing, 153
algorithms, genuinely randomizing, 159
    — , order-preserving, 157
alternate indexes (VSAM), 268
    — — versus inverted files, 279
    — tracks and sectors on disk, 36
AMIGOS software (an alternative to ISAM), 264
archive file, 3
associative key lists, 281
attributes (multiple key processing), 273, 276
audit trail, 330
average direct access time (of storage), 12
    — number in batch, 14
    — seek time, 229
    — sequential access time (of storage), 12
    — service time, 14

backing storage, 11
    — — devices, 20
backout, transaction, 349
backward space block (BSB), 29
    — — file, 29
balanced (of a run), 63
    — (of trees), 223, 224
    — tree, direct link indexing, 224, 225
    — — , example, 224
    — — indexing, 223, 239
batch processing, 13
    — size, 13, 107
batching benefits, 107, 108
BDAM, 279
bit pattern index, 275, 282
binary (logarithmic) search of disk, 219
    — search of disk, 119

block activity, 83, 84, 86, 88
    — — , grouped updates, 86
    — — , random updates, 84
    — — , regular updates, 89
    — hit rate, 84
    — size, effect of, 85, 86, 87
blocked records, 4
blocking factors, 27
    — — , general considerations, 82
    — — , limitations on size, 82
    — — , MVS limit, 83
    — — , optimum, for tapes, 90
blocks on magnetic disk, full discussion, 75
    — — — tape, — — , 71
bounded index exponential hashing, 179
Braegen automated tape library, 48
B-trees, 225
    — , examples, 226, 227
bubble memory, 49
bucket (ICL usage on disk), 71
    — processing in online systems, 351
buffer pool, 98
    — , single, 99
    — , IBM 3480 mass buffer, 98
buffers, double, 101
    — , hardware, 98
    — , multiple, 101
    — , software, 98
bypass procedures, 352

cache memory, semiconductor 'disk', 47
CAFS-ISP (content-addressable file storage), 43, 46
    — — quorum search, 43
care of magnetic media, 51
catastrophic failure, precautions against, 354
CDROM, 49, 50
certifier (tape), 51
chained overflow versus consecutive spill, 192, 193
chaining of direct file overflow, 186
changes file, 2, 3
changing data, 2
check digit usage and examples, 322
checkpoints, 332
    — , data recorded in, 336,
    — , meeting a deadline as reason, 334
    — , saving time overall as reason, 334
    — , theoretical analysis, 337 et seq
    — , when they are taken, 337
choice of file organization, 290, 291
chromium dioxide coating on 3480 tapes, 25, 30
CICS (customer interface control system), 297
    — backout provisions, 349
cleaner (tape), 51
cluster (VSAM file), 266
clustering of primary keys, 160
    — — secondary keys, 160
colliding (of records), 161
comb, access, 33
competing files (for storage space), 89
COMTEN AMIGOS software (alternative to ISAM), 264

416 Index

computer main storage, 10
___ storage, general, 10
consecutive spill, 184
contention on disk, 47
control area, 266
___ ___ split, 268
___ Data 38500 mass storage device, 48
___ interval, 266
___ ___ split, 268
controller (tape), 27
cost per access (diagram), 289
count data disk format, 56, 57
___ key data disk format, 35, 56, 58
cylinder index, 229
___ on disk, 35

data compaction, in 3520 solid state buffer, 31
___ fields, 5
___ format on tape, 56 (diagram), 57
___ formats on disk, 56 (diagram), 57, 244
___ preparation, checks during, 319
___ records, 4
___ security, accuracy and integrity, 318
___ set (VSAM), 266
___ transfer rate, 12, 212
deadline by which a run must be complete, 334
deadly embrace, 348
deblocking, move mode, 59
___ , locate mode, 61
deck (tape), 27
deleted (of records), 2
deletions, 2, 9
descriptor (in multiple key processing), 273
direct file, 7, 144 et seq.
___ ___ , access data, 211
___ ___ , ___ time, average, 12
___ ___ , additions and deletions, 213
___ ___ , 'aging', 210
___ ___ , algorithmic addressing, 153
___ ___ , initializing the file area, 210
___ ___ , key/address relationship, 144
___ ___ , loading, 180
___ ___ , optimum bucket size, 214
___ ___ , preparing a device, 209
___ ___ , processing, 14
___ ___ , ___ modes possible, 144, 212
___ ___ , self-indexing, 145
___ ___ , 'sequential' updating, 313
___ ___ , service times, 212
___ ___ , setting up, 209
___ ___ , statistics, 210
___ ___ , storing and retrieving synonyms, 184
___ ___ , well 'aged', 214
disks, CDROM, 49, 50
___ , laser, 49, 50
___ , magnetic, addressing, 33
___ , ___ , alternate tracks, 36
___ , ___ , blocks on, 75
___ , ___ , content-addressable, 43, 46
___ , ___ , count-key-data format (CKD), 35, 42
___ , ___ , cyclic check bytes, 32
___ , ___ , cylinders, 35
___ , ___ , data reference formats, 33, 35
___ , ___ , ___ storage, 32
___ , ___ , disk organization, 33
___ , ___ , embedded key 42
___ , ___ , fixed, 40
___ , ___ , ___ block architecture, 35, 42
___ , ___ , ___ head, 40

disks, magnetic, floppy, 36
___ , ___ , ___ performance, 37
___ , ___ , free format, 35
___ , ___ , head movement, 41
___ , ___ , minifloppies, 36
___ , ___ , multiple track search, 42
___ , ___ , packs, 33, 37
___ , ___ , physical characteristics, 32
___ , ___ , record transfer time, 41
___ , ___ , rotation time, 41
___ , ___ , rotational position sensing, 35
___ , ___ , searching facilities, 42
disks, magnetic, sector mode, 35
___ , ___ , shortcomings, 46
___ , ___ , spare sectors, 36
___ , ___ , systems considerations, 42
___ , ___ , timing considerations, 41
___ , ___ , 3350 capacity data, 76, 77, 78, 79
___ , ___ , Winchester technology, 38, 39
___ , ___ , 'zero access', 41
___ , optical, 49, 50
___ , semiconductor, 46
___ , ___ , native mode, 47
___ , WORM, 49, 50
distributed free space, 247, (in VSAM), 267
drive (tape), 27
dummy records in IS files, 248
dumping disk to tape, 332
duplication in online systems, 352
dynamic hashing, 178

EDS 8, 30, 60, 100 disks (ICL equipment), 77, 79
EDS 200 disk, 80, 81
effective transfer rate on tape, 28
electronic labels on tape and disk, 328
embedded overflow areas, 221, 230
enable write switch on disk, 328
enquiry handling, 7
environmental advantages of bubble memory, 50
erase head for tape, 27
error checking on tape, 28
exofiles (ICL), 327
extendible hashing, 178

fan in and out ratios, 9
field, data, 5
___ length, fixed and variable, 5
FIA (file information area), 329
file, 1, 2
___ , accessing modes, 8, 9
___ , activity ratio, 9
___ , archive, 3
___ , changes, 2, 3
___ , direct, 7, full discussion 144 et seq.
___ , dynamic, 2
___ , growth rate, 10
___ , historical, 3
___ , hit rate, 9
___ , ___ ratio, 9
___ , indexed sequential, 7, discussion, 219 et seq.
___ , inverted, fully and partial, 276
___ , master, 2
___ , multilist, 281
___ , organization, 6
___ , processing, 12
___ , random, 7, 144 et seq.
___ , reference, 3

Index

file, sequential, 6, full discussion 106 et seq.
— , serial, 6
— , — (multiple key), 274
— , transaction, 3
— , update, 3
— , volatility, 10
filestore, 263, security considerations 327
fixed block architecture (FBA), 58
— length records, 4
floppy disks, 36, performance 37
flush command, in online systems, 349
forced write, 349
format identification burst, 28
— of tape records, 28, 57
formats of records on disk, 57
forward space block (FSB), 29
— — file (FSF), 29
full indexing of an IS file, 219

generation number of a file, 328
GFS (grandfather-father-son) security system, 331
global overflow area in IS files, 230
GCR (group-coded recording) of tape records, 22
growth rate of files, 10

hard errors on disk or tape, 51
hash functions, perfect, 153
— totals, use in data validation, 325
hashing algorithm, 145
— , bounded index exponential, 179
— , dynamic, 178
— , extendible, 178
— , linear, 179
— , use in IS files, 230
heads (on tape), erase, read and write, 27
height of index trees, 223
hierarchy of indexes, 219
historical files, 3
hit rate, 9
— — , block, 84
— — , effect on IS file processing, 255 et seq.
— — , — — sequential media choice, 123
— — , probability calculations, 305
— ratio, 9
home record, 154
Honeywell MTU 0400, 0500, 0600 tapes, 23
housekeeping, 66

IBM 2314 disk, 38
— 3330 — , capacity data, 79, 80
— 3340, 3370, 3375, 3380 disks, 39
— 3350 disk capacity data, 76, 77, 78, 79
— 3420 tape performance data, 26
— 3480 — , 20, 21, 23, 26, 29, 30
— — — solid state buffer and stacker, 31
— 3850 mass storage facility, 48, 49
— 8809 tape 22, performance 26, retries 28
ICL CAFS-ISP 43, 46
— EDS 8, 30/60, 100, capacity details 77, 79
— EDS 200 disk, 80, 81
— MT 320T tape, 23
identifier, record, 1
immediate access storage, 10
independent overflow area, 221, 230
index, balanced tree, 223

index, choice of technique, 228
— , cylinder, 229
— , master, 229
— , n'ary tree, 228
— , optimization in IS files, 229, 230
— , root, 223
— , seek area, 229
— , set (in VSAM), 266
— , trie, 228
— , types, 223
indexed-sequential files, 7, 8, 219 et seq.
— additions, 232
— — techniques, 238
— alternative indexing ideas, 230
— design factors, 261
— direct processing, 258
— dummy records, use of, 248
— full indexing, 219
— hierarchy of indexes, 219
— indexes, general principles, 220
— packing density, 246
— partial indexing, 219
— sequential processing, 249
— software considerations, 263, 264
input-output time, 63
input controls on data, 319
instantaneous data transfer speeds on tape, 25
integrity of data, 318
inter-block gap (IBG) on tape, 23
interpolation search of disk, 120
— — — IS files, 230
inverted files, 276 et seq.
— — , additions and alterations, 283
— — , full and partial inversion, 276
— — , record reference, 281
— — , storage requirements, 284
— — , versus alternate indexes, 279
— — , — multilist files, 281
invoice number and file, 1

journal usage in online systems, 350

key compression in VSAM, 268
— , primary and secondary clustering, 160
— , record, 1
— , secondary, 2

labels on tape and disk, 328
laser disk, 50, 51
leaf of a storage tree, 233
ledger, 1
linear hashing, 179
LIOCS (logical input-output control system), 62, 63
loading of direct files, one and two pass, 180
— , one pass curves and tables, 182, 183
— , two pass curves and tables, 171, 176
— , one versus two pass comparison, 185
locate mode of de-blocking, 61
locking, active and passive, 348
logarithmic (binary) search, 119, 219
logical record, 55
logs in online systems, 350
longitudinal redundancy checking of tape data, 28

magnetic disks, 32 to 46
— — , addressing, 33
— — , alternate tracks, spare sectors, 36
— — , blocking (full discussion), 75
— — , care of, 51
— — , content addressable, 43, 46
— — , floppy and minifloppy, 36, 37
— — , formats, 35
— — , multiple track search, 42
— — , physical characteristics, 32
— — , rotational position sensing, 35
— — , searching facilities, 42
— — , shortcomings, 46
— — , systems considerations, 42
— — , timing considerations, 41
— — , 'zero access', 41
— tape, 20 to 31
— — , automated library, 48
— — , blocking, full discussion, 71, 90
— — , care of, 51
— — , cassettes, 30
— — , data compaction, 31
— — , error checking, 28
— — , format, 28, 57
— — , — identification burst, 28
— — , inter-block gap, 23
— — , optimizing operations, 293, 294
— — , read-opposite recovery, 28
— — , systems functions, 29
main storage, 10
master files, 2
___ index in IS files, 229
mean time between failures, in checkpointing, 337
Memorex 6520 tape cache processor, 31
memory, primary, 10
___ , secondary, 11
minifloppy disks, 36
move mode of de-blocking, 59
multilist file, 280
— — versus inverted file, 281

NCR 7261 tape cassette drive, 30
___ 7330 tape, 25
___ 7560 disk, 39
node of a storage tree, 223
non-first overflow records effects in ISAM, 253
normal operating mode of tapes, 2
NRZI (non return to zero on ones), 21

online transaction processing, 343
Open file checking routine, 329, 330
operating data-transfer rate of tapes, 25
optical disk, 50, 51
optimizing magnetic tape file handling, 110 et seq.
order of a balanced tree, 223
___ of B-trees, 225
___ , purchase handling of, 319
organization, of files, 6, 7, 8
outages, 348
overflow areas, embedded, 221, 230
— — , global, 230
— — , independent, 221, 230
___ records, effect of non-first, 253, 254, 261
___ tracks, 224

pack, disk, 33
page image posting, 349
pages, VSAM, 83
paging of data, 82
partial indexing of IS files, 219
passive locking, 348
password, 354, 355
perfect hash functions, 153
PE (phase encoding) of tape, 22
physical labels on tape and disk, 328
___ record, 55
PIOCS (physical input-output control system), 62, 63
pointers in B-trees, 225
pre-input controls on data, 319
primary clustering, 160
___ memory, 10
___ storage, 10
prime data track, 224
___ index in VSAM, 268
processing, batch, 13
___ , controls, 325
___ , direct, 14
___ , sequential, 13
___ , time, 63
profile, query, 280
progressive overflow, 184
prompts from the system, 346
PSAM (alternative to ISAM), 264

quadratic hashing, 160
___ quotient hashing, 160
query profile, 280
queue time, 212
quorum search on CAFS-ISP, 43

random file, 7
randomization, genuinely randomizing, 159
___ , order preserving, 157
___ , testing for success, 166
randomized file, 145
randomizing algorithm, 145, choice of, 178
RBA (relative byte address), 266
read head of tape, 27
___ opposite recovery, 28
record, 1
___ accessing, 9
___ addition, 8
___ attributes, 273
___ blocked, 4
___ data, 4
___ deletion, 9
___ descriptor, 273
___ fixed length, 4
___ hit, 9
___ home, 154
___ insertion in handling IS files, 238, 251
___ linking (for IS overflow), 241, 254
___ logical, 55
___ physical, 55, 57
___ spanned, 4
___ synonym, 154
___ tagging, 9
___ undefined, 4, 57, 61
___ update, 8
___ variable length, 4, 57, 61, 67
recall, 281
recording density, 23

Index 419

reference file, 3
relative byte address (RBA), 266
___ record addressing, 148, (in VSAM), 266
relevance, 281
removable disk packs, 37
restoring disk from tape, 332
root index, 223
rotational position sensing, 35

SDI (selective dissemination of information), 280
secondary clustering, 160
___ memory, 11
___ storage, 11
___ ___, security considerations, 327, 328
sectioning sequential tape files, 112 to 115
___ ___ ___ ___, example, 291
sector mode on disk, 35
security of data, 318
seek area, and index, 229
___ time, average, 229
seeks per access, 202, 210
self addressing file, 145
___ indexing file, 145
___ organizing list, 119
semiconductor disk, 46; native operating mode, 47
sequence number to verify online updates, 348
___ set, VSAM, 266
sequential access time, average, 12
___ file, 6, 106 et seq.
___ files on DA devices, 116 to 120
___ processing, 13
___ search performance, 6, 109
___ tape files, 110, 111, 112
___ updating run, 13, (diagram), 124
serial file, 6
___ information retrieval files, 274 to 284
shared channels and control units, for tapes, 29
shortcomings of manufacturers IS software, 264
skip-sequential search, 118
soft errors on disk or tape, 51
software functions on tape, 29
sorting, 108
spanned records, 4
staging data on mass storage devices, 48
STAIRS/AQUARIUS, 279
static information, 3
statistical binary search or chop, on disk, 120
STC 4305 and 4325 solid state disks, 46
storage, backing, 11
___, computer, 10
___, immediate access, 10
___, main, 10
___, primary, 10
___, secondary, 11
streaming mode of tapes, 25
synonym records, 154
___ ___, choosing an algorithm, 178
___ ___, how they occur, 154
___ ___, minimizing number and effect, 172
___ ___, storage techniques, 184 to 192

tagging overflow records in direct files, 188
___ records, 9
tape, magnetic, 20 et seq.
___ ___, automated library, 48, 49
___ ___, blocks on, 71
___ ___, care of, 51

tape, magnetic, cassette, 30
___ ___, data compaction, 31
___ ___, effective transfer rate, 71
___ ___, error checking, 28
___ ___, format identification burst, 28
___ ___, inter-block gap, 23
___ ___, physical characteristics, 21
___ ___, read-opposite recovery, 28
___ ___, recording modes, 21
___ ___, streaming mode, 25
throughput, 12, 13
transaction backout, 349
___ files, 3
___ initiation, 344
___ log, 348
___ processing security, 343
trial balance run, 332
two channel switch, 29

undefined records, 4, 61
Unisys tape units, 27
update of a record, 8
UPGRADE, as a VSAM command, 268
user profiles, in information retrieval systems, 281

validation of data on input, 319 et seq.
___ ___ ___ ___ processing, 325
___ ___ ___ ___ output, 326
variable length records, 4, 61
vertical redundancy checking, 28
volatile files, indexed, 226
volatility, 10
VSAM files, 266 et seq.
___ ___, alternate indexes, 268
___ ___, cluster, 266
___ ___, control area and interval, 266
___ ___, ___ ___ ___ ___, splits, 268
___ ___, data set, 266
___ ___, optimization, 268, 270
___ ___, reorganization, 297
VTOC (volume table of contents), 329

wait time, 212
Winchester technology disks, 38
WORM (write once, read many) disks, 49, 50
write head (tapes), 27
___ protect ring, 28, 328